Handbook of Research on Analyzing IT Opportunities for Inclusive Digital Learning

Patricia Ordóñez de Pablos
The University of Oviedo, Spain

Mohammad Nabil Almunawar
Universiti Brunei Darussalam, Brunei

Kwok Tai Chui
The Open University of Hong Kong, Hong Kong

Maniam Kaliannan
Business School, Nottingham University, Malaysia

IGI Global
PUBLISHER of TIMELY KNOWLEDGE

A volume in the Advances in Educational Technologies and Instructional Design (AETID) Book Series

Published in the United States of America by
IGI Global
Information Science Reference (an imprint of IGI Global)
701 E. Chocolate Avenue
Hershey PA, USA 17033
Tel: 717-533-8845
Fax: 717-533-8661
E-mail: cust@igi-global.com
Web site: http://www.igi-global.com

Library of Congress Cataloging-in-Publication Data

Names: Ordóñez de Pablos, Patricia, 1975- editor. | Almunawar, Mohammad Nabil, 1960- editor. | Chui, Kwok Tai, 1991- editor. | Kaliannan, Maniam, 1971- editor.
Title: Handbook of research on analyzing IT opportunities for inclusive digital learning / Patricia Ordenez de Pablos, Mohammad Nabil Almunawar, Kwok Tai Chui, Maniam Kaliannan, Editors.
Other titles: Analyzing information technology opportunities for inclusive digital learning
Description: Hershey : Information Science Referencce, [2021] | Includes bibliographical references and index. | Summary: "The edited book presents a variety of contributed chapters that explore the new demands of labor markets in the digital economy, how educational institutions can respond to these new opportunities and threats, the development of new teaching and learning methods, and finally the development of digital skills and competences"-- Provided by publisher.
Identifiers: LCCN 2020056165 (print) | LCCN 2020056166 (ebook) | ISBN 9781799871842 (Hardcover) | ISBN 9781799871866 (eBook)
Subjects: LCSH: Education--Effect of technological innovations on--Cross-cultural studies. | Distance education--Computer-assisted instruction. | Educational technology--Cross-cultural studies. | Education and globalization. | COVID-19 (Disease)--Social aspects.
Classification: LCC LB1028.3 .A488 2021 (print) | LCC LB1028.3 (ebook) | DDC 371.33--dc23
LC record available at https://lccn.loc.gov/2020056165
LC ebook record available at https://lccn.loc.gov/2020056166

This book is published in the IGI Global book series Advances in Educational Technologies and Instructional Design (AE-TID) (ISSN: 2326-8905; eISSN: 2326-8913)

British Cataloguing in Publication Data
A Cataloguing in Publication record for this book is available from the British Library.

For electronic access to this publication, please contact: eresources@igi-global.com.

Advances in Educational Technologies and Instructional Design (AETID) Book Series

Lawrence A. Tomei
Robert Morris University, USA

ISSN:2326-8905
EISSN:2326-8913

Mission

Education has undergone, and continues to undergo, immense changes in the way it is enacted and distributed to both child and adult learners. In modern education, the traditional classroom learning experience has evolved to include technological resources and to provide online classroom opportunities to students of all ages regardless of their geographical locations. From distance education, Massive-Open-Online-Courses (MOOCs), and electronic tablets in the classroom, technology is now an integral part of learning and is also affecting the way educators communicate information to students.

The **Advances in Educational Technologies & Instructional Design (AETID) Book Series** explores new research and theories for facilitating learning and improving educational performance utilizing technological processes and resources. The series examines technologies that can be integrated into K-12 classrooms to improve skills and learning abilities in all subjects including STEM education and language learning. Additionally, it studies the emergence of fully online classrooms for young and adult learners alike, and the communication and accountability challenges that can arise. Trending topics that are covered include adaptive learning, game-based learning, virtual school environments, and social media effects. School administrators, educators, academicians, researchers, and students will find this series to be an excellent resource for the effective design and implementation of learning technologies in their classes.

Coverage

- Virtual School Environments
- K-12 Educational Technologies
- Instructional Design Models
- Classroom Response Systems
- Adaptive Learning
- E-Learning
- Game-Based Learning
- Web 2.0 and Education
- Digital Divide in Education
- Collaboration Tools

IGI Global is currently accepting manuscripts for publication within this series. To submit a proposal for a volume in this series, please contact our Acquisition Editors at Acquisitions@igi-global.com or visit: http://www.igi-global.com/publish/.

The Advances in Educational Technologies and Instructional Design (AETID) Book Series (ISSN 2326-8905) is published by IGI Global, 701 E. Chocolate Avenue, Hershey, PA 17033-1240, USA, www.igi-global.com. This series is composed of titles available for purchase individually; each title is edited to be contextually exclusive from any other title within the series. For pricing and ordering information please visit http://www.igi-global.com/book-series/advances-educational-technologies-instructional-design/73678. Postmaster: Send all address changes to above address.

Titles in this Series

For a list of additional titles in this series, please visit:
http://www.igi-global.com/book-series/advances-educational-technologies-instructional-design/73678

Acquiring Learning Skills With Digital Technology
Charles Westerberg (Beloit College, USA) and Tom McBride (Beloit College, USA)
Information Science Reference • © 2021 • 148pp • H/C (ISBN: 9781799844266) • US $175.00

Emerging Realities and the Future of Technology in the Classroom
Inaya Jaafar (The Chicago School of Professional Psychology, USA) and James M. Pedersen (Delaware Valley University, USA)
Information Science Reference • © 2021 • 338pp • H/C (ISBN: 9781799864806) • US $195.00

Leading Schools With Social, Emotional, and Academic Development (SEAD)
Tara Madden-Dent (Sierra Nevada University, USA) and Deborah Oliver (National University, USA & Mindful SEAD, USA)
Information Science Reference • © 2021 • 336pp • H/C (ISBN: 9781799867289) • US $195.00

Simulation and Game-Based Learning in Emergency and Disaster Management
Nicole K. Drumhiller (American Public University System, USA) Terri L. Wilkin (American Public University System, USA) and Karen V. Srba (Saint Francis University, USA)
Information Science Reference • © 2021 • 290pp • H/C (ISBN: 9781799840879) • US $195.00

Applications of Work Integrated Learning Among Gen Z and Y Students
Trevor Gerhardt (University of West London, UK) and Paulette J. Annon (London School of Economics, UK)
Business Science Reference • © 2021 • 345pp • H/C (ISBN: 9781799864400) • US $215.00

Career Ready Education Through Experiential Learning
Karen Rasmussen (University of West Florida, USA) Pamela Northrup (University of West Florida, USA) and Robin Colson (University of West Florida, USA)
Information Science Reference • © 2021 • 305pp • H/C (ISBN: 9781799819288) • US $195.00

Advancing the Power of Learning Analytics and Big Data in Education
Ana Azevedo (CEOS:PP, ISCAP, Polytechnic of Porto, Portugal) José Manuel Azevedo (CEOS:PP, ISCAP, Polytechnic of Porto, Portugal) James Onohuome Uhomoibhi (Ulster University, UK) and Ebba Ossiannilsson (International Council for Open and Distance Education (ICDE), Norway & European Distance and e-Learning Network (EDEN), UK & Swedish Association for Distance Education (SADE), Sweden)
Information Science Reference • © 2021 • 296pp • H/C (ISBN: 9781799871033) • US $195.00

IGI Global
PUBLISHER of TIMELY KNOWLEDGE

701 East Chocolate Avenue, Hershey, PA 17033, USA
Tel: 717-533-8845 x100 • Fax: 717-533-8661
E-Mail: cust@igi-global.com • www.igi-global.com

Editorial Advisory Board

Desi Setiana, *Universiti Brunei Darussalam, Brunei*
Graziella Sicoli, *University of Calabria, Italy*
Heru Susanto, *University Technology of Brunei, Brunei*
Jeļena Zaščerinska, *Centre for Education and Innovation Research, Latvia*
Mihails Zascerinskis, *Centre for Education and Innovation Research, Latvia*
María Elena Zepeda Hurtado, *Instituto Politécnico Nacional, Mexico*

List of Contributors

Table of Contents

Detailed Table of Contents

between those who have and those who do not have digital skills, has evolved into the concept of digital inequality. Given these premises, the work investigates after careful analysis, the impact of digital systems on the educational system, such as the emergence of the "digital divide," impacts on training within universities. To verify the "digital divide," the work proposes a quantitative survey carried out through a questionnaire submitted to a sample of students. The subject of the survey is given by the students of the University of Calabria.

The purpose of this study is to gain insights on students' and educators' perspectives of the current unconventional learning and teaching methods carried out during the COVID-19 pandemic. The main data is sourced from BruCERT's online survey of 785 students and 664 educators conducted during the closing downs of educational institutes due to preventive measures imposed by the government of Brunei Darussalam. The result shows that 77.96% of students and 72.14% of educators preferred the conventional classes. The main reasons are due to their inability to acquire good internet connectivity and proper area and time management that best suits online classes. In addition to that, the respondents perceived that the aforementioned problems become the root cause of their low discipline, productivity, and motivation to conduct and attend such classes. This chapter would be beneficial as a guideline to synthesize better teaching and learning strategies in online settings in the future.

There were interesting subjects and future connections between the education sectors and popular views and perceptions of the public for decades between the literature types of the conventional and the technological element. This chapter will analyze the impact on educational areas and the surrounding environment from the interactive learning perspective on how it can enhance learning practices using the augmented reality medium. The purpose of the analysis is to find the direction that the transformation of the knowledge process has evolved over the course of time, and how it supports society and the community through an efficient method of learning diversification.

This study was conducted to investigate e-learning acceptance and factors influencing higher institutions students. Among the factors involved in this study were perceived ease of use, perceived usefulness, self-efficacy, technology availability, and usage and intention to use. Technology acceptance models (TAM) were used as a basis for the study and for hypothesizing the effects of such variables on the use of e-learning. The research methods used were inclined to the use of quantitative methods of online questionnaire surveys that consist of 23 items based on a Likert scale. The findings of this study found that there is significant influence of self-efficacy on perceived ease of use and perceived usefulness while perceived ease of use has direct impact on perceived usefulness and perceived usefulness has influence on intention to use towards e-learning systems.

This study reveals cyberbullying in the information technology age, particularly in student beliefs and behaviours. Cyberbullying has become an issue that's arising with the advancement of technology, which makes it easier for everyone in the world to be connected wirelessly. The result of the study is very interesting. More than half of the participants have reported that they spent most of their free time on social media. Due to that, some of them have experienced cyberbullying, but fewer than half of the students have actually reported the case. Moreover, social networking sites and any chat sites were found to be the platforms where cyberbullying has mostly been occurred, with email, texting on mobile phones, as well as gaming online also used for cyberbullying. Although the majority of the participants have witnessed cyberbullying, they preferred to ignore the issue instead of reporting it. According to the survey and deep interview, most of the students mentioned that there is a lack of support regarding cyberbullying.

The objective of the chapter is to assess distance education in times of COVID-19 through the implementation of the Virtual Plan for Academic Continuity of the Instituto Politécnico Nacional (IPN) in order to identify good educational practices at the postgraduate level. A quantitative methodology with an exploratory-descriptive scope was used. The participants of the study were students who were pursuing a graduate degree during confinement. The main results are a positive assessment of distance education in terms of the incorporation and continuous use of digital resources, the use of continuous evaluation, the usefulness of technological tools, as well as an interaction with the teaching staff to review the academic progress of the student.

The evolution in the field of internet technologies and the spectacular acceptance of the world wide web have shaped a new framework, not only for teachers' training but also for their distant support. This study provides insights into the utilization of Microsoft Teams digital collaboration and communication environment to improve the ways teachers are trained and supported by educational work coordinators (EWCs), through an action research conducted in Peloponnese Regional Educational Planning Center, Greece. Research results reveal that Microsoft Teams can contribute to the improvement of teachers' training and support in many ways, considering how successfully it has been utilized to improve the ways teachers are trained and supported by EWCs since the COVID-19 outbreak. At the same time, however, policy makers and education officials should take specific steps in order to assist EWCs in utilizing Microsoft Teams for teachers' training and educational work support.

Unemployment is the main problem within many countries, and it has been increasing in the past few years especially during pandemic COVID-19, not only concerning for fresh graduates but also for people with disabilities. This study is made to understand the factors leading to job opportunities among people with disabilities, which are education, training, job placement, and internship. The study also aims to find challenges and barriers to job opportunity among people with disabilities. It aims to create awareness regarding people with disabilities to be accepted in the society as differently abled persons with specialties. The study findings shows that there is correlation between education, training, job placement, and internship for both hiring and non-hiring companies. To conclude, research findings show that training and work placement experience are factors of job opportunity for people with disabilities. The main challenges or barriers are communication, attitudes, and perceptions of co-workers towards employees with disabilities.

COVID-19 caused a drastic closure of universities with traditional campus instruction. The university discussed in this chapter is a large institution out of which two campuses were examined for remote faculty

Preface

The outbreak of the pandemic around the world came with national measures to deal with the health emergency that caused and probably will cause important disruption in education for students, teachers, and policy makers.

On July 21, 2020 European leaders agreed on a recovery plan and European long-term budget 2021-2027 (European Commission, 2021). Digital technologies can provide innovative solutions during COVID-19 in order to prevent the negative effects of lockdowns of countries and regions. It is important to analyze digital solutions and experiences for distant learning, know better the available resources and best practices to deal effectively with COVID-19 challenges for learners and academic staff. Countries need to promote digital excellency and explore the opportunities that information technologies can provide to education institutions, especially in the post-COVID-19 scenario and the major transformations it will bring to citizens, economies, and societies (Dascalu *et al.*, 2019; Xi, Liu and Ordóñez, 2014; Xi *et al.*, 2019; Zhang and Yu, 2021).

OBJECTIVE

The book will explore the new demands of labor markets in the digital economy, how educational institutions can respond to these new opportunities and threats, the development of new teaching and learning methods, and finally the development of digital skills and competences.

The book will offer a reference for a wide number of stakeholders interested in how to face the challenges and opportunities offered by COVID-19 in the area of education to transform education (schools and universities) with the support of information technologies and develop a new workforce with the required digital skills, competences and knowledge to fit in the post-COVID-19 labour market.

CONTENTS OF THE BOOK

The book is formed by a collection of 16 book chapters that address new and emerging issues in the field of digital transformation of education and challenges.

The first chapter, titled "Challenges and Opportunities of Online Learning Amidst the COVID-19 Pandemic in Brunei Darussalam" (by Mohammad Nabil Almunawar and Muhammad Anshari Ali), proposes that educational institutions in Brunei have transitioned into an online mode of learning due to the pandemic of COVID 19 that challenged the education system, forcing educators to change their method of teaching. The aim of this research is to investigate the challenges and opportunities risen from online learning during the pandemic. Brunei are one of the few countries that did not enforce lockdown measures but enforced strict measures to contain the pandemic. The pandemic has greatly affected the government, businesses and the educational institutes of the nation. Challenges include digital transformation and educational operability while opportunities emphasize on technological innovations and reassessing the education system.

Chapter 2, titled "Comparative Studies on Inclusive Digital Teaching in Higher Education in Light of COVID-19" (by Andreas Ahrens, Parulkumari Bhati, Alena Leshchenko, Jeļena Zaščerinska, Olga Gukovica, Mihails Zascerinskis, and Anastasija Aleksejeva), states that the pandemic COVID-19 has disrupted the higher education sector which is a critical determinant of a country's economic future. The manuscript aim is to compare the views of teachers and students on inclusive digital teaching in higher education during the pandemic COVID-19. The meaning of "inclusive digital teaching" and "view" is studied. The empirical study was carried out in September-November 2020. 40 respondents from Germany, Latvia, India, Ukraine and South Africa participated in the study. The data were collected via a semi-structural interview. The theoretical findings allow defining inclusive digital teaching and its criteria and indicators. The positive views on inclusive digital teaching in higher education during the pandemic COVID-19 were expressed by the university teachers. The students' views were more negative. The novel contribution of this manuscript is the implications on inclusive digital teaching in higher education. Directions of further research are formulated.

Chapter 3, titled "Knowledge Management and Blended Learning: Towards a Compatibility and Complementarity Model" (by Fahmi Ibrahim and Nena Padilla-Valdez), aims to discuss about the compatibility and complementarity of blended learning and Knowledge Management (KM) and their relationship. Blended learning which combines classroom instruction with e-learning while KM is the process of creating, capturing, disseminating, applying and managing organizational knowledge. This chapter illustrates how attention to two main perspectives exists in KM field, namely: objectivist perspective and practice-based perspective can inform the learning and teaching approach, the deep and surface learning. Yet they are two complementary processes if they are properly integrated. From here, a shift to the need to rethink and restructure the learning and teaching experience occurs and its transformative potential is analysed. This book chapter proposes a TWO-C (Compatible & Complementarity -2C) model which accommodates the blended learning and KM simultaneously. This suggests an integrated approach to provide for a balanced strategy in terms of both blended learning with KM approach can be applied in Higher Education Institution (HEI).

Chapter 4, titled "Business Simulation Games: A Direction in the New Era of Teaching and Learning" (by Chai-Lee Goi), states that a dynamic business environment and changing economic conditions require the reorientation and modification of educational programs. The learning process should focus on strengthening knowledge, skills, behaviours, and attitudes according to market needs and wants. The use of business simulation games in education can overcome this problem and even increase student motivation and engagement. This book chapter covers three main sections: (1) history of business simulation games; (3) types of business simulation games; and (3) the use of business simulation games in teaching and learning.

Chapter 5, titled "The Digital Divide in the World of Education at the Time of COVID-19" (by Giovanni Bronzetti, Graziella Sicoli and Dominga Ippolito), states that education has always been a challenge, today even more so given the difficulties of the moment, to support school in the time of Covid-19. Schools at every level have reorganized the training offer, implementing technological solutions. All this has raised a problem: the division is no longer between those who have access to the network and those who do not, but between those who know and those who do not know these new tools. knowledge support. Thus, lately the concept of digital divide, understood as a gap of opportunity between those who have and those who do not have digital skills, has evolved into the concept of digital inequality. Given these premises, the work investigates after careful analysis of the impact of digital systems on the educational system, such as the emergence of the "digital divide", impacts on training within universities. To verify the "digital divide", the work proposes a quantitative survey carried out through a questionnaire submitted to a sample of students. The subject of the survey is given by the students of the University of Calabria.

Chapter 6, titled "Student and Educator Perspective on Unconventional Online Classes" (by Muhammad Azmi Sait and Hajah Fathiin Najihah binti Haji Mohd Rozaini), aims to gain insights on students' and educators' perspective of the current unconventional learning and teaching methods carried out during COVID-19 pandemic. The main data is sourced from (Brunei Computer Emergency Response Team's online survey responded by 785 students and 664 educators, conducted during the closing downs of educational institutes due to preventive measures imposed by the government of Brunei Darussalam. The result shows that 77.96% of students and 72.14% of educators preferred the conventional classes. The main reasons are due to their inability to acquire good internet connectivity and proper area and time management that suits best to this online classes. In addition to that, the respondents perceived that the aforementioned problems become the root cause of their low discipline, productivity and motivation to conduct and attend such classes. This paper would be beneficial as a guideline to synthesize better teaching and learning strategies in online settings in the future.

Chapter 7, titled "Augmented Reality Towards Informative Educational Environment Digitalizing Interactive Learning" (by Saleem Nazamudeen, Heru Susanto, and Fadzliwati Mohiddin), studies that the impact on educational areas and the surrounding environment from the interactive learning perspective on how it can enhance learning practices using the augmented reality medium. The purpose of the analysis is to find the direction that the transformation of the knowledge process has evolved over the course of time, and how it supports society and the community through an efficient method of learning diversification.

Chapter 8, titled "Three Parties Engagement of Learning Management System: Students-Lecturer Technology Evidence From Brunei" (by Fadzliwati Mohiddin, Heru Susanto and Saleem Nazamudeen), presents the results of a study to investigate e-learning acceptance and factors influencing higher institutions students. Among the factors involved in this study were perceived ease of use, perceived usefulness, self-efficacy, technology availability and usage and intention to use. Technology acceptance models (TAM) were used as a basis for the study and for hypothesizing the effects of such variables on the use of e-learning. The research methods used were inclined to the use of quantitative methods of online questionnaire surveys that consist of 23 items based on a Likert scale. The findings of this study found that there is significant influence of self-efficacy to perceived ease of use and perceived usefulness while perceived ease of use have direct impact to perceived usefulness and perceived usefulness have influence to intention to use towards e-learning systems.

Chapter 9, titled "ICT Emerging Technology Impact Within Learning Ecosystem Cyberbullying Among Students: Facts or Rumors?" (by Desi Setiana and Norainna Besar), reveals cyberbullying perspective of the information technology age particularly in student's beliefs and behaviours. Cyberbullying has become an issue that's arising with the advancement of technology in which it makes it easier for everyone in the world to be connected wirelessly. The result of the study is very interesting. More than half of the participants have reported that they spent most of their free time on social media. Due to that, some of them have experienced cyberbullying but less than half of the students have actually reported the case. Moreover, social networking sites and any chat sites were found to be the platforms where cyberbullying has mostly been occurred, with email, texting on mobile phones as well as gaming online also used for cyberbullying. Although majority of the participants have witnessed number of cyberbullying, they preferred to ignore the issue instead of reporting it. According to the survey and deep interview, most of the students have mentioned that there is lack of supports regarding this cyberbullying.

Chapter 10, titled "Distance Education in Times of COVID-19 in Mexico: The Case of the Instituto Politécnico Nacional at the Postgraduate Level" (by Edgar Oliver Cardoso Espinosa, María Elena Zepeda Hurtado, and Jésica Alhelí Cortés Ruiz), aims to assess distance education in times of COVID-19 through the implementation of the Virtual Plan for Academic Continuity of the Instituto Politécnico Nacional (IPN) in order to identify good educational practices at the postgraduate level. A quantitative methodology with an exploratory-descriptive scope was used. The participants of the study were students who were pursuing a graduate degree during confinement. The main results are a positive assessment of distance education in terms of the incorporation and continuous use of digital resources, the use of continuous evaluation, the usefulness of technological tools, as well as an interaction with the teaching staff to review the academic progress of the student.

Chapter 11, titled "IT Opportunities for Teachers' Training and Support: An Action Research During the COVID-19 Pandemic in Greece" (by Antonios Kokkonos and Maria Korres), states that the evolution in the field of internet technologies and the spectacular acceptance of the worldwide web have shaped a new framework, not only for teachers' training but also for their distant support. This study provides insights into the utilization of Microsoft Teams digital collaboration and communication environment to improve the ways teachers are trained and supported by Educational Work Coordinators (EWCs), through an action research conducted in Peloponnese Regional Educational Planning Center, Greece. Research results reveal that Microsoft Teams can contribute to the improvement of teachers' training and support in many ways, considering how successfully it has been utilized to improve the ways teachers are trained and supported by EWCs since the covid-19 outbreak. At the same time, however, policy makers and education officials should take specific steps in order to assist EWCs in utilizing Microsoft Teams for teachers' training and educational work support.

Chapter 12, titled "Role of Learning Technology Strategies Among People With Disabilities: A Job Opportunities Barrier" (by Heru Susanto, Hamizah Hamid, Saleem Nazamudeen, Fadzliwati Mohiddin, and Desi Setiana), addresses unemployment. In particular, it aims to understand the factors leading to job opportunities among people with disabilities which is education, trainings, job placement and internship. The study also aims to find challenges and barriers to job opportunity among people with disabilities. It aims to create awareness regarding people with disabilities to be accepted in the society as differently able person with speciality. The study findings show that there is correlation between education, education, trainings, job placement and internship for both hiring and non-hiring companies. To conclude research finding shows that trainings and work placement experience are factors to job opportunity for people with disabilities. The main challenges or barrier is communication, attitudes and perception of co-workers towards employee with disabilities.

Chapter 13, titled "Analyzing IT Opportunities for Inclusive Digital Learning: The Largest Academic Project Ever Implemented During the COVID-19 Era" (by Mina Richards), states that COVID-19 caused a drastic closure of universities with traditional campus instruction. The University discussed in this chapter is a large institution out of which two campuses were examined for remote faculty training and student impact. The results from two short surveys for students and faculty are presented. Faculty responses focused on the perspective of facilitating remote courses and what direct impact remote teaching has had on their personal life. The students' responses were mixed. Some participants stated that remote courses positively impacted their self-engagement and performance, and the remaining said that they had noticed a downward trend in performance. Five lessons learned are derived from observations and participants' provided information regarding the lack of communication and faculty engagement in training. By identifying the lessons learned, recommendations for each are provided for future-readiness and insights on how to influence engagement and approach communications and faculty attitude factors.

Chapter 14, titled "Digital Technologies for Teaching and Learning at the BoP: A Managerial Perspective" (by Alessia Pisoni, Alessandra Corti, and Rafaela Gjergji), addresses digital technologies for teaching and learning/ICT for education. The topic under investigation was approached under a managerial perspective, i.e. with the final aim to identify and describe the main factors that enable and/or inhibit successful implementation of digital technologies for teaching and learning at the Bottom of the Pyramid (BoP). First of all, a comprehensive and systemized literature review has been performed outlining/identifying these factors. Then, to robustly grasp our findings, a deeper assessment through a multiple descriptive case study analysis on the key factors behind a successful implementation of ICTs for education at the BoP level has been carried out.

Chapter 15, titled "Study of Blended Learning in Higher Education and the Role of Social Media Applications with Special Reference to Vietnam" (by Thanh Hong Lam, Jaheer KP, Lanh Thanh Le, Hien Le, Nam Nguyen, and Bao Quoc Do), analyses the effect of the combination of learning methods, in which diverse IT resources are applied to facilitate study activities of Vietnamese undergraduate students. The main Focus of this study is that in the blended learning context of Vietnam education, the combination of various communication means such as face-to-face (F2F) and traditional education technologies can enable the level of engagement of students with the blended courses. The study measured the level of students' engagement in the blended learning program, in which physical classrooms and different IT resources are implemented. We distinguish two kinds of IT resources: traditional education technologies and social media applications. It is proposed that while F2F classrooms and traditional education technologies can enable students' engagement, which leads to stronger satisfaction and motivation. Meanwhile, social media applications are believed can intensify those relationships.

Chapter 16, titled "Implications of Knowledge Management Adoption Within Higher Education Institutions: Business Process Reengineering Approach" (by Fadzliwati Mohiddin, Heru Susanto, Fahmi Ibrahim, Saleem Nazamudeen, and Desi Setiana), aims to understand knowledge management system (KMS) practices and perception within HEIs. This research will focus on three main aspects. The first aspect will be on identifying management tools used at the organizational level. Secondly, the supportive and hindrance factors on the adoption of KMS, and the user perception and practices of KMS in the institution. A mix of methodologies is adapted to generate findings for this research. Both quantitative and qualitative methods will be used for this research through a questionnaire approach. The questionnaire is constructed in such a way that close-ended questions and open-ended questions are included. The research has led to several important outcomes for the implementation of KMS in HEIs. This study has proposed a conceptual framework and the support from other research outcomes, i.e. identification of the management tools used, the support and barriers for implementation, and user perception and practices for the KMS implementations.

ACKNOWLEDGMENT

We would like to thank authors for their interest in participation in this book as well as the members of the Editorial Advisory Board and reviewers for the time and efforts they invested in choosing the best collection of chapters for this book. Thank you very much to all of you.

Patricia Ordóñez de Pablos
University of Oviedo, Spain

Mohammad Nabil Almunawar
Universiti Brunei Darussalam, Brunei

Kwok Tai Chui
The Open University of Hong Kong, Hong Kong

Maniam Kaliannan
Business School, Nottingham University, Malaysia

REFERENCES

Chang, W. L., & Yeh, Y. C. (2021). A blended design of game-based learning for motivation, knowledge sharing and critical thinking enhancement. *Technology, Pedagogy and Education*, 1–15. Advance online publication. doi:10.1080/1475939X.2021.1885482

Dascalu, M. I., Bodea, C. N., Mihailescu, M. N., Tanase, E. A., & Ordóñez de Pablos, P. (2016). Educational recommender systems and their application in lifelong learning. *Behaviour & Information Technology*, *35*(4), 290–297. doi:10.1080/0144929X.2015.1128977

European Commission. (2021). *2021-2027 long-term EU budget*. Accessed on March 14, 2021. https://ec.europa.eu/info/strategy/eu-budget/long-term-eu-budget/2021-2027_en

Xi, Z., Liu, L., & Ordóñez de Pablos, P. (2014). *The auxiliary role of information technology in teaching: enhancing programming course using Alice. International Journal of Engineering Education, 30(3).*

Xi, Z., Meng, Y., Ordóñez de Pablos, P., & Sun, Y. (2019). Learning analytics in collaborative learning supported by Slack: From the perspective of engagement. *Computers in Human Behavior*, *92*(March), 625–633.

Zhang, Q., & Yu, Z. (2021). A literature review on the influence of Kahoot! On learning outcomes, interaction, and collaboration. *Education and Information Technologies*. Advance online publication. doi:10.100710639-021-10459-6

Chapter 1
Challenges and Opportunities of Online Learning Amidst the COVID-19 Pandemic in Brunei Darussalam

Mohammad Alif Azizi Abdullah
Universiti Brunei Darussalam, Brunei

Mohammad Nabil Almunawar
https://orcid.org/0000-0001-5296-2576
Universiti Brunei Darussalam, Brunei

Muhammad Anshari Ali
https://orcid.org/0000-0002-8160-6682
Universiti Brunei Darussalam, Brunei

ABSTRACT

Educational institutions in Brunei have transitioned into an online mode of learning due to the pandemic of COVID-19 that challenged the education system, forcing educators to change their method of teaching. The aim of this research is to investigate the challenges and opportunities risen from online learning during the pandemic. Brunei is one of the few countries that did not enforce lockdown measures but enforced strict measures to contain the pandemic. The pandemic has greatly affected the government, businesses, and the educational institutes of the nation. Challenges include digital transformation and educational operability while opportunities emphasize on technological innovations and reassessing the education system.

DOI: 10.4018/978-1-7998-7184-2.ch001

INTRODUCTION

Educational institutions (schools, colleges, and universities) in Brunei Darussalam incessantly practices and are based on traditional systems of learning which is face-to-face interaction within a classroom between students and the teacher (Dhawan, 2020). Although in some cases, blended learning is increasing in application globally, it is difficult to move away from the traditional methods of learning. The unexpected global outbreak of the COVID-19 pandemic sent shocks throughout the world. With social distancing enforced globally, it has negatively impacted learning opportunities in educational institutions where these institutions faced difficulties in coping with the formidable conditions. These conditions have highlighted the importance of scenario planning which are needed for educational institutions. The pandemic has disrupted all aspects of education all the around the world, including in Brunei Darussalam. The difficult state of Brunei in the pandemic offered a stern challenge to the education system of Brunei. This situation forced education personnel of Brunei to transition from traditional methods of teaching to unchartered waters of online learning mode of teaching in a limited time frame. The sudden change of learning modes also impacted other factors that were key in the transition between learning modes which are the students and the parents. Due to the pandemic, educational institutions in Brunei were forced to remain closed temporarily.

While it was uncertain to resume normal teaching in Brunei due to social distancing measures enforced by the government and the ministry of health in hope to combat the pandemic. The sudden transition from face-to-face learning to online learning have posed challenges to students and lecturers. Thus, with social distancing in place, it negatively influences learning options nationwide. Online learning was constantly discussed to address the learning issues due to the pandemic. Few controversies related to e-learning proved to be a valid stumbling block with regards to the current state of Brunei. While the pandemic proved to be a difficult time for educators, students and parents within the education system. It also provided hope of moving forward with the use of technology and innovation for educational institutions. The circumstances require understanding and solidarity of every nations education workers in order to preserve and protect the students, communities, staff and the nation generally.

This objective of this research is to identify the challenges and opportunities of online learning in Brunei with the backdrop of the COVID-19 pandemic. It is interesting to identify these factors that are unique from other nations' struggle towards adapting the online mode of learning. While opportunities from online learning can be used to improve and strengthen the education system of Brunei. The rest of the research is organized as follows: the next section is the literature review supporting the research, research methodology before presenting significant timeline of online learning in Brunei, followed by the challenges and opportunities of online learning. The last section of the research consists of the conclusion and recommendations for future studies.

LITERATURE REVIEW

Online Learning or E-Learning

The progression in technologies and the Internet have considerably altered the way of life of individuals and have produced an immense shift in numerous areas (Nadikattu, 2020). McBrien et al. (2009) argued that the development and innovation in technology have enabled remote learning or education effortless which makes online learning highly applicable to the situation of the pandemic that have affected all aspects of education. Particularly in education institutions, online learning became an important medium to successfully maintain the teaching-learning procedure during the closure of institutions around the world. The world wide web has turned into one of the influential method of learning that gives individuals the chance to access education effortlessly at no cost or lower cost (Noor-Ul-Amin, 2013). Online learning or e-learning comprises of technology supported applications used for learning through learning portal, web pages, YouTube, video conferencing, mobile applications and many more blended learning resources that are available online (Shahzad et al. 2020). Presently, online learning is improving learners and students' knowledge, where academic personnel, experts, and industry workers upgrade their skills online (Adams et al. 2018; Chopra et al. 2019). Online learning or e-learning has turned into a significant feature of education around the world which was due to the COVID 19 pandemic, its usage and importance have rapidly progressed in 2020. Online learning has developed their origin in order to accommodate the demand of modern learners. The phrase web-based learning, online learning and blended learning have a similarity of using a computer linked to a network, that provides the ability to facilitate learning anytime, anywhere, in any occasion and any medium (Cojocariu et al. 2014). Online learning can be referred to as an apparatus in making the process of teaching and learning towards a student-focused, unconventional, and adaptable. Fry (2001) expressed online learning as the utilization of the Internet and other essential technologies to create items for educational reasons, the delivery of guidelines and program management. Hrastinski (2008) mentioned that there are two forms of online learning, particularly asynchronous and synchronous methods of e-learning, but for e-learning to be successful and effective, educators, institutions and organizations need to possess an extensive knowledge of the positive impacts and its constraints. Online learning is determined as the educational experiences in a contemporary or self-paced surroundings using various gadgets (e.g., smartphones, laptops, etc.) connected to Internet access. Singh & Thurman (2019) claimed that within these surroundings, student can be self-reliant in learning and interacting with educators and their peers. This synchronized learning conditions is organized in a way that students participate in lectures in real-time and unrecorded that allows live responses between teachers and students and enables immediate responses. According to McBrien et al. (2009), synchronous learning has the ability to provide many social interaction possibilities. Furthermore, Basilaia et al. (2020) claimed that in the middle of the COVID-19 pandemic, online platforms are required where (a) video conferencing with students of 40-50 is achievable (b) allowing discussions with students to maintain the structure or naturality of lessons (c) stable internet connections (d) classes are made available through smartphones not just laptops, (e) potential to watch pre-recorded classes, (f) immediate feedback from students can be obtained while assignments can be received.

While online platforms is part of a digital transformation in the transition of conducting businesses and services through online mediums or platforms, it has been recently associated with higher education institutions (Kopp et al., 2019; Leszczyński et al., 2018). During the pandemic, teachers and instructors have been employing online learning platforms to broadcast education to their students which the learning method performed via electronic mediums. Soni (2020) claimed that online learning or virtual learning provides an alternative way to share reading resources via the Internet through documents, emails, presentations or webinars. IT (information technology) is an essential component of modern day education that highlights the deep connection of ICT in the current teaching-learning process (Anderson, 2005). According to Felix (2020), lectures are also conducted through WeChat by exchanging audio-visual clips through emails, using various e-learning applications such as Voov, Zoom, Superstar, and g-suite cloud meeting. The advancement of technologies has provided an encouraging area for the teaching-learning system. Thamarana (2016) argued that these applications offer educators to alter their educational method and improve teaching and learning methods.

There are a countless number of technologies made available for online learning but to some extent some of these technologies posed issues for its users. The problems mentioned are mainly due to the issues related to the availability of latest technologies that includes errors, installation problems, login issues, issues with video and audio and other related problems with connectivity. A situation can just be imagined on how time consuming for educators to carry out an online lecture with students experiencing one of these problems which issues can vary through different learning platforms. While online learning demands time and adaptability from students, students consider the poor association, technical issues, and concerns in understanding educational objectives are the significant constraints for online learning (Song et al. 2004). With numerous problems associated with online learning, it could not be ignored in times of the COVID 19 pandemic. Measures should be considered to improve the process of learning to its optimum level of operation. Personal consideration should be given to students to allow better adaptation to the new learning circumstances. The key to a successful learning process with students is the communication between the educator and learner where the teachers should consistently improve the courses or modules taught that can enable students to practice and also improve their personal skills. According to Partlow and Gibbs (2003), online learning should be configured to be innovative, interactive, applicable, learner-centered, and team-based. Teachers should spend their time in building a productive plan to give online instructions. Successful online instructions encourages comments or response from students, stimulates questions from students, and expands the students perspective on content of the course or module (Keeton, 2004). One significant challenge for educational institutions is not only limited to determining latest technology and utilizing it but also reassessing its education, consequently assisting students and academic personnel that requires supervision on digital knowledge.

Sandkuhl and Lehmann (2017) claimed that most of universities and schools have designed plans of digitalization and modern ways to replace their traditional ways in education. However, these digitalization plans and strategies are often limited to converting lecture contents to digital contents and providing access to students' modules through an online website or platform. These features can be found in higher educational institutes in Brunei namely Universiti Brunei Darussalam (UBD) and Universiti *Teknologi* Brunei (UTB) where lectures slide and notes can be found online through a specific platform while modules can be accessed through students' respective accounts. Digital transformation in higher education institutions is a highly relevant matter that causes concern amongst educational stakeholders where the competency to implement ICT in every aspect of life are at a progressive stage, resulting in higher education institutions preparing themselves in developing experts in facing challenges and providing solutions (Bond et al., 2018; Sandkuhl & Lehmann, 2017). This is similar to the case of educational institutes in Brunei during the pandemic where it was made compulsory to adopt technologies and be competent in ICT to facilitate the learning and education process during the pandemic.

Dhawan (2020) states that through online approach of learning makes it readily available to access which can reach remote and rural regions, viewed as a low-cost method of education that projects cost effective transportation, accommodation, and the general cost of inexpensive learning through institutions. Flexibility is another intriguing element of online learning where the learner is able to arrange or schedule convenient time to finish accessible online courses. Merging direct (face-to-face) lectures with technology paved the way for blended learning and flipped classroom where learners are presented with materials at home and doing assignments independently. This form of learning setting has the potential to positively impact the learning capacity of students. Learners or students have the option to learn anywhere and anytime, consequently acquiring new abilities through the process. According to Carey (2020), during the difficult time of the COVID 19 pandemic, the issue surrounding it was more towards on how educational institutions are able to embrace online learning or e-learning in such a significant nature.

Several studies have investigated the effect or impact of COVID 19 pandemic to e-learning in different perspectives. A research by Sathishkumar et al. (2020) investigated student's attitude towards e-learning amidst the enforced lockdown during the pandemic that incorporates students from different schools, colleges, and universities across the world. The research focused on students that are accustomed to online-based technologies where it also assisted in determining solutions to boost students' self-learning capability. Due to the pandemic, teaching staff are forced to consider other learning tools during the lockdown. As a result, it has opened the passage for e-learning and web-based learning to be adopted. The digital world has facilitated the virtual connection between teaching staff and students. E-learning is seen as straightforward to comprehend and implement using laptop, desktop, or smartphones via the Internet that represent the major component used in e-learning. Online learning has progressed rapidly and have shown to be the leading approach in education during the lockdown. The study by Sathishkumar et al. (2020) established that there is positive feedback regarding e-learning among students. Furthermore, there is a good percentage of interest and growing application in online learning applications towards academic purposes. While this may be the case, majority of students does not prefer e-learning than virtual learning (face-to-face). The study concluded that e-learning have grown in stature and popularity among students because of its usability and functionality to enable learning, specifically during the lockdown.

A study by Alhumaid et al. (2020) investigated the perceptions and attitudes of teachers or educators towards online learning during the COVID 19 pandemic. The study aims to explore the teachers' side of perception in relation with e-learning as a replacement to conventional learning. While e-learning has replaced the standard conventional classroom setting all around the world, online learning act as a direct alternative in continuing learning activities. By using the technology acceptance model (TAM), the study carried out multiple regression analysis to reaffirm the hypotheses of the research. Findings discovered a positive correlation between the acceptance of technology and e-learning during COVID 19 in Pakistan. Generally, the respondents showed encouraging views on acceptance of e-learning amidst the lockdown conditions and its influence on students' educational achievements. Though, due to poor infrastructure, the Education Ministry of Pakistan are faced with numerous obstacles in implementing online learning. In conclusion, the study highlights the growing dependence on web-based technology during the COVID 19 outbreak. Individuals around the globe are relying strongly on online platforms to engage in leisure, communicate, and collect information. In the same manner the educational system is relying heavily on technologies to proceed with educational activities.

Online learning is facing numerous issues from students' issues, teachers' issues, and material issues. It can be a challenge for teachers from educational institutions to tempt students and persuade them to be involved in the teaching-learning system. For teachers, it can be a challenge for them to change from traditional teaching to online learning, modifying their way of teaching and their time management. It can be a difficult task to produce teaching materials that does not only cover the syllabus but also demands participation from the students Kebritchi et al. (2017). According to Affouneh et al. (2020), the advantages on the acceptance of online learning should not be given much emphasis during the current COVID 19 situation but emphasis should be given in improving the quality of online education provided in such condition. Online learning is not as easy as it seems, it requires plenty of time and cost which requires a substantial amount of funds for equipment, maintenance, human resource training, and the development of online materials. Thus, an operative and systematic educational structure is needed to convey education via online mode of learning. Dhawan (2020) expressed that assuring digital equity is vital given the current situation, due to not all teachers and students have access to digital gadgets, Internet, and Wi-Fi. Absence of suitable digital equipment, unavailability of internet connections, and unpredictable Wi-Fi connections can cause difficulties from a student's perspective that can cause students to lose the opportunity to learn. Appropriate actions should be taken by educational institutions to guarantee that every student and faculty have access to necessary resources. Educational institutions should also assure that all learning platforms and applications work on smartphones, in the case students do not have access to laptops in which to decrease digital partition between students and online learning.

Although online learning has its challenges, many opportunities has also emerged which was made available due to the swift increase in application around the world as majority of educational institutions have utilized this model. In the present time, educational institutions have the chance to promote their teachers use and their student to learn via online methods. Individuals have always been comfortable and never bothered to explore other alternatives of learning and teaching.

A case study by Ayebi-Arthur (2017) of a college in New Zealand which was heavily impacted due to earthquakes. The study discovered that the college was more resistant to online learning after the natural occurrence where technologies assisted them to overcome the obstacles. It was suggested that a sturdy IT foundation is an essential component for online learning. The base needs to be robust to deliver unobstructed services during and after the occurrence.

A research by Babu & Reddy (2015) examined the e-learning conditions of both developed and developing countries. E-learning or online learning offers students flexibility and a simple environment that costs less and providing a suitable time and place to learn and study. Significant factors such as user perception and readiness play a major role in the effectiveness of e-learning in both developing and developed countries. Besides these factors, government financial assistance, student's motivation and well-educated tutors are vital of achieving effective application of e-learning. In developed countries, e-learning is viewed as the obligation of the government and not only the burden of educational institutions, the UK established a council called quality of assurance agency (QAA) as the guideline for e-learning. While developed countries are encouraging the application of e-learning, the universities are more involved in maintaining their teaching approaches and are not entire dependent on technology. In developing countries, countries rely on traditional methods of teaching rather than online learning for higher education.

METHODOLOGY

The research focuses on secondary data sources consisting of timelines and official statements from government publication (press conferences). The scope of the research emphasizes on data and information from the Ministry of Education Brunei. The research is solely on Brunei Darussalam and its current state of online learning during the pandemic. Data collected from the Ministry of Health will then be analyzed and put into a timeline to provide clarification of relevant regulations that have been implemented to support the transition towards online learning in Brunei. Collection of data also includes other important factors of the research which includes the challenges faced during online learning modes. Analysis of data collected will identify recommendations on the success of online learning with regards to the current state of Brunei's education system with the support of other secondary data sources (online journals, e-books and articles).

Data Collection

Data collection prioritize on the rules and regulations that have been implemented by the Ministry of Education (MOE) in-line with the government's enforced rules on the COVID-19 pandemic. These rules and regulations have been introduced in phases through press conferences since the closure of educational institutions to ensure smooth transition between learning modes. Data of relevant information on rules and regulations from press conferences are then collected to identify challenges and opportunities. Data collected for the timeline within the chapter are gathered from the official website of Ministry of Education Brunei (Ministry of Education, 2021).

IMPORTANT TIMELINE OF ONLINE LEARNING DURING COVID 19 IN BRUNEI DARUSSALAM

Detection of the First Case of COVID 19 Infection in Brunei Darussalam – 9th March 2020

Brunei Darussalam enforced a travel ban for Bruneians travelling to infected countries in a measure to protect the safety of the population from COVID 19. Inessential travel was forced to be deferred to lessen the likelihood of imported case entering Brunei. Individuals returning to Brunei are required to go through 14 days of self-isolation.

The Ministry of Health (MOH) of Brunei Darussalam confirmed an initial test for COVID 19 had returned positive for a 53-year-old male who returned from Kuala Lumpur on 3rd March 2020. The detection of the first case has brought increasing number of cases afterward. The subsequent cases were all related to the Kuala Lumpur cluster. From the first detected case, the whole nation was updated daily through press conferences on the latest situation of COVID 19.

Closure of Educational Institutions Nationwide – 11th March 2020

The closure of schools nationwide was announced one week before the first term school holiday. Activities such as mass gatherings, dining in at restaurants and cafes and social meetings were all prohibited. Social distancing was enforced and personal hygiene were recommended to the population. A one-nation method was implemented by the Brunei government to combat the COVID 19 infection. Sudden closure of schools has prompted the Ministry of Education to reassess other tools to facilitate teaching and learning despite the current situation of the virus in Brunei Darussalam.

Universiti Teknologi Brunei (UTB) Survey on Delivering Online Education Platform Usage during COVID-19 Crisis – 14th March 2020

UTB had considered other emergency situations to curb the spread of the virus while guaranteeing the continuation of research and teaching objectives, including transitioning towards online and remote guidelines. With the situation of the pandemic growing globally as well as in Brunei, UTB prioritizes the health, safety, and the welfare of its community and students in moving forward. The objective of the enforced social distancing measure is to restrain the number of situations where students and lecturers are assembled together in large groups and spending time in close distance with each other in classrooms, labs and common rooms. The aim of the survey is to investigate the possibility of effectiveness of online teaching, students' experiences and satisfaction, and to identify transformational challenges faced when teaching online. From the survey, 670 responses were collected making the response rate of approximately 45 per cent of UTB's student population. The survey indicates that for online application deliverable, 64 per cent of respondents used UTB Learning Management System (MOODLE), 61 per cent, Microsoft Teams, 40 per cent, Zoom, 22 per cent, Skype, four per cent, Google Hangout and nine per cent, other online technologies. The survey suggests that, although in general students were satisfied with the quality of screen sharing, audio, video and presentation slides, they also faced challenges and showed some concerns. A total of 35 per cent respondents are not satisfied with the Internet bandwidth. The survey stated that it is significant to mention that the unfavorable experience would be temporary, at least for the lecturers' issues.

Cancellation of Brunei Cambridge General Certificate of Education (BC GCE) Examination 'O', 'US', and 'A' Level and Brunei Cambridge International General Certificate of Secondary Education (IGCSE) – 25th March 2020

Following the spread of COVID-19, Ministry of Education priorities is to ensure the health and welfare of students and teachers and the public in general. Thus, the Cambridge Assessment International Education (CAIE) has decided not to conduct all international examination for the May/June 2020 session. For the case of Brunei Darussalam, the examinations that will not be conducted are the Brunei Cambridge International General Certificate of Secondary Education (IGCSE), Brunei Cambridge General Certificate of Education (BG GCE) 'O', 'US' and 'A' Level which has been scheduled to start in April until June 2020. The cancellation of the international exam is to ensure no large gatherings in halls for the examinations to take place.

Online Leaning and Teaching (Online) for the Second Term School – 30th March 2020

The Ministry of Education in consultation with the Ministry of Health have informed that the teaching and learning for all primary, secondary, sixth form centers, vocational schools and Brunei Institute of Technical Education (IBTE) under the control of the Ministry of Education and also including schools under the control of the Ministry of Religious Affairs, private schools will start on 30 March 2020 (online learning). For international schools, teaching and learning also to be conducted online that will start on the date set by the respective educational institutions.

To ensure the health and safety of students and assuring their well-being and protected from any possible infection, students are required to stay at home and follow online learning through various platforms according to the capacity of their respective schools either via Email, Google *Docs, WhatsApp, Video Conference, Microsoft Teams and* social media platforms or any suitable telecommunications application. In addition, schools also provide home-pack learning for students who do not have access to the internet. Education through TV shows will also be implemented as additional support for teaching and learning through the mass media.

Educational institution has also activated their Business *Continuity Plan (*BCP) to ensure the well-being of teachers and school people by providing flexibility for school people who fall into the *vulner-*

able category as stated by the Ministry of Health including those who are pregnant, to work from their respective homes (Work *from Home,* WFH).

Continuing Online Learning and Teaching – 9th April 2020

The Ministry of Education in consultation with the Ministry of Health have informed that to ensure the health and safety of students, the Ministry of Education has decided that students remain at home during the school session and the second term to continue the implementation of online teaching and learning for all primary, secondary schools, form six centers, vocational schools and the Brunei Institute of Technical Education (IBTE) under the control of the Ministry of Education including all schools in under the control of the Ministry of Religious Affairs, private schools from 13 April 2020 to 14 May 2020 while international schools are subject to the dates set by their respective educational institutions.

The special school holidays for the month of Ramadhan and Hari Raya Aidilfitri will start on 15 May 2020 to 31 May 2020. Thus, the next second term school session for all primary, secondary, form six centers, vocational schools and the Brunei Institute of Technical Education (IBTE) under the control of the Ministry of Education and also all schools under the control of the Ministry of Religious Affairs, as well as private schools will be started on 02 June 2020. For international schools, it is subject to the date set by the respective institution. However, the date and its implementation are still subject to the development of this COVID-19 pandemic infection.

Ministry of Education Receives a Donation of 100 Tablets – 22nd April 2020

The Ministry of Education received a donation of 100 units of new Lenovo tablets from Digital World Enterprise on the 22nd April 2020. The donation is a joint initiative of Ministry of Education, Ministry of Transport and Info-communications and Authority for Info-communications Technology Industry (AITI) in supporting online learning and to provide assistance to students in need amidst COVID-19 pandemic in the country. The donation drive to collect ICT devices to support online learning for students in need is one of the significant challenges faced by students and parents in Brunei. The absence of digital devices to facilitate online learning of student may well cause student to miss out on learning opportunities.

Computer Equipment Contributed to Five Schools – 30th April 2020

The result of a joint initiative of the Ministry of Education, the Ministry of Transport and Info-Communications and the Information and Communication Technology Industry Authority of Brunei Darussalam (AITI) which currently opens the contribution of computers, laptops and tablets from the public to support online learning and help students in need during the COVID-19 pandemic in the country, the Ministry of Education through the Department of Schools distributed the donation through the Computer Equipment Donation Distribution Counci. For the submission of this contribution, a total of 23 computer units were distributed to five (5) secondary schools.

The handing over of computer equipment to selected students is done in stages to avoid *mass gathering* to prevent the spread of the COVID -19 epidemic. The distribution of this equipment will continue to be further reduced to some schools that have students in need. This time, the distribution has been held using the drive- *thru method* taking into account *social distancing (social distancing)* to prevent and prevent the spread of the COVID-19 epidemic.

The Ministry of Education in collaboration with the Ministry of Transport and Info-communication and AITI have worked together to ensure that the donated computer equipment meets the minimum specifications required to be equipped with the installation of certain software for online learning purposes. Meanwhile, the Distribution Committee, Ministry of Education has identified students who will receive this ICT equipment according to the criteria that have been set.

The cooperation of students and parents and guardians of selected students receiving this equipment is needed to be jointly responsible in ensuring that this equipment is used safely and as best as possible in the use of home learning, and not misused.

Restoration of Teaching and Learning Operations in Primary, Secondary Schools and Six Form Centers in Brunei – 2nd June 2020

With the return of the operational stages of teaching and learning for the second part of School Session of the 2nd Division in all primary schools, secondary schools, colleges, sixth form centers, vocational schools and the Australian Institute of Technical Education under the Ministry of Education and also including all schools under the control of the Ministry of Religious Affairs as well as private schools on 2 June 2020, with this schooling session, learning and teaching physically or '*face to face*' has started in stages.

This first stage has involved students who will sit for the public examination of 23,103 students which is 25.5% of the total number of students in Brunei Darussalam for schools under the Ministry of Education and the Ministry of Religious Affairs who are expected to start their school sessions.

In the first week of school opening, a total of 91.5% of students have attended face-*to-face* at their respective schools. The number has shown the commitment and trust of parents and guardians to the school by sending their children to school even though the country is still in a situation to deal with the COVID-19 pandemic.

In ensuring the well-being of students and school people, the school always emphasizes two important aspects, namely practicing social imprisonment and personal hygiene as well as school premises. In addition, the Ministry also conducts continuous monitoring using on-*line reporting*. As a result of the initial monitoring, it has been found that the seriousness of the school staff (teachers and students) to comply with the guidelines provided by the school in ensuring well-being, safety and health in preventing the spread of the COVID-19 epidemic.

Majority of all schools under the Ministry of Education and the Ministry of Religious Affairs have activated the QR scan code as recommended by the Ministry of Health. The use of QR scan codes can help schools monitor the health status of teachers and school staff and divide them into *Vulnerable* and Non-*Vulnerable* groups. For those who are in the *Vulnerable* category, subject to the discretion of their respective school leaders in planning the teaching schedule of teachers in ensuring the well-being of teachers and school people is guaranteed.

The Ministry of Education and the Ministry of Religious Affairs will monitor the implementation continuously in ensuring the implementation of learning and teaching sessions run smoothly. COVID-19 has changed the pattern of daily work ethic and is no exception in the field of Education. Therefore, the Ministry of Education is confident that the implementation of online learning and teaching is in line with the Industrial Revolution 4.0 era approach and is a future direction for the field of education. Therefore, improvements and strengthening in mastering teaching and learning methods based on technology will continue to be implemented in the post-COVID-19 time later.

CHALLENGES OF ONLINE LEARNING DURING COVID 19 IN BRUNEI

Due to the COVID 19 pandemic, it has emerged that the structure of education is vulnerable to outside hazards (Bozkurt & Sharma, 2020). Ribeiro (2020) accurately indicated that the digital transformation from traditional learning to online learning came with logistical issues and attitude alteration. The challenges of online learning may vary from nation to nation depending on the duration of severity of the pandemic and the duration of educational institutes closure. Challenges discussed are specifically to the case of Brunei that includes digital transformation and educational activities during COVID 19.

Technology

Online learning or e-learning rely heavily on technology and the Internet to provide a good experience, teachers and students with poor Internet connections are likely to be denied the opportunity to learn online. The heavy reliance on smart devices such as tablets and laptops were a big issue to tackle by the Brunei's educational institutions. Students or learners with outdated devices may find it hard to meet the technical requirements for online learning. Students could experience incompatibility to current online learning platforms or browsers required for them to learn. While the absence of personal gadgets or devices also plays a major part in the challenges of online learning. Not every student and teacher possess a personal device to be used for online learning. Majority of students are known to share laptops, tablets and desktop with their other siblings or family. While contributions from government and private sectors and businesses in Brunei have eased the shortage of gadgets during the period of online learning experience in Brunei. It has shown that the sudden transition to online mode of learning have impacted the digital usage of every family in Brunei. Furthermore, it shows proof there is a shortage of digital gadgets of devices among the population to cope with online learning. Access to technology and proper Internet connection provides students with infinite resources online, promoting them to conduct research and training them to be independent. The application of technology in online learning has the ability to motivate students to learn, exposing them to learn and explore through different websites, applications, videos, and educational games. The difference online learning brings compared to a conventional material used in physical classrooms can be used to help student stay engaged through online interaction.

Socio-Economic Factor

As a result of dissimilarity in the socio-economic status among students, some students rely on the computer and free Internet connections n school (Demirbilek, 2014), and due to the closure of educational institutions nationwide for Brunei, these group of students are in low numbers. It becomes unquestionable students with low socio-economic background are surely to experience difficulties in transitioning to online mode of learning initially due to the closure of school. Fishbane and Tomer (2020) research discovered that students that does not have access to the Internet shows that as the level of poverty increases in the community, the internet rate of internet accessibilities declined rapidly and by implications, students with no or low socio-economic power to afford broadband connection are most vulnerable to fall behind or encounter additional challenges to meet up with others in online learning. In the case of Brunei, schools are providing home-pack learning packages for parents and guardian that do not have access to Internet. These group of students may struggle in the initial stage of online learning due to the absence of proper internet connection to learn online.

Digital Competence

Digital competence refers to the group of expertise, understanding, and perspective needed when using ICT and digital gadgets to perform responsibilities, such as problem solving, information management, collaboration with respect to effectiveness, efficiency and ethics (Ferrari, 2012). Students and instructors with low digital competence are liable to lack behind in online learning. Due to digital transformation of instructional activities during this pandemic, libraries are to follow the trend in order to deliver effective services to faculty, students and other stakeholders through digital library, students and faculty with low digital competence might find it difficult to make optimal utilization of the digital library. Computer literacy also exists where teachers, students, and parents may find it difficult using learning management system (LMS) or any other digital tool out of a sudden with additional research and training. Digital competence is a significant factoring in assessing the challenges of implementing and utilizing online learning during the COVID 19 pandemic in Brunei. While higher educational institutes students have a better expected digital competence, they may be susceptible in operating new and latest developments of online learning platforms to be used by instructors and lecturers. However, in primary and lower secondary students may have low digital competence that may require supervision from parents and guardians in order to make their online learning experience a good one. This may be time consuming and can be a distraction to the whole online mode of learning.

OPPORTUNITIES OF ONLINE LEARNING DURING COVID 19 IN BRUNEI

The situation experience by the whole world have forced the education system to shift towards online learning. Online learning has its own benefits, such as its versatility (Smedley, 2010), interactive nature (Leszczyński et al., 2018; Wagner et al., 2008), self-study and opportunities.

Technological Innovations

With technologies and the Internet as the center of attention during the pandemic its usage is rapidly increasing in Brunei Darussalam while its functionality has prompted Internet service providers (ISPs) to acknowledge majority of the nation is connected and using their services. Government and private sectors also saw the opportunity in using technologies and connectivity to improve their operations while also improving the state and functionality of technologies used. For example, Internet packages are specifically crafted to fit the needs of students and educators to assist them to learn and teach during the difficult times.

The pandemic has forced the government and private sectors to develop their infrastructure and make use of digital mediums and digital channels to limit face to face interaction. For example, renewal of identification card and renewal of driving license were introduced during the pandemic to limit mass gathering and practicing social distancing in order to combat the pandemic. The BruHealth Application was also introduced in stages to the population of Brunei where it uses artificial intelligence and modern technologies to help the government with contact tracing as well as providing the nation with relevant information on the current developments of the pandemic.

Reassessing the Education System

The unexpected transition from traditional face-to-face learning to online mode of learning may have caused difficulties initially for educators and learners in Brunei. As it progressed day by day it became a normal practice in the education system of Brunei. The main advantage of online learning is that it allows students to participate from distance and students are able to participate in classes from anywhere in Brunei provided they have access to a digital device and stable Internet connection. The flexibility of online learning provides students with the freedom to juggle their activities and classes where they are not tied down to a fixed schedule.

The benefits of personal and online interaction are significant to consider moving forward in improving the education system of Brunei. Reassessing the education system can be beneficial to Brunei due to the functionality of online learning and it may shape the future of learning of Brunei. The low cost and flexibility of online learning may have the ability to reduce carbon footprints of Bruneians where students of higher educational institutes are able to learn from home and reduce their carbon footprints from going to their respective schools.

RECOMMENDATIONS

The pandemic has changed the way humans accept and transmit education due to the suspension of physical interaction via classrooms or face to face communication. With the rapid adoption and acceptance of technologies globally, innovations and changes are bound to transform educational system through technologies and digital platforms via the Internet which was accelerated due to the pandemic. Some recommendations can be considered include training educational workers (teachers and lecturers) in online learning to better train and prepare them in the future and encouraging teachers and lecturers to create a lesson plan with decreased mental strain and improving interactivity between the students and teachers. By providing proper training and guidance to educational workers, it can enable the transmission of quality education to students. While using technologies and digital learning platforms via the Internet, education can be an enjoyable experience for students motivating them and promoting a feeling of passion towards learning.

CONCLUSION

This research was aimed to investigate the challenges and opportunities of online learning during the COVID 19 pandemic in Brunei. This research contributes the knowledge of the challenges and opportunities arising from the implementation of online learning due to the COVID-19 pandemic in Brunei. Technology plays a significant role in facilitating the interaction between a student and a teacher during the pandemic, as it acts as an intermediary or a gateway for students to learn without the concern of social distancing measures between other students in physical classrooms. Without technology or relevant gadgets, students are hindered from gaining access to education during the pandemic. The importance of online learning during the pandemic are the opportunities it provides students to continue learning at their own convenience and at the safety of their homes with the help of technologies (smartphones, tablets, laptops, and desktops). Online learning is assisted with educational digital tools such as Edmodo and Lark that helps educators to share information, circulate assignments, and communicate with students, coworker, and parents. These digital tools help educational institutions to raise the quality level of education and reduce the challenges in the transmission of knowledge in online learning.

Findings from the timeline included have shown that there is shortage of digital devices to facilitate online learning in Brunei, with government and private sectors contributions have eased the challenges of online learning to be implemented immediately due to the circumstances experienced. Findings from the research also highlights that student from a low socio-economic background may have difficulties in coping with online learning due to the absence of proper Internet connection and digital device to learn online. While challenges of online learning were addressed quite well during the pandemic by providing assistance packs for students without proper Internet connections and contributing digital devices to allow online learning to take place, opportunities also emerged on the implementation of online learning in Brunei. The shift towards online medium in education and government sectors have positively impacted the nation's blueprint in becoming a smart nation as well as achieving a state of digitalization in accordance to the 2025 digital masterplan ultimately moving forward to the '2035 *Wawasan* Brunei'.

By acknowledging these challenges and opportunities, Brunei has the potential to facilitate the development and growth of Brunei's education system to move forward and innovate their current methods of learning and educational curriculum. Analysis of these factors will be able to reveal recommendations on the success of online learning that can guide educational institutions towards a better and progressive education of Brunei.

Potential future research direction includes the study of user acceptance towards online learning during and after the pandemic in Brunei. Employing a quantitative method of research and data collection through surveys can potentially reveal significant findings on user behavior towards online learning. While online learning has not been introduced recently, its usage and application have rapidly risen due to the pandemic situation in Brunei that has forced the educational system to shift towards online learning through technologies and online applications in an unexpected manner. Targeting respondents comprising of students and educational personnel within the education system in Brunei can determine the level of acceptance of online learning. Findings can be used to manage, change or improve the educational system of Brunei and prepare the nation for a better future.

REFERENCES

Adams, D., Sumintono, B., Mohamed, A., & Noor, N. S. M. (2018). E-Learning Readiness among Students of Diverse Backgrounds in a Leading Malaysian Higher Education Institution. *Malaysian Journal of Learning and Instruction*, *15*(2), 227–256.

Affouneh, S., Salha, S., & Khlaif, Z. (2020). Designing Quality E-Learning Environments for Emergency Remote Teaching in Coronavirus Crisis. *Interdisciplinary Journal of Virtual Learning in Medical Sciences*, *11*. Advance online publication. doi:10.30476/ijvlms.2020.86120.1033

Alhumaid, K., Ali, S., Waheed, A., Zahid, E., & Habes, M. (2020). COVID-19 & Elearning. *Perceptions & Attitudes Of Teachers Towards E-Learning Acceptance in The Developing Countries.*, *6*. Advance online publication. doi:10.5281/zenodo.4060121

Anderson, J. (2005). IT, E-Learning and Teacher Development. *International Education Journal, 5*(5), 1–14.

Ayebi-Arthur, K. (2017). E-learning, resilience and change in higher education: Helping a university cope after a natural disaster. *E-Learning and Digital Media, 14*(5), 259–274. doi:10.1177/2042753017751712

Babu, N., & Reddy, D. (2015). Challenges and Opportunity of E-Learning in Developed and Developing Countries-A Review. *International Journal of Emerging Research in Management and Technology, 4*, 2278–9359.

Basilaia, G., Dgebuadze, M., Kantaria, M., & Chokhonelidze, G. (2020). Replacing the Classic Learning Form at Universities as an Immediate Response to the COVID-19 Virus Infection in Georgia. *International Journal for Research in Applied Science and Engineering Technology, 8*(3), 2321–9653. doi:10.22214/ijraset.2020.3021

Bond, M., Marín, V. I., Dolch, C., Bedenlier, S., & Zawacki-Richter, O. (2018). Digital transformation in German higher education: Student and teacher perceptions and usage of digital media. *International Journal of Educational Technology in Higher Education, 15*(1), 48. doi:10.118641239-018-0130-1

BozkurtA.SharmaR. (2020). *Emergency remote teaching in a time of global crisis due to CoronaVirus pandemic. 15*, i–vi. doi:10.5281/zenodo.3778083

Carey, K. (2020, March 13). Everybody Ready for the Big Migration to Online College? Actually, No. *The New York Times*. Retrieved from https://www.nytimes.com/2020/03/13/upshot/coronavirus-online-college-classes-unprepared.html

Chopra, G., Madan, P., Jaisingh, P., & Bhaskar, P. (2019). Effectiveness of e-learning portal from students' perspective: A structural equation model (SEM) approach. *Interactive Technology and Smart Education, 16*(2), 94–116. doi:10.1108/ITSE-05-2018-0027

Cojocariu, V.-M., Lazar, I., Nedeff, V., & Lazar, G. (2014). SWOT Anlysis of E-learning Educational Services from the Perspective of their Beneficiaries. *Procedia: Social and Behavioral Sciences, 116*, 1999–2003. doi:10.1016/j.sbspro.2014.01.510

Demirbilek, M. (2014). *The "Digital Natives" Debate: An Investigation of the Digital Propensities of University Students*. Retrieved December 25, 2020, from https://www.researchgate.net/publication/287248663_The_'Digital_Natives'_Debate_An_Investigation_of_the_Digital_Propensities_of_University_Students

Dhawan, S. (2020). Online Learning: A Panacea in the Time of COVID-19 Crisis. *Journal of Educational Technology Systems, 49*(1), 5–22. doi:10.1177/0047239520934018

Felix, A. (2020). *Awareness of Students towards E-Learning in Education*. Academic Press.

Ferrari, A. (2012). *Digital competence in practce: An analysis of frameworks*. Publications Office. Retrieved from https://data.europa.eu/doi/10.2791/82116

Fishbane, L., & Tomer, A. (2020, March 20). *As classes move online during COVID-19, what are disconnected students to do?* Retrieved December 25, 2020, from Brookings website: https://www.brookings.edu/blog/the-avenue/2020/03/20/as-classes-move-online-during-covid-19-what-are-disconnected-students-to-do/

Fry, K. (2001). E-learning markets and providers: Some issues and prospects. *Education + Training, 43*(4/5), 233–239. doi:10.1108/EUM0000000005484

Hrastinski, S. (2008). *Asynchronous and Synchronous E-Learning*. Retrieved December 20, 2020, from https://er.educause.edu/articles/2008/11/asynchronous-and-synchronous-elearning

Kebritchi, M., Lipschuetz, A., & Santiague, L. (2017). Issues and Challenges for Teaching Successful Online Courses in Higher Education: A Literature Review. *Journal of Educational Technology Systems, 46*(1), 4–29. doi:10.1177/0047239516661713

Keeton, M. (2004). Best online instructional practices: Report of phase I of an ongoing study. *Journal of Asynchronous Learning Networks, 8*(2), 75–100. doi:10.24059/olj.v8i2.1829

Kopp, M., Gröblinger, O., & Adams, S. (2019, March 12). *Five common assumptions that prevent digital transformation at higher education institutions*. Academic Press.

Leszczyński, P., Charuta, A., Łaziuk, B., Gałązkowski, R., Wejnarski, A., Roszak, M., & Kołodziejczak, B. (2018). Multimedia and interactivity in distance learning of resuscitation guidelines: A randomised controlled trial. *Interactive Learning Environments, 26*(2), 151–162. doi:10.1080/10494820.2017.1337035

McBrien, J. L., Cheng, R., & Jones, P. (2009). *Virtual spaces: Employing a synchronous online classroom to facilitate student engagement in online learning*. doi:10.19173/irrodl.v10i3.605

Ministry of Education. (2021). *Ministry of Education, Brunei Darussalam*. Retrieved February 17, 2021, from https://www.moe.gov.bn/SitePages/News.aspx

Nadikattu, R. R. (2020). *Information Technologies: Rebooting the World Activities during COVID-19* (*SSRN* Scholarly Paper No. ID 3622733). Rochester, NY: Social Science Research Network. doi:10.2139srn.3622733

Noor-Ul-Amin. (2013). *An effective use of ICT for education and learning by drawing on worldwide knowledge, research and experience: ICT as a change agent for education (A Literature review)*. Retrieved December 21, 2020, from https://www.researchgate.net/publication/312197085_An_effective_use_of_ICT_for_education_and_learning_by_drawing_on_worldwide_knowledge_research_and_experience_ICT_as_a_change_agent_for_education_A_Literature_review

Partlow, K. M., & Gibbs, W. J. (2003). Indicators of constructivist principles in internet-based courses. *Journal of Computing in Higher Education, 14*(2), 68–97. doi:10.1007/BF02940939

Ribeiro, R. (2020). *How University Faculty Embraced the Remote Learning Shift.* Retrieved December 25, 2020, from Technology Solutions That Drive Education website: https://edtechmagazine.com/higher/article/2020/04/how-university-faculty-embraced-remote-learning-shift

Sandkuhl, K., & Lehmann, H. (2017). *Digital Transformation in Higher Education – The Role of Enterprise Architectures and Portals—Digitale Bibliothek—Gesellschaft für Informatik e.V.* Retrieved December 17, 2020, from https://dl.gi.de/handle/20.500.12116/119

Sathishkumar, V., Radha, R., Saravanakumar, A., & Mahalakshmi, K. (2020). E-Learning during Lockdown of Covid-19 Pandemic: A Global Perspective. *International Journal of Control and Automation, 13*, 1088–1099.

Shahzad, A., Hassan, R., Aremu, A. Y., Hussain, A., & Lodhi, R. N. (2020). Effects of COVID-19 in E-learning on higher education institution students: The group comparison between male and female. *Quality & Quantity*. Advance online publication. doi:10.100711135-020-01028-z PMID:32836471

Singh, V., & Thurman, A. (2019). How Many Ways Can We Define Online Learning? A Systematic Literature Review of Definitions of Online Learning (1988-2018). *American Journal of Distance Education, 33*(4), 289–306. doi:10.1080/08923647.2019.1663082

Smedley, J. (2010). *Modelling the impact of knowledge management using technology*. Retrieved December 25, 2020, from https://www.researchgate.net/publication/220438594_Modelling_the_impact_of_knowledge_management_using_technology

Song, L., Singleton, E. S., Hill, J. R., & Koh, M. H. (2004). Improving online learning: Student perceptions of useful and challenging characteristics. *The Internet and Higher Education, 7*(1), 59–70. doi:10.1016/j.iheduc.2003.11.003

Soni, V. D. (2020). Global Impact of E-learning during COVID 19. SSRN *Electronic Journal, 12*. doi:10.2139srn.3630073

Thamarana, S. (2016, August 27). *Role of E-learning and Virtual Learning Environment in English language learning*. doi:10.13140/RG.2.1.4665.1122

Wagner, N., Hassanein, K., & Head, M. (2008). Who is Responsible for E-Learning Success in Higher Education? A Stakeholders' Analysis. *Journal of Educational Technology & Society, 11*, 26–36.

Chapter 2
Comparative Studies on Inclusive Digital Teaching in Higher Education in Light of COVID-19

Andreas Ahrens
Hochschule Wismar, Germany

Parulkumari P. Bhati
Nirma University, India

Alena Leshchenko
Kherson State Maritime Academy, Ukraine

Jeļena Zaščerinska
https://orcid.org/0000-0003-4664-8593
Centre for Education and Innovation Research, Latvia

Olga Gukovica
Centre for Education and Innovation Research, Latvia

Mihails Zascerinskis
Centre for Education and Innovation Research, Latvia

Anastasija Aleksejeva
Centre for Education and Innovation Research, Latvia

ABSTRACT

The COVID-19 pandemic has disrupted the higher education sector, which is a critical determinant of a country's economic future. The aim is to compare the views of teachers and students on inclusive digital teaching in higher education during the COVID-19 pandemic. The meaning of "inclusive digital

DOI: 10.4018/978-1-7998-7184-2.ch002

teaching" and "view" are studied. The empirical study was carried out in September-November 2020. Forty respondents from Germany, Latvia, India, Ukraine, and South Africa participated in the study. The data were collected via a semi-structural interview. The theoretical findings allow defining inclusive digital teaching and its criteria and indicators. The positive views on inclusive digital teaching in higher education during the COVID-19 pandemic were expressed by the university teachers. The students' views were more negative. The novel contribution of this chapter is the implications on inclusive digital teaching in higher education. Directions of further research are formulated.

INTRODUCTION

The COVID-19 pandemic has spread over the whole world. It was the first identified in Wuhan, China, on December 31, 2019. The first death by COVID19 was the 61-year old man in Wuhan, China, 2020. The World Health Organisation (WHO) declared COVID-19 as a pandemic on 2020. February 11, 2020, WHO proposed an official name of the virus as COVID-19.

The outbreak of COVID-19 in the world has led to the unprecedented changes in people's lives. A lot of people have experienced rapid transformations in many aspects of their lives: working conditions, education, shopping, travelling, finance, etc (Zascerinska, Aleksejeva, Zascerinskis, Gukovica, & Aleksejeva, 2020). The COVID-19 pandemic has compelled the human society to maintain social distancing (Ahrens, & Zascerinska, 2020). The spread of the COVID-19 pandemic has significantly disrupted the higher education sector which is a critical determinant of a country's economic future. The occurrence of COVID-19 has impacted more than 120 crores of students and youths across the planet.

Many people consider the COVID-19 pandemic to be a crisis among others (i.e. political, economic, social, financial, etc) as depicted in Figure 1 adopted from Zaščerinska and Ahrens (Zaščerinska, & Ahrens, 2015).

Figure 1. The relationship between the contemporary situation in the world and crises
Source: (Zaščerinska, & Ahrens, 2015)

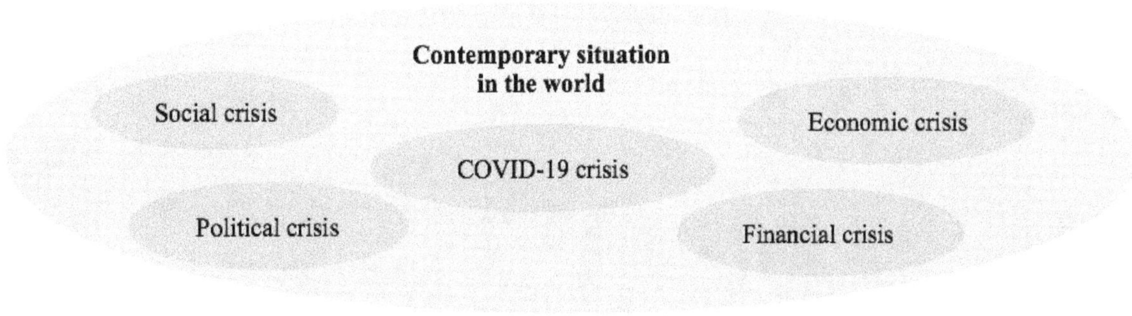

By crisis, a problem situation is meant. The terms *problem situation* (Sokol, 2008), *problem* and *solving a contradiction* (Сорокин, 1977) are considered synonymously (Bassus, & Zaščerinska, 2012). Thereby, a problem situation implies solving a contradiction (Čehlova, 2002). Therein, a contradiction is defined as two incompatible requirements that are set to one element/subject/phenomenon/etc (Sokol, 2008). Contradiction creates contradictory needs: the necessity in change and stability (Grabovska, 2006) as demonstrated in Figure 2 adopted from Zaščerinska and Ahrens (Zaščerinska, & Ahrens, 2015).

Figure 2. Elements of contradiction
Source: (Zaščerinska, & Ahrens, 2015)

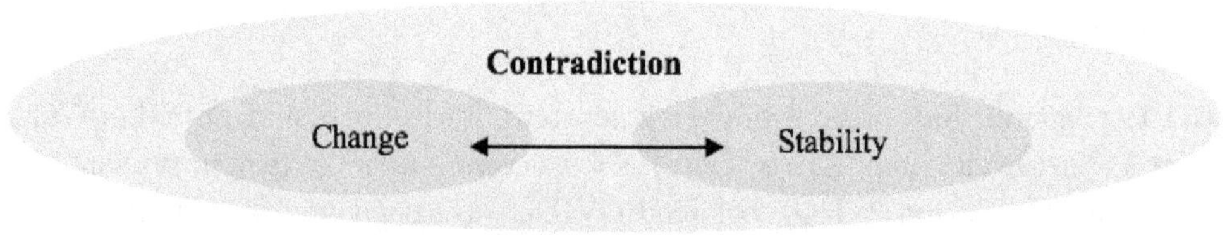

It should be noted that solving a contradiction often demands on the application of non-traditional and innovative solutions. Problem situations emerge in different dimensions of life of the modern world such as pandemic, society, finance, politics, and economy. Thus, a crisis in society is identified as social crisis, in health - pandemic, in finance – financial crisis, in politics – political crisis, and in economy – economic crisis. The COVID-19 crisis is the defining global health crisis and the greatest challenge (Ahrens, & Zascerinska, 2020). The COVID-19 crisis is a cornerstone for the situation development in the world (Zaščerinska, & Ahrens, 2015). By a health crisis or public health crisis, a difficult situation or complex health system that affects humans in one or more geographic areas (mainly occurred in natural hazards), from a particular locality to encompass the entire planet is meant (Gérvas, & Meneu, 2010). Health crises generally have significant impacts on the community health, loss of life, and on the economy (Gérvas, & Meneu, 2010), education system, tourism and others as revealed in Figure 3.

As all the dimensions of life of the modern world are inter-related, problem situations, or, in other words, crises, are inter-dependent, too (Zaščerinska, & Ahrens, 2015). That means that a crisis can be

Figure 3. Life dimensions affected by a health crisis
Source: (the authors)

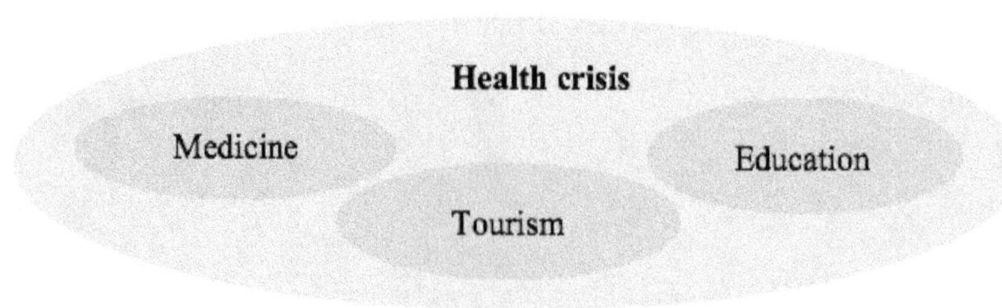

a factor of another crisis. Hence, higher education being a part of education as illustrated in Figure 4, adopted from Zaščerinska and Ahrens (Zaščerinska, & Ahrens, 2015), is formed by a health crisis, too.

Figure 4. The relationship between education and higher education
Source: (Zaščerinska, & Ahrens, 2015)

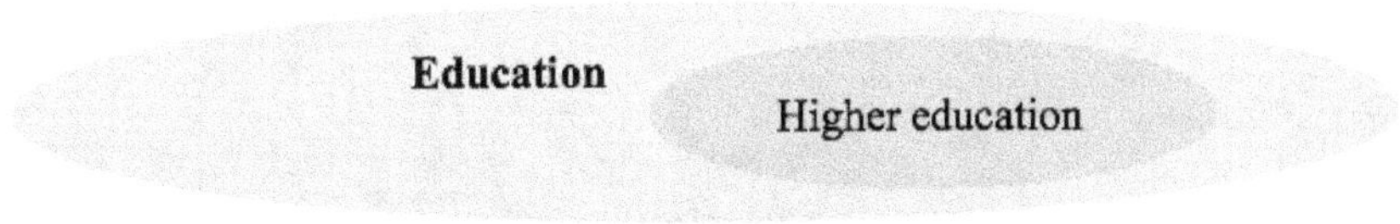

A health crisis has a two-fold influence on higher education as disclosed in Figure 5 (Zaščerinska, & Ahrens, 2015):

- On the one hand, the health crisis has reinforced the value of higher education as
    - educational attainment has always had a huge impact on employability (OECD, 2013) as well as
    - social cohesion (The European Council by the Reflection Group on the Future of the EU 2030, 2010).
- On the other hand, the health crisis has led to the critical importance of expanding access to as many students as possible, increasing the capacity of state institutions to serve students, and refocusing energies on retention and pedagogical research (Galilee-Belfer, 2010).

Figure 5. The relationship between a health crisis and higher education
Source: (Zaščerinska, & Ahrens, 2015)

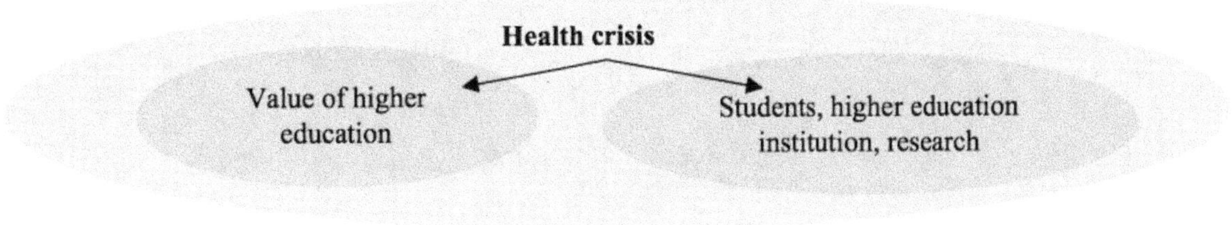

The health crisis changes higher education at the macro, mezzo and micro levels (Tsiligiris, 2012) as shown in Figure 6, adopted from Zaščerinska and Ahrens (Zaščerinska, & Ahrens, 2015).

By the macro level of higher education, a society is meant. The mezzo level of higher education implies a higher education institution. And, as the micro level of higher education, students are identified. It should be noted that all the three levels of higher education are inter-related. It means that shifts in one of the levels of higher education change the other levels of higher education: the health crisis has led to expanding enrollments while severely constraining spending, especially in developing countries, lead-

Figure 6. Levels of higher education
Source: (Zaščerinska, & Ahrens, 2015)

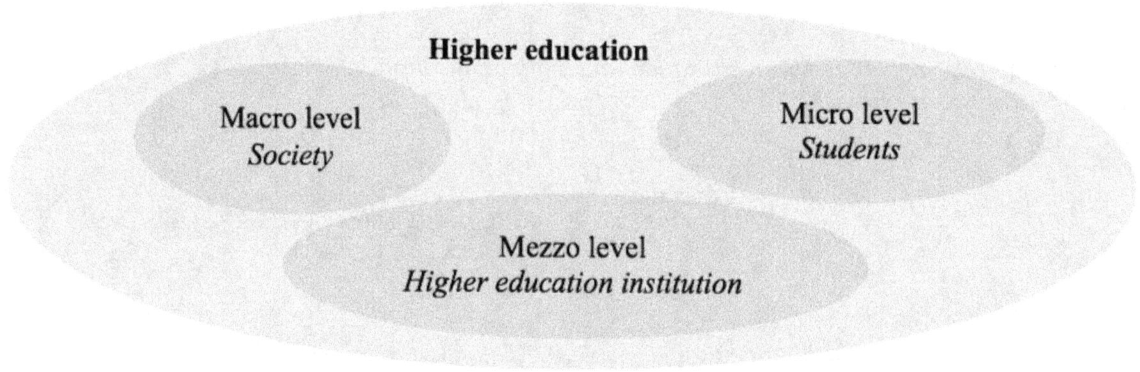

ing to larger classes, less-trained teachers, deteriorating facilities, and less access to textbooks and other learning materials (Klees, 2012). This, combined with the very difficult out-of-school circumstances students face, leads to high rates of repetition and dropouts and little learning for those who manage to stay in university (Klees, 2012).

Moreover, the health crisis strongly influences the mezzo level of higher education *Higher Education Institution* that includes teaching, research and institution autonomy as depicted in Figure 7, adopted from Zaščerinska and Ahrens (Zaščerinska, & Ahrens, 2015).

Figure 7. Dimensions of the mezzo levels of higher education
Source: (Zaščerinska, & Ahrens, 2015)

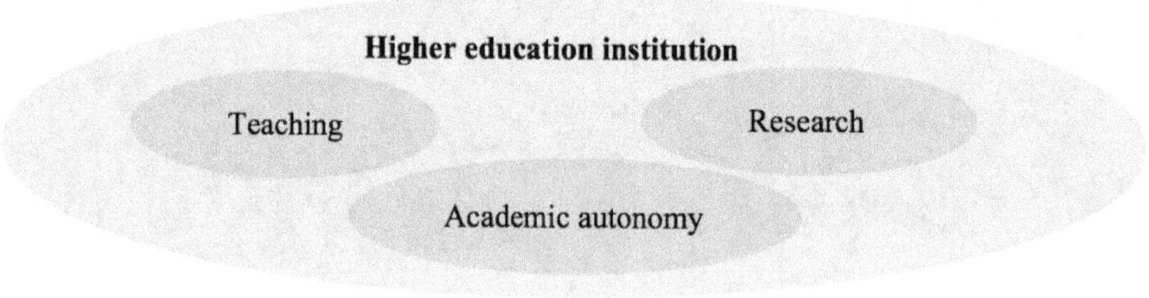

Teaching is, on average, more affected by health crisis than research activities (European University Association, 2011) and academic autonomy. The outbreak of COVID-19 in the world has forced the overnight transformation of teaching practices in universities

- from mostly on-campus
- to only digital teaching.

Teaching facilitates teachers' and students' creation of new products, new patents, new entrepreneurial activities and new jobs as students succeed harder to find a job in the light of the increased enormous socio-economic and unprecedented demographic challenges due to the COVID-19 pandemic. In the lockdown times, the importance of each student participation in the study process significantly increased. For the inclusion of each student in the process of digital teaching, university use diverse digital tool such as ZOOM, Cisco Webex Meetings, Microsoft Teams, etc (Salcenau, 2020). The research was devoted (Salcenau, 2020) to the analysis of

- The adaptation process to this new type of didactic activity and barriers it involves;
- The advantages and disadvantages of the online environment in educational context;
- Students' attitude (fears, emotions, etc).

As university teaching staff plays the key role in the provision of the study process to all the assigned students at universities, inclusive digital teaching has attracted a lot of attention from teaching staff, researchers, academics, university managers and students in order to ensure the engagement of all the students in the university study process.

Against this background, in order to organise inclusive digital teaching within a university study process during the first wave of COVID-19, university teaching staff had to act in accordance with the state policy and university strategy on COVID-19 mitigation measures, availability of IT infrastructure including teaching staff digital teaching skills, students' digital learning skills and other factors.

However, the lack of references to similar crises in the past makes it difficult to predict what may happen in the immediate future (UNESCO IESALC, 2020).

The enabling research questions (RQ) are formulated as following:

RQ1: What is inclusive digital teaching in higher education?

RQ2: What are the views of teachers, students and university management staff on inclusive digital teaching in higher education during the COVID-19 pandemic in selected countries?

The aim of the proposed manuscript is to compare the views of teachers, students and university management staff on inclusive digital teaching in higher education during the COVID-19 pandemic in the selected countries underpinning the elaboration of implications on inclusive digital teaching in higher education.

The novel contribution of this manuscript will be revealed by the implications on inclusive digital teaching in higher education.

The methodological foundation of the present research is formed by the System-Constructivist Theory. The System-Constructivist Theory implies that the world is constructed in modules (Maslo, 2006). New Constructivism supposes that any understanding is not separated from the observer, and reality is socially constructed (Maslo, 2006). Constructing is a creative process that includes a diversity of meaning understanding to offer a variety of opportunities to construct mankind development (Maslo, 2006). Constructive process is always situative (Lamberigts, & Dīpenbroks, 2004). Cognitive process is considered by the Pedagogical Theory of Social Constructivism to be a component: perception is not right or wrong but whether it is relevant to a place or conditions (Maslo, 2006). The System-Constructivist Theory emphasizes that human being's point of view depends on the subjective aspect (Zaščerinska, 2010):

- everyone has his/her own system of the external and internal perspectives that is a complex open system (Osberg, 2008; Rudzinska, 2008),
- experience plays the central role in a construction process (Maslo, 2007).

The remaining part of this contribution is organized as follows: the next section introduces the background of the research, followed by the conceptual framework on inclusive digital teaching in higher education. The associated results of the empirical study will be presented in the following section. Finally, some concluding remarks are provided followed by a short outlook on interesting topics for further work.

Background

The literature review (i.e. Molbæk, 2017; Gruenwald, Pfaffenberger, Zascerinska, & Ahrens, 2017) allows identifying that there are two separate concepts exist as highlighted in Figure 8.

In 2017, inclusive teaching with digital technology was presented by McGlynn-Stewart, Brathwaite, Hobman, Maguire, Mogyorodi, & Park (McGlynn-Stewart, Brathwaite, Hobman, Maguire, Mogyorodi, & Park, 2017). However, the emphasis was put on open-ended tablet applications for teaching English to young children with special learning needs (McGlynn-Stewart, Brathwaite, Hobman, Maguire, Mogyorodi, & Park, 2017).

Figure 8. Elements of inclusive digital teaching
Source: (the authors)

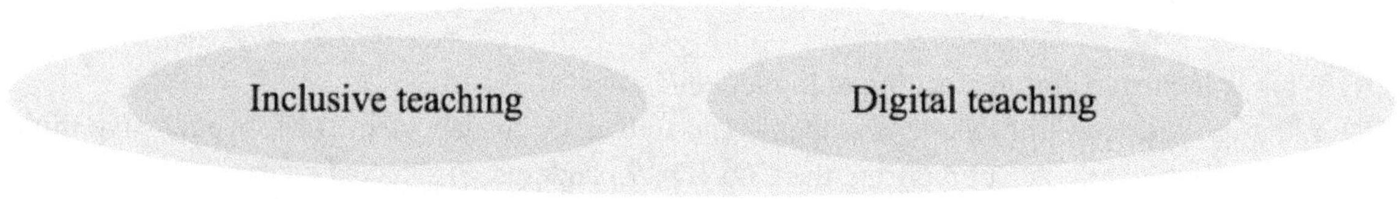

The literature review shows that inclusive digital practice is an emerging research field. The paradigm in the research on inclusive digital practice has shifted from inclusive digital practice for only disadvantaged students to inclusive digital teaching to all the students in diverse underprivileged situations (social and economic problems, language barriers, etc).

MAIN FOCUS OF THE CHAPTER[1]

Conceptual Framework

Against this background, the authors propose inclusive digital teaching to be defined as the combination of three concepts as presented in Figure 9:

- inclusiveness,

- digitalization, and
- teaching.

Inclusive digital teaching centres on the concept of teaching.

Figure 9. Three concepts of inclusive digital teaching
Source: (the authors)

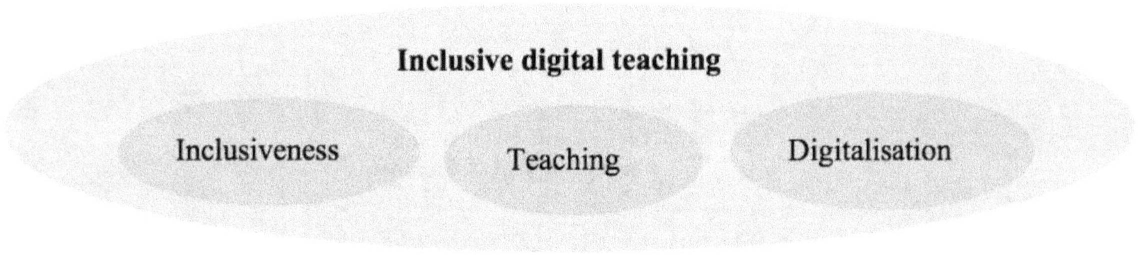

Teaching in formal higher education is defined as a purposefully organized process of teacher's sharing experience (knowledge, skills and attitudes) with students (Zaščerinska & Ahrens, 2013).

By inclusive teaching, an approach to teaching that considers the diverse needs and backgrounds of all the students for the creation of a learning environment where all the students feel valued and where all the students have equal access to learn (i.e. Molbæk, 2017) is identified. By students‘ diverse needs and backgrounds, students' cultural differences, economic obstacles, geographical obstacles, health problems, disability and social obstacles are meant (i.e. Molbæk, 2017).

Digital teaching refers to teaching digitalization and digitization (Gruenwald, Pfaffenberger, Zascerinska, & Ahrens, 2017). Digital teaching includes such dimensions as (Gruenwald, Pfaffenberger, Zascerinska, & Ahrens, 2017)

- media and equipment,
- courses,
- didactics and instructional design,
- Learning Management Systems,
- videoconferencing,
- social networks, and
- e-moderation.

Analysis of inclusive digital teaching as the combination of the concepts of inclusiveness, digitalization and teaching allows defining inclusive digital teaching as a purposefully organized process of teacher's sharing experience (knowledge, skills and attitudes) with students in a digital environment adapted to students' needs.

Inclusive digital teaching proceeds in a certain social cultural environment (Zaščerinska, 2010). The systems constructivist approach reveals that a social cultural environment includes its objective structural component determined as social and cultural aspects of development, namely, opportunities of gaining experience (Tiļļa, 2003). Opportunities as the objective component are the unity of two processes (Tiļļa, 2003) as emphasized in Figure 10:

- experience constructing process as the subjective aspect and
- provision of open variable guaranteed choices of social culture learning organization.

Figure 10. The relationship between inclusive digital teaching in a social cultural environment, opportunity and its structural components
Source: (the authors)

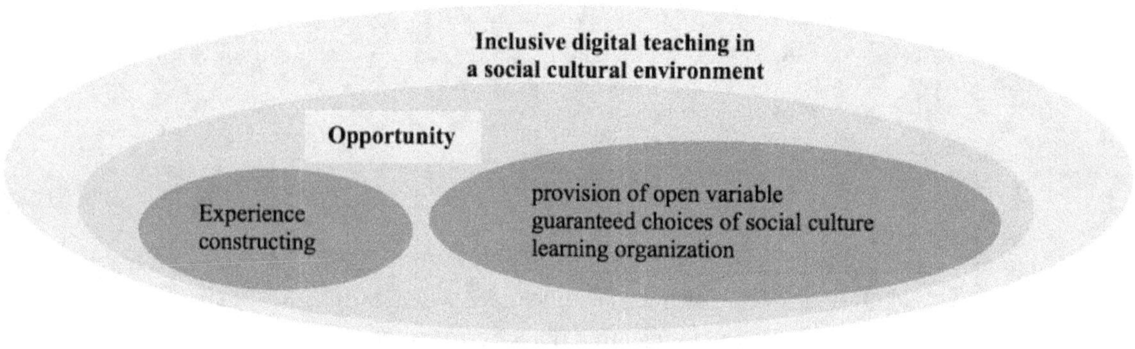

Opportunity is defined as the development of culture of learning, education and interaction in a certain social-cultural environment gaining his/her individual's experience (Tiļļa, 2006). Opportunities to construct knowledge about the world on their own means the availability of social environment (Maslo, 2006):

- teacher,
- other students jointly implement a common teaching/learning task and acquire a new knowledge in pairs and/or groups,
- equal relationships,
- activity relevant to everyone's abilities,
- teacher competence in managing co-operation,
- the improvement of attitudes,
- co-operation supports and strengthens the willingness to learn,
- every individual belongs to a group and is acknowledged by the group,
- the development of communication abilities:
- listening to the opinion,
- making arguments,
- respecting other partners in communication, and
- the evaluation of a joint result.

The emphasis is laid to the objective aspect of opportunities, namely, organizing an environment for student learning (Zaščerinska, 2010).

Literature analysis (i.e. Molbæk, 2017; Gruenwald, Pfaffenberger, Zascerinska, & Ahrens, 2017) allows determining the criteria and indicators of inclusive digital teaching as illustrated in Table 1:

Table 1. Criteria and indicators of inclusive digital teaching

	Criteria	Indicators
Inclusive Digital Teaching	Satisfaction of students' needs	• Satisfaction of students' learning needs. • Satisfaction of students' social needs. • Satisfaction of students' cultural needs, etc.
	Teacher's sharing experience (knowledge, skills and attitudes)	• Teaching materials including digital teaching materials. • Implementation of the teaching process including the digital teaching process. • Enriched students' knowledge, skills and attitudes.
	Digital environment	• Availability of teacher's and students' computers. • Availability of the Internet. • Availability of the software.

Source: (the authors)

Empirical Study

The present part of the manuscript demonstrates (Ahrens, & Zaščerinska, 2014a)

- the design of the empirical study,
- results and
- findings of the study.

More Issues, Controversies, Problems

Figure 11. Elements of the design of the empirical study
Source: (Ahrens, & Zaščerinska, 2014b)

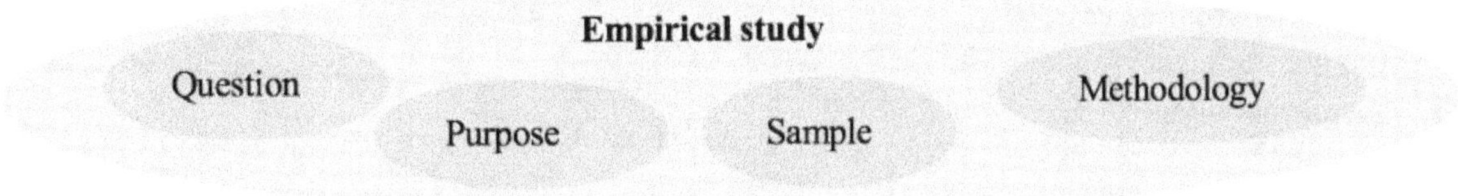

The design of the present empirical study comprised as demonstrated in Figure 11 (Ahrens, & Zaščerinska, 2014b)

- the purpose and
- question,

- sample and
- methodology of the present empirical study.

The empirical study's question was as following: What are the views of teachers, students and university management staff on inclusive digital teaching in higher education during the COVID-19 pandemic in the selected countries?

The empirical study was aimed at comparing the views of teachers, students and university management staff on inclusive digital teaching in higher education during the COVID-19 pandemic in the selected countries.

It should be noted that individual's view is defined as his/her knowledge, skills and attitudes to a phenomenon (Ahrens, Zaščerinska, Hariharan, & Andreeva, 2016). The knowledge, skills and attitude are inter-related (Ahrens, & Zaščerinska, 2015a). The inter-connections between knowledge, skills and attitude allow identifying individual's attitude to be the key element of the individual's view on a phenomenon. Traditionally, attitude is differentiated into positive, neutral or negative as illustrated in Figure 12 (Ahrens, & Zaščerinska, 2014a).

Figure 12. Differentiation of attitude
Source: (Ahrens, & Zaščerinska, 2014a)

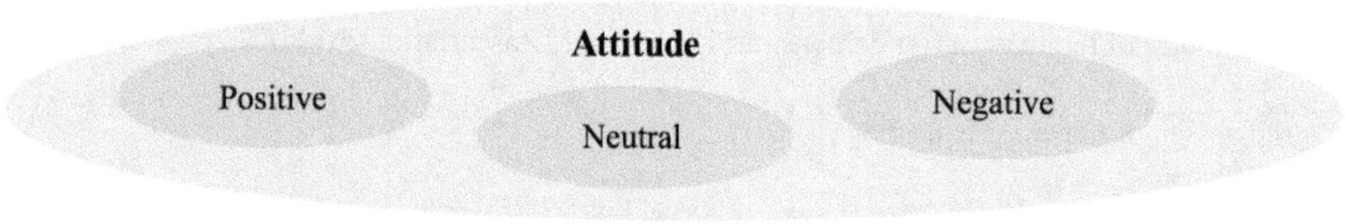

However, for the study purposes, only positive and negative attitude, or, in other words, view will be considered.

The empirical study was carried out in September-November 2020.

The sampling was based on the principles of (Ahrens, & Zaščerinska, 2015b)

- sample appropriateness,
- sample sufficiency, and
- sample confidence.

The sample size was formed by the factors revealed in Table 2 (Ahrens, & Zaščerinska, 2014b).

The present empirical study involved 40 respondents:

- 33 respondents were from Germany,
- two respondents from Latvia
- one respondent from India, and
- one respondent from Ukraine
- three respondents from South Africa.

Table 2. Factors that influence sample size in educational research

Factors that influence sample size in educational research	
External Perspective	Internal Perspective
Surroundings' and resources' factors: - *access to the sample* - *resources:* - *time,* - *personnel and its competences and experiences,* - *technical support,* - *measurement procedures, etc*	Researcher factors: - *aims of research,* - *aims of generalisation,* - *research methodologies,* - *educational research paradigm,* - *motivation,* - *interest,* - *skills, and* - *experience*

Source: (Ahrens, & Zaščerinska, 2014b)

The respondents from Germany were

- university rectors, presidents and chancellors,
- representatives of State Ministry for Science,
- representatives of German Academic Exchange Service,
- university researchers,
- university professors,
- domestic students, and
- international students.

Two respondents from Latvia were university students.

The respondent from India was an assistant professor.

The respondent from Ukraine was a professor.

Two respondents from South Africa were professors.

All the respondents provided the signed letetr of consent.

In order to save the information of the present research confidential, the respondents' names and surnames were coded as

- RGT1 (Respondent 1 is a teaching and/or managing staff member from Germany), etc;
- RGS1 (Respondent 1 is an international student from Germany) etc;
- RL1 (Respondent 1 from Latvia, etc);
- RI1 (Respondent 1 from India);
- RU1 (Respondent 1 from Ukraine);
- RSA1 (Respondent 1 from South Africa, etc).

All the respondents have obtained or were obtaining different degrees in different scientific fields in different countries and cultures. In regard to the international students, it should be pointed that Germany is famous with enrolling students from such countries as India, China, Egypt, etc (Ahrens, Gruenwald, Bassus, Zaščerinska, & Melnikova, 2017; Ahrens, Grünwald, Bassus, Andreeva, Zaščerinska, & Melnikova, 2018; Gruenwald, Ahrens, Zaščerinska, Melnikova, & Andreeva, 2018). International students in Germany have to keep a certain amount of money for living in the country and are allowed to work not more than 20 hours per week. International students in Germany mostly live in a dormitory or rent a flat. The students from Latvia who took part in the study were domestic, mostly they live in the parents' flats and houses. They are allowed to work in accordance with the state legislation (about 40 hours per week) if they can manage to combine studying and working. Working experience of the participating respondents was different, too. The respondents represented different professional cultures such as engineering, banking, education, business, etc. Thus, the respondents' socio-cultural context (age, field of study and work, mother tongue, etc.) was heterogeneous. The number of respondents depends on the heterogeneity: the greater the heterogeneity of the respondents, the fewer the number of participants (Okoli, & Pawlovski, 2004) in the empirical study. As the respondents with different cultural backgrounds and diverse educational approaches were chosen, the sample was multicultural. That emphasizes the significance of the analysis of each individual respondent view (Luka, Ludborza & Maslo, 2009) within the present empirical study. However, whereas cultural similarity aids mutual understanding between people (Robbins, 2007), the respondents' different cultural and educational backgrounds allows examining the process of the construction of the knowledge and opinion (Krueger, & Casey, 2000). In inclusive digital teaching, different cultural and educational backgrounds become an instrument of bringing the teachers and students together more closely under certain conditions such as appropriate materials, teaching/learning methods and forms, motivation and friendly positioning of the educator (Abasheva, 2010).

A generally exploratory and explanatory methodology was applied, the specific balance of which depends on the outcomes of the literature review. Exploratory to answer the sub questions, and explanatory for the main big picture research questions.

Here exploratory relates to being open at the outset of the research and applying a grounded theory approach based on discussions with practitioners and policy makers. This allows flexibility in the classification and assessment of inclusive digital teaching practices in higher education. Explanatory elements relate to identifying common patterns of association relating to the success of embedding inclusive digital teaching practices in higher education.

A confirmatory based methodology may be premature for the main questions given the apparent lack of consensus in the literature (based on a limited review). If the thorough literature review establishes a strong case for a particular pattern, a confirmatory research element may be embedded to establish the extent the literature review identified association generalizes across higher education institutions and countries. A confirmatory methodology may test the extent this association generalizes across the countries and across the range of higher education providers in each country. It may also allow for some independent replication of the findings in the same country as the original study.

The study was carried out in the three main steps:

1. Conceptualisation.
2. Case studies, and
3. Culmination.

The study started with the conceptualisation step (Phillips, 2006) during which a comprehensive literature review was undertaken to inform refined research methodology and case study research tools. This step described in detail inclusive digital teaching practices in higher education in Germany and Latvia, with full attention paid to the local context in terms of its historical, geographical, cultural, political, religious, and linguistic and other features (Phillips, 2006).

The second step was the case studies collecting information and data in interviews with policy makers, teaching staff and students across two states. As part of case study work preparation, a detailed national report on policy, curricula and standards were prepared prior to conducting interviews.

The third step elaborated on the study findings in the form of case studies to feed into the development of implications on inclusive digital teaching practices in higher education for higher education providers, stakeholders, and practitioners.

The data were collected via the semi-structured interview. Semi-structured interviews were used as the researchers had obtained the initial knowledge on the research field (Kroplijs, & Raščevka, 2004). The semi-structured interviews were conducted with the respondents in different times. The semi-structured interviews included the following question: What is your view on higher education during the COVID-19 pandemic. The semi-structured interviews were recorded and detailed notes made. The semi-structured interviews were relatively open and exploratory until novel concepts and ideas stopped emerging. Full transcripts were be made, and thematic analysis was carried out using tools such as Nvivo to elucidate common themes, and topics of discussion.

The collected data were processed via content analysis (Ahrens, Foerster, Zaščerinska, Wasser, 2020). The content analysis included (Mayring, 2000)

- The structuring content analysis, and
- The summarizing content analysis.

The structuring content analysis assists in categorising the data in accordance to the previously determined criteria (Budde, 2005). The summarizing content analysis seeks to reduce the material in such a way that the essential contents are preserved, but a manageable short text is produced (Mayring, 2004, p. 269).

Pedagogical interpretation was applied in the proposed study. Pedagogical interpretive paradigm is characterized by the researcher's practical interest in the research question (Cohen, Manion, & Morrison, 2003). Interpretive paradigm is featured by the researcher's interest in a phenomenon. The interpretive paradigm is aimed at analysing the social construction of the meaningful reality. Meanings emerge from the interpretation. The researcher is the interpreter (Ahrens, Purvinis, Zaščerinska, Miceviciene, & Tautkus, 2018).

Results of the Empirical Study

During the interview, Respondent RGT1 stated that, in order to prepare universities to work in emergency situations, more focus should be put on the elaboration of a strategy, and not on defining separate actions.

Respondent RGT2 agreed that by 2025 universities in Germany have to be able to practice hybrid (partly on campus and partly online) models in regard to teaching, learning, research and other activities.

In terms of teaching, a specific (professional) knowledge within a study programme will be delivered mostly on-line, while the knowledge for personal development of students – face-to-face. It was pointed by Respondent RGT3 that the preparation of a face-to-face lecture requires the same time as for the preparation of an online lecture. It was also noted that online lectures can be given by the university staff without the obligation for the teaching staff to do it from the university campus. Online lectures can be delivered from any place and location.

Lectures for big students' groups were discussed by Respondent RGT4 to become online as the coronavirus pandemic restricted the number of participants per event. Online lectures for big students' groups arise the problem of the use and management of big lecture halls in university buildings.

The transfer to the hybrid model of university studies increases the students' load. The respondents expressed the opinion that students' work within the university studies will only grow. As students' work within the university studies is tightly connected to students' learning, learning will take more and more an individual format. Individual learning will allow students' own pace within the university studies.

The delivery of lectures mostly online raised the issue of the use and management of university buildings. Currently, administrative staff members work in office rooms which are mostly occupied by one person. Respondent RGT5 highlighted a possibility of creation of co-working spaces for administrative staff members at universities.

Another important issue that received a lot of attention was universities' internalization. Respondent RGT6 opined that university internalization should be enhanced as internalisation facilitates the financing of studies and universities. The universities in Germany expect the increase of international team members after the introduction of the vaccine against coronavirus.

Respondent RGT7 pointed an interesting fact that during the first wave of the COVID-19 pandemic, more international students applied for an Erasmus+ exchange in Germany. The respondents assumed that the exchange students wished to stay in Germany during the first wave of the COVID-19 pandemic, despite Germany that time was on the list of the countries with a high infection rate, as Germany has a good health system that is highly ranked in Europe and worldwide. The interview respondents stressed that a new university ranking criteria such as a country's health system will appear in future.

University internalisation was also related to the university networking activities. Networking was concerned in a wider context, not only as part of university internalisation. Respondent RGT8 underlined that a network cannot be established via digital tools, personal contacts and meetings are significant for the network creation and maintenance.

RGS1 explained that his computer broke in the middle of the semester. Due to the COVID-19 pandemic, he could not find any job to earn some money for buying a computer. His parents could not support his buying a new computer.

RGS2 wished to updated his computer as his computer had not enough space for installing a specific software to be used for his engineering studies. The shop staff offered him to join the online queue for a couple of months as the demand for new computers as well as spare computer parts was higher than the offer.

RGS3 also had some computer problems and applied for a scholarship in order to be able to spend the scholarship money for buying a new computer.

Respondents RL1 and RL2 point that the transfer of studies from on-campus format to the digital one requires more computers per family as well as space for taking part in online classes. The respondents explained that if a family has a couple of children who learn at school and/or study at university, the classes usually are given at the same time. Consequently, each family's child, who learns or studies, requires an own computer with the needed infrastructure as well as a separate room. Very often the child's parents also work from home, and the parents need their own computer and equipment for working as well as the room. Both respondents stressed that due to the people who mostly worked from home, the Internet network was overloaded, and, consequently, the connection for the online classes was lost, even for a couple of times per one class. Both respondents could not find any job as many companies in the country were on lockdown, and many employees lost their jobs. In that situation, buying a computer for each family member was a demanding task for the family budget.

Respondent RI1 revealed that occurrence of COVID-19 has impacted more than 120 crores of students and youths across the planet. In India, more than 32 crores of students have been affected by the various restrictions and the nationwide lockdown for COVID-19. As per the UNESCO report, about 14 crores of primary and 13 crores of secondary students are affected which are two mostly affected levels in India. To prevent spread of the COVID-19 pandemic, the Government of India has taken number of preventive measures. The Union Government declared a countrywide lock-down of all educational institutions on 16 March 2020. Similarly, the most of the state Governments and other educational boards postponed examinations due to the outbreak of COVID-19. The Government of India has observed one day nationwide Janta-curfew on March 22 and implemented the lockdown from March 25, 2020 onwards in different phases. The Government of India has been extending lockdown periods from time to time adopting different strategies to fight with the pandemic but educational institutions remained closed continuously. The lockdown 6.0 was declared on June 29, which was effective from 1st July to 31st July 2020 with some less restriction in other sectors except education. Almost all state government ministries have taken measures to ensure that the academic activities of schools and colleges do not hamper during the lockdown period. The lockdown has compelled many educational institutions to cancel their classes, examinations, internships etc. and to choose the online modes. Initially, the educators and the students were quite tangled and did not understand how to handle up with the situation of this sudden catastrophe that forced educational activities. But latter on all realized that the lockdown has taught so many lessons to manage with the emergence of such pandemics. Thus, COVID-19 has challenges and opportunities for the educational institutes to use the Internet and ICT.

There are several ICT initiatives of the Ministry of Human Resource Development (MHRD), University Grant Commission (UGC) and its Inter-University Centres (IUCs) - Information and Library Network (INFLIBNET) and Consortium for Educational Communication (CEC), in the form of digital platforms. These digital platforms can be accessed by the teachers, students, and researchers in Universities and Colleges for learning.

The University Grants Commission of India (UGC India) is a statutory body set up by the Government of India in accordance to the UGC Act 1956 under Ministry of Education, and is charged with coordination, determination and maintenance of standards of higher education. It provides recognition to universities in India, and disbursements of funds to such recognized universities and colleges.

The UGC since then has been coordinating, determining and maintaining standards of university education and teaching in the India and has taken initiatives for various eLearning sources as under.

These ICT initiatives, which cover a broad range of subjects and courses, have been prepared by experts for providing an excellent learning experience to all.

1. SWAYAM Online Courses: SWAYAM Online Courses provides access to teaching-learning resources. These resources were earlier delivered on the SWAYAM platform. Students or learners who registered on SWAYAM (swayam.gov.in) in the January 2020 semester can continue their learning as usual.
2. UG/PG MOOCs: UG/PG MOOCs hosts learning material of the SWAYAM UG and PG (Non-Technology) archived courses.

3. e-PG Pathshala: e-PG Pathshala hosts high quality, curriculum-based, interactive e-content containing 23,000 modules (e-text and video) in 70 Post Graduate disciplines of social sciences, arts, fine arts and humanities, natural & mathematical sciences.
4. e-Content courseware in UG subjects: e-Content courseware in 87 Undergraduate courses with about 24,110 e-content modules is available on the CEC website at http://cec.nic.in/.
5. SWAYAMPRABHA: Swayamprabha is a group of 32 DTH channels providing high-quality educational curriculum-based course contents covering diverse disciplines such as arts, science, commerce, performing arts, social sciences and humanities subjects, engineering, technology, law, medicine, agriculture, etc to all teachers, students and citizens across the country interested in lifelong learning.
6. These channels are free to air and can also be accessed through a cable operator. The telecasted videos/lectures are also as archived videos on the Swayamprabha portal.
7. CEC-UGC YouTube channel: CEC-UGC YouTube channel provides access to unlimited educational curriculum based lectures absolutely free.
8. National Digital Library: National Digital Library is a digital repository of a vast amount of academic content in different formats and provides interface support for leading Indian languages for all academic levels including researchers and life-long learners, all disciplines, all popular form of access devices and differently-abled learners.
9. Shodhganga: Shodhganga is a digital repository platform of 2, 60,000 Indian Electronic Theses and Dissertations for research students to deposit their Ph.D. theses and make it available to the entire scholarly community in open access.
10. e-Shodh Sindhu: e-Shodh Sindhu provides current as well as archival access to more than 15,000 core and peer-reviewed journals and a number of bibliographic, citation and factual databases in

Figure 13. The MOODLE platform at Kherson State Maritime Academy
Source: (the authors)

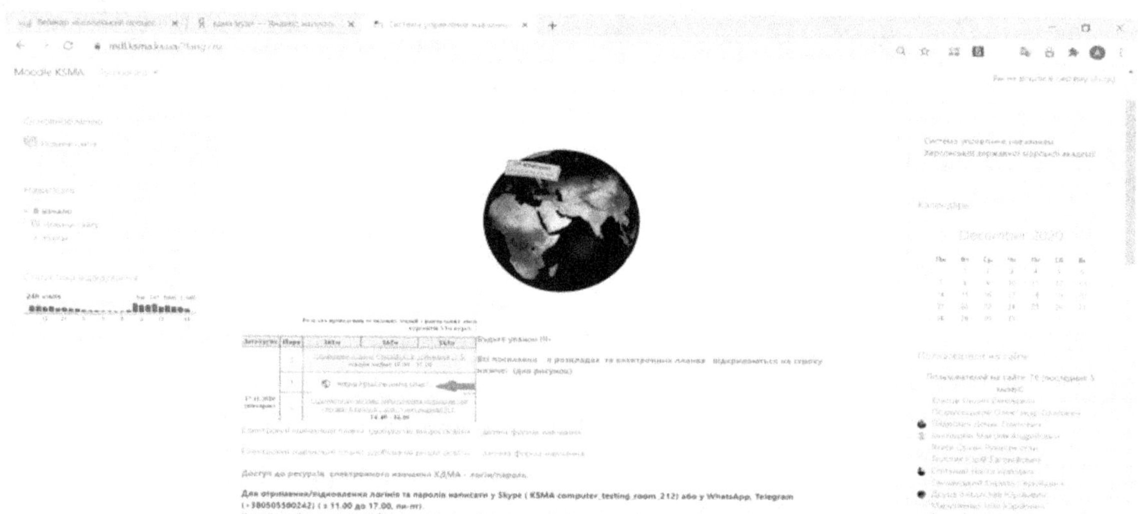

different disciplines from a large number of publishers and aggregators to its member institutions including centrally-funded technical institutions, universities and colleges that are covered under 12(B) and 2(f) Sections of the UGC Act.

11. Vidwan: Vidwan is a database of experts which provides information about experts to peers, prospective collaborators, funding agencies policymakers and research scholar in the country.

On 6th November 2020, the University Grants Commission framed and issued Guidelines for the universities and colleges for reopening their campuses. These Guidelines have been vetted by the Ministry of Health & Family Welfare and approved by the Ministry of Home Affairs and the Ministry of Education. The Guidelines may be adopted by the institutions as per the local conditions and directives of the Government authorities.

Respondent RU1 noted that Ukrainian higher education institutions, like all the world educational institutions, in connection with the spread of the pandemic, are faced with the need to search for new models of the educational process. Hence, various online platforms have been used in the educational process by higher educational institutions in Ukraine. The most used platforms are ZOOM and LMS MOODLE, which make it possible to implement various types of training sessions. Kherson State Maritime Academy (Kherson, Ukraine) actively uses the LMS MOODLE platform as shown in Figure 13, which allows implementing both training sessions and semester knowledge control. On the platform, the student can find all the information s/he is interested in:

- the schedule of classes,
- consultations,
- a list of courses that are planned in his/her individual work plan.

Figure 14. The teacher's page on the MOODLE platform at Kherson State Maritime Academy
Source: (the authors)

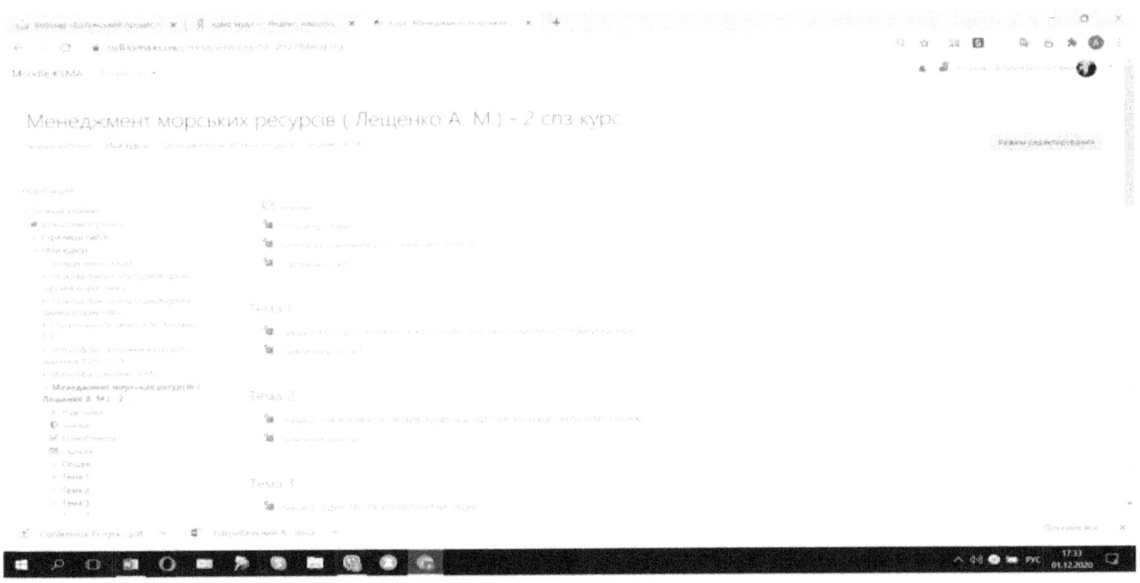

Figure 15. Students' data on the teacher's page on the MOODLE platform
Source: (the authors)

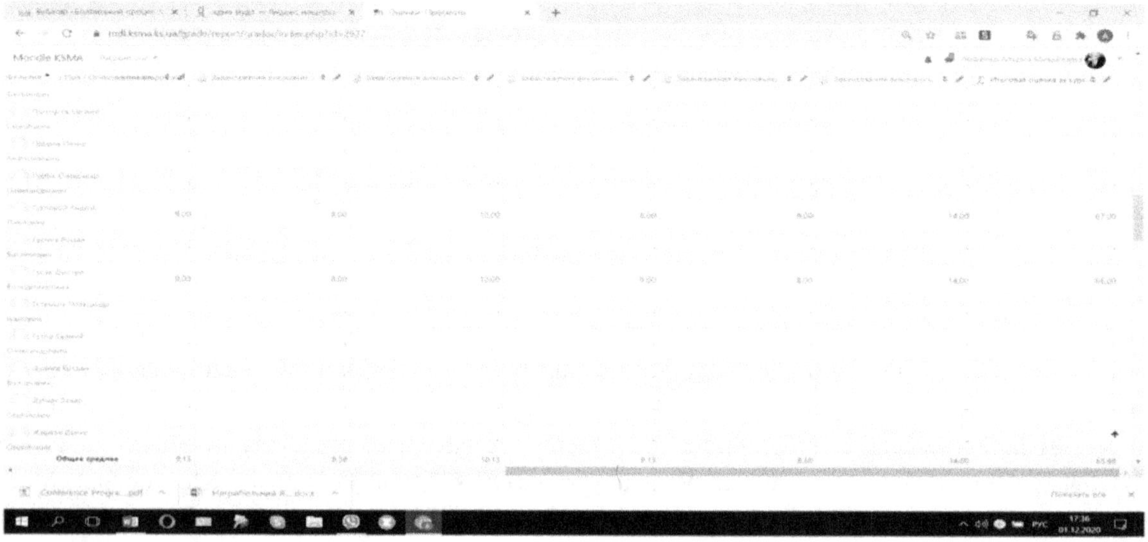

Having a username and password, a student from anywhere in the world can log in and start working on the course.

The use and implementation of the MOODLE platform at the academy began in 2013, therefore, after the announcement of quarantine measures, the teaching staff and management did not face serious problems associated with changing the characteristics of the educational process.

Figure 16. Teaching tools on the MOODLE platform
Source: (the authors)

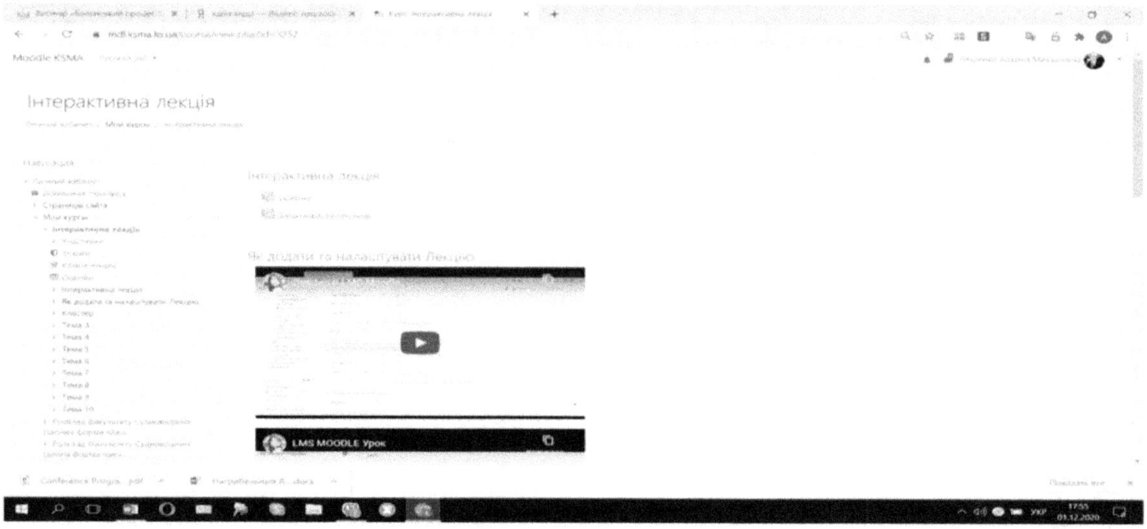

For each teacher, a special page for a course has been created. The teacher can implement some tasks on such a page as illustrated in Figure 14:

- to fill the page out,
- to edit the page,
- to connect to the students,
- to communicate with them via chat and message.

In the teaching process, the teacher can observe as disclosed in Figure 15

- who is on the platform,
- when the student attended the page,
- how much work s/he completed,
- to track his/her progress and answer the questions that s/he had while working on the course.

Additionally, the platform provides the creation of the automatic assessment of a student task that allows the student to immediately receive feedback on the completed assignments.

The platform also offers such tools as gamification of the educational process, augmented reality and others as revealed in Figure 16.

Thus, in the current conditions of the COVID-19 pandemic, the contemporary educational process can actually be completely switched to a mixed learning mode:

- online mode is theoretical material, and
- offline mode is the development of practical competencies,

RSA1 introduced the Collaborative Online International Learning (COIL) at the Durban University of Technology, South Africa. RSA1 underlined that universities had themselves to be adaptive to changes and redesign curricula to respond to rapid changes and the need to ensure the graduates have 21st century skills that can help them respond and adapt, even through tough economic meltdowns. RSA1 gave insight on COIL implications for teaching and learning: “Institutions of higher learning today are faced with the challenge of providing unique academic opportunities used for learning that in many cases use technology, end up as a full online or blended curriculum, however it is not simply offering online or blended courses that matter, but what you do with those technologies that make the difference for students today”.

RSA2 relayed that the global pandemic, COVID-19, has shown everyone how things in the world can change rapidly and how job insecurity, health risks and economic instability can affect the education system, society and the graduates’ chances for employability. The university has over 30 000 students, 95% of these students are undergraduate students, 5% are postgraduate students. The cohort of postgraduate students is an area that we are currently trying to grow. In terms of staffing, currently, the university has 600 identified academics over which 30% have PHDs. So, these statistics are important in the context of COIL, the university defines this platform as one for not just to expose the students, but also different types of teaching and learning experiences; especially in terms of the staff in forming partnerships, learning from each other and enhancing the curriculum.

RSA2 specified the plan of the university to have 15 new COIL projects across the University.

RSA3 gave more context to the contemporary global context and the importance of COIL in international higher education: "The Network of International Education Associations (NIEA) recognises that the COVID-19 pandemic has had an enormous impact on Higher Education and on Internationalisation of Higher Education in particular. She also indicated that at the same time, NIEA believes that the solutions to the challenges posed by the COVID-19 pandemic require international collaboration and reaffirms the importance of international higher education, as international collaboration is essential to finding solutions to global problems, which manifest differently in the local contexts: "Higher education institutions must internationalise their curricula in order to provide an alternative mode of internationalisation that can overcome the limitations inherent in international mobility schemes that remain accessible to a minority of students. COIL offers a creative, relevant, accessible way of engaging in international teaching and learning. Partners working on COIL programmes can share content and methodology, in mutually beneficial ways". RSA3 discussed on the collaboration of students from a university in the USA and a partner university in South Africa. RSA3 also described their COIL projects and student voices.

Findings of the Empirical Study

The data were categorized in accordance to the criteria and indicators of inclusive digital teaching as illustrated in Table 1.

Table 3 shows the results of the structuring content analysis of the semi-structured interviews.

Table 3. Results of the interviews

	Criteria	Indicators	Positive	Negative
Inclusive Digital Teaching	Satisfaction of students' needs	• Satisfaction of students' learning needs. • Satisfaction of students' social needs. • Satisfaction of students' cultural needs, etc.	XXX XXXX X	XXX
	Teacher's sharing experience (knowledge, skills and attitudes)	• Teaching materials including digital teaching materials. • Implementation of the teaching process including the digital teaching process. • Enriched students' knowledge, skills and attitudes.	XXX XXX	X
	Digital environment	• Availability of teacher's and students' computers. • Availability of the Internet. • Availability of the software.	X	XXXXX XX

Source: (the authors)

The university teachers positively evaluated the satisfaction of students' social needs in terms of

- teaching internalisation, and
- organisation of networking.

Also, the university teachers demonstrated a positive view on

- the availability of digital teaching materials as well as
- digital teaching.

The teachers emphasized that there is a variety of software such as MOODLE, ZOOM, etc, for the implementation of inclusive digital teaching. The inclusiveness of digital teaching was highlighted by possibilities to participate in an online class from any location the teacher or student are at.

The students negatively evaluated the availability of computers for the creation of a digital environment. The Internet connection was also a problem.

The summarising content analysis allows identifying that the positive views on inclusive digital teaching in higher education during the COVID-19 pandemic were expressed by the university teachers and managing staff members. The students' views were more negative.

Issues, Controversies, Problems

The empirical study reveals the discrepancy between the teachers' and students' view on inclusive digital teaching in higher education during the COVID-19 pandemic:

- the teachers showed the positive views while
- the students expressed the negative ones.

The present research has *limitations*. The inter-connections between the concepts of inclusiveness, teaching and digitalisation have been set. Another limitation is the empirical study conducted by involving only the teachers and students from the selected countries. The implementation of only semi-structured interviews is a limitation for the data collection, too. Therein, the results of the study cannot be representative for the whole area. Nevertheless, the results of the research – the definition of inclusive digital teaching - may be used as a basis of analysis of inclusive digital teaching in other institutions and countries. If the results of other institutions and countries had been available for analysis, different results could have been attained.

SOLUTIONS AND RECOMMENDATIONS

As students are the key actors in higher education, their views have to be studied in more detail.

Satisfaction of needs of the key actors (teachers and students) in inclusive digital teaching could increase the number of positive views.

The extension of the observation period is also proposed in order to receive a reliable data.

The availability of infrastructure (computers, Internet, software, etc) is the basis of the inclusive digital teaching. However, a teacher is not able to solve this problem for a student. Stakeholders have to be attracted by higher education institutions to provide students with the necessary infrastructure (computers, Internet, software, etc).

FUTURE RESEARCH DIRECTIONS

The contemporary concept of inclusive digital teaching remains as an open point for further research. The inter-connections between the concepts of inclusiveness, teaching and digitalisation will be re-considered.

Research on criteria, indicators and constructs of inclusive digital teaching will be further developed.

Prospects for development include modelling of a favourable inclusive digital teaching and learning environment for the enrichment of students' knowledge, skills and attitude.

Further research tends to focus on the search for relevant methods for evaluation of each criterion of inclusive digital environment.

Students' needs as a criterion of inclusive digital teaching will be further analyzed, too.

Empirical studies in other institutions and countries will be carried out.

A comparative research of more different countries could be beneficial for the scientific community, too.

CONCLUSION

The theoretical findings allow defining inclusive digital teaching. The theoretical analysis facilitated the determination of the criteria and indicators of inclusive digital teaching. Another theoretical finding is that the individual's view on inclusive digital teaching in higher education can be regulated. The individual's view can be increased or decreased according to the situation requirements.

The empirical findings reveal that the positive views on inclusive digital teaching in higher education during the pandemic COVID-19 were expressed by the university teachers and managing staff members. The students' views were more negative. The empirical data allow concluding that the COVID-19 pandemic fastens the shift from the on-campus to inclusive digital teaching.

Validity and reliability of the research results have been provided by involving other researchers into several stages of the conducted research. External validity has been revealed by international co-operation as following:

- the research preparation has included individual interdisciplinary consultations given by other researchers, and
- the present contribution has been worked out in co-operation with international colleagues.

Therein, the findings of the present research are validated by other researchers.

ACKNOWLEDGMENT

This research received no specific grant from any funding agency in the public, commercial, or not-for-profit sectors.

REFERENCES

Сорокин, Н. А. (1974). Дидактика [Didactics]. Издательство "Просвещение" Москва.

Abasheva, C. (2010). Specifics of the English Language Education in the Study Groups with Different Mother Tongues. In *Proceedings of the 5th International Scientific Conference Theory for Practice in the Education of Contemporary Society*. Riga: Riga Teacher Training and Educational Management Academy.

Ahrens, A., Foerster, M., Zaščerinska, J., & Wasser, I. (2020). European Accreditation Agency's View on Kazakhstan's Engineering and Information Technology Higher Education. *Society. Integration. Education Proceedings of the International Scientific Conference, 5*, 15-25. 10.17770ie2020vol1.4861

Ahrens, A., Gruenwald, N., Bassus, O., Zaščerinska, J., & Melnikova, J. (2017). Master Programme "Information and Electrical Engineering" for International Students at Hochschule Wismar: Theoretical Framework. In *Conference Proceedings of 8th Balkan Region Conference on Engineering and Business Education (BRCEBE) and 10th International Conference on Engineering and Business Education (ICEBE) "Creating a mindset for growth and socio-economic development* (pp. 175-182). Lucian Blaga University of Sibiu. 10.1515/cplbu-2017-0023

Ahrens, A., Grünwald, N., Bassus, O., Andreeva, N., Zaščerinska, J., & Melnikova, J. (2018). Impact of Master Programme "Information and Electrical Engineering" for International Students at Hochschule Wismar on Regional Economics: Theoretical Modelling. In *Scientific Printed Works of the 8th International Scientific Conference Perspectives of Economics of Kaliningrad Region and EU Development* (pp. 6-9). Kaliningrad State Technical University.

Ahrens, A., Purvinis, O., Zaščerinska, J., Miceviciene, D., & Tautkus, A. (2018). *Burstiness Management for Smart, Sustainable and Inclusive Growth: Emerging Research and Opportunities*. IGI Global.

Ahrens, A., & Zaščerinska, J. (2014a). Students' Attitude to Interdisciplinary Research. Society, Integration, Education. *Proceedings of the International Scientifical Conference*. Volume I*: Higher Education Institutions Pedagogy, School Pedagogy, Pre-School Pedagogy*, 13-23.

Ahrens, A., & Zaščerinska, J. (2014b). *Factors that Influence Sample Size in Educational Research. In 2014 ATEE Spring University proceedings Changing Education in a Changing Society*. Klaipeda University.

Ahrens, A., & Zaščerinska, J. (2015a). A Comparative Study of Business and Engineering Students' Attitude to Mobile Technologies in Distance Learning. In Assessing the Role of Mobile Technologies and Distance Learning in Higher Education (pp. 29-59). IGI Global.

Ahrens, A., & Zaščerinska, J. (2015b). Principles of Sampling in Educational Research in Higher Education. *Proceedings of the International Scientifical Conference Society, Integration, Education, Volume 1 Higher Education Pedagogy*, 25-35. http://journals.ru.lv/index.php/SIE/issue/view/23

Ahrens, A., & Zascerinska, J. (2020). Post-COVID-19 University Governance in Germany. In Education Reform: Education Content Research and Implementation Problems (vol. 2, pp. 7-16). Rezekne: Rezekne Academy of Technologies. doi:10.17770/er2020.2.5336

Bassus, O., & Zaščerinska, J. (2012). *Innovation and Higher Education*. Mensch & Buch.

Budde, R. (2005). *Mexican and Central American L.A. Garment Workers: Globalized Industries and their economic constraints*. LIT Verlag Münster.

Čehlova, Z. (2002). *Izziņas aktivitāte mācībās* [Cognitive activity in learning]. RaKa.

Cohen, L., Manion, L., & Morrison, K. (2003). *Research Methods in Education*. Routledge/Falmer Taylor & Francis Group.

European University Association. (2011). *Impact of the economic crisis on European universities*. European University Association. https://eua.eu/downloads/publications/impact%20of%20the%20economic%20crisis%20on%20european%20universities%20january%202011.pdf

Galilee-Belfer, M. (2010). *Higher Education and the New Economy: Crisis or Opportunity? Summary and Recommendations*. The University of Arizona College of Education.

Gérvas, J., & Meneu, R. (2010, December). Las crisis de salud pública en una sociedad desarrollada. Aciertos y limitaciones en España. Informe SESPAS 2010. *Gaceta Sanitaria*, *24*, 33–36. doi:10.1016/j.gaceta.2010.06.009 PMID:21094562

Grabovska, R. (2006). *Ilgtspējības principa īstenošana skolotāju izglītībā* [Implementation of principle of sustainability in teacher education] [Unpublished doctoral dissertation]. Univeristy of Daugavpils, Latvia.

Gruenwald, N., Ahrens, A., Zaščerinska, J., Melnikova, J., & Andreeva, N. (2018). Socio-Cultural Adaptation of International Students of Master Programme "Information and Electrical Engineering" at Hochschule Wismar. In *Proceedings of the 5th International Scientific Conference on "Modern Economics"*. University of Wismar.

Gruenwald, N., Pfaffenberger, K., Zascerinska, J., & Ahrens, A. (2017). A Study on Digital Teaching Competence of Trainers from South Africa within the PEESA Project. In *Proceedings of Riga Teacher Training and Educational Management Academy's 12th International Young Scientist Conference*, (pp. 116–124). Riga: Riga Teacher Training and Educational Management Academy.

Klees, S. (2012). *The economic crisis and education: key issues*. Retrieved on June 26, 2014 from http://www.educationincrisis.net/blog/item/403-the-economic-crisis-and-education-key-issues

Kroplijs, A., & Raščevska, M. (2004). *Kvalitatīvās pētniecības metodes sociālajās zinātnēs* [Qualitative research methods in social sciences]. RaKa.

Krueger, R. A., & Casey, M. A. (2000). *Focus Groups: A Practical Guide for Applied Research* (3rd ed.). Sage Publications.

Lamberigts, R., & Dīpenbroks, J.-V. (2004). Aktīvās mācības kooperatīvā mācību vidē: eksperimenta īstenošana un rezultāti [Active learning in cooperative learning environment: conducting of an experiment and its results]. In *Kooperatīvā mācīšanās* (pp. 106–116). RaKa.

Luka, I., Ludborza, S., & Maslo, I. (2009). *Effectiveness of the use of more than two languages and quality assurance in European interuniversity master studies*. Paper presented at the European Conference on Educational Research, University of Vienna. https://www.eera-ecer.de/ecer-programmes/conference/2/contribution/3411/

Maslo, E. (2007). Transformative Learning Space for Life-Long Foreign Languages Learning. In D. Rumpite, K. Makinen, & T. S. Piskozub (Eds.), *International Nordic-Baltic Region Conference of FIPLV Innovations in Language Teaching and Learning in the Multicultural Context*. Rīga: SIA "Izglītības soļi".

Maslo, I. (2006). *No zināšanām uz kompetentu darbību* [From knowledge to Competent Performance]. Latvijas Universitātes Akadēmiskais apgāds.

Mayring, P. (2000). Qualitative Content Analysis. *Forum Qualitative Social Research*, *1*(2), 20.

Mayring, P. (2004). Qualitative Content Analysis. In U. Flick, E. Von Kardoff, & I. Steinke (Eds.), *A Companion to Qualitative Research* (pp. 266–269). SAGE.

McGlynn-Stewart, M., Brathwaite, L., Hobman, L., Maguire, N., Mogyorodi, E., & Park, Y. U. (2017). Inclusive Teaching with Digital Technology: Supporting Literacy Learning in Play-Based Kindergartens. LEARNing Landscapes, 11(1), 199-216.

Molbæk, M. (2017). Inclusive teaching strategies – dimensions and agendas. *International Journal of Inclusive Education*, *22*(3), 1–14. doi:10.1080/13603116.2017.1414578

Ņikiforovs, O. (1994). *Lomu mijiedarbības sistēma „Skolotājs-skolēns" ietekme uz skolēnu tuvākās attīstības zonas kognitīvajiem komponentiem* [Impact of role "teacher-student" in the interaction system on pupil proximal zone of development's cognitive components] [Unpublished doctoral dissertation]. Rīgā, Latvia: University of Latvia.

Okoli, C., & Pawlovski, S. (2004). The Delphi Method as a Research Tool: An example, design considerations and applications. *Information & Management*, *42*(1), 15–29. doi:10.1016/j.im.2003.11.002

Organisation for Economic Co-operation and Development (OECD). (2013). *Education Indicators in Focus*. The Organisation for Economic Co-operation and Development (OECD) Publishing. https://www.oecd.org/education/skills-beyond-school/educationindicatorsinfocus.htm

Osberg, D. (2008) *Education, Emergence and the Idea of "Non- Normative Normativity"*. The European Conference of Educational Research, Gothenburg, Sweden. https://www.eera-ecer.de/ecer-programmes/conference/1/contribution/509/

Phillips, D. (2006). Comparative Education: Method. *Research in Comparative and International Education*, *1*(4), 304–319. doi:10.2304/rcie.2006.1.4.304

Robbins, D. (2007). Vygotsky's and Leontiev's Non-classical Psychology Related to Second Language Acquisition. In *International Nordic-Baltic Region Conference of FIPLV Innovations in Language Teaching and Learning in the Multicultural Context*. Rīga: SIA "Izglītības soļi".

Rudzinska, I. (2008). The Quality of Aim Setting and Achieved Results in English for Specific Purposes-Study Course in Lecturers and Students' Opinion. In *Proceedings of the ATEE Spring University Conference Teacher of the 21st Century: Quality Education for Quality Teaching* (pp. 366-373). Riga, Latvia: University of Latvia.

Salceanu, C. (2020). Higher Education Challenges During COVID-19 Pandemic. A Case Study. *Revista Universitară de Sociologie*, *16*(1).

Sokol, A. (2008). *The Thinking Approach. Introductory Information*. www.thinking-approach.org

The European Council by the Reflection Group on the Future of the EU 2030. (2010). *Project Europe 2030 Challenges and Opportunities*. Luxembourg: Publications Office of the European Union. https://www.consilium.europa.eu/media/30776/qc3210249enc.pdf

Tiļļa, I. (2003). *Development of adolescents' social culture competence within the second foreign language studies* [Unpublished doctoral dissertation]. University of Latvia, Riga, Latvia.

Tiļļa, I. (2006). Sociālkultūras mācīšanās konstruktīvistiskā sistēma [The constructive system of social culture learning]. In I. Maslo (Ed.), *No zināšanām uz kompetentu darbību. Latvijas Universitātes Akadēmiskais apgāds* (pp. 161–170).

Tsiligiris, V. (2012). The impact of the economic crisis on higher education. *University World News,* (213).

UNESCO IESALC. (2020). *COVID-19 and higher education: Today and tomorrow*. UNESCO. http://www.iesalc.unesco.org/en/wp-content/uploads/2020/04/COVID-19-EN-090420-2.pdf

Zaščerinska, J. (2010). Professional Environment for Teacher Professional Development. *Proceedings of 5th International scientific conference Theory for Practice in the Education of Contemporary Society of Riga Teacher Training and Educational Management Academy*. Riga: Riga Teacher Training and Educational Management Academy.

Zaščerinska, J., & Ahrens, A. (2013). E-business Applications to Students' Blended Learning in Higher Education. In *Proceedings of the 4th International Conference on Data Communication Networking (DC NET 2013), 10th International Conference on e-Business (ICE-B 2013) and 4th International Conference on Optical Communication Systems (OPTICS 2013)*. SciTePress - Science and Technology Publications. Printed in Portugal.

Zaščerinska, J., & Ahrens, A. (2015). A Comparative Study of Teacher and Student Use of Social Media for Interaction with Other People. In Impact of Economic Crisis on Education and the Next-Generation Workforce. IGI Global. doi:10.4018/978-1-4666-9455-2

Zascerinska, J., Aleksejeva, L., Zascerinskis, M., Gukovica, O., & Aleksejeva, A. (2020). The Impact of COVID-19 on the Improvement of Teaching Skills on Problem-Solving Learning. *International Journal for 21st Century Education, 7*(1), 42-59. https://www.uco.es/ucopress/ojs/index.php/ij21ce/article/view/13074/12073

ADDITIONAL READING

Grünwald, N., Pfaffenberger, K., Melnikova, J., Zaščerinska, J., & Ahrens, A. (2016). A Study on Digital Teaching Competence of University Teachers from Lithuania and Latvia within the PEESA Project. *Andragogika, 1*(7), 109–123. doi:10.15181/andragogy.v7i0.1380

Sowińska-Milewska, D., Czernicka-Szpakowska, A., Mitzner, M., Aerts, W., Stroobants, I., Glewe, M., Zaščerinska, J., Aļeksejeva, L., Aļeksejeva, A., Gloņina, O., & Zaščerinskis, M. (2016). ICT in Training Room. Hanbook for Trainers. Warsaw: Stowarzyszenie Trenerów Organizacji Pozarządowych (NGO Trainers' Association).

KEY TERMS AND DEFINITIONS

Design of the Empirical Study: The purpose and question, sample and methodology of the present empirical study (Ahrens, & Zaščerinska, 2014b).

Inclusive Digital Teaching: A purposefully organized process of teacher's sharing experience (knowledge, skills, and attitudes) with students in a digital environment adapted to students' needs.

Opportunity: The development of culture of learning, education and interaction in a certain social-cultural environment gaining his/her individual's experience (Tiļļa, 2006).

Semi-Structured Interviews: Used when the researchers had obtained the initial knowledge on the research field (Kroplijs, & Raščevka, 2004).

Structuring Content Analysis: Categorising the data in accordance to the previously determined criteria (Budde, 2005).

Summarizing Content Analysis: To reduce the material in such a way that the essential contents are preserved, but a manageable short text is produced (Mayring, 2004).

Teaching in Formal Higher Education: A purposefully organized process of teacher's sharing experience (knowledge, skills and attitudes) with students (Zaščerinska, & Ahrens, 2013).

View: Individual's knowledge, skills and attitudes to a phenomenon (Ahrens, Zaščerinska, Hariharan, & Andreeva, 2016).

Chapter 3
Knowledge Management and Blended Learning: Towards a Compatibility and Complementarity Model

Fahmi Ibrahim
University of Technologyi Brunei, Brunei

Nena Padilla-Valdez
Universiti Teknologi Brunei, Brunei

ABSTRACT

The purpose of this chapter is to provide a discussion about the compatibility and complementarity of blended learning and knowledge management (KM) and their relationship. Blended learning combines classroom instruction with e-learning while KM is the process of creating, capturing, disseminating, applying, and managing organizational knowledge. This chapter illustrates how attention to two main perspectives exists in KM field; namely, objectivist perspective and practice-based perspective can inform the learning and teaching approach, the deep and surface learning. Yet they are two complementary processes if they are properly integrated. From here, a shift to the need to rethink and restructure the learning and teaching experience occurs, and its transformative potential is analysed. This chapter proposes a Two-C (compatible and complementarity) model which accommodates the blended learning and KM simultaneously. This suggests an integrated approach to provide for a balanced strategy in terms of both blended learning with KM approach can be applied in higher education institution (HEI).

INTRODUCTION

Innovation and technology have incessantly propelled the conditions for which knowledge (KM) management stirs up a new frontier of sophistication in the global arena. In the academic world, the diverse pockets of knowledge do leverage the 21st century innovative outlook of higher educational institutions (Dhamdhere, 2015; Serban and Luan, 2002). Hyped as a method of institutional innovation (Lyman, 2000),

DOI: 10.4018/978-1-7998-7184-2.ch003

KM has been acclaimed to boost institutional credibility in research, curriculum development, student and administrative services, strategic planning, among others (Kidwell et al., 2001). With a positive approach to KM, Higher Education Institutions (HEIs) can transit to a knowledge-based economy, enhance knowledge sharing, improve educational programs, and consequently improve the overall performance of universities (Alhammad et al., 2009; Amayah, 2013; Cheng et al., 2009). The basic challenge, then is to convert the knowledge pool that currently resides in each human talent/unit, and make it widely and easily available to all stakeholders.

KM in HEIs are manifested into two dimensions: academic knowledge and organisational knowledge (Yeh, 2005; Kok, 2007), both of which are enhanced by a set of KM practices and tools that facilitate the development of an environment of knowledge creation, collaboration and sharing and a space of knowledge transformation and application of novelties (Alavi and Leidner, 2001; Bushry and Ranjan, 2011). It simply alludes that knowledge is HEIs' input as well as output, making each institution maintains some distinctive features compared to other institutions and organizations (Omerzel et al., 2011). For instance, Management Information System (MIS) and Business Information System initiatives with web-based portals linking academic units to shared databases and business sites are common platforms used in higher education. Likewise, World Wide Web hosts education courses via Massive Open Online Courses (MOOCs), blended learning, E-learning, and M-Learning, and other virtual or remote instructional deliveries. These initiatives affirm the development of techno-centric institutional infrastructures and wired classrooms in colleges and universities (Metcalfe, 2006). In the end, whatever initiatives HEIs pursue, improvement and promotion of student learning and learning outcomes remain their priority goals (Creemers et al., 2013).

The explosive growth of globalization and to date, the intricacies brought about Covid-19 have driven KM in HEIs into multi-level complexities. To date, education has to be delivered in its varied forms with the basic support of media and technology. Online-blended learning which carries the features of face-to-face classroom in a virtual environment has taken toll to date as the most-sought stop-gap for instruction. Blended learning reaped scrutiny with regard to how it must be designed and transmitted not to be unfairly dismissive of the conventional routine and how it must be efficient and effective in relation to performance (Kim, et al., 2006). But the theoretical and methodological evolution of KM in HEIs carries complicated and challenging transitions as digital technologies become inevitable operational requisites. Its adaption has mounted organizational tensions as HEIs increase their responsive to the needs of global audiences (Kenechukwu et al.,2009). It is thus an overwhelming transition for HEIs to align local initiative with global thrust. Moreover, the implementation of new technologies in an effort to become more efficient, more competitive and most importantly more profitable in this modern world is still on the rise (Skoumpopoulou, et al. 2018). Besides this, the readiness and attitude of the end users (educators and students) and technical staff who are expected to use the new technologies often hinder technology adoption in the workplace (Gedik et al., 2013). Nevertheless, the main issue with the implementation of such Education Management Systems traces back to people's attitudes towards the system as most of them seem reluctant to change (Ibrahim et al. 2020).

Moreover, the fact that HEIs' well of knowledge is emerging from a layer of interactions and network of global connectedness, KM plays a central role in the integration and internal transfer of advancement and development interventions among HEIs. The phenomenal rise of alternative delivery modalities such as blended learning and teaching emerged from a layered interaction involving interactive learning activities (e.g. discussion, simulation, role-playing, experimental, mentoring, interactivity, case studies, games, and support groups) where connectivity and coexistence must thrive (Mahesh et al. (2007).

A scholarly approach to frame the links between the theoretical depth of KM and the methodological breadth of blended learning forms the rationale supporting this chapter. Specifically, it aimed to discuss KM frameworks and perspectives in HEIs; KM concepts on instruction and blended learning. In addition, it examines the convergent points between deep and surface learning as espoused by the constructs of complementarity and compatibility. From the same purview, KM processes and outcomes are mapped and clarified to determine potential stop-gaps and incompatibilities in blended learning implementation.

KNOWLEDGE MANAGEMENT FRAMEWORKS IN HIGHER EDUCATION INSTITUTIONS (HEIs)

Significant work has been existent in the field of KM in HEIs focusing on practices, tools, initiatives, resources and frameworks to manage organisational knowledge and increasing its sharing and its use (Al Kurdi et al.,2018). In particular Ibrahim and Salleh (2019) proposed the so- called hybrid framework which illustrates how attention to two main perspectives exists in the KM field: the objectivist perspective and the practice-based perspective, both of which can expound how surface and deep learning can be achieved. Ibrahim and Ali (2021) further developed a conceptual KMPro framework to provide a comprehensive understanding of the KM practices in HEIs and interrelated mechanisms between knowledge resource (input), KM tools and applications, knowledge types, knowledge process, the institutional support of KM implementation, and knowledge recipient (output). It is important to note that several frameworks have been developed and tested with the aim of enhancing KM in HEIs. These frameworks focus on a variety of perspectives, determinants and constructs according to literature reviews. The Covid-19 pandemic has directly and indirectly changed the landscape of the education system. Through information-based decision-making, the management of the education system seeks to increase the access to and efficiency, effectiveness, quality of holistic education on students (Ibrahim et al., 2020).

Some authors point to the implementation of information systems and others refer to social networks, organisational culture, individual and technological factors, knowledge practices, or organisational methodologies, in order to manage the creation and sharing of structured and unstructured knowledge. In fact, almost all of these frameworks comprise a set of knowledge processes i.e. knowledge creation, acquisition sharing, transfer, codification, application, among others to support and enhance knowledge activities and resources. It is important to note that KM and learning activities can be integrated and how the two can jointly be supported by KM systems (Lytras and Pouloudi, 2006; Lytras et al., 2002).

KM lacks a common framework (Ibrahim and Reid, 2010; Ibrahim and Barr, 2009). This is because there is no consensus of a working definition of KM itself. KM frameworks presented in the literature tend to emphasise different aspects of KM and do not address the hard issues (e.g. IT) and soft issues (e.g. culture) equally. For example, many of the KM frameworks focus on knowledge process (capture, share, storage of knowledge) and, consequently, other elements such as the cultural context, within which KM is developed, are neglected. It is worthy to mention, too that KM provide benefits to HEIs such enhance competitiveness and responsiveness for research scholars, facilitates interdisciplinary research, enhance the quality in curriculum and minimise time spend on research and administrative cost (Nawaz and Gomez, 2014).

KNOWLEDGE MANAGEMENT CONCEPTS IN LEARNING-TEACHING PROCESS

A handful of literature reveals that KM concepts are associated with the learning dimensions. For example, the need for KM in the teaching-learning process in technical educational institutions (TEIs) in India (Bhusry and Ranjan, 2011), the utilization of KM through E -learning (Lytras and Poloudi, 2006; Lytras et al., 2002) and the effects in a blended learning environment with application of KM (Chandavimol et al., 2013; Yeh et. al., 2011; Yeh, 2005) are just a few of the evidences to prove this claim. While the KM concept is potentially related to learning and teaching in HEI, evidences have also shown that it has been applied in industry for knowledge sharing and transfer. For instance, the management consulting firm McKinsey formed internal groups of experts called 'practices' to collect and distil experiences gained in particular fields, such as manufacturing and energy, and to communicate industry and project specific knowledge to others in the firm. Other firms developed collaborative relationships with educational institutions that enable the institutions to provide industry specific training. To add on, Ford, General Motors and Chrysler in conjunction with industry and local university, have established the Michigan Virtual Automotive College, to raise the levels of industry-specific education among automotive industry workers (Probst et al., 2000). British Aerospace has linked with a number of UK universities to both deliver and accredit training from its 'virtual university'. In addition, organisations can arrange for staff to complete distance-based or learning programmes. Where specialist tacit knowledge is required, an expanding role can be envisaged for retired professionals to provide mentoring services to staff in the organisations. On the other hand, granting university qualifications through the new form of work-based learning credential requires partnering arrangements among organisations, universities and individual participants. It involves the recognition of learning that occurs in workplaces in ways that enable the transformation of tacit knowledge, everyday 'know-how' into observable and accessible knowledge (Psarras, 2006). What someone does at work can be turned into areas of learning to acquire academic credits. In summary, these initiatives demonstrate ways of applying KM to learning and teaching in organisations and cultivating KM practices in HEI.

Almost all universities recognize two main approaches of learning; *deep approach* and *surface approach*. Students who take deep approach to learning intend to understand the subject in a way that is personally meaningful, engaging their own experience and previous knowledge in an interactive process with relevant content, logic and existing evidence of the subject. Learning is essentially a transformative experience in which students make or construct personal meaning out of the shared meaning available' (Light et al., 2009,p.52). Their intention is to understand ideas for themselves by constructing their own meaning. Here, knowledge is defined as a 'process' (Lytras and Pouloudi, 2006). On the other hand, students who adopt a surface learning approach intend to use or reproduce the available meanings in an instrumental way to deal with course requirements. The students use meanings, but perceive them as alien and eternally imposed (Light et al., 2009,p.52). As such, they simply approach learning through memorisation or reproducing material course; there is no sustained personal engagement with student's own experience and their previous knowledge. In this respect knowledge is described as 'artefacts' (Lytras and Pouloudi, 2006).

Similarly, universities acknowledge two main conceptions of teaching: teacher-focused and learning-focused. In the first conception, the lecturer regards the practice of teaching as an expert, imparts or transmits information to a passively receptive or compliant student. It is further described 'that the mass of students are passive recipients of the wisdom of single speaker' (Ramsden, 2003, p. 108). Teaching mainly rests on the content of the curriculum (Light et. al, 2009) and knowledge to be transferred to students at this level is seen unproblematic (Ramsden, 2003). Student learning is considered not a central concern of the teacher. Consistent with this view of how learning occurs, lecturers who use this theory of teaching typically attribute any failure to learn to faults in the students (Ramsden, 2003). Biggs (1999) refers this as the 'blame-the-student' theory of teaching. According to Kramer et al. (2010), to promote collaborative learning, educators have to create specific teaching-learning processes within particular learning set ups supported by educational media-technology. Faculty members and institutions discern the need to store the intellectual asset produced by faculty in the course of preparing their lectures and make it available for students and colleagues. However, it is argued that this practice only focuses on explicit knowledge.

The second conception focuses on the learner, and on promoting conceptual change. Teaching is comprehended as a process working cooperatively with learners to help them change their understanding (Ramsden, 2003). It is making student learning possible. Teaching involves finding about students' misunderstandings, intervening to change them and creating a context of learning that encourages students to engage with subject matter (Ramsden, 2003). Therefore, good teaching consists of developing ways to help students improve and change their conceptual understanding (Light et. al, 2009). In developing those practices, it recognizes that meaning and knowledge are outcomes constructed by students in an active dialogue within the socially rich situation of the course and programme. Further, to add value to the lecture materials and textbook content it becomes significant to relate the content with research work, industry interfaces and projects to fully realize the significance and future prospects of subjects. Case studies, simulation games, role plays, brainstorming sessions, interview questions and frequently asked questions (FAQs) along with the theoretical knowledge to enhance comprehension amongst the students and facilitate them to attain improved tacit knowledge of the subject.

In summary, this discussion seeks to map some of the concepts of learning and teaching to the application of KM practices, with a view to setting agenda for the future. Universities have significant level of KM activities and it is important recognise these and use them as foundation for further development particularly in the area of learning and teaching. In today's rapidly-changing economic environment, the role of universities as providers of knowledge is greatly challenged. The important question which now arises is how KM can contribute to the HEI in the new digital economy.

OBJECTIVIST-SUBJECTIVIST KNOWLEDGE MANAGEMENT PERSPECTIVES

For the purpose of this chapter, knowledge is defined based on two broad epistemological camps in the contemporary debate on the nature of knowledge, identified by Hislop (2005:p.14): objectivist perspective (explicit knowledge) and practice-based perspective (tacit knowledge). For example, authors such Cook and Brown (1999) and Asudani (2005), refer to the objectivist perspective as epistemology of possession, where knowledge is regarded as an asset (Empson, 2001), 'stock' (Fahey and Prusak, 1998) and static (Newell et al., 2002). Such knowledge can exist in the form of documents, operating procedures, computer systems or databases. On the other hand, the practice-based perspective conceptualises knowledge as socially constructed and inherently tacit. This perspective is labelled as 'epistemology of practice' (Cook and Brown, 1999) where knowledge is regarded as 'flow' (Fahey and Prusak, 1998) and process (Empson, 2001). The central issue of this perspective is that knowledge resides in the human mind and is dependent on the knower (Venzin et al., 1998). These perspectives, in turn, not only provide an insight into how the nature of knowledge has been conceptualised, but also provides the roots of KM practices, based on the different assumptions of knowledge.

For instance, in the KM practice – objectivist perspective, there is an acknowledgement that much of organisational knowledge may be tacit and it is possible to convert this knowledge into the explicit form. For example, all the instructions for operating machines may not be totally explicit but, with the expertise and experience of workers operating them, it is possible to make all the knowledge explicit and codify it into a complete set of standard operating procedures. The primary role of this kind of KM perspective is to allow knowledge to be shared widely and effectively within or across organisations, so that best practices, problem solutions and procedures can be shared. Technology, includes hardware, software or other means of processing, storing, capturing and organising data or information plays a major role in this KM process. The characteristics of this KM perspective can be defined as the first generation KM (McElroy, 2003,p.xxiv) as there was strong emphasis on IT in many of the earliest KM initiatives. This has become known as the 'supply side of KM' which consists of capturing, codifying, and sharing valuable knowledge, and also involves getting the right information to the right people at the right time.

In contrast to the objectivist perspective, the practice-based perspective conceptualises knowledge not as a codifiable entity, but instead emphasises that knowledge is socially constructed and is inherently tacit. This perspective defines knowledge in dynamic terms, regarding it as a practice of doing or knowing rather than static or objective- knowledge which people possess (Newell et al., 2002,p.7). Cook and Brown (1999) labelled this perspective as an 'epistemology of practice' due to the centrality of human activity to its conception of knowledge. In other words, knowledge resides in mind, body and social systems, which are dependent on the context and the knower (Venzin et al., 1998,p.43). Therefore, the nature of knowledge which is rooted and manifested in the human mind and activity represents the characteristics of knowledge from a practice-based perspective. As noted by Hislop (2005,p.29-34) that tacit and explicit knowledge are inseparable. They are not two ends of a continuum, but two sides of the same coin (Tsoukas, 2005, p.158). The consequence is that there is no such thing as completely explicit knowledge, as all knowledge will have a tacit dimension or will remain tacit, and therefore resistant to articulation or codification (Newell et al., 2002,p.7). Thus, the view of explicit knowledge which stands on its own, would reduce the ineffability of tacit knowledge and narrow all knowledge to only what can be articulated (Tsoukas, 2005,p.158). In view of that, from this perspective, it is impossible to totally codify knowledge into fully explicit form. There will be an element of tacit knowledge which is still embodied in people. The practice-based perspective argues that all knowledge is socially constructed which is purely subjective to interpretations from people. A general model of KM practice-based perspective is focused on knowledge sharing through rich interactions, knowledge sharing culture that motivating people to share knowledge instead of hoarding their knowledge by establishing networked relationship and trust (Davenport and Prusak, 1998). In summary of selected KM literature related to main issues of KM practices in two different perspectives is discussed. This is central in order to provide a theoretical background for developing the proposed conceptual framework.

BLENDED LEARNING: DEEP AND SURFACE LEARNING CONVERGENCE?

Blended learning is rapidly emerging as a domain of practice and of research (Halverson et al., 2013; Güzera and Canera, 2014). Given the evidence that Internet information and communication technologies (ICT) are transforming much of society, there are demands for universities to ''provide for a larger and more diverse cross-section of the population, to cater for emerging patterns on educational involvement which facilitate lifelong learning and to include technology-based practices in the curriculum'' (Hicks, Reid, and George, 2001,p. 143), A source of this transformation stems from the ability of online learners to be both together and apart—and to be connected to a community of learners anytime and anywhere, without being time, place, or situation bound. The trend in HEI since then is to blend text-based asynchronous Internet technology with face-to-face learning—often referred to as simply *blended learning*. Blended learning is both a face–to– face and a technology–based learning platforms which are combined for inclusive and equitable pedagogical access. From the vantage of engagement, it covers a myriad of learning processes bearing the features of a formal education approach in which learning is delivered through and mediated by a mix of non-digital, digital and online media tools (Vanhoucke and Wauters, 2015). It is leaning toward a situated learning where surface and deep thinking and learning processes take place in concrete physical settings and virtual social structures, rendering individuals to explore a gamut of resources and opportunities.

In the midst of a dynamically transforming educational system, teaching and learning can be delivered and channelled into various platforms such as (1) face-to-face or no technology; (2) mixed such as flipped and hybrid; and (3) non-face-to face or online/offline technology-driven schemes- all these highlight the invasive role of technology. It is a common knowledge that face-to-face, by default of human support positioning, is inherently superior against digitalized modalities. But with the emerging technology-mediated learning support that are accessible, learning has become self-directed, flexible and adaptable. Hence, any change in the delivery method via technology must propel intellectually challenging outcomes and allow individuals to do things differently. Thinking as a cognitive process begins when students starts to follow structured learning activities effectively; they are taught how to think skilfully before they are guided to scale in possession of complex skills. Noticeably, surface learning which is often associated with the conventional approach partially leads learners to gain surface understanding of learning materials. In a blended or a mixed learning mode, the pedagogy of mastery learning which is commensurate to surface learning normally commences with the concentration of lower-order cognitive skills derived from rote learning, memorization, and engagement to complete targeted tasks or outcomes and subsequently progresses toward complex skills acquisition. It has to be noted that the acquisition of higher-order cognitive skills demands instructional techniques from which students' learning disposition toward self-regulated learning, an active process of knowledge acquisition and construction in explorative learning environments (Boekaerts, 2002) is definitive of deep learning. By virtue of their inherent features, both surface and deep learning levels thrive in a cognitive continuum, progressively and intermittently honed by carefully managed activities and pedagogical practices in order to develop varied levels of knowledge and skills among diverse learners.

During the advent of new learning approach, blended learning has embraced the concepts of practice-based, team-oriented learning, and open learning which are carried out by integrating face-to-face meetings in diverse groups with online activities in multiple ways to produce and share knowledge and experiences (Kauppinen et al.,2020). These trends reveal that the design principles of blended methods depend how well each method is applied with emphasis on the pedagogical contexts rather than the basis of subject applications and that specifically, personalization of learning and learning engagement are both directive and interactive within a semi-realistic context. Such affordances denote strategic and appropriate redesigning of blended learning activities to encourage a deep learning approach (Machumu and Zhu, 2019). Likewise, interactive engagement which stems from a surface level inevitably expands the learners' mind to metacognition or thinking about thinking, leading to the establishment of a more specific-proactive approach of learning known as thinking-based learning. In this perspective, students are actively involved in learning activities at all levels; they become aware and experience learning processes in a progressing scale.

Blended learning is akin and closely defined as a distance learning community in recognizing the value of synchronous learning activities, like face – to – face interactions with instructor, and collaborative work with peers, as complements to activities performed asynchronously by individual learners (Howard et al., 2006). For example, virtual asynchronous may include lecturing but also inter-group and hands-on task activities with online/direct feedbacking and evaluation to enhance learners' knowledge and practice. From the asynchronous perspective, for instance, collaborative activities with on-campus and off-source/off-line to scaffold online coaching and continuous assessment through feedbacking. The convergence of surface and deep learning from the standpoint of distance learning whether it is supported by partial or full immersive technology ensures adaptive learning with media and digital tools as mainly filling up the learning needs of students. This can be defined as a 'modified blended learning' with tools and methods of active distance learning introduced during the Covid-19 lockdown period (Ozadowicz, 2020) that may become new norm of learning and teaching approach.

A number of investigators have assembled a comprehensive agenda of transformative and innovative research issues for blended learning that have the potential to enhance effectiveness (Garrison and Kanuka 2004; Picciano 2009). Generally, research has found that blended learning results in improvement in student success and satisfaction (Dziuban and Moskal 2011). A case study made by Stockwell et al. (2015) reported improved science education; it was blended learning that contributed a great impact to the students' attendance, satisfaction and improved academic performance. This has showed that interactive learning helped students come to class regularly. However, Ali (2015) believed that the transition from traditional teaching to an online environment is considered a challenge for many teachers in high school education, since traditional teaching was still described as being passive teaching, the resultant of which discouraged students from critically filtering the delivered information (higher-order thinking skills). This is argument pointed to the lack of socialization; the process of converting tacit knowledge from shared experience and analytical thinking proved inactive, rendering students' limited internalization of explicit knowledge and tacit knowledge gained through experimentation and simulations (Ibrahim and Salleh, 2019). This internalization process is related to 'learning by doing' in promoting creativity and innovation.

Although a blended learning is types of courses, there is no formula for aligning time and technology in a precise way (Gülbahar and Madran, 2009). By inserting the blended learning in teaching, students and teachers spent extra interaction in terms of answering the questions and be proactive through the lesson. This claim is supported by Huong (2018) study where a blended learning can be categorized into activity level, course level, program level and institutional level depending to what levels are being implemented. On top of that, Gülbahar and Madran (2009) believed that through communication and collaboration, satisfaction, equity, and autonomy are among those concepts that need to be taken into consideration. In addition, Al-drees, et al. (2015) mentioned that blended learning contributes to the development of interpersonal and communication skills, presentation skills, promotes self – directed learning. Overall, it enhances students' enthusiasm and motivation.

Porter, et al. (2016) believed that before adopting blended learning, educators reported concerns with regard to decreasing the quality of student interaction, the lack of time to prepare online content and activities, and the difficulty of dealing with online interactions. Moreover, Al-Zahrani (2014) studied that some of the school teaching staff lacked adequate training and experience in computer use and technology, thus they had low level of readiness related to technology and its uses. In fact, by not having an internet connection in their offices had showed how generally weak were they in preparing the teaching resources in terms of effective use of digital technologies. Another study by Kim et al. (2009) showed that although many places did recognize the potential of blended learning to bring learning closer between the students and teachers, there were still numerous issues to be addressed in delivering blended learning in workplace learning settings. Inversely, Singla et al. (2018) mentioned that technology is a stimulant for change. This however can be observed as a positive or negative change- resulting from different individuals or groups depending upon their approach with reference to change or acceptance. Though some changes in delivering the lesson, students' acceptance of blended learning took time, denoting whether these changes advanced or stunted the lesson itself.

In line with this, Beaman et al. (2018) also argued that with a better understanding of the diffusion process, how people choose to adopt new technologies could potentially impact social learning especially those strategies that would maximize diffusion. It simply means that drastic changes cultivate innovative capability. For example, providing creative learning spaces help develop students' techniques and skills efficiently thereby increasing learning productivity and reducing waste time in return. In other words, integration of technology approach in delivering the lesson balances students' knowledge, better understanding, and greater efficiency in adapting blended learning in their daily school and personal lives. Moreover, the study by Huda et al. (2018) explained that by attempting to collect big data for innovative learning meant engaging learners to manage and store intangible assets such as report and documents. The study further stressed that with the integration of technology, students can prepare paperwork and notes more efficiently as it could reduce workload in no time. As a result, utilization of Information Communication Technology (ICT) in all dimensions of student life can be generated into data volume within the purview of the human daily needs. However, the majority of e-learning initiatives are limited on the application or the customization of learning platforms that facilitate the delivery of learning content on a predefined, static and sequential way of surface learning approach. The flexibility of such implementations is rather inadequate to support the dynamic nature of deep learning approach.

From the organizational perspective, Aubert et al. (2008) claimed that the benefits from a new technology are not achieved if organizations experience low utilization by the intended users, emphasizing that teachers' and students' exposure to technology while supporting human daily needs increases ICT literacy. Unfortunately, due to the still lacking access to technology such as computers and reliable internet has become a common problem and this in return, has restricted the use of modern technology such as a laptop in the computer lab where the teachers preferred to use the old method or the chalk and talk approach (USAID, 2014). Also, Robert (2005) cited that some of the workforce had never known life without a computer. It is thus right to assume that technology adaptation can bring difficulties to teachers as they are not adept users of newer technology and eventually dent students' satisfaction and lead them to the brink of boredom. With less application of technology and real exposure to digital life, workforce productivity and achievement is doomed to happen. However, number of new applications emerging technology such Cloud Intelligent Systems has been revealed during this Covid-19 pandemic (Susanto et al., 2020) that possibly mitigate the problem.

Vongkulluksn et al., (2018) noted that there were responsive teachers and administrators to the challenges brought about by available technological and organizational resources with full administrative leadership and school culture in support of technology integration. Technology use in blended learning resources such as desktop and/or laptop computers, tablets and connection network for the teachers and students narrows down inequity and digital divide. Once technology integration is achieved, learning technology and digital curriculum can operationalize maximally. Apart from that, due to the rapid changing requirements of job-related tasks, traditional learning and trainings are no longer considered sufficient for acquiring the necessary skills and knowledge (Schumacher, 2018). Here, e-learning provides the flexible learning options for educators, employees and students which then allow them to up -skill more rapidly. Even more, it can also decrease the costs of up-skilling a workforce through reducing travel and time away from work as this is more beneficial for a geographically dispersed work places because it can deliver a consistent training experience (Wang, 2018).

As the foundation of Interactive Learning, blended learning emerged poorly understood but as time went by, teachers introduced several approaches which led to the polarization of technological resources in pursuit of pedagogical innovations such as distance and functional interventions to the space and time limitations of face – to – face lessons. On a similar vein, blended learning reaped advantages; it enhances the learning opportunities and propels learning experiences by means of facilitating learners' access to the resources, motivating learners through communication, collaboration and interaction, and supplementing the course management activities through giving feedback and grading (Yildirim and Kurt, 2018). From the students' perspective, they gained satisfaction from the interaction, technology, classroom management and teaching as they were able to follow, contribute as well as give feedback during the lesson time. More essentially, they felt a boost in their self-confident while they voluntarily engaged in discussion and class activities.

The growth and access of blended learning as a form of the distance learning has brought attention to the felt need for the students to meet face-to-face and later for them to conduct peer-to-peer evaluation for students' interaction (Picciano et al., 2016). It is a recognition that this type of assessment increases students' and teachers' rapport at the same time provide opportunities for socialization and connectivity. Moreover, blended learning which can include interactive online activities through a combination of conferencing tools, electronic whiteboards, cloud storage, among others cultivate motivation and social learning engagement with the present as well as in the future time (Ashton et al., 2014). Interestingly, flipping the classroom in blended learning increases students' motivation, enhances independent learning, and bolsters students-centred classroom strategies as students lead the discussions, and participate in activities such as technology exploration where they display gained skills (Villanueva, 2015). Afterall, there is no difference either face – to – face learning or e – learning in generating better students' performance in a holistic way.

The introduction of the web-based learning system such as the Moodle has helped in the integration of instructional materials via different types of media. Since it acts as a primary means of communication, known as an interaction with learners, students must not fail to use such system as this acts as a supplementary learning tool for traditional classes and therefore, it is important to consider school initiatives, students' perceptions and attitudes, and parents' involvement and assistance towards Moodle in a blended learning in a fully online distance learning context (Yeou, 2016). On a similar vein, the open source Learning Management System (LMS) Moodle, a widely used free, flexibility and customized system contains many standard features and is available in various languages. In other words, it is an easy or user –friendly learning system with tools and provisions for communication, discussion area, group space, and workspace (Umek et al., 2016). All these are observed to make learning more interesting, sustain participation of stakeholders, and increase school and student overall performance.

KNOWLEDGE MANAGEMENT AND BLENDED LEARNING: COMPATIBILITY AND COMPLEMENTARITY

Blended learning provides an extremely challenging research context. The facilitation mixed of learning through technology and face-to-face requires a multi-fold consideration of issues that fall into the categories of technology, cognition, behaviour, attitudes, and pedagogy. KM, on the other hand, poses a critical question to researchers; how do they justify abstractions that provide a systematic way for the management of knowledge which include different characteristics of knowledge perspectives?

Figure 1. Two-C KM-blended learning pedagogy model

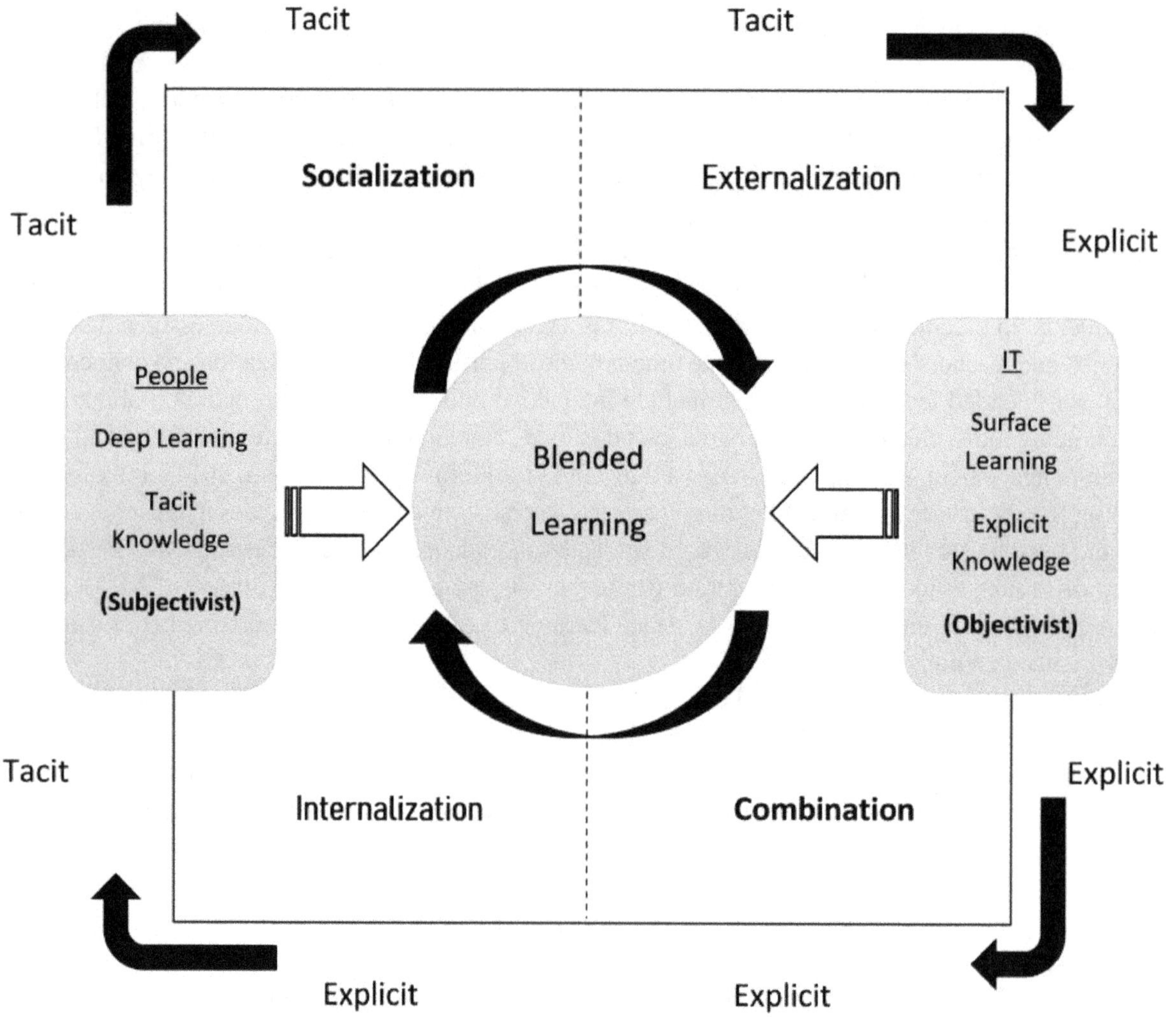

In Figure 1, KM process is presented as a critical mechanism, where a plethora of knowledge objects-types have to be managed and adopted in order to fulfil and further enhance the requirements for learning utilization through blended learning. The issue of learning utilization is not a linear function nor even guided from a well-defined cause-and-effect formula, where learning outcome is directly related to interconnected factors. KM can be utilized in many different ways in the context of blended learning. A first point of argument is the direct linkage of knowledge to learning content and, thus, the need to justify the ways that diverse knowledge types are used in blended learning system in order to provide learning material. The evolution of databases, multimedia technologies, human computer interactivity, adaptive hypermedia, mobile and wireless technologies, and the advent of the Semantic Web have moved the emphasis from the traditional artifact approaches (surface learning) to a process approach (deep learning) to the utilization of unstructured content. Unstructured content that resides such in Google, YouTube, LinkedIn, Blog or other online resource, and peer to peer knowledge sharing which requires unstructured learning approach with tacit knowledge emphasis by removing the typical confinements of a classroom to allow students to learn in unconventional ways. Unstructured learning suggests no formal structure to the learning as it is a more ad-hoc, open-ended, varied, and informal way of learning. In contract, structured content such include in textbooks and modules specifications only requires surface learning approach which is explicit knowledge emphasis. Basically the essence is we learn best by making the most of both approaches based on the objective of the learning outcome, the proficiency of the learner (existing knowledge and skill set), and what stage of the overall learning journey we are at.

The framework provides a sense of understanding the KM implementation by showing the interrelationship mechanisms between blended learning, KM processes in the backdrop i.e. socialization, externalization, combination and internalization; knowledge type i.e. tacit and explicit which are embedded both in deep (people related with subjectivity) and surface learning approach (IT related with objectivity). The illustration is only conceptual based on interpretations from the synthesis of concepts and theories both from blended learning and KM theories. As a starting point, the HEIs should have a 'resource' – knowledge type that must be identified and 'blended' in the learning process. Given to the advantages and disadvantages of both deep-surface learning approaches that focus purely on single dimension of knowledge type, the blended learning is justified to have a balanced view of gaining effective learning approach. The KM applications such LMS, Moodle, MS Teams, Web Boards, eBooks, Email, WhatsApp, are combined with Face to Face Meeting, Brainstorming, Classroom Learning & Teaching in blended learning where the process of knowledge conversion drawing from the work of Nonaka and Takeuchi (1995) of tacit-tacit (socialization), tacit-explicit (externalization), explicit-explicit (combination), explicit-tacit (internalization) knowledge takes place. This is a complementary approach to knowledge both knowledge type and KM perspectives along with deep and surface learning-teaching style.

Pedagogies of practice have demanded and constructed complex collective relations, drawing attention to the processes through which knowledge is created, thus the emergence of productive pedagogies, critical pedagogies, authentic pedagogies, technological pedagogies on top of instructional pedagogy or explicit teaching to name a few (Churchill et al., 2011). Pedagogy is thus a complex and impactful term. If teachers articulate their teaching and learning beliefs- knowledge that is often labelled as tacit, they do regard themselves professional providers. But pedagogy is equally a learning engagement process, which affirms that explicit knowledge or academic knowledge form core part of the various pedagogical variations particularly those drawn on the concept of authentic pedagogy and grounded in constructivist teaching methods. Given the framework's significance, selecting strategies in relation to variable methods, approaches and background of the learners promote intellectual quality which means that connectedness of pedagogical content knowledge and technological pedagogies model how teachers transform and represent current information and content into impactful and meaningful effects through internalization process.

From KM ontological perspective, current efforts to standardize learning resources are centred on the notion of a blended learning as a piece of content that can be reused in diverse educational contexts. The embodiment of instructional design to learning poses new challenges for the standardization process. In blended learning, the key issue is neither the interoperability nor the reusability of content, but rather the support of learning as a cognitive and constructive process. For example, at a university an Assistant Professor holds a number of knowledge resources in knowledge base or repository. These learning objects have to support the educational processes in many ways. The most effective way would be the development of blended learning mechanism that that would facilitate the integration of knowledge stored in various formats i.e. scientific journals, manuscripts etc. combine with specific learning processes for the structured diffusion of knowledge. This demonstrate that the KM is compatible and complement to the blended learning approach. In the similar vein, KM is driver of blended learning and *vice-versa.*

The Two-C KM-Blended Learning Pedagogy model has also shown the interactive processes of those KM process; `activate' the blended learning process mechanisms. Further, the success of KM practices is affected by the factors of learning-teaching approach; deep and surface learning. The illustration of Fig. 1 is meaningful because it integrates the interrelated mechanisms and processes with a balanced view of KM perspectives and knowledge type in a single framework.

CONCLUSION

KM perspective and blended learning is a crucial consideration in enhancing the effectiveness and efficiency of teaching and learning in HEIs. Both KM initiatives blended learning approach in teaching and learning can be used as part of the institutional strategies to create, transform, store and disseminate knowledge according to the needs of the students and learners. The KM concepts are seen as innovative development which complements and is compatible with blended learning that can be applied in HEIs and perhaps it can emerge as a 'new norm or approach' in learning and teaching. This is illustrated in Figure 1 which displays blended learning embedded in KM practices incorporating both perspectives of deep and surface learning approaches. HEI should have strategy to achieve the added value of learning-teaching by utilising both 'IT' (associated with surface approach in learning and teacher-focused in teaching), and 'people' approach (associated with deep approach in learning and, student and learning-focused in teaching) via blended learning mechanisms.

There has indeed been a paradigm shift in HEIs. The teaching-learning process cannot be confined only to the contents in the textbook, the so-called explicit knowledge only. The needs of the industry and competition require academicians and students to be equipped with both 'content and construct' of knowledge of their subjects from cross platform perspectives. The proposed Two-C KM-Blended Learning Pedagogy model can be used as guideline to develop an institutional learning-teaching approach. In sum, to build and develop a robust and thriving knowledge environment in the learning-teaching process, institutions need to foster the overall culture of sharing and managing knowledge. In this context, HEIs will be required to expand flexibility and innovativeness in learning and teaching.

REFERENCES

Al-drees, A. A., Khalil, M. S., Irshad, M., & Abdulghani, H. M. (2015). *Students' perception towards the problem based learning tutorial session in a system-based hybrid curriculum*. doi:10.15537mj.2015.3.10216

Al-Kurdi, O., El-Haddadeh, R., & Eldabi, T. (2018). Knowledge sharing in higher education institutions: A systematic review. *Journal of Enterprise Information Management*, *31*(2), 226–246. doi:10.1108/JEIM-09-2017-0129

Al-Zahrani, A. M. (2014). Challenges and Obstacles to the Effective Integration of Technology : A Qualitative Investigation of the Policymakers Perspective in Saudi Pre-Service Teacher Education. *Saudi Journal of Educational Technology Research*, 1-12.

Alavi, M., & Leidner, D. E. (2001, March). Knowledge Management And Knowledge Management Systems: Conceptual Foundations And Research Issues. *MIS Quaterly*, *25*(1), 107–136. doi:10.2307/3250961

Alhammad, F., Al Faori, S., & Abu Husan, L. S. (2009). Knowledge sharing in the Jordanian universities. *Journal of Knowledge Management*, *10*(3), 1–9.

Ali, A. (2015). Integrating Blended Learning in Higher Education. *Procedia: Social and Behavioral Sciences*, *186*, 600–603. doi:10.1016/j.sbspro.2015.04.086

Amayah, A. T. (2013). Determinants of knowledge sharing in a public sector organization. *Journal of Knowledge Management*, *17*(3), 454–471. doi:10.1108/JKM-11-2012-0369

Andersson, U., Dasi, A., Mudambi, R., & Pederson, T. (2016). Technology, innovation and knowledge: The importance of international connectivity. *Journal of World Business*, *51*(1), 153–162. doi:10.1016/j.jwb.2015.08.017

Ashton, P. B., Koch, L., & Rothberg, A. (2014). The influence of blended learning on student performance in an undergraduate occupational therapy curriculum. *South African Journal of Occupational Therapy*, *44*(1), 75–80. Retrieved November 4, 2018, from http://www.scielo.org.za/pdf/sajot/v44n1/15.pdf

Assudani, R. H. (2005). Catching the chameleon: Understanding the elusive term knowledge. *Journal of Knowledge Management*, *9*(2), 31–44. doi:10.1108/13673270510590209

Aubert, B. A., Barki, H., Patry, M., & Roy, V. (2008). A multi-level, multi-theory perspective of information technology implementation. *Information Systems Journal*, *18*(1), 45–72. doi:10.1111/j.1365-2575.2007.00279.x

Beaman, L., Ariel, B., Jeremy, M., & Musfiq, M. A. (2018). Can Network Theory-Based Targeting Increase Technology Adoption? *Evolution*, 1–14.

Bhusry, M., & Ranjan, J. (2011). Knowledge Collaboration in Higher Educational Institutions in India: Charting a Knowledge management Solution. *International Journal of Computational Science*, *8*(5), 332–341.

Biggs, J. B. (1999). *Teaching for Quality Learning at University*. SRHE and Open University Press.

Boekaerts, M. (2002). Bringing about change in the classroom: Strengths and weaknesses of the self-regulated learning approach. *Learning and Instruction*, *12*(6), 589–604. doi:10.1016/S0959-4752(02)00010-5

Chandavimol, P., Natakuatoong, O., & Tantrarungroj, P. (2013). Knowledge Management and Action Learning in Blended Training Activities. *Creative Education*, *4*(9), 51–55. doi:10.4236/ce.2013.49B010

Cheng, M. Y., Ho, J. S. Y., & Lau, P. M. (2009). Knowledge Sharing in Academic Institutions: A Study of Multimedia University Malaysia. *Electronic Journal of Knowledge Management*, *7*(3), 313–324.

Churchill, R., Ferguson, P., Godinho, S., Johnson, N. F., Keddie, A., Letts, W., Mackay, J., McGill, M., Moss, J., Nagel, M. C., Nicholson, P., & Vick, M. (2011). *Teaching: Making a difference*. John Wiley and Sons.

Cook, S. D. N., & Brown, J. S. (1999). Bridging epistemologies: The generative dance between organizational knowledge and organizational knowing. *Organization Science*, *10*(4), 381–400. doi:10.1287/orsc.10.4.381

Creemers, B., Kyriakides, L., & Antoniou, P. (2013). *Teacher professional development for improving quality of teaching*. Springer Publication. doi:10.1007/978-94-007-5207-8

Davenport, T. H., & Prusak, L. (1998). *Working Knowledge: Managing What Organization Knows*. Harvard Business School Press.

Dhamdhere, S. N. (2015). Importance of Knowledge Management. In *The Higher Educational Institutes, Turkish Online. Journal of Distance Education*, *6*(1), 162–183. doi:10.17718/tojde.34392

Dziuban, C., & Moskal, P. (2011). A course is a course is a course: Factor invariance in student evaluation of online, blended and face-to-face learning environments. *The Internet and Higher Education*, *14*(4), 236–241. doi:10.1016/j.iheduc.2011.05.003

Empson, L. (2001). Introduction: Knowledge Management in Professional Service Firms. *Human Relations*, *54*(7), 811–817. doi:10.1177/0018726701547001

Fahey, L., & Prusak, L. (1998). The eleven deadliest sins of knowledge management. *California Management Review*, *41*(3), 265–276. doi:10.2307/41165954

Garrison, D. R., & Kanuka, H. (2004). Blended learning: Uncovering its transformative potential in higher education. *The Internet and Higher Education*, *7*(2), 95–105. doi:10.1016/j.iheduc.2004.02.001

Gedik, N., Kiraz, E., & Ozden, M. Y. (2013). Design of a blended learning environment: Considerations and implementation issues. *Australasian Journal of Educational Technology*, *29*(1), 1–19. doi:10.14742/ajet.6

Gülbahar, Y., & Madran, R. O. (2009). Communication and Collaboration, Satisfaction, Equity, and Autonomy in Blended Learning Environments: A Case from Turkey. *International Review of Research in Open and Distance Learning*, *10*(2), 1–22.

Güzera, B., & Canera, H. (2014). The past, present and future of blended learning: An in depth analysis of literature. *Procedia: Social and Behavioral Sciences*, *116*, 4596–4603. doi:10.1016/j.sbspro.2014.01.992

Halverson, L. R., Graham, C. R., Spring, K. J., Drysdale, J. S., Curtis, R., & Henrie, C. R. (2014). A thematic analysis of the most highly cited scholarship in the first decade of blended learning research. *The Internet and Higher Education*, *20*, 20–34. doi:10.1016/j.iheduc.2013.09.004

Hicks, M., Reid, I., & George, R. (2001). Enhancing on-line teaching: Designing responsive learning environments. *The International Journal for Academic Development*, *6*(2), 143–151. doi:10.1080/713769258

Hislop, D. (2005). *Knowledge Management in Organisations*. Oxford University Press.

Hislop, D. (2013). *Knowledge Management in Organisations: a critical introduction*. Oxford University Press.

Howard, L., Remenyi, Z., & Pap, G. (2006). Adaptive Blended Learning Environments. *Proceedings 9th International Conference on Engineering*, 11–16.

Huda, M., Maseleno, A., Atmotiyoso, P., Ahamad, R., Nor Muhammad, N. H., Jasmi, K. A., Nasrul Hisyam Nor Muhamad, N. H. N., Mustari, M. I., & Basiron, B. (2018). Big Data Emerging Technology: Insights into Innovative Environment for Online Learning Resources. *International Journal of Emerging Technology in Learning*, *13*(1), 23–36. doi:10.3991/ijet.v13i01.6990

Huong, P. T. T. (2018). Applying Blended Learning Method in Teaching English at the University of Da Nang, Vietnam. *The Educational Review, USA*, *3*(1), 16–21.

Ibrahim, F., & Ali, D. N. (2021). Evaluating Knowledge Management Practices in Higher Education Institutions (HEIs): Towards KMPro Framework Guidelines. In S. Zyngier (Ed.), *Handbook of Research on Knowledge Management Tools in Higher Education* (pp. 221–245). IGI Global.

Ibrahim, F., & Barr, S. (2009). Reconfiguring IT and the Cultural Dimension in Knowledge Management Practices, International *Journal of Knowledge. Culture and Change Management*, *9*(11), 27–43.

Ibrahim, F., & Reid, V. (2010). Unpacking Knowledge Management: Management Fad or Real Business Practice? *Enterprise Risk Management*, *2*(1), 25–38.

Ibrahim, F., & Reid, V. (2010). Integrated Use of Information Technology and People Involvement for Knowledge Management. *International Journal of Technology, Knowledge and Society*, *6*(2), 163–180. doi:10.18848/1832-3669/CGP/v06i02/56086

Ibrahim, F., & Salleh, N. M. (2019). Embedding Knowledge Management Theory in Learning and Teaching Approach. *International Journal of Learning and Development*, *9*(1), 20–40. doi:10.5296/ijld.v9i1.13786

Ibrahim, F., Susanto, H., Haghi, P. K., & Desi Setiana, D. (2020). Shifting Paradigm of Education Landscape in Time of the COVID-19 Pandemic: Revealing of a Digital Education Management Information System. *Applied Systems Innovation*, *3*(4), 1–21.

Kauppinen, M., Kainulainen, J., Hökkä, P., & Vähäsantanen, K. (2020). Professional agency and its features in supporting teachers' learning during an in-service education programme. *European Journal of Teacher Education*, *43*(3), 384–404. doi:10.1080/02619768.2020.1746264

Kenechukwu, M., Newman, C., Kramer, I. I. D., & Pearson, M. (2009). The changing landscape in higher education. In S. Harper & S. J. Quaye (Eds.), *Student engagement in higher education* (pp. 137–154). Springer Publishing.

Kidwell, J. J., Vander Linde, K. M., & Johnson, S. (2001). Applying corporate knowledge management practices in higher education. In G. Bernbom (Ed.), *Information alchemy: The art and science of knowledge management* (pp. 1–24). Jossey-Bass.

Kim, K., Bonk, C. J., & Oh, E. (2008). The present and future state of Blended Learning in Workplace Learning Settings in United States. *Performance Improvement*, *47*(8), 5–16. doi:10.1002/pfi.20018

Kok, A. (2007). Intellectual Capital Management as Part of Knowledge Management Initiatives at Institutions of Higher Learning. *Electronic Journal of Knowledge Management*, *5*(2), 181–192.

Kramer, B. J., Klebl, M., & Zobel, A. (2010). Sharing educational knowledge and best practices in edu-sharing. *Proceedings of the 2010 Second International Conference on Mobile, Hybrid and On-Line Learning*, 53-9. 10.1109/eLmL.2010.27

Light, G., Cox, R., & Calkins, S. (2009). *Learning and Teaching in Higher Education* (2nd ed.). Sage.

Lytras, M. D., & Pouloudi, A. (2006). Towards the development of a novel taxonomy of knowledge management systems from a learning perspective: An integrated approach to learning and knowledge infrastructures. *Journal of Knowledge Management*, *10*(6), 64–80. doi:10.1108/13673270610709224

Lytras, M. D., Pouloudi, A., & Poulymenakou, G. (2002). A framework for technology convergence in learning and working. *Journal of Educational Technology & Society*, *5*(2), 99–106.

Machumu, H., & Zhu, C. (2019). Students' conceptions of learning approaches and their engagement in blended learning environments. *International Journal of Technology Enhanced Learning*, *11*(3), 304–322. doi:10.1504/IJTEL.2019.100490

Mahesh, V., & Woll, C. (2007). Blended learning in high tech manufacturing: A case study of cost benefits and production efficiency. *Journal of Asynchronous Learning Networks*, *11*(2), 43–60.

McElroy, M. (2003). *The New Knowledge Management: Complexity, Learning, and Sustainable Innovation*. Butterworth-Heinemann.

Nawaz, M. N., & Gomez, A. M. (2014). Review of Knowledge Management in Higher Education Institutions. *European Journal of Business and Management*, *6*(7), 71–79.

Newell, S., Robertson, M., Scarborough, H., & Swan, J. (2002). *Managing Knowledge Work*. Palgrave Macmillan.

Nonaka, I., & Takeuchi, H. (1995). *The Knowledge Creating Company: How Japanese Companies Create the Dynamics of Innovation*. Oxford University Press.

Omerzel, D. G., Biloslavo, R., & Trnavcevic, A. (2011). Knowledge management and organisational culture in higher education institutions. *Journal for East European Management Studies*, *16*(2), 111–139. doi:10.5771/0949-6181-2011-2-111

Ożadowicz, A. (2020). Modified Blended Learning in Engineering Higher Education during the COVID-19 Lockdown—Building Automation Courses Case Study. *Education Sciences*, *10*(10), 292. doi:10.3390/educsci10100292

Picciano, A. G. (2009). Blending with purpose: The multimodal model. *Journal of Asynchronous Learning Networks*, *13*(1), 7–18.

Picciano, A. G. (2016). Research in Online and Blended Learning: New Challenge and New Opportunity. In C. Dziuban, A. G. Picciano, C. R. Graham, & P. D. Moskal (Eds.), *Conducting research in online and blended learning environments: New pedagogical frontiers*. Routledge, Taylor & Francis Group.

Porter, W. W., Graham, C. R., Bodily, R. G., & Sandberg, D. S. (2016). Internet and Higher Education A qualitative analysis of institutional drivers and barriers to blended learning adoption in higher education. *The Internet and Higher Education*, *28*, 17–27. doi:10.1016/j.iheduc.2015.08.003

Probst, G., Raub, S., & Romhardt, K. (2000). *Managing Knowledge: Building Blocks for Success*. John Wiley & Sons.

Psarras, J. (2006). Education and training in the knowledge-based economy. *VINE: The Journal of Information and Knowledge Information Systems*, *36*(1), 85-96.

Ramsden, P. (2003). *Learning to Teach in Higher Education* (2nd ed.). Routledge Flamer., doi:10.4324/9780203507711

Robert, S. (2005). On demand learning: Blended learning for today's evolving workforce. *IBM Learning Solutions*, (September), 24.

Schumacher, C. (2018). Supporting Informal Workplace Learning Through Analytics. In D. Ifenthaler (Ed.), *Digital Workplace Learning* (pp. 43–61). Springer., doi:10.1007/978-3-319-46215-8_4

Serban, A. M., & Luan, J. (2002). *Knowledge management: Building a competitive advantage in higher education: New Directions for Institutional Research*. Jossey-Bass.

Serban, A. M., & Luan, J. (2002). Overview of Knowledge Management. In Knowledge Management: Building a Competitive Advantage in Higher Education. Wiley Periodicals. doi:10.1002/ir.34

Singla, A., Sethi, A., & Ahuja, I. S. (2018). A study of transitions between technology push and demand pull strategies for accomplishing sustainable development in manufacturing industries. *World Journal of Science. Technology and Sustainable Development*, *15*(4), 302–312. doi:10.1108/WJSTSD-09-2017-0028

Skoumpopoulou, D., Wong, A. K. L., & Ng, P. M. L. (2018). Factors That Affect the Acceptance of New Technologies in the Workplace: a Cross Case Analysis Between UK and Hong Kong. *Ukais 2018*. http://nrl.northumbria.ac.uk/id/eprint/34489

Stockwell, B. R., Stockwell, M. S., Cennamo, M., & Jiang, E. (2015). Blended Learning Improves Science Education. *Cell*, *162*(5), 933–936. doi:10.1016/j.cell.2015.08.009 PMID:26317458

Susanto, H., Leu, F.-Y., Caesarendra, W., Ibrahim, F., Haghi, P. K., Khusni, U., & Glowacz, A. (2020). Managing Cloud Intelligent Systems over Digital Ecosystems: Revealing Emerging App Technology in the Time of the COVID19 Pandemic. *Applied System Innovation*, *3*(3), 37–55. doi:10.3390/asi3030037

Sveiby, K. E. (1989). *Managing Know how: Add value by Valuing Creativity*. Bloomsbury.

Umek, L., Keržić, D., Aristovnik, A., & Tomaevic, N. (2016). Implications of blended learning on students' performance in public administration education. *Proceedings - 8th International Conference on U- and E-Service, Science and Technology, UNESST 2015*, 39–44. 10.1109/UNESST.2015.18

Vanhoucke, M., & Wauters, M. (2015). Blended learning in project management experiences on busineß games and case studies. *CSEDU 2015 - 7th International Conference on Computer Supported Education Proceedings*, *2*, 267–276.

Venzin, M., von Krogh, G., & Roos, J. (1998). Future research into Knowledge Management, In Knowing in Firms: Understanding, Managing and Measuring Knowledge. Sage Publications. doi:10.4135/9781446280256.n3

Villanueva, J. (2015). Flipped Inclusion Classroom. *Action Research*, 1–16. http://128.171.57.22/handle/10125/40822

Vongkulluksn, V. W., Xie, K., and Bowman, M. A. (2018). The role of value on teachers' internalization of external barriers and externalization of personal beliefs for classroom technology integration. *Computers and Education*, *118*(November), 70–81. doi:10.1016/j.compedu.2017.11.009

Wang, M. (2018). *E-Learning in the Workplace: Performance Oriented Approach*. Springer. doi:10.1007/978-3-319-64532-2

Yeh, Y. C., Huang, L. Y., & Yeh, Y. L. (2011). Knowledge management in blended learning: Effects on professional development in creativity instruction. *Computers & Education*, *56*(1), 146–156. doi:10.1016/j.compedu.2010.08.011

Yeh, Y. M. C. (2005). The Implementation of Knowledge management system in Taiwan's Higher Education. *Journal of College Teaching and Learning*, *2*(9), 35–42. doi:10.19030/tlc.v2i9.1861

Yeou, M. (2016). An Investigation of Students ' Acceptance of Moodle in a Blended Learning Setting Using Technology Acceptance Model. *Journal of Educational Technology Systems*, *44*(3), 300–318. doi:10.1177/0047239515618464

Yildirim, I., & Kurt, S. C. (2018). The Students' Perceptions on Blended Learning. *Educational Sciences: Theory and Practice*, *18*(2), 427–446. doi:10.12738/estp.2018.2.0002

Chapter 4
Business Simulation Games:
A Direction in the New Era of Teaching and Learning

Chai-Lee Goi
https://orcid.org/0000-0003-0131-2818
Curtin University, Malaysia

ABSTRACT

The history of the development of business simulation games started in 3000 BC, and the development of modern business simulation games began in the 1950s. Since the introduction of modern business simulation games, it has grown rapidly and is widely used by corporations, managers, educators, development consulting firms, and collegiate business programs for training and teaching purposes. A dynamic business environment and changing economic conditions require the reorientation and modification of educational programs. The learning process should focus on strengthening knowledge, skills, behaviours, and attitudes according to market needs and wants. The use of business simulation games in education can overcome this problem and even increase student motivation and engagement. This chapter covers three main sections: (1) history of business simulation games, (2) types of business simulation games, and (3) the use of business simulation games in teaching and learning.

INTRODUCTION

The world is changing now (Turns, 2020)

A dynamic business environment and changing economic conditions require the reorientation and modification of educational programs. The learning process should focus on strengthening knowledge, skills, behaviours, and attitudes according to market needs and wants. Students also need to have entrepreneurial intentions to have an in-depth understanding of market dynamics, financial management skills, and exchange methods.

DOI: 10.4018/978-1-7998-7184-2.ch004

Even, Covid-19 pandemic changes the world and global outlook. The education needs to change to better prepare the young generation for what the future might hold. The changes include educating citizens in an interconnected world, redefining the role of the educator, teaching life skills needed for the future, and unlocking technology to deliver education (Luthra & Mackenzie, 2020).

Also, one of the problems in education is the boredom of students in the classroom. The effective use of games can spark interest and enhance active learning in business courses (Ritzko & Robinson, 2006). The use of business simulation games in education can overcome this problem and even increase student motivation and engagement (Zirawaga, Olusanya, & Maduku, 2017). Games offer a unique structure to complement traditional teaching strategies and make learning more enjoyable for students (Boyle, 2011). The role of games in education can be referred to in Figure 1. To this end, business simulation games can play an essential role as a true representation of market operations in a virtual environment (Zulfiqar, Sarwar, Aziz, Chandia, & Khan, 2018).

Figure 1. The use of games in education
Source: (Boyle, 2011)

Since the introduction of modern business simulation games in 1955 (Faria, 1998), it has grown rapidly, and it is widely used by corporations, managers, educators, development consulting firms, and collegiate business programs for training and teaching purposes (Faria, 1987, 1998). Business simulations currently support three types of applications: educational programs, training firms, and evaluating business strategies (Gonen, Brill, & Frank, 2009). Since the late 1960s, over 90% of AACSB business school members have used business simulation games (Faria & Nulsen, 1996).

This book chapter covers four main sections:

- History of business simulation games
- Types of business simulation games
- The Use of business simulation games in teaching and learning
- Visualising bibliometric networks analysis

We have reviewed conference papers, journal articles, books, and online articles to complete this book chapter. Also, to get a clearer picture, visualising bibliometric networks analysis has been conducted. The study undertaken includes areas of discipline, and the purpose of business simulation games are used.

HISTORY OF BUSINESS SIMULATION GAMES

The early history of business games, such as board games and war games has started since 3000 BC in China (Faria, 1996; Wolfe, 1993). Board games have been widely used since the 17th century for entertainment and educational purposes. This includes Round the town (1900), Grand jeu de la tour Eiffel (1889), Il giro del Mondo (1890), L'orient or the Indian travellers (1845), A trip to marks (1920), Walli's new game of universal history and chronology (1840), The new game of human life (1790), Jeu de la revolution francaise (1790), For living a virtuous life – Le jeu des bons infans (1780), to teach how to make a good career – Game of the telegraph boy or merit reward (1888). For the war games, this can be traced back to GO (from China about 400 BC), Chaturanga and Chess (from India about 500 AB) and chess-like tabletop games - Christoph Weickmann's newly incented great king's game (1644). Another example is Brunswick war game (1780) (Kriz, 2017).

In 1903, Monopoly, originally from The Landlord's Game, was created by Lizzie Magie. The game's basic idea demonstrates an economy that rewards wealth creation is better than one where monopolists work under few constraints and promote Henry George's economic theories, particularly taxation (Pilon, 2015).

From 1932 to 1940, over 40 similar exercises related to production and distribution simulations at several different types of businesses were developed by Mary and her team in Leningrad (Faria, Hutchinson, Wellington, & Gold, 2009).

The modern business simulation game was started in 1955 when the Rand Corporation developed a simulation exercise, Monopologs, that simulated part of the air force supply system (Renshaw & Heuston, 1957). The modern business games leverage concepts from military war games, operational research, computer science, and educational theory. During World Wars I and II, complex war games were developed for military purposes. After the war ended, the development of simulations focused more on business games for business education and training (Kim & Watson, 2018). From 1956 to 1957, there were three well-known business game, Top management decision simulation. The first was developed by the AMA for use in management seminars. The second was Greene and Andlinger's business management game, and finally Schreiber's Top management decision game, the first business simulation game used in the business policy class at the University of Washington in 1957 (Faria, 1998).

Capitalism, the first modern business simulation game developed by Trevor Chan in 1995, is considered the best business simulation game. An expanded version of Capitalism II, Capitalism Lab, was released in 2012 and regularly updated with some new features (IGN, 2002).

TYPES OF BUSINESS SIMULATION GAMES

Greenlaw, Herron, and Rawdon (1962), Eilon (1963), and Blazic and Blazic (2015) classified business simulation games according to whether the game is focused on the total enterprise or some particular functionalities; whether the game is interactive or a noninteractive; and whether the game is a computer or a non-computer based. Overall, these classifications can be summarised and defined as the game is part of a general management training program; the game teaches new techniques, or just teaches procedures for selling; the game is intended to be used for conducting research; and the game studies the interactions of individuals within a team.

Wolfe (1993) classified three main fields of business simulation games application: Top-management games, Functional games, and Concept simulation games. Blazic and Arh (2013) classified the evaluation properties into two major groups. First, the technical classification that presents the properties using the technical data that describe the business simulation game. Second, the usability classification that presents a variety of dimensions that describes types of usability characteristics. The details can be referred to in table 1.

Table 1. Classification of the evaluation properties

Properties	Dimension	Description
Technical properties	Web-Based/Desktop	Whether the game can be played via modern browser or with installation package?
	Distribution	Whether the game is free for use, played by license, on CD-ROM, or run by downloaded application/client?
	Year of publishing	The year that game was started to be available for public use.
	Users	How many registered users the game has?
	Label	The name of the development team.
	Single/Multi user	Whether game can be played by one or many players.
	Dimension	Whether game is present in 2D/3D environment.
Usability Properties	The time period simulated	Day/week/quarter/year.
	Industry specific or generic	In industry specific game, the authors attempt to replicate closely the actual industry. In generic games only general business relationships are replicated.
	Degree of complexity	Game decision input variable complexity, or the computer model complexity.
	Functional or total enterprise	Designed to focus specifically on problems of decision-making as seen in one functional area or designed to give participants experience in making decisions at a top executive level and in which decisions from one functional area interact with those made in other areas of a firm.
	Competitive or Non-Competitive	Whether the decisions or participants influence the other participants?
	Feedback system	Whether the results are shown by gained scores, experience points, upgrade level or a summary report?
	Deterministic or stochastic	The stochastic alternative is probabilistic, including chance of elements.
	Briefing systems	The level and usability of briefing screen.
	Learning objectives	Types of learning skills that can be obtained.
	Background knowledge	Whether a basic/advanced or none business knowledge is recommended in order to play a game?
	Interactivity type	In an interactive game participant respond to the questions at the computer, receive an immediate response, and then submit additional decisions. In a non-interactive game decision are submitted to the game administrator.

Source: Adopted from (Blazic & Arh, 2013)

Business simulation games can be classified by subject matter as being available on a web-based platform and a desktop-based platform. Web-based games can be played within the modern web browser and desktop-based games need to be pre-installed in order to play them (Blazic, Ribeiro, Fernandes, Pereira, & Arh, 2012). The Vault Publication (2020) discussed that the development of a good simulation game should manage a balance between a high degree of realism and engagement. Also, it should incorporate the users into the game and allow them to make decisions that can be reflected in the simulation canvas. Jerman and Arh (2013) commented that the game has to be realistic, engaging, motivating, popular and user-friendly and a clear educational objective. There are five types of business simulation games created to meet the needs and appropriateness in the training process as well as teaching and learning. Types of business simulation games can be referred to table 2.

Table 2. Types of business simulation

Type	Description
Total enterprise simulation	This type of simulation deals with modelling most business functions. It is used as graded elements by instructors in business degree capstone policy courses under the assumption that their use enriches the learning experience. There are four categories of Total enterprise simulation: a. Strategic management Strategic simulation involves the strategic management aspect of the business, such as deal with finance, marketing, product design, etc. This category of simulation involves groups of learners interacting with each other. b. Business appreciation This category of simulation helps in developing business acumen and financial knowledge. c. Tactical management This category of simulation covers the tactical management aspect of the business. It allows the learners to experience the daily operation of the entire business. d. Totally simulation This category of simulation replicates the entire operation of the business in totality. It is a combination of the strategic and tactical aspects.
Functional simulation	Functional simulation focuses on a specific function or area by emphasising one of the company's business operations, such as marketing, production, finance, sales, advertising, personnel management etc.
Concepts simulation	This type of simulation emphasises on specific business concepts, for example a new product launch or the operations of a factory unit are types of concept simulation.
Planning simulation	This type of simulation comprises of preparing business plans with what-if models. The users apply what they have learned and explore the dynamics of the business. Even though the overall process is the same, the time that is allocated for the plan is not set and the number is not predefined.
Process simulation	This type of simulation uses mathematical techniques in the game. The users will need to consider the practical aspects. This includes dealing with different kinds of data and finding patterns, discussing the various implications, and producing outcomes.

Sources: Washbush and Gosen (1998); Faria et al. (2009); Blazic and Blazic (2015); and Designing Digitally (2017)

THE USE OF BUSINESS SIMULATION GAMES IN TEACHING AND LEARNING

The use of simulation games has long been regarded as a potentially transformative innovation (Rogmans & Abaza, 2019). Surveys conducted by Faria and Wellington (2004) reported that the simulation game usage at AACSB member schools has increased from 71.1% in 1962 to 97.5% in 1998. Business game usage was highest in strategic management, business policy, management, and marketing disciplines.

The use of business simulation games requires lecturer time to administer and also student time for data analysis and decision-making (Wellington, Hutchinson, & Faria, 2017).

The main advantages of using business simulation games in teaching and learning are it allows a lecturer to bring interactive or dynamic training into the classroom; to enable a lecturer more easily demonstrate the integration of the firm's key functional areas; to enable application theory; and interest and motivate students (Faria & Wellington, 2004).

Business simulation games provide ideas about the future, and the participants gained some knowledge about how future generations might work together and where potential conflicts might be (Lohmann, 2019). In cultivating the spirit of teamwork, students not only improve their concept knowledge but also improve soft skills (Geithner & Menzel, 2016) and management skills (Roungas, Bekius, & Meijer, 2019).

Table 3. The use of business simulation games

References	Finding
Bitrián, Buil, and Catalán (2020)	Business simulation games are increasingly emerging as pedagogical tools for actively motivating and engaging players in the learning experience.
Sierra (2020)	Students perceived the simulation as a very productive tool to develop multiple learning outcomes, such as improving their knowledge acquisition, problem-solving, critical thinking, and interpersonal skills. Also, Role-play activities are an effective way to enhance affective-learning outcomes.
Farrell (2020)	The simulation provided students with opportunities for reflection and the development of an understanding of international marketing's real world, with all its complexities and challenges. The simulation also allowed students to receive feedback, correct mistakes, and appreciate the varied activities that contribute to achieving an objective.
Mesquita and Silva (2020)	Business simulation games is an instrument that transforms the real business world in a simplified model enabling students to make decisions and simulate activities as if they were in a real business environment.
Wang, Wang, and Jian (2020)	Behavioural intention to use business simulation games is influenced by facilitating conditions, hedonic motivation, and price value.
Yen and Lin (2020)	To combine simulation-based learning systems with entrepreneurship education helps create and recognise entrepreneurial opportunities. The challenge-skill balance and playability play a critical role in enhancing flow experience and improving learning performance and entrepreneurial self-efficacy.
Zulfiqar et al. (2021)	Business simulation games build an interactive system and enhance motivation for students and teachers. Business simulation games help students enhance their decision-making abilities and skills, collaborative learning, gain knowledge, think proactively, and performance. Another essential element is to increase students' level of interest as they find it enjoyable.
Román, Román, and Gil (2021)	Students have been able to develop their skills in a real environment and improve their professional skills and ability to make effective decisions in the management of the company.
Palmunen, Lainema, and Pelto (2021)	Business simulation game increases students' understanding of the complex nature of relationships among various business concepts. It helps them to develop more integrated, complex, and accurate mental models of the phenomena illustrated by the business simulation game.
Davis, Fox, DeBode, and Peterson (2021)	Team Learn Goal Orientation (LGO) and Avoid Goal Orientation (AGO) are positively related to objective simulation performance. At the same time, AGO and Prove Goal Orientation (PGO) are related to perceived team effectiveness. It appears students are motivated to avoid negative judgments about their team's competence and not those motivated to learn or demonstrate their superiority, are more likely to perform better across both outcome measures.

A review conducted by Goi (2019) highlighted 30 reasons for the importance of using business simulation games. Among the most popular factors are collaboration, engagement, interaction and discussion of ideas; fun and enjoyment; and effectiveness of teaching and learning. Another few research works published in 2020 and 2021, which can be referred to in Table 3 show the importance of business simulation games used in learning and learning.

VISUALISING BIBLIOMETRIC NETWORKS ANALYSIS

For more insight, a total of 1960 journals were extracted from the Scopus database. The keyword, 'business simulation games' has been used to search for Scopus-indexed journals. These data are analysed using the visualising bibliometric networks method. The results of the analysis can be referenced in figures 1 and 2. This analysis has shown that the use of simulation games in business education not only involves business and commerce areas, but it is also closely related to other areas such as education (for examples medical education, and e-learning), psychology, game theory, and science and technology (for examples telecommunication, distributed computer system, networking, and human-computer interaction) (refer to figure 2).

Figure 2. Areas of discipline using simulation games

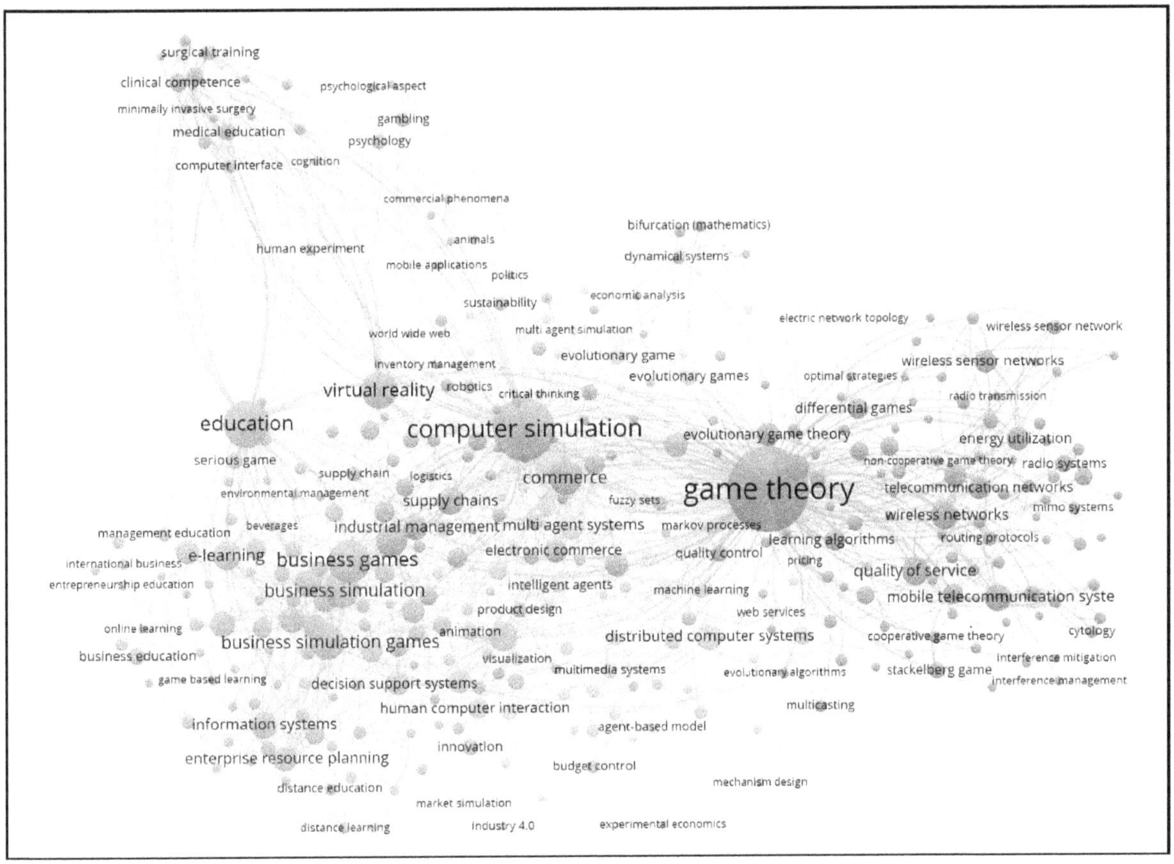

The use of business simulation games is very effective in teaching and learning. It is one of the innovative methods in addition to being able to include gamification elements in teaching and learning. As obtained from the results of this study, business simulation games can train students in terms of (1) apply and translate concepts and pedagogy to real business situations; (2) forecast, research, experiment and planning; (3) decision making; (4) critical thinking; (5) analysis skill, soft skill and managerial skill; (6) business strategy; (7) collaboration, engagement, interaction, and discussion of ideas; (8) gamification; (9) fun and enjoyment; (10) increase motivation in learning; and (11) effectiveness of teaching and learning (refer to figure 3).

Figure 3. The use of business simulation games

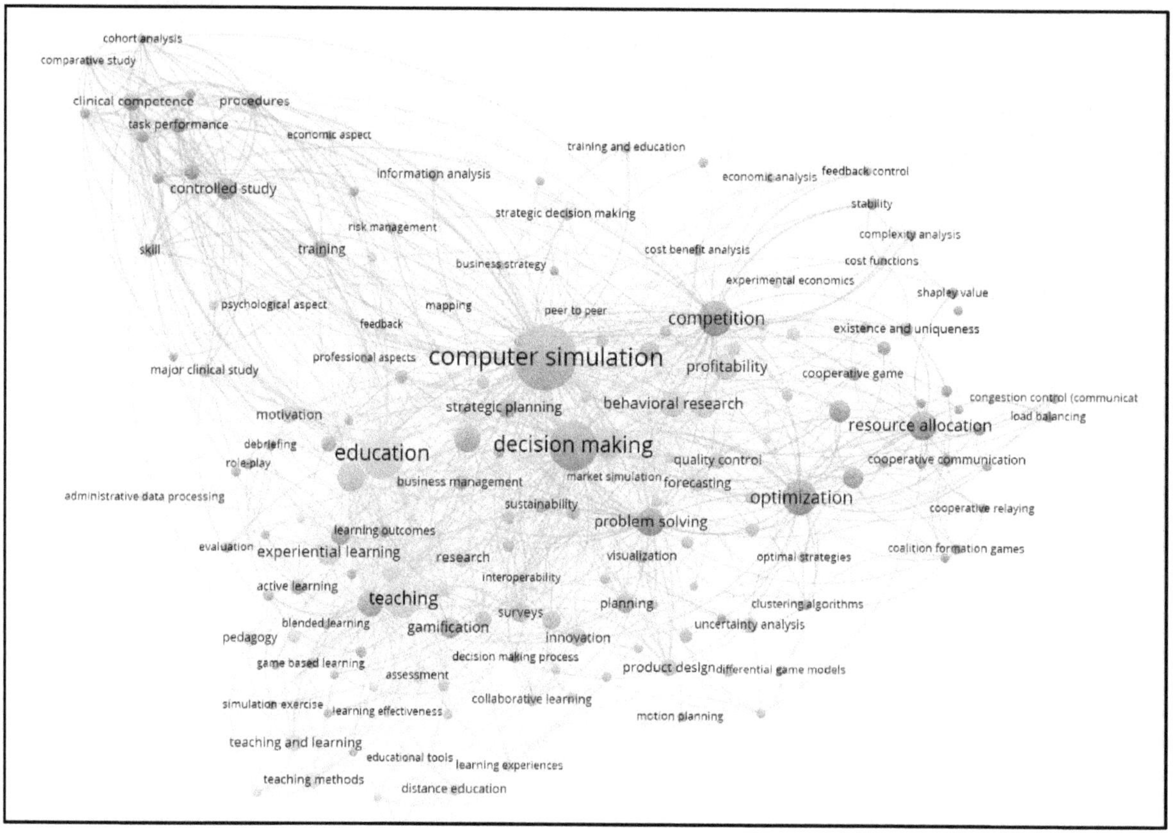

CONCLUSION

The development of business simulation games is according to the suitability and objectives of teaching and learning. The use of business simulation games has positively impacted teaching and learning (refer to figure 4). The early history of business simulation games began in 3000 BC in China and flourished in the 17th and 18th centuries. The development of this game peaked when a modern business simulation game was created in 1955. Overall, there are five types of business simulation games created (total enterprise simulation, functional simulation, concepts simulation, planning simulation, and process simulation) to meet the needs and appropriateness in the training process as well as teaching and learning.

Figure 4. The use of business simulation games and their impact on teaching and learning

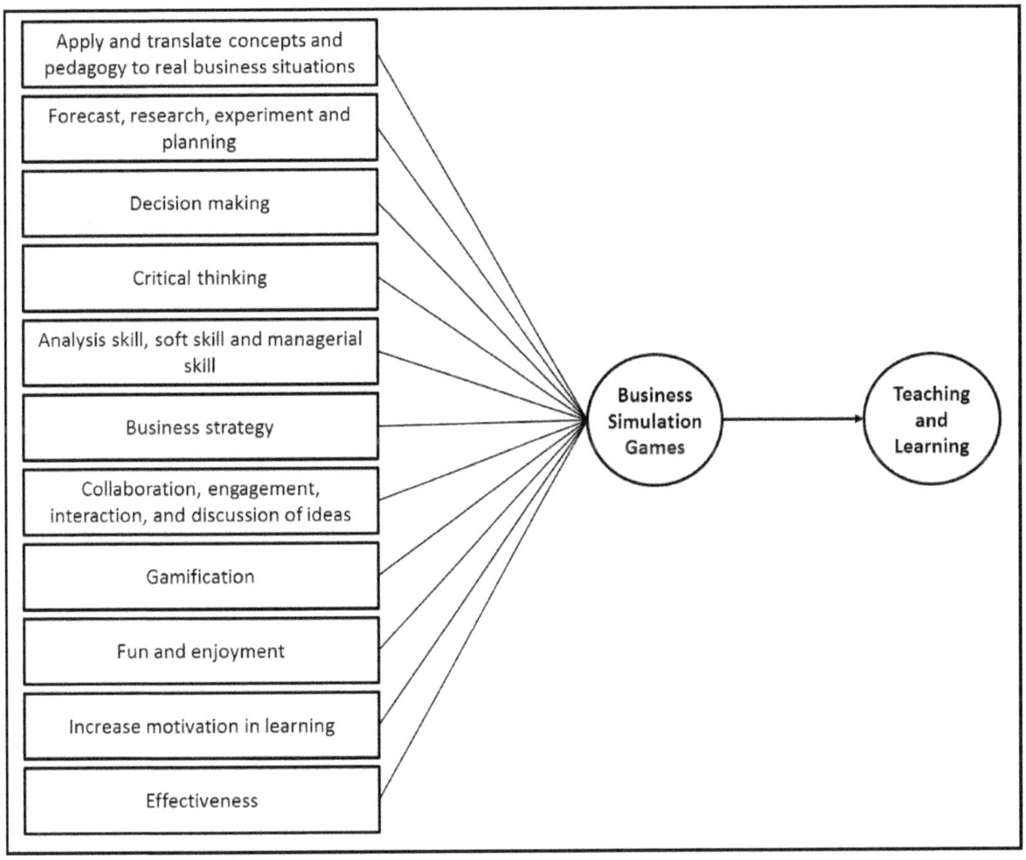

Future research will focus not only on one sector, education, but also other sectors such as services, manufacturing, oil and gas, and tourism. Therefore, comparisons of effectiveness on the use of business simulation games between these sectors can be made. Also, further research will be conducted on the development of business simulation games and their sustainability.

REFERENCES

Bitrián, P., Buil, I., & Catalán, S. (2020). Flow and business simulation games: A typology of students. *International Journal of Management Education*, *18*(1), 100365. doi:10.1016/j.ijme.2020.100365

Blazic, A. J., & Arh, T. (2013). *Immersive business simulation games: An innovative pedagogical approach to e-learning and education*. Paper presented at the 30th Ascilite Conference, Macquarie University.

Blazic, A. J., & Blazic, B. D. J. (2015). Exploring and upgrading the educational business-game taxonomy. *Journal of Educational Computing Research*, *52*(3), 303–340. doi:10.1177/0735633115572959

Blazic, A. J., Ribeiro, C., Fernandes, J., Pereira, J., & Arh, T. (2012). Analysing the required properties of business simulation games to be used in E-learning and education. *Intelligent Information Management*, *4*(06), 348–356. doi:10.4236/iim.2012.46039

Boyle, S. (2011). *Teaching toolkit: An introduction to games based learning*. UCD Teaching and Learning/ Resources.

Davis, P. E., Fox, C. J., DeBode, J. D., & Peterson, L. T. (2021). Is avoiding the appearance of incompetence the key to success? An examination of team goal orientation and performance in a simulation environment. *Journal of Educational Computing Research*, *58*(8), 1562–1585. doi:10.1177/0735633120940955

Eilon, S. (1963). Management games. *The Journal of the Operational Research Society*, *14*(2), 137–149. doi:10.1057/jors.1963.22

Faria, A. J. (1987). 'A survey of the use of business games in academia and business. *Simulation & Games*, *18*(2), 207–224. doi:10.1177/104687818701800204

Faria, A. J. (1996). Business simulation games: Current usage levels - A ten year update. *Developments In Business Simulation & Experiential Exercises*, *23*, 22–28.

Faria, A. J. (1998). Business simulation games: Current usage levels - An update. *Simulation & Gaming*, *29*(3), 295–308. doi:10.1177/1046878198293002

Faria, A. J., Hutchinson, D., Wellington, W. J., & Gold, S. (2009). Developments in business gaming: A review of the past 40 years. *Simulation & Gaming*, *40*(4), 464–487. doi:10.1177/1046878108327585

Faria, A. J., & Nulsen, R. (1996). Business simulation games: Current usage levels - A ten year update. *Developments In Business Simulation & Experiential Exercises*, *23*, 22–28.

Faria, A. J., & Wellington, W. J. (2004). A survey of simulation game users, former-users, and never-users. *Simulation & Gaming*, *35*(2), 178–207. doi:10.1177/1046878104263543

Farrell, C. (2020). Do international marketing simulations provide an authentic assessment of learning? A student perspective. *International Journal of Management Education*, *18*(1), 100362. doi:10.1016/j.ijme.2020.100362

Geithner, S., & Menzel, D. (2016). Effectiveness of learning through experience and reflection in a project management simulation. *Simulation & Gaming*, *47*(2), 228–256. doi:10.1177/1046878115624312

Goi, C. L. (2019). The use of business simulation games in teaching and learning. *Journal of Education for Business*, *94*(4), 342–349. doi:10.1080/08832323.2018.1536028

Gonen, A., Brill, E., & Frank, M. (2009). Learning through business games – An analysis of successes and failures. *Horizon*, *17*(4), 356–367. doi:10.1108/10748120910998434

Greenlaw, P. S., Herron, L. W., & Rawdon, R. H. (1962). *Business simulation in industrial and university education*. Prentice-Hall.

IGN. (2002). *Trevor Chan's Capitalism II*. Retrieved from https://www.ign.com/articles/2002/01/17/trevor-chans-capitalism-ii

Jerman, B. A., & Arh, T. (2013). *Immersive business simulation games: an innovative pedagogical approach to E-learning and education*. Paper presented at the 30th ascilite Conference, Macquarie University.

Kim, J. B., & Watson, E. F. (2018). *Flow in business simulation games: Comparison between online and face-to-face MBA*. Paper presented at the 51st Hawaii International Conference on System Sciences, Hilton Waikoloa Village, HI. 10.24251/HICSS.2018.004

Kriz, W. C. (2017). Historical roots and new fruits of gaming and simulation. *Simulation & Gaming*, *48*(5), 583–587. doi:10.1177/1046878117732845

Lohmann, R. (2019). Taking a Glimpse Into the Future by Playing? *Simulation & Gaming*, *50*(3), 377–392. doi:10.1177/1046878119848133

Luthra, P., & Mackenzie, S. (2020). *4 ways COVID-19 could change how we educate future generations*. Retrieved from https://www.weforum.org/agenda/2020/03/4-ways-covid-19-education-future-generations/

Mesquita, A., & Silva, P. (2020). Are we ready for the job market?: The role of business simulation in the preparation of youngsters. In J.-É. Pelet (Ed.), *Handbook of Research on User Experience in Web 2.0 Technologies and Its Impact on Universities and Businesses* (pp. 19–36). IGI Global.

Palmunen, L.-M., Lainema, T., & Pelto, E. (2021). Towards a manager's mental model: Conceptual change through business simulation. *International Journal of Management Education*, *19*(2), 100460. doi:10.1016/j.ijme.2021.100460

Pilon, M. (2015). Monopoly's inventor: The progressive who didn't pass 'go'. *The New York Times*. Retrieved from https://www.nytimes.com/2015/02/15/business/behind-monopoly-an-inventor-who-didnt-pass-go.html

Renshaw, J. R., & Heuston, A. (1957). *The game Monopologs*. US Air Force Project Rand Retrieved from https://www.rand.org/content/dam/rand/pubs/research_memoranda/2007/RM1917-1.pdf

Ritzko, J. M., & Robinson, S. (2006). Using games to increase active learning. *Journal of College Teaching and Learning*, *3*(6), 45–50.

Rogmans, T., & Abaza, W. (2019). The impact of international business strategy simulation games on student engagement. *Simulation & Gaming*, *50*(3), 393–407. doi:10.1177/1046878119848138

Román, M. P., Román, A. P., & Gil, I. P. (2021). Business simulation as a tool to develop the scenario analysis capacity. *Journal of Management and Business Education*, *4*(1), 1–17.

Roungas, B., Bekius, F., & Meijer, S. (2019). The game between game theory and gaming simulations: Design choices. *Simulation & Gaming*, *50*(2), 180–201. doi:10.1177/1046878119827625

Sierra, J. (2020). The potential of simulations for developing multiple learning outcomes: The student perspective. *International Journal of Management Education*, *18*(1), 100361. doi:10.1016/j.ijme.2019.100361

Turns, A. (2020). *'The world is changing now': why education and climate activism go hand in hand.* Retrieved from https://www.theguardian.com/education/2020/jan/27/the-world-is-changing-now-why-education-and-climate-activism-go-hand-in-hand

Wang, Y. Y., Wang, Y. S., & Jian, S. E. (2020). Investigating the determinants of students' intention to use business simulation games. *Journal of Educational Computing Research, 58*(2), 433–458. doi:10.1177/0735633119865047

Washbush, J. B., & Gosen, J. (1998). Total enterprise simulation performance and participant learning. *Journal of Workplace Learning, 6/7*(6/7), 314–319. doi:10.1108/13665629810236264

Wellington, W. J., Hutchinson, D. B., & Faria, A. J. (2017). Measuring the impact of a marketing simulation game: Experience on perceived indecisiveness. *Simulation & Gaming, 48*(1), 56–80. doi:10.1177/1046878116675103

Wolfe, J. (1993). A history of business teaching games in English-speaking and Post-Socialist countries: The origination and diffusion of a management education and development technology. *Simulation & Gaming, 24*(4), 446–463. doi:10.1177/1046878193244003

Yen, W. C., & Lin, H. H. (2020). Investigating the effect of flow experience on learning performance and entrepreneurial self-efficacy in a business simulation systems context. *Interactive Learning Environments*, 1–16. doi:10.1080/10494820.2020.1734624

Zirawaga, V. S., Olusanya, A. I., & Maduku, T. (2017). Gaming in education: Using games as a support tool to teach history. *Journal of Education and Practice, 8*(15), 55–64.

Zulfiqar, S., Al-reshidi, H. A., Al-Moteri, M. A., Feroz, H. M. B., Yahya, N., & Al-Rahmi, W. M. (2021). Understanding and predicting students' entrepreneurial intention through business simulation games: A perspective of COVID-19. *Sustainability, 13*(4), 1–27. doi:10.3390u13041838

Zulfiqar, S., Sarwar, B., Aziz, S., Chandia, K. E., & Khan, M. K. (2018). An analysis of influence of business simulation games on business school students' attitude and intention toward entrepreneurial activities. *Journal of Educational Computing Research, 57*(1), 106–130. doi:10.1177/0735633117746746

Chapter 5
The Digital Divide in the World of Education at the Time of COVID-19

Giovanni Bronzetti
Università degli studi di Palermo, Italy

Graziella Sicoli
Università della Calabria, Italy

Dominga A. Ippolito
Università della Calabria, Italy

ABSTRACT

Education has always been a challenge, today even more so given the difficulties of the moment, to support school in the time of COVID-19. Schools at every level have reorganized the training offer, implementing technological solutions. All this has raised a problem: the division is no longer between those who have access to the network and those who do not, but between those who know and those who do not know these new tools. Lately the concept of digital divide, understood as a gap of opportunity between those who have and those who do not have digital skills, has evolved into the concept of digital inequality. Given these premises, the work investigates after careful analysis, the impact of digital systems on the educational system, such as the emergence of the "digital divide," impacts on training within universities. To verify the "digital divide," the work proposes a quantitative survey carried out through a questionnaire submitted to a sample of students. The subject of the survey is given by the students of the University of Calabria.

DOI: 10.4018/978-1-7998-7184-2.ch005

INTRODUCTION

The disruptive event of the Covid-19 pandemic has altered social, work and study habits in every country in the world. In this scenario, completely unexpected in educational research (Hall et al., 2020), technology has become an essential tool to slow down and manage the crisis and mitigate its consequences. The crisis has accelerated the digitalization of education, but has also contributed to increasing the digital divide among students, a phenomenon that has been dragging on for years (Portillo et al., 2020). The new digital tools have avoided total paralysis of the economy by allowing millions of people to continue to carry out their activities and millions of students to continue learning and teaching through distance learning. However, there was no lack of inevitable delays attributable on the one hand to the limited digital infrastructures available and, on the other, to the scarce, and sometimes absent, technical skills necessary to use them.

The term distance learning means a teaching method that has allowed students and teachers to continue their training and learning path even if they are "physically" distant. All this required the adoption of new "digital" standards both in terms of instrumentation and specific skills. In particular, many academic institutions that were earlier reluctant to change their traditional pedagogical approach had no option but to shift entirely to online teaching – learning. In this context, the adoption of e-learning was immediately inserted, which is the direct result of the integration of education and technology and is considered a powerful means for learning (Al-Fraihat, Joy and Sinclair, 2017).

The race towards "technological innovation" has inevitably accelerated the digital divide, that is the exclusion from the benefits dictated by technological progress and innovation with an inevitable negative effect on those who are excluded from it. Digital inequalities certainly feed school inequalities and educational poverty between those who have the tools available to communicate, work, study, being able to react to the moment of crisis, and those who do not.

In light of this premise, the idea of the work takes shape which, after a careful theoretical analysis of the impact of digital systems on the education system, investigates how the "digital divide" aggravated by the Covid-19 pandemic impacts on education and on the provision of services within universities. The work proposes a quantitative survey carried out through the administration of a questionnaire to a sample of students from the University of Calabria who, starting from March 2019, have been engaged in the provision of online teaching.

The purpose is mainly to investigate the perception and satisfaction of students with respect to new forms of digital learning and with respect to the tools put in place by the university that have ensured the restart of the university through the e-learning platform. Subsequently, the work aims to understand whether the aid put in place by the university, especially in favor of the weakest, have been used and if used, if they have been effective, thus avoiding that no one is left behind.

LITERATURE REVIEW

The advent of the pandemic on a global level has led to a systemic revolution in different sectors, including education, paving the way for a new way of teaching. The world of education has fully opened up to the digital world and technology; this has allowed the academic activity not to suffer slowdowns and/or sudden braking, but to continue in its educational and cultural activities, ensuring a more innovative use.

The sudden adaptation that the new needs of the moment have imposed together with the rapid application times required high investments and also new ways of sharing knowledge. All of this involved inevitable difficulties and it was not at all easy. In this situation there is an urgent need of unity. Because it's necessary to protect and save our students, faculty, academic staff (Rieley, 2020). Only by acting in this direction has it been possible to make a virtue of necessity. Schools of all levels have been forced to review and reorganize their educational offer by implementing solutions developed by the digital technology systems available on the market. (Selwyn, 2015). In its embryonic stage, the efforts undertaken by teachers in the first weeks of distance learning were defined as "emergency distance teaching" (Hodges et al., 2020). There were some critical issues already partially known especially with reference to our territorial context, namely the digital device.

Re-education towards the world of digitization has brought out some very relevant problems such as the scarce equipment available to students accompanied by the often-limited skills necessary for their use. Having their own personal devices, an adequate connection in the home environment and digital skills that allow them to be able to use and produce learning content is not always simple and immediate. This is what the Istat (Italian Statistic Institute) report published in 2019 "Istat citizens and ICT" also shows, with reference to Italy, from which it emerges that Italy is a poorly digitized country. Families who have a broadband connection are 74.7%, while the percentage of respondents who said they used the internet at least once in the 3 months prior to the survey was 67.9%. Numbers up compared to the previous year but which are still not very exciting (https://www.istat.it/it/archivio/236920).

The advent of e-learning accelerated by the Covid-19 pandemic has inevitably had its repercussions in the world of education. Thus, within the academic world, the role of technology and the availability of digital and always connected classrooms has become a priority. (Dhawan, 2020; Hess, Leal, 2001; Alspaugh, 1999; Owens, Hersholt, 1996; Rosen and Weil, 1995). Having the availability of digital classrooms, even more so in times of crisis such as the current one, becomes a tool capable of fully guaranteeing the right to education. Combining face-to-face lectures with technology gives rise to blended learning. Students can learn anytime and anywhere, thereby developing.

However, this cannot neglect the inevitable digital inequality that arises since in education 3.0 students and families are forced to face the challenge of the digital divide on a daily basis, also in terms of complexity and cost that the implementation of new technologies requires. Even with internet access, the quality of learning could be affected by the number of internet-enabled devices available in the family (Frenette, 2020). Some argue that online mode of learning is easily accessible and can even reach to rural and remote areas. It is considered to be a relatively cheaper mode of education in terms of the lower cost of transportation, accommodation, and the overall cost of institution-based learning. Flexibility is another interesting aspect of online learning; a learner can schedule or plan their time for completion of courses available online.

All this has been possible thanks to the technology that has supported universities in the implementation of distance education (McBrien et al., 2009). While many studies highlight the positive effects associated with distance education, assisted by technology and digitization (Barron et al., 1999; Christmann, Badgett, 1999; Fitzgerald and Werner, 1996), on the other hand they highlight the digital divide between different population groups. Cole and Griffin (Cole and Griffin, 1987) firmly argue that technology must be an integral part of a well-planned pedagogy for students, ensuring fair access to teaching.

The use of IT platforms and new intelligent technologies to support e-learning increasingly require additional training for teachers so that they can implement what is required of them efficiently and correctly, obtaining the expected results (Srivastava et.al., 2018).

At the same time, it is also necessary to invest in students, who have to shape their skills with a view to learning. In fact, the implementation of e-learning requires students a certain degree of "self-sufficiency". This aspect has a more or less significant influence on their different level of satisfaction as well as on their interaction in continuing to use online teaching (Hayashi, Chen, Ryan, Wu, 2004).

Parkes et al., For example, show in their studies that students are poorly prepared in terms of specific skills on the use of e-learning and also find low-level preparation regarding the use of learning management systems (Parkes et al., 2014). Song et Al., On the other hand, believe that the lack of community and relationship together with the problems linked to any connection problems represent the main barriers for adequate online learning (Song et al., 2004). Dhawan, on the other hand, highlights the desire expressed by students in terms of bidirectional interaction and underlines that the way in which institutions behave, also enhancing the didactic quality offered especially in times of crisis, shows their ability to adapt, facing the e-learning challenge (Dhawan, 2020). The bidirectional challenge continues to affirm the author can be considered overcome provided that, on the one hand, an adequate technological structure is implemented for students useful for planning and designing their course of study and therefore the level of learning itself; on the other hand, an adequate technological structure for teachers in order to provide them with adequate skills in the use of learning tools and platforms (Ningshi, Mulyono, 2019).

The challenge therefore is not just to find a new technology and implement it, but to reinvent education itself, helping students and learners towards a new digital literacy. Only by following this approach will the implemented online teaching and learning methods be increasingly able to produce quality teaching (Carey, 2020; Srivastava et.al., 2018).

DIGITAL DIVIDE

Digital divide is known to be linked with digital literacy and the limitations experienced by people in the use of IT. The digital divide terminology, which has evolved over time (Di Maggio et al., 2004; Van Dijk, 2017; Bentivenga, 2009) was first coined by Warschaver (Ziemba, 2016) and more generally indicates the gap between those who have access suitable for the Internet and has the tools and skills useful to access and take advantage of the opportunities offered by technology and those who do not have it, whether voluntarily or not, and therefore remain excluded. The tools refer to the network coverage in the territory and therefore to the availability of the connection (technological profile of the digital divide); skills instead are represented by computer literacy (cultural profile of the digital divide) (Van Dijk, 2020)

This inevitably causes a number of disadvantages related to the missed "possibilities" that the digital world offers and therefore to the possible socio-economic damage that those affected suffer. The digital divide is a real phenomenon that is destined to remain in developed countries, but it is worse in developing countries, not only in terms of the first digital divide (internet access), but also in terms of attitude, skills, use (second digital divide) and internet results / benefits (third digital divide) (Mpungose, 2020; Van Deursen, Van Dijk, 2019).

Haythorthwaite (Haythorthwaite, 2007) defines three types of groups existing in the digital divide:

1. temporary, those rapidly closing the digital gap;
2. ever evolving delays, those that catch up momentarily but soon fall back again;
3. delay and exclusion, those groups that will never catch up.

Digital divide is a problem that affects students from all over the world to a greater or lesser extent. Therefore, scientists have tried to analyze this phenomenon at different stages of a student's life in an attempt to discover the underlying problems and seek explanations and possible solutions. For example, Waycott, Bennett, Kennedy, Dalgarno and Gray (Gray, 2010) identified differences in the use of technology in higher education and inthe daily lives of teachers and students in Australia.

Brown and Czerniewicz (Brown and Czerniewicz, 2010) state that the so-called "digital natives" are an elite lot because of their familiarity and experience in the use of IT rather than because of their age.

In recent times, the digital divide has extended to access to the world of IT and the necessary skills that are needed to stay connected. A high level of digital skills allows the user to take advantage of the use of the network and therefore improve their economic and social position as well as allowing a more active participation in the civil world (Hargatti, 2008) thus contributing to enriching human capital. of a country (Argentin, Gui; Tamanini, 2013). The use of the network, in fact, has a significant impact on the methods of socialization and the construction of social identity, and also on the same way of thinking, putting in place new logics in the learning processes.

The lack of possibility or the will to access the internet is to be considered a new form of social inequality that is added to the existing ones, representing an impediment not only to cultural growth and interaction processes, but to the development of new forms of democracy based on higher levels of participation in social, political and civil life, through the spread of forms of democracy and government.

Given the significant importance of digital skills, the topic has not gone unnoticed at an institutional level. In fact, the European Parliament has included digital competence among the eight key competences at the service of the education and training system. In this sense, Europe faces the challenges of globalization by giving a specific definition of digital competence, such as knowing how to use information society technologies with familiarity and a critical spirit, for work, communication, education and free time (European Parliament, 2006). A more recent part of the doctrine has recognized the existence of a real "damage from the digital divide", caused by the violation of the individual's right of access to the regular exercise of their rights online. This aspect takes the form of a particular type of prejudice, which can be qualified as damage to the person in the form of loss of chances of inclusion (see: agendadigitale.eu).

As Mansell (Mansell, 2017) argues, that linked to the digital divide is an issue to be considered ethical, since it highlights the equality of citizens under different forms of social inequality and technological stratification, with repercussions in the relational world and therefore in work. As it happens in a number of different realities, including the world of education, digital integration involves the different roles at play; in the case of the education sector, educators and students are involved in the continuous use of technology as a tool to complete the course of study undertaken and a means to promote the development of higher-order skills. This approach to technology has appeared as useful as it is.

It must be borne in mind that a segment of the population still has economic limitations for the purchase of adequate digital devices, while there are also those who lack digital skills among them. Goode (Goode, 2010). Furthermore, many students who do not have sufficient resources and experience probably miss the opportunity that in this pandemic period is the only alternative in terms of training opportunities. As Hwang, Chu, Lin and Tsai argue, teachers must provide strategies for students to guide training through new digital tools (Hwang, Chu, Lin and Tsai, 2011). At the same time, universities must provide initiatives to mitigate inequalities among students by providing them with digital mobile devices, increasing lesson times, increasing the quality and bandwidth of the Internet signal, etc. Students should also be provided with digital support in terms of lessons in order to reduce the existing asymmetries.

What the world of education tries to break down, especially in times of crisis we are experiencing, is precisely this gap that unfortunately still characterizes the academic population today. In fact, a series of initiatives and investments are promoted by the academic world aimed at shortening the digital distance between students, both in terms of "instrumental equipment" and in terms of skills, although the latter aspect is less rooted in the "millennial" generation (see: https://www.pewresearch.org/fact-tank/2019/09/09/us-generations-technology-use/).

OBJECTIVE OF THE RESEARCH

Starting from the concept of digital divide applied to the world of education, the work through the administration of a questionnaire made available online to a sample of students from the University of Calabria, aims to respond to the two research hypotheses listed below:

1. **Hypothesis One:** was the digitization and provision of online education a valid investment tool during Covid-19? What is the perception and the degree of satisfaction of the student in this sense?
2. **Hypothesis Two:** have the actions promoted by the University mitigated the digital divide by supporting students in the use of e-learning?

METHODOLOGY

The survey carried out in October 2020 was aimed at a sample of students of the University of Calabria, enrolled in three-year, master's or single-cycle degree courses, struggling with online teaching for a few months, now with the aim of detecting whether the digitization undertaken during the lock down period was a valid investment and whether the skills and equipment technology necessary for the use of online teaching have proved effective. With reference to this last point, the research analyzed whether the quality of the innovative services offered by the university have supported students by bridging where there are inevitable inequalities in terms of digitization, thus ensuring continuity and the right to study for the entire academic community.

The technological platform used to create the questionnaire is Google Forms, an online tool that allowed us to create the questionnaire and monitor the responses in real time. Our sample is made up of 2300 students who participated in filling out the questionnaire through the main social channels that put students in contact with the academic community of the university on a daily basis.

The totally anonymous questionnaire is made up of 35 multiple choice questions and is divided into four sections of questions: socio-demographic profile, preliminary knowledge of the support related to teaching, preliminary evaluation of tools related to distance learning, evaluation of teaching experiences on -line. In total, 1008 responses were collected. The main information received is summarized in the search results.

RESEARCH RESULTS

From the survey carried out, the first section of questions regarding socio-demographic data reveals preliminary aspects such as gender, age, nationality, region of residence, as well as membership in a three-year or master's degree course and the possession of adequate equipment in support of e-learning.

Table 1. Socio-demographic aspects

Gender	Male	51.20%
	Female	48.80%
Age	19 - 23	87.70%
	24 - 28	9.10%
	over 28	3.20%
Nationality	Italian	98%
	Other	2%
Region of residence	Calabria	98.80%
	Other	1.20%
Degree course	Triennial	83.70%
	Masterful	14.30%
	Single cycle	2%
Off-site student	Yes	65.10%
	No	34.90%
Who are you currently living with?	Family	72.60%
	Friends / colleagues	21.80%
	Alone	5.60%
How often do you usually go to university?	Daily basis	31.70%
	At least once a week	9.50%
	Several times a week	23.80%
	At least once a month	6%
	Several times a month	3.60%
	For exams only	25.40%
How do you get to university?	Car	34.50%
	Public transport	40.50%
	On foot	36.50%
	Other	0.40%

SOURCE: (OUR ELABORATION)

It was found that 51.2% of the students who took the questionnaire were male, while 48.8% were female; the predominant age group is the youngest, ranging from 19 to 23 (87.7%) with a predominance of students of Italian origin residing in Calabria. About 84% of students are enrolled in a three-year

Table 2. Preliminary knowledge of teaching aids

What device do you use to follow the online lessons?	Computer	9.50%	
	Laptop Computer	88.10%	
	Tablet	14.70%	
	Smartphone	29.40%	
	Smart tv	0.40%	
	Other	0%	
Satisfaction with the e-learning device	Computer	Very	76
		Quite	84
		Little	60
		For Nothing	44
	Laptop computer	Very	364
		Quite	460
		Little	56
		For Nothing	12
	Tablet	Very	80
		Quite	120
		Little	60
		For Nothing	40
	Smartphone	Very	116
		Quite	176
		Little	92
		For Nothing	52
	Smart tv	Very	28
		Quite	28
		Little	44
		For Nothing	80
Do you think there are more efficient devices to follow distance learning?	Yes	33.70%	
	No	34.50%	
	I do not know	31.70%	
If so, which ones?	Computer	35.90%	
	Laptop Computer	62.60%	
	Tablet	31.30%	
	Smartphone	4.60%	
	Smart tv	9.90%	
	Other	9.20%	
Internet connection in possession	ADSL	21.80%	
	FIBRA	39.70%	
	Wi-Fi mobile	16.70%	
	Hotspot	18.70%	
	Other	3.20%	
Have you taken advantage of the university incentives for the purchase of a computer?	Yes	15.10%	
	No	84.90%	
Have you taken advantage of the university incentives for the purchase of a modem?	Yes	36.50%	
	No	63.50%	
Are there other people you share your device (s) with?	Yes	29.40%	
	No	70.60%	
If so, does this affect your distance learning?	Yes	31.30%	
	No	59.70%	
	I do not know	9%	
How long the device can be used over a day	Computer	Up to an hour	64

continued on following page

Table 2. Continued

		2 to 5 hours	80
		More than 6 hours	96
		Never	192
	Laptop computer	Up to an hour	24
		2 to 5 hours	240
		More than 6 hours	580
		Never	24
	Tablet	Up to an hour	56
		2 to 5 hours	100
		More than 6 hours	120
		Never	200
	Smartphone	Up to an hour	24
		2 to 5 hours	112
		More than 6 hours	468
		Never	12
	Smart tv	Up to an hour	44
		2 to 5 hours	76
		More than 6 hours	40
		Never	196
Would you be willing to buy a new device?	Yes	43.70%	
	No	28.60%	
	I do not know	27.80%	

SOURCE: (OUR ELABORATION)

degree course and the majority of students state that they are off-site students (65.1%) and currently live with a family (72.6%). The sample of students interviewed declared that, in normal situations, they go to the University every day (31.7%), usually using public transport (40.5%).

As regards the section dedicated to the preliminary knowledge of teaching aids, the data collected shows that the majority of students declare that they use the laptop as a device (88.1%), followed by the use of the common means of use among young people, that is the smartphone (29.4%). The satisfaction recorded with regard to the device used to take advantage of the online lessons found satisfactory data

Table 3. Preliminary evaluation of students for distance learning

Connection quality	1 to 5	21.50%
	6 to 10	78.50%
Quality e-learning platform	1 to 5	15.50%
	6 to 10	84.50%
Image quality	1 to 5	21.90%
	6 to 10	78.10%
Audio quality	1 to 5	17.10%
	6 to 10	82.90%
Teacher narrative quality	1 to 5	10.80%
	6 to 10	89.20%
Interactivity E-learniing	1 to 5	24.30%
	6 to 10	75.70%

SOURCE: (OUR ELABORATION)

with regard to the laptop and smartphone. In fact, 460 students said they were quite satisfied with the use of the laptop and 176 with the smartphone. The computer and smartphone are the two most used digital tools by the student community which, however, declares itself not fully satisfied in its entirety by the use of the same. In fact, 33.7% of students think that there are more efficient tools for using online teaching. In terms of internet connection, on the other hand, only 39.7% declare they use Fiber, while less efficient means such as portable Wi-Fi and hotspot reach 16.7% and 18.7% respectively; these data reveal a not completely efficient technological equipment on the part of the students, in line with the main criticalities that characterize the phenomenon of the digital divide. As for the policies implemented to support students, to mitigate and bridge any digital divide that characterizes the world of education, the data are quite positive. In fact, 15.1% of students declare that they have taken advantage of the incentives put in place by the University of Calabria, for the purchase of a computer; 36.5% declared that they had taken advantage of the incentives for the provision of a modem for the internet connection.

Regarding the use of the devices owned by students, the majority of them declare that they do not share their use with other family members (70.6%). The residual part declares to share the devices in possession with the members of their family (29.4%). Those who share the device answer the consequential question aimed at investigating the negative influence that sharing the device can generate on online education. Of all the students who answered this question, only 31.3% declared that this sharing influences the use of distance learning. Analyzing the time that students spend in front of digital devices to enjoy the lessons it emerges that the majority of students use the laptop for more than six hours, followed by the smartphone for the same amount of time. No accessibility in terms of time is recorded for the smart TV (196 students say they never use it) and for the tablet (200 students never use it).

With regard to a qualitative assessment of the different facets of distance learning, Table 4 summarizes the main data relating to the quality of the connection, the platform, audio, images, interactivity and teacher support. For each aspect, all students assigned a score higher than six (from sufficiency to excellence) to each section investigated. In particular, the teacher's narrative is well rated by a percentage of students equal to 89.20%, followed by the quality of the platform used by the university which is positively evaluated by a percentage of students equal to 84.50%. These results show how, after eight months, the university has managed to implement an e-learning system which, in its various facets, satisfies the majority of the student community.

From the last section of the survey, with reference to students' experiences with regard to e-learning activities, it is important to focus on the perceptions of students deriving from the distance learning experience. A good percentage of students feel quite satisfied with the support offered by the university in providing distance learning (63.5% of students are quite satisfied). The majority of the students interviewed found little difficulty in using distance learning, implemented by the university. Still, 44% of students rate the courses held electronically as satisfactory enough, comparing them with the courses held in the classroom. Finally, e-learning activities are considered a positive tool for dealing with the pandemic crisis. As can be seen from table 5, about 76% evaluate e-learning as a suitable tool aimed at guaranteeing the right to study, during the emergency period linked to the spread of Covid-19, also hoping for a potential continuation in the future. The analysis can be concluded by arguing that in general the data processed show a positive feeling of acceptance towards the digitization of the lessons, although there are still critical issues with regard to digital divide.

The results that emerged confirm the research hypotheses initially mentioned. In fact, to the first research question: has digitization turned out to be a valid investment tool for the academic world in this time of crisis? The students consider the digitization implemented by the University as a valid tool

Table 4. Distance teaching experiences

Main teaching method	Live lessons	29.80%	
	Recorded lessons	1.20%	
	Live and recorded lessons	69%	
Do the teachers provide support material?	Yes	95.60%	
	No	3.60%	
	I do not know	0.80%	
If so, which one do you prefer?	Slides	Very	556
		Quite	356
		A little	48
		For nothing	8
	Academic articles	Very	88
		Quite	260
		A little	276
		For nothing	100
	Video	Very	312
		Quite	260
		A little	124
		For nothing	96
	Chapters of books	Very	288
		Quite	312
		A little	168
		For nothing	56

SOURCE: (OUR ELABORATION)

to address the problems that the Covid-19 pandemic has caused. In fact, in relation to the current context, the experiences of students in relation to DAD seem to highlight a positive feedback, source of the perception of the help offered by the university for the continuity of teaching, aimed at guaranteeing the right to study and 'learning.

On the second hypothesis: have the investments made by the University mitigated the effects of digital, divide by supporting students in the use of e-learning? The students' response brought out important considerations.

The student team confirms that the University of Calabria immediately implemented a series of different initiatives, especially in support of disadvantaged students; think, for example, of the equipment on loan for use of hardware instrumentation and modems for surfing the net in order to allow an adequate connection to those who did not have one.

The university immediately promoted activities aimed at tackling the digital divide, to prevent it from becoming an obstacle in the use of online lessons. There are also many and different activities promoted in favor of students to guarantee them adequate preparation in terms of "digital knowledge". This has allowed the entire academic community to be able to adequately follow the lessons delivered, mitigating the digital divide thanks to the many frontal initiatives delivered in streaming.

The research conducted confirms the university's commitment to mitigate and, when possible, eliminate any digital divide through the implementation of e-learning platforms that can also be exploited in the future and usable by everyone regardless of where they are, trying to harmonize the operational context and interaction at each level as much as possible.

CONCLUSION

Online learning is commonly defined as a learning experience in synchronous and asynchronous environments (Singh, Thurman, 2019; Dhawan, 2020) implemented through the use of different technological devices. In this environment, students can take advantage of teaching wherever they are, shortening physical distances, learning, interacting and relating to each other.

The difficult moment caused by the spread of Covid-19 has seen the world of education committed to restarting precisely from the digitization of online training to guarantee the right to education. We start from innovation and the virtual, even if with some critical issues related above all to the different possibilities of access to technology by everyone.

The technological digital divide, essentially linked to network coverage in the national territory, is evident in every wall of the territory with the inevitable consequence that a wider possibility to access the web, to operate consciously, exploiting the wealth of knowledge available, is an indispensable prerequisite. to take advantage of the benefits of online teaching.

The problem related to the digital divide manifests itself differently, from inadequate digital equipment, to the lack of skills to access it, giving rise to a form of general exclusion from technological progress and innovation. Those who are excluded inevitably lose the advantages, suffering social, economic and above all cultural damage.

The problems and difficulties related to the use and access to technologies can be solved by focusing on interactivity and dynamism between the individuals involved, carrying out the necessary activities in support of the educational world, trying to harmonize the operational context as much as possible. It is necessary to fill in the disparities that access to distance learning has inevitably brought out; it is necessary to act in a timely manner by promoting digitally adequate and possibly accessible solutions and initiatives by everyone.

Since the beginning of the pandemic caused by Covid-19, the University of Calabria has embraced the challenge, promoting digitalization and at the same time mitigating the gap. This was possible thanks to the implementation of e-learning platforms through which it was possible to ensure didactic continuity throughout the crisis period. The digital divide has been mitigated by transferring the right digital skills to teachers and students. In the crisis, the university has seen an opportunity to innovate more in terms of digitalization of knowledge for a cultural change that starts from the bottom, therefore from the student component, opening the classrooms to virtual reality.

Finally, from the results that emerged, the need for a continuous interest of the Universities certainly emerges, aimed at improving student satisfaction, continuing to carry out promotion and investment activities in technological innovation, aiming at breaking down the digital divide.

REFERENCES

Al-Fraihat, D., Joy, M., Masa'deh, R., & Sinclair, J. (2017). Identifying success factors for e-learning in higher education. In *International conference on e-learning* (pp. 247-255). Academic Conferences International Limited.

Alspaugh, J. W. (1999). The Relationship between the Number of Students per Computer and Educational Outcomes. *Journal of Educational Computing Research, 21*(2), 141–150. doi:10.2190/RBRX-39G9-LHAP-7DT3

Argentin, G., Gui, M., Tamanini, C. (2013). Ascuola di competenza digitale. Il ruolo degli insegnanti nell'uso delle ICT degli student. *Scuola democratica, 1.*

Barron, A., Hogarty, K., Kromrey, J., & Lenkway, P. (1999). An Examination of the Relationships between Student Conduct and the Number of Computers per Student. *Journal of Research on Computing in Education, 32*(1), 108–127. doi:10.1080/08886504.1999.10782271

Bentivenga, J. (2009). Escenarios mundiales de la educaciòn superior: Anàlisis global y estudios de casos. *Propuesta Educativa (Buenos Aires)*, 31.

Carey, K. (2020). Is everybody ready for the big migration to online college? Actually no. *The New York Times*. http://www.nytimes.com

Christmann, E., & Badgett, J. (1999). A Comparative Analysis of the Effects of Computer-Assisted Instruction on Student Achievement in Differing Science and Demographical Areas. *Journal of Computers in Mathematics and Science Teaching, 18*, 135 43.

Cole, M., & Griffin, P. (Eds.). (1987). *Contextual Factors in Education: Improving Science and Mathematics Education for Minorities and Women*. Wisconsin Center for Education Research.

Czerniewiez, L., & Brown, C. (2010). *Born into the digital age in the South of Africa: the reconfiguration of the "digital citizen". Proceedings ot the 7th International Confernces on Networked Learning 2010.*

Dhawan, S. (2020). Online learning: A panacea in the time of Covid-19 crisis. *Journal of Educational Technology Systems, 49*(1), 5–22. doi:10.1177/0047239520934018

Di Maggio, P., Hargittai, E., Celeste, C., & Shafer, S. (2004). Digital inequality. From unequal access to differentiated use: A literature review and agenda for research on digital inequality. In *Neckerman K. (a cura di), Social inequality*. Russell Sage.

Fitzgerald, G., & Werner, J. (1996). The Use of the Computer to Support Cognitive Behavioral Interventions for Students with Behavioral Disorders. *Journal of Computing in Childhood Education, 7*, 127–148.

Frenette, M., Frank, K., Deng, Z. (2020). School closures and the online preparedness of children during the Covid-19 pandemic. *Economic Insights, 103.*

Goode, J. (2010). Mind the gap: The digital dimension of college access. *The Journal of Higher Education, 81*(5), 583–618. doi:10.1080/00221546.2010.11779068

Gray, L., Thomas, N., & Lewis, L. (2010). Teachers' us of educational technology in U.S. Public Schools: 2009 (NCES 2010-040) National Center for Education Statistic. Institute of Education Sciences, U.S. Development of Education.

Hall, T., Connolly, C., Ó Grádaigh, S., Burden, K., Kearney, M., Schuck, S., Bottema, J., Cazemier, G., Hustinx, W., Evens, M., Koenraad, T., Makridou, E., & Kosmas, P. (2020). Education in precarious times: A comparative study across six countries to identify design priorities for mobile learning in a pandemic. *Information and Learning Sciences*, *121*(5/6), 433–442. doi:10.1108/ILS-04-2020-0089

Hargittai, E. (2008). *The digital reproduction of inequality, Social Stratification, a cura di D. Grunsky*. Westview Press.

Hayashi, A., Chen, C., Ryan, T., & Wu, J. (2004). The role of social presence and moderating role of computer self efficacy in predicting the continuance usage of e-learning system. *Journal of Information Systems Education*, *15*(2).

Haythornthwaite, C. (2007). Digital Divide and Elearning. In R. Andrews & C. Haythornthwaite (Eds.), *Handbook of Elearning Research*. Sage.

Hess, F. M., & Leal, D. L. (2001). A shrinking "Digital Divide"? The provision of classroom computers across urban school system. *Social Science Quarterly*, *82*(4), 765–778. doi:10.1111/0038-4941.00058

Hodges, C., Moore, S., Lockee, B., Trust, T., & Bond, A. (2020). The differences between emergency remote teaching and online learning. *Educause Review*. Available at: https://er.educause.edu/article/2020/3/the-difference-between-emergency-remote-teaching-and-online-learning

Hwang, G., Chu, H., Lin, Y., & Tsai, C. (2011). A knowledge acquisition approach to developing mindtools for organizing and sharing differentiating knowledge in a ubiquitous learning environment. *Computers & Education*, *57*(1), 1368–1377. doi:10.1016/j.compedu.2010.12.013

Mansell, R. (2017). Inequality and digitally mediated communication: divides, contradictions and consequences. *Javnost- the Public*, *24*(2), 146-161.

McBrien, J. L., Cheng, R., & Jones, P. (2009). Virtual spaces: Employing a synchronous online classroom to facilitate student engagement in online learning. *The International Review of Research in Open and Distributed Learning*, *10*(3), 1–17. doi:10.19173/irrodl.v10i3.605

Mpungose, C. B. (2020). Emergent transition from face- to-face to online learning in a South African University in the context of the Coronavirus pandemic. *Humanties and Social Sciences Communications*, *7*(1), 113. doi:10.105741599-020-00603-x

Ningsih, S. K., & Mulyono, H. (2019). Digital assessment resources in primary and secondary school classrooms. Teachers' Use and Perceptions. IJIM, 13(8).

Owens, E., & Hersholt, W. (1996). Differences among urban, suburban, and rural schools on technology access and use in Eighth- Grade mathematics classrooms. *Journal of Educational Technology Systems*, *24*(1), 83–92. doi:10.2190/PAP0-HJTM-95JU-RE2W

Parkes, M., Stein, S., & Reading, C. (2014). Student preparedness for university e-learning environments. *The Internet Higher education*, *25*, 1–10. doi:10.1016/j.iheduc.2014.10.002

Parlamento Europeo. (2006). Raccomandazione del Parlamento Europeo e del Consiglio del 18 dicembre 2006 relativa a competenze chiave per l'apprendimento permanente. *Gazzetta Ufficiale dell'Unione Europea.*

Portillo, J., Garay, U., Tejada, E., & Bilbao, N. (2020). Self-perception of the digital competences of educators during the Covid-19 pandemic: a cross- analysis of different educational stages. *Sustainability, 12*, 1-128.

Rieley, J. B. (2020). *Corona virus and its impact on higher education.* Research Gate.

Rosen, L., & Weil, M. (1995). Computer Availability, Computer Experience, and Technophobia among Public School Teachers. *Computers in Human Behavior, 11*(1), 9–31. doi:10.1016/0747-5632(94)00018-D

Save the Children. (2014). *No child left behind, Education in crisis in the Asia-Pacific Region Victoria.* Author.

Selwyn, N. (2015). The discursive construction of education in the digital age. In R. H. Jones, A. Chik, & C. A. Hafner (Eds.), *Discourse and digital practices: Doing discourse analysis in the digital age* (p. 226). Routledge.

Singh, V., & Thurman, A. (2019). How many ways can we define online learning? A systematic literature review of definitions of online learning (1998-2018). *American Journal of Distance Education, 33*(4), 289–306. doi:10.1080/08923647.2019.1663082

Song, L., Singleton, E. S., Hill, J. R., & Koh, M. H. (2004). Improving online learning: Student perceptions of useful and challenging characteristics. *The Internet and Higher Education, 7*(1), 59–70. doi:10.1016/j.iheduc.2003.11.003

Srivastava, S., Malik, H., Sood, Y. R., & Ahmad, A. (2018). *Applications of artificial intelligence techniques in engineering. In Sigma* (Vol. 1). Springer.

Van Deursen, A. J., & Van Dijk, J. A. (2019). The first- level digital divide shifts from inequalities in physical access to inequalities in material access. *New Media & Society, 21*(2), 354–375. doi:10.1177/1461444818797082 PMID:30886536

Van Dijk, J. (2017). Digital divede: impact of access. In P. Rossler (Ed.), *The International Encyclopedia of Media Effect.* Wiley. doi:10.1002/9781118783764.wbieme0043

Van Dijk, J. (2020). *Il Digital Divide Cambridge*, Polity Press. *Communication, 2020.* Advance online publication. doi:10.1515/commun-2020-0026

Ziemba, E. (2016). Factors affecting the adoption and usage of ICT's within polish household. *Interdisciplinary Journal of Information. Knowledge and Management, 11*, 89–113.

KEY TERMS AND DEFINITIONS

Digital Divide: Inequality exists between those who have access to information technologies (also in terms of skills) and those who are totally or partially excluded.

Digital Learning: Is any type of learning that is accompanied by technology or by instructional practice that makes effective use of technology.

Digitization: Business operations and activities carried out with the aid of digital tools.

E-Learning: Use of digital technologies for distance learning through the aid of an internet connection.

Innovation: Success of innovative and creative ideas that have introduced something new and useful.

Intelligent Technology: Is various approach and means which use knowledge to reach concrete purpose in efficiency.

Platform: IT structure responsible for the provision of technological tools and services for the distribution of digital services, free or paid.

Technological Innovation: The evolution, growth, and improvement of technical and scientific knowledge suitable for the creation of products, services and technologies.

Technology: Application and study of everything that can be functional to the resolution of practical problems and business strategies to achieve a goal.

Chapter 6
Student and Educator Perspective on Unconventional Online Classes

Muhammad Azmi Sait
https://orcid.org/0000-0002-5175-6436
Universiti Brunei Darussalam, Brunei

Hajah Fathiin Najihah binti Haji Mohd Rozaini
Universiti Brunei Darussalam, Brunei

ABSTRACT

The purpose of this study is to gain insights on students' and educators' perspectives of the current unconventional learning and teaching methods carried out during the COVID-19 pandemic. The main data is sourced from BruCERT's online survey of 785 students and 664 educators conducted during the closing downs of educational institutes due to preventive measures imposed by the government of Brunei Darussalam. The result shows that 77.96% of students and 72.14% of educators preferred the conventional classes. The main reasons are due to their inability to acquire good internet connectivity and proper area and time management that best suits online classes. In addition to that, the respondents perceived that the aforementioned problems become the root cause of their low discipline, productivity, and motivation to conduct and attend such classes. This chapter would be beneficial as a guideline to synthesize better teaching and learning strategies in online settings in the future.

INTRODUCTION

In this unprecedented time of COVID-19 pandemic, developing countries such as Brunei Darussalam has to close down its public premises including educational institutes, mosques, restaurants and many others, in the effort to contain the virus outbreak within the community. With reportedly hundreds of cases of community spread in the South East Asia region within short period of time, "Social Distancing", "Movement Control Orders", "Lockdowns" are few of the many notions that are prominently heard

DOI: 10.4018/978-1-7998-7184-2.ch006

of in countries that are affected by the pandemic. This newly imposed social restrictions by the governments has pressured their public and private sectors to adapt towards the "new normal" as well as to find alternative ways to stay operational and relevant without the need of being present in the workplaces.

In the domain of education, the students and educators (i.e., teachers, lecturers, tutors) from primary to tertiary levels finds utmost challenge to adapt to the new unprecedented learning and teaching environment via internet connectivity, thus giving rise to the notion, "learning from home" for the students and "teaching/working from home" for the educators (also refers to as "teachers"). This unconventional way of learning and teaching is quite unfamiliar to developing countries such as Brunei Darussalam as its educational system been accustomed to the traditional learning and teaching methods. The process of adapting to the "new normal" for the students and educators alike, are believed to be mediated by their familiarity towards the new learning and teaching environments (Wang et al., 2013), intrinsic motivations to interact with each other as well as the sets of standard guidelines imposed to facilitate the learning outcomes of the classes (Song & McNary, 2011)

Therefore, this study aims to explore general insights on students' and teachers' perspective of the unconventional online learning and teaching method conducted during this pandemic in Brunei Darussalam. The followings are the objectives of this research:

1. To investigate the learning methods that students and educators preferred during this pandemic;
2. To identify the challenges and its effects faced by the students and educators in participating and conducting online classes respectively;
3. To recommend better learning and teaching strategies that would aid the students and educators alike for online classes in the future.

The rest of the paper will be structured as follows: next section will cover on the literature reviews on the social restrictions during this pandemic, brief insights on the learning and teaching methods deployed in unconventional class as well as the new unfamiliar environment. Then, it will be followed by the methodology that is being deployed for this research. Then, next will be on the results and discussion section and lastly ended with conclusion, limitation and recommendation of this study.

LITERATURE REVIEW

Unconventional Learning and Teaching Method

Unconventional method in the context of class settings, refers to the type of classes that is unfamiliar and unheard of, as well as the type that has never been conducted in the past. Conventionally, traditional classes comprised of the teachers and the students physically present at the same location or place at a given dedicated of period of time (Odhaib, 2018). This traditional class setting is believed to allow for a better conducive learning environment as it enables interactions and communication via instant real-time feedbacks and discussions which in turn will initiate trusts between the students and teachers (Nazarenko, 2015; Sarrab et al., 2014). Given the social restrictions imposed during this time of pandemic, the traditional classes are needed to be conducted unconventionally, particularly in online setting, but still required to deliver the same level of knowledge dissemination as the conventional method.

In overcoming this issue, online class is deemed as the most suitable choice because it only require the students and teachers to be present in the virtual world at the comfort of their homes, through means of Web 2.0-based applications that supports knowledge sharing such as video conferencing and class discussions (e.g. Zoom, Skype, Microsoft Team), sharing of documents (e.g. Gmail, Hotmail) as well as distributions of learning materials (i.e. Canvas) (Amin et al., 2016) (Mulyani et al., 2019; Razzaq et al., 2018). In its essence, online classes in the perspective of students is more familiar to be known as "e-learning" method. e-Learning is an integration of traditional learning style with the utilization of ICT for the means of online learning, teaching as well as research (Alsulimani & Kaabi, 2018).

Through e-learning, the students agreed that they have the privilege of the flexibility of time and place to learn; able to study at their own paces as well as cost effective as they don't have to spend their money, time and energy to go to their respective schools and educational institutions (Alsaaty et al., 2016; Guragain, 2016). On the other hand, the educators view online teaching ease their deliverability of classes through the ability of creating interactive learning materials by utilizing graphics, sounds, and illustrations which would else cannot be done on a plain whiteboard or blackboards (Li et al., 2018).

However, e-learning can be disadvantage to both the students and the teachers. In the aspect of students, they may be prone to over-procrastination, if they are not being motivated by their teachers to learn the materials that are given due to the fact that the students have the control of their own learning paces (Guragain, 2016). On the other hand, the teachers may become unmotivated because they are not able to control the learning progress of their students as they cannot observe them in person (Anshari et al., 2017). In addition to that, online classes require good internet connectivity. Inability to acquire good internet connectivity becomes the main factor to the ineffectiveness of online class deliverability. This would then cause the students' inability to successfully interact with their teachers and cause their deteriorating participation and motivation in the learning process (Husniyah, 2019).

Unconventional Learning and Teaching Environment

Online classes in education domain, is believed to be the start of the notion 'learning from home' for the students and 'work from home' for the educators. Learning is inevitably part of students' work scope as much as teaching is part of teachers. Thus, learning and working shall be made non-distinguishable in its nature of outcome. The notion 'from home' is significantly similar to 'teleworking' which certainly meant the work are to be done far away from the supervision of the teachers (for the students) and the superiors (for the teachers), facilitated by virtual communication tools i.e. video conferences, teleconferences, remote access to intranets, to name a few (Coenen & Kok, 2014). This type of work setting is believed to increase productivity as it mitigates distractions from other colleagues and time can be maximized to do works which would otherwise be spent for commutation from home (Gunderman, 2019). However, a study by Kazekami (Kazekami, 2020) argues that there is no linear relationship between productivity and teleworking because there is a threshold to the significant productivity when time is made as the mediator. Moreover, the absence of superiors entails the idea that working or learning hours can be flexible to suit to the workers' (teachers and students) lifestyle (Hill & Holmes, 2019).

In addition to that, working and learning from home is believed to facilitate better team communication, but not necessarily replace the actual physical interactions. It may give the utmost opportunity of knowledge sharing, cross-functional cooperation and interorganizational involvement in the delivering a task, but the participants need to have good relationships prior to it (Coenen & Kok, 2014). Moreover, online classes may cause confusions and conflicts to the physical and mental states of the students and teachers. Working and learning from home may carry the benefit of having more time to spend on with the family at home, but it may inevitably diminish the distinctive differences between home and work-place or class (Gunderman, 2019).

In the human psychological perspective, a place may exist as only one distinctive salient identity: either a place is a home or an office or a school. Merging the boundaries between a home domain and a work domain proven to be difficult for a healthy human to perform (Capitano & Greenhaus, 2018). Thus a study confirms that it is very common to experience unproductivity when performing office or school tasks at home due to the high salient identity of home that prevents tasks-related permeation into the home domain, dubbed "Protection Effect" (Capitano et al., 2017).

Context of Study

COVID-19 was first reported in Brunei on 9th March 2020 in Tutong district (Abu Bakar, 2020). In response to this first confirmed COVID-19 case, the government has taken fast, strict and proactive preventive measures whilst tightening restrictions. These measures were taken in accordance to the guidance that was provided by the World Health Organisation (WHO) in order to find, isolate, test and treat confirmed COVID-19 cases (WHO, 2020). In addition to the preventive measure, the government provided guidelines for businesses to abide, such as wearing face masks and monitoring customer's temperature in hope to lessen the spread of COVID-19 to more places (Han, 2020).

As of recently, the nation has fortunately managed to combat the rapid spread of COVID-19, and this has been proven by the Ministry of Health (MOH) that as of 3rd November 2020, Brunei has recorded zero local transmission cases and the last local case reported was 181 days ago with a total of 144 recovered patients (Ministry of Health, 2020). As a result, this allows for the de-escalation plan to be slowly implemented by enforcing the plan in five different phases depending on the current COVID-19 situation in the country (Han & Abu Bakar, 2020). Currently Brunei is at the final phase of de-escalation plan, as stated by the Minister at Ministry of Health on 27th July 2020 (Han & Abu Bakar, 2020) where mass gathering and physical distancing guidelines have been modified to ease previous restrictions.

The general education system in Brunei Darussalam began from the primary, secondary, post-secondary education (sixth form) up until tertiary level. Bruneian locals have the perks of enjoying subsidized education from primary to tertiary levels, which includes free public examinations i.e. GCE O'Level, A'Level, etc. In addition to that, Brunei's National Education Policy also emphasized on giving all Bruneian children with opportunities to achieve at least an upper secondary or vocational education in order to develop their potential with hopes that their skills will help benefit the development of the country in the future.

Higher education comprises all post-secondary education, training and research guidance at education institutions such as universities that are authorized as institutions of higher education by state authorities (Herrington, 2006). Crucially it consisted of additional processes that are taking place, bringing about in the individual student a special level of personal development. Higher education is more than just a subset of the education system. They carry certain values and aims which are intrinsic to educational processes and which warrant the description of 'higher education' (Barnett, 1990). Historically, institutions of higher education exist to educate students for lives of public service, to advance knowledge through research, and to develop leaders for various areas of the public service Today's universities, however, are required to prepare graduates with the knowledge, skills, and ethical responsibility to meet the future workforce needs of society and to participate fully in the new global economy (Spellings, 2006).

According to UNESCO Institute of Statistics, as of 2018, Brunei Darussalam is among one of the countries in Southeast Asia with a high literacy rate of 97.21 percent for females and males aged 15 years and above. To date, there are currently four major public higher education institutions in Brunei which offer courses from Diplomas to PhDs. The four major higher institutions in Brunei are Universiti Brunei Darussalam (UBD), Universiti Teknologi Brunei (UTB), Universiti Islam Sultan Sharif Ali (UNISSA) and Politeknik Brunei (Tibok & Hiew, 2019). On top of that, one of its local universities, Universiti Brunei Darussalam, is also ranked in the top 100 among universities in Asia at 86th place (Sowter et al., 2017).

METHODOLOGY

The type of research conducted in this study is an exploratory research with the main aim to gain insights on students' and educators' perspective of the online learning and teaching method conducted during this pandemic in Brunei Darussalam. To achieve the objectives of this study, secondary data from BruCERT quantitative and qualitative online survey entitled, "Survey on Learning/Working from Home" is used (Brunei Computer Emergency Response Team (BruCERT), 2020). This survey was conducted from 17th to 23rd April 2020, with 3,000 respondents with the purpose to understand the local experience of studying or working from home due to COVID-19 restrictions that was imposed by Ministry of Health, Brunei Darussalam.

In addition to that, the literature review for this study is obtained by utilising search engines such as Google Scholars, ScienceDirect, Emerald Insights and Wiley Online Library to name a few, to search for keywords that comprises of 'online learning challenges', 'e-learning issues to students and educators', 'barriers to new learning systems, 'hybrid or blended learning', 'psychological effect of new learning environment', 'digital literacy and digital gap', 'opportunities to e-learning' and any keywords related to this research topic. Only journal articles and past research papers from 2001 onwards, in Malay and English languages were used in this paper. Multiple systematic literature reviews from the same period of time, revolving around the aforementioned keywords were extensively used to construct the basic understanding of this study.

RESULTS AND DISCUSSIONS

A total of 3,000 respondents took part in this online survey conducted over a duration of one week from 17th to 23rd April 2020 conducted by BruCERT. The total of 785 (26.17%) students and 664 (22.13%) educators (i.e. teachers, tutors, lecturers) participated in this survey. In the aspect of acquired devices, majority of the students and educators uses laptops (students – 78.34%, educators – 91.87%) and mobile phones (students – 80.51%, educators – 89.76%). Approximately only 2.42% of students and 0.15% of teachers do not have internet access in their homes respectively.

This shows that majority of the students and educators in Brunei Darussalam are able to acquire electronic smart devices and only a minority of them do not have internet access in their homes to conduct and participate in online classes. This has positively shown that Brunei students and teachers do not have major obstacles in acquiring such devices and internet connectivity, thus proving that Brunei has only a small digital gap within its population and proven the successful implementation of transition towards working and learning from home. In terms of the students' and educators' acceptability of online classes, majority of them prefers their classes to be conducted traditionally in their respective educational institutes i.e. schools, colleges and university. A total of 77.96% of students and 72.14% of educators approves of this statement. This has shown that both the students and educators are facing challenges and issues in online class settings. Inevitably, this has also shown that the population as a whole in the domain of education, is not ready towards the transition of online education system.

Table 1. Preference for working/learning at school or educational institutes

	Response
Students	77.96%
Educators (i.e. teachers)	72.14%

There are few major issues and challenges faced by both students and educators that becomes the root of their perceived unproductivity and demotivation during this pandemic. The top four issues are their challenges in acquiring good internet speed and performance; the affordability of the current internet cost in Brunei; coping up with the distractions in their new working and learning environments as well as incapability to manage time to perform their office/class works as well as home duties. The table below shows the aforementioned issues as well as the responses made by the students and educators.

Table 2. Issues and challenges faced by students and educators in online work/learn settings

	Issues	Student Responses	Educators Responses
1	Internet speed and performance	79.36%	69.58%
2	Distractions from Home Environment	68.28%	51.96%
3	Cost of Internet Connection	60.25%	52.41%
4	Time Management	57.2%	43.52%

In the aspect of internet speed and performance, both students and teachers agree that they have utmost challenges in getting a good internet speed and performance. As being mentioned, internet connectivity is very crucial in ensuring the successful implementation and deliverability of online classes. Inability to acquire stable internet connection would cause demotivation and thus unproductivity to both aspects of the students and teachers (Husniyah, 2019).

Although the impact is heavily eccentric towards the students (79.36%) compared to the teachers (69.58%), the teachers are quick to comment that they are significantly frustrated on this new way of teaching method because of the difficulties to communicate with their students due to the underwhelming internet connectivity, causing them to feel unmotivated to do work. In addition to that, the affordability of internet connection shows a more significant impact towards the students (60.25%) compared to the teachers (52.41%). This may root from the fact that the teachers are being paid to work and thus able to acquire a better internet connection compared to students.

This can be reflected back to the first challenge where the students (79.36%) are significantly impacted by internet speed and performances compared to the teachers (69.58%). In the aspect of challenges due to environmental settings, both the students and teachers are affected. The new environmental setting that differs significantly from their initial work settings have become a challenge for both the entities to adapt. The students (68.28%) pointed out that they have lack of discipline as well as low motivation because they perceived that the absence of teachers cause them to be unable to perform their daily tasks and concentrate in the online classes. This is agreed upon by a study that states the absence of superiors will cause the perceive idea of working hours flexibility that suits their lifestyles (Hill & Holmes, 2019).

Moreover, the students also address the fact that they are facing difficulties to concentrate during online classes because of the absence of proper area to study in their homes. As being stated in a past study, psychological effect dubbed "Protection Effect" felt by workers working from home causes this phenomena (Capitano et al., 2017). The lack of life experiences of students to interchangeably adapt to new environments may be the cause of this psychological conflict that inevitably causes their demotivation and unproductivity. This case is different for teachers, where they only slightly affected by the new teaching environment (51.96%) compared to the students (68.28%). The teachers also felt that their home suddenly becomes a workplace, causing similar psychological conflicts that revolves around the "Protection Effect" where they are unable to distinguish the indifferent salient identities of their homes and workplaces (Capitano & Greenhaus, 2018)(Capitano et al., 2017).

Lastly, the students (57.2%) and teachers (43.52%) are facing challenges in managing their working hours. The students commented that they are prone to over-procrastinating and thus missed most of their classes. This was agreed by a study that said online learning (or e-learning) may give the privilege of learning at students' pace, but they also may encounter inability to keep-up with the learning materials that are required to be studied by their education facilitators (Hubackova, 2015). The teachers pointed out that the new working environment has no proper policy in place, addressing the fact that they are bombarded by requests from parents and students in the odd hours, causing them to feel burnout due to the extended working hours.

CONCLUSION AND RECOMMENDATION

To conclude this paper, students and educators in Brunei Darussalam in general are majorly do not prefer the unconventional method of teaching and learning conducted during this time of pandemic. The few main reasons that become the root cause of this lack of support is the challenges faced in acquiring suitable internet speed and performances, the affordability of stable internet connection, struggles to cope with distractions in the new work or learn settings as well as the inability to manage time productively. In the aspect of technology, this paper would like to recommend implementation of fast, low latency and stable internet connectivity that can be achieved via implementation of the cutting-edge 5G network infrastructure in Brunei Darussalam in the years to come. In the aspect of policy, it is hoped that the educational authorities impose a new regulatory framework that acts as guidelines for educational institutes in the domains of online learning for the students and educators. Lastly, in the aspect of home environment, to mitigate the psychological conflicts and confusion, it is suggested that there should be a proper area for study that secludes the home environment from the working environment under the same roof. It is hoped that this paper would be beneficial for the policy makers and relevant stakeholders in the area of education in implementing conducive environment for online learning and teaching for both the students and teachers alike.

REFERENCES

Abu Bakar, R. (2020). *Brunei reports first COVID-19 case*. Retrieved from https://thescoop.co/2020/03/09/brunei-reports-first-COVID-19-case/

Alsaaty, F. M., Carter, E., Abrahams, D., & Alshameri, F. (2016). Traditional versus online learning in institutions of higher education: Minority business students' perceptions. *Business and Management Research*, *5*(2), 31–41. doi:10.5430/bmr.v5n2p31

Alsulimani, T., & Kaabi, H. (2018). The effect of E-Learning on Teachers' Motivation: A case study in Jeddah University. *International Journal of Management and Information Technology*, *14*(1), 3316–3327.

Amin, N. A. H. N., Hasnan, A. S., Besar, N. N., & Almunawar, M. N. (2016). Knowledge Sharing Using Web 2.0: Preferences, Benefits and Barriers in Brunei Darussalam's Tertiary Education. *International Journal of Asian Business and Information Management*, *7*(4), 1–18. doi:10.4018/IJABIM.2016100101

Anshari, M., Almunawar, M. N., Shahrill, M., Wicaksono, D. K., & Huda, M. (2017). Smartphones usage in the classrooms: Learning aid or interference? *Education and Information Technologies*, *22*(6), 3063–3079. doi:10.100710639-017-9572-7

Barnett, R. (1990). *The idea of higher education*. McGraw-Hill Education.

Brunei Computer Emergency Response Team (BruCERT). (2020). *Survey on Learning / Working from Home*. Author.

Capitano, J., DiRenzo, M. S., Aten, K. J., & Greenhaus, J. H. (2017). Role identity salience and boundary permeability preferences: An examination of enactment and protection effects. *Journal of Vocational Behavior*, *102*, 99–111. doi:10.1016/j.jvb.2017.07.001

Capitano, J., & Greenhaus, J. H. (2018). When work enters the home: Antecedents of role boundary permeability behavior. *Journal of Vocational Behavior*, *109*, 87–100. doi:10.1016/j.jvb.2018.10.002

Coenen, M., & Kok, R. A. W. (2014). Workplace flexibility and new product development performance: The role of telework and flexible work schedules. *European Management Journal*, *32*(4), 564–576. doi:10.1016/j.emj.2013.12.003

Conceição, P. (2019). Human Development Report 2019. United Nations Development Program.

Gunderman, R. B. (2019). *Educating Learners about the Pros and Cons of Telework*. Elsevier Science Inc.

Guragain, N. (2016). *E-learning benefits and applications*. Helsinki University of Applied Sciences Thesis.

Han, S., & Abu Bakar, R. (2020). Brunei proceeds to final phase of de-escalation plan on July 27. *The Scoop*. Retrieved from https://thescoop.co/2020/07/23/brunei-proceeds-to-final-phase-of-de-escalation-plan-o n-july-27/

Herrington, J. (2006). Authentic e-learning in higher education: Design principles for authentic learning environments and tasks. *E-Learn: World Conference on E-Learning in Corporate, Government, Healthcare, and Higher Education*, 3164–3173.

Hill, E. J., & Holmes, E. K. (2019). Families and workplaces. In *APA handbook of contemporary family psychology: Applications and broad impact of family psychology* (Vol. 2, pp. 379–395). American Psychological Association. doi:10.1037/0000100-024

Hubackova, S. (2015). History and perspectives of elearning. *Procedia: Social and Behavioral Sciences, 191*, 1187–1190. doi:10.1016/j.sbspro.2015.04.594

Husniyah, A. I. (2019). *Blended Learning in Efl Classrooms With Slow Internet: Insights From Teachers and Students*. https://www.researchgate.net/publication/330400197_BLENDED_LEARNING_IN_EFL_CLASSROOMS_WITH_SLOW_INTERNET_INSIGHTS_FROM_TEACHERS_AND_STUDENTS

Kazekami, S. (2020). Mechanisms to improve labor productivity by performing telework. *Telecommunications Policy, 44*(2), 101868. doi:10.1016/j.telpol.2019.101868

Li, S., Yamaguchi, S., & Takada, J. I. (2018). The influence of interactive learning materials on self-regulated learning and learning satisfaction of primary school teachers in Mongolia. *Sustainability (Switzerland), 10*(4), 1–19. doi:10.3390u10041093

Ministry of Health. (2020). *The Current Situation of the COVID-19 Infection in Brunei Darussalam* [Press Release]. Retrieved from http://www.moh.gov.bn/SitePages/pressreleaseCOVID-19.aspx

Mulyani, M. A., Razzaq, A., Ridho, S. L. Z., & Anshari, M. (2019). Smartphone and Mobile Learning to Support Experiential Learning. *2019 International Conference on Electrical Engineering and Computer Science (ICECOS)*, 6–9. 10.1109/ICECOS47637.2019.8984501

Nazarenko, A. L. (2015). Blended learning vs traditional learning: What works?(a case study research). *Procedia: Social and Behavioral Sciences, 200*, 77–82. doi:10.1016/j.sbspro.2015.08.018

Odhaib, M. F. (2018). Does E-Learning Give a Better Result than Traditional Learning? *International Journal of Computer Science and Mobile Computing, 7*(9), 29–36.

Putterman, L. (2013). Institutions, social capability, and economic growth. *Economic Systems, 37*(3), 345–353. doi:10.1016/j.ecosys.2012.12.002

Razzaq, A., Samiha, Y. T., & Anshari, M. (2018). Smartphone habits and behaviors in supporting students self-efficacy. *International Journal of Emerging Technologies in Learning, 13*(02), 94–109. doi:10.3991/ijet.v13i02.7685

Reddy, P., Sharma, B., & Chaudhary, K. (2020). Digital literacy: A review of literature. *International Journal of Technoethics, 11*(2), 65–94. doi:10.4018/IJT.20200701.oa1

Sarrab, M., Alzahrani, A., Al Alwan, N., & Alfarraj, O. (2014). From traditional learning into mobile learning in education at the university level: Undergraduate students perspective. *International Journal of Mobile Learning and Organisation, 8*(3–4), 167–186. doi:10.1504/IJMLO.2014.067014

Song, L., & McNary, S. W. (2011). Understanding students' online interaction: Analysis of discussion board postings. *Journal of Interactive Online Learning*, *10*(1), 1–14.

Sowter, B., Reggio, D., & Hijazi, S. (2017). QS World University Rankings. *Research Analytics: Boosting University Productivity and Competitiveness through. Scientometrics*, 121–136.

Spellings, M. (2006). *A test of leadership: Charting the future of US higher education*. US Department of Education.

Tibok, R. P., & Hiew, W. (2019). Higher Education Systems and Institutions. Academic Press.

Wang, C. H., Shannon, D. M., & Ross, M. E. (2013). Students' characteristics, self-regulated learning, technology self-efficacy, and course outcomes in online learning. *Distance Education*, *34*(3), 302–323. doi:10.1080/01587919.2013.835779

World Health Organization. (2020a). *Coronavirus disease (COVID-19) pandemic*. Retrieved from https://www.euro.who.int/en/health-topics/health-emergencies/coronavirus-COVID-19/n ovel-coronavirus-2019-ncov

World Health Organization. (2020b, September 17). *COVID-19 in Brunei Darussalam*. Retrieved from https://www.who.int/brunei/emergencies/coronavirus-disease-(COVID-19)-in-brunei

World Health Organization. (2020c, September 16). *WHO Coronavirus Disease (COVID-19) Dashboard*. Retrieved on November 03, 2020 from https://COVID19.who.int/

Chapter 7
Augmented Reality Towards an Informative Educational Environment:
Digitalizing Interactive Learning

Saleem Nazamudeen
Univeristy of Technology Brunei, Brunei

Muhammad Ridhauddin
Univeristy of Technology Brunei, Brunei

Heru Susanto
https://orcid.org/0000-0002-1823-357X
Univeristy of Technology Brunei, Brunei & The Indonesian Institute of Sciences, Indonesia

Fadzliwati Mohiddin
https://orcid.org/0000-0002-7332-209X
Univeristy of Technology Brunei, Brunei

ABSTRACT

There were interesting subjects and future connections between the education sectors and popular views and perceptions of the public for decades between the literature types of the conventional and the technological element. This chapter will analyze the impact on educational areas and the surrounding environment from the interactive learning perspective on how it can enhance learning practices using the augmented reality medium. The purpose of the analysis is to find the direction that the transformation of the knowledge process has evolved over the course of time, and how it supports society and the community through an efficient method of learning diversification.

DOI: 10.4018/978-1-7998-7184-2.ch007

INTRODUCTION

The overview and objectives throughout this chapter will be further clarified in this page. The study's background and objectives will be on a different agenda to explain the research processes in more detail. Problems with the existing information collection process and the proposed solution that will inspire the study result will be addressed. Interactive digital learning usually involves a variety of methods such as reading, theoretical interaction or realistic involvement with advanced technology. This research will focus solely on the advanced method of technology. The collaborative method is to encourage people to communicate and connect with each other on the subject matter. This initiates the enthusiasm and depth of thought, having to do more if this helps, an incentive for them to grow in the creative dimension and the inventive side direction for any part of problem-solving. (Renner, 2018)

The aim of this project is to extract information and data from various source materials and find the impact if the implementation of interactive learning would be beneficial to society and even to the education system. This study will allow people and users to gain knowledge on how experiences through technological aspects in a new learning concept of learning adaptation. The completion of the work is based on the self-study knowledge and a skill throughout the university's given time period. Users and learners will explore a whole new level of getting information and academic performance from entertainment through Augmented Reality with the intention of introducing a fun and engaging new learning concept Developing this research is very challenging from the basics of Augmented Reality because it is based on individual learning and not being given by the university.

Problem Statement

The concept of incorporating the use of Augmented Reality for interactive learning would help create a platform that can engage people through Augmented Reality and different other learning concepts, to gain knowledge and educate them about their learning skills. It's because people just obtain the knowledge to be helpful to their school, tests and book use can be ignored as the idea of execution would be held in a type of technology or program which students and faculty can install and use. Since the old period through the modern age, culture has experienced a major transition and is now fusion into what concept is called as the digital age. In reality, today's education structures at various rates have been influenced by these dramatic changes. It was seen as undergoing major difficulties at the beginning of the century. This has proven to be an important problem for all individuals who need knowledge and are entitled to access it as quickly as practicable to be resolved in the 21st century. Educational institutions have attempted by designing innovative methods to address these problems. There is more interactive learning concept that actually need to look upon but the issue to be addressed is to accumulate the data needed to use Interactive Learning in the educational environment. Accessible from the public or private sector are restricted assets. It would be difficult to have the capacity to collect data with the right amount of data and it would take a lot of time and resources to reach various agencies and even university. To address this issue, research will be extended to help contribute the right data to the project by looking for more proof of success across specific target group and valuable assets from country-approved confirmed areas. (Besar, 2009)

Aims

Aims of developing the project research:

- Gaining access to the local community, extending awareness regarding improving educational experience and discovering the world of Augmented Reality not only unique to universities, but also to the public concerned.
- Contribute and support people of all ages by understanding and engaging through the technical dimension of the learning system from the diverse forms of learning result.

Objectives

Objective of this project research are:

- To study the interactive learning methods by finding out the impact towards the society.
- To explore the motivation of interactive learning which could lead to potential contribute for the education environment.
- To analyze the awareness of the digital learning usage for adaptation on the learning concept.
- To learn and evaluate the values of interactive learning that may lead to the transition of the present, current and future aspects of learning concept based on the perceptions.

Project Scope

The explanation for the plan is to merge local data using Augmented Reality would transform people's point of view as a part of progressing and innovating in the future. With the data and information presented inside the framework, it will allow users to learn the facts when interacting the navigation system enables them to build an interactive experience of learning. People will experience a 3D environment without physically contacting the real thing through their cell phone or devices. Users are therefore more drawn to carry in more and try new things from the basic generic quality of information in the mainstream. (NewGenApps, 2017) (Marr, 2018)

Technical Opportunity and User Needs

The result of collisions between technical opportunity and user needs will be innovative developments. Researchers recognize that individual innovations can be purely caused by 'accidents', but that is not the usual pattern. This means that the innovation situation needs not only access to technical knowledge but also relevant data on user requirements. However, knowledge on user needs differs in complexity and economic suitability, but that the information is always provided at a certain cost and effort. It is of central importance for the results to assume that information about users needs is not an asset to the public. The needs for education act from innovating units will be defined in the first part of the next chapter. (Lundvall, 2016)

Behavioural Assumptions

The research does not depend on any precise behavioral conclusions. It can be used for units that are rationally and uncertainly optimized under limited conditions and for fulfilling units. However, take into account full information and unlimited rationality, and also reject the possibility of completely irrational behavior. It is believed that the units analyzed here have clear, perhaps undefined targets, providing that they make a fairly economical attempt to achieve such objectives. This suggests that the shifts in market costs and cost-cutting technologies can affect them. It may take a long time to influence actual conduct and may be weak in comparison with other working forces. However, stricter assumptions would be necessary for a more accurate analysis of the influence of user-producer relations. (Lundvall, 2016)

LITERATURE REVIEW

Resources in this section must suit the relevant and acceptable methodologies to be applied throughout the system's implementation techniques specification. The section will provide proof of research and reasoning that is relevant to the proposed project from other assets. Interactive learning illustrates the importance of creativity in different approaches to reporting, restoration and conservation. This will make it possible for generations to come to an absolute and accurate reconstruction. The enhancement of social learning and cultural knowledge through the use of the ICT system would boost the heritage's growth and study. Technology typically has great impact by partnerships of different types of technological devices through the material. As of now, various intriguing projects anticipate parts of the less represented by digital media to societies. The goal is to make and help the process of learning through the application of digital technology, and one of the forms is the excellent Augmented Reality. (Gilmore, 2015) (Adzaho, 2013)

Learning Basis

Learning is a path to an end for any industry. In general, that aim is to improve the performance of the workforce, reflecting its value, better goods and services, lower cost, more competitive market position, more innovation, better productivity, greater market share and so on. In the business context, learning is the mechanism by which people acquire new skillset in order to better their performance. Industries want retailers to learn innovative selling strategies to boost sales efficiency that goes straight to the bottom line of the company. A hotel needs its employees to know about customer support and provide customers with quality facilities, while allowing the hotel and improve occupancy levels and strengthen client loyalty. Learning allows individuals or groups of people to work faster, better and smarter to benefit their businesses and their organizations. Education and instruction in different forms may be delivered in the classroom, on the web, via device or broadcast through different kinds of medium. Different teaching methods, including seminars, case studies, scenarios, drills, classroom and small group research, are used to do the task. (Rosenberg, 2000). The online revolution gives companies an extraordinarily valuable ability to immediately and continuously update content. Now, students won't need to depend on so called 'student guides' in classes rapidly growing old and dated. Nor do companies have to worry that people can act on information from last week or last month, believing they are still true and accurate. Online tools, including instructional materials, can be held up to date and are far more valuable for learners in the foreseeable future. (Rosenberg, 2000).

Broadening the Perspective

This strengthens the role of learning in the corporation. Notwithstanding a stronger focus on technology, most training agencies, commercial colleges and even organizations which have started to shift from learning and teaching to success are still mostly educated. By way of design or legacy, they have almost exclusively concentrated their resources in the education field. E-learning offers us the chance to broaden a certain point of view. Providing access to information containing the institution's collective knowledge can be a powerful addition to learning. (Rosenberg, 2000). Learners need; access is key, comprehensive approach and balance. What a learner needs are some key factors that may affect their adaptation towards the interactive learning: access, approach as well as the balance within the information and knowledge. (Rosenberg, 2000)

Nothing that exists without exposure to information. Students need access to information, whenever and wherever they need to do their job. Access has four dimensions: technical, as with the infrastructure for information connection; empowerment, as with authority or consent for information retraction; flexibility, as with adaptation of the learners schedules and not trainers' schedules; and time as with time to gather the information, review it, absorb it, and learn it. In other terms, because people cannot understand it, are not able to use so, will re-arrange their existence, or have little ability to do it, there is a basic question in control, which needs to be overcome first. (Rosenberg, 2000)

After evaluation is established, students expect a comprehensive, reliable, accurate, finalize, structured and marked approach to information for ease of use. (Rosenberg, 2000). The essential argument is a complementary connection between preparation and knowledge. Many types of information are not required in a course and other skills or knowledge must be delivered as continuing education. One aspect of progress is that distinguish within. They lose the energy and money as they ask people to wait through instruction to know what they can understand more quickly. At the other side, merely directing people to a work service or a platform will not be appropriate because actually had to educate people on a specific talent or competency. Brand experience, for example, may also be given as knowledge. But at least some official preparation and experience is needed in order to know how to offer CPR. One of the greatest errors' practices create is the contradictory skill criteria by instruction and certain skill conditions, such as finding knowledge or utilizing task-taking resources, so people don't actually have to master them. (Rosenberg, 2000).

Educational Foundation

Augmented reality can make a standard class an enjoyable experience. AR technology offers simulated models and supports classroom resources with entertainment elements. This increases the interactivity of classes. AR allows students to more thoroughly interpret the knowledge they have already heard. But beyond this latest technical dimension of learning are certain influences and foundations. This chapter explores in depth the contradictions between education and technology. (Victoria, 2019). Throughout the context of education technologies, advancement in technology is primarily guided instead by development in recognizing human thinking and the creation by skills. The inability of instructional philosophy to direct development of technology-based learning environments may have led, as all of us had expected, to the inability of machines to transform current teaching activities. Learning technology has become evident as it comes to a modern idea of what the learning experience will be. This will help transform the educational setting. A few scholars in the field are actually attempting, as the contributions to the present volume demonstrate quite well, to use cognitive theory to build fresh and creative learning environment. It addresses some of the consequences for the creation of new technology-supported learning experiences from recent cognitive science work. The issues to be answered involve the usage of practical instructional activities that promote the learner 's productive behavior and lead to a meta-conceptual understanding and the versatility of cognition (Vosniadou, 1994)

New learning research has brought into doubt the common belief that intelligence is a subject composed of decontextualized ideas that can be transmitted by teaching to students ' minds. Engagement cannot be isolated from experience and what is taught is an essential part of how it is understood and implemented. Such strategies, defined as scenarios or anchored, highlight the necessity to create learning spaces that involve students in culturally significant, purposive and genuine experiences that utilize the physical and social framework purposefully. (Vosniadou, 1994)

Although school activities will certainly not be substituted completely by what is considered genuine practices, more can be accomplished to close the present gap. Technology may benefit, as it helps learning scenarios to be generated that represent what takes place in the actual world in ways impossible to do in a classroom. For example, the student is more likely to apply this knowledge to similar situations in the real world by learning basic math in situations such as a bank or food shopping. Similarly, abstract data and ideas, which will inevitably be discarded by the end of the academic year, should be supplemented by immersive learning experiences that enable students to observe what sorts of things specialists are going to be involved in such that in science and economics, history and geography. (Vosniadou, 1994)

The purpose of anchored teaching is to use practical video challenges to create the nuanced analysis and reasoning required to overcome the types of problems that actual experts sometimes have to tackle. Computer simulations offer powerful ways in which students can engage with complex thinking and problem solving in true learning situations which offer students the kind of knowledge easier to apply to real life situations. (Vosniadou, 1994)

A theory that could be checked is the future beneficial learning results that certain condition can have. While these conditions preclude such problems linked to the transmission of information posed in conventional teachings, they themselves are not clear of problems. Students must still realize how the simulations they were exposed to in the multimedia environments are similar and different from the real task of life. Furthermore, students must be prepared to have the more theoretical concepts widely offered at school rather than the other way around interpreted by the individual cases they learn. Only after such settings are built and checked on multiple students can the possible benefits and drawbacks of the system be apparent. (Vosniadou, 1994).

Augmented Reality and Technology Relation

Augmented Reality is described as an invention which takes up the extensive atmosphere and adds artificial content on top which provides the immediate or backhanded vision of the physical world with superimposed PC objects generated over a user's perspective of this present reality henceforth improving one's existing understanding of reality (Marr, 2018).

Augmented reality comes in many directions, but using mobile apps allows it more noticeable as its application. Most of it centers on the general use of either gaming or entertainment purposes. The camera interface is the most important part of an Augmented Reality app to function. The real-life world has to be seen and understood. It is used well in the improvisation of objects and people experiences because the simulation generated by the Augmented Reality experience is what makes users get the excitement. Augmented reality based on projection can also be mapped to sensors that are somewhat related to the project system being proposed (Sumra, 2018). It is portrayed as an invention which takes the encompassing atmosphere and contains artificial material top which gives the immediate or backhanded view of the actual real-world situation with superimposed PC generated picture over a user's perspective of this present reality, thus enhancing one's view of reality. (NewGenApps, 2017)

How Multimedia Enhance Learning

Without considering the impact of multimedia no discussion of learning or e-learning would be complete. For educational scenarios, visual components, such as illustrations, animation, animations, audio and video have long been included. Computer technologies offer the opportunity for learners to interact with various media technologies. Multimedia focused teaching is how media promote technology as an interactive design problem. Such that these scenarios will certainly be used for the augmented reality features for learning purposes. More essential than technologies are how utilize multimedia to understand. (Woolfolk, 2014). Multimedia will bring benefit but incorporating multimedia obviously does not slowly improvise a poor learning system. The resources and the immersive design of multimedia are essential if students are to encounter circumstances that bring true reality and effect in their learning. However, intrinsically poor curriculum style cannot be remedied for any digital worldwide. Appropriate focus should be given to multimedia. For example, back then people thought they had finally discovered the technologies as CD-ROMs became widely available, which would allow them to integrate instruction and multimedia on a storage unit which could hold so much data that they were free of floppy disk constraints. Unfortunately, in comparison to new technologies such as cloud computing, nothing is enough nowadays. The multimedia often has trouble accessing and uploading pace. For short-form video artists, Augmented Reality is a potentially exciting opportunity but is unlikely to be used on short notice in mainstream filmography. The technology is still not able to substitute VFX, while technology firms use Augmented Reality to build simple enjoyable and informative environments for their customers. Hence why it might be a good start for the education environment to implement and start focusing on new learning concept. (Woolfolk, 2014) (Scammell, 2020)

Thanks to its capabilities Augmented Reality Technologies can be used to improve video conferences services, synchronous and async content distribution channels and traditional classes, mixing actual footage with 3D objects that users can view and control. This contributes to the creation of innovative and improved ways through which digital information is shared and exploited, including interactive collaboration and e-learning technologies, which have immense potential and will be addressed in more depth in the following pages. (Lobo, 2014)

The complexity of multimedia can be incorporated without compromising its exposure, consistency or pace when utilized correctly and carefully in the learning environment. Augmented Reality is one of the innovations studied in education later. Education usage of augmented reality is a new frontier, although it is still common in diverse sectors and markets. Within this paper, authors look more closely at the position of the increased truth within education, including its benefits, patterns and specific instances. The need for solid content behind e-learning is not eliminated by the use of good multimedia or by the critical value that educational design plays in shaping how the media are used. Given a solid instructional design, great instructions without multimedia can be more effective than great multimedia. Perhaps the strongest term that comes to mind when discussing multimedia is balance. Relation between the principles of output and teaching. Balance between sincerity and glitz. Costs and return balancing. Moreover, the goal was to balance education and entertainment with learning. Multimedia will be an outstanding approach to studying and inspiring students. As technology, however, digital flaws are known as an e-learning technique where it is used inappropriately. (Woolfolk, 2014)(Program Ace, 2020)

Learning Interactive Concepts

Education has always been based on the traditional model of pursuing learning by books or locations like the library, college or any kind of field trips. Other than that, people get to know through a chat process through blogs or workshops by witnessing the real-life scenario. Thankfully, today's technology makes it possible to secure extraordinarily fragile structures and objects from further deterioration, given the re-establishment of verifiable information by keeping track of a current database system. Current day technology means the skill does not restrict the pleasure of seeing the job of individuals. (Danielle, 2013)

Different users can connect or understand as much knowledge the program can provide through diverse practice. On these lines, ensuring that consumers are interested in the way they research literature, as well as in safeguarding their point of view. (Danielle, 2013). Augmented reality will render classrooms engaging and allow students to focus more on realistic rather than theory. AR allows students to train skills by using physical appliances by adding virtual objects to the real world. But students and trainees will finally get to learn by utilizing the headphones and goggles instead of just reading books or listening to lectures. This enhances commitment and improves academic perspective (Victoria, 2019)

Moreover, these three activity links; learning, forgetting and remembering are consider the key processes in the learning industry in changing knowledge. What is a fair decision though is not obvious because certain improvements in information shift the basis on which reasonable decisions will depend. When the discussion knowledge changes, it is more relevant to think about communicative and interactive processes than about rational choice of resources at certain times. (Lundvall, 2016). Nearly all research is interactive but there are various learning techniques, which require varying degrees of social contact, which can be found useful. Clearly, the imprinted perception of immediate memory encounters is clear, individual and unique, but definitely not the most significant mode of learning. Rote learning is also feasible; practice frequently, so they don't need to grasp what they do. It usually includes studying and knowing about others rather than merely superimposing and therefore requires further interpersonal contact. Much is learned through feedback, which involves even more interaction. Throughout the end, there is a systemic and coordinated quest for new knowledge, for instance throughout colleges, academic institutes and R&D divisions. Technical transition often involves discussion, interaction or conversation; information and expertise sharing sequences through multiple organizations and at various stages, within businesses and across businesses. The more innovations are advanced technologically or scientifically, the more complex the interaction processes are usually required. (Lundvall, 2016).

It is a core aspect of the learning system because it improves the capacity to learn progressively. New entrants also pursue new expertise of manufacturing as new technologies or new products of order to look systematically and organically. This process is constrained and evolutionarily conserved in numerous forms. Firstly, to the point that the technological shift is a competition-oriented rent-seeking operation, the process must often take place to a certain degree, such that the learning outcomes of one business are not instantly available to other businesses. Secondly, an creative approach would influence, including the challenges occurring, approaches selected and the alternatives found, the mixing knowledge, experience, expertise and expertise classification that define the R&D workers of a company. Third, the searching is likely to pursue different strategic trajectories due to the unique technological possibilities and slowdowns in the company's product field. Fourthly, the prevailing technical and socioeconomic model influences research and exploration in culture at all stages. Researchers are told how to address challenges and how they select approaches by thinking patterns generated by the prevailing Paradigm and often lead to potential solutions. (Lundvall, 2016) (Woolfolk, 2014). Awareness of economic practices that are not directly or primarily aimed at the generation is also acquired. The student learning routine procurement, production and marketing activities and normal communication between companies for example are often associated with learning. This is, however, just a by-product of events coordinated for certain purposes. (Lundvall, 2016). In the learning environment, the contrast between deliberate learning; schooling, training, development and growth, market analysis and learning as a by-product of routine economic activities; learning in relation to, via and engaging with, regular manufacturing processes and marketing by firms is significant. However, research learning and production learning are not mutually exclusive activities. They are interdependent, and there are a lot of mixed forms in between. Routine searches on the one hand are definitely an opportunity in modern manufacturing, especially in manufacturing areas with well defined technical trajectories. Patterns of behaviour are critical testing elements. Repetitive development may on the other side be tracked and regulated in a deliberate and organized way to encourage innovation. It can be organized to increase the possibilities of learning. (Lundvall, 2016) (Woolfolk, 2014)

Although at first, these days, Augmented Reality was intensely based on diversions as it was introduced to the video game sector, it has the opportunity to increase some support in the area of teaching and data management as it provides a dynamic education approach. This immersive teaching approach will enable users to learn to interact with collaborative knowledge by being ready to embrace the usage through the appearance of the cell phone screen. It is one of the ways to set up a great scenario in a kind of social learning context. The 3D objects and the development of motion capture technology with the help of the cell phones will pick up the system's data components. High-level companies have pushed their digital and advanced Augmented Reality to the market, enabling the public as a whole to have the potential to get to and bring in more the focus on the enhanced Augmented Reality already built up. Augmented Reality is better represented as a concept if linked in the educational field, as opposed to a particular blend of technology that can improve the development of immediate, scientifically significant experiences with Augmented Reality. (Lopez, 2016) (Miller, 2015)

Technology and digital innovations are popular because people still usually read books in practical situations, rather than facing screens and textbooks. The Augmented Reality textbooks are another fascinating use of this technology. These books are typically printed but point to the book with a webcam that contains visuals and ability to interact. Special software can be installed on a computer, using special mobile applications or a website. This technology makes it possible to develop any emerging book into an augmented reality edition once it is being published. Simulations of various forms of encounters utilizing 3D artifacts and images, diverse devices and creative technology is the best way to link the two separate worlds. By the use of the augmented reality, textbooks become flexible sources of data in published book pages. This allows people who have no device background to have a rich immersive element experience. (Kesim, 2012)

Wikitude World Browser: Information Based System

Wikitude World Browser is one of the applications that use cell phones to execute the Augmented Reality. It gives user the view format of a genuine physical environment where it is extended by a generally called computer-generated imaging virtual CGI. Through imaging software, CGI makes an animated object with a visual substance. This offers a dynamic graphical representation that the 3D drawings must conceive of. What Wikitude World Browser is doing is filtering the encompassing territory to display information with reactions to places and spots that are considered as useful as reasonably expected. This assembles data and information via local content distributors so that the right type of information is provided to consumers. It also offers consumers with the Position Aware App, as it allows people to examine items and locations within the area for a specific target. This needs Compass, Accelerometer, GPS and Camera to work properly within the cell phone's transparency. The weight of using this item is that you really need to think about the location information in the territory. (Hauser, 2010) (Rouse, 2016)

Genesis Augmented Reality: Gaming Reality

The experimental discovery that has been brought in was the mobile code of Genesis Augmented Reality. The game idea is a battle zone interaction. A fantasy novel communicated to' reality' with the aid of Virtual Image using Augmented Reality. It is a card game which shares Augmented Reality which helps the user to combat the battles on whatever nearby screen or surface it can run. Player can move the character using the joystick feel like customers are given movement and functional catches to connect with their diversion of character. The problem it had was that it needed to play with a perfect and compatible game as it lags behind a few devices as the activity is high graphics and this application focuses on movement. This concept is similar to the project which begins with the use of the 3D marker point picture by Genesis Augmented Reality to get the entity to understand the augmented reality world. (Wang, 2018)

Sun-Keeper: GPS System

Sun Seeker is an application obsessively planned design in view of a certain thing of idea which is the tremendous star position in the focal point of the close planetary system. The application gives both a level view compass and a 3D, Augmented Reality view, each specifying the's sun oriented way, most extreme height, its hourly interims, and its ascent and set occasions, among other important information. Besides, the application exhibits the sun's winter and summer solstice ways and enables users to rapidly see the sun's position in the sky, finish with checked hour focuses. With users being able to browse around any place on Earth, the software often takes advantage of the GPS and magnetometer of the cell phone, delivering useful information for plant experts, photographers and reporters, designers, and anyone else who hopes to find optimal lighting conditions and relative sunlight dependent plots for a given area. However, for a specified date, users can even experience the sun-oriented style. (Ajnaware, 2009). This segment will be related to acknowledging the contribution to research finding and creation by ensuring that every study exploration achieved in is better for the current implementation of informative and entertaining use of the Augmented Reality environment. For growth, by organizing lifestyle learning through a creative dimension, providing accurate information and ensuring effective program implementation.

Management Usage of Technology

For over four decades electronic data and information infrastructure for production and processing has grown and has achieved exceptional speeds. The IT revolution has influenced employees, managers and their organizations significantly. For millions of businesses and people, it has generated various issues and constraints. Particularly high were the challenges to introduce and implement the technology. In a knowledge-based world, enterprise and every area of research will understand, while overcoming the many challenges associated with rapid technical developments, to optimize the advantages that information technology provides. (Frenzel, 2004)

The balance of control between people, organizations and authorities is dramatically changed by the wide spring of essential knowledge. Power bases focused on knowledge are being produced, transformed and lost as vital information spreads with little constraints across the globe. The way many people operate has shifted, and the essence of operate in developed nations is altered, by Information Technology (IT). Management was heavily impacted. Managers must be competent in modern methods and strategies to survive in the rapidly evolving world. (Frenzel, 2004)

Over the last 50 years, the technology transition facing today has grown. Many people who enter the workplace have already experienced and perhaps acknowledge the technological phenomenon directly. On the other end, the whole continuum of incidents has been witnessed by people who have accomplished their jobs throughout their lives. The rise in computer technology was an unequivocal gift for many people. Technological innovation played an important role in formal education and technological mastery is both a key part of the career process and an important element in future success. To some, IT became a complicating element, creating apprehension or direct uncertainty. Either or not digital technology has been embraced, it has improved enormously with many lives. People in contemporary institutions or organizations have visions and expectations about what technology are doing for people but may not fully appreciate their potential impacts on the innovation but cannot fully appreciate its effect on them. (Frenzel, 2004) (DMS Team, 2015)

Modern organizations, to help those they represent, using increasing forms of tools. Money, qualified personnel, intelligence, physical property and time are the most important means by which organizations conduct their tasks. Such services must be integrated, their interest balanced in achieving the purpose of the company, and their primary duty will be to produce superior returns for the partners of the company. (Frenzel, 2004). The creative mix of knowledge and people will be a key force in delivering excellent performance in today's information-intensive setting. outstanding principles for stakeholders, staff and consumers are expected to attract skilled, committed people backed by well-developed information structures that reach and broaden existing demands or create new ones and accomplish or surpass demanding targets. The integration of qualified personnel and state-of-the-art computer technologies has revolutionized industry and business and transformed the definition of management. (Frenzel, 2004). IT transforms the relational and operational structure of the workforce forever and irreversibly, changing the essence of the job for managers and non-management alike. It means more than adding impersonal technical appendages to the current office equipment to adopt new information technology. Technological innovation distributes expertise across all workers and removes conventional, proprietary information access-based control structures. (Frenzel, 2004). In today 's thriving knowledge-based world, the gathering and processing of information continuously involves. Improved worker accountability and academic commitment are expected. Since a lot of information is shared and collectively used, employees are increasingly aware that they are jointly responsible for organizational success. (Roblyer, 2014).

Computerized IT applications have two types of application. Throughout daily processes, they can complement human efforts and thus improve efficiency and organizational consistency. Around the same period, they will provide valuable knowledge regarding the automatic procedure and that can be used for more enhancements. As a result, evolving and increasingly widespread technology deployments lead to improved processes, benefiting from all of this, increasing accountability for the technology facilitators and users, and constantly changing social and professional relationships both between many companies. (Frenzel, 2004) (Roblyer, 2014)

Similar systems have continuously been updated over the last few decades. New technologies can manage transactions quicker and more efficiently than ever. Clunky text displays that have no details have been substituted and graphical user interfaces became a standard. The production of these modern technologies is quicker than ever, due to increasing development strategies. In contrast to modifying the conventional conceptions of managerial authority through wider knowledge, IT encourages workers to become more knowledgeable, and provides them input on success from even more outlets. This transition contributes to an increasingly interdependent, less hierarchical system of management hierarchy. (Roblyer, 2014) (Frenzel, 2004)

Companies must develop and support new technologies in conjunction with people and dept. to gain the many important advantages of information technology. The creation of these policies and proposals is performed and executed in several organizations through specialist IT teams. Because IT is commonly broadly dispersed, the IT team also advises and helps other agencies with their policies, proposals and deployment of technologies. As a consequence, much of the practices that most businesses conduct Their organizations have become increasingly significant. (Frenzel, 2004) (Roblyer, 2014)

The involved, positive essence of the information development phase is stressed in recent learning strategies. The learner should be an aggressive, productive translator or context rather than a passive knowledge receiver. The notion that instructional systems continue to help the actions of students after the case doesn't adhere to the epistemological expectations of the conventional computer-assisted instruction (CAI) or Intelligent Tutoring System (ITS) paradigm where a lot of the instructional tech community's research and development progress has been concentrated. Whilst Intelligent Tutoring Systems can be too organized, testing environments can be too flexible and not ideal for usage where a lot of fresh material has to be added. What exploratory environments do best is to enable student to learn something they already know at a theoretical level and thus create a clear level of knowledge and perspective. Systems that enable students to control their learning process, but also provide guidance and advice when required seem to be necessary. (Rosenberg, 2000)

Students also established a broad and powerful information framework, focused on an understanding of the everyday life in the physical, financial, and cultural sense, before being subjected to formal instruction. Student interpretations of this fact provide descriptions that sometimes vary considerably from the types of descriptions that our society generally embraces and teaches in classrooms. A research study in the research facilities showed that, when information is submitted which does not comply with what already exists on their knowledge base, the information either becomes confusing and internally inconsistent or misrepresents it in ways that make it compatible with current statements. (Rosenberg, 2000). One of the basic reasons for these misunderstandings or distortions is that students do not have a metaconceptual conscience of the theoretical constructs and theoretical opinions that restrict their efforts to gain new understanding. If children were aware of the conceptual, hypothetical nature of their opinions, they would often ask, challenge or say that they do not understand opposing viewpoints. (Rosenberg, 2000). The development of a learning environment to extent and analyze current meanings will facilitate conceptual progress and help establish metaconceptual knowledge. To achieve so, it is necessary to provide the students with educational interactions that make them aware that their theories, which they that accept into account as true facts about the world, are assumptions whose adequacy can be questioned and substituted by alternate and more appropriate explanations. Technology-based learning experiences may allow educators and help students to alter their current academic awareness in a number of ways. These academic experiences allow students to express their thoughts and analyze them critically. This helps the students to reflect on, analyze and alter the hidden meanings of these presentations. (Rosenberg, 2000) (Kurdi, 2019)

As students learn of concepts and knowledge dependent interpretations, model-driven teaching can have a greater probability of generating comprehension than simplistic memorization instead of a verbal or quantitative one. Rather than standard approaches, technology-based learning frameworks deliver model-based teaching. (Rosenberg, 2000). Model-free and model-based algorithms tackle the same question of optimizing long-term incentives and varies in their learning and knowledge. The difference between model-free and model-based learning also is clear, as it is necessary yet again for learners to take steps that have provided the previously satisfying outcomes. Model-based algorithms are, therefore, forward-looking and versatile and thus capable of integrating new knowledge (Rosenberg, 2000) (Kurdi, 2019). Unexpected objects and processes using technology or computers to enhance students' experiences, understand the need to construct different types of representations and provide clear and clear examples of scholarly clarifications that currently are being accepted, thereby minimizing the possibility of misconception. For starters, through the use of a computer could show how the earth looks both from an earthly human and from a theoretical observer from a moon's point of view. The model-based learning can lead the students to restructure their early navigational models gradually in qualitative models used by professional developers. One challenge with standard teaching is that students are guided too easily to memorize and implement structured quantitative regulations in problems without being taught the relational frameworks that experts use to help their qualitative analysis. (Rosenberg, 2000).

However, model-based instructions may not be without issues themselves. Sometimes the patterns to use or to decide how the students view them are hard to evaluate. In fact, it is necessary to explain the relations between teaching methods and the actual world in hopes for model-based teaching to help the students alter their current interpretations. Where simulation is portrayed as distinct instances of an ambiguous connection of everyday interactions, the students are motivated instead of having them restructure their original interpretations to build different systems of information about the two contexts – what occurs in the physical world versus what takes place on machines. Further work is needed in these settings in order to understand their benefits and increasing inherent limitations. (Rosenberg, 2000) (Kurdi, 2019)

The point was that establish a vision of the current educational framework where expect technology to help and build technologically based teaching experiences which will change established activities rather than becoming assimilated. Four characteristics of a theoretically significant educational environment;

1. The value of identifying practical and appropriate instructional activities to fill the divide between schooling and daily life.
2. The need for students to improve their involved, positive involvement in learning by allowing students to monitor their instructional experiences but also to be supported if appropriate.
3. The value of having a means of encouraging students to convey their own perceptions on circumstances in such a manner that they learn the meanings and versatility of their use.

4. Concentrate on the significance of utilizing templates that concretize complex and unknown concepts or processes in order that the students using them will recognize their behavior.

Technology enables the development of education experiences that more than conventional teaching materializes the ramifications of cognitive theory. In addition, technology-supported learning frameworks generate unique learning conditions that may offer additional intellectual perspective into the nature of learning within. (Kurdi, 2019) (Rosenberg, 2000). Augmented Reality technology has the best growth and has become increasingly popular as predicted and forecast to keep this development. In comparison to a augmented environment with the ability to be a mainstream resource for education, Augmented Reality technology has been listed by educational organizations as one of the most exciting innovations embraced by the education sector during the years ahead. Preserving and securing cultural heritage assets is becoming extremely vital for efficient generations. For situations where valuable objects are missing or damaged, knowledge and networking technology will increasingly be seen as a means of remedy. (Tzima, 2019) (Rodriguez, 2020). These findings are widely believed that augmented reality has the ability to offer various learning experiences with numerous learning and teaching advantages. Augmented reality systems may also boost the learning cycle, incentive for effective learning and performances. Augmented reality triggers learning interest and participation, improves learning motivation, provides student creativity in an enjoyable way, and allows participants to learn from experience in the field in a significant way. Some research and comprehensive evaluations often indicate that Augmented reality apps promote academic efficiency, help users concentrate on actual tasks, inspire participants, allow new learning opportunities and minimize workload for educators in the lab and save time as they will take students to have already completed their tasks, that use equipment more precisely. (Tzima, 2019) (Rodriguez, 2020).

METHODOLOGY

The idea that a researcher wants to contribute to the end of analysis applies to a theoretical framework. Therefore, a theoretical framework involves the implementation of a principle or a collection of theories originating from one and the same definition to provide the interpretation of an occurrence. This also means that it acts as the structure that guides the research by forming a proper and formal theory based. (Imenda, 2014)

The structure and vision of a study is unclear, without a theoretical framework, much like a house that cannot be built without a plan. By comparison, a study strategy incorporating a theoretical structure enables the research analysis to be stable and structured from one chapter to another in a structured flow.

Research Questions

The study will be based on these questions:

1. How does interactive learning can contribute towards the educational techniques?
2. Will the introduction of Augmented Reality be accepted among the community?
3. Are the people aware of the usage of interactive learning via augmented reality?
4. How does interactive learning provide value to the educational system?

Figure 1. Dependent and independent variables

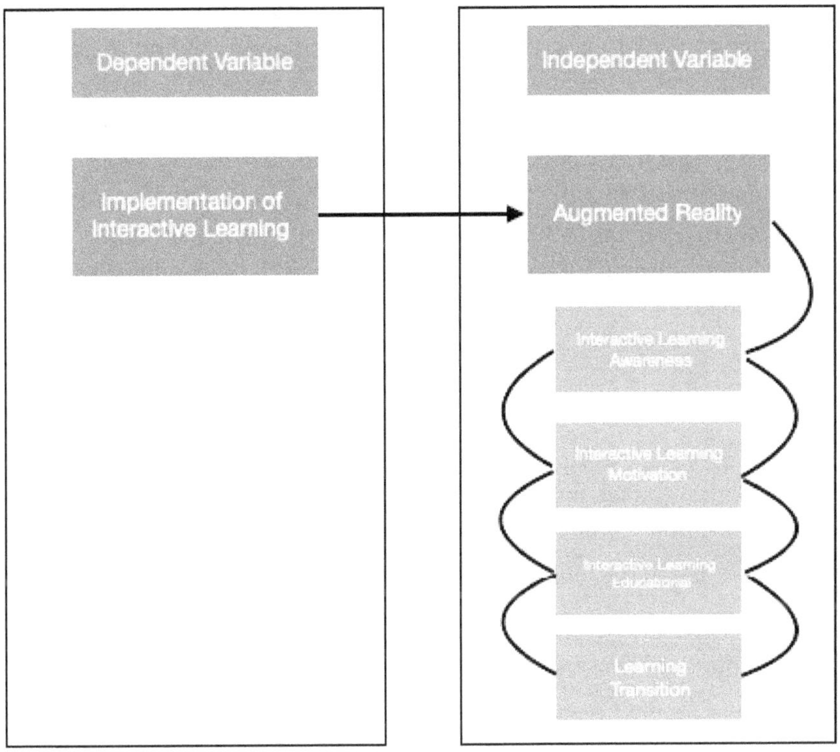

Statement of Proposition

1. P1: People are aware of the technology-based that exist in their daily usage of devices.
2. P2: The Interactive Learning technique effectively used in the educational area.
3. P3: The adaptation of augmented reality will be based on the motivational factors.
4. P4: The acceptance of transition of old and new would be based on the perceptions of people.

Research Type: Description Approach

By doing descriptive approach, it is not limited to the quantitative or qualitative methodologies as both elements will be explored throughout this research project. This will involve in collecting descriptive data to be able to observe and analyze the impact that it held accountable on the usage of digital interactive learning via augmented reality approach. The three main purposes would have to describe, explain and validate the findings. This is to ensure that three purposes are aligning with the research development outcome. Survey and interview technique may be used to collect data for improving teaching strategies as this is applicable to the education officers.

Information gain can be gain directly from the firsthand sources such that surveys, observation will be used as primary data for this research. While Secondary data will always be available throughout the studies from various publication data such as books, journals and website. It is best to ensure that these studies collect both ways as this research requires the outcome from original and unique data that will be provided and directed collected from different source in prior to the study and topic provided. As opposed to the latter data collection can be depending on quality research that can be found elsewhere.

This research technique would make proper use of the sampling method to establish a community focused on the educational environment within the Brunei area mainly on the district of Brunei Muara due to accessibility to the representative of the population. For this research, the target audience will gain priority over the population of that is still under university and college supervision. Data collected from other educational level sectors will be included but will only be available to educational officers as the respondent to the survey will either be distributed via social media or platform such as the Google Form. In order to generate some quality content, audiences from the general public will also be included randomly in order to contrast with all respondents ' reference and opinion.

RESULT

This chapter presents and examines in depth all of the study findings of the survey questionnaire research. There is an explanation of both the effect on the study of perception as well as the knowledge of augmented reality & interactive learning, and various implications for design will be discussed.

Table 1. Individuals respondent background

		Number of respondents	**Percentage (%)**
Gender		80	100
	Male	13	16.3
	Female	67	83.8
Age		80	100
	10-15	0	0
	16-25	32	40
	26-35	22	27.5
	36-45	11	13.7
	45 and above	15	18.8
Occupation		80	100
	Students	34	42.5
	Lecturers/Teachers/Educational Officer	29	36.3
	Others	17	21.3
Area of Field		80	100
	Public Sector	48	60
	Private Sector	20	25
	Others	12	15

Table above shows the individual respondent background for the survey questionnaire that was been given towards the procedure of the research progress. The profile includes the gender, age, occupation and as well as their area of field. Data collected for the project consist of 80 respondents. Two genders; 13 respondents are male and 67 respondents are female, 16.3% for male while 83.8% are from female respectively. There are 5 options given for the age group; 10-15 years old, 16-25 years old, 26-35 years old, 36-45 years old as well as 45 years old and above. There were no respondents received from the 10-15 years old age group due to some limitation that will be discussed in the limitation chapter of this research work. A big amount comes from the 16-25 years old category which has 32 respondents with a 40% among the 80 respondents. From the age group of 26-35, there are 22 respondents with a 27.5%. The age group of 36-45 consist of 11 respondent with the 13.7% while the age group from 45 years old and above has 15 respondent with a 18.8%. The age group shows that the group of respondent belongs to the student within or above the secondary level as well as the tertiary level. This also shows that the age group belongs to the public whether is in the public sector, private sectors or belongs to the others group of occupation. 3 options were given within the occupation group; students with 34 respondents of 42.5%, Lecturers, teachers & educational officers belongs to a group of 29 respondents with a 36.3% while 17 respondents with the 21.3% belongs to the group of people who answered others. Others category can also mean that they belong to the publics' perception. Three are of fields were given, public sector, private sector and others. Public sector belongs to the private companies, organization whether or not it be in the educational industries or not. Same applies to the public sector which also means that it belongs to the public school, or the government side. Others section might as well mean that it is under the publics' perception. There are 48 respondents with a 60% that answers from the public sector, 20 respondents with a 25% that goes for the private sector while 12 respondents with a 15% are from the other areas of field.

This profile shows that there are majority belongs to the educational areas as the heavy percentage weights more than the publics' perception. It can be seen that from the occupation section, combined respondents from the educational sides are 63 respondent with a 78.8%, while the rest belongs to the publics' perception. Therefore, answer from the educational sector will be seen to be useful for the future references of the next few chapters for evaluation.

Figure 2. Application graphs

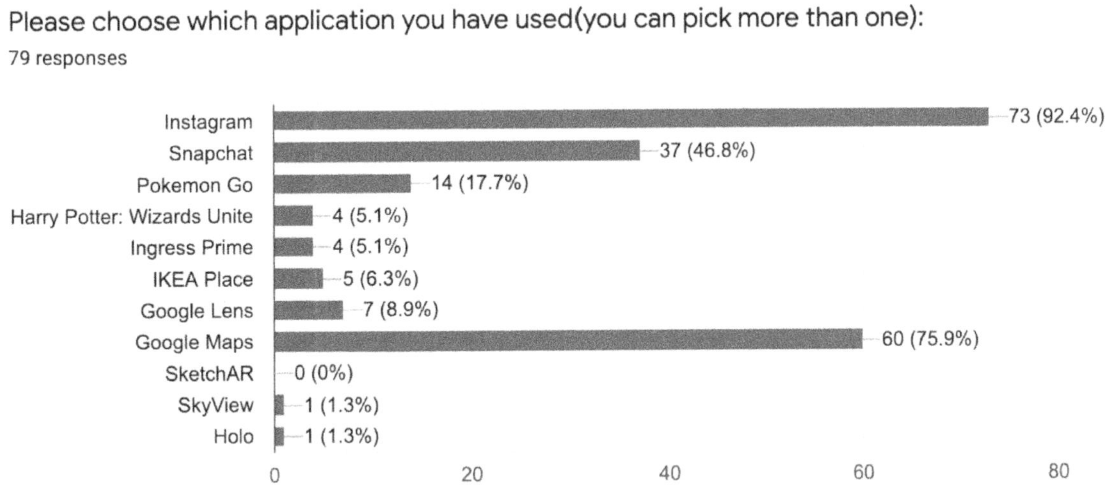

Technology Awareness

The challenge was to figure out based on how the perception of the technological awareness can be found in the region as part of the data collection. The data collected will be then use for evaluation of this research.

Eleven applications for smartphone devices were given for the respondents to be chosen from. This is to ensure that respondent would be able to familiarize with the application or software that they use are considered having an augmented reality system embodied with the application. This will also unintentionally made to ensure that users and respondents are aware that the creation of the interactive augmented reality is useful in any sort of platform provided by the organization that created the application for the smartphones. Each respondent are able to pick more than option based on what application that they used. Among those options, 73 responded out of 80 uses Instagram which leads to a 92.4% of usage on the application. Snapchat has 37 respondent with a 46.8%, Pokemon Go has 14 respondents with a 17.7%, Harry potter: Wizards Unite has 4 users that brings to 5.1%, same statistics with Ingress Prime with 4 respondents usage of 5.1%, IKEA Place application has 5 respondents with a 6.3%, Google Lens application has 7 respondents with a 8.9%, Google Maps application is well known as users are able to track location by using this application which lead to a 60 respondents with a 75.9% second in lead in compare with Instagram, null user uses SketchAR, SkyView has a 1 respondent with a 1.3% as well as Holo has a 1 respondent with a 1.3%.

Based on the statistics shown above, it shows that respondents use these applications as part of their social media medium as well as the usage for their convenience of the application created.

Figure 3. Augmented reality awareness chart

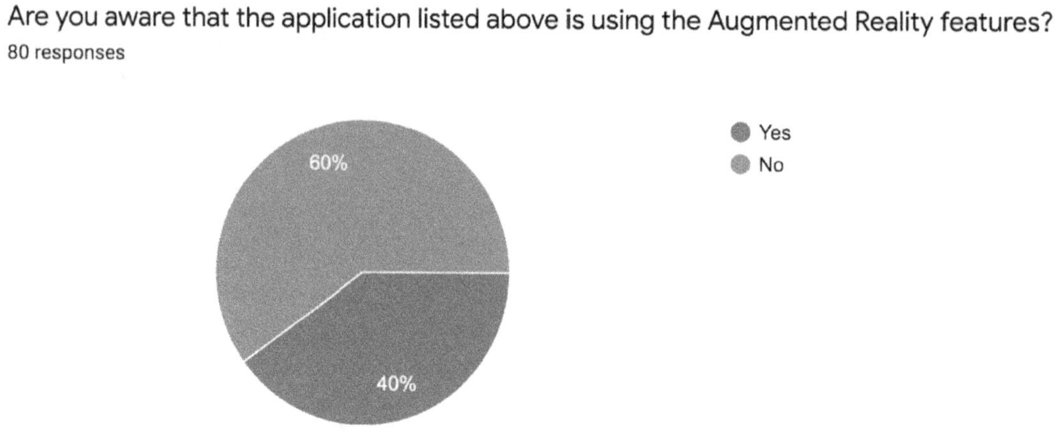

Chart above shows that the awareness of the respondents that uses the application from the previous question whether or not that the respondent is aware of the implementation of Augmented Reality features exist within the application that they used. Above shows that 32 respondents with a 40% are well-aware of the features being implemented on their application, while the rest of 48 respondents are not aware

Figure 4. AR featured application graph

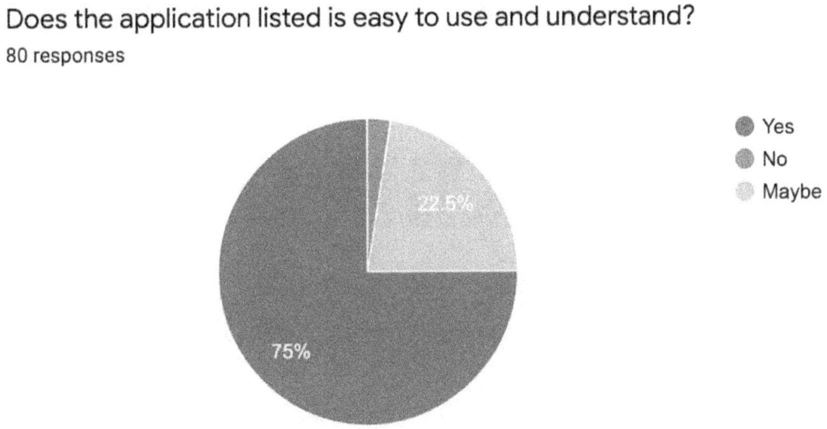

that the feature exist on their application usage with a 60% saying No. this shows that majority uses the technology on their devices without the existence of the augmented reality features.

This chart has the purpose to ensure that respondents are able to know the user-friendly system of the implementation of the augmented reality, this allow the respondent to know that without the awareness of the feature, it will and can let respondent know that the feature is actually being used without their knowledge of understanding what the augmented reality features can do. Out 80 respondent, 60 respondent from the 75% believes that the application used can be seen as easy to understand and comprehend, while 2 respondent says no with a small amount of 2.5% and lastly 18 respondents answer 'Maybe' with a 22.5% which allow respondent to contemplate with their decision and behavioral knowledge regarding the augmented reality features.

Figure 5. Augmented reality convenience

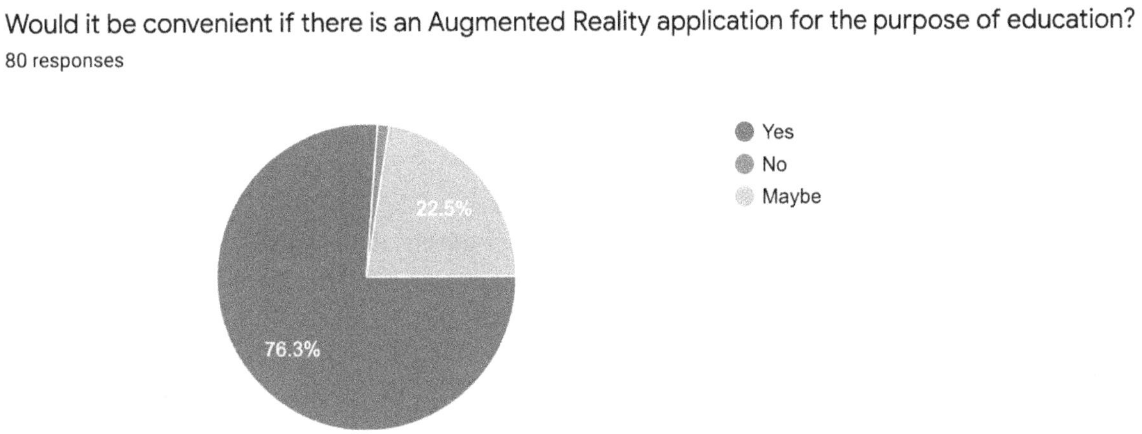

Figure 6. Learning tools option

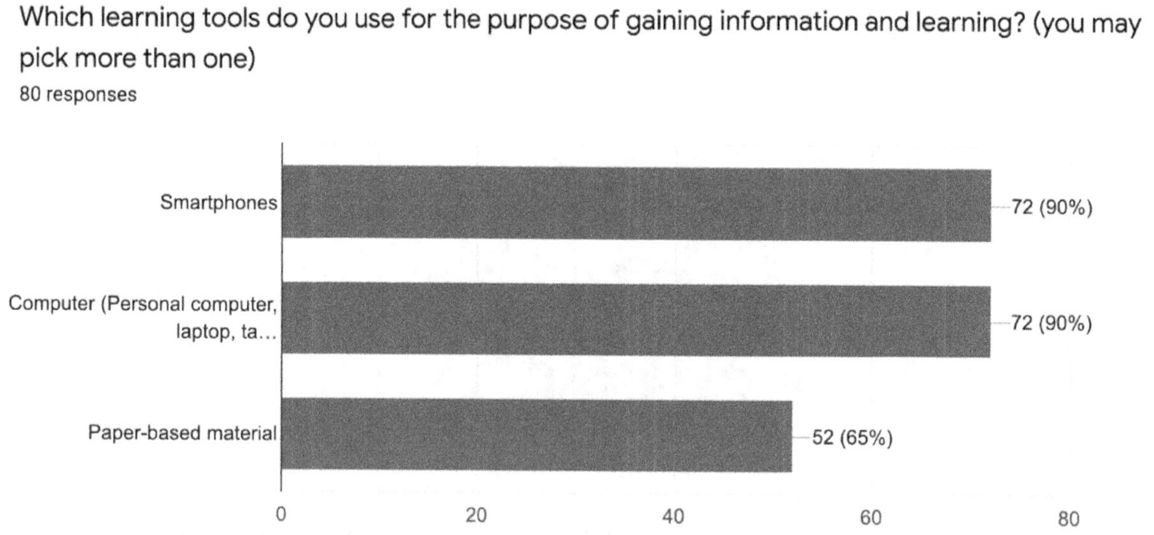

Interactive Learning

In recent decades, numerous practitioners and researchers have developed rational theories and implementations for the adoption of AR in academic and business world. Through these experiments, some of AR's inventions were created and used to improve students' and employee education and training efficiency. In fact, multiple experiments will boost the reliability and applicability of AR in real life. (Lee, 2012)

At the result, technology is not disconnected, nor effectively incorporates the functionality it provides. One of the first step would come from the awareness that it can create and hence it always starts with education. The question relates to the convenience of the augmented reality features to be used in part of the interactive learning, to be used for the educational field. Majority votes 'yes' with a 76.3% from 61 respondents. 22.5% of 18 respondents picks 'maybe' as their answer due to some uncertainty by the respondent, while 1.2% would say 'no' coming from 1 respondent. The reason of having no as answer would probably cause by the transitional factor, which will be discussed in the next chapter.

Above results shows the learning tools that is being used by the respondents when they decided to gain information and study based on their own experienced and perspective. 3 options were given for the respondent; Smartphones, Computer as well as the traditional paper-based material. Respondents are able to pick more than one of the choices as it can be predicted that respondent may use more than one learning tools as their sources of studying or information. 72 respondents answer smartphones with a 90% out of the 80 respondent, another 72 respondents has the same 90% of using computers as their sources of information and knowledge, while 52 respondents prefers the paper-based material with 65%.

Some learning types and methods work well with others, while some would prefer to stay true to the traditional conventional methods. But with the 80 respondents, the graphs show that most of them are aware with the advantage of using different learning methods for their learning process. It shows that 71.3% from 57 respondents uses both ways; the traditional/conventional methods that consists of books, paper, physical tools etc., and as well as prefer using the interactive learning on using technology medium such as online material and other multimedia. 23.8% of 19 respondents specifically chose

Figure 7. Learning method options

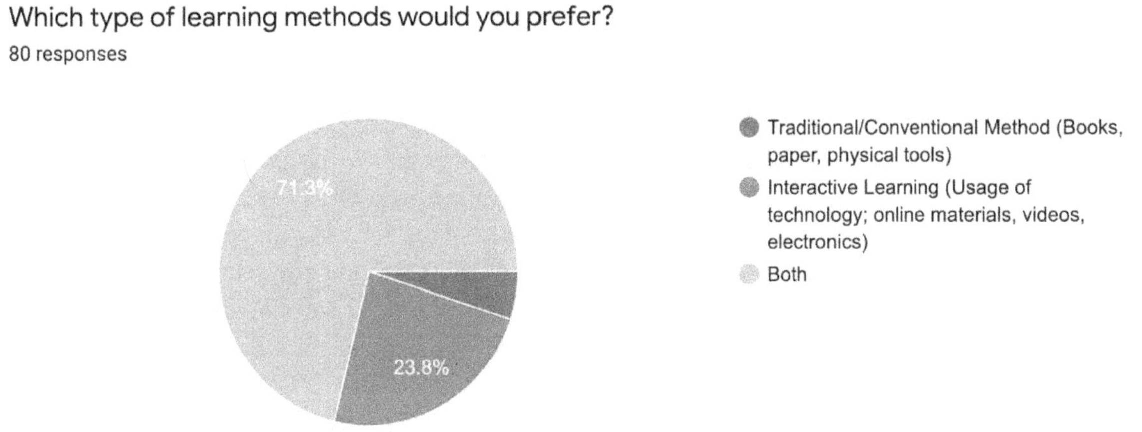

Interactive Learning as their learning process, which shows that they are aware and expose to the aspect of using technology for their ease of use. While there are 5% with 4 respondents still prefer the traditional conventional methods for their learning methods and procedures.

DISCUSSION

1. P1: People are aware of the technology-based that exist in their daily usage of devices.
2. P2: The Interactive Learning technique effectively used in the educational area.
3. P3: The adaptation of augmented reality will be based on the motivational factors.
4. P4: The acceptance of transition of old and new would be based on the perceptions of people.

The purpose of this discussion is to interpret and describe the relevance of the results in the light of the research problem that is being investigated and to explain any new understanding or insight into the problem after the findings have been taken into account.

The correlation between P1 and findings indicates that the respondent utilizes the application as their everyday usage, but it also demonstrates that certain respondents are not completely informed that through the framework and applications that usage, the augmented reality capabilities are being developed. That aspect allows users to be unsure of the product who may not have been acknowledged due to the assumption that the implementation technology is not widely established or respondents are still being brought with the system and have not noticed that it needs a particular feature that helps the program to work properly.

The results related to P2 shows that the drive and enthusiasm to evolve to a better side of the technical element can be seen as most respondents giving the answer to understanding that it will help users in the educational field for better use. Within this section this discussion will be explained to show that respondents finding interactive learning would benefit the educational environment in order to shift to a new concept of learning.

The study relates more towards P3 as the survey also revealed that due to their awareness, motivational factors come to part as respondents are willing to learn on how the augmented reality will affect the educational scenery as it most of the applications that the respondents uses have benefit them in many ways as respondent not realizing that respondents actually find that the adaptation towards augmented reality has been existed, except that the knowledge on that area is quite lacking.

The results and findings that are base towards P4 would be depending on the perception of the individuals as well as the contributing factors. Respondents answer leaning towards the transition based on how it actually would work and how the new system will carry the old system in ensuring that similar concept would be present into the new learning concept. This shows that respondents believe the transition can be done by ensuring that the progress can be done but the process of it will takes time to adapt.

Some results show that the introduction of augmented reality would be welcoming, but keeping the traditional method that needs to be incorporated to keep the essence of learning concept, as what some of the few respondents answered;

1. The interactive learning can boost the students' interests and motivation. The lesson will be more interactive, active and alive. The traditional method can still be applied in the presence of emergency cases such as no electrical supply, last minute lesson replacement etc. The traditional can also cater the different needs of students especially the kinaesthetic learners who usually need concrete materials to help them in learning.
2. I choose both because it depends on the situation. In university, to summarize notes from lectures, I'd prefer using pen & books as well as revision for exams. As for doing assignments, research & go through notes (lecturers who teach online) then, I'd choose interactive learning. To add, when doing assignments, to sort things out, like.. to jot down or list down on what to write for an essay, I still use paper & pen then afterwards I'll just elaborate more on Microsoft Word (laptop). It's actually up to the individual's situation & comfort.
3. Depends on what i am teaching, but interactive learning is more interesting and easy to make the students understand better rather than traditional methods. But our problems always not enough the technology at our school.
4. As educator, they need blended use of paper based as the core for learning to achieve lesson objective. On the other hand, Interactive learning such as augmented reality is a good opportunity for students' engagement in the classroom.
5. In the world of a new technological era, its best to have an integration between traditional manuals plus technology and together helps in better understanding of anything complex

Answers from these selected respondent shows that there is a need of blending the learning concept methods to ensure that students and educators can have access to both to allow them to have more significant and polishing their skills. However, it also shows that lack of the support materials which is quite hard to achieve if the awareness of the concept has not been established. There is already a lot to learn. The creation of meaningful curriculum material that is utilized in classrooms would be important in particular for a comprehensive assessment of the realistic utility of education methods such as ours.

CONCLUSION

To derived back on the research, this project is in regards on the study on the use of augmented reality features through an interactive learning concept, on how informative and education environment that includes industry and organization, that can be the main factors in ensuring in finding the impact of the potential future usage. Several literature reviews have been argued and compared that most conventional and traditional learning methods is still popular, but the results show that this method can be implemented within the modernized version of learning concept. Hence, interactive learning considers a modern-day technique, but with the incorporation of augmented reality, it helps this study to analyze that technology usage towards educational aspect would create a positive impact throughout the educational environment.

The opportunity is to improve instructional effectiveness and preparation in academia and industry by presenting knowledge at the right time and location by delivering computer-based 3D graphics with compelling content. AR that call for constructivist conceptions of education where students take care of their own education and can provide more substantive learning and training. That being said, this study shows more in depth on how interactive learning plays a bigger role in the IT industry as well as the educational environment. There are factors such that the behavioral, motivation, awareness as well as how there is a need a study on the educational psychology plays vital in terms of the factors mentioned in allowing the mindset and the perceptions of people are shifted to a positive outcome towards the innovative change. However, the ability of Augmented Reality function needs detailed reflection in order to be successful for education. The problem isn't that Augmented Reality is helpful in order to improve learning or not.

RECOMMENDATION

To reflect back upon the research objective, this research study has the purpose to ensure that the study of interactive learning through the augmented reality would actually create an impact to the old and new learning system. Through different outcome and inputs received from the findings and discussion, it can be seen that interactive learning is consider one of the best techniques that is widely used in the educational field. However, the shifting of the conventional/traditional method is still being carried out until the current days. This shows that the awareness of using the technology i.e. augmented reality can be seen through the application and software used in some other areas or major industry but not in the perspective of education. To argue the point, knowledge of the feature is quite lacking in the educational aspect as students are not really exposed to different kinds of techniques and ways of learning and as well as teaching.

Many ideas are challenging to grasp and are much more complicated to properly interpret and present in a textbook. The augmented reality, however, serves as a new medium for achieving it much easier. The prediction impact results is positive, but the initiation phase of introduction might take longer as to the motivation to change is quite low compared to the methods that are still being used for generations. People are able to learn and adapt but requires a proper tools and equipment in order for the development of interactive learning criteria of using augmented reality needs to be established in the coming future. Looking at the examples, human gullibility knows no limit and growing truth is just the technology required to render schooling more productive and involved throughout. The technology already contains so many success stories and the number are growing further. The upward trend is clear, which makes it sure one of the major environments in the coming decade in which app developers, schools, universities and other educational institutions invest. (Program Ace, 2020)

ACKNOWLEDGMENT

Saleem Haja Nazamudeen as lead author; Heru Susanto as main contributor; Muhammad Ridhauddin, Fadzliwati Mohiddin as contributor. All authors review and approved final version of this manuscript.

REFERENCES

Adzaho, G. (2013, December 19). *Diplo*. Retrieved from Can technology help preserve elements of culture in the digital age: https://www.diplomacy.edu/blog/can-technology-help-preserve-elements-culture-digital-age

Ajnaware. (2009, October 6). *Ajnaware's Weblog*. Retrieved from Sun Seeker – Seeing the Light with Augmented Reality: https://ajnaware.wordpress.com/2009/10/06/sun-seeker-seeing-the-light-with-augmented-reality/

Besar, N. A. (2009). *Impact in ICT in Brunei Darussalam System of Education*. Universiti Brunei Darussalam.

Bhatia, M. (2018, September 5). *Human of Data*. Retrieved from Your Guide to Qualitative and Quantitative Data Analysis Methods: https://humansofdata.atlan.com/2018/09/qualitative-quantitative-data-analysis-methods/

Kurdi, B. (2019, March 26). *PNAS*. Retrieved from Model-free and model-based learning processes in the updating of explicit and implicit evaluations: https://www.pnas.org/content/116/13/6035

Lee, K. (2012). *Augmented Reality in Education and Training*. University of Northern Colorado. doi:10.100711528-012-0559-3

Leu, F.Y., Liu, C.Y., Liu, J.C., Jiang, F.C., & Susanto, H. (2015). S-PMIPv6: An intra-LMA model for IPv6 mobility. *J. Netw. Comput. Appl.*, *58*, 180–191.

Liu, J. C., Leu, F. Y., Lin, G. L., & Susanto, H. (2018). An MFCC-based text-independent speaker identification system for access control. *Concurr. Comput. Pract. Exp.*, *30*(2), e4255. doi:10.1002/cpe.4255

Lobo, R. A. (2014). *Augmented Reality for educative and collaborative environments*. Bogoto: University Pompeu Fabra.

Lopez, L. L. (2016, March 24). *L3*. Retrieved from Virtual Reality And Augmented Reality In Education: https://elearningindustry.com/virtual-reality-augmented-reality-education

Miller, D. R. (2015). *The University of Arizona*. Retrieved from Implementing Augmented Reality in the Classroom: https://journals.uair.arizona.edu/index.php/itet/article/view/18601/18526

NewGenApps. (2017, November 23). *newgenapps*. Retrieved from Know the Augmented Reality Technology: https://www.newgenapps.com/blog/augmented-reality-technology-how-ar-works

Program Ace. (2020, February 7). *Program Ace*. Retrieved from Augmented Reality in Education: The Future is Already Here: https://program-ace.com/blog/augmented-reality-in-education/

Roblyer, M. (2014). *Integrating Educational Technology into Teaching*. Pearson.

Rodriguez, D. R. (2020, April 28). *aim*. Retrieved from Augmented Reality And The Future Of Education: https://analyticsindiamag.com/augmented-reality-and-the-future-of-education/

Rosenberg, M. J. (2000). e-Learning. McGraw-Hill.

Rouse, M. (2016, July). *TechTarget*. Retrieved from CGI (computer-generated imagery): https://whatis.techtarget.com/definition/CGI-computer-generated-imagery

Scammell, R. (2020, February 27). *Verdict*. Retrieved from Augmented reality media trends: https://www.verdict.co.uk/augmented-reality-media-trends/

Sumra, H. (2018, April 25). *wareable*. Retrieved from Augmented reality explained: What is AR and what's coming next?: https://www.wareable.com/ar/everything-you-need-to-know-about-augmented-reality

Susanto, H. (2017). Electronic Health System: Sensors Emerging and Intelligent Technology Approach. In *Smart Sensors Networks* (pp. 189–203). Elsevier. doi:10.1016/B978-0-12-809859-2.00012-7

Susanto, H. (2018). Smart mobile device emerging Technologies: An enabler to Health Monitoring system. In *High-Performance Materials and Engineered Chemistry* (pp. 241–264). Apple Academic Press. doi:10.1201/9781315187860-8

Susanto, H., & Almunawar, M. N. (2015). Managing Compliance with an Information Security Management Standard. In *Encyclopedia of Information Science and Technology* (3rd ed., pp. 1452–1463). IGI Global. doi:10.4018/978-1-4666-5888-2.ch138

Susanto, H., & Almunawar, M. N. (2018). *Information Security Management Systems: A Novel Framework and Software as a Tool for Compliance with Information Security Standard*. CRC Press. doi:10.1201/9781315232355

Susanto, H., Almunawar, M. N., Leu, F. Y., & Chen, C. K. (2016). Android vs iOS or Others? SMD-OS Security Issues: Generation Y Perception. *International Journal of Technology Diffusion*, *7*(2), 1–18. doi:10.4018/IJTD.2016040101

Susanto, H., & Chen, C. K. (2017). Information and Communication Emerging Technology: Making Sense of Healthcare Innovation. In *Internet of Things and Big Data Technologies for Next Generation Healthcare* (pp. 229–250). Springer. doi:10.1007/978-3-319-49736-5_10

Susanto, H., Chen, C. K., & Almunawar, M. N. (2018). Revealing Big Data Emerging Technology as Enabler of LMS Technologies Transferability. In *Internet of Things and Big Data Analytics Toward Next-Generation Intelligence* (pp. 123–145). Springer. doi:10.1007/978-3-319-60435-0_5

Susanto, H., Leu, F.-Y., Caesarendra, W., Ibrahim, F., Haghi, P. K., Khusni, U., & Glowacz, A. (2020). Managing Cloud Intelligent Systems over Digital Ecosystems: Revealing Emerging App Technology in the Time of the COVID19 Pandemic. *Appl. Syst. Innov.*, *3*(3), 37. doi:10.3390/asi3030037

Tzima, S. (2019). *Augmented Reality Applications in Education: Teachers Point of View*. University of Patras.

Victoria. (2019, January 18). *RubyGarage*. Retrieved from Use Cases of Augmented Reality in Education and Training: https://rubygarage.org/blog/augmented-reality-in-education-and-training

Vosniadou, S. (1994). *Technology-Based Learning Environments*. Springer. doi:10.1007/978-3-642-79149-9

Wang, A. (2018, April 16). *Gearbrain*. Retrieved from Genesis Augmented Reality — your one stop shop for warriors, beasts and gods: https://www.gearbrain.com/genesis-augmented-reality-app-review-2556535762.html

Woolfolk, A. (2014). *Educational Psychology*. Pearson Education Limited.

ADDITIONAL READING

Danielle. (2013, April 27). *ChurchMag*. Retrieved from Technology plays a role in keeping cultures alive: https://churchm.ag/technology-plays-a-role-in-keeping-cultures-alive/

Frenzel, C. W. (2004). *Management of Information Technology*. Course Technology.

Gilmore, L. (2015, November 25). *tnw*. Retrieved from How technology is preserving the past: https://thenextweb.com/insider/2015/11/24/how-technology-is-preserving-the-past/

Hauser, A. (2010, August 9). *Wikitude*. Retrieved from Wikitude World Browser: https://www.wikitude.com/wikitude-world-browser-augmented-reality/

Imenda, S. (2014). Is There a Conceptual Difference between Theoretical and Conceptual Frameworks? KwaDlangezwa: University of Zululand. doi:10.1080/09718923.2014.11893249

Kaufmann, H. (2003). *Collaborative Augmented Reality in Education*. Vienna University of Technology.

Marr, B. (2018, July 30). *forbes*. Retrieved from 9 Powerful Real-World Applications Of Augmented Reality (AR) Today: https://www.forbes.com/sites/bernardmarr/2018/07/30/9-powerful-real-world-applications-of-augmented-reality-ar-today/#149486222fe9

Team, D. M. S. (2015, December 5). *Decision Management Solutions*. Retrieved from The Disadvantages of Traditional Information Systems: http://www.decisionmanagementsolutions.com/14831/

KEY TERMS AND DEFINITIONS

Assistive Technology: Is assistive, adaptive, and rehabilitative devices for People with disability or the elderly population. People with disability often have difficulty performing activities of daily living (ADLs) independently, or even with assistance. ADLs are self-care activities that include toileting, mobility (ambulation), eating, bathing, dressing, grooming, and personal device care. Assistive technology can ameliorate the effects of disabilities that limit the ability to perform ADLs. Assistive technology promotes greater independence by enabling people to perform tasks they were formerly unable to accomplish, or had great difficulty accomplishing, by providing enhancements to, or changing methods of interacting with, the technology needed to accomplish such tasks.

Augmented Educational Foundation: Augmented reality can make a standard class an enjoyable experience. AR technology offers simulated models and supports classroom resources with entertainment elements. This increases the interactivity of classes. AR allows students to more thoroughly interpret the knowledge they have already heard.

Augmented Reality Technology Relation: An invention which takes up the extensive atmosphere and adds artificial content on top which provides the immediate or backhanded vision of the physical world with superimposed PC objects generated over a user's perspective of this present reality henceforth improving one's existing understanding of reality.

Information Technology Apps for Learning: The Apps enable students to acquire lecture materials, take online quizzes or assessments, submit tutorials or assignments, view results, view course materials, see news and announcements, online interaction, anytime and anywhere without any geographical or time barriers. However, the key to effective apps -learning is not from its multimedia, design or user-friendliness, but on how the individuals are engaged by the content. Although the use of apps-learning provides notable benefits for students as a whole, the effectiveness of the use of the system depends on the level of acceptance and use of students. The goals of apps-learning will not be achieved if there is lag and resistance to the use of new technology. The process of implementing apps-learning in the institution might face several factors that constraints the effective use of apps-learning as a learning medium, such as infrastructure issues, the willingness and readiness of the institutions and students.

Interactive Learning: Education has always been based on the traditional model of pursuing learning by books or locations like the library, college or any kind of field trips. Other than that, people get to know through a chat process through blogs or workshops by witnessing the real-life scenario. Today's technology makes it possible to secure extraordinarily fragile structures and objects from further deterioration, given the re-establishment of verifiable information by keeping track of a current database system.

Technology Management Usage: For over four decades electronic data and information infrastructure for production and processing has grown and has achieved exceptional speeds. The IT revolution has influenced employees, managers, and their organizations significantly. For millions of businesses and people, it has generated various issues and constraints. Particularly high were the challenges to introduce and implement the technology.

Chapter 8
Three Parties Engagement of Learning Management System:
Students-Lecturer Technology Evidence From Brunei

Fadzliwati Mohiddin
https://orcid.org/0000-0002-7332-209X
Univeristy of Technology Brunei, Brunei

Heru Susanto
https://orcid.org/0000-0002-1823-357X
Univeristy of Technology Brunei, Brunei & The Indonesian Institute of Sciences, Indonesia

ABSTRACT

This study was conducted to investigate e-learning acceptance and factors influencing higher institutions students. Among the factors involved in this study were perceived ease of use, perceived usefulness, self-efficacy, technology availability, and usage and intention to use. Technology acceptance models (TAM) were used as a basis for the study and for hypothesizing the effects of such variables on the use of e-learning. The research methods used were inclined to the use of quantitative methods of online questionnaire surveys that consist of 23 items based on a Likert scale. The findings of this study found that there is significant influence of self-efficacy on perceived ease of use and perceived usefulness while perceived ease of use has direct impact on perceived usefulness and perceived usefulness has influence on intention to use towards e-learning systems.

INTRODUCTION

With recent development of information technology, e-learning has become one of the important technology's tools in higher educational institutions today. In implementing an information system in an institution, it is necessary to consider the user acceptance. Implementation of the information system is said to fail if there is inability and resistance to the use of the information system. The purpose of this

DOI: 10.4018/978-1-7998-7184-2.ch008

report is fourfold. First, to clarify objectives and purpose of conducting this study. Second, to discuss detailed literature reviews on the conceptualization of e-learning. Third, to analyze and develop detailed theoretical discussion on data collection and hypothesis. Last but not least, to provide recommendations to overcome challenges of current adoption of e-learning.

Problem Statement

Today, the utilization of electronic learning systems is no stranger to educators and students. However, the use of electronic learning systems among students has not reached the maximum level for their learning purpose. There are a number of factors that have been identified in the use of electronic learning systems such as lack of students' knowledge to the importance of using electronic learning systems in the learning process, low levels of motivation among students and problems related to the use of electronic learning systems among students due to lack of technological preparation and encouragement in the study area.

The existence of e-learning in Brunei is relatively new compared to other developed countries where e-learning has become a basic method of learning to aid smooth traditional learning process more conventionally. The implementation is still relatively new, most are just blended learning where e-learning is simply the facilitator or support for the conventional teaching and learning process. As a result, many local higher institutions are yet to fully implement the use of e-learning. For an example, lecturers only use e-learning for a specific purpose such as downloading notes to websites, making important announcements, answering student e-mails, forums, etc. There is no current institution in the country that practices e-learning as an alternative to creating opportunities for more students as e-learning can be a platform to facilitate the process of distance learning.

The growth of today's e-learning in education in terms to fully utilize its advantage and efficiency in education will not completely maximize if students or teachers do not accept the use of the system. Therefore, the success of e-learning systems depends on the institution's stakeholders willingness to adopt and accept the technology. E-learning implementation is not only a technological solution but also involves processes of different factors such as individual factors, organizational factors and social factors.

In today's advanced technological world, the use of information and communication technology for educational purposes has increased, and the spread of network technologies has caused learning practices to develop and change significantly (Kahiigi et al, 2008). With recent development of information technology, e-learning has become one of the important technology's tools in higher educational institutions today.

Electronic learning (E-learning) has become a forefront for Higher education institutions to keep up with the current technology and advanced education. E-learning defines as a learning system or education program that involves the use of information technology such as computers, laptops or smartphones. In order to meet the educational goals and demands of students, the system development of electronic learning has emerged to be a catalyst for today's educational institutions (Alsabswy et al, 2013 & Docimini & Palumbo, 2013).

In the current global competitiveness, the favourable outcome of the country relies heavily on people's knowledge, skills and competencies. E-learning provide significant benefits that include improved access to quality education, electronic communication and collaboration and learning flexibility. In line to Brunei Vision 2035 of well educated and highly-skilled people, the electronics learning system is an important medium for creation of effective learning and quality education. Even though there are significant benefits in the use of e-learning systems, not all are fully utilized and adopted by students in assisting their study, thus the use of e-learning systems in Brunei is still less than optimal.

E-learning systems enable students to acquire lecture materials, take online quizzes or assessments, submit tutorials or assignments, view results, view course materials, see news and announcements, on-line interaction, anytime and anywhere without any geographical or time barriers. However, the key to effective e-learning is not from its multimedia, design or user-friendliness, but on how the individuals are engaged by the content. Although the use of e-learning provides notable benefits for students as a whole, the effectiveness of the use of the system depends on the level of acceptance and use of students. The goals of e-learning will not be achieved if there is lag and resistance to the use of new technology. The process of implementing e-learning in the institution might face several factors that constraints the effective use of e-learning as a learning medium, such as infrastructure issues, the willingness and readiness of the institutions and students, the power to use technology and so on.

To understand students' acceptance behavior toward technology, this study used Technology Acceptance Model (TAM) developed by Davis which is an adaptation of the Theory of Reasoned Action (TRA). "TAM is an intention-based model developed specifically for explaining and/or predicting user acceptance of computer technology" (Hu et al., 1999). According to Davis, technology acceptance of an individual is based on two variables; *perceived usefulness*, the extent to which an individual believes that using a technology will improve work performance and *perceived ease of usage*, the extent in which the use of technology requires no effort and easy to use (Fred D Davis, 1985). Both variables significantly affect behavioral intention to use which therefore affect the actual system utilization.

Purpose

The purpose of this study is to investigate the e-learning acceptance and factors influencing higher institutions students in Brunei Darussalam by determining perceived ease of use and perceived usefulness of e-learning along with the intention to use towards e-learning. The basic framework of the study is the Technology Acceptance Model (TAM), which was appropriate for obtaining the research aims. Additionally, the study is carried out to investigate the external factors such as availability and usage of technology, self-efficacy that may have significant influence on the perceptions of students regarding the adoption of the E-learning system.

Scope of the Study

The scope of this study is limited to assess the acceptance behavior of students in higher institutions in Brunei. This paper concentrates on studying the students' perception, intention to use and external factors of TAM towards e-learning approach. In the next section of this paper, we will discuss the literature review followed by further explanation of methodology and analysis. Subsequently in the last section, recommendations to overcome the current findings issue will be addressed.

Objectives

In order to concisely achieve the research study, several research objectives are listed as follow:

- To investigate whether technology availability and usage and users' self-efficiency have a significant influence on users' perceived usefulness and perceived ease of electronic learning systems.
- To investigate whether users' perceived usefulness and perceived ease use have a significant influence on the intention to use electronic learning systems.
- To assess users' perception on ease of use, usefulness, self-efficiency, intention to use and technology availability and usage.
- To analyse the relationship between perceived ease of use, perceived usefulness, self-efficiency, intention to use and technology availability and usage in the use of electronic learning systems among higher institution stakeholders.

LITERATURE REVIEW

E-learning defines as a learning that occurs when information technology is used to facilitate, convey and enable the learning process over the internet (Bullen & Janes, 2007). As stated to Yahaya & Ning (2011) states the main purpose universities implementing online learning is to provide a centered learning platform for students that promote self-learning. Liu & Wang (2009) stated that electronic learning system processes are characterized by the use of the internet, source of information and flexibility. In addition, electronic learning was created to overcome practical limitations of time and space. Furthermore, the main benefit of e-learning such as Moodle's where the design is based on constructivism approaches that provide opportunities for students to build and gain knowledge through sharing of information and online discussion. Moreover, e-learning overcomes the limitations of time and space an individual faced with the use of technology (Sun et al., 2007). Love and Fry (2006) indicated that e-learning has become crucial in higher institution education. Institutions of higher learning are competing to advance their online system capability in today's technological market.

Figure 1. Technology acceptance model (Davis, 1989)

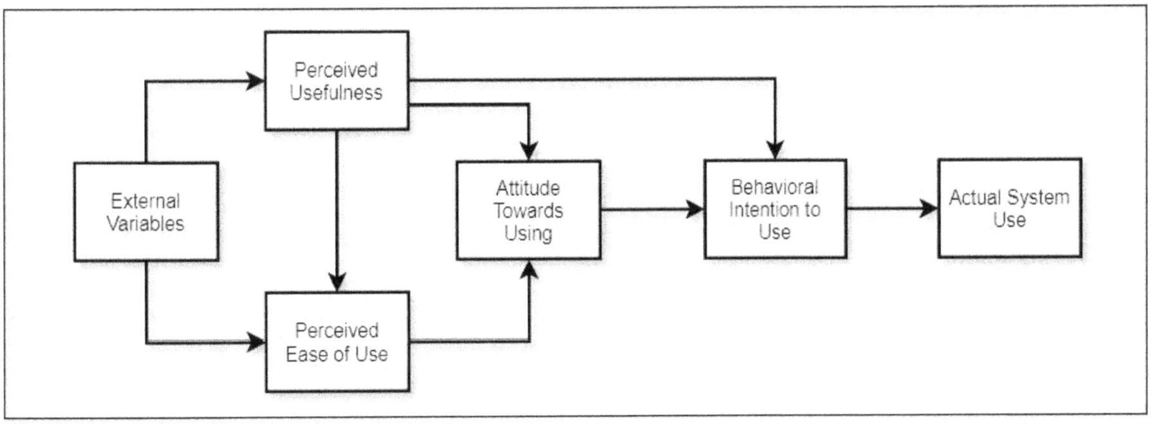

Technology Acceptance Model (TAM)

Technology Acceptance Model (TAM) was first introduced by Fred D. Davis in 1986. TAM is an adaptation of the TRA (Theory of Reasoned Action) which was first developed by Fishbein and Ajzen in 1980 made specifically for modelling the acceptance of the use of information systems. TAM is one of many research models influencing determinants e-learning acceptance. TAM is widely used to predict user acceptance and usage based on perceptions of ease of use of e-learning. To date, TAM has been considered the most relevant theory in predicting the desire and readiness for adopting technology (Chuttur, 2009).

The Technology Acceptance Model was invented to extend the construction of additional behaviour to increase the understanding of new technology. In the TRA model, it can be concluded that the beliefs and behaviour of each individual is influenced by intentional behaviour. As for behavioural intention, it is caused by two things, first is the attitude towards behavioural intention and the second is the subjective norm of each individual.

In contrast to TRA model, Technology Acceptance Model (TAM) is a model built to analyse and understand the factors that influence the acceptance and the use of information technology. TAM aims to explain and estimate user acceptance of an information system. TAM provides a theoretical basis in significance and predicts the factors that influence the acceptance of a technology in an organization. TAM explains the causal relationship between belief and the behaviour, goals and needs, and the actual use of users of an information system. Davis et al. argues that people's acceptance of new technology is determined through two perceptions: perceived usefulness and perceived ease of use.

The TAM models users' in Figure 1 shows the acceptance of e-learning systems in learning explained by the perceived usefulness and ease of use of the system. The perceived usefulness and perceived ease of use components represent users' cognitive responses to the use of technology. These then influence the users' attitude toward using the technology. The users' attitude then subsequently became the significant drivers of the behavioral intention to use toward technology (BurtonJones & Hubona, 2005). Figure 1 shows the main components of the original TAM, that include perceived ease of use, perceived usefulness, attitudes toward using, and behavioral intention to use that predict the users' actual system usage.

However, according to the IS Success model, system quality refers to measurement of technical success and information quality measures semantic success (DeLone & McLean, 2003). Both of these factors are expected to promote the use of the system and to influence the acceptance of the system and ultimately to the satisfaction of the user and the organization.

Perceived Usefulness (PU)

The TAM model is a theory in information systems about how system users can accept and use technology. This model shows that when users are introduced to new technology, a number of factors influence their decisions; one of the factor is Perceived Usefulness (PU), to an extent which believes that the use of a system or technology can increase performance (Fred D Davis, 1985).

In online learning context, perceived usefulness refers to the learner's belief that the online learning will enhance their performance in the course (Lee, Cheung, & Chen, 2005). For instance, students who have the knowledge, use and motivation in an e-learning system would know the usefulness of the system and have the desire to use the e-learning system properly. Perceived usefulness reflects the user's subjective probability of using specific technology that increases or influences the user's expectation.

There are six indicators to measure the construct of usefulness; efficiency, performance, productivity, effectiveness, facilitation and usefulness (Fred D. Davis, 1989). PU encourages the actual use of the system.

Perception Ease of Use (PEOU)

Meanwhile, Perception Ease of Use (PEU) refers to the degree where an individual believes how effortless it would be in using a particular system (Fred D Davis, 1985). Individuals tend to use technology or systems which they believe will enhance their performance, efficiency and accuracy. In the application of information systems, TAM has been successfully used by many researchers to predict the behaviour and intentions of users in the use of information technology (Legris, et al, 2003). In an online learning context, it refers to the learner's belief that the online learning system will be easy to use. There are six indicators to measure this construct, namely: the ease of the system to learn, the ease of the system to be controlled, the interaction with the system that is easily understood and clear, flexibility of interaction, ease of ability to be skilled at using the system and easy to use (Davis, 1989).

Intention to Use (ITU)

In TAM, the use of technology is actually equivalent to the term behavior in the Theory of Reasoned Action (TRA) but for use in a technological context. This construct is directly influenced by intensity and usability. As studied by Walker (2002), behavioral intention to use is the extent of an individual readiness to carry out particular actions. The use of e-learning depends on the user's attitude and level of confidence on believing that the e-learning system will increase learning objectives. The user's interest is directed to the use of e-learning which is considered to provide benefits to the learning process and ease of use.

Self-Efficacy

Researchers of TAM have assessed the influence of users' e-learning self-efficacy on technology acceptance (Grandon, Alshare, & Kwan, 2005; Park, 2009). E-learning self-efficacy refers "beliefs in one's capabilities to organize and execute the courses of action required to produce given attainments" (Bandura, 1997, p. 3). It refers to the personal confidence and skills to perform particular tasks or findings within the e-learning system. In addition, Gradon (2005) analysed that e-learning self-efficacy has an indirect impact on students' intention through perceived ease of use.

Park (2009) argues that access to technology and equipment have influence on the acceptance of an individual to e-learning systems. Learners often have difficulties in perceiving technologies because the equipments to carry out tasks is not readily accessible. He added that external equipments accessibility outside the organization or university such as software and hardware assist in supporting one's belief and enhance outcome expectations. The external equipment added a sense of convenience for an individual that allows access to the system outside the organization or university. Thus, both benefits of convenience and accessibility contribute to the positive attitude to the use of e-learning systems where they are inclined to accept it and learn it. As a result, users will tend to be more engaged in self-motivating mechanisms and contribute to the perception of ease of use of the e-learning system.

Despite the convenience and benefits of using new technology, a vast number of researchers support the fact where people appear to resists against the use of information systems. Siegel (2008) views that resistance to technology illustrates a reluctance to embrace an initiative and perception towards the use of technology. Nonetheless, it is vital for an organisation to overcome resistant behavior by understanding the reason for technological resistance of an individual.

Berna-Martinez and Macia-Perez (2012) mentioned that factors such as culture, technology, process and business structure influence the resistance and rejection of new technology. However, they added that the opposition to technology can be overcome through training and assistance. As eloquently stated by Rivard and Lapointe (2012), they added that they view technology resistance as a vital issue in IT implementation that can lead to organisational problems.

In the opinion of Selvaganapathi and Raja (2012), they referred to the feeling of anxiety in using new technology as 'technophobic'. They had suggested that this feeling is the reflection of nervousness and constant feeling of dissatisfaction and uneasiness. These feelings are very common in the present because of the use of technology in every aspect of life.

A study published by Universiti Brunei Darussalam on 'e-Learning and Knowledge Society', January 2016, stated about sixty-four per cent (64%) of the respondents showed interest in online learning. The survey involved 856 respondents of local Bruneians aged 10 to 40 years old. The results showed 67 per cent agreed that online learning makes learning easier, 53 per cent certain that it would improve their academic performance and 87 percent believe online learning enables flexibility. In addition, 67 per cent believe that online learning would improve individual project quality and 53 per cent perceived it as a medium to information sharing and discussion.

The authors said that online learning can benefit educational institutions through 'Big Data' that can optimize data collection opportunities. The author added that not only it benefits the institution, it also benefits the student's individual needs by providing service and knowledge personalization and customization. Hence, due to large amounts of data being received on a daily basis, big data could become the future direction of online learning.

METHODOLOGY

The study is inclined to the use of a quantitative approach that uses questionnaire survey. Google forms survey was used to obtain the research data, and the survey was shared and distributed through various mediums such as Whatsapp and email. On the whole, 101 responses were obtained from the survey and these were used to test the hypotheses. The hypotheses were developed on the basis of existing theories that are in line with the e-learning context. Demographic section will be analyzed by frequency and percentage while other sections data were analyzed based on descriptive statistics of mean, standard deviation, reliability test and regression analysis.

Study Design

This section demonstrates the study design and instruments used as the part of the study. The survey questions are developed based on Technology Acceptance Model framework (TAM). The questionnaires for the survey were designed based on the hypotheses from the literature review conducted to reach the research objectives. The first part of the survey compromised questions related to the respondents' personal information. This section is intended to capture the background of the subject of the study.

Among the items that are collected for personal data are gender, age, institution name, educational level, utilization of e-learning systems.

Respondents were needed to answer six sections of the questionnaire; on personal information, perceived ease of use of the e-learning system, perceived usefulness of the e-learning system, self-efficiency of the e-learning system, intention to use the e-learning system and technology availability and usage. There are six sections in the survey. The first section consists of the personal data of the participants and the utilization of e-learning systems. There are five questions in the second section which signify the present e-learning systems perceived ease of use. There are two questions in the third section which signify the e-learning system perceived usefulness. Six questions in the self-efficiency section and two questions in intention to use section. The final section comprising eight questions which covers the area of technology availability and usage. Figure 3 shows a list of questions used in the study. To measure the 23 questions, a five-point Likert scale has been used; *strongly agree (5), agree (4), neutral (3), disagree (2), and strongly disagree (1).*

As the questionnaire involves items using a Likert scale and multiple choices, it is considered closed ended questions (Sekaran and Roger, 2016). Closed ended questions enable quick decisions and ease to code information easily for subsequent analysis.

Google form was used for the online survey, as it was deemed to be appropriate to collect data during pandemic situation. The online survey is designated to be completed in approximately four to five minutes. Therefore, it is assumed that the time to complete would be sufficient to garner a response from participants. No questions should be avoided as participants were not allowed to go to the next questions without answering previous questions or sections. This action will avoid missing data in the main study. All respondents' answers are entitled to privacy and ethical issues such as informed consent and confidentiality were prior, during and after data collection.

The target demographic of this study is the students enrolled at various higher institution in Brunei (i.e, Universiti Teknologi Brunei (UTB), Universiti Brunei Darussalam (UBD) Sultan Sharif Ali Islamic University (UNISSA), Politeknik Brunei, etc) who are actively involved in the use of e-learning systems.

Hypothesis

Based on TAM, a number of hypotheses have been developed. The hypothesis of the study is as follows:

H1: Self-efficacy (SE) has a significant positive effect on perceived ease of use (PEOU).
H2: Self-efficacy (SE) has significant positive effect on perceived usefulness (PU).
H3: Technology availability and usage (TAU) has a significant positive effect on perceived ease of use.
H4: Technology availability and usage (TAU) has a significant positive effect on perceived usefulness (PU).
H5: Perceived ease of use (PEOU) has significant positive effect on perceived usefulness (PU).
H6: Perceived ease of use (PEOU) has significant positive effect on intention to use (ITU).
H7: Perceived usefulness (PU) has significant positive effect on intention to use (ITU).

Research Model

Based on the hypothesis above, the research model is created and presented below (Figure 2):

Figure 2. Research model

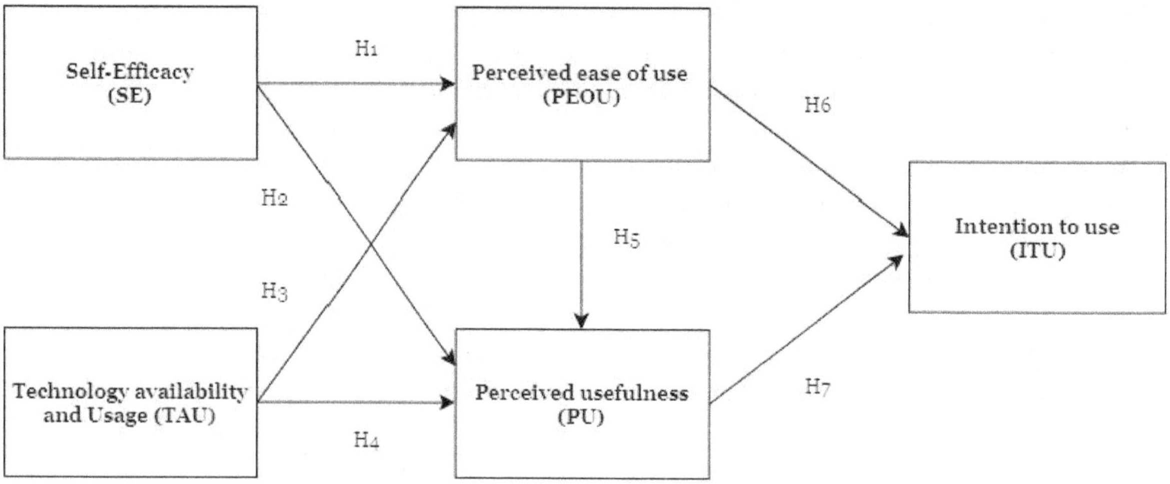

Pilot Study

Prior to conducting the survey, a pilot study was carried out to measure the reliability and usability of the questionnaire. Three students were selected for this study. All respondents were able to answer the questionnaire questions without any consent. Therefore, assuming all questions were reliable, and hence, surveys are used in the final study.

Following tables represent all the questions that were used for the questionnaire survey for this study. Total of 23 questions were prepared that are categorized into five sub-section.

Perceived Ease-of-Use (PEOU)

1. I find the e-learning system is easy to use.
2. The features of the e-learning system are easy to understand.
3. The design and user interface of the e-learning system are attractive and customizable.
4. There are difficulties in adapting the use of e-learning systems.
5. There are guidance and training given on the use of e-learning.

Perceived Usefulness (PU)

1. I am able to use the e-learning system for my learning with ease.
2. The e-learning system is useful to fulfill my learning needs.

Self-Efficiency

1. I support the implementation of e-learning in my institution.
2. I believe that e-learning can enhance the quality of education.
3. I believe that using e-learning can increase my productivity.
4. I believe that e-learning enables me to effectively learn more than the traditional classroom-based approach.
5. I believe that e-learning enables students and lecturers to communicate and interact better with one another.

6. I believe that e-learning platforms ease the submission of all related task (assignments, curriculum, forms).

Intention to Use

1. I am willing to use e-learning throughout my semester.
2. I am willing to access my e-learning system daily to check announcements, schedule as well as interaction between teachers and students.

Technology Availability and Usage

1. I have access to the internet whenever I need.
2. The speed and stability of the internet access in the institution is satisfactory.
3. The hardware facilities provided in the institution are sufficient.
4. The hardware facilities provided in the institution are up-to-date.
5. I have access to electronic technology (e.g. Computer, Mobile Phone, laptop, tablet) whenever I need.
6. I frequently use the internet.
7. I use the internet as a source of information.
8. I can use computers confidently.

RESULT AND DISCUSSION

Capitalize the Use of Technology among Institution

With the world facing a pandemic outbreak today, the trend of using technology in this situation should be taken advantage of among educational institutions. The adoption of online learning strategies are competent to improve the quality of learning and learning outcomes of different individuals; can use new techniques, methods or learning models and new technologies to improve teacher performance and overall improve the quality of education. The benefit of online learning is, it provides flexibility, particularly in terms of time. Online learning facilitates the learning process to be done anywhere and anytime where internet connection is available. Thus, this enhances students' motivation compared to traditional classroom approaches. In addition, it is very effective and efficient for the students as they don't have to go back and forth to college but only open their devices or laptop at home.

Technology Training

In general, training plays a crucial part to improve an individual's performance and skills. In a learning context, training ensures students are able to understand and use the technology or system. Training in the use of technology is called technology training. Technology training of e-learning involves the transfer of knowledge and guidelines about the specific online learning software or system that will be used by the institution as the platform for e-learning. Training can be conducted internally or externally through departments or courses. According to Agarwal & Prasad (1998), external or internal training is positively related to technology acceptance. Training acts as a forerunner to a positive attitude to technology where it eliminates negative effects such anxiety of performing new things that is unpredictable. Thus, training facilitates learners' acceptance towards the system or technology consequently leads to a positive attitude of using the technology specifically e-learning system.

Furthermore, a study by Lee (2008) found that technology training is positively related to perceived ease of use and perceived usefulness of the technology. Take into consideration, a student who is new to a specific computer program and those who have difficulties in using technology, a training makes it possible to facilitate the use of the computer as well as perceives its usefulness.

Technical Support Availability

Technical support is considered an important component in promoting learners' belief of new technology and making the system effective. The availability of technical support ensures that obstacle or technical problem learners encountered such as system down or bug error, are brought into solution in a matter of time. Failure to provide support will frustrate users and therefore negatively impact technology. Thus, learners will likely perceive a new learning system as easy to use and useful for their learning when system assistance is readily available through their use of the system.

In addition, lecturers or staff play an important role in encouraging students to use the e-learning system. Waheed and Hussain (2010) mentioned that the lecturers' characteristics factors can contribute to the acceptance of the satisfaction of the students in system use. Moreover, the success of the e-learning system depends on the lecturer's attitude towards e-learning. Not only the attitude towards the system, but the role of lecturers in the management of e-learning, the dissemination of information, the teaching style, the provision of relevant and quality information and content that influence and influence the acceptance of e-learning among students. Sun et al. (2008), in turn, suggested that lecturers' attitudes toward learning can influence e-learning acceptance among students.

Demographics

Based on Figure 4 shows that most of the participants were mainly male (*54.5%*) while female (*45.5%*). Most of the respondents were in the age group of 19-30 years (*93.1%*) followed by below 18 years and below (*5.0%*), 31-40 years (*1.0%*) and 40 years and above (*1.0%*). *77.2%* of the respondents were undergraduate students, *12.9%* were higher students and *2.0%* e-learning systems. national diploma students, followed by *7.9%* were post-graduate were diploma students. All respondents (*100%*) institutions utilize

Based on respondent answers on what systems or applications they used for their e-learning, various application or systems are used in facilitating their e-learning are such as Moodle, Canvas, Politeknik website LMS, Tencent, Microsoft Team, Office 365, Google hangout, Zoom, Whatsapp, Webex, Youtube, Edmodo, Google classroom, Telegram, Skype, Zoology. From the findings, Moodles was the popular e-learning platform used amongst the respondents.

Data Analysis

Table below (Figure 5) shows the summary statistics and frequency distributions were calculated for each of the 23 items of the construct. Means for the items range between 2.14 and 4.54 and standard deviations of items are less than 1.336.

The first variable Perceived ease of use (PEOU) shows a minimum mean of 2.14 and maximum mean of 3.18. The results show that guidance and training followed by the interface of e-learning are relatively poor. Davis (1989) in his study revealed that usability in the TAM model has positive effects on e-learning. This is because the easy-to-use aspect is one of the factors that leads to the actual use of

Table 1.

		Frequency	Percentage
Gender	Male	55	54.5%
	Female	46	45.5%
Age	18 and below	5	5.0%
	19-30	94	93.1%
	31-40	1	1.0%
	40 and above	1	1.0%
Educational Level	Post-Graduate	8	7.9%
	Undergraduate	78	77.2%
	Higher National Diploma	13	12.9%
	Diploma	2	2.0%
Does your institution utilize e-learning system?	Yes	101	100%
	No	0	0.0%

the lesson system. Therefore, when technology training is absent and the interface is complex, thus, this affects the ease of use of the system, leading to poor performance in using the system.

The second variable (Perceived Usefulness), the average records a fairly above average mean of 3.06. Although it is satisfactory, these variables are impacted by first variables as when e-learning is difficult to use thus affecting the usefulness of using the e-learning system that the person perceives. (F. Abdullah, R.Ward & E.Ahmed, 2016).

The third variable (Self-efficacy) represents the minimum mean of 3.06 and highest mean of 4.00. The lowest mean of these variables shows that e-learning of communicating over the internet is not as effective as physical interaction, where students preferred face to face communication to gain more consensus. However, the students are assertive that e-learning eases the submission of all tasks with a mean of 4.00. This is because e-learning enables paperless submission that can be done anytime and anywhere thus saving time and cost.

The finding of the fourth variable (Intention to use) shows significant willingness by the student in using e-learning throughout their semester with a mean of 3.73 and records mean of 3.34 for using it on a daily basis. This results shows that students are willing to use the e-learning system in assisting in their daily learning activities.

In the variable of Technology availability and usage, records the lowest mean of 2.68 and highest mean of 4.54. The highest shows that most of the students' have access to the internet and can use computers with confidence. These results can be a positive result in the use of e-learning as students are comfortable with the use of technology and seamlessly have access to electronic equipment and the internet. Contrary, the infrastructure provided by the institution shows poor mean value. This can be based on where infrastructure provided in the institution is inadequate, outdated and has very poor maintenance. Infrastructure plays an important role in supporting the effectiveness of e-learning as it contributes to the ease of use and access.

Table 2.

Item description		*Mean*	*Std. deviation*
Perceived ease of use (PEOU)			
PEOU1	I find the e-learning system is easy to use	3.02	1.149
PEOU2	The features of the e-learning system are easy to understand.	2.94	1.094
PEOU3	The design and user interface of the e-learning system are attractive and customizable.	2.75	1.043
PEOU4	There are difficulties in adapting the use of e-learning systems.	3.18	0.994
PEOU5	There are guidance and training given on the use of e-learning.	2.14	0.906
Perceived usefulness (PU)			
PU1	I am able to use the e-learning system for my learning with ease.	3.06	1.231
PU2	The e-learning system is useful to fulfill my learning needs.	3.06	1.085
Self-Efficiency (SE)			
SE1	I support the implementation of e-learning in my institution.	3.41	1.336
SE2	I believe that e-learning can enhance the quality of education.	3.85	0.932
SE3	I believe that using e-learning can increase my productivity.	3.49	0.976
SE4	I believe that e-learning enables me to effectively learn more than the traditional classroom-based approach.	3.16	0.956
SE5	I believe that e-learning enables students and lecturers to communicate and interact better with one another.	3.06	0.947
SE6	I believe that e-learning platforms ease the submission of all related task (assignments, curriculum, forms).	4.00	0.980
Intention to use (ITU)			
ITU1	I am willing to use e-learning throughout my semester.	3.73	1.048
ITU2	I am willing to access my e-learning system daily to check announcements, schedule as well as interaction between teachers and students.	3.34	1.032
Technology availability and usage (TAU)			
TAU1	I have access to the internet whenever I need.	4.05	1.062
TAU2	The speed and stability of the internet access in the institution is satisfactory.	2.82	1.117
TAU3	The hardware facilities provided in the institution are sufficient.	2.69	1.075
TAU4	The hardware facilities provided in the institution are up-to-date.	2.68	0.979
TAU5	I have access to electronic technology (e.g Computer, Mobile Phone, laptop, tablet) whenever I need.	4.09	0.981
TAU6	I frequently use the internet.	4.54	0.843
TAU7	I use the internet as a source of information.	4.48	0.715
TAU8	I can use computers confidently.	4.08	0.924

Reliability Statistics

Construct reliability was tested to ensure that the results are reliable and consistent. Cronbach alpha is used to calculate each of the factors and for the entire scale (Cronbach alpha = 0.808) which measures the internal consistency of the scale as shown in table 3. Internal consistency measures the inter-relatedness of the items used by indicating how a set of items are closely related as a group (Moola and Bisschodd, 2012). Hair et al (2003) recommended Cronbach's alpha values of 0.6 to 0.7 as the limit of satisfaction whilst Streiner (2003) recommended a maximum threshold of 0.09. A very high value for alpha indicates that some items are redundant. However, Nunnally (1967) suggests that a Cronbach alpha value of 0.7 is still acceptable, with a slightly lower value might sometimes be acceptable.

Table 3. Cronbach alpha

Factors	*Cronbach's Alpha*
Perceived ease-of-use (PEOU)	0.586
Perceived usefulness (PU)	0.889
Self-Efficiency	0.714
Intention to use	0.616
Technology accessibility and usage	0.759
Total (23 items)	**0.808**

If all variables in the questionnaire show a high level of reliability, an accurate study results can be obtained. The results of the reliability test (Cronbach Alpha) of the total factors is 0.808 shows a high correlation coefficient. The independent variable was that of the perceived ease-of-use recorded 0.586 values, the perceived usefulness records 0.889 values, the self-efficiency had 0.714 values while the intention to value was 0.616 and lastly the technology accessibility and usage had values of 0.759. Cronbach alpha of total variables (CR=0.808) for the construct used in the current study indicates that it can be used for further analysis.

Correlation

According to Cohen and Manion (1985), the use of correlation test statistics is to understand the relationship or influence of one factor to another. It is essential to confirm reliability and correlation as they are all the underlying assumptions for conducting regression analysis on data. Perceived ease-of-use (PEOU), Perceived usefulness (PU), Self-Efficiency, Intention to use, Technology accessibility and usage were checked for correlation among the variables.

Based on figure 3, there was high correlation among anticipated perceived ease-of-use and perceived usefulness of 0.749, 0.304 correlation among perceived ease-of-use and self-efficiency, 0.184 correlation among perceived ease-of-use and intention to use and -0.032 correlation among perceived ease-of-use and technology accessibility and usage.

Perceived usefulness had 0.392 correlation with self-efficiency, 0.273 correlation with intention to use and 0.162 correlation with technology accessibility and usage. Self-Efficiency had 0.742 correlation with intention to use and 0.101 correlation witH technology accessibility and usage. The intention to use had 0.246 correlation with technology accessibility. This level of correlation is appropriate among the variables and shows that there is a relationship that is present among the variables and also confirming that independent variables are not too highly correlated as that help to avoid the problem of multicol-

Figure 3. Pearson's correlation coefficient

Correlations

		PEOUs	PUs	SEs	ITUs	TAUs
PEOUs	Pearson Correlation	1	.749**	.304**	.184	-.032
	Sig. (2-tailed)		.000	.002	.066	.751
	N	101	101	101	101	101
PUs	Pearson Correlation	.749**	1	.392**	.273**	.162
	Sig. (2-tailed)	.000		.000	.006	.105
	N	101	101	101	101	101
SEs	Pearson Correlation	.304**	.392**	1	.742**	.101
	Sig. (2-tailed)	.002	.000		.000	.315
	N	101	101	101	101	101
ITUs	Pearson Correlation	.184	.273**	.742**	1	.246*
	Sig. (2-tailed)	.066	.006	.000		.013
	N	101	101	101	101	101
TAUs	Pearson Correlation	-.032	.162	.101	.246*	1
	Sig. (2-tailed)	.751	.105	.315	.013	
	N	101	101	101	101	101

**. Correlation is significant at the 0.01 level (2-tailed).
*. Correlation is significant at the 0.05 level (2-tailed).

linearity. Avoiding multicollinearity problems in regression analysis is important because the least squares estimation method assumes that the independent variables are not correlated with each other.

Table 4. Summary of regression analysis

Hypothesis	*Independent variable*	*Dependent variable*	*β*	*Standard error*	*t*	*p*	*Hypothesis supported*
H1	Self-efficiency	Perceived ease of use	0.315	0.099	3.176	0.002	yes
H2	Self-efficiency	Perceived usefulness	0.236	0.056	4.242	0.000	yes
H3	Technology availability and usage	Perceived ease of use	-0.030	0.093	-0.318	0.751	no
H4	Technology availability and usage	Perceived usefulness	0.087	0.053	1.634	0.105	no
H5	Perceived ease of use	Perceived usefulness	0.435	0.039	11.265	0.000	yes
H6	Perceived ease of use	Intention to use	0.133	0.071	1.862	0.066	no
H7	Perceived usefulness	Intention to use	0.340	0.120	2.822	0.006	yes

Regression Analysis

A regression analysis was conducted to test all the seven hypotheses to determine relationship between variables whether it is supported or not. The hypothesis was tested by the *Statistical Package for Social Sciences (SPSS) version 19* software.

Table 4 summarises the results obtained from the regression analysis testing. Overall, four out of five hypotheses are supported. In the next paragraph, a results of the hypothesis are discussed.

***H1**: Self-efficacy (SE) has a significant positive effect on perceived ease of use (PEOU).*

For the first **hypothesis (H1)**, regression analysis was conducted for testing where self-efficiency (SE) was an independent factor while perceived ease of use (PEOU) was a dependent factor. Regression analysis gave a p-value of 0.002 ($p<0.05$), which indicates the existence of a significant relationship between the factors SE and PEOU. Thus, SE has impacts on PEOU and hypothesis (H1) is supported.

H2: Self-efficacy (SE) has significant positive effect on perceived usefulness (PU).

Similarly, **hypothesis two (H2)** was also tested, where self-efficiency (SE) was an independent factor while perceived usefulness (PU) was a dependent factor. Regression analysis gave a p-value of 0.000 ($p<0.05$), which also implies the existence of a significant relationship between the factors SE and PU. Thus, SE has impacts on PU and this hypothesis (H2) is supported.

Self-efficacy represents the judgement of one's belief or capability to perform a particular job or task across a variety of different situations (Bandura, 1997). Self-efficacy is a critical role in influencing behavior. When students perceive their ability to use the system, the easier they find in using the system. As studied by Park (2009) with a sample of 628 university students has found that self-efficacy of e-learning predicted both perceived ease of use and perceived usefulness of e-learning systems in the university. It is believed that individuals with high self-efficacy are able to perform new tasks with ease compared to those who are not. This is because they have higher expectations and confidence in the skills and ability they have in using the e-learning system which they assume the system is easy to use. In contrast, those who have lack of confidence tend to avoid the use of e-learning systems.

Conversely, e-learning self-efficacy through perceive of use has significant effects on behavioral intention, in which, the more interest and self-driven the individual possesses on performing specific tasks the more they perceive the usefulness of new technology. Due to the perception of usefulness on the new technology is believed to be able to enhance performance.

***H3**: Technology availability and usage (TAU) has a significant positive effect on perceived ease of use.*

As for **hypothesis three (H3)**, a regression analysis was conducted where Technology availability and usage (TAU) was an independent factor while perceived ease of use (PEOU) was a dependent factor. The analysis gave a p-value of 0.751 ($p>0.05$) which displays there is no significant influence on PEOU. Thus, this hypothesis (H3) is rejected.

***H4**: Technology availability and usage (TAU) has a significant positive effect on perceived usefulness (PU).*

As for **hypothesis four (H4)**, where technology availability and usage (TAU) was an independent factor while perceived usefulness (PU) was a dependent factor, the regression result gave a p-value of 0.105 ($p>0.05$) which also shows there is no significant influence on PU and thus, the hypothesis (H4) is rejected.

Based on the results above, it can be supported by numerous researchers. Martins and Kellermanns (2004) argued that there was no significant relationship between system accessibility and perceived ease of use of system in which the measures does not involve separation of internal and external technology access but overall general access. In contrast, Lee (2008) contested the accessibility of internal and external technology which he described internal technology as equipment provided by the organization and external technology as equipment outside an organization. However, there was no provided evidence for a relationship between technology accessibility and perceived usefulness, and no support for a relationship between perceived ease of use and internal technology accessibility.

***H5**: Perceived ease of use (PEOU) has significant positive effect on perceived usefulness (PU).*

For the **fifth hypothesis (H5)**, where Perceived ease of use (PEOU) was an independent factor while perceived usefulness (PU) was a dependent factor, the regression result gave a p-value of 0.000 ($p>0.05$) which also reveals there is significant influence on PU and thus, the hypothesis (H5) is accepted.

Based on the TAM model, perceived ease of use has positive impacts on perceived usefulness of an information system (Davis, 1989). When an individual perceives the use of e-learning is easy and hassle free, they are likely inclined to believe that it will improve their performance. In other words, if students perceive that the e-learning system is easy to use, students will deemed the system useful. The reasoning is that individuals deemed e-learning as useful when they know how to utilize the system. A research study conducted by Lee (2008) of 1,100 student's participants showed that there is a positive and notable relation between student's perceived ease of use of online systems and the perceptions of usefulness of online learning systems.

E-learning ease of use can be improved through the revamping of interface or design The design and requirement of the system must meet the expectation of the users in terms of its user-friendliness, navigation, aesthetic, access and security. Easy access to the system also plays an important part to provide easy accessibility. A poor design and complicated functionality may cause complications to the use of the system.

***H6**: Perceived ease of use (PEOU) has significant positive effect on intention to use (ITU).*

As shown in table x, **hypothesis six (H6)**, the perceived ease of use (PEOU) has no influence on Intention to use. The regression result gave a p-value of 0.066 ($p>0.05$), therefore the hypothesis (H6) is rejected

***H7**: Perceived usefulness (PU) has significant positive effect on intention to use (ITU).*

However, the last **hypothesis (H7)**, indicates that perceived usefulness (PU) has significant influence on intention to use (ITU). The regression result gave a p-value of 0.006 ($p>0.05$) thus, the hypothesis (H7) is accepted

In this study, the perceived ease of use does not have direct influence on the intention to use of e-learning system, although it has direct influence on perceived usefulness. This demonstrates perceived usefulness has significance in e-learning system acceptance. In other words, although e-learning systems are inconvenient. The institutions provided training by formal and informal ways, such as; one module as common subject through e-learning and also provided blended learning, between e-learning and offline learning. Therefore, a system with a high level of perceived usefulness will induce positive attitudes. Opposingly, if the e-learning system is easy to use but does not bring any benefits to the students, then they will not use it. Consideration of the desire to use technology or not, will depend on the level of ease in learning its use. The easier the technology is, the higher the interest of individuals to use it. The more difficult the technology is, the lower the interest of individuals to use it, and the slower individuals and community groups will adopt it. To overcome this, training and guidance availability should be considered to support and influence the student to the use of e-learning systems.

Research has supported that the higher the individual perceived usefulness and ease of use of using new technology, the more positive the attitude toward the new technology, leading to greater intention to use the system. Lee (2008) argues that easy access and perception of convenience provide a positive effect on the online learning system where in turn, users become more likely to accept it and learn it. Because e-learning itself can be accessed anywhere and anytime and is very convenient, thus perception of usefulness will further encourage students to use e-learning systems.

CONCLUSION

To conclude, e-learning is a way forward in today's world that enables quality education service in Brunei Darussalam. E-learning will not reach its objective and benefits if students refuse or are unable to use the system. This study represents the applicability of TAM to investigate and explain the students' behavior towards e-learning technology. Therefore, an understanding of student acceptance behavior toward the system and technology availability is important in order to improve the online learning environment. A research model and hypothesis were developed based on TAM and evaluated using data collected of 101 students studying at several higher institutions in Brunei. This study is inclined to the use of quantitative methods. Descriptive analysis were performed to analyse the data using Statistical Package for Social Science (SPSS) Version 19 software. Two TAM external variables are used; Self-efficacy and Technology availability and usage which plays a role in influencing the students' intention to use.

Based on the data analysis, four out of seven hypotheses were supported. First, self-efficacy had significant influence on both perceived usefulness and perceived ease of use of e-learning systems. On the other hand, technology availability and usage had no significant impact on perceived usefulness well as the perceived ease of use of e-learning systems. Perceived ease of use has a major impact to perceive usefulness. Moreover, the perceived ease of use does not have influence on the intention to use of e-learning system, while perceived usefulness has influence on intention to use. Overall, the determinants of e-learning adoption in higher institutions are Self-efficacy, Perceived ease of use, Perceived usefulness and Intention to use. Furthermore, it was recommended that institutions should provide training and technology support to neuter attitude and acceptance of students towards effective e-learning.

RECOMMENDATION

With the world facing a pandemic outbreak today, the trend of using technology in this situation should be taken advantage of among educational institutions. The adoption of online learning strategies are competent to improve the quality of learning and learning outcomes of different individuals; can use new techniques, methods or learning models and new technologies to improve teacher performance and overall improve the quality of education. The benefit of online learning is, it provides flexibility, particularly in terms of time. Online learning facilitates the learning process to be done anywhere and anytime where internet connection is available. Thus, this enhances students' motivation compared to traditional classroom approaches. In addition, it is very effective and efficient for the students as they don't have to go back and forth to college but only open their devices or laptop at home.

In general, training plays a crucial part to improve an individual's performance and skills. In a learning context, training ensures students are able to understand and use the technology or system. Training in the use of technology is called technology training. Technology training of e-learning involves the transfer of knowledge and guidelines about the specific online learning software or system that will be used by the institution as the platform for e-learning. Training can be conducted internally or externally through departments or courses. According to Agarwal & Prasad (1998), external or internal training is positively related to technology acceptance. Training acts as a forerunner to a positive attitude to technology where it eliminates negative effects such anxiety of performing new things that is unpredictable. Thus, training facilitates learners' acceptance towards the system or technology consequently leads to a positive attitude of using the technology specifically e-learning system.

Furthermore, a study by Lee (2008) found that technology training is positively related to perceived ease of use and perceived usefulness of the technology. Take into consideration, a student who is new to a specific computer program and those who have difficulties in using technology, a training makes it possible to facilitate the use of the computer as well as perceives its usefulness.

Technical support is considered an important component in promoting learners' belief of new technology and making the system effective. The availability of technical support ensures that obstacle or technical problem learners encountered such as system down or bug error, are brought into solution in a matter of time. Failure to provide support will frustrate users and therefore negatively impact technology. Thus, learners will likely perceive a new learning system as easy to use and useful for their learning when system assistance is readily available through their use of the system.

In addition, lecturers or staff play an important role in encouraging students to use the e-learning system. Waheed and Hussain (2010) mentioned that the lecturers' characteristics factors can contribute to the acceptance of the satisfaction of the students in system use. Moreover, the success of the e-learning system depends on the lecturer's attitude towards e-learning. Not only the attitude towards the system, but the role of lecturers in the management of e-learning, the dissemination of information, the teaching style, the provision of relevant and quality information and content that influence and influence the acceptance of e-learning among students. Sun et al. (2008), in turn, suggested that lecturers' attitudes toward learning can influence e-learning acceptance among students.

LIMITATION TO STUDY

On 12th March 2020, the World Health Organization (WHO) declared COVID-19 a pandemic, following its outbreak reaching hundreds of thousands of cases worldwide. The WHO's pandemic declaration led to aggressive prevention initiatives from various parties. Brunei has taken drastic steps that include closure of various educational institutions. Prior to this announcement, several educational institutions took proactive steps by limiting teaching practices, avoiding face-to-face lectures and encouraging the use of technology in teaching and learning as a medium of intermediary. Due to this situation, several data collections were aborted such as interviews and distribution of manual survey form. Thus, data collection was limited to online surveys.

There are also limitations in evaluating the results of this study. First, this study focuses only on five factors - perceived ease of use of the e-learning system, perceived usefulness of the e-learning system, self-efficiency of the e-learning system, intention to use the e-learning system and technology availability and usage. This study does not take into account other factors such as experience, learning satisfaction, user acceptance, culture, subjective norm, etc. Therefore, the results of this study are limited to these five factors only.

Second, this study used samples that are biased in which the respondents are from students of Universiti Teknologi Brunei (UTB). The results of this study may be different if samples are equally distributed. Evidently, the results of this study is not gathered as the representative of students in all the different institutions of higher learning.

ACKNOWLEDGMENT

Heru Susanto as main contributor, and Fadzliwati Mohiddin, Saleem Haja Nazamudeen as contributors. All authors reviewed and approved the final version of this manuscript.

REFERENCES

Abdullah, F., Ward, R., & Ahmed, E. (2016). Investigating the influence of the most commonly used external variables of TAM on students' Perceived Ease of Use (PEOU) and Perceived Usefulness (PU) of e-portfolios. *Computers in Human Behavior*, *63*, 75–90. doi:10.1016/j.chb.2016.05.014

Abdullah, F., Ward, R., & Ahmed, E. (2016). Investigating the influence of the most commonly used external variables of TAM on students' Perceived Ease of Use (PEOU) and Perceived Usefulness (PU) of e-portfolios. *Computers in Human Behavior*, *63*, 75–90. doi:10.1016/j.chb.2016.05.014

Agarwal, R., & Prasad, J. (1998). A conceptual and operational definition of innovativeness in the domain of information technology. *Information Systems Research*, *9*(2), 204–215. doi:10.1287/isre.9.2.204

Bandura, A. (1997). *Self-efficacy: The exercise of control*. W.H. Freeman.

Barhoumi, C. (2016). User Acceptance of the e-Information Service as Information Resource: A New-Extension of the Technology Acceptance Model. *New Library World*, *117*(9/10), 626–643. doi:10.1108/NLW-06-2016-0045

Berna-Martinez, J. & Maciá Pérez, F. (2012). Overcoming resistance to change in business innovation processes. *IACSIT International Journal of Engineering and Technology*, *4*, 148.

Burton-Jones, A., & Hubona, G. (2005). Individual differences and usage behavior: Revisiting a Technology Acceptance Model assumption. *ACM SIGMIS Database*, *36*(2), 58–77. doi:10.1145/1066149.1066155

Chuttur, M. (2009). Overview of the Technology Acceptance Model: Origins, Developments and Future Directions. *Sprouts: Working Papers on Information Systems, 9*.

Cohen, L., & Manion, L. (1985). *Research Methods in Education*. Croom-Helm.

Davis, F. D. (1985). *A Technology Acceptance Model for Empirically Testing New End-User Information Systems: Theory and Results (Ph.D in Management Disertation)*. Massachusetts Institute of Technology, Sloan School of Management.

Davis, F. D. (1989). Perceived usefulness, perceived ease of use, and user acceptance of information technology. *Management Information Systems Quarterly*, *13*(3), 319–340. doi:10.2307/249008

Delone, W. H., & McLean, E. R. (2003). The Delone and McLean Model of information systems success: A Ten-Year update. *Journal of Management Information Systems*, *19*(4), 9–30. doi:10.1080/07421222.2003.11045748

Dominici, G., & Palumbo, F. (2013). How to Build an E-Learning Product: Factors for Student/Customer Satisfaction. *Business Horizons*, *56*(1), 87–96. doi:10.1016/j.bushor.2012.09.011

Durodolu, O. (2016). *Technology Acceptance Model as a predictor of using information system to acquire information literacy skills*. Academic Press.

Grandon, E., Alshare, O., & Kwan, O. (2005). Factors influencing student intention to adopt online classes: A cross-cultural study. *Journal of Computing Sciences in Colleges*, *20*, 46–56.

Hu, P. J., Chau, P. Y. K., Sheng, O. R. L., & Tam, K. Y. (1999). Examining the technology acceptance model using physical acceptance of telemedicine technology. *Journal of Management Information Systems*, *16*(2), 91–112. doi:10.1080/07421222.1999.11518247

Jr, H., Celsi, M., Money, A., Samouel, P., & Page, M. (2015). *The essentials of business research methods* (3rd ed.)., doi:10.4324/9781315716862

Kahiigi, E., Ekenberg, L., Hansson, H., Tusubira, F., & Danielson, M. (2008). Exploring the e-Learning State of art. *The Electronic Journal of e-Learning, 6*.

Lapointe, L., & Rivard, S. (2005). A Multilevel Model of Resistance to Information Technology Implementation. *Management Information Systems Quarterly*, *29*(3), 461–491. doi:10.2307/25148692

Lee, J., Burnett, G., Vandegrift, M., Baeg, J. H., & Morris, R. (2015). Availability and accessibility in an open access institutional repository: a case study. *Information Research, 20*(1). Retrieved from http://InformationR.net/ir/20-1/paper661.html

Legris, P., Ingham, J., & Collerette, P. (2003). Why do people use information technology? A critical review of the technology acceptance model. *Information & Management*, *40*(3), 191–204. doi:10.1016/S0378-7206(01)00143-4

Leu, F.Y., Liu, C.Y., Liu, J.C., Jiang, F.C., & Susanto, H. (2015). S-PMIPv6: An intra-LMA model for IPv6 mobility. *J. Netw. Comput. Appl., 58*, 180–191.

Liu, J. C., Leu, F. Y., Lin, G. L., & Susanto, H. (2018). An MFCC-based text-independent speaker identification system for access control. *Concurr. Comput. Pract. Exp., 30*(2), e4255. doi:10.1002/cpe.4255

Liu, Y., & Wang, H. (2009). A comparative study on e-learning technologies and products: From the East to the West. *Systems Research and Behavioral Science, 26*(2), 191–209. doi:10.1002res.959

Love, N., & Fry, N. (2006). Accounting Students' Perceptions of a Virtual Learning Environment: Springboard or Safety Net? *Accounting Education, 15*(2), 151–166. doi:10.1080/06939280600609201

Susanto, H. (2017). Electronic Health System: Sensors Emerging and Intelligent Technology Approach. In *Smart Sensors Networks* (pp. 189–203). Elsevier. doi:10.1016/B978-0-12-809859-2.00012-7

Susanto, H. (2018). Smart mobile device emerging Technologies: An enabler to Health Monitoring system. In *High-Performance Materials and Engineered Chemistry* (pp. 241–264). Apple Academic Press. doi:10.1201/9781315187860-8

Susanto, H., & Almunawar, M. N. (2015). Managing Compliance with an Information Security Management Standard. In *Encyclopedia of Information Science and Technology* (3rd ed., pp. 1452–1463). IGI Global. doi:10.4018/978-1-4666-5888-2.ch138

Susanto, H., & Almunawar, M. N. (2018). *Information Security Management Systems: A Novel Framework and Software as a Tool for Compliance with Information Security Standard.* CRC Press. doi:10.1201/9781315232355

Susanto, H., Almunawar, M. N., Leu, F. Y., & Chen, C. K. (2016). Android vs iOS or Others? SMD-OS Security Issues: Generation Y Perception. *International Journal of Technology Diffusion, 7*(2), 1–18. doi:10.4018/IJTD.2016040101

Susanto, H., & Chen, C. K. (2017). Information and Communication Emerging Technology: Making Sense of Healthcare Innovation. In *Internet of Things and Big Data Technologies for Next Generation Healthcare* (pp. 229–250). Springer. doi:10.1007/978-3-319-49736-5_10

Susanto, H., Chen, C. K., & Almunawar, M. N. (2018). Revealing Big Data Emerging Technology as Enabler of LMS Technologies Transferability. In *Internet of Things and Big Data Analytics Toward Next-Generation Intelligence* (pp. 123–145). Springer. doi:10.1007/978-3-319-60435-0_5

Susanto, H., Leu, F.-Y., Caesarendra, W., Ibrahim, F., Haghi, P. K., Khusni, U., & Glowacz, A. (2020). Managing Cloud Intelligent Systems over Digital Ecosystems: Revealing Emerging App Technology in the Time of the COVID19 Pandemic. *Appl. Syst. Innov., 3*(3), 37. doi:10.3390/asi3030037

Tabak, F., & Nguyen, N. T. (2013). Technology Acceptance and Performance in Online Learning Environments: Impact of Self-Regulation. UBD study shows Bruneians interested in online learning. *Brunei Times*. https://btarchive.org/news/national/2016/02/06/ubd-study-showsbruneians-interested-online-learning

Ünal, Y., Alır, G., & Soydal, İ. (2013, September). Students readiness for e-learning: an assessment on Hacettepe University Department of Information Management. In *International Symposium on Information Management in a Changing World* (pp. 137-147). Springer.

Waheed, M., & Hussain, M. F. (2010). Empirical study of e-learner contentment towards e-Learning: Influential role of key factors. *The 2010 MIT LINC Conference in Stratton Center on the MIT Campus.*

Walker, S. (2002). *Insight: Distance education learning environments survey.* https:// insight.southcentralrtec.org/ilib/delesa/delesainfo.html

Woen, A.,, Sylvia, C.,, & Handoko, H., & Abdurachman, E. (2018). E-learning acceptance analysis using technology acceptance model (Tam) (case study: Stmik mikroskil). *Journal of Theoretical and Applied Information Technology, 96*, 6292–6305.

ADDITIONAL READING

Mohammadi, H. (2014). Investigating users' perspectives on e-learning: An integration of TAM and IS success model. *Computers in Human Behavior, 45*, 359–374. Advance online publication. doi:10.1016/j.chb.2014.07.044

Moolla, A., & Bisschoff, C. (2012). Validating a Model to Measure the Brand Loyalty of Fast Moving Consumer Goods. *J. Soc Sci, 31*(2), 101–115. doi:10.1080/09718923.2012.11893019

Nunnally, J. C. (1978). *Psychometric Theory* (2nd ed.). McGraw-Hill.

Park, S. Y. (2009). An analysis of the technology acceptance model in understanding university students' behavioral intention to use e-learning. *Journal of Educational Technology & Society, 12*(3), 150–162. http://www.ifets.info/journals/12_3/14.pdf

Streiner, D. L. (2003). Being inconsistent about consistency: When coefficient alpha does and doesn't matter. *Journal of Personality Assessment, 80*(3), 217–222. doi:10.1207/S15327752JPA8003_01 PMID:12763696

Sun, P. C., Tsai, R. J., Finger, G., Chen, Y. Y., & Yeh, D. (2008). What drives a successful e-Learning? An empirical investigation of the critical factors influencing learner satisfaction. *Computers & Education, 50*(4), 1183–1202. doi:10.1016/j.compedu.2006.11.007

KEY TERMS AND DEFINITIONS

Assistive Technology: Is assistive, adaptive, and rehabilitative devices for People with disability or the elderly population. People with disability often have difficulty performing activities of daily living (ADLs) independently, or even with assistance. ADLs are self-care activities that include toileting, mobility (ambulation), eating, bathing, dressing, grooming, and personal device care. Assistive technology can ameliorate the effects of disabilities that limit the ability to perform ADLs. Assistive technology promotes greater independence by enabling people to perform tasks they were formerly unable to accomplish, or had great difficulty accomplishing, by providing enhancements to, or changing methods of interacting with, the technology needed to accomplish such tasks.

Awareness Training: Helps employees to understand risks and identify potential attacks they may encounter as they receive email and use the web. Awareness training also acquaints emplyees with best practices for avoiding risk.

Information Technology Apps for Learning: The Apps enable students to acquire lecture materials, take online quizzes or assessments, submit tutorials or assignments, view results, view course materials, see news and announcements, online interaction, anytime and anywhere without any geographical or time barriers. However, the key to effective apps -learning is not from its multimedia, design or user-friendliness, but on how the individuals are engaged by the content. Although the use of apps-learning provides notable benefits for students as a whole, the effectiveness of the use of the system depends on the level of acceptance and use of students. The goals of apps-learning will not be achieved if there is lag and resistance to the use of new technology. The process of implementing apps-learning in the institution might face several factors that constraints the effective use of apps-learning as a learning medium, such as infrastructure issues, the willingness and readiness of the institutions and students.

LMS Support Availability: LMS is considered an important component in promoting learners' belief of new technology and making the system effective. The availability of technical support ensures that obstacle or technical problem learners encountered such as system down or bug error, are brought into solution in a matter of time. Failure to provide support will frustrate users and therefore negatively impact technology. Thus, learners will likely perceive a new learning system as easy to use and useful for their learning when system assistance is readily available through their use of the system.

Self-Efficacy: Is the belief we have in our own abilities, specifically our ability to meet the challenges ahead of us and complete a task successfully. General self-efficacy refers to our overall belief in our ability to succeed, but there are many more specific forms of self-efficacy as well (e.g., academic, parenting, sports).

Technology Acceptance Model (TAM): Is an information systems theory that models how users come to accept and use a technology. The actual system use is the endpoint where people use the technology. Behavioral intention is a factor that leads people to use the technology. The behavioral intention (BI) is influenced by the attitude (A) which is the general impression of the technology.

Technology Training: Technology training of e-learning involves the transfer of knowledge and guidelines about the specific online learning software or system that will be used by the institution as the platform for e-learning. Training can be conducted internally or externally through departments or courses. Training acts as a forerunner to a positive attitude to technology where it eliminates negative effects such anxiety of performing new things that is unpredictable. Thus, training facilitates learners' acceptance towards the system or technology consequently leads to a positive attitude of using the technology specifically e-learning system.

Chapter 9
ICT Emerging Technology Impact Within Learning Ecosystem Cyberbullying Among Students:
Facts or Rumors?

Desi Setiana
The Southern Jakarta Correctional Center, Ministry of Law and Human Right, Indonesia & University of Brunei Darussalam, Brunei.

Norainna Besar
https://orcid.org/0000-0002-4833-2018
University of Brunei Darussalam, Brunei

ABSTRACT

This study reveals cyberbullying in the information technology age, particularly in student beliefs and behaviours. Cyberbullying has become an issue that's arising with the advancement of technology, which makes it easier for everyone in the world to be connected wirelessly. The result of the study is very interesting. More than half of the participants have reported that they spent most of their free time on social media. Due to that, some of them have experienced cyberbullying, but fewer than half of the students have actually reported the case. Moreover, social networking sites and any chat sites were found to be the platforms where cyberbullying has mostly been occurred, with email, texting on mobile phones, as well as gaming online also used for cyberbullying. Although the majority of the participants have witnessed cyberbullying, they preferred to ignore the issue instead of reporting it. According to the survey and deep interview, most of the students mentioned that there is a lack of support regarding cyberbullying.

DOI: 10.4018/978-1-7998-7184-2.ch009

INTRODUCTION

Nowadays, the majority of students have their access to a new connected cyber world through internet and several uses of other information and communication technologies (ICT) which include mobile phones and computers. There are many benefits that students can get from the advancement of ICT; it acts as an educational tool for students to seek knowledge, to maintain social contacts and so forth. However, ICT does not only give students some sort of advantages but also several disadvantages. One of them is cyberbullying; it is a new practice of bullying with distinct differences in form, personality, and response. In addition to this, there are many electronic communication devices where cyberbullying can occur. For examples, through emails, social networking websites such as Facebook, Twitter, Instagram or it can be through online games. here is a substantial number of students becoming victims of cyberbullying. By looking at this, it leads to a realization that cyberbullying is slowly becoming a serious matter (Cross, 2008; Li, 2006a, 2006b; Llard, 2004a). Furthermore, Cyberbullying is one of the emerging issues amongst students since their ICT accessibility is becoming part of their daily university life.

According to Tokunaga (2010), cyberbullying is defined as 'any behaviour performed through electronic or digital media by individuals or groups that repeatedly communicates hostile or aggressive messages intended to inflict harm or discomfort on others'. Moreover, Calvete, et al (2010) has also stated that cyberbullying was significantly linked with the use of proactive aggression, justification of violence, exposure to violence, and less perceived social support of friends. In addition to this, there are several other reasons for cyberbullying such as envy, prejudice and intolerance for disability, gender, religion, shame, guilt, anger and pride. Some of the examples for cyberbullying are as follows (Hoff & Mitchell, 2009; Jones, Manstead, & Livingstone, 2011):

- Sending emails, instant messages or text messages using a mobile phone in which the contents are threatening and mean.
- Manipulating the messages and the contents of emails so that students convey their personal information and later, the personal information is forwarded to others.
- Creating fake accounts at social networking websites such as Facebook, Myspace, etc. without owner's permission.
- Posting embarrassing or inappropriate pictures of other people in public.
- Making harassing phone calls using mobile phones.

Cyberbullying is an extension of traditional bullying. In this modern era, where technology is most commonly been used, a new element of the internet has been added to the old kind of bullying. Based on thisstudies, traditional bullying can even start at a very young age. This study had emphasized that there are 50 students from Primary, secondary and higher institutions who have been bullied several times or more. An example of traditional bullying incident can be seen at parking areas, school, or even at local malls while cyberbullying can be done on computers with the help of the internet, for instance, through emails, instant messaging (IM), social networking websites such as MySpace and Facebook.

In terms of parents ways to handle the issue of bullying differ between traditional bullying and cyberbullying. There is a high chance that cyberbullying can be reduced in the long-run. This can be done if parents and other parental guidance have control of their children's activities. The parents and other guidance can block as well as monitor their children's accounts. At least, they can act to defend their children if cyberbullying is to take place. However, traditional bullying is too difficult to handle. This is because when bullying happens, there is a high possibility that no one is around to lend help to the victim. In addition to this, the victims cannot do anything as they cannot simply go offline and ignore what they can do if they were being cyberbullied. Furthermore, it is the traditional bullying that gives more impacts towards students, to compare with cyberbullying. Cyberbullying does not need any confrontation. In other words, the person who is bullying and the victim do not meet or see each other. It is only the power of words used that might affect the victim. Therefore, the consequences of cyberbullying are more towards students' emotions and mental aspect; not the students' physical aspect. However, confrontation exists in traditional bullying. The person who is bullying and the victim are seeing each other. Moreover, the victims might get affected both physically and psychologically. Thus, this makes the traditional bullying more dangerous than cyberbullying. However, in recent years, cyberbullying has become a centre of attention. Several cases involve bullying online and it gives risky consequences upon the victims. One of the consequences for experiencing cyberbullying is it affects the victims psychologically. Studies by Selkie et all in 2015Students who have been cyberbullied have mentioned that they have a higher level of depression and lower self-confidence. Furthermore, the victims are more likely to show hostility and delinquency. Kowalski & Limber in 2013 has found that academically, students who have experienced cyberbullying has reported that they usually would score lower grades and faced other problems related to their studies.

LITERATURE REVIEW

Characteristics of Cyberbullying

Victims

A few other kinds of research have been identified the similarity between the characteristics of victims of traditional bullying and cyberbullying (Hutcherson, 2012; Kowalski & Limber, 2013; Resett & Gamez-Guadix, 2017). Therefore, it is essential to study the characteristics of the bullying-victims to understand the students' beliefs and behaviours associated with cyberbullying. By identifying the real risk factors of cyberbullying, individuals or any relevant authorities can prevent or intervene in new techniques in helping the potential victims.

Difference

According to Hutcherson (2012) the individual who is different from the majority groups prone to be the victims of cyberbully as there is power imbalance on personality or social strength. For example, students who change to new schools, students who are most likely to be the teachers' favourite and even students who stand out for being excellent. Weber and Pelfrey (2014), in their study of 3,403 middle and high school students that participated in Safe Schools and Healthy Students Program in 2009, victims stated that their appearance, the way they communicate, the poor family background and the uniqueness of the first or last names are the main factors which could harm them. As cited by a female middle school participant said that in her old school a girl picked on an overweight girl by posting comments on the social media such as Facebook saying, "she is going to blow up if she keeps eating." She kept posting and the overweight girl eventually just ignored the postings.

Physically Weak

Individuals who are physically weak and act anxiously tend to be targeted by the cyberbully (Kokkinos, Antoniadou, & Markos, 2014). They tend to have poor social and communication problems which also lead to the risk of peer rejection or often left out of social situations. A survey of 931 students in grades 6 through 12 at two schools in a rural community of Pennsylvania shows that the anxiety, depression, self-esteem, physical well-being correlates with cyberbullying. Hence, these factors also lead to poor school attendance and academic performance to the victims of cyberbully (Kowalski & Limber, 2013).

Provocative

Sometimes the victims do not realize their actions which encourage them to be targeted to be bullied. Amin Al Haadi (2013) stated that being natural provocative individuals highly risk to the cyberbully. They always say and act according to their perceptions or opinions. This encourages the rise of negative feelings among their group members or communities. However, in the present study of 146 Greek junior high school student by Antoniadou, Kokkinos & Markos (2016), students are high sensation seekers who are most aggressive and have challenging behaviours. They find entertainment by socializing with strangers and post provocative materials while online. Besides, Roth and Hammelstein (2012) found that an inclination of motivation such romantic motivation encourages them to be sensation seekers. While Görzig and Frumkin (2013) examined a random stratified sample of 25,142 children from 25 European countries, aged 9 to 16, students are mostly sensation seeking. They have high sensation-seeking tendencies which are more likely to experience cyber-victimization.

Personality

The typical bully-victim is likely to be individuals who have low self-esteem and noticeably rejected or isolated by their peers (Brito & Oliveira, 2013). They do not dare to fight back or report the issues to the relevant authority. Research by Antoniadou, Kokkinos & Markos (2016) also stated that antisocial personality is one of the factors which can trigger the predators of a cyberbully. The chances of being attacked by the cyberbully are higher if they are most likely to spend their time on the computer. In contrast, a study made on the emergence of the cyberbullying in childhood, an introvert child has the most risk to be cyberbullied (Monks et al, 2016). Besides, gender and age have a significant impact on cyberbullying. Lindfors (2012) studied on population-based of cyberbullying among 5516 Finnish boys reported less experience than girls in cyberbullying and a higher proportion of 14-year-olds and lowest among 18-year-olds of both genders.

Gender

Bullying occurs to both male and female genders. According to Kowalski, Limber and Agatston, (2012), males are most likely to be bullied physically by their peers. Where else, females are bullied mentally through sexual comments and rumour spreading. Since 1970 the meta-analysis of 153 studies showed that males are bullied more than females. But as time changes to the new digital age, it created a shift that females are bullied more than males. That is because of the internet world creating a new type of bullying which is cyber-bullying. Sexual comments and rumour spreading has increased drastically especially through the use of social media. It is important to understand that males usually bullied by other males and females are usually bullied by both male and female.

Age

Kowalski, Limber and Agatston, (2012) stated that the most bullied victims are from the primary school groups. For secondary school groups have lesser bullies than primary school groups and for higher education groups have lesser bullies than secondary school groups. Youth ages 6-12 from primary schools has the highest rates experience of physical bullying. Secondary schools have the second-highest rates experience of physical bullying. The least to experience physical bullying is higher education group. Youth aged between 6 to 12 years old have the highest rates for emotional bullying compared to the other age groups. Traditional bullying is likely to decrease as the youth age matures and progress through secondary school and higher education level. But cyberbullying is at its peak during secondary school (Hinduja and Patchin, 2010).

Race and Religion

The minority groups are less powerful for offline bullying. However, minority groups can be powerful online. Which means that cyberbullying victims are from the majority group and the minority groups are the cyberbullies since they have not much power offline, they will tend to bully on cyberspace. These minority groups are usually groups of people who are unpopular at school that they would hide their identity in the digital world so they will not be exposed that they are the cyberbullies (Hinduja and Patchin, 2010).

Anonymity

Unlike the conventional bullying method, cyberbullying remains discreet in cyberspace. The main factors of why it has become widely spread are typically bullying often happen without knowing whom the harasser is, theoretically, they would hide behind the monitor screen; thus, prevents from being known and punished. Access to free email accounts, fake social media account and other web-based application gives the harasser power to stalk other people, threaten and spread rumours without any implications. According to Yun-yin Huang and Chien Chou (2010), bullying victims are those who are socially outcast and of the minority, and physically stronger people amongst the crowds often are those who bully. However, research has shown that cyberbullying reverses the relationship between bully and victim. The bully-victim relationship role has shifted in cyberspace as the platform unlocks the door for minority and outcasts to fight back and take revenge. The assumptions that cyberbullying is anonymous in cyberspace suggest that users are aware of cyberbullying behaviours and know the action taken. Anonymity provides a perfect cover in cyberspace, however not all cyberbullying uses it or successfully implement it. Even though the act of cyberbullying is often discreet and anonymous, students don't tend to try and hide their identity (similarly to not wearing a mask during face to face confrontation) as the most bullying act, based on student's perspective, is not taken seriously and might not be viewed by teachers or parents. However, that is not often the case, as online materials are quite public in comparison to the typical bathroom or classroom bullying. Parents and teachers are aware of this behaviour even though actions have not been taken. Thus, research also suggests that cyberbullying and traditional bullying have no distinct differences in the literature (Yun-yin Huang & Chien Chou, 2010) and provides inconsistent findings.

Social Media Cyberbullying

Apart from IM text messaging and harassment via text and phone call, social media have also contributed to cyberbullying through social media sites such as Facebook, Twitter and Instagram. As of 2008, young people between the ages of 12 to 17 have spent more time online than other activities besides sleeping (Chandrashekhar, A., Muktha G. S., & Anjana D. K., 2016). Facebook has contributed to one million young people suffering from harassment and any form of cyberbullying. Majority of these individuals have chosen to ignore that form of behaviour. 55 per cent have reported witnessing cyberbullying in various networking sites. The statistics from the Pew Research study of 2013, close to eight out of ten teens have shared information about themselves to social media. These include contact information such as email & phone number and personal status in terms of videos, images and location (Chandrashekhar, A., Muktha G. S., & Anjana D. K., 2016).

Based on the studies conducted by Elizabeth and Robin (2015) on Cyberbullying Via Social Media, it has reported that people spend at least 1 to 6 hours a day using the Internet; 45.1% of people spend around 3 – 4 hours and 25.8% spend between 5 – 6 hours. The most common technological social communication tools used in social media is Facebook (86.5%), followed by YouTube (75.1%). Furthermore, 18.2% have reported having been a victim to cyberbullying at least within the last year. Responses to cyberbullying events vary following different individuals, which included doing nothing (25.0%), reporting (31.8%) and asking to stop (29.5%). According to Elizabeth Whittaker & Robin M. Kowalski (2015), the venue to engage in cyberbullying in social media reflect upon the technological tools used by the individual. In summary, there is a correlation between the technology used by individuals and cyberbullying. Study shows that as new modes of technology emerge and made known in public (i.e. social media platforms, devices, programs, software, etc.), a new form of cyberbullying will exist. Therefore, as technology progresses, so does individual creativity to implement cyberbullying tactics. This varies according to the level of an institution among students; for instance, Year 9 student technological tools may differ from an undergraduate student. When social networking sites becomes dominant, the evolution of cyberbullying shift from the traditional modes (i.e. sending threatening messages, emails and phone calls) to current modes (posting images and videos on Instagram, Facebook and YouTube). The implication of these modes has a significant impact, not in terms of how it occurs but the effects and responses that it generates. Online communications need no longer be direct such as phone calls and instant messaging, rather indirect and public. The most common responses based on the study by Elizabeth & Robin (2015) for secondary students when they experience cyberbullying was to do nothing; very common in adolescence. However, college/university graduate's that faced with cyberbullying tend to block the person from social media and report the action. This shows the level of awareness in young people on the appropriate responses from a different level of the institution.

Cyberbullying in the Gaming World

The violent video game is a contributing factor to harassment which includes offensive words, stereotyping, sex-role portrayal, inappropriate and aggressive languages. A study by National Sun Yat-sen University shows that children who spend time playing this gaming may result in cyberbullying (Chandrashekhar, A., Muktha G. S., & Anjana D. K., 2016). This suggests how women are portrayed in video games. They are seen as a sex symbol. An act of treating women more as an object rather than people can influence the behaviour of young individuals that relates to cyberbullying. Students are more often being cyberbullied if they play online games. This could be measure through a statistic within 3 months period a group of Korean and Chinese were observed. 38% of Korean students are bullied at least once on the digital gaming world compared to 33% Chinese students. 9.8% of Korean students are bullied more than 16 times in online mobile game and Chinese only 5.8% (Jin, 2017). This shows that the gaming world is the place where students are high to experience cyberbullies. Jin (2017) stated that online mobile game is one of the main platforms for students to experience cyberbullying.

METHODOLOGY

Participants

Participants were selected from different levels of education; primary, secondary and higher institution in Depok (West Java) and Lenteng Agung (South Jakarta) and client's The Southern of Correctional Center Ministry of Law and Human Right, Indonesia. 40-50 survey papers were given to each level of the institution. The survey study gathered a total of 150 participants. Among the 150 respondents, there were a total of 54.7% male and 45.3% female taking part in this study. The majority were from Malay race (80%), followed by Chinese (10%), Indian/ Middle East (1%) and others (9%).

Procedure

The questionnaire was distributed to the representative from each level of the institution by hand and collected before the end of the week. Using a stratified random sampling technique, questionnaires were given to students at a random where participants were not specifically from the same class or taking the same major. While for the interview, purposive sampling technique was implemented as the only selected participant took part for an in-depth interview in Correctional Center Ministry of Law and Human Right.

Measure

Participants were requested to complete a questionnaire inquiring how often they use social media and their experiences to negative behaviour or harassment ever since they are in the institution; primary, secondary or higher. In the questionnaire, the participants were given a definition of cyberbullying as "willful and repeated harm inflicted through the use of computers, cell phones, and other electronic devices". The key areas focused in the questionnaire are whether (a) they have been cyberbullied, (b) witness to someone being cyberbullied, (c) whether an action is taken by them once being cyberbullied or witnessing a cyberbullied situation. Additionally, the questionnaire also provided participants with a section on solutions to prevent cyberbullying. The participants were also asked to report their background in terms of ethnicity and gender.

FINDINGS

Findings from the questionnaires suggest that 78% of the students often use social media, 17.3% of students use it moderately and 4.7% rarely use it. Table 1 shows students experience according to the level of institutions (primary, secondary, higher). The results stated that among the students that experience cyberbullying, 14.8% were from primary level, 54.3% secondary level and 30.9% from a higher institution. While result from students that state that they have witnessed cyberbully, 2.5% from primary education, 63.3% secondary and 34.2% from higher education.

Table 1. Cyberbullying experience according to institutions

Level of Institution	Experience Cyberbullying	Witness Anyone Cyberbullied
Primary (12 years old & below)	14.8%	2.5%
Secondary (13 – 17 years old)	54.3%	63.3%
Higher (18 & above)	30.9%	34.2%

Table 2 shows the occurrences of harassment and cyberbullying among participants. Based on the results, the study indicated that 22% of students from all institutions experience cyberbullying. Of these students, only 9.1% of them decided to talk to someone. The research also shows that 84.7% of the students in all institutions have reported to witnessing someone being cyberbullied. However, only 2.7% of the students reported the cyberbully, 29.3% chose only to intervene and 68% of students decided to ignore.

Discussions

Victims to Cyberbully

According to the research conducted in different levels of the institution, the majority of the students (68%) that experience cyberbullying refused to report or seek support from anyone. Victims do not have the skills to socially engage with people and manage them properly. Furthermore, the victims are afraid of getting into trouble by the bully if they were to report it. As a result, they are more likely to perceive the situation as less changeable. Due to the inability to express their feelings and emotions, they will have very little resources to cope with the problem. They perceived the problem as uncontrollable and will emphasis on acceptance as a probable solution. This will result in application to emotion-focused coping which takes the form of an escape, avoidance, hopelessness and depression. Social media may also be a concern especially to students from a secondary and higher institution. Majority of them (78%) spend most of their time in social media, sharing videos and images and displaying their personal information to the public. Without knowing, the information shared can be used to engage in any form of cyberbullying activities. This correlates to their inability to seek support from people. With access to technology, a cyberbully has the power to share personal information (images and videos) to close family and friends and exercise more control over victim which lead to the feeling of hopelessness and depression.

Table 2. Occurrences of harassment and cyberbullying behaviours

<table>
<tr><th colspan="7">Entire Sample from All Institutions</th></tr>
<tr><th colspan="3">Experience Cyberbullying</th><th colspan="2">Talked to Someone</th><th colspan="2">Did Not Talk to Anyone</th></tr>
<tr><td colspan="2">Yes</td><td>No</td><td colspan="2">9.1%</td><td colspan="2">90.9%</td></tr>
<tr><td colspan="2">22%</td><td>78%</td><td colspan="2">N/A</td><td colspan="2">N/A</td></tr>
<tr><td>Male</td><td>Female</td><td></td><td colspan="2"></td><td colspan="2"></td></tr>
<tr><td>30%</td><td>70%</td><td></td><td colspan="2"></td><td colspan="2"></td></tr>
<tr><td colspan="3">Witness Anyone Cyberbullied</td><td>Ignore</td><td colspan="2">Intervene</td><td>Report</td></tr>
<tr><td colspan="2">Yes</td><td>84.7%</td><td>68%</td><td colspan="2">29.3%</td><td>2.7%</td></tr>
<tr><td colspan="2">No</td><td>15.3%</td><td>N/A</td><td colspan="2">N/A</td><td>N/A</td></tr>
</table>

Females are the most targeted gender as a victim of the cyberbully according to the findings that showed 70% of those people who have experienced being bullied in the digital world are females. These female victims of cyberbully are mostly groups from the secondary school level. According to the open-ended questions from the questionnaires, these victims of female groups mostly from secondary school are bullied online by being sexually attacked digitally. These online bullies would send the victims adult content videos or pictures and would ask the victims sexual favours. This act of disrespect may cause mental health problems and traumas. If the sexual favour is rejected by the victim, the bully would usually say rude things to the victim. The worst case would be the victim's personal information and photos will be used by the cyberbullies to make a fake account. Those fake accounts would be used to shame the victims and ruin the victim's social status. To avoid this, schools and parents should educate their children way to encountered cyberbullies such as protecting their social accounts that have personal information. Likewise, stricter laws should also be implemented to punish cyberbullies.

Findings from the questionnaires show that education level and age does play a role in cyberbullying. As people age, they grow wiser and becoming more mature. For primary school students aged 12 years and below, they have not gone through puberty and hormonal changes. Also, some do not own any devices and do not have easy accessibility to the online world. For this reason, primary school students experience less cyberbullying activity which in our findings shows only 14.8% have been cyberbullied and only 2.5% have witnessed cyberbullying. Compared to secondary school students' group of ages 13 - 17 years old, secondary students experienced the highest cyber bullying activity which is 54.3% experienced cyberbullying and 63.3% have witnessed cyberbullying. The reason why secondary students have the highest rate amongst primary and higher education students is that secondary students are at the stage of age where they are experiencing hormonal changes and puberty. Also, these group of students now own some devices of their own and have online accessibility discovering new things in the online world. These groups of secondary students are active on social media and online gaming. Since they are active in the digital world, they have a higher risk to be cyberbullied or be the cyberbullies. These groups of secondary students are still new in the digital age where they are still not educated or experienced to give good manners and behaviours online or know how to react to online misunderstandings and bad online behaviours. Mostly they would respond negatively to online misunderstandings and bad behaviour due to the low level of maturity and emotionally unstable at that stage of age which they usually want to always win until they would take revenge causing bigger cyberbullying problems.

Unlike Higher education students ages 18 and above, they are already stable emotionally due to maturity and would act professionally to bad online behaviours and online misunderstandings. This explained the drop in the number of students that experienced cyberbully at a mature age with only 30.9% and witness cyberbullying at 34.2%. They only experienced cyberbullying mostly during their secondary school days. When they reached a higher-level education, they would mostly use social media or go online to do school assignments, research and purposeful activities. In this study, it can be identified that in higher education level there are a diverse group of nationality and different ethnic groups nevertheless has a lower cyberbullying experience compared to the secondary school level groups. The secondary school level groups only have two ethnic groups which majority of them are Malay and the minority are Chinese which is not as diverse as the higher education level groups. This shows that ethnic, nationality and religion is not effective towards cyberbullying with higher education level groups ages 18 and above. The reason might be the level of maturity and professionalism when students reach higher education learning.

The Motive for Cyber Bullying

Both online and offline types of bullying have similarities. There are reasons why people are bullying. The main motivation for bullying is mostly personal motivations such as:

1. The need for power and dominance
2. The bullies find satisfaction in people's suffering and injuries.
3. The behaviour is rewarded in terms of materials or psychological such as social status

Encouragement and influence from peers motivated bullies especially if they are being rewarded with social status. Cyberbullies may come from a family with parents who do not provide warmth and love or implement good discipline towards their children that resulted in bullying behaviour where they feel satisfaction seeing others suffer.

Impact of Cyberbullying on Adolescent Health

Cyberbullying can have a significant impact on young adolescence. Both bully-victim and victims reported to suffer from depression, social anxiety, loneliness, worried, hopelessness, angry and experience stress more than non-victims. Furthermore, lower self-esteem, interpersonal, behavioural and physical problems are some of the symptoms faced by these individuals as cyberbullying have detrimental impact compared to the traditional form of bullying. As the impact may lead to young adolescence to consider committing suicide and do commit suicide. The cyberbullying-victims can be categories as passive victims and aggressive victims. Passive victims are thoughtful, sensitive and doubtful and tend to avoid aggression and confrontations with their peers. In contrast with aggressive victims, they tend to play the role of provocative victims or bully-victims. However, most of the cyberbullying victims especially children and adolescents usually experience short-term or long-term negative health effects after being attacked. In a short-term period, the victims may show several physical symptoms such as headache, abdominal pain, tiredness, dizziness, muscular pain and poor appetite. Then it may lead to several negative psychological effects such as insomnia, anxiety, emotional reactivity and nightmare. Hence, it has often resulted in students becoming more withdrawn as they are having difficulty in giving full attention in the class. Then they will drop in school motivation and performance which lead to the refusal to go to school. There was a high correlation of academic performance with bullying-victims. After a long period being controlled, the cyberbully-victims may suffer the psychological impairment which can lead to depression, self-harm and worse to suicide. For example, a study on Cyberbullying victimization and symptoms of depression and anxiety conducted on 489 Chinese adolescents from an ordinary junior high school in Wuhan (in central China) showed that the cyberbullying victimization depression and anxiety were much stronger for adolescents with lower self-compassion was depression and anxiety. The impacts of cyberbullying have been dominatingly investigated in the territory of young people's emotional well-being. In general,he connection between the contribution of cyberbullying and youths' propensity to the disguise issues for instance, forlornness, nervousness, dejection, self-destructive ideation etc. Finding from interview that cyberbullying has been conceptualized as a stressor. It is set that cyberbullying is more distressing than customary bullying, maybe due to the unknown identity of the cyberbully. In contrast to the traditional bullying, victims of cyberbullying are more averse to know their culprits.

Anonymity Correlation to Social Media

According to the questionnaire conducted, electronic communication provides the platform for the likelihood of a student being cyberbullied as only 4.7% of the students rarely use social media and 95.3% of students either often or moderately use social media. Anonymity allows the students to be more discreet and very difficult to punished by the school. Majority of the event that happens is likely to occur outside of school. According to some of the responses from the open-ended question, there is a close relationship between the person who bullies in real life and cyberbullying. The act often carries forward from real life to cyberspace. Some student still receives threat and verbal harassment from Facebook, IM, WhatsApp and other networking software from the students who bully them in school. They are more likely to know the person who bully them and unable to seek any assistance. This is because a student that experience bullying in school often continues that experience beyond the school compound and beyond jurisdiction and care from teachers and committee members of the school. Although some student seeks help from counselling provided by the school; the boundaries, effects and support from counselling members do not go beyond that. Threats, harassment and verbal abuse (such as name-calling) still occur online and other social networking platforms. Cyberbullying often amplifies the act of the bully further and intensify the experience of the victims. Therefore, cyberbullying need to be focused more closely not as an independent entity but as a probable extension of a real-life bully. Therefore, the techniques or solutions to prevent bully must also expand and further amplify to social media platforms via spreading awareness, online counselling and other methods; as both acts of bully and cyberbully are quite similar, but just in different domain.

Cyberbullying in the Gaming World

According to the data collected from the questionnaire, the majority of students in Depok- West Java and South Jakarta District claimed that they had played online games such as PUBG, Rules of Survival and League of Legends. These games can connect students with other people around the world and make interactions using text or headsets voice communication with other players. Everyone that played online game experienced cyberbullying because some people always want to mentally cause negative impact to their competitions online such as the use of vulgar rude languages, an attack on personal identity and discrimination. In some cases, cyberbullying can cause suicide to the victims. There is no evidence and case yet in South Jakarta and Depok- west java District about suicide due to online gaming.

Taking into account that most students can connect to the internet and play online games, especially with their smartphones, the risk of being cyberbullied is high. Students might think the games are fun but online gaming may lead to mental health problems not just because of addiction but also for the reason of cyberbullies. There will be a high risk of being cyberbullied if there is an interaction with other live online players during gameplay. Cyberbullies would do anything to make the victim lose the game and sabotage them by using verbal words and touch on sensitive topics such as race, religion or nationality.

Witness to Cyberbullying

Based on the questionnaire conducted, 68% of those people who witness cyberbullying have chosen to ignore it. A prevalent idea suggests that an act of reporting is solely not their responsibility nor their business and seen as a "no big deal". Cyberbullying is seen as an affair between the bully and the victim, where the general public will constitute to privacy concern if involved. From the questionnaire data, of the 68% students that witness cyberbullying, only 2.7% of them have reported to their parents and teachers. According to the open-ended questions, an act of reporting is seen as their inability to handle the situation by themselves and a sense of incompetence to ask for assistance and social support. This is more likely true among male student as reporting to teachers make them appear as "the weak ones". Based on the reasons provided, the students (in secondary school) did not believe that teachers would address the problems effectively; mainly to prevent triggering concern to parents and dealing with the overwhelming complaints. Furthermore, many students feel powerless and afraid to voice out concerns regarding cyberbullying and decide not to report it to anyone. This has especially happened among female students. Students in this study also feel that by addressing their concerns to the parents and teachers, it will limit their access to internet and smartphone privileges. They believe restrictions to smartphone devices in school during class is enough rather than to restrict the uses at home entirely. To others who feel the need to report to their parents are afraid that parents would advise them to ignore the situation (as "it is of no importance" or "unfamiliarity" to cyber world environment), scolded for inappropriate use of internet privileges, or intervene (further escalating the conflict and complexity of the situation). These are some of the reasons as to how ignorance might be a better option in the perception of the bully-victim.

Early Prevention and Intervention

Based on findings from this study, several suggestions and potential solutions can be implemented to reduce, tackle and lessen the effects of cyberbullying issue. Therefore, it is essential to highlight the importance of how the school environment relates to cyberbullying. Building a relationship between staff members and students are a crucial point in providing support to cyberbullying. Early prevention and intervention are needed to combat against cyberbullying. Schools need to established a system that monitors the usage of computers in school, mainly to the primary and secondary institution; and set up a restriction towards certain websites that may pose threat or encourage cyberbullying. Teachers need to equip their students with critical tools (e-safety and netiquettes) for them to understand the complexity of cyberworld; attain the benefits of the Internet as a whole (e.g. educational purpose (online lectures/ tutorials), communication (social awareness), creativity & inspiration (art & language); and be aware of the risk associate with it (e.g. violent video games, R-rated movies, deep dark web, online hacker, inappropriate use of language in music and videos, etc).

The importance of parents' involvement in working together with their children is crucial. They play an important role for children in terms of setting the age-appropriate limit to certain websites. Parents need to be able to monitor networking sites because poor parental monitoring will lead to the risk of young adolescence involved in cyberbullying. Attention is also needed to evaluate the behaviour of their children. Parents should also be aware of the signs and symptoms of cyberbullying behaviours such as anxiety of using smartphone devices, insomnia, and change in mood/behaviour, social isolation and possibly sign of harm to themselves (suicidal thought). Parents need to seek outside support such as therapy for their children, online counselling, expert's opinions and another website that provides information regarding cyberbullying behaviour. Cyberbullying defence campaign could also be done to help to reduce the risk of cyberbully attacks on victims. It can aim to educate society on how to secure personal identity and react towards cyberbullies. In Depok-West Java and South Jakarta District, there is still not much awareness of cyberbullying. Most students can easily show and share their identity compared to Singaporean students where they are educated and trained to protect their identity to prevent harm.

CONCLUSION

In conclusion, cyberbullying is a serious matter since the majority of students nowadays are more exposed to technological advancement. Reference to the survey that has been distributed, cyberbullying usually happened at the secondary level. Certain characteristics can help identify whether the students are being cyberbullied or not; it can be in terms of their personality, appearances and so forth. Anonymity is one of the characteristics too. Other aspects such as age, gender and race can also be considered to characterize cyberbullying. In addition to this, there are several platforms where cyberbullying can take place such as through social networking websites or even in the gaming world. Of course, cyberbullying can give massive impacts on the victims; cyberbullying can affect them emotionally, psychologically, academically and so on. Moreover, following the survey that has been shown in the result section, different students will have different responses when witnessing cyberbullying. But, the majority of them has ignored the cyberbullying act. Since cyberbullying is now becoming an emerging issue, therefore, cyberbullying need to be tackled. Different parties should perform their responsibilities to stop or decrease cyberbullying. First and foremost, students need to be extra careful when communicating with strangers in the cyber world. Students are the key group to tackle cyberbullying. They need to know the use of technology. Furthermore, students are advised to be aware of the possible negative consequences when they misuse the technology so that they can control their behaviour online at an early age. Also, students need to learn how to respond to cyberbullying appropriately.

Subsequently, parents' guidance also plays an important role in the mission of reducing cyberbullying. Parents should know their children's activities whenever they access the internet. They need to ensure that the children are not disclosing their details or any privacy as these can be used for cyberbullying purposes. Other than that, parental education can also be the key to preventing cyberbullying. Bullying has hit its way into the technological age; it gives negative impacts on the lives of students as well as educators. Cyberbullying has no stress-free solution. Several strategies such as policies, programs and education need to be considered and the endless efforts of the whole university community are required to develop, execute and evaluate those strategies. Based on the research conducted, the questionnaire might also be a limitation to our report. Knowing what questions to ask the students would enable us to addresses the issues in cyberbullying further. Additional open-ended questions would shed more light towards the experiences that students faced, problems that needed to be addressed and further mitigate it by understanding the core aspects of cyberbullying.

ACKNOWLEDGMENT

Desi Setiana and Norainna Besar as Main Contributor and Lead Author, where Marlina Nasution and Tiroana as contributor. We would like to thanks to all staff of *Bimbingan Klien Anak, Balai Pemasyarkatan Klas I, Jakarta Selatan, Kementrian Hukum dan Hak Azasi Manusi, Republik Indonesia,* helping us on data collection and interview over the respondents and participants.

REFERENCES

Aftab, P. (2010). *Stop cyberbullying: What's the parent's role in this?* Retrieved June 22, 2010, from http://www.stopcyber bullying.org/prevention/parents_role.html

Agatston, P., Kowalski, R., & Limber, S. (2007). Students perspectives on cyberbullying. *The Journal of Adolescent Health, 41*(6), S59–S60. doi:10.1016/j.jadohealth.2007.09.003 PMID:18047946

Antoniadou, N., Kokkinos, C. M., & Markos, A. (2016). Possible common correlates between bullying and cyber-bullying among adolescents. *Psicologia dell'Educazione, 22*(1), 27–38. doi:10.1016/j.pse.2016.01.003

Brito, C. C., & Oliveira, M. T. (2013). Bullying and self-esteem in adolescents from public schools. *Jornal de Pediatria, 89*(6), 601–607. doi:10.1016/j.jped.2013.04.001 PMID:24029549

Calvete, E., Orue, I., Estévez, A., Villardón, L., & Padilla, P. (2010). *Cyberbullying in adolescents: Modalities and aggressors' profile*. Academic Press.

Kokkinos, C. M., Antoniadou, N., & Markos, A. (2014). Cyber-bullying: An investigation of the psychological profile of university student participants. *Journal of Applied Developmental Psychology, 35*(3), 204–214. doi:10.1016/j.appdev.2014.04.001

Kowalski, R., Limber, S., & Agatston, P. (2012). Cyber Bullying: Bullying. In *The Digital Age* (2nd ed., pp. 27–39). John Wiley & Sons.

Kowalski, R. M., & Limber, S. P. (2013). Psychological, Physical, and Academic Correlates of Cyberbullying and Traditional Bullying. *The Journal of Adolescent Health, 53*(1), S13–S20. Advance online publication. doi:10.1016/j.jadohealth.2012.09.018 PMID:23790195

Leu, F. Y., Chiang, P. J., Susanto, H., Hung, R. T., & Huang, H. L. (2020). Mobile Physiological Sensor Cloud System for Long-term Care. *Internet of Things*.

Leu, F. Y., Ko, C. Y., Lin, Y. C., Susanto, H., & Yu, H. C. (2017). Fall Detection and Motion Classification by Using Decision Tree on Mobile Phone. In Smart Sensors Networks (pp. 205-237). Academic Press.

Leu, F. Y., Susanto, H., Tsai, K. L., & Ko, C. Y. (2020). A channel assignment scheme for MIMO on concentric-hexagon-based multi-channel wireless networks. *International Journal of Ad Hoc and Ubiquitous Computing*, *35*(4), 205–221. doi:10.1504/IJAHUC.2020.111462

Li, Q. (2010). Cyberbullying in High Schools: A Study of Students Behaviors and Beliefs about This New Phenomenon. *Journal of Aggression, Maltreatment & Trauma*, *19*(4), 372–392. doi:10.1080/10926771003788979

Lindfors, P. L., Kaltiala-Heino, R., & Rimpelä, A. H. (2012). Cyberbullying among Finnish adolescents – a population-based study. *BMC Public Health*, *12*(1), 1027. Advance online publication. doi:10.1186/1471-2458-12-1027 PMID:23176715

Monks, C. P., Mahdavi, J., & Rix, K. (2016). The emergence of cyberbullying in childhood: Parent and teacher perspectives. *Psicologia dell'Educazione*, *22*(1), 39–48. doi:10.1016/j.pse.2016.02.002

Selkie, E. M., Kota, R., Chan, Y. F., & Moreno, M. (2015). Cyberbullying, depression, and problem alcohol use in female college students: A multisite study. *Cyberpsychology, Behavior, and Social Networking*, *18*(2), 79–86. doi:10.1089/cyber.2014.0371 PMID:25684608

Susanto, H. (2017). Electronic Health System: Sensors Emerging and Intelligent Technology Approach. In Smart Sensors Networks (pp. 189-203). Academic Press.

Susanto, H. (2018). Smart mobile device emerging Technologies: an enabler to Health monitoring system. In *High-Performance Materials and Engineered Chemistry* (pp. 241–264). Apple Academic Press.

Susanto, H., & Almunawar, M. N. (2015). Managing Compliance with an Information Security Management Standard. In *Encyclopedia of Information Science and Technology* (3rd ed., pp. 1452–1463). IGI Global.

Susanto, H., & Almunawar, M. N. (2016). Security and Privacy Issues in Cloud-Based E-Government. In *Cloud Computing Technologies for Connected Government* (pp. 292–321). IGI Global.

Susanto, H., & Almunawar, M. N. (2018). *Information Security Management Systems: A Novel Framework and Software as a Tool for Compliance with Information Security Standard.* CRC Press.

Susanto, H., Almunawar, M. N., Leu, F. Y., & Chen, C. K. (2016). Android vs iOS or Others? SMD-OS Security Issues: Generation Y Perception. *International Journal of Technology Diffusion*, *7*(2), 1–18.

Susanto, H., & Chen, C. K. (2017). Information and Communication Emerging Technology: Making Sense of Healthcare Innovation. In *Internet of Things and Big Data Technologies for Next Generation Healthcare* (pp. 229–250). Springer.

Susanto, H., Chen, C. K., & Almunawar, M. N. (2018). Revealing Big Data Emerging Technology as Enabler of LMS Technologies Transferability. In *Internet of Things and Big Data Analytics Toward Next-Generation Intelligence* (pp. 123–145). Springer.

Susanto, H., Ibrahim, F., Nazmudeen, S. H., Mohiddin, F., & Setiana, D. (2020). Human-Centred Design to Enhance the Usability, Human Factors, and User Experience Within Digital Destructive Ecosystems. In *Global Challenges and Strategic Disruptors in Asian Businesses and Economies* (pp. 76–94). IGI Global.

Susanto, H., Leu, F. Y., Caesarendra, W., Ibrahim, F., Haghi, P. K., Khusni, U., & Glowacz, A. (2020). Managing Cloud Intelligent Systems over Digital Ecosystems: Revealing Emerging App Technology in the Time of the COVID19 Pandemic. *Applied System Innovation, 3*(3), 37. doi:10.3390/asi3030037

Susanto, H., Leu, F. Y., & Chen, C. K. (2019). *Business Process Reengineering: An ICT Approach.* CRC Press.

Susanto, H., Leu, F. Y., Chen, C. K., & Mohiddin, F. (Eds.). (2019). *Managing Human Capital in Today's Globalization: A Management Information System Perspective*. CRC Press.

Susanto, H., Yie, L. F., Rosiyadi, D., Basuki, A. I., & Setiana, D. Data Security for Connected Governments and Organisations: Managing Automation and Artificial Intelligence. In Web 2.0 and Cloud Technologies for Implementing Connected Government (pp. 229-251). IGI Global.

Susanto, H., Yie, L. F., Setiana, D., Asih, Y., Yoganingrum, A., Riyanto, S., & Saputra, F. A. (2020). Digital Ecosystem Security Issues for Organizations and Governments: Digital Ethics and Privacy. In Web 2.0 and Cloud Technologies for Implementing Connected Government (pp. 204-228). IGI Global.

Yie, L. F., Susanto, H., & Setiana, D. (2020). Collaborating Decision Support and Business Intelligence to Enable Government Digital Connectivity. In *Web 2.0 and Cloud Technologies for Implementing Connected Government* (pp. 95–112). IGI Global.

ADDITIONAL READING

Chandrashekhar, A., Muktha G. S., & Anjana D. K. (2016). Cyberstalking and Cyberbullying: Effects and prevention measures. *Imperial Journal of Interdisciplinary Research, 2*(3).

Chu, X., Fan, C., Liu, Q., & Zhou, Z. (2018). Cyberbullying victimization and symptoms of depression and anxiety among Chinese adolescents: Examining hopelessness as a mediator and self-compassion as a moderator. *Computers in Human Behavior, 86*, 377–386. doi:10.1016/j.chb.2018.04.039

Cyberbullying. (2018). Cyberbullying Research Center. Retrieved 21 August 2018, from https://cyberbullying.org/what-is-cyberbullying

Faucher, C., Jackson, M., & Cassidy, W. (2014). Cyberbullying among University Students: Gendered Experiences, Impacts, and Perspectives. *Education Research International, 2014*, 1–10. doi:10.1155/2014/698545

Görzig, A., & Frumkin, L. A. (2013). Cyberbullying experiences on-the-go: When social media can become distressing. *Cyberpsychology (Brno), 7*(1). Advance online publication. doi:10.5817/CP2013-1-4

Hoff, D. L., & Mitchell, S. N. (2009). Cyberbullying: Causes, effects, and remedies. *Journal of Educational Administration, 47*(5), 652–665. doi:10.1108/09578230910981107

Hoff, D. L., & Mitchell, S. N. (2009). Cyberbullying: Causes, effects, and remedies. *Journal of Educational Administration, 47*(5), 652–665. doi:10.1108/09578230910981107

Hutcherson, A. N. (Ed.). (2012). *Psychology of victimization*. Retrieved from https://ebookcentral.proquest.com

Ibrahim, F., Susanto, H., Haghi, P. K., & Setiana, D. (2020). Shifting Paradigm of Education Landscape in Time of the COVID-19 Pandemic: Revealing of a Digital Education Management Information System. *Applied System Innovation*, *3*(4), 49. doi:10.3390/asi3040049

Jin, D. (2017). *Mobile Gaming in Asia*. Springer. doi:10.1007/978-94-024-0826-3

Whittaker, E., & Kowalski, R. M. (2015). Cyberbullying Via Social Media. *Journal of School Violence*, *14*(1), 11–29. doi:10.1080/15388220.2014.949377

KEY TERMS AND DEFINITIONS

Assistive Technology: Is assistive, adaptive, and rehabilitative devices for People with disability or the elderly population. People with disability often have difficulty performing activities of daily living (ADLs) independently, or even with assistance. ADLs are self-care activities that include toileting, mobility (ambulation), eating, bathing, dressing, grooming, and personal device care. Assistive technology can ameliorate the effects of disabilities that limit the ability to perform ADLs. Assistive technology promotes greater independence by enabling people to perform tasks they were formerly unable to accomplish, or had great difficulty accomplishing, by providing enhancements to, or changing methods of interacting with, the technology needed to accomplish such tasks.

Behavioral Psychology: Behavioral psychology is the study of the connection between our minds and our behavior. Sometimes you will hear behavioral psychology referred to as behaviorism. The researchers and scientists who study behavioral psychology are trying to understand why we behave the way we do and they are concerned with discovering patterns in our actions and behaviors. The hope is that if we can use behavioral psychology to help us predict how humans will behave, we can build better habits as individuals, create better products as companies, and develop better living spaces as communities.

Cyberbullying: Is an extension of traditional bullying, where technology is most commonly been used, a new element of the internet has been added to the old kind of bullying. Based on some research studies, traditional bullying can even start at a very young age.

Information Technology Apps for Learning: The Apps enable students to acquire lecture materials, take online quizzes or assessments, submit tutorials or assignments, view results, view course materials, see news and announcements, online interaction, anytime and anywhere without any geographical or time barriers. However, the key to effective apps-learning is not from its multimedia, design or user-friendliness, but on how the individuals are engaged by the content.

Mental Health: Mental health includes our emotional, psychological, and social well-being. It affects how we think, feel, and act. It also helps determine how we handle stress, relate to others, and make choices. Mental health is important at every stage of life, from childhood and adolescence through adulthood.

Technology Management Usage: For over four decades electronic data and information infrastructure for production and processing has grown and has achieved exceptional speeds. The IT revolution has influenced employees, managers, and their organizations significantly. For millions of businesses and people, it has generated various issues and constraints. Particularly high were the challenges to introduce and implement the technology.

Peer Group: A peer group is both a social group and a primary group of people who have similar interests, age, background, or social status. The members of this group are likely to influence the person's beliefs and behavior. Peer groups contain hierarchies and distinct patterns of behavior. In a high school setting for example, 18 year olds are a peer group with 14 year olds because they share similar and paralleled life experiences in school together. In contrast, teachers do not share students as a peer group because teachers and students fall into two different roles and experiences.

Chapter 10
Distance Education in Times of COVID-19 in Mexico:
The Case of the Instituto Politécnico Nacional at the Postgraduate Level

Edgar Oliver Cardoso Espinosa
https://orcid.org/0000-0001-7588-9439
Instituto Politécnico Nacional, Mexico

María Elena Zepeda Hurtado
Instituto Politécnico Nacional, Mexico

Jésica Alhelí Cortés Ruiz
https://orcid.org/0000-0002-5459-4874
Instituto Politécnico Nacional, Mexico

ABSTRACT

The objective of the chapter is to assess distance education in times of COVID-19 through the implementation of the Virtual Plan for Academic Continuity of the Instituto Politécnico Nacional (IPN) in order to identify good educational practices at the postgraduate level. A quantitative methodology with an exploratory-descriptive scope was used. The participants of the study were students who were pursuing a graduate degree during confinement. The main results are a positive assessment of distance education in terms of the incorporation and continuous use of digital resources, the use of continuous evaluation, the usefulness of technological tools, as well as an interaction with the teaching staff to review the academic progress of the student.

DOI: 10.4018/978-1-7998-7184-2.ch010

INTRODUCTION

With the emergence of the pandemic, the population has seen its family, professional and work stability altered, which has led to an environment of uncertainty about what happens and will happen when the confinement stage ends. In the same way, from one moment to another, in a disruptive way, the use of technology became present and necessary in society, as well as nationally and internationally because it went from being used as fun and a source of information and communication, to become a work tool and a means to deliver the educational service.

According to IESALC (2020a), 75% of Higher Education Institutions (HEIs) have the technological and pedagogical capacity to offer online education, as well as 76% of students has access to technological platforms and tools. In addition, as educational systems have entered distance education, the digital divide in connectivity, access to devices and levels of digital training of citizens are strategic elements that influence student learning. Additionally, the diversity of access to connectivity and the type of mobile device has been identified, which is why both the phenomenon of the digital and academic divide has increased (UNESCO, 2020; OECD, 2020a).

Particularly in Latin America, COVID-19 has generated a variety of immediate, medium and long-term impacts for the education system of each of the countries. For the teachers, they have had to integrate situations into the technological tools and platforms in their classes. However, there are other teachers with a lack or with a limited use and who have to attend the educational service. Also, the diversity of the teaching profiles in terms of the domain of digital skills has been manifested. In the same way, for educational centers it has implied a commitment to guarantee the continuity of academic training by providing both technological resources and open access to databases and bibliographic data and the adjustment of calendars to give continuity to the educational process (Martin & Furiv, 2020).

In the case of students, they have been forced to experience their classes at a distance, as well as to modify their non-academic activities, which have influenced their academic performance. Also, the variable of connectivity in their homes has been added, which influences both their availability and the time of use to continue with their academic training. The above situations have led not only to changes in the educational trajectory of the student body by not being able to continue attending distance courses, but also to dropping out of school due to not feeling safe, with the appropriate technological tools or the effectiveness of fulfilling the academic tasks (Wang , Cheng, Yue and McAleer, 2020).

In this way, the coronavirus has forced to reconvert and adapt face-to-face classes to distance sessions, showing various limitations in both students and teachers with respect to their digital training coupled with different conditions in which they live during confinement, which has impacted in attitudes, skills and disposition to carry out a transformation of the educational process with the main purpose of continuing with the academic training of students (Cabrera, 2020). To achieve this, educational television was implemented and a loan of laptops was carried out in various countries to continue educational care (Gewin, 2020; Boursicot, 2020). Also, it has been necessary to venture into the use of immediate communication tools such as WhatsApp as a usual way with the student body, especially in higher education (Zafra, 2020).

Faced with this educational transition process caused by COVID-19, IESALC (2020b) establishes the importance of introducing efficient mechanisms for evaluating and monitoring student learning; document pedagogical changes and their impacts; detect the areas of opportunity for distance education coupled with generating an analysis of results that enable the incorporation of a renewed teaching and learning model. Besides, Murillo and Duk (2020) indicate that the impact generated by the closure of schools and other social restrictions in the countries, motivated the development of distance education studies in order to obtain and systematize useful information on the practices employed by the teachers, which enable the formulation and establishment of short and long-term educational strategies that help to face the return to face-to-face classes after the health emergency has ended.

In the case of Mexico, COVID-19 exposed the needs and shortcomings as a nation, as well as the creativity, responsibility, desires and responsibilities for teachers to continue teaching and students to continue learning in person. The untimely closure of schools due to the pandemic gave a guideline to the continuity of the educational work, diversifying both the training modalities and the tasks of the actors involved: teachers, students, authorities, parents, society in general. In the case of Mexico, as of March 2020, more than 30 million students and two million teachers faced the situation generated by the coronavirus (SEP, 2019; ANUIES, 2020a).

To continue with the educational service, ANUIES (2020b) established that the strategies to continue with the substantive functions (teaching, research and dissemination of culture) will be carried out through the development of platforms and digital resources to continue the learning of students; the delivery of training courses for online learning aimed at students, academics and managers; free access to digital libraries, resource collections, specialized magazine sites and publications; strengthening of information platforms and systems to provide services to teachers and students online.

In the same way, the long-awaited change in paradigms and roles in the educational work of teachers and students also happened in an untimely way so that in order to achieve the training objectives by the teacher, a modification in communication strategies was required together with assuming the role of facilitator of learning in cooperative and flexible environments. Moreover, the Mexican educational system had to make changes in the teaching practice incorporating information and communication technologies (ICTs) as support resources, so it is relevant to carry out studies on the methodologies and didactic materials used in order to identify both coverage and satisfaction in the educational service coupled with determining its impact on the academic training of students. Therefore, related studies are required on these problems at each educational level caused by the health emergency of COVID-19.

From this context of the coronavirus pandemic, the Instituto Politécnico Nacional (IPN, 2020) implemented the Virtual Plan for Academic Continuity organized by a series of technologies, resources and tutorials in order for educational actors to use them to continue the educational service. Thus, the educational activities were carried out through virtual classrooms (Google Classroom); Workspaces and collaboration (Microsoft Teams) coupled with work rooms by videoconference (Zoom).

Based on the above, the postgraduate level saw the need to carry out changes in educational practices incorporating ICTs as tools. In this sense, it is relevant to carry out studies on the methodologies and teaching materials used at this level in order to identify both coverage and satisfaction in the educational service provided. Also, these investigations will allow assessing the impact of the Virtual Plan for Academic Continuity on the academic training of students in times of COVID-19.

Therefore, this chapter is dedicated to the research of the technological resources that students have available to access and continue their academic training during confinement, for which the adaptation to the *National Survey on Availability and Use of ICT in Homes (ENDUTIH),* generated by the National Institute of Geography and Information Statistics (INEGI, 2020), was used for the organization and analysis of the information. The relevance of this survey is due to the fact that it was carried out by sending surveyors to households in order to collect updated data on ICTs for the decision-making in national education policy and administration. Said instrument was limited using the specific section of section IV called ICT equipment at home, to determine what technological tools a student has, such as equipment and internet access at home.

Consequently, the objective of the chapter is to assess distance education in times of COVID-19 through the implementation of the Virtual Plan for Academic Continuity of the IPN in order to identify good educational practices at the postgraduate level.

PREVIOUS LITERATURE

Since the appearance of the coronavirus worldwide, its evolution has led to consequences at multiple levels that include the social, economic, psychological and educational in a global and fulminant form (Zaar and García, 2020). In this sense, for the educational field, three main objectives have been established: 1) To make the educational service more flexible; 2) Adapt educational practices to a non-face-to-face environment and 3) Formulate alternatives to both teaching and evaluation to continue with the student's academic training (González, Marco and Medina, 2020).

In the same way, it is important to note that teachers have had to use their means, their personal effort, their experience in teaching face-to-face classes and their available skills to continue with the educational service that most of them had not experienced before. Hence, this process of change forced by the pandemic is recommended to be implemented as far as possible based on the principles and good practices of a virtual modality (Castillo and Castillo, 2021).

Thereby, to determine the level of adaptation of the educational service to an online context there is a central element, which is the incorporation and continuous use of technological tools (González, Infante and Infante, 2020). Thus, their importance is to be considered as means to modernize the academic and administrative management processes of educational systems, as well as an opportunity for educational innovation, which is why they have been established as alternatives to contribute to the improvement of education and generate transformations in student learning, overcoming the traditional paradigm where greater autonomy is now generated in the training process and in knowledge management by accessing a diversity of information sources, which is why the development of the digital competence is relevant (UNESCO , 2014).

Prior to the appearance of the coronavirus, the vertiginous advance of technological and cultural changes in society has created a dynamic scenario for teaching that requires the integration of ICTs in the curricular learning of students (Cabero, Marín and Castaño, 2015). Against this background, the work of the teaching staff takes place in a complex context that requires the combination of didactic, curricular and technological knowledge to develop meaningful teaching practices in the student body (Castaño, Redecker, Vuorikari and Punie, 2014). To achieve this, teachers are required to plan activities that promote collaboration, reflection, analysis and argumentation on the contents to be developed in a subject, together with integrating ICTs as tools in educational strategies (Escudero, 2018; Gutiérrez, 2014).

Furthermore, the introduction of technological tools enables not only the exchange of knowledge but also a new way of interacting between individuals and organizations both nationally and internationally (Hayes, 2010). In this sense, the World Bank (2003) established the relevance of having adequate, up-to-date and functioning information and communication technologies (ICTs), since they have the potential to speed up and reduce the activities of institutions; expand the access and improve educational quality and significantly increase access to information and databases not only nationally but globally. Similarly, Akareem and Hossain (2012), mention that ICTs generate a new social space and, therefore, a new educational space known as virtual education. Consequently, virtual education is a modality based on formal education institutions, where the learning group is separated and has interactive telecommunications systems that are used to create the connection between the student body, the resources and the teaching body (Pérez, 2017).

While Ng (2018); McCallum, Schultz, Sellke and Spartz (2015); Álvarez (2012); postulate as regulatory principles of distance education: 1) The responsibility of students for the review of previous materials using technological tools; 2) The use of self-evaluation and hetero-evaluation; 3) Provide opportunities for students to interact in order to promote collaborative work and, 4) Encourage active participation of students, which also generates satisfaction with learning.

The main causes that originated it were: the distancing from higher education centers, the limited availability of time of the students or that they have some type of disability that prevents them from accessing the face-to-face option (Silvio, 2006 and Bourne and Moore, 2003). Meanwhile, Pérez (2017) establishes that its main characteristics are:

1. The access to a set of information about a subject
2. The information is presented in multimedia form
3. The format of organization and use of the information is hypertext
4. Interpersonal communication takes place both in real time and delayed
5. The creation and management of spaces for sending activities

For the implementation of the online educational modality, it is necessary to design and use digital teaching resources, which are defined as the set of support materials that facilitate the understanding, interpretation and appropriation of information in an interactive environment, with multimedia support and easy access (Pérez, 2017). On the other hand, Quirós (2009) conceptualizes them as the set of interactive media that promote collaborative work, participation, creativity and the development of critical thinking.

Moreover, Cabero (2013) establishes that the design of quality online activities considers as basic principles:

- Variability: diversified activities and use of teaching material in different formats;
- Dosage: Organization of activities progressively to allow the student to adapt according to his learning style;
- Temporary organization: Establishment of activities based on their level of achievement to determine the time for their resolution and thus comply in a timely manner;
- Formulation of individual and group activities: During the course, it is important to encourage collaborative and individual work;
- Performance standards: Determine the criteria and guidelines to be met for the performance and delivery of learning activities and,
- Specify the evaluation: Establish the evaluation criteria of the course.

On the other hand, Mohamedbhai (2020) establishes that quality online learning requires the teaching material to be prepared based on the characteristics of the subject, educational level and learning styles of the students, in addition to the fact that both the teachers and the students are trained to navigate content in virtual environments using digital tools simultaneously and mostly in asynchronous scenarios. Similarly, an online educational modality encourages the development in students of other competencies such as critical thinking, creativity and decision-making in a collaborative environment where participants argue their solution strategies (Mevarech and Bracha, 2017).

Based on the foregoing and in the context originated by the pandemic, to continue with academic training it is important for it to be carried out through different didactic strategies by the teacher; transversal content such as gender equity, sustainability, recent scientific advances and human rights is incorporated; the linking of content with the productive and service sector is encouraged, as well as providing an interdisciplinary vision (Chehaibar, 2020).

In the same way, López and Andrés (2020) recommend the following emerging measures to HEIs:

1. Provide information to students and teachers about the process to follow regarding the use of digital platforms and tools, changes in school calendars, as well as the academic and administrative procedures to be used;
2. Identify the competencies of the teaching staff and students regarding the use and disposition of technological resources to implement manuals and tutorials to provide the educational service;
3. Prepare the didactic planning for an online environment integrating digital materials to support the academic training of the student body;
4. Promote an efficient communication between teachers and students through virtual means with the intention of resolving doubts in a timely manner, as well as providing the respective support and,
5. Detect those educational actors that lack the technological resources that allow them to continue with distance education, so it will be necessary to be flexible to solve these cases.

Besides, another important element to consider in academic training in times of COVID-19 is the evaluation of student learning. In this sense, García, Corell, Abella and Grande (2020) established the following lines of action for this component:

- Implement a continuous assessment for each of the subjects based on the type of competencies to be developed in the students;
- Establish flexibility for students who face emergent situations due to the pandemic both in the preparation and delivery of evaluation evidence;
- The preparation of the evidence is carried out through the use of office applications;
- Diversify the evaluation activities to generate a system that weights in a distributive way to obtain the final grade;
- In addition, the resolution of a final test;
- Carry out the resolution of projects with their presentation individually or in groups using videoconference tools and generate as evidence the recording and,
- For the cases in which the presentation and defense of a thesis at the postgraduate level are carried out, they are developed through an online presentation, registering the minute and respective recording of this process.

Also, it is important to consider the scenario on the actions that will have to be carried out by the HEIs once the health contingency has ended and which will be the following according to López and Andrés (2020):

- Prepare a diagnosis of the activities carried out during quarantine to determine the level of achievement of the expected learning in the student body;
- Implement regularization strategies for students who did not have the means to continue with their distance training;
- Identify the good practices of the distance educational service that serve as information for academic flexibility in the future and,
- Make adjustments to the school calendars for the conclusion of school periods in terms of administrative processes to give continuity to the trajectory of the students.

Finally, the conception of educational evaluation as an improvement process focused on the achievements of student learning is continued. Additionally, it considers the academic flexibility in terms of carrying out the activities, as well as focusing on the cognitive processes and strategies used by the student in addition to promoting collaborative work, which has been enhanced from the use of active methodologies such as project-based learning, flipped classroom, case studies, and problem-based learning.

Panorama of the Educational System in Mexico in Times of the Coronavirus

The only certainty in the world is that countries were not prepared for the health or educational emergency, which brought changes in daily life, school and work. In this sense, both the OECD (2020b) and Rogero (2020) have concluded that educational systems are not adapted for the generalization of distance learning, although they establish that it will be a requirement in the short term worldwide. In addition to the fact that moving face-to-face content to the virtual does not necessarily imply a true digital transformation (Llorens, 2020).

In Mexico, the Secretary of Public Education (SEP, 2020), to give continuity to basic education, implemented the programs called *Back to Classes Learn at Home I* (from March to September 2020) from the beginning of the closure of schools to the end of the school year and *Learn at Home II* (August to date) to begin the 2020-2021 school year. Said programs are based on the use of free textbooks delivered at the beginning of each school year, integrating television programs as the main tool, to which 94% of Mexican families have access; another tool used is the radio, especially in indigenous communities where classes will be broadcast in 22 different indigenous languages; printed educational materials from the Educational Development Council (CONAFE) in the most isolated communities, and online with content that is available at all times.

Derived from the previous programs, the scheduling carried out on television was provided at the basic level (preschool, primary and secondary) in order to expand the dissemination of the expected learning per day and per week so that the information was accessible to parents and teachers, with the aim of supporting the student. To follow up on the learning experiences, the *Experiences Folder* was integrated as evidence that would allow the student's evaluation to be carried out. The portfolio is made up of stories and products generated at the TV school. The accounts of the experiences include everyday narratives focused on educational, emotional and playful situations of the student. The TV school integrates the activities that are carried out in the notebook or in the textbooks indicated or guided through the television programs to be carried out at the time of the session or as homework.

In detail, in figures 1, 2 and 3, the main characteristics of the *Experiences Folder* are shown.

These three pieces of evidence prepared by the students and integrated into the folders, were delivered to teachers for various purposes: to monitor learning, qualify and certify, that is, to monitor the partial

Figure 1. Stories of experiences to write

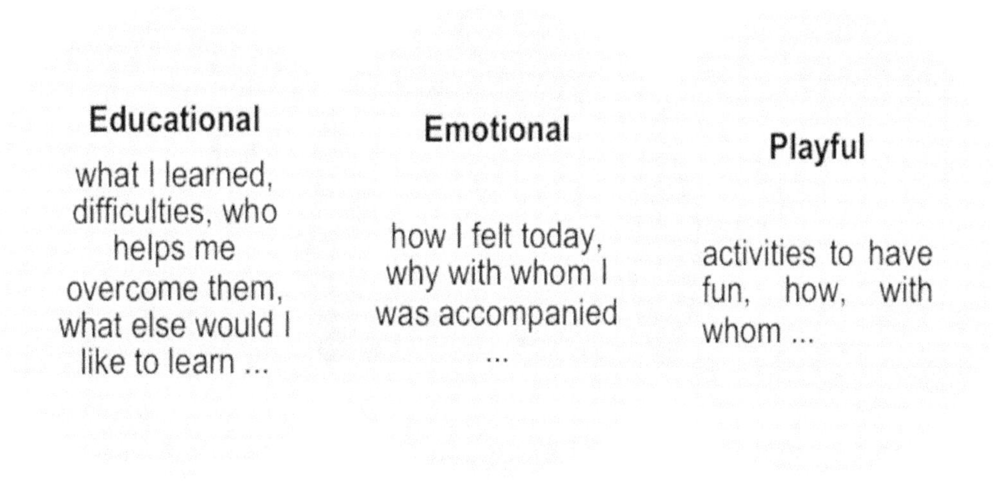

summative evaluation (unit, month, bimester) or final (semester or annual in the case of the basic level that includes primary and secondary).

Educational Actions at the Upper Secondary Level

For the case of the upper secondary level, the information that was considered was that carried out by the two main public institutions in Mexico, which are the Universidad Nacional Autónoma de Mexico (UNAM) and the Instituto Politécnico Nacional (IPN). For the first institution, the College of Sciences and Humanities (five schools in Mexico City and one in the periphery) and the high schools (nine schools distributed only in Mexico City) are institutions belonging to the UNAM, which provide comprehensive education through the general baccalaureate modality that is studied in three years or in six semesters.

Figure 2. TV School

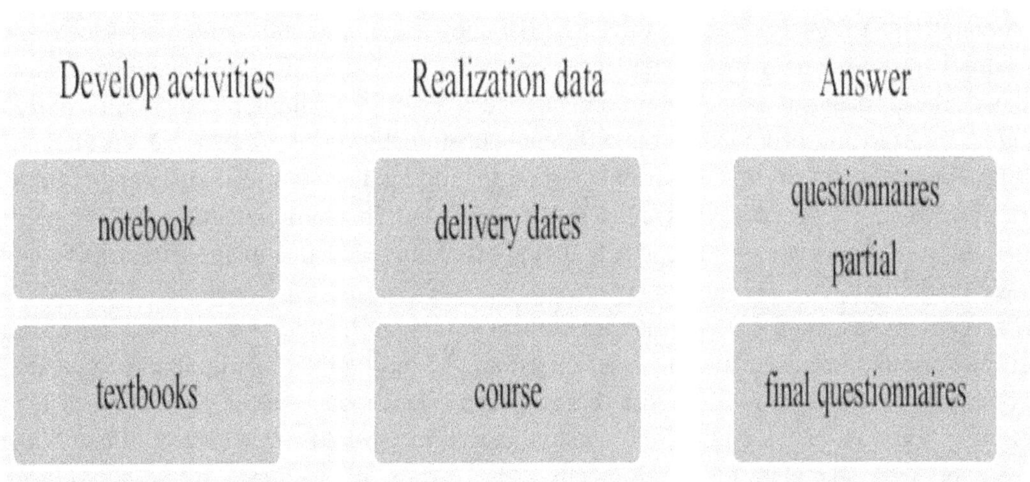

Figure 3. Identification of tasks to be added to the folder

These institutions announced that the start of face-to-face teaching activities will only take place if the epidemiological traffic light is green, otherwise the distance teaching and learning tasks will continue (CCH, 2020). In the same way, it is important to point out that the UNAM has a digital repository made up of a series of resources such as videos, audios, texts and websites that are considered open for consultation, which have been important because students have used them to give continuity to school activities.

Furthermore, the UNAM (2020) published the document called *Recommendations for the transition to non-face-to-face teaching* in which 16 suggestions are organized in three blocks to facilitate online work. The blocks address the following topics: 1) Adapt your teaching plan to the remote mode: prioritize the learning objectives, promote activities for self-management, varied and not excessive activities, consider the infrastructure conditions of the students and take advantage of the available resources of the institution 2) Accompany students in the non-face-to-face mode, which includes: accompanying students, establishing an atmosphere of trust, identifying students who are in trouble, continuously reviewing the teaching plan and if necessary, making the respective changes, and 3) Personal and professional development as a teacher, which implies being attentive in the emotional, physical and mental spheres in order to design innovation strategies and thus learn about distance education. These recommendations have been considered as the guidelines UNAM is currently working with.

With regard to the IPN, the institution has 18 upper secondary level study centers, which teach the bivalent baccalaureate in both the face-to-face and virtual modalities, that is, at the same time a general baccalaureate and a technical career, in three areas of knowledge: physical-mathematics, biological and social-administrative sciences, is studied in three years or six semesters. To continue with the educational service once the coronavirus pandemic was declared, the IPN (2020a) implemented the *Virtual Plan for Academic Continuity* in April 2020 for the different educational levels it offers: upper secondary, higher and postgraduate courses to provide virtual support to study plans and programs, generating learning environments where support materials and activities are found. In addition, there is the so-called Multi-virtual Classroom which is a digital space that supports both teachers and students in the non-school and mixed modalities.

The so-called Classroom 4.0 was also implemented, which includes digital teaching resources to support the various modalities (face-to-face, mixed and virtual) which intention was to create virtual classrooms, Google Classroom, Microsoft Teams, Zoom, on the web pages of each school. The purpose of Classroom 4.0 was the generation of a teaching space in virtual form where the materials created by the teachers were shared for the development of the learning units of each of the school programs.

METHODOLOGY

The type of study used was a quantitative methodology with an exploratory-descriptive scope due to the fact that the academic training of students in times of the coronavirus is a new social phenomenon, which is why its basic purpose is to formulate questions that allow giving rise to new research in the future coupled with the fact that the information collected allows the identification of good practices during confinement (Hernández, Fernández & Baptista, 2010).

The study population was the students who were studying a postgraduate degree in administration taught by the Instituto Politécnico Nacional (IPN) during the COVID-19 pandemic. The sample was of a non-probabilistic type, with the criterion of convenience made up of the following programs: Master of Science in Business Administration (MAN); Master of Sustainable Business Administration (MAES); Master of Administration in Public Policies (MAPP).

The main characteristics of the participants were the following: For gender, an equitable participation of men (51%) and women 49% was identified. With regard to age, it was found that the 25 to 29 year-old intervals presented the highest participation with 73%. Regarding the semester in which they are enrolled during the pandemic, it was determined that 25% study the first, 40% the second, 25% the third and the remaining 10% the fourth. Regarding the participation of students by educational program, it was found that 50% corresponds to MAN; 30% to MAES and the remaining 20% to MAPP.

Meanwhile, the instrument used was a questionnaire based on a Likert scale with the following structure: 1) Socio-labor data; 2) Levels of assessment of academic training in the students with items that were measured through a scale ranging from 1 (totally disagree) to 5 (totally agree). The purpose of this instrument was to collect information from the students' perception regarding the characteristics of the distance academic process originated by COVID-19 at the postgraduate level.

The questionnaire designed in its initial version was subjected to content validity using the expert judgment technique for its analysis in the aspects of clarity, congruence and bias of the items, which allowed the necessary adjustments to be made and the final version of the instrument was prepared (Corral, 2009). Afterwards, Cronbach's alpha coefficient was calculated to measure its reliability, giving a value of 0.803, which was interpreted as a good reliability index for the magnitude and for the relevant elements of the research (George and Mallery, 2011).

The instrument was applied by e-mail, in which the relevance and objective of the study was indicated, as well as the confidentiality of the information obtained was guaranteed for the subjects who participated in the research. Once the information was obtained, it was organized with the SPSS version 25 program, in which descriptive statistics were used to carry out the analysis and interpretation of the results based on the use of percentages, the mean and standard deviation (SD).

RESULTS

Results on the Characteristics, Conditions and Availability of Technological Resources

This section considers the results obtained by the *National Survey on Availability and Use of ICTs in Homes (ENDUTIH)* generated by the National Institute of Geography and Information Statistics (INEGI, 2020), which is the body responsible for regulating and coordinating the National System of Statistical and Geographical Information, as well as to capture and disseminate information about Mexico regarding the territory, resources, population and economy, which allows people to know the characteristics of the country and help decision-making.

According to the National Institute of Geography and Information Statistics (INEGI), ICTs determine new forms of work, learning, participation and entertainment, which contribute to a new paradigm: the Information and Knowledge Society. This organism characterized mobile phones as the device that promotes the sense of inclusion, belonging and closeness among the members of a family; the Internet as a tool to support education, training and research by facilitating, for example, the remote consultation of bibliographic catalogs of almost any library; whereas the computer allows the creation of electronic documents or the processing of data in previously unmanageable volumes.

Based on the foregoing, the INEGI periodically applies the survey aimed at people aged six or more who reside in private homes, covering the following topics:

- ICT home equipment
- Internet connection means
- Household limitations for Access to ICTs
- Ability to use computer, internet and cellphone
- Electronic banking and commerce experience
- Ways to use the internet
- Mobile internet access

The results found at the national level on the aforementioned topics are as follows, considering that the population of the country according to the last population census in Mexico in 2015, for which the INEGI officially reports a total of 119,938,473 people.

The survey applied by the INEGI is analyzed below and the results directed at the population of households with information and communication technology equipment, and are considered according to the type of equipment from 2017 to 2019, which are concentrated in table 1.

Table 1. ICT equipment in homes

Year	Computer (%)	Internet connection (%)	Television (%)	Pay TV (%)	Telephony (%)	Radio (%)	Electric power (%)
2017	45.4	50.9	93.2	49.5	91.9	58.6	99.4
2018	44.9	52.9	92.9	47.3	92.2	56.2	99.3
2019	44.3	56.4	92.5	45.9	92.5	53.9	99.5

Source: INEGI (2020)

The results of the last three years are distinguished by the high percentage of equipment to which there is more access, which are: electric power 99.4%, television 92.86% and telephony 92.2%. Also, it is important to highlight that households have a computer (45.4%), pay TV with 47.3%, internet connection with 52.9% and radio with 56.2%; the reasons why households do not have the equipment have also been identified, which are concentrated in table 2.

Table 2. Reasons why there is no equipment in homes

Year	Lack of financial resources	They're not interested in it	They don't know how to use it	They use a smartphone or other device to connect to the Internet	It is broken
2017	58.2	18.3	14.4	5.2	NA
2018	57.1	20.2	13.9	5.4	1.6
2019	53.3	20.9	16.5	5.6	1.6

Source: INEGI (2020)

Based on table 2, the main reason why Mexican homes do not have equipment is due to the lack of economic resources, the use of a smartphone or other device to connect to the Internet, they are not interested or do not know how to use it, or it is broken.

The Academic Training of the Students of the Instituto Politécnico Nacional at the Postgraduate Level

The IPN (Communiqué 053, 2020b) reported that the tools used for access were the following: 60% using mobile devices, 33% using desktop or laptop computers and the remaining 7% using other devices. It also stands out that 40% of users went to Google Classroom or Microsoft Teams after seeing the tutorials to create their Virtual Classrooms and collaboration spaces or to use a video conference room on the Zoom platform. Another percentage stayed on the portal (30%) or in the Multi-virtual classrooms (30%) to consult material and download content. These results allow us to confirm what is suggested by the World Bank (2003) regarding the availability of ICTs that are up-to-date and operate correctly.

Additionally, according to the results of the same institution, the purpose of using the previous tools was as follows: 75.5% for access to information; 49.9% for content creation; 37% for the diversity of methodologies; 46.9% for evaluation and self-evaluation; 71.3% for time flexibility and 54.6% for the publication of information.

With these platforms and tools that were already available before the pandemic, they had a boom at the time the schools were closed, within the strategies indicated to continue the school year, so that once the confinement had begun, the teachers were requested to carry out the following: create a directory of students, consult the resources available within the portals, create and participate in virtual learning environments using the technological tools Google Classroom and G-suite Microsoft Teams, Zoom, among others. Thus, these results confirm what is established by González, Infante and Infante (2020) in that a central element to operate an educational service in the online context is to count and continuously use these technological tools.

With regard to the situations faced by students during the COVID-19 pandemic, the following stand out: In 85% they were of a logistics nature (organization and distribution of time for work, family and academic activities); in 82% of a socio-emotional nature (manifestation of sadness, frustration, anxiety and demotivation) and for 48% of an educational nature (comply in a timely manner with carrying out and sending the activities at a distance). Based on this finding, it is relevant to note that the presence of the coronavirus has also generated consequences in the socio-affective aspect, as mentioned by Zaar and García (2020), where the participants acknowledged having experienced feelings of sadness, anxiety, insecurity and uncertainty due to what they were experiencing while attending to work, family and academic activities.

With respect to the information collected from the instrument developed for the study, the main results regarding the characteristics of access, time and connection of the students during the coronavirus pandemic show that the main access to technological devices was the laptop with 60%; while the daily time allocated to academic training during the pandemic was three or more hours with 85% of those surveyed. Regarding the Internet connection available to the student body, it is mostly fixed with 90%. On the other hand, the results of the assessment of distance academic training according to the postgraduate level participants are organized in tables 3, 4, 5 and 6.

Table 3. Technological dimension

Distance education allowed	Mean	SD
Employ teaching strategies mediated by digital tools	4.05	0.81
The diverse use of digital teaching resources for learning achievement	4.67	0.17
Expand the usefulness of technology tools	4.32	0.33

Based on table 3, the main findings related to the technological tools had a positive assessment regarding the diversification of digital resources to achieve the learning goals of the course with an average of 4.67; expand the usefulness of technological tools with an average of 4.32, while these tools were used to implement teaching strategies from the teacher with an average of 4.05. These results confirm what is indicated by both Castaño, Redecker, Vuorikari and Punie (2014) and Cabero, Marín and Castaño (2015) regarding the fact that the teaching activity takes place in a complex context, such as the COVID-19 pandemic, that requires the permanent use of technological tools to develop the curricular learning of the students.

Table 4. Planning dimension

Distance education allowed	Mean	SD
Adapt the course work plan to this modality	4.06	0.53
Adapt the thematic contents to this modality to continue with their training	4.11	0.67
Achieve the objectives of each subject	4.07	0.73
Recognize that the training received is useful	4.14	0.89

From Table 4, concerning the adaptation to the online modality during the COVID-19 pandemic at the postgraduate level, the participants valued it positively, in which they recognized that the training received during confinement was useful with an average of 4.14 points. This element is explained from what is indicated by the students in regard to the adjustment made by the teaching staff for the contents of each subject with an average of 4.11, which in turn allowed achieving the objectives of each course with an average of 4.07 points. These results are corroborated based on the positive score of the students regarding that the teaching work plan was adapted to a distance modality with an average of 4.06. These results also confirm what is suggested by Cabero (2013); López and Andrés (2020) respecting the redesign of the didactic planning for an online environment integrating digital materials, as well as the academic activities being diversified, dosed, with a temporary organization and including the evaluation criteria.

Table 5. Evaluation dimension

Distance education allowed	Mean	SD
A responsibility for my academic training	3.86	0.97
Develop the capacities of analysis, argumentation and synthesis	3.81	0.85
Interact with the faculty to check my academic progress	4.31	0.46
Use continuous assessment	4.54	0.19

Source: Own elaboration

Based on Table 5, the assessment of the responsibility of the participants for their academic training during confinement was positive with a mean of 3.86; while the development of analysis, argumentation and synthesis capacities was also positive with an average of 3.81. These findings corroborate what was established by Mohamedbhai (2020); Escudero (2018) and Gutiérrez (2014) on the importance of teachers' commitment to planning and delivering distance sessions that promote various cognitive and non-cognitive skills.

In the same way, for the element of evaluation during the COVID-19 pandemic, it was found that the students valued the continuous type positively with an average of 4.54, as well as the follow-up in academic progress with an average of 4.31. These results confirm what was suggested by García, Corell, Abella and Grande (2020); Ng (2018); McCallum, Schultz, Sellke and Spartz (2015); Álvarez (2012) on the relevance of establishing an evaluation process for each of the courses integrating a series of evidences carried out in the various office applications.

Table 6. Flexibility dimension

Distance education allowed	Mean	SD
Academic flexibility respecting learning styles	3.72	0.91
Flexibility regarding access and use of digital tools	3.93	0.95
A flexibility for learning assessment	4.15	0.48
Administrative flexibility for the educational path	3.74	0.62

Based on Table 6, the postgraduate level participants rated the flexibility on the part of the teaching staff and educational institution as positive; the learning evaluation with an average of 4.15; the access and use of digital tools with an average of 3.93; the administrative type with an average of 3.74; and the academic one with an average of 3.72 points. These results confirm what is recommended by López and Andrés (2020), as well as by García, Corell, Abella and Grande (2020) in relation to establishing flexibility for the student body during the coronavirus pandemic.

DISCUSSION

With reference to the basic level that includes primary and secondary, the *Learn at home I and II* has been complicated, the authority has complied with the coverage trying to reach the school population through television and radio programs; however, leaving these homework assignments or tasks at home under the responsibility of the parents has been an arduous and difficult task because, on the one hand, there is not the time, space and training for a parent to replace the teacher; and on the other hand, the little technological infrastructure makes it difficult to send the homework with the internet, limiting it to textbooks and notebooks, which has generated a variety of doubts both in its implementation and in its monitoring when they are sent to teachers, who have to prepare the evidence folders that allow verifying the way in which the students are evaluated.

In this sense, another situation has been generated with respect to the delivery of the evidence folder either in digital, electronic or physical form, which collects the learning products, leaving the question of how the student is supported in the construction of these, that is, what guides the learning process, and that, on the one hand, the experience, whether exercise, play, etc., can be considered synonyms of learning and of what type. Regarding the subsequent level, which is the baccalaureate, the problems are the same and virtual materials are also made available on institutional platforms. Nonetheless, for both the UNAM and the IPN, little is said about the didactic monitoring and accompaniment, as well as the learning results obtained and the training actions aimed at students that have been implemented for this level.

In addition, the circumstances faced by both teachers and students until January 2021 have been complicated due to the fact that they have to communicate from their respective homes under different conditions and resources, such as internet use and computer use. These differences in technological resources identified empirically by teachers during confinement have shown the existence of a great difference in equal opportunities for students to continue learning. However, it coincides with what is indicated by Castillo and Castillo (2021) who emphasize that the teachers have used their means, their personal effort, their experience in teaching face-to-face classes and their available skills to continue with the educational service which, in their most, had not experienced before.

Therefore, the previous findings confirm what is established by Martin and Furiv (2020) with regard to the diversity of situations faced by the main educational actors: students and teachers related to access and use of technological tools and platforms due to the diversity of mastery levels in digital training. In this sense, it confirms what is stated by UNESCO (2014) in that technological tools are considered as means to modernize the academic and administrative management processes of educational systems, so they are an area of opportunity to integrate in the case of Mexico because they allow transforming student learning by promoting greater autonomy and collaborative work.

Besides, concerning the fact that each educational institution, to continue with the academic service, needed to reformulate the school calendars and provide various technological resources coupled with providing free access to digital libraries, specialized magazines, and publications and information systems to provide care to teachers and students online so it coincides with what is recommended by ANUIES (2020b). In the same way, what is established by both the OECD (2020a) and IESALC (2020a) is confirmed with relation to the diversity of access to connectivity and the type of mobile device with which educational actors access to continue with the academic service. In this sense, for Mexico, the digital and academic divide has manifested itself to a greater extent.

Consequently, the long-awaited change in paradigms and roles in the educational work of teachers and students also happened unexpectedly, so that to achieve the training objectives by the teacher, a modification in communication strategies was required by introducing tools such as WhatsApp, coupled with assuming the role of facilitator of learning in cooperative and flexible environments, as indicated (Zafra, 2020). The foregoing confirms what was stated by Cabrera (2020) regarding the fact that the coronavirus forced a transition to distance education, evidencing limitations in educational actors, which has generated obstacles to maintaining academic training.

Nevertheless, the presence of the coronavirus in the educational system also has to be addressed as an area of opportunity that allows the incorporation of a renewed teaching and learning model as established by IESALC (2020b). Therefore, this study provides relevant information on actions aimed at academic training, evaluation and monitoring of student learning at the postgraduate level that allow the formulation of educational strategies that contribute to the return of face-to-face sessions after the pandemic as pointed out by Murillo and Duk (2020).

CONCLUSION

This radical change caused by the pandemic in the world in all areas of life: economic, political, social and cultural, has exposed two educational gaps. The first in terms of the technological infrastructure that exists in the country regardless of educational level, and the second, related to the digital training that teachers have in the domain of technological skills, as well as the curricular design, which has a planning, development and evaluation of didactic sequences with defined characteristics and implemented through various modalities (in person, mixed or virtual) and on various platforms.

Moreover, it is important to recognize the efforts of both authorities, families, teachers and students to continue with the teaching and learning process, so that the results of this period of confinement, which seems endless, will be known when the experiences of the various actors involved are systematized, not only programmatic learning but also those that this life experience has left in each human being.

In this sense, the Virtual Plan for Academic Continuity implemented by the IPN (2020) has worked at the postgraduate level because the assessment of the student body has been positive, highlighting strengths such as the incorporation and continuous use of digital resources, the use of evaluation, the usefulness of technological tools, as well as the interaction with the teaching staff to review the student's academic progress. Also, what is indicated by Zaar and García (2020) is confirmed regarding the fact that said Virtual Plan at the postgraduate level has considered the flexibility of the educational service, the adaptation of educational practices in a non-face-to-face environment, as well as the design of methodological alternatives and evaluation elements by the teacher that have allowed the students to continue with the academic training.

ACKNOWLEDGMENT

This research was supported by the Instituto Politécnico Nacional, México [SIP number 20210598 and SIP number 20211263].

REFERENCES

Akareem, H., & Hossain, S. (2012). Perception of education quality in private universities of Bangladesh: A study from students' perspective. *Journal of Marketing for Higher Education, 22*(1), 11–33. doi:10.1080/08841241.2012.705792

Álvarez, B. (2012). Flipping the Classroom: Homework in class, lessons at home. *Journal of Education Digest: Essential Readings Condensed for Quick Review, College Student Personnel, 77*(8), 18–21. Retrieved from https://eric.ed.gov/?id=EJ982505

Asociación Nacional de Universidades e Instituciones de Educación Superior. (2020a). *Acuerdo Nacional por la Unidad en la Educación Superior frente a la emergencia sanitaria provocada por el covid-19.* Retrieved from http://www.anuies.mx/media/docs/avisos/pdf/200424155500Acuerdo+Nacional+frente+al+COVID-19.pdf

Asociación Nacional de Universidades e Instituciones de Educación Superior (2020b). *Anuarios estadísticos de la educación superior, ciclo escolar 2018-2019. Licenciatura y posgrado.* ANUIES.

Banco Mundial. (2003). *Construir sociedades de conocimiento: Nuevos desafíos para la educación terciaria.* Banco Mundial. Retrieved from http://siteresources.worldbank.org/TERTIARYEDUCATION/Resources/Documents/Constructing-Knowledge-Societies/CKS-spanish.pdf

Bourne, J., & Moore, J. (2003). *Elements of Quality Online Education.* Babson College.

Boursicot, K., Kemp, S., Ong, T., Wijaya, L., Goh, S., Freeman, K., & Curran, I. (2020). Conducting a high-stakes OSCE in a COVID-19 environment. *MedEdPublish, 9*(1). Advance online publication. doi:10.15694/mep.2020.000054.1

Cabero, J. (2013). *Nuevos modelos, recursos y diseño de programas en la práctica docente.* Ediciones CEF.

Cabero, J., Marín, V. & Castaño, C. (2015). Validación de la aplicación del modelo TPACK para la formación del profesorado en TIC. *Revista d´innovació Educativa Universitat de Valéncia, 14,* 13-22. doi:10.7203/attic.14.4001

Cabrera, L. (2020). Efectos del coronavirus en el sistema de enseñanza: Aumenta la desigualdad de oportunidades educativas en España. *Research in Sociology of Education, 13*(2), 114–139. doi:10.7203/RASE.13.2.17125

Castaño, J., Redecker, C., Vuorikari, R., & Punie, Y. (2014). Open Education 2030: Planning the future of adult learning in Europe. *Open Learning, 28*(3), 171–186. doi:10.1080/02680513.2013.871199

Castillo, J., & Castillo, A. (2021). El impacto de la COVID-19 en el profesorado de educación superior y sus concepciones sobre la evaluación. *Campus Virtuales, 10*(19), 89-101. Retrieved from http://www.uajournals.com/campusvirtuales/journal/18/7.pdf

Chehaibar, L. (2020). Flexibilidad curricular. Tensiones en tiempos de pandemia. In H. Casanova (Coord.), Educación y pandemia. Una visión académica (pp. 83-91). UNAM.

Colegio de Ciencias y Humanidades. (2020). *Cuadernillo de orientaciones 2020-2021.* https://www.cch.unam.mx/sites/default/files/Cuadernillo_Orientaciones_2020-2021.pdf

Corral, Y. (2009). Validez y confiabilidad de los instrumentos de investigación para la recolección de datos. *Revista Ciencias de la Educación, 19*(33), 229-247. http://servicio.bc.uc.edu.ve/educacion/revista/n33/art12.pdf

Escudero, A. (2018). Redefinición del "aprendizaje en red" en la cuarta revolución industrial. *Apertura (Guadalajara, Jal.), 10*(1), 149–163.

García, F., Corell, A., Abella, V., & Grande, M. (2020). La evaluación online en la educación superior en tiempos de la COVID-19. *Education in the Knowledge Society, 21*(0), 1–26. doi:10.14201/eks.23013

George, D., & Mallery, P. (2011). *SPSS for Windows Step by Step: A simple guide and reference.* Allyn y Bacon.

Gewin, V. (2020). Five tips for moving teaching online as COVID-19 takes hold. *Nature, 580*(7802), 295–296. doi:10.1038/d41586-020-00896-7 PMID:32210377

González, C., Infante, A., & Infante, J. (2020). Implementation of e-proctoring in online teaching: A study about motivational factors. *Sustainability, 12*(8), 3488. Advance online publication. doi:10.3390u12083488

González, C., Marco, E., & Medina, T. (2020). *Informe de iniciativas y herramientas de evaluación online universitaria en el contexto del COVID-19.* Ministerio de Universidades.

Gutiérrez, I. (2014). Perfil del profesor universitario español en torno a las competencias en tecnologías de la información y la comunicación. *Pixel-Bit. Revista de Medios y Educación, 44*, 51–65.

Hayes, H. (2010). *Curriculum 21: Essential education for a changing world.* ASCD.

Hernández, R., Fernández, C., & Baptista, P. (2010). *Metodología de la investigación.* McGraw-Hill.

IESALC. (2020a). *Coronavirus COVID-19 and Higher Education: Impact and recommendations.* UNESCO. Retrieved from http://www.iesalc.unesco.org/en/2020/03/09/coronavirus-covid-19-and-higher-education-impact-and-recommendations/

IESALC. (2020b). *COVID-19 and higher education: Today and tomorrow. Impact analysis, political responses and recommendations.* UNESCO. Retrieved from http://www.iesalc.unesco.org/en/wp-content/uploads/2020/04/COVID-19-EN-090420-2.pdf

Instituto Nacional de Estadística y Geografía. (2020). *Encuesta Nacional sobre la Disponibilidad y Uso de las Tecnologías en los Hogares.* México: INEGI. Retrieved from https://www.inegi.org.mx/programas/dutih/2019/

Instituto Politécnico Nacional. (2020a). *Plan virtual de continuidad académica.* Retrieved from https://elementosdeaprendizaje.ipn.mx/

Instituto Politécnico Nacional (2020b). *Comunicado 53. Registra alrededor de 166 mil visitas virtuales la plataforma de continuidad académica del IPN.* Author.

Llorens, F. (2020b). *Transformación digital versus digitalización.* Universidad. Retrieved from https://www.universidadsi.es/transformacion-digital-versus-digitalizacion/

López, M., & Andrés, S. (2020). Trayectorias escolares en la educación superior ante la pandemia ¿continuar, interrumpir o desistir? In H. Casanova (Coord.), Educación y pandemia. Una visión académica (pp. 66-74). UNAM.

Martin, M., & Furiv, U. (2020). *COVID-19 shows the need to make learning more flexible.* University World News. Retrieved from https://www.universityworldnews.com/post.php?story=20200324115802272

McCallum, S., Schultz, J., Sellke, K., & Spartz, J. (2015). An Examination of the Flipped Classroom Approach on College Student Academic Involvement. *International Journal on Teaching and Learning in Higher Education, 27*(1), 42–55. https://www.isetl.org/ijtlhe/pdf/IJTLHE1880.pdf

Mevarech, Z., & Bracha, K. (2017). *Matemáticas críticas para las sociedades innovadoras. El papel de las pedagogías metacognitivas.* OECD – IPN. doi:10.1787/9789264273078-es

Mohamedbhai, G. (2020). *COVID-19: What consequences for higher education? University World News.* Africa Edition. Retrieved from https://www.universityworldnews.com/post.php?story=20200407064850279

Murillo, J. & Duk, C. (2020). El Covid-19 y las Brechas Educativas. *Revista latinoamericana de educación inclusiva, 14*(1), 11-13. doi:10.4067/S0718-73782020000100011

Ng, E., & Lai, Y. (2012). An exploratory study on using wiki to foster student teachers' learner-centered learning and self and peer assessment. *Journal of Information Technology Education: Innovations in Practices, 11*, 71–84. https://eric.ed.gov/?id=EJ971761

OECD. (2020a). *A Helping Hand: Education Responding to the Coronavirus Pandemic.* Retrieved from https://oecdedutoday.com/education-responding-coronavirus-pandemic/

OECD. (2020b). *Education Disrupted - Education Rebuilt: Some Insights from PISA on the Availability and Use of Digital tools for Learning.* Retrieved from https://oecdedutoday.com/coronavirus-education-digital-tools-for-learning/

Pérez, I. (2017). Creación de recursos educativos digitales: Reflexiones sobre Innovación Educativa con TIC. *The International Journal of Social Education, 6*(2), 244–268. doi:10.17583/rise.2017.2544

Quirós, E. (2009). Recursos didácticos digitales: Medios innovadores para el trabajo colaborativo en línea. *Revista Electrónica Educare, 13*(2), 47–62. doi:10.15359/ree.13-2.4

Rogero, J. (2020). *Ficción educativa en tiempos de confinamiento.* El Diario de la Educación. Retrieved from https://eldiariodelaeducacion.com/2020/03/25/ficcion-educativa-en-tiempos-de-confinamiento/

Secretaría de Educación Pública (2019). *Principales cifras del Sistema Educativo Nacional, 2018-2019.* México: SEP.

Secretaría de Educación Pública. (2020). *Boletín No. 239 El sector educativo se impuso a los efectos de la pandemia: Esteban Moctezuma Barragán.* Retrieved from https://www.gob.mx/sep/articulos/boletin-no-239-el-sector-educativo-se-impuso-a-los-efectos-de-la-pandemia-esteban-moctezuma-barragan?idiom=es

Silvio, J. (2006). Hacia una educación virtual de calidad, pero con equidad y pertinencia. *Revista Universitaria y Sociedad del Conocimiento, 3*(1), 1–14.

UNESCO. (2014). *Políticas TIC en los sistemas educativos de América Latina*. UNESCO.

UNESCO. (2020). *Consecuencias negativas del cierre de las escuelas*. Retrieved from https://es.unesco.org/covid19/education-response/consecuencias

Universidad Autónoma de México. (2020). *Recomendaciones para la transición a la docencia no presencial.* Retrieved from https://cuaieed.unam.mx/descargas/Recomendaciones-para-la-transicion-a-la-docencia-no-presencial.pdf

Wang, G., Cheng, Z., Yue, X., & McAleer, M. (2020). Risk Management of COVID-19 by Universities in China. *Journal of Risk and Financial Management*, *13*(2), 36. doi:10.3390/jrfm13020036

Zaar, M., & García, M. (2020). El COVID-19 en España y sus primeras consecuencias. *Espaço e Economia*, *17*(17). Advance online publication. doi:10.4000/espacoeconomia.10142

Zafra, I. (2020). La desesperada búsqueda de los alumnos que se han quedado desconectados del sistema educativo. *El País*. Retrieved from https://elpais.com/sociedad/2020-04-12/la-desesperada-busqueda-de-los-alumnos-que-se-han-quedado-desconectados-del-sistema-educativo.html

Chapter 11
IT Opportunities for Teacher Training and Support:
An Action Research During the COVID-19 Pandemic in Greece

Antonios Kokkonos
Hellenic Open University, Greece & University of Peloponnese, Greece

Maria Pavlis Korres
https://orcid.org/0000-0001-6390-4013
Aristotle University of Thessaloniki, Greece & Hellenic Open University, Greece

ABSTRACT

The evolution in the field of internet technologies and the spectacular acceptance of the world wide web have shaped a new framework, not only for teachers' training but also for their distant support. This study provides insights into the utilization of Microsoft Teams digital collaboration and communication environment to improve the ways teachers are trained and supported by educational work coordinators (EWCs), through an action research conducted in Peloponnese Regional Educational Planning Center, Greece. Research results reveal that Microsoft Teams can contribute to the improvement of teachers' training and support in many ways, considering how successfully it has been utilized to improve the ways teachers are trained and supported by EWCs since the COVID-19 outbreak. At the same time, however, policy makers and education officials should take specific steps in order to assist EWCs in utilizing Microsoft Teams for teachers' training and educational work support.

INTRODUCTION

The technological advances, especially those achieved during the last decade, and the exponential progress in the field of internet technologies have created new conditions and established direct communication, interaction, collaborative action and social networking as core elements of a new reality, as these concepts are closely related to fundamental quality characteristics of the way people learn, create, share,

DOI: 10.4018/978-1-7998-7184-2.ch011

collaborate, support each other, make decisions, critique etc. (Selwyn, 2014, cited in Benkler, 2014, pp. 191-216; Chen, 2016, cited in Kadry & El Hami, 2016, pp. 114-117).

This study provides insights into the utilization of a digital collaboration and communication environment to improve the ways teachers are trained and supported by Educational Work Coordinators (EWCs), through an action research conducted in Peloponnese Regional Educational Planning Center (REPC), Greece. Subsequently, the action research investigates EWCs' school principals' and teachers' views, perceptions, experiences and personal stories on key issues regarding the utilization of Microsoft Teams digital collaboration and communication environment for teachers' training and educational work support in circumstances requiring distance teachers' training and support, as is the case with the covid-19 pandemic. The reasons for choosing Microsoft Teams for the purpose of this action research were the fact that it was already in use by the Peloponnese REPC since September 2019 for communication and collaboration with remote school units and the fact that its use was free for EWCs and teachers through their academic license.

The first section of this study focuses on the theoretical background of the above-mentioned action research. In this context, the notions of distance education, adult learner characteristics, teacher training and educational work support, e-learning and types of e-learning are clarified. Emphasis is placed on the analysis and documentation regarding the use of advanced internet technologies for teachers' training and support of educational work. Moreover, the core elements and functions of Microsoft Teams collaboration and communication environment as well as a literature review regarding the use of Microsoft Teams in workplaces and school and/or academic contexts are presented.

In the second section of this study, the research methodology and the results of the action research we conducted over a period of five months are presented; we investigated "if" and "how" a digital collaboration and communication environment, such as Microsoft Teams, can be utilized to improve the ways teachers are trained and supported by EWCs. The action research was carried out in the region of Peloponnese, Greece, during the period between December 2019 and April 2020, and study participants included four (4) EWCs, twelve (12) primary or secondary school principals and thirty-two (32) teachers in primary and secondary schools.

According to the findings of the action research, there is strong evidence suggesting that Microsoft Teams digital collaboration and communication environment can contribute in many ways to the improvement of teachers' training and educational work support by EWCs, especially for schools that are dispersed in different or inaccessible regional units, or when circumstances require distance teachers' training and support. The results of the action research also reveal that, since the outbreak of the covid-19 pandemic, Microsoft Teams has been utilized to improve the ways teachers are trained and supported by EWCs in an innovative, productive and efficient way.

Furthermore, research participants pointed out that policy makers and the Peloponnese REPC should take specific steps in order to assist EWCs in utilizing digital collaboration and communication environments, such as Microsoft Teams, for teachers' training and educational work support, given that, at the time the research was carried out, epidemiologists underlined that covid-19 pandemic's second wave was "knocking at the door".

THEORETICAL BACKGROUND

Important issues regarding the consideration of advanced internet technologies as learning technologies - including the ideas that: a) learning can be achieved without the need of face-to-face contact between teachers and learners, b) each learner can learn by following their own learning path and c) a large number of learners can be trained independently and through differentiated time scheduling - have been exhaustively discussed, tested and confirmed in practice in the field of distance education for a long time (Horton, 2001; Horton & Horton, 2003).

Distance education is the educational process in which teachers and learners are not physically present at the same place (Sewart, Keegan, & Holmberg, 1988; Perraton, 1988, 1993; Moore & Kearsley, 2012). The fact that learners are not on the same premises as teachers and the educational organization is a core issue, not only due to the physical distance created between teachers and learners, but also because of its strong impact on interpersonal interactions and the results of the entire educational process (Moore, 1983; Saba & Shearer 1994; Saba, 2005; McLaughlin & Talbert, 2006; Webster-Wright, 2009; Burns, 2011; Moore & Diehl, 2019).

Distance education that takes place in primary, secondary, postsecondary and adult education is founded in the belief that the distance education paradigm serves learning as effectively as the face-to-face education paradigm (Simonson, Schlosser & Orellana, 2011; Simonson, Smaldino & Zvacek, 2015; Moore & Diehl, 2019). Subsequently, learners seem to consider their distance training experiences as successful and effective as those they acquired through the face-to-face training paradigm (Simonson et al., 2015).

The importance of the above becomes of greater value especially in the case of covid-19 pandemic, where the measures for social distancing dictate the necessity of distance learning paradigm both for the day to day learning process and the teachers' training and the support of their educational work (Daniel, 2020; Huang, Liu, Tlili, Yang, Wang, et al., 2020; Jackson & Keirstead, 2020; Reimers & Schleicher, 2020).

Teachers as Adult Learners

Theorists agree that adult learners have special characteristics that differentiate them as learners from children or young learners (Knox, 1977; Brookfield, 1986; Williams, 1996; Knowles, 1998).

Rogers, (2001), Pavlis-Korres, Karalis, Leftheriotou & Garcia Barriocanal (2009) and Pavlis-Korres & Leftheriotou (2016) summarize specific characteristics of adult learners as follows: a) they participate in educational programs in order to meet concrete goals and expectations related to their real -explicit or inexplicit- needs and the acquisition of knowledge and skills they are motivated to acquire, b) they have knowledge and experience stemming from a variety of life experiences and family, professional and social roles they assume, c) they have developed a personal path and style of learning, based on their own skills, experiences, pace and personality, d) they favor active involvement, as adulthood is associated with the tendency of adults to be self-directed learners and to participate in all stages of a training program's lifecycle, e) they face barriers during the learning process, usually due to family, professional, social or mental factors and they tend to develop defense or resignation mechanisms.

Teachers who participate in training programs are adult learners that -in addition to the above-mentioned characteristics- have a variety of teaching-learning experiences and are involved in a continuous reflection and negotiation process regarding the experiences they acquired as students, education practitioners and adult learners in their lifetime, as they are aware that these teaching-learning representations and experiences are core elements of teachers' professional identity.

Teachers' Training and Support

Teachers' support in combination with the opportunities they have to be trained, are perceived as key factors for the success of their work (Smith & Gillespie, 2007; Timperley, 2008; Whitcomb, Borko & Liston, 2009; Webster-Wright, 2009), as these factors are closely related to their personal and professional development, the effective implementation of curricula and the improvement of teaching practices, learning outcomes and educational work (Fullan & Hargreaves, 1992; Borko, 2004; Darling-Hammond et al., 2009; Wei, Andree & Darling-Hammond, 2009).

Subsequently, teachers' distant support is perceived as a supportive process during which, EWCs and teachers are not in physically present at the same place. As mentioned above, the distance that separates them overemphasizes the physical distance between the two parties -those who support and those who are supported- and strongly influences the interpersonal interactions between them (McLaughlin & Talbert, 2006; Webster-Wright, 2009; Burns, 2011; Moore & Diehl, 2019).

However, the evolution in the field of internet technologies and the spectacular acceptance of the worldwide web have formed a totally new framework not only for teachers' training but also for their distant support and they have given rise to a wide range of infrastructures, services and tools that enable direct communication, interaction, collaborative action and exchange of information between EWCs and teachers, and facilitate teachers' personal and professional development, by assisting them in effectively implementing curricula and improving their teaching practices, learning outcomes and educational work.

The Concept of Electronic Learning

The exponential growth and acceptance of educational programs that utilize internet technologies and are offered through the worldwide web, created the conditions for the emergence of new, dynamic ideas and the gradual emergence of the concept of electronic learning (e-learning) (Sangra, Vlachopoulos & Cabrera, 2012).

Since the early 2000s, an extensive discussion began, regarding the definition of e-learning and its utilization in an efficient way (Sanders, 2001; Masie, 2001; Kirschner & Pass, 2001; Rosenberg, 2001; Broadbent, 2002; Clark & Mayer, 2003; Beetham, 2004; Koper, 2004; Van Dam, 2005; Bermejo, 2005; Liao & Lu, 2008; Gonella & Panto, 2008; Li, Lau & Dharmendran, 2009; Ellis, Ginns & Piggott, 2009; Rupesh-Kumar, 2009; Cedefop, 2014) but this topic still remains open to discussion, as there are many e-learning definitions that refer to the multiple, complex and multifaceted nature of the concept of e-learning and -at the same time- reflect the difficulty that still exists in formulating a definition that can indisputably include all the aspects of the e-learning concept.

Significant research efforts and mainstream design practices of e-learning programs were initially focused on the "content" and "the way" it would be delivered to each learner. However, the way each learner actually interacted with the e-learning content became a key issue that greatly influenced the e-learning program design process and thus interest was gradually shifted from the "content" to the teaching-learning "process" - especially towards "learning activities" performed during this process and "interactions" that take place between everyone involved in teaching-learning process (Koper & Olivier, 2004; Beetham, 2004; Beetham & Sharpe, 2007).

In this study, we perceive the concept of e-learning as the learning for the individual aspects of which -achievement, extension, support, management and assessment- interconnected computer systems (via internet, intranets or other types of networks) that provide appropriately designed learning experiences to individual learners or group of learners, play a major role.

Synchronous and asynchronous communication technologies serve as a criterion for breaking down e-learning experiences in two types, synchronous and asynchronous (Urdan & Weggen 2000; Hrastinski, 2008; Simonson, Smaldino, Albright, & Zvacek, 2012).

The synchronous e-learning paradigm is related to the potential offered by two-way communication and interaction between teachers and learners in real time, as well as to the use of audiovisual clips, audio clips, instant messaging, chat conversations, file sharing, etc. (Mason & Rennie, 2006). In practice, teachers and learners use the learning environment in real time, each-one from a different location or space, and they communicate, interact, and exchange ideas through videoconferencing, audio, chat conversations, file sharing etc. According to Hrastinski (2008) learners involved in a synchronous e-learning process develop personal motivation and commitment, exhibit a non-reflective type of participation that is more suitable for approaching less complex issues, for planning tasks or getting acquainted. Teachers act as facilitators, providing guidance and feedback, and encouraging interaction, positive interdependence, and collaborative action (Diaz & Entonado, 2009).

The asynchronous e-learning paradigm is strongly related to internet use in order to access an e-learning environment at any time and from any place each learner is located (Mason & Rennie, 2006). Learners involved in an asynchronous e-learning process study e-content and perform training activities at their own pace - as there is no dependency on other learners (Mui, 2016, cited in Kadry & El Hami, 2016, pp. 96-97; Chen, 2016, cited in Kadry & El Hami, 2016, pp. 128-137; Pavlis-Korres, 2017) - demonstrate increased cognitive participation, tend to process complex issues in a reflective way (Hrastinski, 2008), develop interactions with their co-learners, provide feedback to their co-learners and act reflectively insofar as they have achieved the goals they have set and the expected training outcomes (Er et al., 2009; Harris, Mishra & Koehler, 2009; Simonson et al., 2012). In this context, teachers focus on the development and facilitation of learners' e-learning experiences through the development of asynchronous collaborative action that facilitates a critical - reflective approach of educational objectives and a knowledge synthesis process (Diaz & Entonado, 2009; Garrison & Kanuka, 2004; Bonk & Zhang, 2006).

Advanced Internet Technologies Utilization for Teachers' Training and Support

Advanced internet technologies have shaped a new framework not only for teachers' training but also for their distant support, as well as digital collaboration and communication environments that support synchronous and asynchronous communication, integrate tools for meetings, social networking and educational content sharing (Wenger, McDermott & Snyder, 2002; Glazer & Hannafin, 2006; Hou, Chang & Chang, 2010; Liu, Macintyre & Ferguson, 2012), allow the formulation of dynamic social structures (Brooks, 2010) and can undoubtedly be used to facilitate teachers' personal and professional development, and assist them in effectively implementing curricula and improving their teaching practices, learning outcomes and educational work (Fullan, 1991; Fullan & Hargreaves, 1992; Fullan, 1995; Borko, 2004; Darling-Hammond et al., 2009; Wei et al., 2009; Hutchison & Colwell, 2012), especially in the case of a large number of schools that are dispersed in different regional units of Peloponnese, Greece, or in circumstances requiring distance teachers' training and support, as is the case with the covid-19 pandemic (Daniel, 2020; Huang, Liu, Tlili, Yang, Wang, et al., 2020; Jackson & Keirstead, 2020; OECD, 2020; Reimers & Schleicher, 2020).

De Janasz and Godshalk (2013) and Trust (2015) argue that, within digital environments, where people communicate, interact, and share ideas and practices, it is possible: a) to develop interpersonal relationships and receive instant feedback to the benefit of both interacting parties -those who support and those who are supported- and b) for the support process to become effective. In the same direction, the results of an empirical research conducted by Alemdag and Erdem (2017) show that, within a digital environment, where individuals do not accept support in a passive and silent way but provide guidance and support to their peers, cooperation and effective support is achieved.

Allan, Hunter and Lewis (2006), Vaughan and Garrison (2006) and Brooks' (2010) research findings highlight the positive role of learning communities and communities of practice, as they combine face-to-face and digital environment's interactions, they enable participants' interaction without space-time limits, they build interpersonal relationships and promote participation and collaborative action. Additionally, the results of an empirical research conducted by Trust and Horrocks (2017) suggest that the extension of participants' face-to-face training activities involving communication and collaboration through the use of advanced internet technologies created a wide range of formal or informal opportunities for learning, support and enhanced cooperation.

Owen (2014) argues that a supportive online community of practice can significantly contribute to the establishment of a culture of trust and subsequently impact personal knowledge and promote success, while McLoughlin, Brady, Lee and Russell (2007) point out that the participation in a community of practice and the interconnection with other professionals can act as a catalyst to individual performance improvement, change and professional development.

In conclusion, the evolution in the field of advanced internet technologies and the increasing familiarity that more and more people have with instant communication, interaction and social networking, combined with the acceptance and growing popularity of social media indicates, according to Wilbanks (2014), that face-to-face support can -and should be- complemented with support through digital tools and services, or offered exclusively through digital collaboration and communication environments that -as mentioned above- can be used to improve teachers' training and educational work support by EWCs, especially in cases of large number of schools that are dispersed in different or inaccessible regional units, or in circumstances requiring distance teachers' training and support, as is the case with the covid-19 pandemic (Daniel, 2020; Huang et al., 2020; OECD, 2020; Reimers & Schleicher, 2020).

Microsoft Teams Digital Collaboration and Communication Environment

Microsoft Teams is perceived as a collaboration hub (Hubbard & Bailey, 2018; Ilag, 2018), that provides a unified communication, interaction, collaboration and support workspace, enables synchronous and asynchronous communication between users, the use of meeting tools, social networking, file and application sharing, and also shapes a framework for the creation and development of dynamic social structures, such as professional learning communities and communities of practice (Brooks, 2010). The discussion and research in the context of this section focus on the free version of Microsoft Teams and on "how" the latter can be used for teachers' training and educational work support.

Microsoft Teams digital collaboration and communication environment integrates a set of tools, services and applications that utilize advanced internet technologies in a flexible and efficient way with a coherent workspace, and is accessible through the worldwide web (see: https://teams.microsoft.com)

using a web client, desktop clients (Windows, Mac or Linux) or mobile apps for iOS, Android and Windows Phone devices. The core elements of Microsoft Teams' free version are: a) overview of users' activity, b) conversations and chats, c) teams and channels for teamwork, d) calls and meetings, e) file storage, editing and sharing, and f) external applications integration (Figure 1).

Figure 1. Microsoft Teams free version's core elements

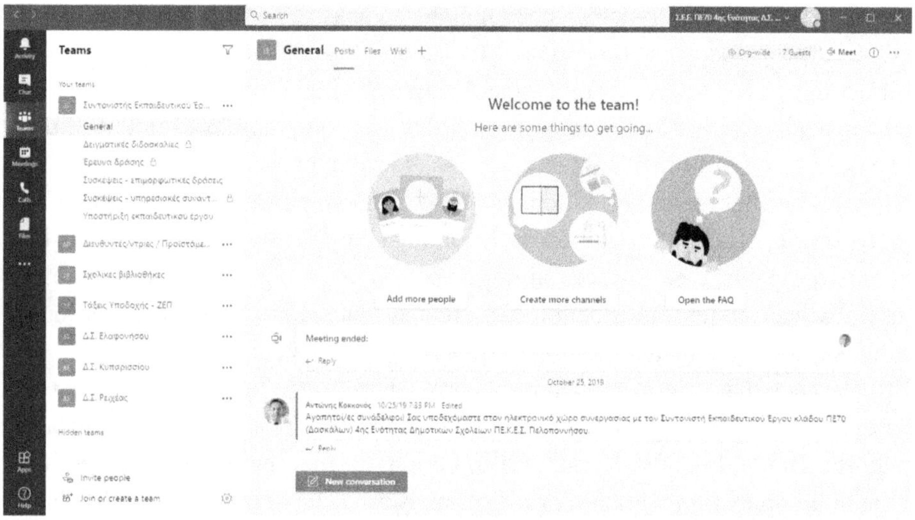

After performing a literature review, we discovered that only a handful of papers have been included in scientific journals and conferences, and only two academic books have been published regarding the functions and/or utilization of Microsoft Teams in the workplace and educational – academic contexts. Similarly, Sankey, Campbell and Poulsen (2019) note that, upon conducting a literature review, they were able to find only two papers included in scientific journals and four papers in conferences regarding the Microsoft Teams environment.

Benke (2019) points out that innovative collaboration apps such as Microsoft Teams have revolutionized the working environment, as they combine the functions of communication, collaboration and coordination in a unified environment that promotes and facilitates teamwork.

As part of an ongoing research project taking place in an organization with over thirty-one thousand (31,000) employees in forty-eight (48) countries, Lansmann, Schallenmuller and Rigby (2019) investigate "how" Microsoft Teams impacts the way employees collaborate and communicate during daily activities and "if" and "why" they perceive this environment as beneficial (or not). The initial findings of this research project indicate that the Microsoft Teams environment is the most important tool for everyday communication and collaboration, because it is easy to use and makes the job easier, efficient and more productive.

The results of a research study conducted by Buchal and Songsore (2019) among undergraduate students suggest that: a) Microsoft Teams is an effective environment to provide scaffolding for collaborative knowledge building, b) students -using Microsoft Teams- can provide constructive feedback without worrying if their contribution will be brought to the attention of teachers, c) Microsoft Teams was found to be more effective than other tools the authors had used, and d) at the end of the activity, students rated their collaboration skills to be good to excellent.

Martin and Tapp (2019) studied aspects of Microsoft Teams use for teaching undergraduate students and argued that: a) Microsoft Teams is associated with the paradigm of social constructivism as far as the teaching-learning process is concerned, b) collaborative learning was developed during the student interaction process, c) the initial research results and feedback received from students were particularly positive; and d) they planed extensive qualitative research on the effectiveness of Microsoft Teams as an environment that supports collaborative learning.

An empirical research study by Mazzola (2019) notes that Microsoft Teams is utilized by world leading organizations to create digital communities of practice (CoP) and there is evidence suggesting that Microsoft Teams is suitable for and accessible to teachers and learners. In this context, this digital environment can provide opportunities for collaborative and social learning based on peer interaction. Furthermore, the research study shows that Microsoft Teams is a flexible environment that can support both formal and informal communication between teachers and learners and that *communication* and *file sharing* were most frequently observed among participants during the empirical research.

Ilag (2019) argues that Microsoft Teams provides the appropriate framework to bring professional learning community's members together, so they can share ideas and content, discuss, learn and grow professionally.

In conclusion, Microsoft Teams' free version provides organizations with a unified workspace for communication, interaction and collaboration that - by using teams and channels - combines and integrates, dynamic elements, such as: a) an overview of individual and group activity, b) synchronous and asynchronous communication through conversations and chats, c) synchronous collaboration through meetings, d) synchronous communication through calls, e) file storage, sharing and collaborative documents editing and f) external applications integration. Furthermore, as we already have documented, these dynamic elements can be utilized to improve the ways teachers are trained and supported by EWCs, to facilitate teachers' personal and professional development, to assist them in effectively implementing curricula and to improve their teaching practices, learning outcomes and educational work, especially in the case of a large number of schools that are dispersed in different regional units or in circumstances requiring distance teachers' training and support, as is the case with the covid-19 pandemic.

RESEARCH METHOD

The main scope of this research was to investigate "if" and "how" a digital collaboration and communication environment, such as Microsoft Teams, can be utilized to improve the ways teachers are trained and supported by the Educational Work Coordinators of Peloponnese REPC, Greece. Subsequently, this research investigated EWCs' school principals' and teachers' views, perceptions, experiences and personal stories on key issues regarding the utilization of Microsoft Teams digital collaboration and communication environment for teachers' training and educational work support. To this end, the research questions were formed as follows:

Research Question 1: Can a digital collaboration and communication environment, such as Microsoft Teams, contribute to improving the ways teachers are trained and supported by EWCs, and if so, how can this be achieved?

Research Question 2: How did the EWCs of Peloponnese REPC utilize the digital environment Microsoft Teams to improve their practices in the context of teachers' training and support?

Research Question 3: What steps can be taken by the Peloponnese REPC, Greece, in order to support EWCs in using a digital collaboration and communication environment, such as Microsoft Teams, for teachers' training and educational work support?

The methodology that was chosen for the design and development of this research is that of action research. Action research design is the most appropriate, as it is best suited for our study, considering that it enables members of a school community or an educational organization to approach and investigate their practices regarding specific educational issues from an inner perspective – by exploring participants' views, perceptions, experiences and personal stories, as acting persons. They subsequently follow a process of reflective communication and collaborative action and -at the same time- they encourage change and introduce innovation to the school community or the educational organization (Creswell, 2015).

Participation and improvement are the two basic pillars of action research designs (Grundy & Kemmis, 1988; Mills, 2011; Creswell, 2015). In particular, improvement regarding the applicable educational interventions and practices, teachers' professional identity and the context of interventions' implementation is sought, as well as participation through research participants' – members of the school community or an educational organization - active involvement in all stages of action research (Grundy, 1987).

The entire process of the action research we conducted is based on the action research interacting spiral (Stringer, 2013), which, through the basic action research routines "look", "think" and "act", provides a powerful action research framework. Creswell (2015) supports that Stringer's action research interacting spiral most accurately reflects the process of action research. In this context, each "observation", "thought", and "action" set serves as the basis for the next one and this recycling set of activities indicates that action research is not a linear process (Figure 2); rather, it works as a flexible framework that allows participants to review and reflect on activities, routines, procedures, interpretations, steps or stages of each cycle.

Figure 2. Action research interacting spiral (Stringer, 2013) Source: Stringer, 2013

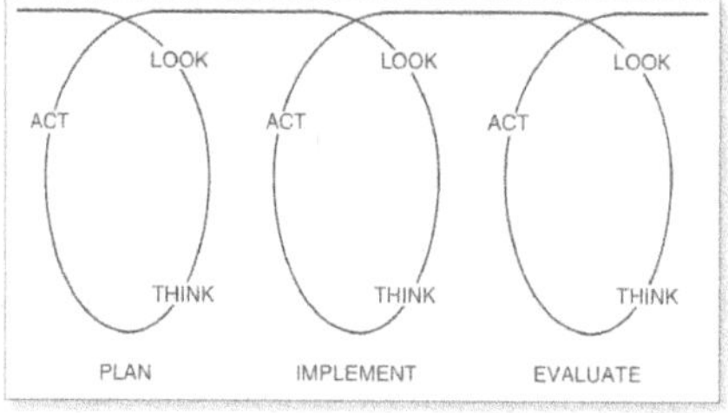

The above-mentioned action research interacting spiral provides opportunities for interaction between EWCs, school principals and teachers participating in the conducted action research, it highlights the collaborative - participatory aspects of the entire research process (Creswell, 2015) and it serves participation and improvement that are key elements of an action research design (Grundy & Kemmis, 1988; Mills, 2011; Creswell, 2015). Additionally, participation, collaboration and interactive communication of all those involved in the research process are perceived as core elements of an educational action research (Grundy 1987; Stringer, 2013; Creswell, 2015).

Action Research Context

The action research was carried out in the region of Peloponnese, Greece, during the period between December 2019 and April 2020. Four (4) EWCs, twelve (12) primary or secondary school principals and thirty-two (32) teachers in primary and secondary schools interacted and collaborated as participants. Having the Peloponnese REPC as a starting point, the interacting spiral process of the conducted action research attempts to investigate how a digital collaboration and communication environment, such as Microsoft Teams, can be utilized to improve the ways teachers are trained and supported by EWCs of Peloponnese REPC, especially in the case of a large number of schools that are dispersed in remote - inaccessible regional units or in circumstances requiring distance teachers' training and support.

The first cycle of the interacting spiral research process focuses on the internal environment of Peloponnese REPC, on a small number of schools and on specific groups of teachers. This cycle is followed by a new one, in which the participants in the action research "look again", "reanalyze", "modify their actions" and implement their elaborated action or intervention in the internal environment of the Peloponnese REPC, in a larger number of schools and in specific groups of teachers in the second cycle of the interacting spiral research process.

More specifically, the first cycle of the interacting spiral research process (December 2019 to mid-February 2020) includes a set of activities through which, ECWs participating in the action research -but also any other ECW- get acquainted with Microsoft Teams digital environment's use and utilization, as they are involved in activities regarding the daily internal collaboration and communication between Peloponnese REPC's EWCs, and also in distance training and support activities involving a small number of schools and specific groups of teachers that are dispersed in remote or inaccessible regional units of the Peloponnese region.

The second cycle of the action research (mid-February 2020 to April 2020) includes a new set of actions for Peloponnese REPC and distance training actions for a larger number of schools and specific groups of teachers that are dispersed in different or inaccessible regional units of the Peloponnese region. It is worth noting that after the outbreak of the covid-19 pandemic in Greece in late February 2020, the action research activities were adapted to the new context, as teachers now participate in distance school education programs' (synchronous and asynchronous) and there is a pressing demand for teachers' distance training and educational work support by EWCs.

To this end, all EWCs of Peloponnese REPC get acquainted with Microsoft Teams digital collaboration and communication environment's functions, learn how to incorporate the platform in everyday synchronous communication and collaboration with school principals and teachers of their district through the use of the Microsoft Teams' meeting tool, and use it for distance training and support of their work in the same way.

The second cycle of the interacting spiral research process is followed by semi-structured interviews with fifteen (15) action research participants (three EWCs, four school principals and eight teachers), aimed at investigating their views, perceptions, experiences and personal stories on key issues regarding the utilization of Microsoft Teams for teachers' training and educational work support.

Data Collection and Analysis Method

Considering the fact that action research is or can be a really complex process, researchers select and utilize a wide range of data collection, analysis and interpretation methods and techniques in order to ensure a clear understanding and interpretation of the questions under investigation, as well as of perceptions, ideas, experiences and personal stories expressed by the participants -as acting persons- in the research process (Stringer, 2013; Creswell, 2015).

Thus, for the collection, analysis and interpretation of the results, the use of qualitative research methods was opted. Qualitative data are collected using different data collection methods, such as: a) discussions between researcher and action research participants, b) researcher's personal diary, c) Microsoft Teams chat conversations and d) semi-structured interviews with fifteen (15) action research participants. The choice of these data collection methods was guided by the context and orientation of the action research, as well as the selective affinity and methodological convergence between action research and qualitative research methods.

The analysis of qualitative data collected from an empirical research (e.g. interview transcripts, personal diary notes, chat conversations, etc.) is related to the process of constructing and attributing meaning to this data and to answers to research questions (Willig, 2013).

In the context of this action research and based on the type of data collected, on the research questions and on our personal research perspective, thematic analysis was selected as the most appropriate qualitative data analysis method. Due to the volume of interview data, the conceptual definition of the simplest meaning units that, as conceptual constructions, express the data of each interview in the form of descriptive or/and interpretive type "codes" (Braun & Clarke, 2012), is provided through the use of the open source software TAMSAnalyzer for Mac, version 4.49b5, and follows the process of organizing these "codes" into similar "thematic categories" which are related to both the research questions and the conceptual schemes that have emerged from the literature review.

Furthermore, the methodological triangulation, that is, the collection of data through different methods (discussions, chat conversations, semi-structured interviews, researcher's personal diary) and data triangulation, that is, the action research data collection from different groups of participants (by EWCs, school principals and teachers), contribute to the enhancement of action research data validity (Denzin 1989; Cohen, Manion & Morrison, 2000; Altrichter et al., 2008; Creswell, 2015).

ACTION RESEARCH FINDINGS AND DISCUSSION

First Research Question

According to the findings of the action research, there is strong evidence that a digital collaboration and communication environment such as Microsoft Teams can contribute in many ways to the improvement of teachers' training and educational work support by EWCs. More specifically, with respect to the first research question, the majority of the fifteen participants in the semi-structured interviews (EWCs, school principals and teachers), firmly believe that this contribution can be achieved in a variety of ways, namely: a) with flexibility in organization of teachers' distance training, b) with communication immediacy, c) with educational resource and practice sharing, d) by overcoming obstacles posed by physical distance and other factors (time, place, etc.), e) by encouraging participation, interaction and collaboration, and f) by providing autonomy and flexibility in terms of time, place and pace, especially for schools that are dispersed in different or inaccessible regional units, or when circumstances require distance teachers' training and support, as is the case with the covid-19 pandemic. The excerpts quoted below are suggestive of the views expressed:

"... I feel that if we did not have the opportunity to take advantage of these (digital) environments, we would not be able to accomplish everything we have achieved in the short period of time we have been here ... in such a remote school ..." (interviewee 6)

"... (a digital communication environment) could contribute efficiently to the enhancement of teachers' communication and support. It could also support teachers, because the time available for communication is significantly increased ..." (interviewee 4)

"... (a digital communication environment) could facilitate the sharing of educational material, the exchange of ideas and good practices among the members of the educational community..." (interviewee 15)

These results are in accordance with findings of the literature review, as they show that advanced internet technologies have formed a new framework not only for teachers' training but also for their distant support, as well as digital collaboration and communication environments that support synchronous and asynchronous communication, and integrate tools for meetings, social networking and educational content sharing (Wenger et al., 2002; Glazer & Hannafin, 2006; Hou, Chang & Chang, 2010; Liu et al., 2012). They also enable the formulation of dynamic social structures (Brooks, 2010) and can undoubtedly be used to facilitate teachers' personal and professional development, and to assist them in effectively implementing curricula and improving their teaching practices, learning outcomes and educational work (Fullan, 1991; Fullan & Hargreaves, 1992; Fullan, 1995; Borko, 2004; Darling-Hammond et al., 2009; Wei et al., 2009; Hutchison & Colwell, 2012).

Second Research Question

Regarding the second research question, the results of the action research reveal that Microsoft Teams has been utilized to improve the ways teachers are trained and supported by EWCs, especially: a) for the implementation of teachers' distance training program using meetings tool, b) for the development of synchronous and asynchronous communication, interaction and collaboration between EWCs, school principals and teachers, c) for sharing educational resources, ideas and practices, and d) for supporting many aspects of teachers' and school principals' educational work after the outbreak of covid-19 pandemic in an innovative, productive and efficient way. As one of the teachers characteristically said:

"... I would say that it has been utilized to a large extent because, through this environment, and in addition to training meetings, educational resources, ideas and practices have been shared, and our EWC very often posts educational content and instructions regarding the ways we can approach the teaching-learning process ..." (interviewee 9)

Two (2) EWCs note that they utilized Microsoft Teams to a small or very small extent, especially for synchronous communication, interaction and collaboration, and for the implementation of teachers' distance training program using Microsoft Teams' meetings tool. The remaining two (2) EWCs utilized Microsoft Teams to an extent that it is deemed -by EWCs themselves and by school principals and teachers- from satisfactory to great, for the development of synchronous and asynchronous communication, interaction and collaboration between EWCs, school principals and teachers, for sharing educational resources, ideas and practices, for the implementation of teachers' distance training program using meetings tool, and for supporting many aspects of teachers' and school principals' educational work in a productive and efficient way, especially after the outbreak of the covid-19 pandemic. The excerpts quoted below are suggestive of the views expressed:

"... a new paradigm in educational work's support has been introduced, based on continuous communication, interaction and collaboration through a digital environment ... I also provide my support and guidance as a school principal regarding educational leadership's issues ..." (interviewee 7)

"... it has contributed to the improvement of training and support practices because it encourages immediacy in collaboration and communication, even in the case of remote schools such as ours ..." (interviewee 14)

Furthermore, the action research findings show that EWCs, school principals and teachers argue that Microsoft Teams digital environment's use has contributed to the improvement of the ways teachers are trained and supported by EWCs, mainly for the following five (5) reasons.

The first reason is that it introduces a new paradigm in educational work support that is founded on cooperation, interaction, communication and change in the relationship between EWCs and teachers. These findings are in accordance with those of De Janasz and Godshalk (2013) and Trust (2015), who note that, within digital environments, where people communicate, interact, share ideas and practices, it is possible for interpersonal relationships to be developed, for instant response or feedback to be provided to the benefit of both interacting parties -those who support and those who are supported- and for the support process to become effective. In the same direction, Benke (2019) points out that digital environments, such as Microsoft Teams, have revolutionized the educational landscape, as they combine the functions of communication, collaboration and coordination in a unified workspace that promotes and facilitates teamwork.

A second reason is that Microsoft Teams ensures immediacy in communication and support/provision of a framework for a regular and substantive contact and collaboration between EWCs and teachers. As regards this finding, the literature review suggests that there is exponential progress in the field of internet technologies, which have established direct communication, interaction, collaborative action and social networking as core elements of a new reality, as these concepts are closely related to fundamental quality characteristics of the way people learn, create, share, collaborate, support each other, make decisions, critique etc. (Selwyn, 2014, cited in Benkler, 2014, pp. 191-216; Chen, 2016, cited in Kadry & El Hami, 2016, pp. 114-117). In addition, Mazzola (2019) points out that Microsoft Teams is a flexible digital environment that can support both formal and informal communication between teachers and learners.

A third reason is that Microsoft Teams enables the organization and coordination of training, along with supportive interventions that fulfil the requirements/needs of schools or groups of teachers' in an extremely flexible way through the use of the internet. In the same direction, Ilag (2018) as well as Hubbard and Bailey (2018) point out that Microsoft Teams integrates a set of tools, services and applications that utilize advanced internet technologies and are accessible through the worldwide web into a coherent workspace.

A fourth reason is that Microsoft Teams is a highly functional environment that offers the appropriate context for teachers' support. This finding is in accordance with the initial research findings of Lansmann et al. (2019), which indicate that Microsoft Teams is on its way to becoming the most important tool for everyday communication and collaboration, as it is easy to use and makes the job easier, efficient and productive. Ilag (2019) also argues that Microsoft Teams provides the appropriate framework for bringing the professional learning community's members together, allowing them to share ideas and content, discuss, learn and grow professionally. In addition, a study by Trust and Horrocks (2017) concluded that an increase in participants' engagement in communication and collaboration activates achieved through the use of advanced internet technologies has helped to promote formal and informal learning and support and to consolidate cooperation.

A fifth reason is that, by using Microsoft Teams digital collaboration and communication environment, obstacles posed by the physical distance and other factors (e.g., time, space, number of EWC visits in schools) are surmounted. In the same direction, Allan et al. (2006), Vaughan and Garrison (2006), Mason and Rennie (2006), as well as Leftheriotou and Pavlis-Korres (2016) report that digital collaboration environments help to overcome space-time barriers.

Furthermore, the action research findings show that there is a number of issues regarding the utilization of Microsoft Teams digital environment to improve the ways teachers are trained and supported by the EWCs that concern the action research participants (EWCs, school principals and teachers), such as: a) the hesitation or reluctance of some teachers, b) teacher's skills, attitude and degree of familiarity with the platform, c) the negative attitude of some education officers -including EWCs in some cases, d) the absence of legal provisions concerning the time context of teachers' training and support in secondary education and -subsequently- the obstacles this lack poses and e) the security of personal data and the possibility of using data on the daily use of Microsoft Teams digital environment for the evaluation process of teachers.

These issues, as presented in points a, b and c in the previous paragraph, are related to the findings of a study by Pavlis-Korres (2017), which concluded that learners' and trainers' ability to interact with the digital environment's interface is perceived as important, because it affects other types of interaction such as learner-content interaction and the interaction between users of the digital environment. In the same study it is pointed out that, in adult education programs, it is important to take into account the degree of educators' and learners' familiarity with digital technologies, and to ensure there is ample time to get learners acquainted with the digital environment and its use. The age of those involved is an important factor, as -according to Prensky (2001)- younger people are more familiar with advanced internet technologies, are natural speakers of the "digital" and "internet" language and are thus perceived as "digital natives", while older people are perceived as "digital immigrants" in the digital world.

Third Research Question

"... many steps have been taken; research interest has been expressed by some EWCs; the idea that we should move on to distant support ... this is required, given the fact that some schools and teachers are dispersed in remote locations ..." (interviewee 3)

Regarding the third research question, the results of the action research show that the Peloponnese REPC has taken several steps to enable and support EWCs in the utilization of Microsoft Teams for the improvement of teachers' training and educational work support. The acceptance and support of this action research, EWCs' internal training in order to become familiar with Microsoft Teams digital environment's functions and use, and the academic license acquisition for Microsoft Teams are the main steps in this direction.

The main themes regarding the specific steps the Peloponnese REPC should take, as these emerged though the thematic analysis, were: a) providing training to EWCs in the management of teachers' training and support issues through the utilization of Microsoft Teams digital collaboration and communication environment, b) providing training to EWCs in adult education issues, c) staffing the Peloponnese REPC with digital technologies support experts, d) supplying technological equipment and appropriately distributing it to Peloponnese REPC's offices and e) further encouraging EWCs to utilize Microsoft Teams for the improvement of teachers' training and educational work support, given that, at the time the research was carried out, epidemiologists underlined that covid-19 pandemic's second wave was "knocking at the door". The excerpts quoted below are suggestive of the views expressed:

"...I believe that the Peloponnese REPC should significantly help the education of EWCs and the teachers through seminars on ICTs. For the EWCs in particular the knowledge of adult education principles is a mandatory prerequisite..." (interviewee 12)

"...the EWCs should be encouraged towards generalized and systematic use of Microsoft Teams for teachers' support and training..." (interviewee 13)

The themes which emerged from the answers to the third research question are in line with the international discussion and concern on how the education responds to the covid 19 pandemic, including the creation of mechanisms for the professional development of teachers and online learning strategies that foster teacher collaboration and support (Reimers & Schleicher, 2020; Huang et al., 2020; OECD, 2020; Safi, Wenzel & Trimble Spalding, 2020).

FUTURE RESEARCH DIRECTIONS

Given that the aim of this action research was not to generalize results but to investigate a specific educational situation in depth and to improve the quality of the actions performed in the context of this situation (Cohen et al., 2000; Creswell, 2015), future research should expand the investigation of how a digital collaboration and communication environment, such as Microsoft Teams, can be utilized in other formal or non-formal educational contexts, such as primary, secondary, post-secondary or adult education, in order to create and support a learning and/or practice community that promotes communication, reflection and collaborative action between education practitioners and -at the same time- acts as a catalyst to improve their performance, and professional development.

CONCLUSION

This research study has provided insights into the utilization of a digital collaboration and communication environment to improve the ways teachers are trained and supported by EWCs. Results suggest that the evolution in the field of internet technologies and the spectacular acceptance of the worldwide web have formed a totally new framework not only for teachers' training but also for their distant support, and they have given rise to a wide range of infrastructures, services and tools that enable direct communication, interaction, collaborative action and exchange of information between EWCs and teachers, and facilitate teachers' personal and professional development, by assisting them in effectively implementing curricula and improving their teaching practices, learning outcomes and educational work.

The action research was conducted in Peloponnese REPC, Greece, and it explored EWCs', school principals' and teachers' views, perceptions, experiences and personal stories on key issues regarding the utilization of Microsoft Teams digital collaboration and communication environment for teachers' training and educational work support in circumstances requiring distance teachers' training and support, as is the case with the covid-19 pandemic.

According to the results of the action research, there is strong evidence that Microsoft Teams digital collaboration and communication environment can contribute to the improvement of teachers' training and educational work support by EWCs in many ways, such as by providing flexibility in the organization of teachers' distance training, by fostering communication immediacy, by offering educational resources and facilitating practice sharing, by overcoming obstacles posed by the physical distance and other factors, by encouraging participation, interaction and collaboration, and -finally- by providing autonomy and flexibility in terms of time, place and pace, especially for schools that are dispersed in different or inaccessible regional units, or when circumstances require distance teachers' training and support, as is the case with the covid-19 pandemic.

As per our findings, Microsoft Teams has been utilized to improve the ways teachers are trained and supported by EWCs, especially with regard to the implementation of teachers' distance training program for the development of synchronous and asynchronous communication, interaction and collaboration between EWCs, school principals and teachers through the use of the meetings tool, for sharing educational resources, ideas and practices, and for supporting many aspects of teachers' and school principals' educational work in an innovative, productive and efficient way since the outbreak of the covid-19 pandemic.

Furthermore, participants in the action research pointed out that policy makers and the Peloponnese REPC should take specific steps in order to assist EWCs in utilizing a digital collaboration and communication environment such as Microsoft Teams, for teachers' training and educational work support, given that, at the time the research was carried out, epidemiologists underlined that covid-19 pandemic's second wave was "knocking at the door".

REFERENCES

Alemdag, E., & Erdem, M. (2017). Designing an e-mentoring program for novice teachers in Turkey and investigating online interactions and program outcomes. *Mentoring & Tutoring*, *25*(2), 1–28. doi:10.1080/13611267.2017.1327394

Allan, B., Hunter, B., & Lewis, D. (2006). Four years on: a longitudinal study assessing the impact of membership of a virtual community of practice. In *Fifth International Conference on Networked Learning*. Lancaster University.

Altrichter, H., Feldman, A., Posch, P., & Somekh, B. (2008). *Teachers investigate their work; An introduction an action research across the professions* (2nd ed.). Routledge.

Beetham, H. (2004). *Review: developing e-learning models for the JISC practitioner communities: A report for the JISC e-pedagogy programme*. Joint Information Systems Committee (JISC).

Beetham, H., & Sharpe, P. (2007). *Rethinking Pedagogy for a Digital Age: Designing and delivering e-learning*. Routledge. doi:10.4324/9780203961681

Benke, I. (2019). Social Augmentation of Enterprise Communication Systems for Virtual Teams using Chatbots. *Proceedings of 17th European Conference on Computer-Supported Cooperative Work - Doctoral Colloquium. Reports of the European Society for Socially Embedded Technologies, 2*(3).

Bermejo, S. (2005). Cooperative electronic learning in virtual laboratories through forums. *IEEE Transactions on Education, 48*(1), 140–149. doi:10.1109/TE.2004.837045

Bonk, C., & Zhang, K. (2006). Introducing the R2D2 model: Online learning for the diverse learners of this world. *Distance Education, 27*(2), 249–264. doi:10.1080/01587910600789670

Borko, H. (2004). Professional development and teacher learning: Mapping the terrain. *Educational Researcher, 33*(8), 3–15. doi:10.3102/0013189X033008003

Braun, V., & Clarke, V. (2012). Thematic analysis. In H. Cooper, P. M. Camic, D. L. Long, A. T. Panter, D. Rindskopf & K. J. Sher (Eds), APA Hand- book of Research Methods in Psychology, Vol. 2: Research Designs: quantitative, qualitative, neuropsychological and biological (pp. 57-71). Washington, DC: American Psychological Association. doi:10.1037/13620-004

Broadbent, B. (2002). *ABCs of e-learning: Reaping the benefits and avoiding the pitfalls*. Jossey-Bass.

Brookfield, S. D. (1986). *Understanding and Facilitating Adult Learning*. Jossey-Bass.

Brooks, C. F. (2010). Toward 'hybridized' faculty development for the twenty-first century: Blending online communities of practice and face-to-face Meetings in instructional and professional support programmes. *Innovations in Education and Teaching International, 47*(3), 261–270. doi:10.1080/14703297.2010.498177

Buchal, R., & Songsore, E. (2019). Using Microsoft Teams to support collaborative knowledge building in the context of sustainability assessment. *Proceedings of the Canadian Engineering Education Association (CEEA-ACEG) Conference*.

Burns, M. (2011). *Distance Education for Teacher Training: Modes, Models, and Methods*. Education Development Center.

CEDEFOP. (2014). *Terminology of European education and training policy. A selection of 130 key terms* (2nd ed.). Retrieved from: http://www.cedefop.europa.eu/ en/publications-and-resources/publications/4117

Chen, T. F. (2016). E-learning 3.0: Technologies, applications, benefits, trends and challenge. In S. Kadry & A. El Hami (Eds.), E-Systems for the 21st Century: Concept, Developments, and Applications - Volume 2: E-Learning, E-Maintenance, E-Portfolio, E-System, and E-Voting (pp. 105-176). New York: Apple Academic Press.

Clark, R., & Mayer, R. (2003). e-Learning and the Science of Instruction. San Francisco CA: Jossey-Bass/Pfeiffer.

Cohen, L., Manion, L., & Morrison, K. (2000). *Research Methods in Education* (5th ed.). Routledge Falmer.

Creswell, J. W. (2015). *Educational Research: Planning, Conducting, and Evaluating Quantitative and Qualitative Research*. Pearson.

Daniel, S. J. (2020). Education and the COVID-19 pandemic. *Prospects, 49*(1-2), 91–96. doi:10.100711125-020-09464-3 PMID:32313309

Darling-Hammond, L., Wei, R. C., Andree, L. A., Richardson, N., & Orphanos, S. (2009). *Professional learning in the learning profession: A status report on teacher development in the US and abroad*. National Staff Development Council.

De Janasz, S. C., & Godshalk, V. M. (2013). The role of e-mentoring in proteges' learning and satisfaction. *Group & Organization Management, 38*(6), 743–774. doi:10.1177/1059601113511296

Denzin, N. K. (1989). *The Research Act: A theoretical Introduction to Sociological Methods*. Prentice-Hall.

Diaz, L. A., & Entonado, F. B. (2009). Are the functions of teachers in e-learning and face-to-face learning environments really different? *Journal of Educational Technology & Society, 12*(4), 331–343.

Ellis, R. A., Ginns, P., & Piggott, L. (2009). E-learning in higher education: Some key aspects and their relationship to approaches to study. *Higher Education Research & Development, 28*(3), 303–318. doi:10.1080/07294360902839909

Er, E., Ozden, M., & Arifoglu, A. (2009). A blended e-learning environment: A model proposition for integration of asynchronous and synchronous e-learning. *International Journal of Learning, 16*(2), 449.

Fullan, M., & Hargreaves, A. (1992). Teacher development and educational change. In M. Fullan & A. Hargreaves (Eds.), *Teacher Development and Educational Change* (pp. 1–9). Falmer Press.

Fullan, M. G. (1991). *The new meaning of educational change* (2nd ed.). Teachers College Press.

Fullan, M. G. (1995). The limits and the potential of professional development. In T. R. Guskey & M. Huberman (Eds.), *Professional development in education: New paradigms and practices* (pp. 253–267). Teachers College Press.

Garrison, D. R., & Kanuka, H. (2004). Blended learning: Uncovering its transformative potential in higher education. *The Internet and Higher Education, 7*(2), 95–105. doi:10.1016/j.iheduc.2004.02.001

Glazer, E. M., & Hannafin, M. J. (2006). The collaborative apprenticeship model: Situated professional development within school settings. *Teaching and Teacher Education, 22*(2), 179–193. doi:10.1016/j.tate.2005.09.004

Gonella, L., & Panto, E. (2008). Didactic architectures and organization models. *eLearning Papers*. Retrieved from: https://www.researchgate.net/publication/28264179_Didactic_architectures_and_organization_models_a_process_of_mutual_adaptation

Grundy, S. (1987). *Curriculum: Product or Praxis?* The Falmer Press.

Grundy, S., & Kemmis, S. (1988). Educational Action Research in Australia: The state of the art (an overview). In St. Kemmis & R. McTaggart (Eds.), *The Action Research Planner* (pp. 321–335). Deakin University Press.

Harris, J., Mishra, P., & Koehler, M. (2009). Teachers' technological pedagogical content knowledge and learning activity types: Curriculum-based technology integration reframed. *Journal of Research on Technology in Education, 41*(4), 393–416. doi:10.1080/15391523.2009.10782536

Horton, W. (2001). *Leading e-Learning*. American Society for Training and Development.

Horton, W., & Horton, K. (2003). *E-learning tools and Technologies: A consumer's guide for trainers, teachers, educators, and instructional designers*. Wiley Publishing.

Hou, H. T., Chang, K. E., & Chang, Y. T. (2010). What kinds of knowledge do teachers share on blogs? A quantitative content analysis of teachers' knowledge sharing on blogs. *British Journal of Educational Technology, 41*(6), 963–967. doi:10.1111/j.1467-8535.2009.01040.x

Hrastinski, S. (2008). Asynchronous & synchronous e-learning. *EDUCAUSE Quarterly, 31*(4), 51–55.

Huang, R. H., Liu, D. J., Tlili, A., Yang, J. F., & Wang, H. H. (2020). *Handbook on Facilitating Flexible Learning During Educational Disruption: The Chinese Experience in Maintaining Undisrupted Learning in COVID-19 Outbreak*. Smart Learning Institute of Beijing Normal University.

Hubbard, M., & Bailey, M. J. (2018). *Mastering Microsoft Teams: End User Guide to Practical Usage, Collaboration, and Governance*. Apress. doi:10.1007/978-1-4842-3670-3

Hutchison, A., & Colwell, J. (2012). Using a wiki to facilitate an online professional learning community for induction and mentoring teachers. *Education and Information Technologies, 17*(3), 273–289. doi:10.100710639-011-9159-7

Ilag, B. N. (2018). *Introducing Microsoft Teams: Understanding the New Chat-Based Workspace in Office 365*. Apress. doi:10.1007/978-1-4842-3567-6

Jackson, C., & Keirstead, C. (2020). *Schools' first and forever responders: Preparing and supporting teachers in the time of COVID-19*. National Comprehensive Center at Westat.

Kirschner, P., & Paas, F. (2001). Web-enhanced higher education: A Tower of Babel. *Computers in Human Behavior, 17*(4), 347–354. doi:10.1016/S0747-5632(01)00009-7

Knowles, M. (1998). *The Adult Learner: The Definitive Classic in Adult Education and Human Resource Development*. Gulf Publishing Company.

Knox, A. B. (1977). *Adult development and learning*. Jossey-Bass.

Koper, R. (2004). Learning technologies: an integrated domain model. In *W. Jochems, J. Van Merrienboer & R. Koper, Integrated eLearning: Implications for Pedagogy, Technology and Organization* (pp. 64–79). Routledge.

Koper, R., & Olivier, B. (2004). Representing the learning design of units of learning. *Journal of Educational Technology & Society*, *7*(3), 97–111.

Lansmann, S., Schallenmuller, S., & Rigby, M. (2019). Teams Everywhere - Investigating the Impact of Microsoft Teams on Knowledge Worker. *Proceedings of the Pre-ICIS 2019, 8th International Workshop on The Changing Nature of Work.*

Li, F. W., Lau, R. W., & Dharmendran, P. (2009). A three-tier pro ling framework for adaptive e-learning. *Proceedings of the 8th International Conference on Advances in Web Based Learning*, 235-244.

Liao, H. L., & Lu, H. P. (2008). Richness Versus Parsimony Antecedents of Technology Adoption Model for E-Learning Websites. In F. Li, J. Zhao, T. K. Shih, R. Lau, Q. Li, D. McLeod (Eds.), Advances in Web Based Learning - ICWL 2008. ICWL 2008. Lecture Notes in Computer Science, (vol. 5145). Berlin: Springer.

Liu, H., Macintyre, R., & Ferguson, R. (2012). Exploring qualitative analytics for e-mentoring relationships building in an online social learning environment. In *Proceedings of the 2nd International Conference on Learning Analytics and Knowledge* (pp. 179-183). ACM. 10.1145/2330601.2330646

Martin, L., & Tapp, D. (2019). Teaching with Teams: An introduction to teaching an undergraduate law module using Microsoft Teams. *Innovative Practice in Higher Education*, *3*(3), 58–66.

Masie, E. (2001). *E-Learning: If we Build It, Will They Come?* American Society for Training and Development.

Mason, R., & Rennie, F. (2006). *Elearning: The Key Concepts*. Routledge. doi:10.4324/9780203099483

Mazzola, C. (2019). *Microsoft Teams as Digital Community of Practice in Higher Education?* Retrieved from: https://www.researchgate.net/publi-cation/333451072

McLaughlin, M. W., & Talbert, J. (2006). *Building school-based teacher learning communities: Professional strategies to improve student achievement*. Teachers College Press.

McLoughlin, C., Brady, J., Lee, M. J., & Russell, R. (2007). *Peer-to-peer: An e-mentoring approach to developing community, mutual engagement and professional identity for pre-service teachers*. Australian Association for Research in Education (AARE) Conference, Fremantle, Australia.

Mills, G. E. (2011). *Action research: a guide for the teacher researcher* (4th ed.). Pearson/Allyn & Bacon.

Moore, M. G. (1983). On a theory of independent study. In D. Sewart, D. Keegan, & B. Holmberg (Eds.), *Distance education: International perspectives* (pp. 68–94). Croom Helm, St. Martin's Press.

Moore, M. G., & Diehl, W. (2019). *Handbook of Distance Education*. Routledge.

Moore, M. G., & Kearsley, G. (2012). *Distance education: A systems view of online learning* (3rd ed.). Wadsworth Cengage Learning.

OECD. (2020). *Teachers' training and use of information and communications technology in the face of the COVID-19 crisis. Teaching in Focus, No. 35*. OECD Publishing. doi:10.1787/696e0661-

Owen, H. (2014). Putting the PLE into PLD: Virtual Professional Learning and Development. *Journal of Educators Online, 11*(2). Advance online publication. doi:10.9743/JEO.2014.2.1

Pavlis-Korres, M. (2017). The Positive Effect of Evaluation on Improving E-learning Courses Addressed to Adults: A Case Study on the Evolution of the GSLLLY Courses in Greece over a Decade. *Journal of Education and Training Studies, 5*(1), 1-11. doi:10.11114/jets.v5i1.1940

Pavlis-Korres, M., Karalis, T., Leftheriotou, P., & Garcia Barriocanal, E. (2009). Integrating adults' characteristics and the requirements for their effective learning in an e-learning environment. In M. D. Lytras, P. Ordonez de Pablos, E. Damiani, D. Avison, A. Naeve, & D. G. Horner (Eds.), *Best practices for the knowledge society. Knowledge, learning, development and technology for all. WSKS 2009* (pp. 570–584). Springer. doi:10.1007/978-3-642-04757-2_61

Pavlis-Korres, M., & Leftheriotou, P. (2016). Building interaction in adults' online courses: A case study on training e-educators of adults. In L. Kyei-Blankson, J. Blankson, E. Ntuli, & C. Agyeman (Eds.), *Handbook of research on strategic management of interaction, presence and participation in online courses* (pp. 185–215). IGI Global. doi:10.4018/978-1-4666-9582-5.ch008

Perraton, H. (1988). A theory for distance education. In D. Sewart, D. Keegan, & B. Holmberg (Eds.), *Distance education: International perspectives* (pp. 34–45). Routledge Press.

Perraton, H. (Ed.). (1993). *Distance education for teacher training*. Routledge Press. doi:10.4324/9780203304075

Prensky, M. (2001). Digital Natives, Digital Immigrants Part 1. *On the Horizon, 9*(5), 1–6. doi:10.1108/10748120110424816

Reimers, F. M., & Schleicher, A. (2020). *A framework to guide an education response to the COVID-19 Pandemic of 2020*. The Harvard Graduate School of Education, OECD.

Rogers, R. R. (2001). Reflection in Higher Education: A Concept Analysis. *Innovative Higher Education, 26*(1), 37–57. doi:10.1023/A:1010986404527

Rosenberg, M. (2001). *E-learning: strategies for delivering knowledge in the digital age*. McGraw-Hill.

Rupesh Kumar, A. (2009). E-Learning 2.0: Learning Redefined. *Library Philosophy and Practice (e-journal)*. Retrieved from: https://digitalcommons.unl.edu/libphilprac/284/

Saba, F. (2005). Is distance education losing its identity? Or what should our field be called these days? *XXth Annual Conference on Distance Teaching and Learning*.

Saba, F., & Shearer, R. L. (1994). Verifying key theoretical concepts in a dynamic model of distance education. *American Journal of Distance Education, 8*(1), 36–59. doi:10.1080/08923649409526844

Safi, F., Wenzel, T., & Trimble Spalding, L. A. (2020). Remote Learning Community: Supporting Teacher Educators During Unprecedented Times. *Journal of Technology and Teacher Education, 28*(2), 211–222.

Sanders, K. (2001). *Fast Path to Success with Centra*. Centra.

Sangra, A., Vlachopoulos, D., & Cabrera, N. (2012). Building an inclusive definition of elearning: An approach to the conceptual framework. *International Review of Research in Open and Distance Learning, 13*(2), 145–159. doi:10.19173/irrodl.v13i2.1161

Sankey, M., Campbell, C., & Poulsen, S. (2019). The semi-formal benchmarking of TEL practice: Helping the TEL community get its act together. In Y. W. Chew, K. M. Chan & A. Alphonso (Eds.), Personalized Learning. Diverse Goals. One Heart. ASCILITE 2019 Singapore (pp. 541-545). ASCILITE.

Selwyn, N. (2014). The Internet and Education. In Y. Benkler (Ed.), *Change: 19 Key Essays on How the Internet Is Changing Our Lives*. Turner Publicaciones.

Sewart, D., Keegan, D., & Holmberg, B. (Eds.). (1988). *Distance education: International perspective*. Routledge.

Simonson, M., Schlosser, C., & Orellana, A. (2011). Distance education research: A review of the literature. *Journal of Computing in Higher Education, 23*(2), 124–142. doi:10.100712528-011-9045-8

Simonson, M., Smaldino, S., Albright, M., & Zvacek, S. (2012). *Teaching and learning at a distance: Foundations of distance education* (5th ed.). Pearson.

Simonson, M., Smaldino, S., & Zvacek, S. (Eds.). (2015). *Teaching and learning at a distance: Foundations of distance education* (6th ed.). Information Age.

Smith, C., & Gillespie, M. (2007). Research on professional development and teacher change: implications for adult basic education. In J. Comings, B. Garner & C. Smith (Eds.), Review of Adult Learning and Literacy, Volume 7: Connecting Research, Policy and Practice (pp. 205-245). Lawrence Erlbaum Associates.

Stringer, E. T. (2013). *Action research* (4th ed.). Sage Publications.

Timperley, H. (2008). *Teacher professional learning and development*. International Academy of Education.

Trust, T. (2015). Deconstructing an online community of practice: Teachers' actions in the edmodo math subject community. *Journal of Digital Learning in Teacher Education, 31*(2), 73–81. doi:10.1080/21532974.2015.1011293

Trust, T., & Horrocks, B. (2017). I never feel alone in my classroom: Teacher professional growth within a blended community of practice. *Professional Development in Education, 43*(4), 645–665. doi:10.1080/19415257.2016.1233507

Urdan, T. A., & Weggen, C. C. (2000). *Corporate e-learning: Exploring a new frontier*. WR Hambrecht.

Van Dam, N. (2005). *The Business Impact of e-Learning* (PhD Thesis). Nyenrode Business University.

Vaughan, N., & Garrison, D. R. (2006). How blended learning can support a faculty development community of inquiry. *Journal of Asynchronous Learning Networks, 10*(4), 139–152.

Webster-Wright, A. (2009). Reframing Professional Development through Understanding Authentic Professional Learning. *Review of Educational Research, 79*(2), 702–739. doi:10.3102/0034654308330970

Wei R. C., Andree, A., & Darling-Hammond, L. (2009). How nations invest in teachers. *Educational Leadership: Journal of the Department of Supervision and Curriculum Development, 66*(5), 28-33.

Wenger, E., McDermott, R., & Snyder, W. (2002). *Cultivating Communities of Practice*. Harvard Business School Press.

Whitcomb, J., Borko, H., & Liston, D. (2009). Growing talent promising professional development models and practices. *Journal of Teacher Education, 60*(3), 207–212. doi:10.1177/0022487109337280

Wilbanks, J. E. (2014). E-mentoring: Examining the feasibility of electronic, online, or distance mentoring. *Journal of Higher Education Theory and Practice, 14*(5), 24.

Williams, E. (1996). *So... you want to teach adults*. Pippin Publishing Corporation.

Willig, C. (2013). *Introducing qualitative research in psychology: Adventures in theory and method* (3rd ed.). McGraw-Hill Education.

KEY TERMS AND DEFINITIONS

Advanced Internet Technologies: Digital technologies that use a system of interconnected computer networks to form a global communication and information exchange network.

Digital Collaboration and Communication Environment: A digital environment that integrates a set of communication and collaboration tools, services and applications that utilize advanced internet technologies in a flexible and also efficient way with a coherent workspace and is accessible through worldwide web.

Educational Action Research: A research design that enables members of a school community or an educational organization to approach and investigate their practices regarding a specific educational issue or problem from an inner perspective, following a process of reflective communication and collaborative action.

Electronic Learning: Is the learning for the individual aspects of which -achievement, extension, support, management, and assessment-interconnected computer systems (via internet, intranets, or other types of networks) that provide appropriately designed learning experiences to individual learners or group of learners, play a major role.

Microsoft Teams: A digital hub that provides a unified communication, interaction, collaboration and support workspace and is accessible through the worldwide web.

Teachers' Distance Training and Support: A training and support process in which teachers and their trainers -for most of the process- are not in the same room. The fact that trainees are not on the same premises as teachers is a core issue, not only due to the physical distance created between trainers and trainees, but also because of its strong impact on interpersonal interactions and the results of the entire educational process.

Chapter 12
Role of Learning Technology Strategies Among People With Disabilities:
A Job Opportunities Barrier

Heru Susanto
https://orcid.org/0000-0002-1823-357X
University of Technology Brunei, Brunei & The Indonesian Institute of Sciences, Indonesia

Hamizah Hamid
University of Technology Brunei, Brunei

Fadzliwati Mohiddin
https://orcid.org/0000-0002-7332-209X
University of Technology Brunei, Brunei

Desi Setiana
The Southern Jakarta Correctional Center, Ministry of Law and Human Right, Indonesia & University of Brunei Darussalam, Brunei

ABSTRACT

Unemployment is the main problem within many countries, and it has been increasing in the past few years especially during pandemic COVID-19, not only concerning for fresh graduates but also for people with disabilities. This study is made to understand the factors leading to job opportunities among people with disabilities, which are education, training, job placement, and internship. The study also aims to find challenges and barriers to job opportunity among people with disabilities. It aims to create awareness regarding people with disabilities to be accepted in the society as differently abled persons with specialties. The study findings shows that there is correlation between education, training, job placement, and internship for both hiring and non-hiring companies. To conclude, research findings show that training and work placement experience are factors of job opportunity for people with disabilities. The main challenges or barriers are communication, attitudes, and perceptions of co-workers towards employees with disabilities.

DOI: 10.4018/978-1-7998-7184-2.ch012

INTRODUCTION

To be employed implies to participate in an occupation, a collaboration of working partner with others and a working identity. Individuals wanted to be acknowledged by others that in their own eyes and the eyes of others what they do is important. These aspects are perhaps much more important for people with disabilities, particularly when these individuals become a disadvantaged community in existing high demands for employment, accessibility and productivity (Baker & Jacobs, 2003, pp. 53 – 61). Person with disabilities do have a special place in the society as a motivation for all for their strength and courage as well as for their valuable contribution to the development of a dynamic, compassionate and inclusive society without racial discrimination ("Asia & the Pacific", 2019). Government of Brunei Darussalam, through various agencies has been endlessly taking care of the welfare of individuals with different needs in other words people with disabilities (PWD) by maintaining through the provision of an unlimited and inclusive healthcare support facilities, integrated education system, better allocation of financial aid scheme, participation of different investors for the development of infrastructure and facilities that are friendly to people with disabilities (Hazair, 2018). Throughout the on-going commitment and succeeding the pledge, it has been arranged by the government of Brunei in organising an action plan for people with disabilities in addressing the issues related to people with disabilities, the former Minister of Culture, Youth and Sport announced at the opening ceremony of the 2016 International Day of PWD, "It is a policy document compromising concrete measures that need to be adopted by different organisations, departments and ministries who are members of the National Social Issues Council Special Committee. It is a platform for addressing issues of special needs through approaches from the entire government and society as a whole". The former minister also expressed appreciation for the active participation of the organisations of the special needs in the country who work together alongside with the government of Brunei in increasing awareness and the standard of living of the special and unique people in particular by providing them the chance to participate in the society (Hazair, 2018).

Brunei Darussalam Profile

Brunei Darussalam, it is a nation that is located on the Borneo island which consists of four districts namely Brunei-Muara, Tutong, Kuala Belait and Temburong. The easiest way to reach Brunei is by air, land and sea (Figure 1). Brunei Darussalam is positioned at 13th out of 42 Asia-Pacific countries and ranked above the national and global averages with its country economic freedom rating score is 66.6 and their economy in 2020 index on the 61st at large (Figure 2).

Brunei Darussalam gross domestic product growth (GDP) percentage has been increasing since the year 2018 from 0.1% to 1.9% in 2020 ("OECD", 2019). The combined costs of products and services produced and imported equivalent to 93.9% of Brunei's GDP. As Brunei government continuously reducing its reliance to oil and gas exports, the economy remains open to foreign investment and the small financial area is led by banking industry ("OECD", 2019) (Figure 3).

With the comprehensive application of IT in Brunei, it allows the flow of knowledge for government, people and industries to become more transparent and better improvement as well as understanding of decision making ("The ASEAN post", 2018). Internet access in Brunei can be easily accessed in most cafes and restaurants and Brunei has been providing free hotspots at several buildings for people to access but within a time limit of one hour. According to the International Monetary Fund, in 2017 Brunei is one of the most stable nation in ASEAN with gross domestic product (GDP) per capita. Nevertheless,

Figure 1. Brunei Darussalam map (adapted obtained from Worldometer)

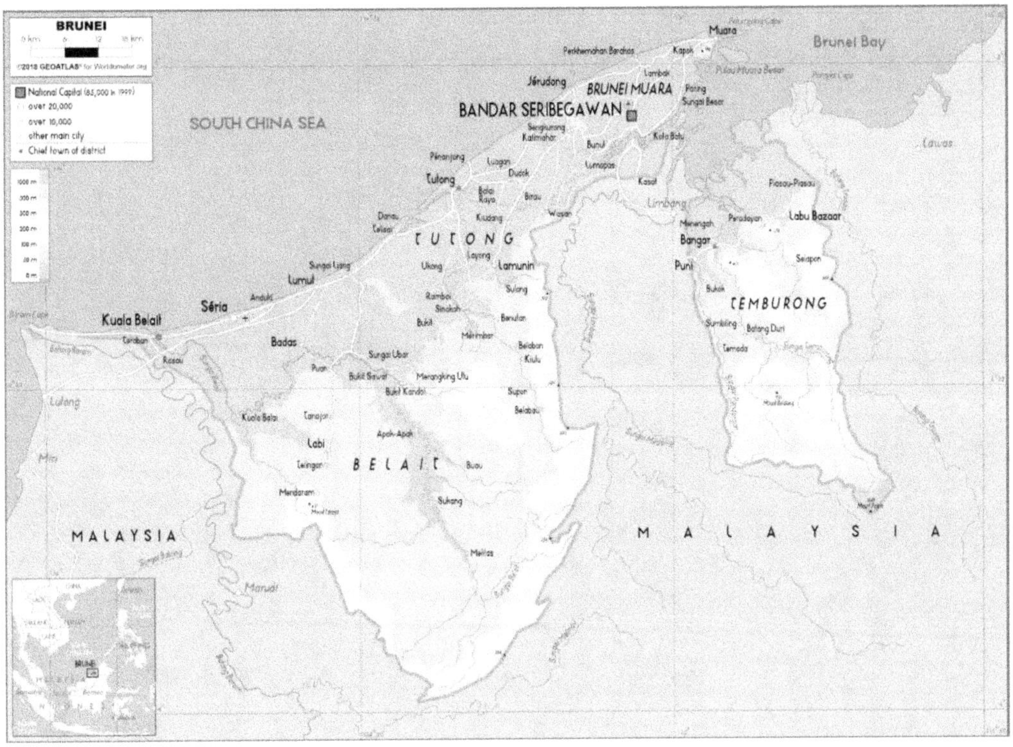

the revenue is unequally disseminated among its citizens, especially those with disabilities (PWDs), who are in risk of slipping through the breaks of the government policy (The ASEAN post", 2018).

During 14th Legislative Council meeting in March 2018, Haji Aminuddin Ihsan, Minister of Culture, Youth and Sports said that out of 9,282 PWD registered with the ministry and only 56 of them had jobs, representing PWD employment rate of just 0.6% ("The ASEAN post", 2018). If this is stated that unemployment for PWD, this figure is likely to be under report of actual PWD unemployment rate in Brunei, as many of people with disabilities are remain unregistered with the Job Centre. NGO in Brunei have been working hard in aiming to provide job opportunities for people with disabilities. The first bistro and café in the country with employing autistic adults, was open officially by Smarter Brunei back in December 2018. It was launched and opened on International Day of Disabled Persons and part of the café initiative in providing training for autism-supported adults on the job, the café is located at Sg. Hanching selling foods such as nasi katok, baked items and coffee beans imported from ASEAN countries.

It is a disappointment to see today's competitive labour market and increasing unemployment rate, it is challenging and virtually impossible to secure a job for disabled person (Rasidah, 2018). With adults autism graduating from their centre, Smarter has put in a career plan categorised into four categories: internships, shared work, encouraged work and open jobs with each group have specific roles and responsibilities. For individuals with open work needed less supervision and they can operate in all cafeterias areas, whereas students grouped under encouraged work who needs greater visual support and structure, but are still expected to perform kitchen and house task. Other task will be carried out by category fall under shared work such as labelling and wrapping paper bags, recycle products such as plastic bottles

Figure 2. Brunei index economic freedom score (obtained from The heritage foundation)

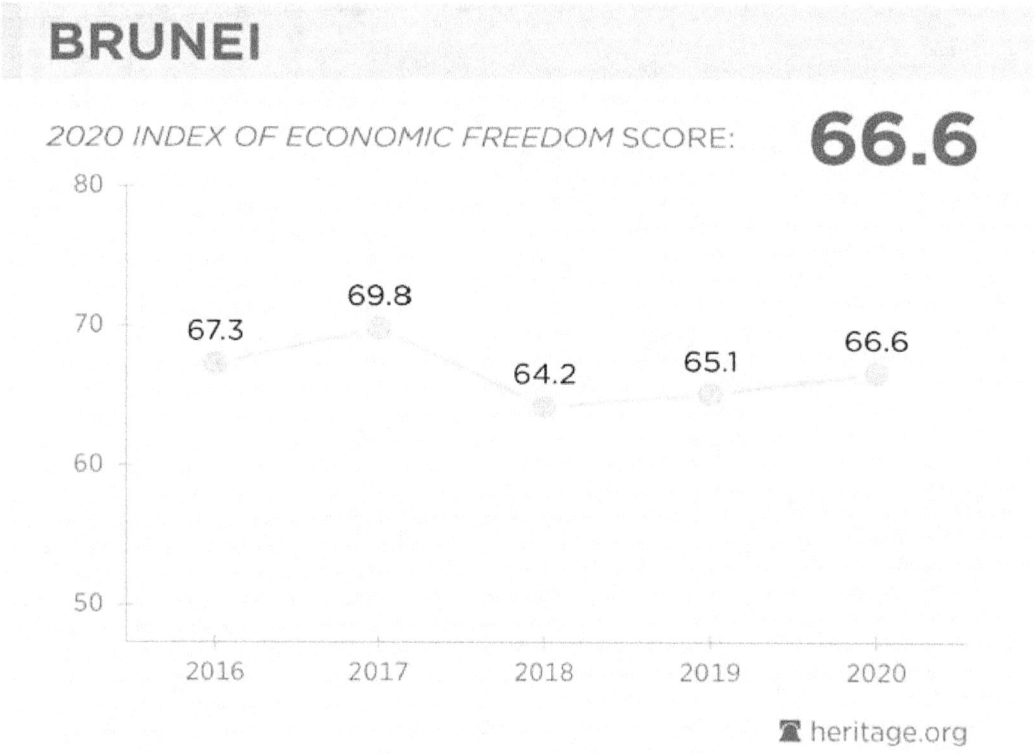

that need to be returned to the cupboards. The complexity of their work is not focused on one target this is due to avoiding students from any job stress.

Research Aims

The aims of this research is to identify the factors of employer perceptions relating to job opportunities for PWD. To identify the issues and challenges or barriers which hinders the job opportunities in Brunei Darussalam focusing on PWD. As well as to focus on what necessities needed for them to be ready in working life with the society, by taking into account the education and trainings provided. Another objective is to study the labour market for people with disabilities, to promote equal participation in the workplace same as non-disable workers. To look for opportunities that can be fit in by people with disabilities in the job sector, on how do they apply for job and the criteria a company or organisation take into account before hiring PWD.

Significant of the study

The significant of the study is to increase awareness on the right of PWD that they should be accepted in the society, given equal rights as same as the normal people so that they do not feel left out because of the different ability that they have. It is not they are fully incapable of doing the job but they have their

Figure 3. Brunei GDP growth rates adapted from OECD. (2019). Economic Outlook for Southeast Asia, China and India 2019 – Update: Responding to Environmental Hazards in Cities. OECD Publishing, Paris.

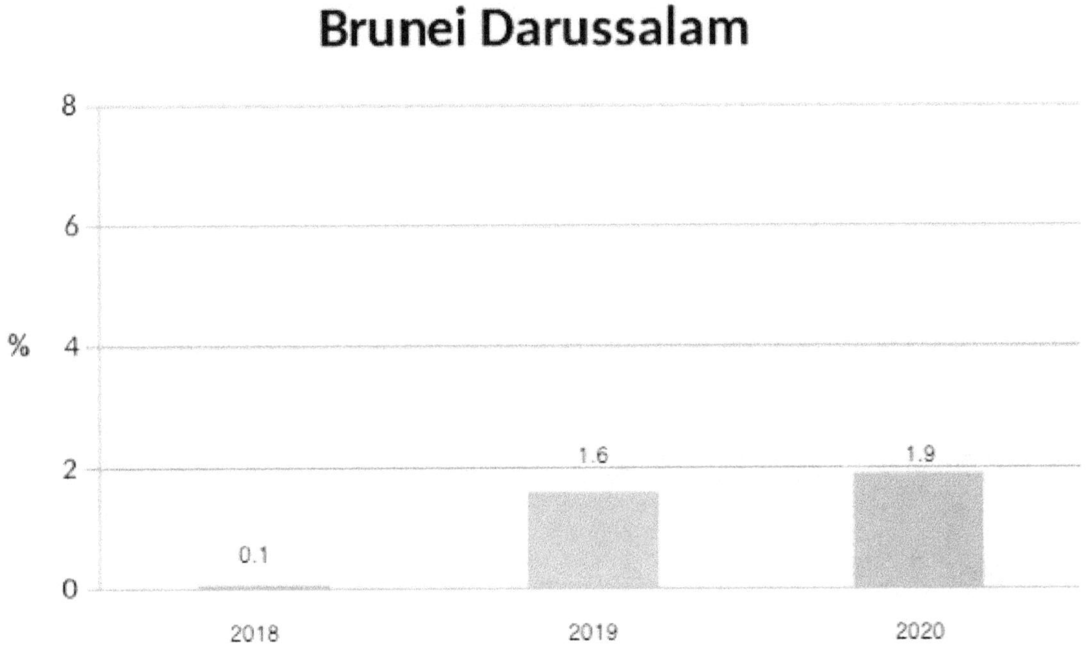

own specialty in a different interpretations. This research is to change public attitudes towards people with disabilities, in support to the society which PWD can have the rights to be employed and having the opportunity to full-fill their potential capabilities. Because, some may believe that people with disabilities may not be able to do works like normal people and the perceptions towards people with disabilities are always negative. Thus, to change the negative perceptions, this research will help to reach out the society especially the employers that people with disability have their own strength or speciality in terms of completing their task or job. This research is to help PWD to focus on the necessities needed and finding the best fit for them to be ready towards future employment. Disabled people need to be equipped with knowledge and skills that might enabled them to be enrolled or employed to the vacancy advertised. To accomplish Brunei Masterplan 2025 which to empower PWD, Brunei has joined the ASEAN Member States in supporting the implementation of ASEAN Enabling Masterplan 2025: Integrating the Rights of PWD, one of the documents to be adopted by the ASEAN Heads of State or Government at the forth-coming 33rd ASEAN Summit. The master plan aims to enable differently abled person in the areas of sport, recreation, cultural events, quality health care, easy information access, universal quality education access, equal access to sustainable growth, more comprehensive disability and disaster-resilient climate. It is stressed by the minister that by empowering the master plan it mirrors the ASEAN people as being caring, sharing community, trustworthy and empathic to the society. Four key goals that the minister outlined that can be discussed in adding value to the implementation of the plan are:

- Smart implementation through 'ASEAN-wide' method by aligning existing national visions and action strategy while addressing gaps and working together with stakeholders
- Integrated authorization through broader opportunities by opening up more programmes for PWD

- Showing the achievements and roles of people with disabilities in the creation of the respective ASEAN Member States and county-wide
- Enabling PWD to be heard collectively, in particular on their rights issues

Research Objectives

The objective of this research study is to understand the barrier that hinder in creating job opportunities for PWD in Brunei Darussalam which can be a challenge for disable person in obtaining a secure occupation for themselves. This is because people with disabilities need to be independent while blending in with the society to prove that they can also be an independent person despite the deficiency or special ability that they have. Another objective is to focus on the factors leading to hiring PWD where this factors is the reason in creating job opportunity for special or disabled person. By defining the factors, the study could have a better understanding of the scope of job market available in Brunei Darussalam for people with disabilities. In this research objective, the main factors of the research will focus on the education, training provided and the internship or work experience of the disabled people.

LITERATURE REVIEW

People with Disability

Up to 12% of the population is projected by the United Nations to be people with disabilities in Brunei in 2016, nevertheless, it is hard to come across clear and specific statistics on people with disabilities recruitment in ASEAN due to the lack of priority given to the problem by the governments ("The ASEAN post", 2018). Disability is a concept that encompasses impairments, behaviour disability is a challenge that a person faces in performing a task or an action, while involvement limitation is a problem that a person experiences while participating in life circumstances. Hence, disability is not only a healthiness problem. It is a complex phenomenon which reflects the interaction between the personality traits of a human body and the characteristics of the society where he or she lives, mentioned World Health Organisation ("World Health Organisation", 2018). PWD are a group that have different abilities, specialties and needs, they are not homogenous group and they also contributed to the community but in a different ways. In time of crisis, they may be vulnerable to judgement, mistreatment and violence while facing several barriers to accessing humanitarian assistance. They are an individual that has activity limitation and difficulty encountered in executing task or action, while participation restriction is a problem experienced by an individual involvement in life situation. There are many types of disabilities, three of them are; acquired disabilities, where this type of disabilities that the person is not born with; invisible disabilities, where their disability is not noticeable; and temporary disabilities, where the disability is expected to resolve over time, human resources categories of disabilities are:

Autism

Autism also known as autism spectrum disorder (ASD) which includes in difficulties with communications and behaviour ("Autism Spectrum Disorder: MedlinePlus", n.d.). People that is diagnosed with autism have difficulties in communicating and have trouble in understanding what other people think and feel ("Autism Spectrum Disorder: Communication Problems in Children", n.d.). Through the struggles that they encounter, it is hard for them to express themselves, either with speech, gestures, facial expressions and touch (Jeanne et al., 2019). People that is suspected with autism might have learning difficulty as their skills developed irregularly. For example; they could have hard time in communicating but be unusually good at art, music, mathematics which involves their memory, thus they might do well on test of analysis or problem solving.

Deaf

Deaf is characterised as the lack of functional hearing and is dependent on visual or auditory communication. Visual contact involves sign languages, reading the lips, interpreting speech as well as reading and writing. Whereas hearing aids and tools provide visual means of communication ("Definition of "Deaf" – Canadian Association of the Deaf, 2015).

Hearing Impairment

Hearing impairment which known as loss either partial or absolute hearing capacity. Hearing loss can occur in one or both of the ears to cause hearing impairments. As for people with the disability condition, it can cause difficulties in terms on social interaction at work, particularly children which can restrict their ability to learn spoken languages. Same as deaf people, hearing impairment also use hearing aids or devices to help them in hearing but not all devices can fully help them to hear fully (Thierry, 2016).

Specific Learning Disability

A specific learning disability, usually affects students with a disability to listen, think, speak, write, spell or do mathematical calculations. This can be known as a slow learner or sloe development disabilities, they may have struggles with writing, reading or calculating but when they are guided carefully from basic they slowly able to read and write even their level are not up to their age ("A Guide to Specific Learning Disabilities I Special Education Guide", n.d.).

Speech or Language Impairment

Speech and language impairments is a communication disorder such as stuttering, impaired articulation, a language impairment, or a voice impairment that harmfully affect a person performance to communicate with others ("Speech and Language Impairments Defined I Special Education Guide", n.d.). If they does not have sign language education which makes it difficult for them to communicate and lead to slow communications.

Visual Impairment (Including Blindness)

Visual impairment is when they have the capacity to see a degree that creates difficulties which cannot be overcome by the use of spectacles, visual impairment is also known as vision loss ("Vision impairment", 2015). Some may also include those who have a significantly lower viewing ability because they do not have access to eye-glasses or contact lenses where they can't help to improve their vision as well.

Job Opportunity

Job opportunity basically applies to students graduating from high school, college and universities where they decided to find job and be employed. It depends on the country on how many job opportunities provided that can fit to employ local people once they applied for the vacancy. Job opportunity does not only applies for those non-disable people who are actively seeking for a job, but also for those who are PWD. Although some of them might not know where is the appropriate channel to register and apply for a vacancy. Job opportunity arises when there is vacancy being adverted through newspapers, websites, social media for any job seekers to apply. It is an opportunity for those who are no longer interested to further their studies instead trying to look for a permanent job. Some nations use lower tax rates to incentivise the employment of people with disabilities. Corporation tax breaks could also provide incentives for companies that hire disabled individuals, as an incentive of job opportunity from the government which would likely to create job opportunities among people with disabilities ("ASEAN Today", 2018) But in Brunei, as a tax free country, the country does not levy any tax to individuals other than contributing 5% and 3.5% of their basic salary as part of the pension scheme to the state-manage provident fund.

Education for PWD

Education is one of the first steps to ensure that people with disabilities have the right to be treated equally among with non-disable people. As mention earlier not all of people with special needs are unable to learn certain things, it is because they have their own speciality that needed to be verbalised and by helping them with education may lead to their future success. Rozan (2012) said that equitable access is offered to everyone in education, including inclusive education without separating schools for special needs with qualified teachers and Centres of Excellence for specially disabled students who succeed in their studies through modes of inclusive schools ("The Daily Brunei Resources", 2012).

The special education unit has produced variety of programs throughout its objectives, including the learning assistance programme, the program for pre-professional training and the national skilled training programme. The program contributes to the development of special initiative education in the fields of literature, digitalization, communication, braille, sign languages, Islamic knowledge and morals, sports, crafts and aid technology ("Ministry of Education – Special Education Unit, 2018).

Trainings for PWD

Trainings for people with disabilities is one of the important role before they can be employed. This is to ensure that people with disabilities are fully equipped and ready to be hired and to fill in the vacancy. Trainings has been made efficient for people with disabilities, by using different methods to help them develop personal ways of accomplishing various tasks, in other words, from training they are able to do multitasking jobs with appropriate instructions. The results of training given can be seen through self-satisfaction and high self-esteem shown when those PWD got hired while developing specific skills that they acquired during training. Training can help PWD with more confidence with themselves, as well as to prepare them being independent without the help of family, guardian or their educators, altogether they are capable of accomplishing tasks on their own. The Community Development Department as well as non-governmental organisations (NGOs) in Brunei provide trainings and jobs, vocational skills training and work-related programmes ("The Daily Brunei Resources", 2012). It shows that there is increase in public awareness on the capabilities of people with disabilities being employed either in public and private sectors.

NGO of PWD

KACA Association

Kaca association is one of Brunei non-profit organisation established on the 27th October 1986 (Ref No: BPD 25/807). The organisation aims to increase the welfare of the disabled children in Brunei Darussalam who have not received any formal guidance and training. Kaca provides special mentoring and training programs for children to be self-reliant and able to continue their education in government primary schools, which is to achieve mainstream education. KACA currently has 3 branches, one in Brunei Muara, Tutong and Belait district. The main of the program adapted by KACA Centre in all districts is to provide a benchmark for all programs or activities to establish as a special training institute that will provide rehabilitation and education facilities based on the Early Development Program and Education (Special Education) from undergraduate level to pre-school (year 1 to year 6). KACA receives funding from private companies, charities and voluntary organisations locally and abroad as well as individuals. In addition to raising funds for KACA's, several activities such as walkathons, jogathons, charities were held from time to time. All KACA centres serve as centres of conferences, forums, seminars, courses, briefings and official events at regional and national levels, especially in areas related to the care and learning of disabled children. The establishment of KACA centre proves that KACA has strong social vision and commitment. KACA is able to identify and seize every opportunity to enhance the quality and image of the special education system which always has room for exploration through intellectual and mental creativity.

Smarter BACA

Smarter Brunei Autism Centre for Adults (BACA) is a G.I.F.T centre where the special children can be themselves and smarter Brunei also provide a S.A.F.E environment for individuals with autism to have an E.D.G.E to their P.A.T.H.S their L.I.F.E. Smarter Brunei is also a non-profit organisation operated by a support network for the family, particularly for autism-only parents and family members. Smarter Brunei seeks to work closely between parents, relatives, therapists and other practitioners to help children strengthen their ability to travel independently. Smarter currently has 2 centre located in Brunei Muara and Belait district. Smarter is an autism-oriented support group for children and adults, and is designed to help build awareness about autism. In order to create employment opportunities, smarter offer training services and skill-based training (CBT). Smarter also offers detailed information about autism at their resource and research centre. Smarter Brunei has met the international standards of (Autism Program Quality indicator, New York, 2001 and Colorado Autism Task Force, 2010). According to Debra Smith, Disability Studies Finders University South Australia, Smarter is a leading regional body which offers high qualiry services worldwide (6th February 2015). Smarter also obtained the highest scores in gold stars in all 14 areas of the A.P.Q.I (Autism Program Quality Indicator):

- Evaluation of individuals
- Development of the Individualised Education Program (IEP)

- Curriculum
- Instructional activities
- Instructional methods
- Instructional environments
- Performance analysis of development and outcome
- Commitment and support for the family
- Inclusion
- Planning the transfer from one location to another
- Challenging conduct
- Community partnership group
- Personnel
- Program assessment

Pusat Ehsan Al-Ameerah Al-Hajjah Maryam

Pusat Ehsan Al-Ameerah Al-Hajjah Maryam is a non-government organisation and charity that provides quality education, therapy and trainings for individuals with special needs. They have preparation and resources for the special needs in order to understand their social potential. The plan assists individuals with special needs for the acceptance and empowerment of society and for necessary interventions to accomplish the mission of the organisation. Pusat Ehsan vision is to allow group with special needs to experience productive social life. Whereas their mission is providing training, support and care for individuals with special needs to achieve their full approach in developing in the society. Pusat Ehsan supports all citizens who have special needs through school in providing education, training and physical rehabilitation. Pusat Ehsan understand that such individuals must me independent members of the society and that is necessary to carry out suitable activities to attain their mission. Pusat Ehsan believe that the network of family, caretakers, volunteers and the community can be implemented to achieve mission. Pusat Ehsan is very proud to introduce their students to the society. Their corporate dream is getting individual with special needs into functional society has been accomplished in various private areas such as food and beverages, hotels and banks. This initiative emphasizes and promotes the engagement of people with special needs.

Pusat Ehsan believes that it is important to include students into mainstream education, as several students who started to leave the centre are now in mainstream schools and more assistance is offered if required. For all therapy sessions, a therapeutic and psycho-social method is implemented by incorporating a medical technique. A patient centred approach is provided by Pusat Ehsan Physical Rehabilitation Unit. Both patients may have limitations on their activities and limits on their community involvement, cultural and family considerations are taken into account as requirement for the treatment. Pusat Ehsan aims to extend its operation to a wider scope and more number of people joining. The centre currently has over 190 students, trainees and patients. They estimated that in few years' time there will be an increase of four times after their master plan to accommodate the new service. The future Pusat Ehsan will have a high-quality infrastructure to accommodate individuals with disabilities.

Challenges and Barriers to Job Opportunities for PWD

People with disabilities have lower employment rates as mention earlier, this is because people with disabilities may face multiple challenges that led to difficulties in securing a job. Some challenges to employment opportunities for people with disabilities is employer misconception of the ability in hiring a person with disability.

Physical Barrier

Physical limitations can take the form of structural problems within the surroundings that hinder the function for disabilities, for example; the absence of a wheelchair ramp or elevator or no longer providing equipment that permits people with disability to perform in the position. Such as if a person has intense dyslexia or visual impairments, they need to be provided with a computer or aids that is capable of reading the display screen to them.

Attitudes and Stereotyping

Attitudes and stereotyping are perceptions regarding disabled people that can often discourage them from being employed or treated positively in the working environment. Such behaviour and stereotypes can be harmful, stigmatic and discriminatory this is due to a person might think that all their surroundings must be up to their expectation, however they might forget that some people may have speciality in expressing attitudes which create a negative or bad perception on people with disabilities. While this can be the problem and challenges it can be a factor to barrier in securing a job. For example; a person can be disregarded assets because the employer no longer believes that he or she has an unlawful disability.

Communication Challenges

Communication barriers can create a lack of ability to speak, write, study or recognise effectively what is needed in a job. There may be some examples such as:

- Inability to use a phone due to hearing problem
- The absence of braille printed objects
- Words are too technical for people with intellectual disabilities who are incompetent

By offering a large print version of manuals for people with vision problems and closed-listing videos which may help disabled people to get up and be competent while doing their work, for instance, should be taken into consideration of the obstacles of disabled workforces and steps should be taken to eliminate the impact. It is important that communication should not be a barrier for people with disabilities but society makes it difficult for them due to lack of awareness.

Technology Challenges

Technology have been one of the challenges faces by people with disability, one of it is the challenges in accessing the internet and applications which is mostly not user friendly to people with disability.

When accessing the internet people with visual impairment might find it difficult to access the internet or application if their device is not compatible to voice command. People with no motor skill will find it hard to use technology due to the screen in the application is too small for them to click the buttons and require and additional device which will cost them to buy.

Since nowadays most medium of communication based on technology, it is important that people with disabilities are able to use technology at least as part of communicating with the society and be able to understand on the uses of technology as part of the benefit that people with disabilities will get.

METHODOLOGY

In this chapter will further discuss the methodology used for this study which includes the design of the study, data collection and data analysis. In this research it develops a review of relevant literature review in exploring the factors of influencing job opportunities for people with disabilities (PWD). The methodology will be based on few methods after generating framework of the author's research study.

Data Collection

Therefore, for the purpose of this research, the author decided to perform an interview with several non-government organisations such as;

1. Kaca Association
2. Smarter Brunei
3. Pusat Ehsan Al-Ameerah Al-Hajjah Maryam
4. Learning Ladders Centre Brunei
5. Uniklearn by An-Nur Harapan
6. Special Education Unit, Ministry of Education

Survey

Therefore, the author of the research paper considered quantitative approach method to employ in this study due to several limitations. Thus, online survey as a tool is best chosen by authors because it is one of approachable methods to reach most private companies. It also helps authors in aims to prove hypothesis in providing conclusions.

Sampling

Random sampling which is common in qualitative research technique, the author decided to distribute the survey based on private companies in Brunei of various industries whether the companies has the experience in hiring people with disabilities or not, the purpose of the sampling is to get the information on what are the factors that a company looking for in hiring people with disabilities.

Deductive and Inductive

There are two types of approaches that researches can use to conduct their research studies which is either the inductive and/or deductive research method (Bryman and Bell, 2007). The researchers also concluded a conclusion based on what is known as a deductive process in a broad field area, it can be defined as hypothesis operational and researchable papers. Hypothesis also shows whether or not the hypothesis is correct and valid and deductive analysis refers to the method of evaluation in theory and the test findings (Bryman and Bell, 2007). Based on the theory mention above, this research chose to approach research problem of the paper as deductive approach is recognized as the most suitable as the factors to job opportunities is based on what the companies think that is suitable as part of recruitment. Aim of the author is to test the establish theories by using hypothesis which is guided by data collection and author will end up with conclusions to solve problems.

RESULT

Data survey analysis collected the percentage of private companies in terms of hiring people with disabilities within private companies in various industries whether they have been hiring PWD. However, this research successfully grabs 25 companies that also respond to the survey. Figure 4 shown the location of the survey distribution in Brunei Darussalam where 60% of the survey is from Brunei Muara, 32% from Kuala Belait, 8% from Tutong and 0% from Temburong. Figure 5 shown data survey analysis collected, 60% of the data is companies who do not hire people with disabilities and 40% of the data are companies that hiring PWD. This indicates that 20% of the respondents are the companies that does not or never hire employees with disabilities.

Figure 6 shown the percentage of mediums of companies that recruit job applicants who are people with disabilities. 40% of the respondents saying that posting at a job employment center such as Job Center enable them to recruit employee with disabilities. 90% of the respondents says that they hire employee with disabilities by contacting PWD non-government organisations in Brunei. 6% of the respondents saying that by doing partnership with disability-related organisations. 1% of the respondents choose to contact school, college and university career centre to recruit employee with disabilities. All the respondents (100%) agree by establishing internship and mentoring programs enable them to create more hiring for people with disabilities. The rest that have 0% voting is posting at publications, posting at job fairs and posting at websites or social media which include hiring people with disabilities.

Reliability Test

Reliability test in statistics is to measure the overall consistency of data collections. Cronbach Alpha is the most common measures of internal consistency. It is most common used when you have multiple Likert scale questions that from the scale the author determines if the scale is reliable. The authors have conducted reliability test of the factors related to retaining customer loyalty. The results of Cronbach alpha analysis shows that when μ^{3} .7 it is an acceptable reliability test.

Table 1 above shows the reliability in terms of hiring people with disabilities related posting at job employment centre, contacting PWD non-government organisations in Brunei to hire people with disabilities, partnership with disability-related organisations, contacting school, college and university career

Figure 4. Location of survey distributions

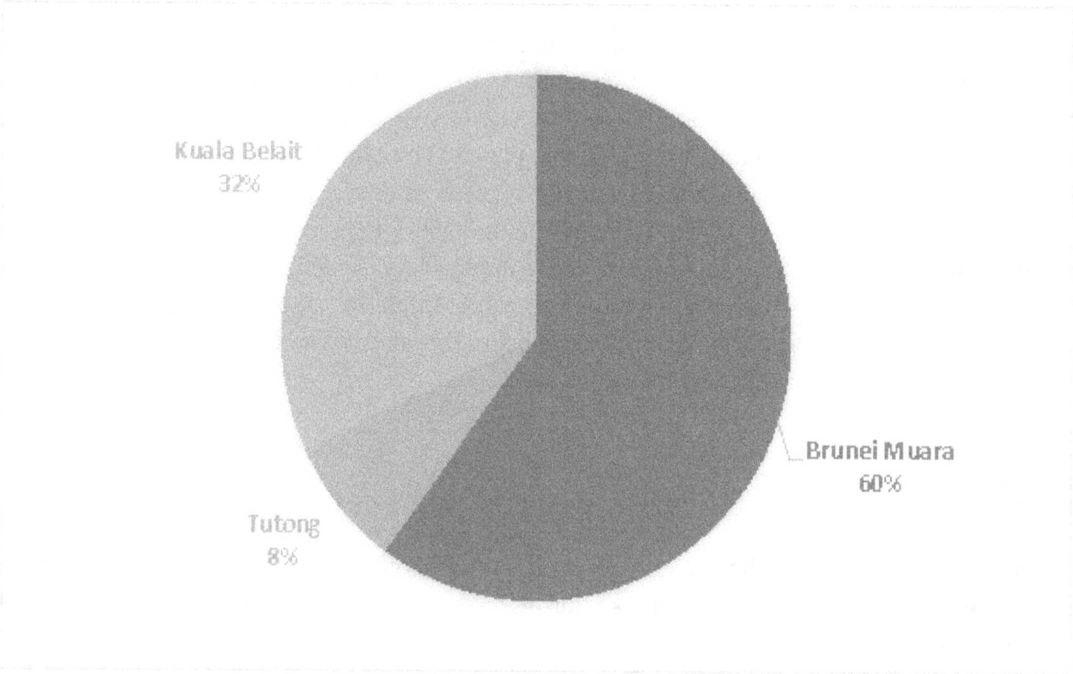

centre, posting at publications (include PWD hiring), posting at websites or social media (include PWD hiring), posting at job fairs (include PWD hiring), establishing internship and mentoring programs. Also include concern factors in hiring people with disabilities where, it costs more to employ workers with disabilities, workers with disabilities has lack in skills and experience, PWD may not be as productive

Figure 5. Private companies in Brunei

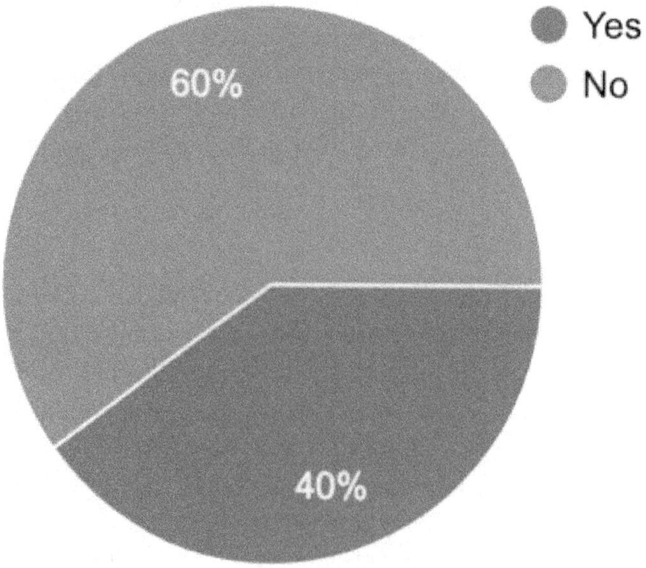

Figure 6. Medium of recruiting PWD

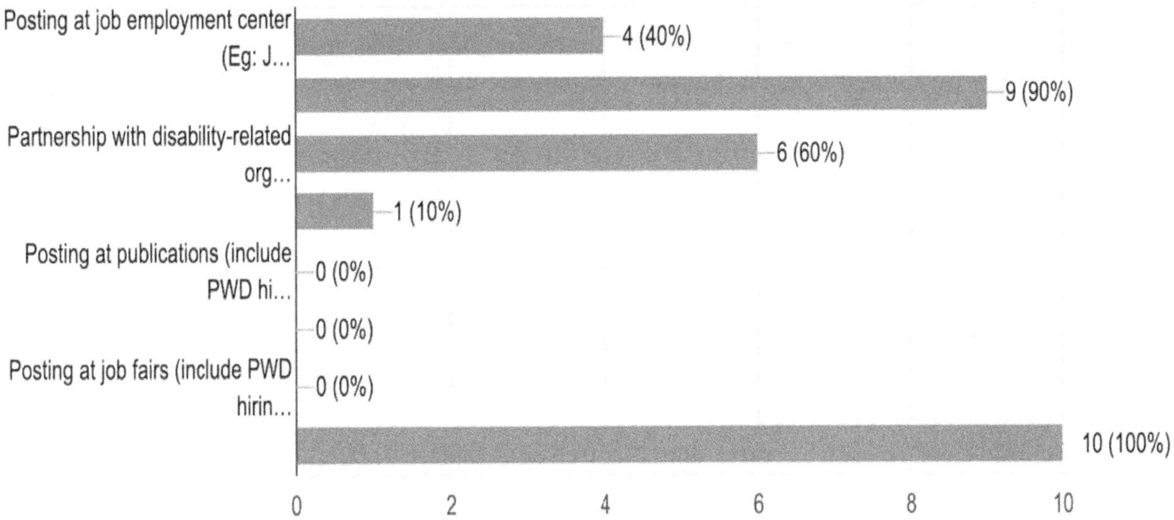

Table 1. Reliability in terms of hiring people with PWD

Reliability Statistics	
Cronbach's Alpha	N of Items
.867	32

Table 2. Reliability for factor concerning companies that do not hire PWD

Reliability Statistics	
Cronbach's Alpha	N of Items
.782	22

as other workers, taking disciplinary action, evaluating employee with disabilities, communicating with employee with disabilities, comfortable in managing workers with disabilities. Other factor in hiring challenges which is nature of work, cannot find qualified people with disabilities, actual cost of accommodating people with disabilities, concern about cost of workers compensation, concern about the cost of disability workers health coverage, lack of knowledge or information, attitudes of customers, attitudes of co-workers and discomfort or unfamiliar working environment. Last but not least, factors to retention challenges for employees with disabilities which is finding a way to return employees to work, Lack of advancement potential (skills, goals, attitudes, commitment), cost of accommodating people with disability, customers attitude and co-workers attitude. A Cronbach's Alpha is being tested among the factors in hiring, challenges in hiring and retention challenges, where it shows that alpha coefficient of the 32 items is .867 where α is ^{3} .7 suggesting that this item has good consistency.

Table 2 above shows reliability test for companies that does not hire employee with disabilities considering the factors that is important to the companies if they were to hire people with disabilities. Which includes, satisfactory job performance, satisfactory job attendance, increase company productivity, benefit to the company, people with disabilities with education, people with disabilities with training (vocational or industrial), PWD with experience in internship or working experience, testimonials from school, institute or previous work, cost concern in hiring people with disabilities, education, disability awareness training, mentoring, assistive technology, using a specialized recruiting source for PWD, flexible work schedule, training existing staff, short-term on the job assistant, long-term on the job assistant, disability internship program, developing recruitment program. A Cronbach's Alpha is being tested among companies that does not hire employee with disabilities considering the factors that is important to the companies if they were to hire people with disabilities, where it shows that alpha coefficient of the 22 items is .782 where α is ^{3} .7 suggesting that this item has good consistency.

Table 3. Reliability factor for hiring PWD

Reliability Statistics	
Cronbach's Alpha	N of Items
.780	11

Table 3 above shows reliability test for factors in hiring people with disabilities which include education, disability awareness training, mentoring, assistive technology, using a specialized recruiting source for PWD, flexible work schedule, training existing staff, short-term on the job assistant, long-term on the job assistant, disability internship program, developing recruitment program. A Cronbach's Alpha is being tested for factors in hiring people with disabilities, where it shows that alpha coefficient of the 11 items is .780 where α is ^{3} .7 suggesting that this item has good consistency.

Goodness-of-Fit Test

Goodness-of-fit test is to test non-parametric data to find out how the observed data is statistically significant different from the expected value, it is a statistical hypothesis test to see how well sample data fit into the distribution. In this test the author is using Chi-Square goodness-of-fit test to define the

Table 4. Goodness-of-fit test for concern factor in hiring PWD for non-hiring company

Test Statistics			
	PWD with education	**PWD with training**	**PWD with internship or work experience**
Chi-Square	4.800[a]	.067[b]	14.600[c]
df	2	1	3
Asymp. Sig.	.091	.796	.002

non-parametric test of the data. The p-value is to determine whether to reject or fail to reject the null hypothesis. Usually a significance level when p £ .05 which means the p-value is less than or equal to the significance level, the null hypothesis is to be rejected. However if p is > .05, it is fail to reject the null hypothesis.

Table 4 above shows the results of goodness-of-fit test for company that does not hire employee with people with disabilities but were ask the important factors that they would consider when hiring PWD which includes education, training and internship or work experience. However, Table 5 above shows the results of goodness-of-fit test for company that hire employee with people with disabilities but were ask regarding the important factors regarding their hiring strategies with PWD which includes education, training and internship and workers with skills and work experience.

Table 5. Goodness-of-fit test factors of hiring for hiring companies

Test Statistics			
	Workers with disabilities has skills and experience	**Education**	**Disability internship program**
Chi-Square	9.800[a]	2.600[a]	3.600[b]
df	2	2	1
Asymp. Sig.	.007	.058	.002

Correlation Test

The statistical correlation is a statistical technique which indicates whether there is a relationship between two variables. The relationship between variables will indicates its use to understand if the relationship is positive or negative that defines the relationship intensity. Spearman rho rank correlation is a non-parametric test that is used to measure the degree of association and monotonic relationship between two variables. It is developed by Spearman; thus it is called the Spearman rank correlation. Data analysis below shows the correlation coefficient relationship testing using Spearman rho and altogether testing null hypothesis using chi-square correlation hypothesis test.

Table 6. Relationship test for company does not hire PWD

Correlations				
			PWDwitheducation	**PWDwithtraining**
Spearman's rho	PWD with education	Correlation Coefficient	1.000	.726**
		Sig. (1-tailed)	.	.001
		N	15	15
	PWD with training	Correlation Coefficient	.726**	1.000
		Sig. (1-tailed)	.001	.
		N	15	15

Table 6 above shows the Spearman's rho correlation coefficient relationship for company that does not hire PWD, dealing with question "What are the factor that would encourage your company to recruit people with disabilities?". This is to test the relationship importance factor based on ratings concerning people with disabilities between two variables which is education and training. This test was taken using one tail test for distribution of 15 companies out of 25 companies. With correlation coefficient for both variable *r* values, $r = .726$, $p < .05$.

Table 7. Relationship test for company does not hire PWD

Correlations				
			PWD with education	**PWD with internship or work experience**
Spearman's rho	PWD with education	Correlation Coefficient	1.000	.614**
		Sig. (1-tailed)	.	.007
		N	15	15
	PWD with internship or work experience	Correlation Coefficient	.614**	1.000
		Sig. (1-tailed)	.007	.
		N	15	15

Table 7 above shows the Spearman's rho correlation coefficient relationship for company that does not hire PWD, dealing with question "What are the factor that would encourage your company to recruit people with disabilities?". This is to test the relationship importance factor based on ratings concerning people with disabilities between two variables which is education and work experience. This test was taken using one tail test for distribution of 15 companies out of 25 companies. With correlation coefficient for both variable *r* values, $r = .614$, $p < .05$.

Table 8. Relationship test for company does not hire PWD

Correlations				
			PWD with internship or work experience	**PWD with training**
Spearman's rho	PWD with internship or work experience	Correlation Coefficient	1.000	.648**
		Sig. (1-tailed)	.	.005
		N	15	15
	PWD with training	Correlation Coefficient	.648**	1.000
		Sig. (1-tailed)	.005	.
		N	15	15

Table 8 above shows the Spearman's rho correlation coefficient relationship for company that does not hire PWD, dealing with question "What are the factor that would encourage your company to recruit people with disabilities?". This is to test the relationship importance factor based on ratings concerning people with disabilities between two variables which is work experience and training. This test was taken using one tail test for distribution of 15 companies out of 25 companies. With correlation coefficient for both variable *r* values, $r = .648, p < .05$.

Table 9. Relationship test for company does not hire PWD

Correlations				
			Education	**Disabilityinternshipprogram**
Spearman's rho	Education	Correlation Coefficient	1.000	.505**
		Sig. (1-tailed)	.	.005
		N	25	25
	Disabilityinternshipprogram	Correlation Coefficient	.505**	1.000
		Sig. (1-tailed)	.005	.
		N	25	25

Table 9 above shows the Spearman's rho correlation coefficient relationship for company that hire and does not hire PWD, dealing with question "What are the strategies factor that would be helpful in hiring people with disabilities?". This is to test the relationship importance based on ratings concerning people with disabilities between two variables which is education and internship program or work experience. This test was taken using one tail test for distribution of all 25 companies participated. With correlation coefficient for both variable *r* values, $r = .505, p < .05$.

Table 10. Relationship test for company that hire and does not hire PWD

Correlations				
			Disabilityinternshipprogram	**Education**
Spearman's rho	Disabilityinternshipprogram	Correlation Coefficient	1.000	.625*
		Sig. (1-tailed)	.	.027
		N	10	10
	Education	Correlation Coefficient	.625*	1.000
		Sig. (1-tailed)	.027	.
		N	10	10

Table 10 above shows the Spearman's rho correlation coefficient relationship for company that hire and does not hire PWD, dealing with question "What are the strategies factor that would be helpful in hiring people with disabilities?". This is to test the relationship importance based on ratings concerning people with disabilities between two variables which is education and internship program or work experience. This test was taken using one tail test for distribution of 10 companies out of 25 companies participated. With correlation coefficient for both variable *r* values, $r = .625$, $p < .05$.

Challenges in Hiring PWD

Figure 7 shown histogram graph for hiring companies regarding their concern in recruiting people with disabilities. By using importance ratings of "1" being not important, "2" for slightly important, "3" being moderately important, "4" being very important and "5" as extremely important. From the graph above shows that:

- *"it cost more to employ workers with disabilities" being rated as moderately important;*
- *"Workers with disabilities has lack in skills and experience" rated as very important;*
- *" PWD may not be as productive as other workers" rated as slightly important;*
- *"Taking disciplinary action" as not important;*
- *"Evaluating employee with disabilities" as moderately important;*
- *"Communicating with employee with disabilities" rated as very important;*
- *"Comfortable in managing workers with disabilities" rated in between moderately important and very important.*

Figure 7. Concern in hiring PWD

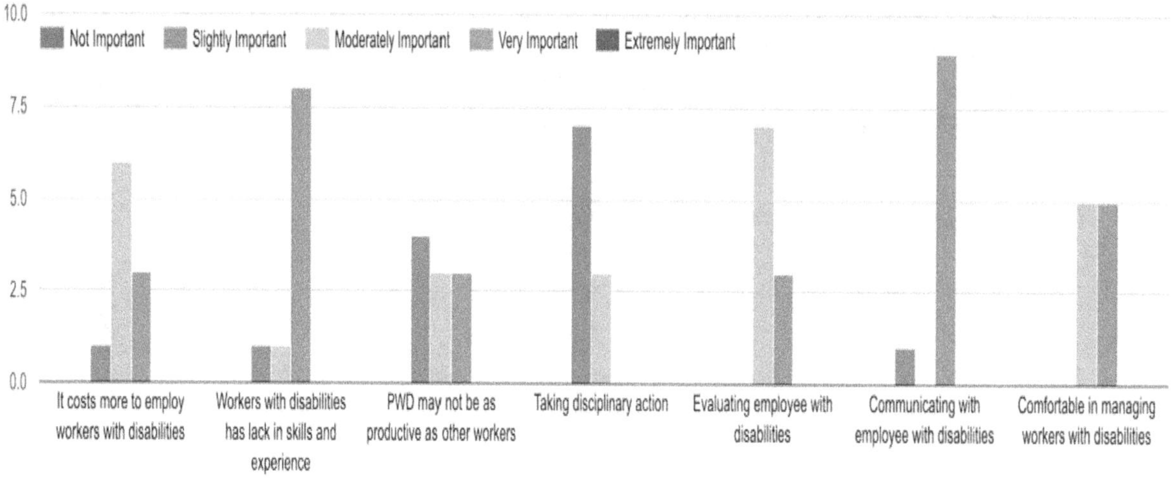

From this importance evaluations it shows that most companies hiring people with disabilities believe that communication with employees are very important because people communicate every day and miscommunication may lead to misunderstanding between employer and the employee which is not good for the company. By having skills and experience is also one of the important concern a company would look into, with experience it is easy for employee to work under less supervision.

Figure 8 Challenges in hiring PWD

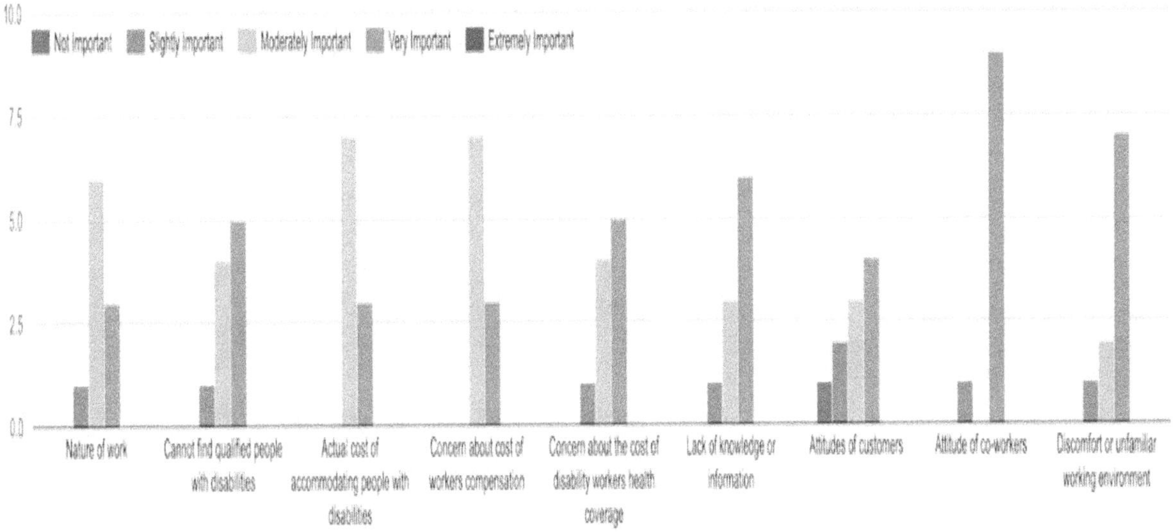

Figure 8 shown histogram graph for hiring companies regarding their challenges in recruiting people with disabilities. By using importance ratings of "1" being not important, "2" for slightly important, "3" being moderately important, "4" being very important and "5" as extremely important. From the graph above shows that:

- *"Nature of work" rated as moderately important;*
- *"Cannot find qualified people with disabilities" rated as very important;*
- *"Actual cost of accommodating PWD" rated as moderately important;*
- *"Concern about workers compensation" rated as moderately important;*
- *"Concern about the cost of disability workers health coverage" rated as very important;*
- *"Lack of knowledge or information" rated as very important;*
- *"Customers attitudes" rated as very important;*
- *"Colleagues attitudes" rated as very important;*

Figure 9. Retention challenges

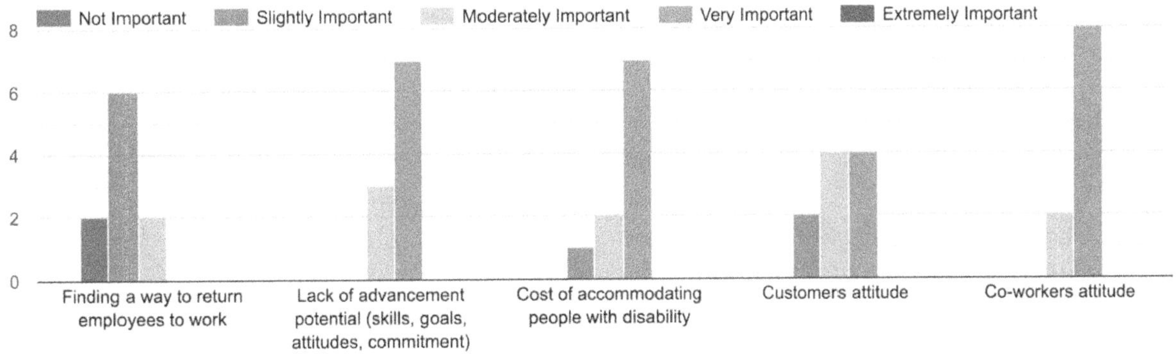

- *"Discomfort or unfamiliar working environment" rated as very important.*

From this importance evaluations it shows that most companies hiring challenges for people with disabilities as very important is qualified PWD that can suit with the job offered, the cost in preparing health coverage which may cost extra for hiring companies, absence of knowledge and information regarding their work, the importance of attitudes of customer and colleague towards PWD and an unfamiliar working environment which could create discomfort for PWD employees.

Figure 13 shown histogram graph for hiring companies regarding their retention challenges in recruiting people with disabilities. By using importance ratings of "1" being not important, "2" for slightly important, "3" being moderately important, "4" being very important and "5" as extremely important. From the graph above shows that:

- *"Finding a way to return employees to work" rated as slightly important;*
- *"Lack of skills, goals, attitudes and commitment" rated as very important;*
- *"Cost of accommodating PWD" rated as very important;*
- *"Customers attitude" rated in between moderately important and very important;*
- *"Colleague attitude" rated as very important.*

From this importance evaluations it shows that most companies retention challenges for people with disabilities are the importance of having skills, goals, attitude and commitment towards their work, cost of accommodating employee may be expensive and attitudes of customers and colleagues that make it difficult to keep PWD employee as they think that being looked down to their capabilities may not lead to employee being devoted to the company.

Hiring Strategies

In this study, the authors found the hiring strategies in order to create job opportunities for people with disabilities.

Figure 10 shown histogram graph for strategies that will be helpful in recruiting people with disabilities. By using importance ratings of "1" being not important, "2" for slightly important, "3" being moderately important, "4" being very important and "5" as extremely important. From the graph above shows that:

- *"Education" rated as moderately important;*
- *"Disability awareness training" rated as moderately important;*
- *"Mentoring" rated as very important;*
- *"Assistive technology" rates as moderately important;*
- *"Using a specialised PWD recruiting source" rated as moderately important;*
- *"Flexible work schedule" rated as slightly important;*
- *"Training existing staff" rated as moderately important;*
- *"Short-term on the job assistant" rated as moderately important;*
- *"Long-term on the job assistant" rated as not important;*
- *"Disability internship program" rated as very important;*
- *"Developing recruitment program" rated as moderately important.*

Figure 10. Hiring strategies

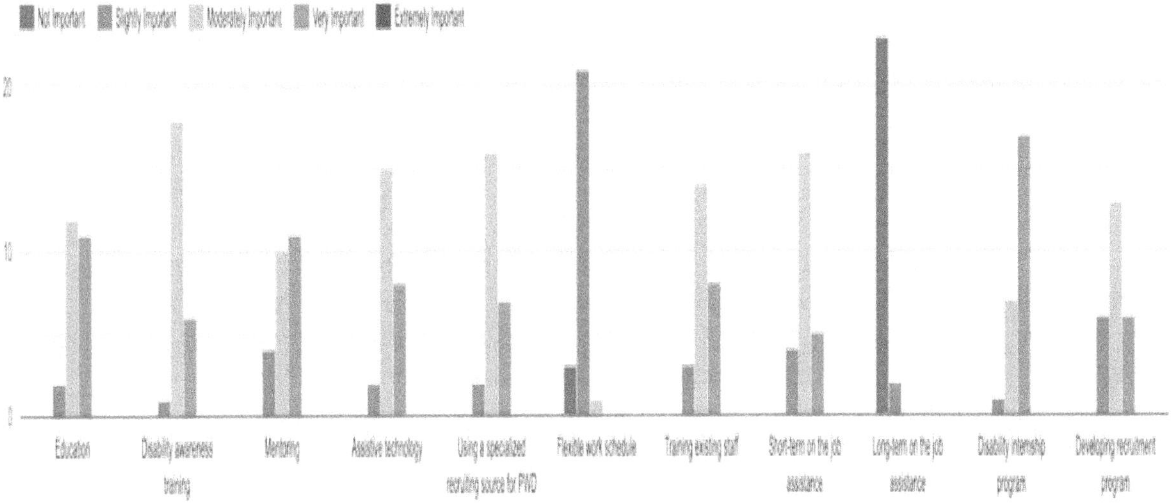

From this importance evaluations it shows that helpful strategies in hiring for people with disabilities are mentoring PWD regarding the scope of job and having an internship program which could help PWD with hands on real working life so that they will understand on how to be independent and to have the capability like others.

Goodness-of-Fit Findings

In this research study, data analysis found the goodness-of-fit test for company that does not hire employee with people with disabilities dealing with question "What are the factor that would encourage your company to recruit people with disabilities", specifically the importance of education, training and work.

The results shows that:

- People with disabilities with education is not statistically significant; (2) = 4.800, $p = .091$,
- People with disabilities with training is not statistically significant, ; (1) = .067, $p = .796$,
- People with disabilities with internship or work experience significant, ; (3) = 14.600, $p < .05$.

Goodness-of-fit findings in table 5 above shows, the statistical Chi-Square methods of test that describe the remainder and shows the total difference between data and hypothesis. The higher the value, the less data "fits" the null hypothesis. The degrees of freedom (df) specify the distribution of Chi-square and Asymp. Sig. that refers to the p value and null hypothesis will be rejected if $p <.05$. Data analysis found for company that hire employee with people with disabilities but were ask regarding "What are the strategies factor that would helpful in hiring people with disabilities?" specifically for skills and experience, education and training or internship. The results shows that:

- Employee with PWD with skills and experience is statistically significant, ; (2) = 9.800, $p < .05$,
- Employee with PWD with education is not statistically significant; (2) = 2.600, $p = .058$,
- Employee with PWD with internship or training is statistically significant, ; (1) = 3.600, $p <.05$.

Correlation Findings

In this study, data analysis found the relationship and significant of people with disabilities in terms of educations, trainings, internship or work experience. Correlation findings using Spearman rho calculate statistical relationship between two variables where coefficient of correlation (r) indicates the relationship measurement of the variables developed by Spearman and significant indicates p value where relationship to be statistically significant when $p < .05$. The N indicates the distribution of the survey tested. Table 6, 7 and 8 shown the correlation coefficient was made for company that does not hire PWD dealing with question "What are the factor that would encourage your company to recruit people with disabilities", specifically the relationship of education, training and work experience. The results shows that:

- People with disabilities with education, has strong positive correlation between people with disabilities with trainings, which was statistically significant, $r = .726$, $p < .01$
- People with disabilities with education, has strong positive correlation between people with disabilities with internship or work experience, which was statistically significant, $r = .614$, $p < .01$
- People with disabilities with internship or work experience, has strong positive correlation between people with disabilities with trainings, which was statistically significant, $r = .648$, $p < .01$

Table 9 above shows the correlation coefficient was made for both company that hire and does not hire PWD dealing with question "What are the strategies factor that would be helpful in hiring people with disabilities?", specifically with the relationship between education and internship program. The result shows that:

- People with disabilities with education, has strong positive correlation between people with disabilities with internship program, which was statistically significant, $r = .505$, $p < .01$

Correlation coefficient was made for both company that hire PWD dealing with question "What are the strategies factor that would be helpful in hiring people with disabilities?", it is the relationship between education and internship program. The result shows that:

- People with disabilities with education, has strong positive correlation between people with disabilities with internship program, but was not statistically significant, $r = .505$, $p > .01$

DISCUSSION

In the research findings shows the importance concern in hiring people with disabilities is workers based on the conceptual framework related to job opportunities for PWD that has lack of skills and experience this is due to the task that will be given to the employee that needs them the experience to execute the task. This is because some companies believe that when employee with disabilities does not have the skill in doing the task may lead to less productive. It shows that employers that had not previously employed PWD had great concerns regarding productivity, proper job fit (i.e. having suitable menial or repetitive tasks for PWDs to perform), accidents or injuries on the job, and worker's compensation claims. Other concern is regarding communication with workers that has disability especially those with hearing impaired that uses sign language as their communication channel, as for employee or co-workers that are not trained to understand how sign language works may find it difficult to understand what is being said by the disabled employee. Visually impaired disabilities also one of the concern when the company is not equipped with aids for visually impaired disabilities which led to cost in preparing the aid for one worker.

This also gives influence to work productivity within the organisation, because failure in providing effective and appropriate communication with people with disabilities may lead to major barrier. There are also few challenges that has been acquired by companies that hire people with disabilities, one of them is to hire qualified people with disabilities, it is not easy to find qualified employee with disabilities as rate of graduates of people with disabilities especially in Brunei is low thus it creates competition between other graduates who has more advantage compared to graduates with disability. Being graduates with disabilities is difficult to some job applicants because it is not easy to disclose their disability during job interview to potential employers because some employees with disability might consider in asking for flexible working hours which made it difficult for the company to hire the graduates. Accommodating the cost of disability workers health coverage is also one of the main concern as part of the challenges in hiring people with disabilities, because as a worker with health issues makes a gap in creating job opportunities for people with disabilities, the extra cost of medical check and insurance that need to be covered by the company lead to employee hiring the non-disabled workers as they are sure that they have good health condition. Worker with disability especially autism, hearing impaired and visual impaired is not a short-term disability that can be easily covered by insurance as this workers tend to be more vulnerable compared to other workers.

Attitudes of customers towards employee with disabilities, this is due to customers that is not aware of employee with disabilities. Customers may thought that the workers may not able to entertain them properly not knowing that the workers have disability for example; providing a slow service at a hotel reception may lead to customers in giving bad feedback in terms of their front line services. Once the worker keep getting low rate feedback which led to employee not able to retain its disable workers and could not create to more job opportunities for people with disabilities. Attitudes of co-workers towards employee with disabilities may also be one of challenges and barriers to job opportunity or hiring people with disabilities, as some co-workers might find people with disability being contagious and dangerous especially those having severe autism as they might not be able to control their own mind and body when they are in anger especially. People with disabilities sometimes were given negative perception as they are the most protected workers because they were regarded as fragile. Having a discomfort or unfamiliar working environments is also one of the challenges faced by people with disabilities, for example in practising an office job because not all employers are willing to do changes especially when hiring people with disabilities. Having skills, goals, attitude and commitment may lead to the retention of PWD employee in a company, which will create trust between employee and employer, despite of the disability that PWD has but with commitment, company can see the potential of PWD in trying to secure the job and being loyal to the company because in Figure 14 shows that it is a challenge to retain workers who has lack of skills, goals, attitude and commitment. When it comes to requesting unique accommodations for disability, which presents another issue this said that, workers with disabilities need to adjust themselves to be as independent as other workers. From the findings in figure 15 above shows that having either short-term or long-term assistance for workers with disabilities is not important to them, as it will add to additional cost in hiring assistant or making other worker to do extra tasks in being the peer of disable worker.

PWD Professional Competencies

Based on the conceptual framework related to job opportunities for PWD from the correlations coefficient test shows that for companies that does not hire people with disabilities in terms of education, trainings, internship or work experience shows strong positive correlation between the three variables being tested. It shows that all education, trainings, internship or work experience has link to each other in order for job opportunity for people with disabilities to happen event though for non-hiring company fail to reject null hypothesis in chi-square test, it was statistically significant with strong relationship both trainings and education variable. Based on the author correlation factor model in figure 7 shown having a relationship of training and education proves that job opportunity is depending on this two variable this is due to the selection of recruiting employee by accepting and giving priority to those with knowledge as they may be able to work independently.

For companies that is hiring workers with disabled employee, the test was run to prove that they company agrees that education and internship has strong relationship between two variables. However, the result shows that both variable has strong relationship but not statistically significant thus is strengthen the chi-square test fail to reject null hypothesis of education has no relationship to job opportunity. However, for companies that has already hired person with disability in their organisation consider that education may not be an important variable for job opportunity to be created shows that the relationship in correlation factor model for education does not lead to job opportunity to people with disabilities, what the company are looking for is those that have the skills and experience to execute task efficiently and possibly the company might be looking into the qualification of disabled person in order to fill in the vacancy according to recruiting guidelines from human resource.

Last but not least, correlation coefficient test was run for both company that hire and does not hire PWD but were ask regarding factor of hiring strategies in hiring people with disabilities, shows strong positive relationship and statistically significant. This shows that most test related to "internship" having strong relationship according to correlation factor model in figure 7 with other variables as one of the factor of hiring people with disabilities to create job opportunities for PWD. Internship is part of working experience process by which it is a practical or hands on working experience. Job opportunity for people with disability will only be an advantage to those who has acquired internship, this is because after finishing the internship, testimonial will be provided to ensure that, people with disabilities that has gone through internship has positive comments on how they handle their job. This testimonials have been assessed by professional recruiters in the human resource department thus adapting internship can also create job opportunity for person with disability for the company itself, this is due to the internship program that they hosted for PWD, the company itself does not have to recruit new employee and has to go through collection of unemployed curriculum vitae, thus employing their interns to be part of their full-time workers.

However, having education does not give an impact to people with disabilities as it is not a major factor in creating job or recruiting employee with disabilities as the findings shows no significant results. As for work experience, has relationship with job opportunity in order for disabled person to be hired by a company the effect of this experience create more productivity as experience play a role in the company and altogether bring benefit to the company itself. Training aims to eliminate barriers to employment of people with disabilities, thus creating more people with disabilities in jobs and raising awareness of the fact that PWD is part of hiring companies for example the trainings of using aid devices will help to boost their confidence to communicate with the society as communication is one of the barrier to job opportunities for disabled people. As for internship the impact to the disable person can add more knowledge and improve skills that the disabled person has, the company need to always ensure that their employee are able to observe the disable person in providing the right assistance so that the experience in real working situation and if they needed help, the employee are able to make configurations to the task given.

CONCLUSION

To conclude the author research study findings shows the barrier of job opportunity in Brunei Darussalam for people with disabilities which is the attitudes and communication barrier encountered by people with disabilities. This is due to specific people with disability is not fully disable of performing work or task given to them. They are often mention as differently abled person because they are special and they also wanted to be accepted as part of the society as normal human beings with special characters. In the research study findings shows same hypothesis fail to reject by both hiring and non-hiring companies is education relates to job opportunity for people with disability even though looking into correlation coefficient test shows education has strong relationship but it is not significant that it can lead to job opportunities. At the end of the day, quality that company will look for employee either people with disabilities or vice versa is the person that has skills, experience and trainings. Nowadays, providing training to employee will increase additional cost to the company sending their workers for trainings. By sending employees to free training regarding people with disabilities, free courses has been provided by Brunei Darussalam National Association of the Blind and Ministry of Education under Special Education Unit, can be learned in Brunei which is the sign language course and braille reading course. Brunei should provide disability awareness on how to handle differently abled people especially those with autism.

However, by giving out training may benefit to the company as well as it can create more productive employee thus learning new things every day. For example; when the company provide sign language training as an additional language because the company is hiring people with hearing aid, it is better to train and create awareness about sign language so it can add skills to the existing employee thus, eliminate the barrier of communication in the future and more job opportunity for hearing impaired person in the job market. Last but not least, it depends on the view of the company itself on how and what are the criteria that they are looking for an employee to secure a job in the company as getting different results from both companies of hiring and non-hiring PWD since survey is just part of their idea in providing strategies in creating job opportunities for people with disabilities. This is due to the applicants need to be hired not based on what is written on paper such as testimonial form previous employment because applicants have to go through screening of interview, from the interview then the employer can identify whether the person is suitable to be hired for the vacancy.

RECOMMENDATION

Further recommendation is for the company together with their employee and society create awareness as from the research study above also involved in the concern of lack in knowledge and information, such as information on how to hire people with disabilities and getting the right channel to hire employees. Brunei has been providing computer generated website to apply for jobs such as PSC recruitment and

Job Centre. However, not all people with disabilities are computer literate. Remembering the author last visit to Kaca association, having a conversation with one of the parents of different abled students, saying that her son has been applying several jobs but is always rejected because he is unable to understand on how to fill in the application form. It is a disappointment to see that this people are eager to start a career but due to several constraints they are not able to apply for the vacancy. As part of the recommendation, to promote equal rights for people with disabilities, in classes that they attend they are required to learn the use of technology such as how to log in to a website and find the right medium for job application as technology is also an issue to this group mostly concerning to slow learner disability. The speed of their learning is not as fast as others, they may understand but it will take time. By teaching them the steps of using technology can create the confidence as they usually have a low self-esteem. Another recommendation is creating a user-friendly application for people with disabilities, this application will help them identify which job best suits them based on their qualification, skills and experience. Not just the society are able to plan their future career but for people with disabilities, they also have their own career dream but being different than others made them feel that they cannot achieve their dream. By having this application will help people with disabilities to be career ready. The application provided must have simple interface and easy for them to understand and can be used by different type of disability from hearing impairment to visual impairment especially for the blind. This is because the technology used by the blind or visual impairment might be limited to voice only comparing to hearing impairment disability, they still can read and write. With voice assistant like Apple Siri enable them to navigate easily using the application.

Recommendation in creating job opportunity in hiring people with disabilities is by creating an inclusive culture, by creating a talent teamwork to enhance employees creativity including those with disability, this is like a teambuilding not limited to healthy employee only but all employee should be included but activities included must enable all employee to join as a roleplay for example; guessing games using sign language thus create awareness for deaf and hearing impaired disability, other than that teambuilding in understanding braille using flashcard without looking at the card and the employee will have the ability to add skills . By having this culture will eliminate bias in negative perception towards people with disability and altogether accepted in the company. Giving access in making sure that the building is accessible for all, such as for those using wheelchair, it is mention in the literature review that Brunei government is providing easy access for people with disabilities but it can be seen that not all buildings in Brunei have the accessibility for people with wheelchairs to no navigate the stairs or the doorways, lift might be provided but limited. By sending employees to free training regarding people with disabilities, so far free courses that can be learned in Brunei is the sign language course and braille reading course. Brunei should provide disability awareness on how to handle differently abled people especially those with autism. For mild autism it is easy to handle their emotions however, it is better for the company to be aware on how to handle and communicate with differently abled colleague. By having recruiters that is trained to maximise engagement in providing opportunities and accommodation for candidates of all abilities including PWD and trained to be ensure that recruiters know how to engage with those who are differently abled.

ACKNOWLEDMENT

Heru Susanto and Hamizah Hamid as main contributors. The remains, Fadzliwati Mohiddin and Saleem Haja Nazamudeen as contributors. All authors review and approved final version of this manuscript.

REFERENCES

AmadeoK. (2020). Retrieved from https://www.thebalance.com/what-is-unemployment-3306222

Amu, A. (n.d.). *Smarter Brunei*. Retrieved from https://www.smarterbrunei.com/

ASEAN Today. (2018, April 30). Retrieved from https://www.aseantoday.com/2018/04/bruneis-equal-opportunities-problem/

Asia & the Pacific. (2019, December). Retrieved from https://www.asia-pacific.undp.org/content/rbap/en/home/blog/2019/ensuring-an-accessible-future-for-people-with-print-disabilities.html

Attorney General's Chambers. (2019). Retrieved from http://www.agc.gov.bn/Theme/Home.aspx

Autism Spectrum Disorder: Communication Problems in Children. (n.d.). Retrieved from https://www.nidcd.nih.gov/health/autism-spectrum-disorder-communication-problems-children

Autism Spectrum Disorder: MedlinePlus. (n.d.). Retrieved from https://medlineplus.gov/autismspectrumdisorder.html

Azaraimy, H. (2017). *3G modasys*. Retrieved from https://3g.modasys.net/index.php/news-events/around-brunei/local-news/29409-centre-for-capacity-building-to-begin-training-programmes-in-september.html

BakarR. (2019). Retrieved from https://thescoop.co/2019/01/02/unemployment-in-brunei-rises-to-9-3-higher-among-men/

Bakar, R. H. (2019). *The Scoop*. Retrieved from https://thescoop.co/2019/01/02/unemployment-in-brunei-rises-to-9-3-higher-among-men/

Baker, N., & Jacobs, K. (2003). The nature of working in the United States: an occupational therapy perspective Work. In *A journal of Prevention* (pp. 53–61). Assessment and Rehabilitation.

International Labour Office. (1990). *Economically active population, employment, unemployment and hours of work (household surveys)*. Author.

JAPEM. (n.d.). Retrieved from http://www.japem.gov.bn/Themed/english/FAQ/Alternative%20Channels%20to%20Provide%20Contribution%20to%20People%20with%20Special%20Needs.htm

Kelly, K., Clark, B., & Vivienne Brown, J. S. (2003). Good practice in the conduct and reporting of survey research. *International Journal for Quality in Health Care, 15*(3), 261–266. doi:10.1093/intqhc/mzg031 PMID:12803354

KentonW. (2019). Retrieved from https://www.investopedia.com/terms/o/one-tailed-test

Khan, A. U. (2020). *The ASEAN post.* Retrieved from https://theaseanpost.com/article/bruneis-youth-facing-unemployment

Kothari, C. (2004). *Research Methodology: methods & techniques* (Vol. 1). New Age International (P) Ltd.

Lawrence. (2019, June). Retrieved from https://www.helpguide.org/articles/relationships-communication/nonverbal-communication.htm

Leu, F.Y., Liu, C.Y., Liu, J.C., Jiang, F.C., & Susanto, H. (2015). S-PMIPv6: An intra-LMA model for IPv6 mobility. *J. Netw. Comput. Appl., 58*, 180–191.

Liu, J. C., Leu, F. Y., Lin, G. L., & Susanto, H. (2018). An MFCC-based text-independent speaker identification system for access control. *Concurr. Comput. Pract. Exp., 30*(2), e4255. doi:10.1002/cpe.4255

Malhotra, N. K. (n.d.). *Marketing Research: An applied orientation, Sixt Edition.* Pearson Education Inc.

Malhotra, N. K., & Birks, D. F. (2003). *Marketing Research; an applied approach* (2nd European Edition). Pearson Education.

Ministry of Education. (2018). *Brunei Darussalam - Special Education Unit.* Retrieved from http://www.moe.gov.bn

Ministry of Religious Affairs. (2015). Retrieved from http://www.mora.gov.bn/Lists/Titah/NewDisplayItem.aspx?ID=176

N, A. (2019). Retrieved from http://nda.ie/Resources/Accessibility-toolkit/Provide-disability-equality-training-to-staff/

NAEDS. (n.d.). Retrieved from https://www.neads.ca/en/about/projects/inclusion/guide/pwd_01.php

OECD. (2019). *Economic Outlook for Southeast Asia, China and India 2019 – Update: Responding to Environmental Hazards in Cities.* OECD Publishing.

Patton. (1990). *Qualitative evaluation and research methods* (2nd ed.). Academic Press.

Persatuan KACA Brunei. (n.d.). Retrieved from http://kacabrunei.blogspot.com/

Pusat Ehsan Al-Ameerah Al-Hajjah Maryam. (n.d.). Retrieved from https://www.pusatehsan.org.bn/

Rasidah. (2018, December 4). *The Scoop.* Retrieved from https://thescoop.co/2018/12/04/smarter-brunei-launches-employment-programme-new-bistro-cafe/

Rasidah. (2019). Retrieved from https://thescoop.co/2019/01/09/moe-wants-to-introduce-work-quotas-for-individuals-with-disabilities/

Smarter Brunei. (n.d.). Retrieved from https://www.smarterbrunei.com/

Speech and Language Impairment Defined | Special Education. (n.d.). Retrieved from https://www.specialeducationguide.com/disability-profiles/speech-and-language-impairments/

StadlerD. (2019). Retrieved from https://www.shrm.org/resourcesandtools/hr-topics/behavioral-competencies/global-and-cultural-effectiveness/pages/4-ways-to-hire-more-people-with-disabilities.aspx

Susanto, H. (2017). Electronic Health System: Sensors Emerging and Intelligent Technology Approach. In *Smart Sensors Networks* (pp. 189–203). Elsevier. doi:10.1016/B978-0-12-809859-2.00012-7

Susanto, H. (2018). Smart mobile device emerging Technologies: An enabler to Health Monitoring system. In *High-Performance Materials and Engineered Chemistry* (pp. 241–264). Apple Academic Press. doi:10.1201/9781315187860-8

Susanto, H., & Almunawar, M. N. (2015). Managing Compliance with an Information Security Management Standard. In *Encyclopedia of Information Science and Technology* (3rd ed., pp. 1452–1463). IGI Global. doi:10.4018/978-1-4666-5888-2.ch138

Susanto, H., & Almunawar, M. N. (2018). *Information Security Management Systems: A Novel Framework and Software as a Tool for Compliance with Information Security Standard.* CRC Press. doi:10.1201/9781315232355

Susanto, H., Almunawar, M. N., Leu, F. Y., & Chen, C. K. (2016). Android vs iOS or Others? SMD-OS Security Issues: Generation Y Perception. *International Journal of Technology Diffusion*, *7*(2), 1–18. doi:10.4018/IJTD.2016040101

Susanto, H., & Chen, C. K. (2017). Information and Communication Emerging Technology: Making Sense of Healthcare Innovation. In *Internet of Things and Big Data Technologies for Next Generation Healthcare* (pp. 229–250). Springer. doi:10.1007/978-3-319-49736-5_10

Susanto, H., Chen, C. K., & Almunawar, M. N. (2018). Revealing Big Data Emerging Technology as Enabler of LMS Technologies Transferability. In *Internet of Things and Big Data Analytics Toward Next-Generation Intelligence* (pp. 123–145). Springer. doi:10.1007/978-3-319-60435-0_5

Susanto, H., Leu, F.-Y., Caesarendra, W., Ibrahim, F., Haghi, P. K., Khusni, U., & Glowacz, A. (2020). Managing Cloud Intelligent Systems over Digital Ecosystems: Revealing Emerging App Technology in the Time of the COVID19 Pandemic. *Appl. Syst. Innov.*, *3*(3), 37. doi:10.3390/asi3030037

Tabung Amanah Pekerja. (n.d.). Retrieved from www.tap.com.bn

The ASEAN post. (2018a, June 17). Retrieved from https://theaseanpost.com/article/bringing-inclusivity-brunei

The ASEAN post. (2018b, october 27). Retrieved from https://theaseanpost.com/article/bruneis-unevenly-distributed-income

The ASEAN post. (2018c). Retrieved from https://theaseanpost.com/article/digitalising-brunei

ADDITIONAL READING

Brudirect. (2019). Retrieved from Retrieved from https://www.brudirect.com/news.php?id=19379

Bryman, A., & Bell, E. (2007). *Business research method.* Oxford University Press.

YB Dato Hj Aminuddin Ihsan. (2019, december 3). *The Scoop.*

Denzin, N. K., & Lincoln, Y. S. (2011). *The handbook of qualitative research.* SAGE Publications Incorporated.

DINF. (n.d.). *Disability Information Resources.* Retrieved from https://www.dinf.ne.jp/doc/english/intl/bf/index_e.html

Disabilities. (2019). Retrieved from https://www.who.int/topics/disabilities/en/

Faisal, F. (2018, October 6). *Asia News Network.* Retrieved from https://annx.asianews.network/content/brunei-masterplan-2025-aims-empower-people-disabilities-83269

HazairH. (2018, March 26). Retrieved from https://thescoop.co/2018/03/26/disability-rights-activists-equal-opportunity-employment/

The Daily Brunei Resources. (2012, October 29). Retrieved from http://bruneiresources.blogspot.com/2012/10/rights-for-persons-with-disabilities-in.html

The heritage foundation. (n.d.). Retrieved from https://www.heritage.org/index/country/brunei

ThierryM. (2016, March). Retrieved from https://kidshealth.org/en/teens/hearing-impairment.html

Trading Economics. (n.d.). Retrieved from https://tradingeconomics.com/brunei/gdp-growth-annual

Uniklearn. (2019). Retrieved from http://uniklearn.com/

World, D. (2013). *Disabled World.* Retrieved from https://www.disabled-world.com/disability/accessibility/websitedesign/tech-challenge.php

World population review. (n.d.). Retrieved from https://worldpopulationreview.com/countries/brunei-population/

Worldometer. (n.d.). Retrieved from https://www.worldometers.info/maps/brunei-darussalam-map/

Xinhua. (2019). Retrieved from http://www.xinhuanet.com/

KEY TERMS AND DEFINITIONS

Assistive Technology: Is assistive, adaptive, and rehabilitative devices for People with disability or the elderly population. People with disability often have difficulty performing activities of daily living (ADLs) independently, or even with assistance. ADLs are self-care activities that include toileting, mobility (ambulation), eating, bathing, dressing, grooming, and personal device care. Assistive technology can ameliorate the effects of disabilities that limit the ability to perform ADLs. Assistive technology promotes greater independence by enabling people to perform tasks they were formerly unable to accomplish, or had great difficulty accomplishing, by providing enhancements to, or changing methods of interacting with, the technology needed to accomplish such tasks.

Autism: Also known as autism spectrum disorder (ASD) which includes in difficulties with communications and behaviour ("Autism Spectrum Disorder: MedlinePlus", n.d.). People that is diagnosed with autism have difficulties in communicating and have trouble in understanding what other people think and feel ("Autism Spectrum Disorder: Communication Problems in Children", n.d.). Through the struggles that they encounter, it is hard for them to express themselves, either with speech, gestures, facial expressions and touch (Jeanne et al., 2019). People that is suspected with autism might have learning difficulty as their skills developed irregularly. For example; they could have hard time in communicating but be unusually good at art, music, mathematics which involves their memory, thus they might do well on test of analysis or problem solving.

Awareness Training: Helps employees to understand risks and identify potential attacks they may encounter as they receive email and use the web. Awareness training also acquaints emplyees with best practices for avoiding risk.

Deaf: Characterised as the lack of functional hearing and is dependent on visual or auditory communication. Visual contact involves sign languages, reading the lips, interpreting speech as well as reading and writing. Whereas hearing aids and tools provide visual means of communication.

Hearing Impairment: Which known as loss either partial or absolute hearing capacity. Hearing loss can occur in one or both of the ears to cause hearing impairments. As for people with the disability condition, it can cause difficulties in terms on social interaction at work, particularly children which can restrict their ability to learn spoken languages. Same as deaf people, hearing impairment also use hearing aids or devices to help them in hearing but not all devices can fully help them to hear fully.

Information Technology Apps for Learning: The Apps enable students to acquire lecture materials, take online quizzes or assessments, submit tutorials or assignments, view results, view course materials, see news and announcements, online interaction, anytime and anywhere without any geographical or time barriers. However, the key to effective apps -learning is not from its multimedia, design or user-friendliness, but on how the individuals are engaged by the content. Although the use of apps-learning provides notable benefits for students as a whole, the effectiveness of the use of the system depends on the level of acceptance and use of students. The goals of apps-learning will not be achieved if there is lag and resistance to the use of new technology. The process of implementing apps-learning in the institution might face several factors that constraints the effective use of apps-learning as a learning medium, such as infrastructure issues, the willingness and readiness of the institutions and students.

People With Disabilities: All persons with disabilities *including* those who have long-term physical, mental, intellectual, or sensory impairments which, in interaction with various attitudinal and environmental barriers, hinders their full and effective participation in society on an equal basis with others. However, this minimum list of persons who may claim protection under the Convention does not exhaust the categories of the disabilities which fall within the it nor intend to undermine or stand in the way of wider definition of disabilities under national law (such as persons with short-term disabilities). It is also important to note that a person with disabilities may be regarded as a person with a disability in one society or setting, but not in another, depending on the role that the person is assumed to take in his or her community. The perception and reality of disability also depend on the technologies, assistance, and services available, as well as on cultural considerations.

Specific Learning Disability: A specific learning disability, usually affects students with a disability to listen, think, speak, write, spell or do mathematical calculations. This can be known as a slow learner or sloe development disabilities, they may have struggles with writing, reading or calculating but when they are guided carefully from basic they slowly able to read and write even their level are not up to their age.

Visual Impairment: Visual impairment is when they have the capacity to see a degree that creates difficulties which cannot be overcome by the use of spectacles, visual impairment is also known as vision loss. Some may also include those who have a significantly lower viewing ability because they do not have access to eye-glasses or contact lenses where they can't help to improve their vision as well.

Chapter 13
Analyzing IT Opportunities for Inclusive Digital Learning:
The Largest Academic Project Ever Implemented During the COVID-19 Era

Mina Richards
California State University, Los Angeles, USA

ABSTRACT

COVID-19 caused a drastic closure of universities with traditional campus instruction. The university discussed in this chapter is a large institution out of which two campuses were examined for remote faculty training and student impact. The results from two short surveys for students and faculty are presented. Faculty responses focused on the perspective of facilitating remote courses and what direct impact remote teaching has had on their personal lives. The students' responses were mixed. Some participants stated that remote courses positively impacted their self-engagement and performance, and the remaining said that they had noticed a downward trend in performance. Five lessons learned are derived from observations and participants' provided information regarding the lack of communication and faculty engagement in training. By identifying the lessons learned, recommendations for each are provided for future-readiness and insights on how to influence engagement and approach communications and faculty attitude factors.

INTRODUCTION

In response to COVID-19, higher education pushed faculty to quickly identify digital learning solutions to transform classrooms into remote learning. Critically to faculty was if there were significant differences using online tools to emulate traditional classrooms. Combined with this concern was the lack of professional faculty development, learning engagement, and facilitation requirements. The pandemic caused many universities to jump on the concept of repurposing teaching, adopting video-conference

DOI: 10.4018/978-1-7998-7184-2.ch013

solutions for business meetings. While technology was available, academic institutions' negative impact was the lack of adequate faculty training and ample time to prepare for teaching continuity.

Although crises can lead to inclusive turning points, these opportunities could be costly if the institution does not consider prior situational knowledge and lessons learned. The University to be discussed in this chapter is a large public university residing in the United States, which required shifting to remote learning in one week. The only exceptions were lab-intensive courses which required face-to-face instruction to about 10% of the students. This chapter discusses the steps and sudden development to convert face-to-face courses to a remote environment in one of the largest public university systems. Two campuses are introduced to sample the faculty preparation before teaching remote and the students' reaction to distant learning.

The first section examines the challenges for tech-enabled inclusive education worldwide. The faculty learning frameworks to empower students to remote learning are discussed. The next sections review the faculty training plans and teaching models to enhance faculty course design, pedagogy, and technology use. The chapter describes two local surveys administered to faculty and students to gain their perspectives and beliefs on remote courses. Lastly, it glances over the areas for improvement during the transition to remote classes through a series of lessons learned and recommendations.

BACKGROUND

According to Moe and Rajendran (2020), the online learning pool has changed from 30% pre-coronavirus to almost 90% on a global scale. Densely populated schools have the option to teach online during a health crisis; however, there could be many obstacles to implementing online courses not only from individualized teaching but also from students' expectations and available technology. Heldt et al. (2021) conducted faculty perception studies to measure attitudes towards remote learning while taking a three-months online training course during the pandemic. They found that 68% of the trainees and 61% of the faculty preferred in-person training. Both groups felt that after returning to in-person, some lectures could be delivered effectively online. Professional development has always been a concern to faculty for training effectiveness, sponsorships, and practical application.

Baldiris Navarro et al. (2016) propose that inclusive learning is challenging, but recipients can be productive if faculty access Open Educational Resources for curriculum development. A great deal has been written about inclusive learning, but technology becomes a mediator to learning when it is considered. Therefore, inclusive digital technologies can enhance learning opportunities for all and overcome geographical challenges in a wide spectrum and conceptual way. Many of the universities worldwide have scrambled to put courses online in a matter of days. A similar scenario has played among American universities. For many institutions after the transition, the challenges have resulted in budget cuts, decreased enrollments, and student lawsuits asking for tuition reimbursement. Witze (2020) believes that in the long term, remote learning options will still be available even after in-person classes resume for some universities.

Digital Learning and Competence around the World

Academic leadership is critical to ensure remote teaching, and procedures and policies to support efficacy and continuity must be in place. According to Mazey and Richardson (2020), the United States ranked first in pandemic preparedness in the 2019 Global Health Security Index. Although the US ranked 83.5/100 out of 195 countries, it does not translate into having the utmost policy and adequate measures to deal with pandemic outbreaks. Aside from health security conditions, not all sectors measured the same leadership and preparedness. For example, the education sector suffered many difficulties, including the online teaching infrastructure, faculty training for online, technology gap, and transition policies to remote teaching and learning.

The call to action to migrate face-to-face teaching to remote learning has confronted many challenges worldwide. In the case of underdeveloped countries, they were not prepared to make the transition to remote education or even had the infrastructure. For instance, Egypt did not have the technical learning platforms to support online teaching (Sobaih et al., 2020). Similarly, other countries in Latin America have suffered from financial losses from declining enrollment and budget. Only one-third of 50 universities have transitioned to online mode, according to studies conducted by Hershberg et. al. (2020). That is an alarming revelation, and more broadly, the move to online in these countries did not anticipate the digital divide with lower socioeconomic living standards. These institutions have learned that returning to in-person learning as before the pandemic will take years before solving their pressing economic issues. Studies from Bhm-Carrer and Lucero (2018) found a concerning difficulty with online students that did not know how to look for information on the Internet and were confused or did not know the available academic tools to attend class. That condition accounts for the lack of digital training on the student population.

Latin American and the Caribbean are known for high unemployment and poverty, and the opening of these institutions to maintain virus safety and student support would require additional investment (Latin America, 2020). On the other hand, European countries classify the pandemic educational crisis as causal disparities in learning, threatening the learning opportunities of many children and diminishing decades of nationwide progress and richness (United Nations, 2020). A study of 80 public and private European universities established that half of the faculty had deficient technology use levels and that digital competencies rated low results (Portillo et al., 2020). Sobaih et al. (2020) discuss the critical shifts in higher education to serve students remotely in Asian universities. Many countries have adopted social media channels such as Facebook, WhatsApp, YouTube, and accessible learning tools ranging from Zoom to Google Classrooms. For instance, El Salvador lacks a robust technology infrastructure and relates that students climb on trees to get a stronger Wi-Fi reception. According to the United Nations, in 2020, 3.6 billion people still do not have Internet (Portillo et al., 2020) or reliable connections.

Other evidence has been reported in countries with initiated planning to improve the ability to serve students remotely. China is an example of innovation and emergency preparedness in unprecedented situations (Ning & Corcoran, 2020). It was one of the first countries with COVID-19, and universities were resilient and proactive in sustaining inclusive digital learning. Yang (2020) asserts that Chinese universities took precise measures to survive the crisis and worked with the government with a high degree of coordination and trust as only the Chinese government can facilitate. On the shift to digital, the transition also experienced teacher's gap in technology and poor networks, leading to formulating policies and resource allocations during and after the crisis. Mazey and Richardson (2020) convey that crisis management, as experienced in education, must be anticipatory and not reactive to deal effectively with massive disruptions.

Additional research on online learning has focused on comparing sustainability to Learning Management Systems (LMS) in terms of economic and social sustainability (Alharti et al., 2019). Human and environmental sustainability as well as encompass a more comprehensive online course delivery and green data centers. Sustainability in learning is distinct because it considers newer concepts in sociability and extends to boundaries addressing the digital divide. The next challenge is for online sustainability to assess the degree of interaction between the course materials, students, and other actors. The interaction component has been instrumental in hybrid learning, but it is not entirely successful yet in asynchronous courses.

As an observation, Moe and Rajendran (2020) believe that the pandemics have led to online utilization in e-commerce and the eLearning space. The authors support that the SARS outbreak and Internet penetration in China pushed E-commerce from 2.1% to 11% growth faster than pre-SARS and expect a similar growth for online learning post-disease era. The digital learning growth presents opportunities for developing new learning platforms and learning modalities to improve course delivery.

Digital Technologies Interacting with Education

Online learning has been evolutionary not only on teaching techniques but also in the appreciation for learning. There is a gradual acceptance that online students can reach higher academic achievements almost as close to those attained through face-to-face. With the sudden change to online learning, online teaching is as effective as face-to-face-learning, as more traditional schools offer online courses. Over 20 years ago, teaching math and technical courses online did not have the proper infrastructure; however, with technology and third party providers, more STEM courses are online to date. There are still challenges not well adapted to the current remote model, even with cutting edge technology. For example, students' access to reliable devices and long Internet sessions were some of the reasons student completion of MOOC courses was 6.8% worldwide in 2013, and only 5% earned certificates at Harvard and MIT (Rai, 2018). Although MOOC courses attracted students worldwide, MOOC universities and designers ignored low bandwidth requirements in the context of learning.

In response to COVID-19, higher learning identified solutions to transform traditional education into digital teaching and learning. Many universities jumped on the concept to repurpose teaching, adopting video conferencing platforms that made sense in the short run and have proven to work for business meetings. Remote learning forced teaching institutions to embrace innovation and new pedagogy alongside technology to support learning. Maybe this notion should have existed all along; however, in the past, traditional universities considered technology at the edge of education to improve course delivery. During the 2020 experience, education transitioned with technology and educational tools elevated to primary activities converting the face-to-face components to distance learning. While academics did not widely accept online learning before the pandemic, it quickly convinced everyone to run online entirely. COVID-19 has opened alternate ways to service education, giving practical solutions. More importantly, it has proven that with imagination, any online class is possible without consequences.

Universities have differed in implementing remote learning using various LMS versions, but all modalities must include technology and pedagogy for effectiveness. For over two decades, distance learning as a way of education is divided into synchronous and asynchronous modes. Synchronous refers to real-time meetings relying on Zoom or similar conferencing systems, and it is less flexible in time. On the other hand, asynchronous has been a model for transforming education into a more interactive and lively teaching method. Online can be blended or hybrid, hyflex, open schedule, and fixed-time online courses using video conferencing systems. The latest form hyflex has hybrid characteristics but meets students on-demand and as required. All modes are available to geographic boundaries but need a solid technical infrastructure at the offering university; therefore, distance learning has replaced physical classroom space with large servers and cloud services. The hybrid modality is the most popular and trendy option among students and faculty.

To improve the quality of learning through meaningful collaboration, inclusive teaching is traditionally associated with enhanced programs for special needs students attending mainstream classes. Conversely, inclusive digital learning goes one step above as seen through a holistic lens of technology and faculty perspective. Inclusiveness in digital learning must facilitate a dominant design and extend to learning communities in general. For globalization to take place, digital technologies must be widespread and constitute a necessity for socio-economic development in industry and governments, and education (Njenga, 2018). There are several frameworks to discuss inclusiveness in learning, such as Differentiated Instruction and the concept of Universal Design for Learning (UDL), which finds its roots in teaching strategy. UDL ensures that learners find flexibility in how information is presented and how students demonstrate skills and engagement (Mitchell, 2014). UDL must conform to content, process, and products for instructors, out of which the last two components suit all learners and use technology. The principle of "inclusive learning" nurtures the right for equal learning while giving a cost break to all. There are many ways for faculty to promote inclusive learning through digital technologies. Mitchell (2014) considers two risks in inclusive education that can limit its effectiveness, such as using digital technologies for partial learning and inadequate faculty training to administer those technologies.

Faculty Interacting with Digital Technologies

Baldiris-Navarro et al. (2016) conveyed specific guidelines and checkpoints to adhere faculty to core values and competency opportunities as shown in the Competence Framework of Inclusive Teachers. In relation to inclusive digital learning, the Competence Framework is incomplete because it does not engage faculty with technology. As shown in Table 1, technology brings new complexity to the model adding UDL for inclusion, tool selection, access to course materials, and tracking students' performance. Therefore, technology inclusion should consider affixing a new core value and competence areas for faculty to think digitally.

Table 1. Competence framework of inclusive teachers (Adapted from Watkins, 2012)

Core Values	Competence Areas
1. Value Learner Diversity: Learner differences is considered as a resource and an asset to education	1.1 Conceptions of inclusive education 1.2 The teacher's view of learner difference
2. Supporting All Learners: Teachers have high expectations for all learners' achievements	2.1 Promoting academic, practical, social, and emotional learning for all learners 2.2 Effective teaching approaches in heterogeneous classes
3. Working with Others: Collaboration and teamwork are essential approaches for all teachers	3.1 Working with parents and families 3.2 Working with a range of other educational professional
4. Personal Professional Development: Teaching is a learning activity, and teachers take responsibility for their lifelong learning	4.1 Teachers are reflective practitioners 4.2 Initial teacher education as a foundation for ongoing professional learning and development
5. Technology Adoption: Teaching tools in the classroom and for distance learning	5.1 Engage with Learning Management Systems and UDL 5.2 Test, evaluate, and select tools to enhance inclusive digital learning

A universal approach to professional development must consider Mezirow's transformative learning theory to examine the connection between faculty engagement and resource perceptions to improve instructional practices. Mezirow theorized that teaching and adult learning uses reflection to associate learning with past experiences to adjust their thinking and perceptions (Fleming, 2018). According to Nielson, (2018), professional development empowers educators to design high-quality programs if collaboration is consistent and supportive among faculty with similar expertise and teaching roles.

In addition to the issues raised in professional development, digital competency efficacy seems to draw a pattern of weaknesses in faculty development, digital skills, and logistic planning (Portillo et al., 2020). In their research, the authors found that teachers show higher competency using digital tools for personal use but are less confident to teal those tools to others. This chapter operationalizes inclusive digital learning as the process to create equal and adequate opportunities in learning by including people, technology, and pedagogy at the center of remote learning.

The following sections provide a magnified view discussing the University's details to appreciate the effort and extent of professional development, digital skills, and training support.

THE "UNIVERSITY" INFRASTRUCTURE AND TRAINING MODELS

The section provides a closer look at the American University transitioning to remote learning and experiencing the theory of inclusiveness, technical competence, and professional development perceptions. Unlike academics, the University support functions were a non-event because relocation happened with the same technical processes and protocols; however, for the teaching community, it was very different. The faculty was confused and needed lots of training to master the LMS and other distance learning platforms.

The majority of faculty had challenges migrating to the LMS and Zoom conferencing systems. There were also conflicting views if courses would be synchronously or partially hybrid online. Adding to the complexity were numerous training meetings to assist faculty in the transition. Instructors familiar with online and hybrid courses were able to adapt to remote teaching quicker than instructors with only face-to-face teaching experience. The latter group required more time to adjusting online. The process of creating full online courses required a solid knowledge of the online infrastructure, adaptable learning, and limitations for "without in-person instruction."

The Center for Faculty Effectiveness rolled out several training initiatives within one month after the University's closure. Because faculty has busy schedules researching, teaching, and services duties, the Center offered multiple levels of LMS training and remote teaching formats. All training was self-paced, using short videos. Also, remote meetings focused on promoting teaching ideas and suggesting best practices and student's care and flexibility. Helpful to the University was a previous experimental rollout of online courses for a handful of classes. That project shared the course infrastructure in place and disseminated brief knowledge and tips about online learning; however, some facts were unknown during the pandemic, such as student access to technology at home. According to Lieberman (2020), most schools are not aware of students' percentage without computers or Internet connectivity at home, making it difficult to plan for remote learning overnight. Since technology is essential to remote learning, the University bridged the digital divide by using funds allocated to the Coronavirus Aid, Relief, and Economic Security (CARES) Act to buy laptops and hotspots for needing students.

In the past, the University implemented courses online using the low bandwidth model as a recommendation from the teaching community. The concept of low bandwidth was introduced in the late 1990s and continues to be well-executed among online courses. Johnson et al. (2007) relate that online courses replaced correspondence courses, but learning management systems became dominant over time and became dominant, relying on complex technologies. Although the concept of online synchronous and asynchronous learning is a few decades old, innovative ideas have surfaced in the last few years such as new tools and functions. The hardware and software requirements for online learners are defined as having an Internet connection, mobile devices, and laptops. With the massive shift to online, cameras, microphones, and speakers are needed to attend classes. Rai (2018) points out that the likelihood of successfully finishing an online course is lower if students are frustrated with partial visibility of course materials and quizzes due to intermittent connections and outages. Having this insight, the course designer must test mobile devices and Internet compatibility before adding multimedia course delivery and interactive materials.

Faculty Training and Strategies for Remote Education

Both campuses at the University offered several professional development opportunities to improve remote delivery over the next academic year. In addition to weekly meetings to use technology and remote teaching techniques, faculty engaged in several workshops for effective teaching. Professional development programs focused on best practices for creating remote courses and offering strategies to make classes a better experience for the students and faculty. Most programs were 4-6 week courses, and faculty could attend as many programs as they wished. Participants received a stipend or professional development funds to support their time and effort to complete the summer program and deliverables during that timeframe.

The Flipped Classroom

The flipped lecture was one of the models introduced for digital learning, and it considers flipping the activities between home and class. This training was another pedagogical strategy for teaching both online and hybrid. The one week course covered discussion forums, assignments, and overall class presentation. Faculty viewed this training as an opportunity to join the unique collection of workshops to earn a prestigious online teaching certification. Woodall (2020) considers that endless meetings and ongoing training of teaching models create cognitive overloads for anxiety in specific ways such as confusion.

To implement a flipped classroom, it requires an open-mind and an understanding of the pros and cons of the model including the way students learn. The numerous activities force faculty to design lectures way in advance and follow up with improvements. For example, most classroom activities include watching videos and working on sample problems leading to high-stakes assignments. Class time is also devoted to questions and answers, and debates about the topics learned from readings. For classes with third party textbooks and ready course materials, the flipped classroom is possible. Third-party publishers offer a variety of hands-on online exercises that are exceptionally suited for math and science courses. Those exercises are navigated on the Internet, require no setup time, and are subscription-free; however, in courses with textbooks only, faculty has to build all related course materials.

Hussain (2013) refers that one of the common barriers to student success is "not knowing" the student ahead of time when course materials are being prepared. The faculty attending those workshops had several observations in this regard. The first concern was the uncertainty of selecting materials too easy or too difficult for the student. If the materials are easy, some students will lose interest in the subject. If the material is difficult, the lack of instructor presence could also discourage the students from learning. The second issue was trust if the students will use their study time to study and understand the materials. Aside from time management, prioritization and cramming were also a concern. Because there is significant work creating a flipped classroom, its adoption is strategic to allow for ample course development time.

For the reasons mentioned, the faculty was not successful in this training. Other obstacles discussed were instructor knowledge of technology, willingness to make progressive changes, and Bloom's taxonomy application. Those obstacles were more prevalent on faculty with set ways to teach a course. Because designing content was essential, some instructors fell behind and withdrew from training.

Quality Matters (QM)

Quality Matters is a system based on instructors' teams to deliver a culture of best practices and constant improvement for online courses (Quality Matters, 2020). The organization offers exclusive rubrics, standards, certifications, peer reviews, and professional development. The motto is to frame, expand, and reinforce best practices. QM is one of the most popular frameworks adopted in the United States to improve student learning, contributing to engagement. There are many articles about validating QM practices in the classroom, and the standards align the course learning outcomes to materials and course assessments.

Although QM courses are extensive and time-demanding, for that reason, very few instructors completed the coursework. For faculty wanting to acquire qualifications to teach hybrid and online courses, QM is exceptional. For faculty interested in conducting internal course reviews, advanced credentials are available. It is important to note that faculty who took QM courses had an easier time switching to remote teaching during the fall semester.

Remote Course Design

The Remote Course Design (RCD) training workshop was the most popular course, although faculty chose to take either the RCD or the ACUE modules as discussed later. The RCD guided faculty using a "Design-Build-Teach-Improve" process based on the QM framework and a course design process for faculty with basic to remote intermediate experience. This course included optional activities such as contributing to discussion boards and faculty course reviews and critiques. Table 2 outlines the deliverables to indicate completion in asynchronous courses.

Best Practices for Remote Teaching

This training was a three-week intensive experience course based on the University Quality Teaching & Learning Framework. Modules within this option were a blend of RCD, QM, and flipped classrooms. It was designed for faculty with basic to remote intermediate teaching, although some modules could appeal to more advanced experienced faculty. This course was another training option, but due to faculty attendance, only a handful finished.

Table 2. RCD deliverables adapted from RCD curriculum (2020)

Steps	Deliverables
Set-Up	Create a well-developed "Start here" section for your course, including syllabus
Design	Build out the first two modules/weeks of your fall course as entirely as possible, even if you plan asynchronous courses. a. Learning objectives articulated for each module or topic. b. Activities and assignments are fully available and ready to go. c. Lectures, if used, at least outlined. If you plan to do video lectures, it is optimal to have the videos ready. d. For activity courses, performance courses, labs, etc., the same or similar items are needed.
Build	Add learning objectives and draft ideas for activities & assessments for the remaining modules of your course (get a head start, in other words).
Teach	Demonstrate your completion of the above 1-3 by contributing to a discussion board with screenshots or other evidence.
Improve	Self-assess your course with a comprehensive rubric that includes consideration of equitable and inclusive practices.

Source: (RCD, 2020)

ACUE Micro-Credential Courses

The micro-credentialing courses for faculty were six modules taught in eight-weeks. The Association of College & University Educators (ACUE) offers courses, including the micro-credential "Promoting Active Learning Online." For this course, trainers were selected at the University from those who have gone through the entire 25-module ACUE credential course and had experience in remote teaching. The second option, "Creating an Inclusive and Supportive Online Learning Environment," was also taught internally for faculty already experienced in online or hybrid education. Those modules include teaching practices selected from ACUE member universities.

ACUE training was considered essential because of the critical learning objectives and standards shared for best practices (ACUE, 2020). Faculty learned that classroom techniques must measure student success and that ACUE is a resource to consult with other faculty across the nation. These courses were released quickly, giving practical advice to use student learning outcomes to redesign courses. Table 3 provides an overview of the Online Toolkit used to assist instructors through six topic areas. It is estimated that over half of the faculty trained took ACUE training as well as the RCD workshop previously described.

Faculty Training on Low Bandwidth eLearning Model

The low bandwidth model was recommended for remote continuity to ease the learning environment and find alternatives to video and synchronous activities. Johnson et al. (2007) as the originators, proposed a model to conceptualize the teaching criteria to meet low-bandwidth e-learning systems. These include the following.

- The learner is the primary user
- Prioritize the student view
- Recognize the University as a learning community
- Provide an environment to adapt to the learning task

Table 3. Adapted from ACUE useful online teaching practices modules

Topic Areas	Practices
Welcoming student to the online environment	• Create a welcome video to let students know that "we are in this together." • Create a Q&A forum and social forum to answer course questions and to connect students with one another. • Create an online orientation video for course navigation and expectations.
Manage your online presence	• Establish clear expectations of teaching presence: post frequent announcements; offer virtual hours; create chat opportunities; provide timely and strategic feedback.
Organize your online course	• Organize course content from the students' point of view. • Provide a module roadmap and consistency of module design. • develop a predictable rhythm through weekly pace and modules.
Planning and facilitating quality discussions	• Provide a rubric with clear expectations for participation. • Assign reflective discussion to evaluate their participation. • Provide strategic feedback to ensure quality discussions.
Recording effective micro-lectures	• Create a 6-minute structured recording to provide explanations about assignments, key concepts, or skill sets.
Engaging students in reading micro-lectures	• Provide guiding questions, ask for annotations, prepare discussion forums. • Administer skeletal outlines asking questions about the lecture about the topic, learning materials, and pending questions.

Source (Quality Matters, 2020)

- Design as an information system
- Design for reusability at the course, author, and student level
- Consider alternative delivery technologies
- Evaluate for functionality, usability, and accessibility

The low bandwidth was the primary model to administer courses in terms of several tactical operations and student flexibility. Designing a good learning experience for students, including those with poor Internet connectivity, it is centered on Johnson et al. model. The low bandwidth model is just one example to accommodate online learning, but other authors also have acknowledged the fundamental shift to adult-learning education in terms of digital learning (Moe & Rajendran, 2020). Table 4 compares school activities before and after COVID-19. Based on this division, Goodall (2020) observes that educators and health promoters have contributed significantly during crisis and human disasters to advanced levels of digital learning. Those occupations have self-redefined with new processes and continue to perform under extreme pressures.

Faculty Adapting to the Learning Task

University classes were interrupted for only one week to allow faculty to redesign courses for remote teaching. Daily discussions and faculty meetings reviewed best practices using the LMS and other tools to administer virtual courses. Additionally, the Center for Faculty Effectiveness established the Teaching Continuity site to post several training videos, quick start guides, and workshops. There were daily video postings to support faculty with pedagogical resources, collaborative events, and FAQs.

Because students were struggling with lost jobs, illness, and crowded-living at home, faculty training emphasized flexibility and kindness. Faculty workshops underlined the importance of reaching out to

Table 4. Adapted from Moe and Rajendran school activities before and after Covid-19

Teaching Before COVID-19	Teaching During COVID-19
Face-to-Face instruction	90% remote instruction
Daytime and evening classes	Anytime and anywhere classes
Live lectures	Zoom and recorded lectures
Partial or no use of the Learning Management System	Full use of the Learning Management System
Classes with 25-40 students	Classes with 60-150 students
Personalized assignment grading	Frequent use of automated grading
Optical Projector in classroom	Zoom conferencing
Review Syllabus due dates in class	Email due date reminders
Classroom office hours	Virtual office hours
Live student presentations	Zoom student presentations
Student attention observed in class as focused	Student attention observed in zoom meetings as playing apps, emailing, etc.

Source: (Moe & Rajendran, 2020)

students frequently with cheerful weekly check-ins and reminders. Many professors felt overwhelmed with information from a dozen different sources, giving teaching tips, using the technology, and sharing ideas, questions, and strategies with other faculty. That effort was intense and needed a personal plan for handling information overload.

The University as a Learning Community

The incorporation of faculty training showed to have beneficial effects in course formats in several dimensions. The class format identified what assignments would work to meet the learning objectives, what other activities will demonstrate learning, and how feedback would impact student learning. Faculty courses investigated the right tools and course materials for faculty who attended remote training to help students succeed. Similarly, students' feedback also required a reflection on areas for improvement. Considering the intense faculty training and faculty who did not train, classroom courses are all working well up to date.

Designing for Resources

Sayer and Braun (2020) discussed that socioeconomic marginalization among urban districts causes a gap in readiness to move immediately to remote learning. Because public systems have socially-disadvantaged students and high immigration status, not all students could readily attend online classrooms but could communicate using mobile devices. For those reasons, low bandwidth resources were the choice for remote teaching at the University. Also, Zoom meetings include synchronous sessions for questions and to create a social environment with students and instructors. Discussion forums have helped to discuss short case studies and share peer-review feedback on assignments. Other ways to use discussions were to invite conversations on designated topics and assign bonus points through LMS Chatrooms. All of these options and activities can be done asynchronously and therefore support low bandwidth requirements.

Facilitating courses synchronously and recording class sessions or specific instructions for missing attendees has created a new teaching model mixing asynchronous, synchronous, and hybrid components.

Quizzes and exams have required new strategies and re-thinking. Testing in quizzes and exams curriculum has become lower-stakes assignments with fewer points and more often than regular classroom assessments. That meant creating a series of quizzes to be delivered weekly with fewer questions. Textbook publishers have been useful in creating online quizzes with auto-grading options.

Alternative Learning through Videos

Instead of recording full lectures, faculty recorded audio lectures with accompanying slides and notes to facilitate low bandwidth teaching. There are plenty of low bandwidth resources and alternatives like YouTube videos that can be linked to class content for ease of use. For class interaction and collaborative work, Google Docs have worked well to enhance the variety of course materials for students' learning.

Additionally, many instructors have opted for lectures with interactive activities, which required different planning and strategies. For example, the instructor could devise the questions or allow students to create questions and discuss the possible answers in an online forum. Students could also meet in small Zoom breakout rooms and regroup in the primary classroom later to discuss the answers and solutions. Interactive and collaborative activities have required a lot of planning in the short time allowed after faculty training. Also, the University has introduced many workshops for accessibility through image captions and section headings for slide content and text documents. In addition to Microsoft programs with accessibility checkers, built-in software in LMS also provided tools to detect if documents needed corrections. Document accessibility is a QM requirement, and therefore, both Universities campuses have adopted the Quality Matters template to make the LMS easy to navigate and include links of interest.

REMOTE IMPLEMENTATION CHALLENGES

Given the crisis and showdown, the pressing goal was to transfer 93% of all courses to remote teaching in one week. That directive presented a substantial challenge, threatening the quality of education that would be delivered and the faculty's well-being. Although both University sites lined up resources in days, remote faculty training was not mandatory for faculty. That meant that some faculty adhered to remote teaching, defining their own rules. The short time and lack of clarity in the transition shifted the pressure to faculty and IT personnel. With those pressures, a group of professors with Zoom and LMS expertise took on the role to virtually train other faculty. The reset time was too short for formal faculty training. It was a daunting task with the uncertainty of going to some new place and embracing immediate change while faculty and students adjusted.

The CARES program received in May helped invest in professional development for faculty. The primary goal was to align pedagogy to remote courses through a series of best practices, learning models, and digital technology. For a University that did not believe in online learning, it made a smooth transition. It is worth noting that remote education remains strong, and both Universities sites are performing well in light of some areas that could be improved.

A support structure for students has been at the center to sustain their financial and mental well-being and personal values to help them persist and succeed in school. Student support has been an opportunity to empathize with their situations creating a more robust social bond. Similarly, it has been an opportunity to prioritize health and safety and build partnerships with mobile service providers.

Perceptions of Remote Learning at the University

This section discusses the perceptions of success with remote courses and whether the students and teaching community adapted to remote inclusive learning. To analyze the perceptions, three surveys with open questions and convenience sampling are used. Because there was no single point to measure remote teaching success, faculty within the colleges had random discussions with Chairs on the progress made during summer training. Those conversations centered on remote practices and witnessed solutions addressing the online challenges; however, they did not investigate teaching or student success. That effort would need appropriate survey instruments to measure remote teaching success criteria. As a result, faculty conducted several informal surveys measuring the effectiveness of faculty-led training. Nearly every survey asked on the design and content delivery of courses using technology. There was also a pulse survey launched in September asking faculty how the pandemic affected their research productivity since publications would have a drastic impact on accrediting profiles.

Every project needs measurements in terms of utility and success. This section introduces explicitly three surveys taking at different times during October at the two University sites. The subject pool for this study consists of 103 faculty members from various disciplines at one University site and 96 undergraduate students taking business courses attending the two University sites. The purpose of sampling faculty was to conduct a well-check test during September and explore faculty perceptions of remote learning and adaptation. The study shows that in addition to community participation, faculty are always aligning to models and survey questions to establish some control analyzing concerns and resolving issues as a group. Conversely, the student survey investigated if remote courses in the fall were attractive and allowed for student collaboration and engagement. The data gathered from these samples are presented in a simple form with the total number of answers only.

Faculty and Students Opinions

The first is a faculty survey collected from institutional emails originated at the Center for Faculty Effectiveness. The purpose was to gather faculty opinions about their experiences with remote courses and the impact to their personal lives. The faculty pool included full and part-time instructors with doctoral and master's degrees spread through all University fields. Since the data was obtained as an informative email, the responses were not rigorously coded because there is no way to know the number of responses per category. There were four open questions, out of which the most common answers are in Table 5.

The criteria for measuring student success with remote engagement should take precedence over faculty expressing opinions. To sample the student population, the researcher created a questionnaire to explore the reasons for taking remote courses and what activities students like best in these courses. The two University sites provided two different student sets to gather various responses splitting the population between 46 and 50 correspondently. The researcher posted a three points bonus questions in the LMS for students to answer and indicate their course preferences. The sample characteristics were students from a four year university attending a management course in the business school. The questions included multiple-choice and open-ended questions to allow students to express their opinions and personal experiences with remote learning. As shown in Table 6, the first question asked if remote

Table 5. Mid-semester faculty check

Question	Most Common Answer	Second Common Answer
Q 1. How are you doing generally?	• Overwhelmed and exhausted	• Pretty good to great
Q 2. What is something that's making faculty life easier right now?	• No commute and no parking struggles • Having done a lot of prep and training over the summer	• Certainty regarding remote spring although it is not what we wanted
Q 3. What's something that's making faculty life harder right now?	• Online teaching takes far more work • Having to give lots of small low stakes assessments and then grade them	• None of the other work expectations have diminished despite the overwhelming workload of remote teaching • Overwhelmed by email
Q.4 What's something you hope will be available in the near future, however you define that time frame? (No promises, just gathering ideas.)	• A vaccine and safe return to campus • A better learning management system, like Canvas	• Better access to hardware for remote teaching • Funding for other home-based teaching infrastructure

Source: Personal Email (2020)

courses encourage students to perform better. Although nine students did not respond, 48 students felt that remote courses enticed them to perform better academically, while 39-students did not find the motivation to improve academic achievements. Nine students did not answer the question.

Table 6. Remote course preferences

Question	Students Do Better	Student Do Less	No Response
Do remote courses encourage you to perform better?	48 responses	39 responses	9 students

The student survey included two more questions to explore the reasons for students attending remote courses. Table 6 shows that 42 students attended remote because of convenience, whereas 54 students attended to finish their degree sooner. Additionally, Table 7 shows the final question indicating the students' favorite activities in remote courses. The students 'choices were Zoom breakouts rooms, team projects, and the use of third party materials respectively. The first three choices also imply that students enjoy communicating with fellow students through online activities.

Table 7. Remote description activities

Questions	Convenience and Flexibility	Finish Degree	Discussion Questions*	Zoom Breakouts*	Team Projects*	Third-Party Materials*
What motivates you to attend remote courses?	42	54				
What activities do you enjoy in remote courses (Students could select multiple activities)			64	36	42	9

The emphasis given on student preferences to engage socially poses a challenge because the social gap in remote courses is difficult to bridge. Distant learning is less likely to increase in popularity after the pandemic because students miss the face-to-face contact. The fundamental problem is that students looking for social interaction in college do not fulfill the social need through online activities. Specifically, the students' data indicates that students are uncertain and have difficulty deciding which virtual engagement option is better. It is unclear if establishing collaboration through remote technology is less effective due to the lapse in responses, short time interacting, or communicating in writing versus verbally. Alharthi et. al. (2019) explain that social sustainability is not optimal for eLearning systems in terms of learning activities and materials.

The short surveys and results discussed in this section provide evidence that remote course quality influences student attendance and fosters engagement across various activities. Faculty responses focused on the perspective of facilitating remote courses and what direct impact remote teaching has had so far. The students' responses were mixed. Some participants stated that remote courses positively impacted their self-engagement and performance, and the remaining said that they had noticed a downward trend in performance. There is potential to investigate further if the theories applied to remote courses such as the flipped classroom, low bandwidth, QM, and others are significant to student learning and meet student expectations in the COVID-19 era. Similarly, listening to student needs and recommendations could also prove a valuable resource to revise course design for remote learning.

FACULTY LESSONS LERNED AND RECOMMENDATIONS

Lessons Learned Analysis

While many universities worldwide have survived and self-restructured their teaching product, this section presents the lessons learned emerged from a large American university training its faculty to sustain inclusive digital instruction beyond the face-to-face timeline. The lessons learned and recommendations are forward-thinking, drawing on several observations discussed in the chapter to institutionalize a campus network and support faculty and students during a crisis. The section proposes lessons learned and University recommendations to proactively define the faculty roles, processes, and infrastructure before a crisis occurs again.

Lesson 1: Recognize that Faculty Training was Reactive and not Proactive

Based on discussions, faculty expressed reactions confirming that during the pandemic faculty training was primarily reactive versus proactive within their colleges. In the first month, there was a lack of formal training, and faculty rapidly introduced peer training meetings to address the basic use of remote technology. Like many other schools, faculty had to respond to new teaching and learning forms, creating stress and pressure to be ready in one week after campus closures. Faculty feedback has been consistent regarding acknowledging that teaching during crisis mode requires a more proactive approach and planning. Repetto and Trentin (2011) analyzed that faculty resist training due to burnout, work overload, and lack of support systems; however, they found evidence that communication and technology can enhance higher education learning if faculty showed motivation to use it.

Feedback shows that faculty reactions to remote teaching rushed information training because of two reasons. While most academic instruction at universities is face-to-face, switching to remote teaching caused faculty to reflect on their teaching techniques and skills needed to manage online platforms. Faculty recognized that something must change to align them on track, whether rethinking the way to teach or reaching out to technology delivery. The second reason relates to faculty transitioning to new forms of assessment and recording lectures from home without the technical know-how. Administrators worked hard to identify if faculty needing training were within specific disciplines only or across colleges. The best solution was to launch short training workshops during mid-spring and a 6-week training session in the summer. Since formal training was not quickly settled, the confusion resulted in faculty relaxing assignments and passing everyone with a good grade at the end of the spring semester.

Even when faculty attended short training workshops, there were inconsistent approaches in training administration. In the quest for quick training, some colleges released 2-5 minute videos blending remote skills and technology; however, faculty wanted to introduce more tangible training rapidly. Some of the faculty self-organized to share best practices, put together Zoom and Kaltura training and presented what they believed to be the best teaching solutions. The remaining faculty expressed that they did nothing and waited for a proper direction. This inconsistent approach illustrates that faculty training and direction should be proactively implemented in a timely and consistent manner. All appropriate steps must be taken prior to deployment to avoid uncertainty.

Lesson Learned: Identify close alignment between faculty roles and crisis management to maintain equal faculty engagement at the forefront.

Lesson 2: Faculty and Administration Teams Lack of Communication

A commonality found in administration is that stakeholders are cautious with the information received and saw it as insufficient or confidential to discuss with faculty. The lack of communication showed that Chairs and Deans were passive and did not openly discuss ideas for remote courses or weaken student experiences. Some faculty arrived at their conclusions while other faculty reacted differently and was frustrated questioning the lack of information and the rationale for keeping quiet.

Only a handful of emails came from the President and Provost announcing the training available; however, occasional emails originated from the Center for Faculty Effectiveness, mainly promoting faculty training programs, content, and start dates. During the remote transition, the communication gap identified opportunities for the administration to improve communication and disseminate plans during crises to the varying teams. Studies from Sutherland (2017) showed that school administrators tend to respond to crises in a complex rather than simplistic form. They revealed that understanding trust in crisis mode leads the stakeholders to protect and preserve themselves, preventing them from learning and growing from the crisis.

Lesson Learned: Although communication flows can be restricted due to confidentiality, providing friendly and transparent support during a crisis can go a long way with faculty and help in any buy-in process.

Lesson 3: Training for Remote Teaching and Learning was Ad-Hoc and Optional but not Mandatory

While remote teaching was an option to continue the academic year, it was the only option for teaching institutions. Since remote instruction radically altered the learning process and faculty collaboration, it has become a paradigm shift in concept. Remote teaching has conditioned the way students learn in academic life; however, having the space to discuss the importance of this change did not happen at a minimum to be heard or evaluated. Although administrators have always expressed their willingness to have open-door policy, it is common knowledge that only on rare occasion faculty reaches out. To make training enticing, the University offered monetary incentives to those attending the 6-week course in summer to help align face-to-face courses to remote teaching. There were only a handful of technology choices for faculty, including the online platform, Zoom, and Kaltura.

The top-down flow of communication shared a consistent message that training was optional or on- the-job-learning. Whereas remote training was optional for faculty, students did not have alternatives, received informational training, or had how-to videos. Students not familiar with online platforms also experienced a learning curve and only had the instructor for relevant training during class. Mazey and Richardson (2020) argue that unpreparedness generally leads organizations to be hesitant in their response to crises.

When faculty responded informally about what techniques they could carry over in the switch to remote, most shared in the feeling that they were clueless. Therefore, a formal training process needed implementation to create more flexible courses and adaptable to remote teaching thoughtfully. The communication flow under Lesson 2 ties directly to Lesson 3 in that students and faculty specifically were not influenced to attend training. The small stipend offered to faculty was not a reword but only the result of the CARES grant, but it was a factor to attend training. Even with allocating the stipend, faculty also showed low engagement in training and a high level of demotivation due to exhaustion with teaching loads and little time to spare on new training.

Lesson Learned: Therefore, a pre-crisis formal process must be in place to evaluate remote learning risks, faculty loads, back up plans, and student experience across the board.

Lesson 4: Remote Learning Transition Impact Faculty Motivation and Engagement

The remote transition demonstrated shortcomings in the overall direction and leadership to support teaching and learning. Despite a generally held with view that lack of direction, faculty stood alone to deal with the lack of support and decision on teaching issues or how they should be addressed. Department Chairs were quiet and could not explain even the differences between teaching remote, online, and asynchronous courses. Often most roadblocks were either discussed with the Center for Faculty Effectiveness or peer-faculty to find answers. There were many shortfalls in clarification, leaving a sense of uncertainty and fragmentation among faculty. Petillion and McNeil (2020) confirmed that faculty and students experienced struggles to keep up the same levels of motivation, productivity, and well-being when face-to-face courses are canceled.

Although the support obtained from peer-faculty was positive, it did not entice a greater motivation and engagement because it was informal. Yet, given the newness of remote learning, some faculty felt that the administration did what they could to support faculty with the limited resources and training available.

Lesson Learned: There is a need for strong leadership to lead by example and hold accountability for enthusiastic support and openness during disasters and crisis times.

Lesson 5: Faculty Engagement Responding to Crisis Change

Schwarzer and Luszczynska (2008) state that information received from others helps mitigate people's similar problems. As discussed earlier, knowledge sharing and faculty cross-training was identified as an essential task by faculty who believe that they could assume the leadership and confidence to train others. Using peer to peer skillsets and open collaboration created a sense of belonging among faculty. A drawback is that departments often implement best practices or procedures without standardizing them, which later pose a risk of inconsistent application or silos. The emphasis on attending training was optional but helped analyze that faculty engagement in remote training was a personal decision. Therefore, not even a crisis forced faculty to attend remote training.

While the number of courses also decreased due to budgets, Chairs and Deans were not always aware of the faculty who attended remote training. Most important, in the fall, Chairs did not readily consider offering course loads to adjunct faculty with remote training certification. It was not always the main deciding factor. Chairs provided a different insight into the topic by emphasizing adjunct tenure contracts over remote teaching readiness.

Lessons Learned: This lesson derives from a combination of lessons learned 1-4, which provides a multi-level viewpoint of the influences of faculty engagement and top down communication as a response to COVID-19 crisis change.

The lessons learned gathered from faculty provide a sequence of competence areas revealing that faculty used the core values adapted to the Competence Framework of Inclusive Teachers Watkins (2012) to ensure courses met inclusive digital learning. UDL was one of the most difficult tasks to achieve during the transition because it was done haphazardly and with minimal expertise and guidance. These findings also indicated that faculty with high motivation and initiatives to engage in professional self-development and made use of networking and collaboration to maximize resources and training.

Recommendations

The short surveys and faculty lessons learned indicate that the University will benefit from recommendations to help navigate future disasters and address shortcomings or areas needing direct communication flows. The recommendations are broken down by lessons to allow for alignment and to help build employee engagement following crises.

Recommendation #1

The observations show the need to create an "Event Committee" by colleges to proactively outline step-by-step actions to restore teaching practices and infrastructure following emergency situations. Formal procedures should be documented and revised each year to include new processes or new compliance. The committee can review these documents or appoint a designated group to keep the information current.

Recommendation #2

Although not all details can be shared with faculty, it is recommended that the administration be more transparent with faculty and give sufficient information behind decisions and changes in crisis. Looking back, faculty would have appreciated personal invitations to explore the benefits of taking the short remote workshops and the summer training course.

Recommendation #3

Faculty showed that openness would help them be better engaged and prepared if all remote training benefits were explained beforehand. The additional information would lead to more transparency and allow faculty to be more involved in training, ask questions, and possibly share their best practices and feel more valued. Similarly, advocating technology acceptance would help faculty align their perception of usefulness to inclusive learning.

Recommendation #4

With the way faculty self-organized before the formal training, the creation of similar faculty groups for idea submission and plans during disasters or emergencies is recommended. That initiative would benefit faculty and staff readiness and lead to a more formal process for idea submission and disseminating procedures for routine tasks. At a minimum, faculty will be empowered beyond the teaching capabilities. Once faculty groups are formed during non-event times, they can be involved in short pilot drills each year after all appropriate directions and procedures are approved and made official.

Recommendation #5

Having a formal process between the Event Committee and faculty groups will centralize college efforts and help streamline and track the various documents and decisions in one place. The process will also promote faculty engagement and empowerment to cross-communicate with other colleges to enhance readiness before crises. If this initiative moves forward, even college staff could be involved in the project and build skillsets, which would result in higher community engagement. The idea is similar to business continuity planning conducted in organizations to pro-actively plan business as usual operations and reduce impact during and after disruptions.

Also, to build on the concepts of emergency preparedness and inclusive learning, training programs could be designed for faculty development and certifications and cross-college communication. The primary recommendation would focus on emergency best practices, social responsibility, technology adoption, and sustainable training for teaching faculty. Yearly accreditation can be done asynchronously through a series of short workshops and a quiz to certify the individual. The practical value would be to have procedures ready and address the shortcomings encountered during the 2020 remote teaching implementation. While time and resources may not be available to conduct more formal training, it is feasible to collect how specific processes and training were conducted in 2020. The Event Committee and faculty groups could collaborate and share practices and stories that worked for faculty during the pandemic. This training would keep all faculty having the same understanding and consistency. As new ideas arise, they can be incorporated into the program. Producing a one-way forward short to long-term plan would preserve the quality of university education. Guidelines would be compiled to ensure a safe and healthy learning environment cycling through remote teaching and returning to in-person instruction. The preparedness program should also recognize the need for additional coordination with other university departments for a comprehensive strategy.

CONCLUSION

Adapting to an extreme event during the pandemic and reacting to change in days has been the experience of many learning institutions and businesses in general. Perhaps this situation is no longer unique, but it gives thought to study the cycle of change during an intense crisis. The emergency transition to remote learning at the University was stressful for faculty and frustrated for students. The switch to remote learning happened so unexpectedly that it was impossible to predict the extent of change and prepare for the unknown. Yet, it provided a broader understanding and consciousness to integrate change quickly using the low bandwidth model, Inclusive Online Learning, Remote Course Design, and other frameworks; however, voluntary professional development significantly affected the attitudes towards faculty engaging in more training courses.

Although faculty shared several lessons learned, there are still many issues pending such as addressing training engagement and communication flow. Engagement is essential and should assist in improving learning. Engagement and communications should be seen as specific requirements of equal importance as course design. The lack of readiness to prepare for remote teaching is still a concern, and it has been troublesome for many of the faculty. This chapter emphasized the importance of forward-thinking a university network to prepare faculty and support students for remote instruction during a transitory or extended crisis. Capturing lessons learned has been an ongoing opportunity through the pandemic. This chapter aimed to look at faculty and student perceptions of remote learning and compiled the lesson learned during the past months to explore a possible implementation of improvements emphasizing faculty readiness.

There are unanswered questions if the remote experience and the transition effort will have a lasting change after reaching some normalcy again. There is no assurance that the protocols developed will last long or be included in contingency plans, or be modified for future-readiness or simulations. Therefore, the switch to remote is guaranteed to survive until classrooms can be safely open; after that, new situations could force teaching and learning plans to be redefined and re-invented all over again given the future conditions. By building on lessons learned in collaboration with faculty and students, those experiences can be preserved and provide a first-hand account for future and similar applications. Inclusive learning and professional development have proven their effectiveness during the pandemic and must bring digital competence at the core to advocate educational resilience as the fundamental response.

REFERENCES

Alharthi, A. D., Spichkova, M., & Hamilton, M. (2019). Sustainability requirements for eLearning systems: A systematic literature review and analysis. *Requirements Engineering*, *24*(4), 523–543. doi:10.100700766-018-0299-9

Association of Colleges and University Educators. (2020). *Effective online teaching practices*. https://acue.org/programs/catalog/

Baldiris-Navarro, S., Zervas, P., Gesa, R., & Sampson, D. (2016). Developing teachers' competences for designing inclusive learning experiences. *Journal of Educational Technology & Society*, *19*(1), 17–27. https://csula-primo.hosted.exlibrisgroup.com/permalink/f/117sn1j/TN_cdi_csuc_recercat_oai_recercat_cat_2072_324273

Giovanis, K. (2015). Keep it simple: Challenges, solutions, and best practices for global eLearning initiatives. *International Journal of Advanced Corporate Learning*, *8*(2), 47–49. doi:10.3991/ijac.v8i2.4622

Heldt, J. P., Agrawal, A., Loeb, R., Richards, M., Castillo, E. G., & DeBonis, K. (2021). We're not sure we like it but we still want more: Trainee and faculty perceptions of remote learning during the COVID-19 pandemic. *Academic Psychiatry*. Advance online publication. doi:10.100740596-021-01403-4 PMID:33594628

Hershberg, E., Flinn-Palcic, A., & Kambhu, C. (2020). The COVID-19 pandemic and Latin American universities. *Center for Latin America & Latino Studies*. https://www.american.edu/centers/latin-american-latino-studies/upload/la-higher-ed-covid-final.pdf

Hussain, J. (2018). Three common barriers to success in the flipped classroom model. *Teach Thought*. Retrieved from https://www.teachthought.com/learning/3-common-barriers-to-success-in-a-flipped-classroom-model/

Johnson, R., Kemp, E., Kemp, R., & Blakey, P. (2007). The learning computer: Low bandwidth tool that bridges digital divide. *Journal of Educational Technology & Society*, *10*(4), 143–155.

Latin America. (2020). Retrieved from american.edu

Lieberman, M. (2020). Coronavirus prompting e-learning strategies. *Education Week*, *39*(24), 11.

Mazey, S., & Richardson, J. (2020). Lesson-Drawing from New Zealand and Covid-19: The need for anticipatory policy making. *The Political Quarterly*, *91*(3), 561–570. doi:10.1111/1467-923X.12893 PMID:32836413

Mitchell, D. (2014). *What really works in special and inclusive education: Using evidence-based teaching strategies* (2nd ed.). Routledge. doi:10.4324/9780203105313

Moe, M., & Rajendran, V. (2020). Dawn of the age of digital learning: An acceleration of trends that have building for year. *GSV Ventures*. https://medium.com/gsv-ventures/dawn-of-the-age-of-digital-learning-4c4e38784226

Nielsen, N. J. (2018). *Community college professors' engagement and perceptions of professional development in remote environments*. ProQuest Dissertations Publishing.

Ning, A., & Corcoran, B. (2020). How China schools are getting through COVID-19. *Ed Surge Global Education*. Retrieved from https://www.edsurge.com/news/2020-04-20-how-china-s-schools-are-getting-through-covid-19

Njenga, J. K. (2018). Digital literacy: The quest of an inclusive definition. *Reading & Writing (Cape Town, South Africa)*, *9*(1), 1–7. doi:10.4102/rw.v9i1.183

Petillion, R. J., & McNeil, W. S. (2020). Student experiences of emergency remote teaching: Impacts of instructor practice on student learning, engagement, and well-being. *Journal of Chemical Education*, *97*(9), 2486–2493. doi:10.1021/acs.jchemed.0c00733

Portillo, J., Garay, U., Tejada, E., & Bilbao, N. (2020). Self-Perception of the digital competence of educators during the COVID-19 pandemic: A cross-analysis of different educational stages. *Sustainability. (Basel, Switzerland)*, *12*(10128), 10128. doi:10.20944/preprints202011.0426.v1

Quality Matters. (2020). *Why QM*. Retrieved from https://www.qualitymatters.org/why-quality-matters/impact

Rai, L. (2018). Offline sport model for low bandwidth users to survive in MOOCs. *International Journal of Emerging Technologies in Learning*, *13*(10), 270–277. doi:10.3991/ijet.v13i10.8595

Repetto, M., & Trentin, G. (2011). *Faculty training for web enhanced learning*. Nova Science, Incorporated.

Sayer, P., & Braun, D. (2020). The disparate impact of COVID-19 remote learning on English learners in the United States. *TESOL Journal*, *11*(3). Advance online publication. doi:10.1002/tesj.546

Schwarzer, R., & Luszczynska, A. (2008). Reactive, anticipatory, preventive, and proactive coping: A theoretical distinction. *Prevention Researcher*, *15*(4), 22.

Singh, G., & Hardaker, G. (2014). Barriers and Enablers to Adoption and Diffusion of ELearning. *Education + Training*, *56*(2/3), 105–121. doi:10.1108/ET-11-2012-0123

Sobaih, A., Elnasr, E., Hasanein, A. M., Elnasr, A., & Ahmed, E. (2020). Responses to COVID-19 in higher education: Social media usage for sustaining formal academic communication in developing countries. *Sustainability. (Basel, Switzerland)*, *12*(16), 6520. doi:10.3390u12166520

Sutherland, I. E. (2017). Learning and growing: Trust, leadership, and response to crisis. *Journal of Educational Administration*, *55*(1), 2–17. doi:10.1108/JEA-10-2015-0097

United Nations. (2020). *Policy brief: Education during COVID-19 and beyond*. Retrieved from https://www.un.org/development/desa/dspd/wp-content/uploads/sites/22/2020/08/sg_policy_brief_covid-19_and_education_august_2020.pdf

Witze, A. (2020). Universities will never be the same after the coronavirus crisis. *Nature*, *582*(7811), 162–164. doi:10.1038/d41586-020-01518-y PMID:32504014

Woodall J. (2020). COVID-19 and the role of health promoters and educators. *Emerald Open Res, 2*(28).

Yang, R. (2020). China's higher education during the COVID-19 pandemic: Some preliminary observations. *Higher Education Research & Development*, *39*(7), 1317–1321. doi:10.1080/07294360.2020.1824212

KEY TERMS AND DEFINITIONS

Asynchronous Courses: Virtual instruction using an online platform to make lectures and assignments available to students anytime and anywhere.

Continuity Planning: An ongoing effort to plan for process resiliency and disaster recovery to strengthen crisis readiness.

Faculty Engagement: Teaching strategy to continuously improve curriculum, course delivery, and student learning success.

Inclusive Digital Learning: A strategy to include technology and access to facilitate education equally to all learners.

Inclusive Learning: A process to provide equal teaching and opportunities to learners.

Lessons Learned: Repository of learning experiences classified as failures or successes for future use and consideration on projects or process improvements.

Pandemic: A disease outbreak, usually fatal, that spreads without boundaries and affects worldwide populations.

Remote Teaching: Distance learning methodology using online platforms, multimedia, and teaching techniques to immerse students in academic learning.

Student Engagement: Student interest and motivation to participate in the learning process by collaborating and sharing ideas with class peers.

Synchronous Course: Live sessions where instructor and learners meet at the same time through an online platform and web-based systems.

Chapter 14
Digital Technologies for Teaching and Learning at the BoP: A Managerial Perspective

Alessia Pisoni
University of Insubria, Italy

Alessandra Corti
University of Insubria, Italy

Rafaela Gjergji
Università Cattaneo, Italy

ABSTRACT

This chapter focuses on digital technologies for teaching and learning/ICT for education. The topic under investigation was approached under a managerial perspective with the final aim to identify and describe the main factors that enable and/or inhibit successful implementation of digital technologies for teaching and learning at the bottom of the pyramid (BoP). First of all, a comprehensive and systemized literature review has been performed outlining/identifying these factors. Then, to robustly grasp the findings, a deeper assessment through a multiple descriptive case study analysis on the key factors behind a successful implementation of ICTs for education at the BoP level has been carried out.

INTRODUCTION

Digital technologies are assuming a disruptive effect in redefining how economy and society works (Autio, 2017; Autio et al., 2018). The Covid-19 pandemic crisis has intensified the debate around the so called "digital economy", and the promise of "digital transformation" in changing how value is created, delivered and captured in society and economy. Moreover, the Covid-19 reminds us also about the so-

DOI: 10.4018/978-1-7998-7184-2.ch014

called "digital divide" (Norris, 2001; Warschauer, 2004). The latter, refers to the physical availability/access to computers and connectivity (digital/ICT infrastructures) as well as to the complementary resources providing people with the use of technologies and related benefits, thus supporting social inclusion (Warschauer, 2004). International organizations, such as the World Bank, the UNDP and the UNESCO, have continuously revealed promising hope on the impact of ICT in overcoming disparities around the world, especially when referring to inequalities in accessing technologies for improving education opportunities. More precisely, United Nations (UN) member states targeted to achieve by 2015 – among the others - the second goal of the UN Millennium Development Goals (MDGs), "*achieve universal primary education*"; at the same time also the "Education For All" (EFA) initiative was created by UNESCO members, aiming at improving learning opportunities for children, youth and adults, and therefore also contributing to the pursuit of MDG2. Nowadays, the call to action to ensure "quality education" is under the fourth UN Sustainable Goal (SDGs).

The chapter focuses on ICTs for education (ICT4E), which are considered as relevant for promoting learning. Though ICT4E, digital technologies as well as the stronger commitment of nations in ensuring the diffusion of quality education have acquired an increasing importance in recent years, there is not a clear-cut picture in the literature on the specific factors that may affect the successful implementation of these technologies (Cabrol and Severin, 2010). More specifically, this chapter aims at contributing to the debate around "digital technologies for teaching and learning" at the Bottom of the Pyramid (BoP) from a managerial perspective, i.e., *with the final aim to identify and describe the main factors that enable and/or inhibit successful implementation of digital technologies for teaching and learning at the Bottom of the Pyramid (BoP)*. The concept of the BoP was first introduced by Prahalad in 2004, thus identifying communities and populations with an almost null income and living in resource constrained settings. These constraints avoid the achievement of the main development goals concerning the access to education and healthcare, poverty reduction and the life expectancy (Wilkinson and Pickett, 2009).

The remainder of the Chapter is structured as follows. First, we present the systematic literature review approach adopted. Second, we discuss results on the main factors that enable and/or inhibit successful implementation of ICTs for education at the BoP level. Thirdly, a multiple descriptive case study analysis focused on ICTs4E has been carried to add robustness to our research findings. Lastly, concluding remarks and suggestions for future research directions complete the chapter.

DIGITAL TECNOLOGIES FOR TEACHING AND LEARNING AT THE BOP: A SYSTEMATIC LITERATURE REVIEW APPROACH

As previously pointed out, our aim is to devote a deeper assessment in understanding the specific factors that enable and/or inhibit the successful implementation of digital technologies for teaching and learning at the BoP. Accordingly, a wide literature review, adopting a multistep systematic approach (Tranfield et al., 2003), has been performed to provide a comprehensive framework able to shed new light on the proposed issue and to provide guidance for future research directions. Thus, our purpose was threefold: 1) to investigate the state of the art (and the progress) of a specific stream of research by analyzing authors' contributions to a specific topic; 2) to identify factors that enable and/or hinder ICTs implementation and to develop a framework as well; 3) and, to provide future research directions.

In order to perform the review process, the authors, basing on prior experience and preliminary assessment of the existing literature, identified a broad range of keywords such as: "inclusive innovation", "digital innovation", "primary education", "mobile learning", "ICT", "ICT4E", "ICT4D", "BoP" and "developing countries" (George et al., 2012; 2016; Ale et al., 2017; Halloluwa et al., 2014; Viswanathan and Blom, 2010). We searched for these concepts on title, abstract and/or keywords in Scopus (Elsevier), which is the most comprehensive database of peer-reviewed journals in the fields of management, organization, and social science. Moreover, Web of Science and Google Scholar were used too, to identify other possible contributions.

A set of inclusion and exclusion criteria such as:

- document type: both articles and conference papers,
- only contributions written in English, to facilitate comparison of different works,
- only contributions published in the last twenty years, as we are interested in the latest studies on the topic,

  were considered as well.

The results were then combined with those emerging both from a further snowballing search and from cross-references. All materials were labelled and stored, and duplications (i.e., journal articles that may appear more than once when searching different keywords) were deleted. Overall, we read 91 abstracts and we discarded those papers not considered relevant to our research. In doing so, we ended up with 39 papers considered relevant to enhance our understanding on the key factors as well as the obstacles that hinder a successful implementation of digital solutions in education at the BoP level.

The next step involved the in-depth analysis of each article. Each one of the 39 contributions were read and coded according to the following categories: article type (empirical/conceptual/review), methodology (qualitative/quantitative), type of data collected/analyzed (survey/interview/secondary data/sample size/geographic scope) and exploratory factors studied. Furthermore, data regarding the objective of the analysis and key findings were collected and treated as qualitative information to describe the key aspects under investigation and to provide future research directions in this stream of research.

Factors Affecting the Successful Implementation of Digital Technologies for Teaching and Learning at the BoP

Assuming that social inclusion in education is of crucial importance for children at the BoP, the process to reach a successful implementation and diffusion of ICTs4E appears complex. Based on our literature review, several aspects emerged to be crucial. Indeed, starting from the role of the teacher and the learner and moving towards more exogenous variables, such as the context, this paragraph aims at describing the enablers and obstacles affecting the successful implementation of digital technologies for teaching and learning at BoP.

The Role of Teachers and Learners

As concern the role of the teacher and the learner, skills-related deficits – either on teachers and/or learners' side - have been clearly identified as being one of the major obstacles in the successful implementation of digital solutions in education (Ale et al., 2017; Conger et al., 2015; Halloluwa et al., 2014; Pruet et al., 2016). Indeed, teachers are the traditional key figure in the school context and therefore the prime actors in implementing ICT (Cavas et al., 2009). Yet, in developing countries, this is not to be taken for granted. ICT is a rather "new arrival" in the field of education and used as an educational support or main tool, that often requires a pedagogical change. It frequently happens, for many reasons, that teachers are technology illiterate or have very little knowing of technology and are therefore not able to exploit its full potential. Consequently, they need to be trained and assisted.

Scholars highlight the importance of having a properly trained teacher (Ale et al., 2017; Cavas et al., 2009), and with personal attitudes towards ICT (Conger et al., 2015) to ensure the success of the project. *Teacher training and attitude* are intercorrelated enablers of success (Potter and Naidoo, 2009). Hence, teachers who do not feel confident about their ICT skills may not actively and efficiently implement ICT during their classes to prevent embarrassment and failure (Conger et al., 2015). Thus, pre- and in-service training is essential to ensure that teachers acquire or strengthen ICT competences to understand how to effectively integrate ICT in education (Li et al., 2019). By involving teachers in the decision process (Tedre et al., 2011) and in all stages of the implementation they will understand the advantages of the technological approach over the traditional one and really feel part of the project (Cavas et al., 2009). In doing so, teachers could also feel more confident when using technologies in class and support students as well. In this respect, teachers' involvement also affects their willingness to cooperate and revise teaching methods and pedagogical approaches (Tedre et al., 2011). A participatory approach is therefore essential for the success of the project (Halloluwa et al., 2018).

Though, technology is mostly seen as helping the teaching process rather than the learning one (Viswanathan and Blom, 2010), the innovation should transform the style of both teaching and learning, i.e. the *pedagogical approach* (Cavas et al., 2009). The traditional authority figure of the teacher is transformed into the one of a friendly facilitator, when technology is proactively used to teach (Halloluwa et al., 2018). Traditionally, classes are teacher-led with limited teacher-child interaction. Instead, digital innovations promote a collaborative learning space and the possibility for learners to interact with their peers (Pruet et al., 2016). Collaboration and flexibility in the learning environment are obtained through participatory teaching strategies, which can include, among others, classroom discussion, group work, Q&A. Technology facilitates the creation of this environment while giving more space to individual self-learning experiences (Viswanathan and Blom, 2010) to which the teacher indirectly participates through the monitoring of the results obtained by children and providing assistance when needed. The school and class environment shift into a more student-focused one, where the main idea should be "*get students doing instead of teacher talking*" (Tedre et al., 2011). Both in school and out-of-school environments, whether at home, in a community centre or wherever, as mobile devices allow the creation of a ubiquitous learning space, technologies are focusing on the child himself/herself, promoting personalised self-learning (Pruet et al., 2016).

The *learner* is therefore at the centre of the educational process (Viswanathan and Blom, 2010) with a technology that has been created for his/her own needs and is usually outcome-based, so that nobody is left behind, even when there is no teacher monitoring the progress of children. In this respect, scholars agree on the fact that a successful integration of ICT in education enable the teacher to transform education from teacher-centred to *learner-centred* (Ferreira et al., 2016; Halloluwa et al., 2014, 2018; Hollow and Masperi, 2009; Iahad et al., 2004; Kim, 2018; Li et al., 2019; Liyanagunawardena et al., 2014; Mohapatra and Roy, 2009; Mridha et al., 2013; Viswanathan and Blom, 2010; Wang and Li, 2010) improving children interactions with their peers and the teacher as well. Moreover, given the high level of ICT illiteracy in developing countries, despite the digitalisation trend that is characterising also the developing world (Heeks, 2008; 2020), *learners training* can be useful to guide the child during his/her first approach with the new technology (Conger et al., 2015; Kivunja and Wood, 2012; Mawere and

Sai, 2018; Ogembo et al., 2012), avoiding in turn initial frustration (Conger et al., 2015; Halloluwa et al., 2014, 2018; Mridha et al., 2013). Aside from instructions provided by the teacher or by trainers, and therefore delivered according to the traditional way, the preferred and most used method of learners training is the embedding of instructions, or a virtual "guide", in the software of the digital tool for education. This is especially useful in case of self-learning approach (Halloluwa et al., 2018).

Providing children with the information on how to use technology in order to enhance their capabilities/attitudes is crucial for ensuring the learner's satisfaction towards a new approach (Niyigena et al., 2018), entailing a positive effect on continuous use (Glood et al., 2018). Acceptance of an innovation involving ICT is usually gradual and incremental (Potter and Naidoo, 2009), but generally speaking, the implementation and use of new technologies are positively related to higher level of school attendance, engagement and enthusiasm (Hollow and Masperi, 2009).

The Context

Specific characteristics of the context in which the digital technology is introduced need to be considered as well. Indeed, every context is unique, and goals should be defined accordingly (Tedre et al., 2011). A proper *contextualization* of the digital tool for education should always start from a deep knowledge of the socio-cultural environment in which the learner lives (Ale et al., 2017; Conger et al., 2015; Halloluwa et al., 2014). Contextualisation is a multifaceted and complex procedure, which should be carefully planned. When creating a technology aimed at working in the education system of a developing country, creators should consider that learning communities differ all around the world. Therefore, the creation of locally relevant content, which considers socio-cultural factors and target specifics needs, demand and interest of local children is essential (Mridha et al., 2013).

One fundamental element is the availability of the *digitalized contents in local language* (Ale et al., 2017; Ferreira et al., 2016; Liyanagunawardena et al., 2014). Most children in developing countries, and especially in rural areas, are not literate enough to use an all-English, or in general foreign language, -based ICT system (Mridha et al., 2013). Education should be in the child's native tongue and then where appropriate also in an additional language, (e.g. in English). Moreover, it is important that learning materials are translated and maybe also created by local content experts which know and experience it first-hand (Tedre et al., 2011).

Lastly, literature review also reveals that *compatibility between technology and local context* is a goal that must be achieved (Ale et al., 2017; Conger et al., 2015; Glood et al., 2018; Halloluwa et al., 2014; Prince Machado et al., 2016; Tabira and Otieno, 2017; Viswanathan and Blom, 2010). Not only should innovation be "localised", but it would be optimal if also updated and scaled locally (Casany et al., 2012) to ensure a good understanding and appreciation of the local context (Pruet et al., 2016).

The Project: Implementation and Management

Project management related issues are an important aspect when considering the success/failure in the implementation/diffusion of new technologies for education (Kim, 2018; Liyanagunawardena et al., 2014).

In this regard, there are several aspects to be considered:

- *Learner–device ratio*. The organisation, company or institution managing the implementation of the project should be able to quantify learners, ideally corresponding to the number of students enrolled (Kim, 2018; Mawere and Sai, 2018; Wang and Li, 2010), and identify typology of ICT equipment (Mridha et al., 2013). However, if this is not possible due to cost-related infrastructural problems, alternative solutions should exist. In this regard, Budoya et al. (2019) suggest the use of devices owned by parents and/or communities. In particular, mobile devices, and more precisely mobile phones, seem to be the best choice as turnkey tool for initiating ICT in primary schools at an affordable cost (Ogembo et al., 2012). Another possibility foresees the shared usage of devices, which still ensures good learning outcomes (Tabira and Otieno, 2017).

- *Assistance and technical support.* Mere deployment of technology, even if well-contextualised, is not efficient and likely to result in failure without assistance and technical support (Hollow and Masperi, 2009; Kim, 2018; Lyanagunawardena et al., 2014; Mawere and Sai, 2018). Strategies for deployment should be integrated with support, regular update and maintenance (Tedre et al., 2011). On top of that, it is also important to help school administrators and teachers involved in the ICT implementation by providing the necessary tools that gradually enable them to manage the technology and potential problems (Ogembo et al., 2012).
- *Monitoring and Evaluation.* When thinking about success, the variable is usually linked with improved learner performances and better scholastic results. The final goal of the technology is the delivery of quality education to learners. Therefore, a systematic monitoring and evaluation framework is essential to gather data, to understand how the project is advancing and what can/should be improved (Hollow and Masperi, 2009; Karim and Hussain, 2019; Tedre et al., 2011). In this respect, scholars underline the importance of ICTs that offer an integrated Learning Management System (LMS) enabling teachers to understand and monitor the progress of each student, so that no one is left behind (Casany et al., 2012; Hallulowa et al., 2014).

In addition to these aspects, implementing an ICT-based education system in resource-constrained areas can be challenging for many reasons. First, once the project is started, it is important to bear in mind as ultimate goal, that is the *sustainability* of the project, achieved through a *long-term* and carefully planned path of implementation (Casany et al., 2012; Glood et al., 2018; Hollow and Masperi, 2009; Tabira and Otieno, 2017). According to Tedre et al. (2011), different aspects of sustainability should be taken into account, such as the environmental, social and economic sustainability and, in detail, self-sustainability, i.e. the project should be able to run independently. Moreover, given the difficulty of achieving sustainability, and then later scalability of an innovation, few authors have also stressed the importance of *post-assistance*. In case of problems, from technical to human to relational, the company, organisation or institution that has managed the project should remain available to provide further assistance (Glood et al., 2018; Meza-Cordero, 2017).

Literature review also reveals the importance of *engagement* with local actors for the successful implementation of the project. *Institutional involvement and support* are in this respect recommended. A systemic educational change requires strong political and administrative support (Mohapatra and Roy, 2009; Tedre et al., 2011). Institutional support can derive from the creation of tailored policies, which ensure the achievement of statements (Ogembo et al., 2012) or through funds to support the project (Stratton et al., 2019). When the government is not the one implementing technology for education, it is better to do everything is possible to involve it anyway, to ensure a better outcome (Glood et al., 2018; Karim and Hussain, 2019; Li et al., 2019; Mridha et al., 2013; Tabira and Otieno, 2017). Another important aspect is the *involvement of communities and families* by engaging local motivation and participation (Casany et al., 2012), and specifically by obtaining parental or more in general family agreement and support (Mridha et al., 2013; Niyigena et al., 2018; Tedre et al., 2011). Acceptance and understanding of the project and of the technology and its advantages can lead to an increase in the value placed on schools, teachers and the role of education within the community (Hollow and Masperi, 2009).

Financial-, Infrastructural- and Cultural-Related Issues

Financial-, cultural- and infrastructural-related issues should be carefully considered when dealing with the BoP. It is acknowledged that BoP markets are characterized by *financial-related issues* at the customers' end (in our case, the learner). Even if many cost-effective frugal innovations have been created to tackle limited financial possibilities at the BoP, the *cost of the device itself and its maintenance* may hinder a successful implementation – and the sustainability in the long run - of the digital innovation for education (Casany et al., 2012; Kabir and Kadage, 2017; Li et al., 2019; Mawere and Sai, 2018; Meza-Cordero, 2017; Mridha et al., 2013). Families' incomes are too low for purchasing a computer or a mobile device to use in school (Liyanagunawardena et al., 2014; Mridha et al., 2013). As previously pointed out, when discussing about the "learner-device ratio", sometimes the devices are shared within the family or within the community (Budoya et al., 2019). Most of the times, the cost of devices is borne either by the government or by NGOs or sponsor companies, that support/fund the project. This, in part solves the problem, because someone should still manage costs of maintenance of the device (Chikumba, 2011). In addition, the *cost of connectivity* may hinder the potentials of the diffusion of the digital tool (Halloluwa et al., 2014; Li et al., 2019; Liyanagunawardena et al., 2014). For many schools, given their limited budget (Li et al., 2019), it is impossible to have stable internet connection, since high data charges make it unaffordable (Budoya et al., 2019; Casany et al., 2012; Halloluwa et al., 2018; Kabir and Kadage, 2017; Mawere and Sai, 2018; Mridha et al., 2013).

Moreover, country-specificities, such as infrastructural deficits, are to be considered determinant in affecting the success of the technological solutions (Ale et al., 2017, Liyanagunawardena et al., 2014; Ogembo et al., 2012). More specifically, *inadequate ICT infrastructure* is a diffused problem in developing countries (Budoya et al., 2019; Chikumba, 2011; Conger et al., 2015; Glood et al., 2018; Halloluwa et al., 2018; Kabir and Kadage, 2017; Kim, 2018; Kivunja and Wood, 2012; Liyanagunawardena et al., 2014; Mawere and Sai, 2018; Mohapatra and Roy, 2009; Mridha et al., 2013; Niyigena et al., 2018; Rodrigo, 2003; Tabira and Otieno, 2017; Viswanathan and Blom, 2010; Wang and Li, 2010). There is lack of access to electricity and to internet, rundown buildings not properly equipped, e.g. few desks (Ogembo et al., 2012). Schools have no textbooks, no libraries and no resources to improve their condition, also given the very high number of children that structures usually host (Ale et al., 2017). Despite the importance of distance education in reducing geographical distances by connecting remote learners and teachers (Hepp and Laval, 2003; Iahad et al., 2004; Liyanagunawardena et al., 2014) and the digital divide existing between urban and rural areas (Niyigenia et al., 2018; Mozelius, 2014; Schulte, 2015), additional cultural specificities may also hinder the success and the sustainability of the project over the long run. *Cultural specificities* such as *scepticism and mistrust towards technology* may led to a sort of reluctancy in integrating ICT in education (Casany et al., 2012; Karim and Hussain, 2019; Li et al., 2019; Niyigena et al., 2018). Digital innovations are sometimes seen pedagogically suspect (Viswanathan and Blom, 2010). That's why, community, family, institutional involvement and support need to be gained in advance.

ICT4E: CASE STUDIES

Table 1. Factors affecting the successful implementation of digital technologies for teaching and learning at BoP[1]

Factors	Specificities	References
Teacher	• Lack of digital skills • Teachers training and attitude • Teachers involvement in the project and in the decision process • Pedagogical approach	Ale et al., 2017; Budoya et al., 2019; Cavas et al., 2009; Conger et al., 2015; Halloluwa et al., 2018; Hollow and Masperi, 2009; Karim and Hussain, 2019; Kim, 2018; Kivunja and Wood, 2012; Li et al., 2019; Mohapatra and Roy, 2009; Mridha et al., 2013; Ogembo et al., 2012; Prince Machado et al., 2016; Potter and Naidoo, 2009; Rodrigo, 2003; Tedre et al., 2011; Viswanathan and Blom, 2010; Wang and Li, 2010.
Learner	• Lack of digital skills • Learners training and attitude • Learner-centred approach	Cavas et al., 2009; Conger et al., 2015; Ferreira et al., 2016; Glood et al., 2018; Halloluwa et al., 2018; Hollow and Masperi, 2009; Iahad et al., 2004; Kim, 2018; Kivunja and Wood, 2012; Li et al., 2019; Liyanagunawardena et al., 2014; Mawere and Sai, 2018; Mohapatra and Roy, 2009; Mridha et al., 2013; Ogembo et al., 2012; Potter and Naidoo, 2009; Pruet et al., 2016; Tedre et al., 2011; Viswanathan and Blom, 2010; Wang and Li, 2010.
Context	• Contextualization of the digital tool in the socio-cultural environment in which teachers and learners live • Coherence with the local curriculum • Content in local language • Compatibility between technology and local context	Ale et al., 2017; Casany et al., 2012; Conger et al., 2015; Ferreira et al., 2016; Glood et al., 2018; Halloluwa et al., 2014, 2018; Hollow and Masperi, 2009; Karim and Hussain, 2019; Li et al., 2019; Liyanagunawardena et al., 2014; Meza-Cordero, 2017; Mohapatra and Roy, 2009; Mridha et al., 2013; Prince Machado et al., 2016; Potter and Naidoo, 2009; Pruet et al., 2016; Schulte, 2015; Tabira and Otieno, 2017; Tedre et al., 2011; Wiswanathan and Blom, 2010.
Project	Implementation and management: • Learner-device ratio • Assistance and technical support • Monitoring and evaluation Sustainability over the years: • Long-term focus • Post-assistance Engagement with local institutions, communities and families	Budoya et al., 2019; Casany et al., 2012; Glood et al., 2018; Halloluwa et al., 2014; Hollow and Masperi, 2009; Karim and Hussain, 2019; Kim, 2018; Li et al., 2019; Liyanagunawardena et al., 2014; Mawere and Sai, 2018; Meza-Cordero, 2017; Mohapatra and Roy, 2009; Mridha et al., 2013; Niyigena et al., 2018; Ogembo et al., 2012; Stratton et al., 2019; Tabira and Otieno, 2017; Tedre et al., 2011; Wang and Li, 2010.
Financial-related issues	Financial constraints at the learners' end: • Cost of device and its maintenance • Cost of connectivity	Budoya et al., 2019; Casany et al., 2012; Chikumba, 2011; Halloluwa et al., 2018; Kabir and Kadage, 2017; Li et al., 2019; Liyanagunawardena et al., 2014; Mawere and Sai., 2018; Meza-Cordero, 2017; Mridha et al., 2013.
Infrastructural specificities	• Infrastructural deficit (lack of electricity, rundown buildings, lack of desks, books, etc.) • Geographical distance and internal digital divide	Ale et al., 2017; Budoya et al., 2019; Chikumba, 2011; Conger et al., 2015; Glood et al., 2018; Halloluwa et al., 2018; Hepp and Laval, 2003; Iahad et al., 2004; Kabir and Kadage, 2017; Kim, 2018; Kivunja and Wood, 2012; Liyanagunawardena et al., 2014; Mawere and Sai, 2018; Mohapatra and Roy, 2009; Mozelius, 2014; Mridha et al., 2013; Niyigena et al., 2018; Ogembo et al., 2012; Rodrigo, 2003; Tabira and Otieno, 2017; Viswanathan and Blom, 2010; Wang and Li, 2010.
Cultural specificities	• Scepticism and mistrust towards technology	Casany et al., 2012; Kabir and Kadage, 2017; Karim and Hussain, 2019; Li et al., 2019; Niyigena et al., 2018; Viswanathan and Blom, 2010.

Research Design

In the following paragraph, an exploratory multiple-case study analysis, as to add robustness to our literature review, has been carried out. In detail, we analyzed 6 digital technologies, at an advanced stage of implementation, which were deployed at the BoP in different areas of the world with the aim to improving the quality of primary education. A purposeful sampling procedure (Patton, 2014) was followed. The "logic and the power of purposeful sampling lies in selecting information-rich cases for in-depth study" (Patton, 2014, p. 264). The latter are useful for learning about key issues relating to the "purpose" of the inquiry/research (Patton, 2014). Moreover, to obtain a homogeneous sample (Patton, 2014), we targeted innovations introduced in the field of primary education included in the Global Innovation Exchange (GIE)[2] database. Case studies have been selected according to the area of implementation (i.e., low- and middle-income countries) and their stage of development (i.e., only "Stage 4 - Transition to Scale", "Stage 5 – Scaling", "Stage 6 - Sustained Scale"); while secondary data have been collected from different sources, i.e., companies' website, press releases, research reports, case studies (see Appendix 1 for the detailed list of sources). In Table 2, the main characteristics of each case study are presented.

Case Overviews

Case 1: KitKit School

KitKit School is a comprehensive learning platform designed by Enuma, a startup based in California, and includes: a game-based learning app, a library and a set of music and art tools. The game-based learning app uses a child-centred and intuitive interface. Every child can succeed in his/her independent learning based on a comprehensive progressive curriculum, aimed at building foundational literacy and numeracy skills. Learner training is included via short tutorials on how to use and care for the tablet, on which the app works, or on the rules and commands of the game. The app tries to deliver an engaging user experience, which overcomes cultural boundaries. Hence, three case studies (i.e., Tanzania, Kenya and Rwanda) were analysed carried out in different situations, with students, learners without access to schools and also with refugees. Case studies results show that in the scholastic context the figure of the teacher disappears, as the rationale of the project is to understand whether children can learn without the instructions given by parents, facilitators or teachers. The project implementation, though itself not culturally specific, is regionally tailored in order to be scalable and sustainable, being the latter a "must" for the company.

Case 2: Can't Wait to Learn

Can't Wait to Learn is a digital game-based app designed by the NGO War Child Holland. It is a cost-effective solution, built to operate in resource-constrained areas, both in school and out of school. The content matches the governmental curriculum and the app is extremely children-directed. Indeed, it is not only designed for children but also by children, because their life stories, feedbacks and drawings are used for the graphics. Accordingly, children are immersed in a familiar world and they can immediately focus on learning, always at their own pace, since progress is linked with performance. Thus, Can't Wait to Learn pays much attention to the context as it is co-created with the children involved in the project. Such a peculiarity is specific to this app and not found in other innovations. Moreover, the teacher-training program offered by the company, besides offering instruct on technical aspects or child-friendly approaches, involves teacher too in playing the educational game to understand how it works, thus fighting scepticism and mistrust. This involvement approach toward teachers seems to facilitate a more proactive attitude to the technology.

Case 3: School BeLL

School BeLL (School Basic e-Learning Libraries) is a platform created by Open Learning Exchange Ghana, a Ghanaian NGO, within the project Ghana Reads. OLEG installs and supports School BeLL, a digital library, in elementary schools. The innovation offers high quality open education resources aimed at increasing children literacy. Given financial and structural deficits of schools, School BeLL works offline and is regularly updated with new resources by a so-called "Ghana National BeLL". This latter also copies available data on use, comments and ratings on the effectiveness of the resources in improving students' achievement, collected through a general platform. If on one hand, Ghana Reads project provides teacher training, helping them deliver a more interactive, activity-based curriculum, on the other it encourages communities to use the BeLL, e.g. to produce their own local newspaper. Thus, although the project focuses on children, it also offers to community and/or adults new working opportunities.

Case 4: Ubongo Kids

Ubongo Kids is an educational tv show produced by Ubongo, a non-profit social enterprise based in Tanzania. The cartoon program uses engaging storylines in local language and is delivered through TV, radio, and mobile devices, using IVR technology or applications. Through test monitoring, Ubongo observed that children watching its show outperform their classmates by a number of improved capabilities, and this was also perceived by parents. Thus, in collaboration with Silverleaf Academy, a Tanzanian chain of primary schools, Ubongo Kids was integrated into schools, with a weekly 30-minute lesson for every class by including also teacher training and classroom management methods. For children in rural communities, instead, was created Ubongo Kids Club, where episodes on DVD were shown to children by a community ambassador (CA), a person trained to facilitate the club and collect attendance data. Appointing a CA facilitated community involvement and made a sort of monitoring possible.

Case 5: OER2GO

OER2GO is a repository of downloadable websites created by World Possible, a Californian non-profit organisation. It is a collection of educational websites available both online and offline so that it can be used in areas where internet access is limited, expensive or non-existent, tackling financial and structural obstacles. OER2GO can be installed on computers or on a RACHEL, a plug-and-play server, which allows any device to access it through (offline) wi-fi. World Possible is affiliated with other organisations, called chapters, who bring RACHEL to communities and villages. Chapters ensure the contextualisation of OER2GO, as they gather suitable locally relevant content, provide teacher training, and technical support. It is interesting that this innovation is deployed and implemented by mediators, ensuring a well localised product as mediators are people who live in the area of implementation. The 60 million girls Foundation designed a Mobile Learning Lab project, to provide quality learning materials to children in remote villages in Sierra Leone using OER2GO through RACHEL. The strong involvement of the community, from the beginning of the project, and the positive impact of the Lab, contributed to the successful implementation of the technology. Indeed, learners continued to use the latter even after the end of the program outlining the relevance of how local engagement can be useful to ensure self-sustainability of the ICT.

Case 6: Broad Class – Listen to Learn

Broad Class – Listen to Learn is an interactive radio instruction program created by Power99 Foundation, a Pakistani non-profit organisation. The program offers lessons and teacher training, providing ubiquitous low-cost education reaching also the poorest and remotest communities. It promotes child-centred practices, such as cooperative learning, and is well contextualised, ensuring social and cultural relevance of the content and their matching with the national curriculum. Moreover, Power99 Foundation, by offering capacity building measures through a well-formulated teacher guide, empowers teachers to increase in confidence and competence in the delivery of child-focused instruction methods. Also, parents are satisfied and express appreciation for the way the program foster overall children development. In the attempt to tackle the frequent lack of resources and infrastructural problems, Power99 Foundation deploys wooden radios to classes. The project involves all stakeholders at every step of implementation, to facilitate future continuity and sustainability.

Analysis and Discussion of Case Findings

The case studies described in the previous section provide a clear picture of how teaching and learning have been transformed by the introduction of digital innovations in education at the BoP. These changes pose important pedagogical issues to be considered, especially in developing countries where, both the external and internal digital divide is higher (Halloluwa et al., 2018). Indeed, as emerged by the case studies, each project adopts a different innovation tool used for educational purposes. For example, Ubongo Kids used an educational TV show, Kit Kit school a game-based learning app accessible through mobile devices and so forth. Hence, when referring to "ICT-enabled" or "digital" teaching and learning instruments on which the innovation works, different categorization can be considered. In this regard, scholars distinguish among "T-learning /T-teaching", "E-learning/ E-teaching" and "M-learning/ M-teaching" (Halloluwa et al., 2014, 2018).

More specifically:

- T-learning /T-teaching refers to the use of TV or radio for educational purposes. In this respect, the term "edutainment" (also educational entertainment or entertainment-education) defines a form of entertainment designed to educate as well as to amuse.
- E-learning/teaching refers to the acquisition and use of knowledge, distributed and facilitated primary by electronic means (Mridha et al., 2013). The new methods of teaching and learning, created through the use of ICT and digital technologies, are transforming the school environment and also bringing new opportunities to those children who cannot normally attend school. At first, the main device was the computer and then all the mobile devices, laptops, tablets, mobile phones, to which we will refer in the next bullet point.
- M-learning and teaching refers to education delivered or enhanced by means of a mobile device. It is a subfield of e-learning, but these will be considered as two different typologies given the

Table 2. ICTs4E: selected case studies

N. Cases	Product	Type of product	Company (business entity)	Year of establishment	Headquarters	Country of implementation
Case 1	Kitkit School	App	Enuma (Startup)	2012	California	Bangladesh, Kenya, Rwanda, Tanzania, Uganda
Case 2	Can't Wait to Learn	SG App	War Child Holland (NGO)	1993	Holland	Jordan, Lebanon, Sudan and Uganda
Case 3	School BeLL	App	Open Learning Exchange Ghana (NGO)	2007	Ghana	Ghana
Case 4	Ubongo Kids	Tv show	Ubongo (Non-profit social enterprise)	2013	Tanzania	Kenya, Malawi, Nigeria, Rwanda, South Africa, Tanzania, Uganda and Zambia
Case 5	OER2GO	PC Platform	World Possible (Non-profit organization)	2009	California	Ghana, Guatemala, Kenya, Sierra Leone and Tanzania
Case 6	Broad Class – Listen to Learn	Radio Program	Power99 Foundation (Non-profit organization)	1984	Pakistan	Pakistan

importance acquired by M-learning in the last decades, but also given the fact that is considered as the next form of e-learning, substituting the first one (Glood et al., 2018; Kabir and Kadage, 2017).

Nowadays, these devices, and especially mobile phones, are the most prevalent form of ICT in developing countries (Kabir and Kadage, 2017). They offer many advantages for education, such as relatively lower cost compared to other ICTs and the creation of an ubiquitous learning environment (Glood et al., 2018; Schulte, 2015). Nowadays, the context of M-learning/teaching is the most addressed one by education projects at the BoP, also considering that developing countries have almost skipped the computer-era to directly jump into the mobile one (Viswanathan and Blom, 2010). Among M-learning solutions, one can find traditional educational software, in the form of application, but also exploiting game-based learning and gamified products. Game-based learning refers to the use of a game as part of the learning process. In particular, the most used kind of game is serious games, in which education is the primary goal, rather than entertainment, and which use pedagogy to incorporate learning experience while keeping entertainment intact (Halloluwa et al., 2014). On the other side, gamification refers to the usage of game design elements in non-game contexts, e.g. rewards (Halloluwa et al., 2018).

Figure 1 provides a classification of selected case studies according to the digital support on which they are offered. Where innovations work on more than one typology of device, they have been classified according to the one on which they were first meant to work and were created for.

Moreover, after an in-depth analysis of the data collected it was possible to identify the factors that affect the implementation of these projects and to summarize them into Table 3 according to the categories we identified in the literature review. Almost all the cases fill all the identified categories.

Figure 1. ICTs4E case studies classified by digital learning approach

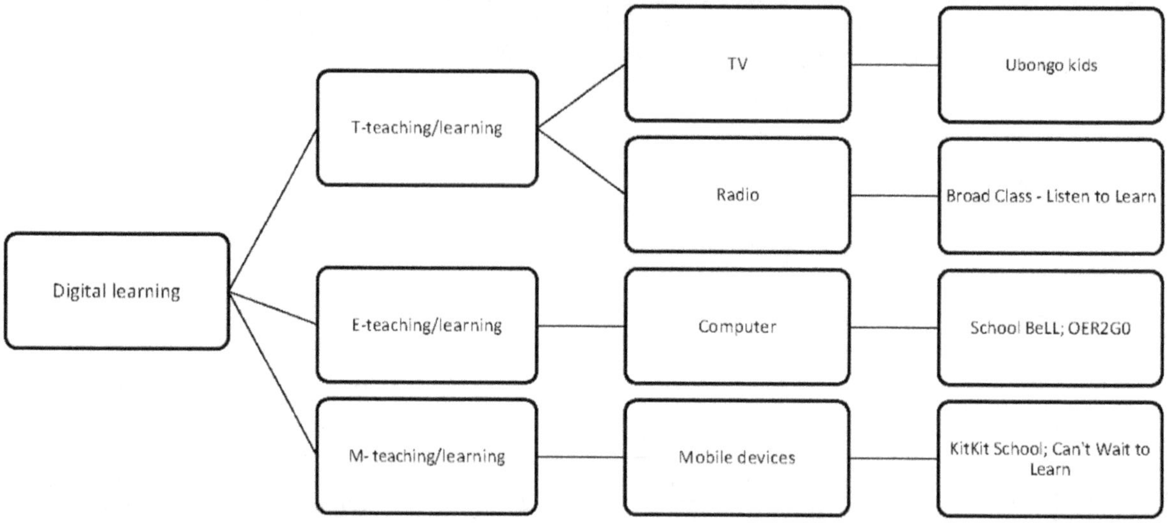

Teachers and learners training is the starting point to overcome the obstacles related to the lack of skills, and to fight technology illiteracy. This has been reported by each of the analyzed company/organization beyond the typology of technological solution adopted for promoting education. More specifically, it was possible to notice how KitKit School, which aims at enabling children to learn without the external support of teachers or parents, is the only one tool providing learner training through in-app explanations. All the other digital technologies provide training to teachers or community facilitators, which are then supposed to help children in getting confident and starting using the technology, either "in" or "outside" the school context. As said, the teacher – considering primary school education – is traditionally playing the role of mediator between knowledge and children. The concept of self-learning promoted by technology is quite recent and therefore still in its infancy and needs to be further explored and exploited. Moreover, though the learner-centred approach is a rather new approach, most of the digital technologies are increasingly paying attention to the learners' attitude, as he/she is the final user of the product. In this respect, Can't Wait to Learn co-creates the tool with the children, thus trying to avoid the initial scepticims and mistrust towards the technology. As regards the contextualization of digital tools in the socio-cultural environment, it is worth noting how all the companies/organization pay a lot of attention to this aspect. In this sense, the above-mentioned co-creation approach implemented by Can't Wait to Learn could be considered as useful to tailor-made and to adapt the project to specific local needs during its implementation. While Broad Class – Listen to Learn decides to match their programmes with the national curriculum to ensure the social and cultural relevance of the contents. Ubongo Kids' cartoon after being conceived for the TV has been later integrated also into schools. OER2GO decides to gather suitable locally relevant content to better contextualize its tool. In doing so, OER2GO also provides teachers training and technical support. Moreover, they also chose to involve the local community from the beginning of the project through "labs". School BeLL too encourages the local communities' involvement - besides the educational programs for kids – by promoting their own local newspaper and pushing everyone to contribute on that. These are also relevant examples/best practices, since the local community's involvement has often been cited as a crucial element to gain legitimacy and in doing so ensuring a successful outcome for the project.

As regards the main obstacles identified in the literature review, almost all the analysed case studies report the need to face at least one of them during project implementation. Kids at the BoP live in conditions of extreme poverty, so we can take financial constraints at the learners' end for granted. All the case studies refer to the "device management and cost" and to the "cost of connectivity" which they face by reducing the features of the product and by adopting frugal approaches. In this respect, it is worth noting how product's "innovative" features were added to overcome specific challenges, e.g. lack of connectivity or very high data charges: OER2GO developed RACHEL and School BeLL use National School BeLLs to always offer up-to-date and new contents. Innovative technologies can also overcome proper limits of devices, such as the unidirectionality of TV, integrating new devices or encouraging participation, as Ubongo does. The other most recurrent obstacle is related to the poor ICT infrastructure that characterize developing countries. To counter-face this obstacle some features of the tools have been adapted to work in "extreme conditions" of resource-constraints, but the need to involve institutions at local or international level to support these infrastructural deficits are of paramount importance to further boost the potential of the projects.

CONCLUSION AND FUTURE RESEARCH DIRECTIONS

Social inclusion in education is of crucial importance for children at the BoP. Though ICTs for education, digital technologies as well as the stronger commitment of nations in ensuring the diffusion of quality education have acquired an increasing relevance in recent years, the process to achieve a successful implementation and diffusion of ICTs4E appears to be a complex issue.

The main goal of this chapter is to provide an attempt of systematization of the contributions published in the field of ICT4E and, in doing so, to provide a clear-cut picture on specific factors – enablers and obstacles - that may affect the successful implementation of these technologies for teaching and learning at BoP. Despite the limitations that systematic literature reviews typically present (selected database of records, keyword selection, qualitative analysis of literature key findings, framework systematization) our study provides a useful contribution to existing knowledge by shedding new light on the obstacles that organizations should face as concern education at the BoP. The literature review, first of all, reveals how skills-related deficits have been clearly identified as being one of the major obstacles in the successful implementation of digital solutions in education (Ale et al., 2017; Conger et al., 2015; Halloluwa et al., 2014; Pruet et al., 2016). The importance of having properly trained teachers (Ale et al., 2017; Cavas et al., 2009) - trained in advance about how to effectively integrate ICT in education (Li et al., 2019), and with personal attitudes towards ICT (Conger et al., 2015) - is, in this respect, of crucial importance to overcome such obstacles. In doing so, also the initial frustration of the learner in approaching the new technology could be avoided (Conger et al., 2015; Halloluwa et al., 2014). The adoption of a learner-centred approach – instead of a teacher-centred one - is also recommended (Halloluwa et al., 2014; Iahad et al., 2004; Liyanagunawardena et al., 2014; Viswanathan and Blom, 2010). Aside from the instructions provided by the teacher or by trainers, it is also recommended to grant children the possibility to interact with their peers.

Second, as regards the project implementation, financial, cultural and infrastructural specificities should be carefully considered. Financial-related issues at the learners' end, such as the cost of the device

Table 3. Factors affecting the successful implementation of digital technologies for teaching and learning at BoP – Evidence from case studies

Factors	Specificities	Observed case studies
Teacher	• Lack of digital skills • Teachers training and attitude • Teachers involvement in the project and in the decision process • Pedagogical approach	Can't Wait to Learn; School BeLL; Ubongo Kids; OER2GO; Broad Class – Listen to Learn
Learner	• Lack of digital skills • Learners training and attitude • Learner-centred approach	Kitkit School; Can't Wait to Learn; School BeLL; Ubongo Kids; OER2GO; Broad Class – Listen to Learn
Context	• Contextualization of the digital tool in the socio-cultural environment in which teachers and learners live • Coherence with the local curriculum • Content in local language • Compatibility between technology and local context	Kitkit School; Can't Wait to Learn; School BeLL; Ubongo Kids; OER2GO; Broad Class – Listen to Learn
Project	Implementation and management: • Learner-device ratio • Assistance and technical support • Monitoring and evaluation Sustainability over the years: • Long-term focus • Post-assistance Engagement with local institutions, communities and families	Kitkit School; Can't Wait to Learn; School BeLL; Ubongo Kids; OER2GO; Broad Class – Listen to Learn
Financial-related issues	Financial constraints at the learners' end: • Cost of device and its maintenance • Cost of connectivity	Kitkit School; Can't Wait to Learn; School BeLL; Ubongo Kids; OER2GO; Broad Class – Listen to Learn
Infrastructural specificities	• Infrastructural deficit (lack of electricity, rundown buildings, lack of desks, books, etc.) • Geographical distance and internal digital divide	Kitkit School; Can't Wait to Learn; School BeLL; Ubongo Kids; OER2GO; Broad Class – Listen to Learn
Cultural specificities	• Scepticism and mistrust towards technology	Can't Wait to Learn; Broad Class – Listen to Learn

and its maintenance, but also the cost of connectivity may hinder the potentials of the diffusion of the digital tool (Halloluwa et al., 2014; Li et al., 2019; Liyanagunawardena et al., 2014). Moreover, cultural specificities such as scepticism and mistrust towards technology may lead to a sort of reluctancy in integrating ICT in education (Li et al., 2019). Country-specificities, such as infrastructural deficit, but also geographical distance to be covered to achieve specific learning goals, are to be considered as dramatically affecting the success of the technological solutions (Ale et al., 2017, Liyanagunawardena et al., 2014; Ogembo et al., 2012). In this respect, the "contextualization of the project" should be properly planned. As said, every context is unique, and goals should be defined accordingly. The literature reveals how a proper contextualization of the digital tool for education should always start from a deep knowledge of the socio-cultural environment in which the learner lives (Ale et al., 2017; Conger et al., 2015; Halloluwa et al., 2014). That's why, community, family and institutional involvement and support need to be gained in advance to partially mitigate these obstacles and enhance the odds of success of the project.

Hence, in such a context, the descriptive approach of the multiple case study adopted, stress the importance to overcome the obstacles for implementing ICTs for education at BoP by adding robustness to our literature review. As shown, companies/organizations identify their "own best way" to implement their project. Common to all investigated case studies is the process through which teachers and learners' training obtain successful outcomes. The increasing importance of contextualizing the contents of the digital tools and the adoption of a learner-centred approach are to be considered as "enablers" of these outcomes. Yet, self-learning approaches seem to have not been fully exploited, mainly because of mistrust about the new technology. In this respect, teachers, learners and communities' involvement is a crucial aspect to avoid scepticisms. Furthermore, more efforts – either at national and international level – are needed to reduce infrastructural deficits, to support the sustainability and scalability of projects and, to create a real impact by bringing effective changes in the primary education field at the BoP.

To conclude, some limitations of this study must be noted. The findings deriving from the case-based study, are limited to the qualitative research approach (e.g., case selection) and rely on secondary data. Therefore, one should be cautious in generalizing results beyond the analyzed digital solutions. Findings need to be further tested concerning the number of cases, evolution of projects over time and investigated context (in terms of geographical scope, i.e., countries/regions where the technology is implemented). Moreover, a thorough and deeper knowledge of the support system of technological innovations in BoP primary education/schools demand critical inclusion for discussion. In this respect, future empirical studies should focus on collection of primary data through face-to-face interviews – with founders or project's executives – as well as on longitudinal case study analysis to better explore the dynamics of how these factors may evolve over time.

REFERENCES

Ale, K., Loh, Y. A.-C., & Chib, A. (2017). Contextualized-OLPC education project in rural India: Measuring learning impact and mediation of computer self-efficacy. *Educational Technology Research and Development, 65*(3), 769–794. doi:10.100711423-017-9517-2

Autio, E. (2017). *Digitalisation, ecosystems, entrepreneurship, and policy*. Perspectives into topical issues in society and ways to support political decision making. Government's Analysis, Research and Assessment Activities. Helsinki, Policy Brief, 20/2017.

Autio, E., Szerb, L., Komlósi, E., & Tiszberger, M. (2018). *The European Index of Digital Entrepreneurship Systems*. JRC Technical Reports. Publications Office of the European Union.

Budoya, C. M., Kissaka, M. M., & Mtebe, J. S. (2019). Towards Developing Interactive Content for Enhancing Life Skills Education in Tanzania: Possibilities and Pitfalls. *IFIP Advances in Information and Communication Technology, 552*, 374–385. doi:10.1007/978-3-030-19115-3_31

Cabrol, M., & Severin, E. (2010). *ICT to improve quality in education—A conceptual framework and indicators in the use of information communication technology for education (ICT4E). In Assessing the effects of ICT in education*. Publications Office of the European Union.

Casany, M. J., Alier, M., & Barcelo, M. (2012). Integration of M-learning and LMS: A sustainability approach. In *2012 International Symposium on Computers in Education (SIIE 2012)* (pp. 1-6). Andorra la Vella.

Cavas, B., Cavas, P., Karaoglan, B., & Kisla, T. (2009). A study on science teachers' attitudes toward information and communication technologies in education. *The Turkish Online Journal of Educational Technology*, *8*(2), 20–32.

Chikumba, P. A. (2011). Student performance in computer studies in secondary schools in Malawi. In R. Popescu-Zeletin, I. A. Rai, K. Jonas, & A. Villafiorita (Eds.), *E-Infrastuctures and E-Services for Developing Countries. AFRICOMM 2010. Lecture Notes of the Institute for Computer Sciences, Social Informatics and Telecommunications Engineering* (Vol. 64). Springer. doi:10.1007/978-3-642-23828-4_11

Conger, S., Krauss, K., & Simuja, C. (2015). Human Factors Issues in Developing Country Remote K-12 Education. *Procedia Manufacturing*, *3*, 1566–1573. doi:10.1016/j.promfg.2015.07.441

Ferreira, S. M., Gouin-Vallerand, C., & Hotte, R. (2016) Game based learning: A case study on designing an educational game for children in developing countries. In *2016 8th International Conference on Games and Virtual Worlds for Serious Applications, VS-Games*. Barcelona: IEEE.

George, G., Howard-Grenville, J., Joshi, A., & Tihanyi, L. (2016). Understanding and tackling societal grand challenges through management research. *Academy of Management Journal*, *59*(6), 1880–1895. doi:10.5465/amj.2016.4007

George, G., McGahan, A. M., & Prabhu, J. (2012). Innovation for inclusive growth: Towards a theoretical framework and a research agenda. *Journal of Management Studies*, *49*(4), 661–683. doi:10.1111/j.1467-6486.2012.01048.x

Glood, S. H., Hussein, R. M., & Kamil, W. A. (2018). The effects of information quality, service quality, and compatibility on continue use of M-learning among students in the public universities of Iraqi. *Journal of Theoretical and Applied Information Technology*, *96*(12), 3739–3755.

Halloluwa, H. K. T. C., Usoof, H., & Hewagamage, K. P. (2014). Stimulating learners' motivation in primary education in Sri Lanka - A literature review. *International Journal of Emerging Technologies in Learning*, *9*(1), 47–52. doi:10.3991/ijet.v9i1.2964

Halloluwa, T., Vyas, D., Usoof, H., & Hewagamage, K. P. (2018). Gamification for development: A case of collaborative learning in Sri Lankan primary schools. *Personal and Ubiquitous Computing*, *22*(2), 391–407. doi:10.100700779-017-1073-6

Heeks, R. (2008). ICT4D 2.0: The next phase of applying ICT for International Development. *Computer*, *41*(6), 26–31. doi:10.1109/MC.2008.192

Heeks, R. (2020). ICT4D 3.0? Part 1—The Components of an Emerging 'digital-for-Development' Paradigm. *The Electronic Journal on Information Systems in Developing Countries*, *1*(1), 1–15. doi:10.1002/j.1681-4835.2016.tb00563.x

Hepp, P., & Laval, E. (2003). ICT for rural education: A developing country perspective. *IFIP Advances in Information and Communication Technology*, *113*, 115–125. doi:10.1007/978-0-387-35668-6_12

Hollow, D., & Masperi, P. (2009). An evaluation of the use of ICT within primary education in Malawi. In *Proceedings of the 3rd international conference on Information and Communication Technologies and Development (ICTD 2009)* (pp. 27-34). IEEE. 10.1109/ICTD.2009.5426707

Iahad, N., Dafoulas, G. A., Milankovic-Atkinson, M., & Murphy, A. (2004). E-Learning in developing countries: Suggesting a methodology for enabling computer-aided assessment. In *Proceedings of the 4th IEEE International Conference on Advanced Learning Technologies* (pp. 983-987). IEEE. 10.1109/ICALT.2004.1357734

Kabir, F.S., & Kadage, A.T. (2017). ICTS and Educational Development: The Utilization of Mobile Phones in Distance Education in Nigeria. *The Turkish Online Journal of Distance Education, 18*(1), 63–76.

Karim, A., & Hussain, F. (2019). 'When will you start teaching the REAL curriculum?': Challenges and innovations in education for Rohingya Refugees. In P. Nielsen & H. C. Kimaro (Eds.), *Information and Communication Technologies for Development. Strengthening Southern-Driven Cooperation as a Catalyst for ICT4D* (pp. 675–686). Springer. doi:10.1007/978-3-030-18400-1_55

Kim, Y. (2018). The Framework of cloud e-learning system for strengthening ICT competence of teachers in Nicaragua. *International Journal on Advanced Science, Engineering and Information Technology, 8*(1), 62–67. doi:10.18517/ijaseit.8.1.2700

Kivunja, C., & Wood, D. (2012). Multigrade pedagogy and practice: Accelerating millennium development goals for sub-saharan Africa. *International Journal of Learning, 18*(11), 17–32. doi:10.18848/1447-9494/CGP/v18i11/47811

Li, S., Yamaguchi, S., Sukhbaatar, J., & Takada, J.-I. (2019). The influence of teachers' professional development activities on the factors promoting ICT integration in Primary Schools in Mongolia. *Education Sciences, 9*(2), 78. doi:10.3390/educsci9020078

Liyanagunawardena, T. R., Adams, A. A., Rassool, N., & Williams, S. A. (2014). Developing government policies for distance education: Lessons learnt from two Sri Lankan case studies. *International Review of Education, 60*(6), 821–839. doi:10.100711159-014-9442-0

Mawere, T., & Sai, K. O. S. (2018). An investigation on e-resource utilisation among university students in a developing country: A case of Great Zimbabwe University. *South African Journal of Information Management, 20*(01), 1–7. doi:10.4102ajim.v20i1.860

Meza-Cordero, J. A. (2017). Learn to Play and Play to Learn: Evaluation of the One Laptop per Child Program in Costa Rica. *Journal of International Development, 29*(1), 3–31. doi:10.1002/jid.3267

Mohapatra, S., & Roy, R. (2009). Impact of ICT on primary education. *World Academy of Science, Engineering and Technology, 38*, 1316–1324.

Mozelius, P. (2014). Education for all by ICT4D hubs: A Sri Lankan case study. In *Proceedings of the European Conference on e-Learning (ECEL 2014)* (pp. 354-361). Academic Conferences and Publishing International Limited.

Mridha, M., Nihlen, G., Erlandsson, B.-E., Khan, A. A., Islam, M. S., Sultana, N., Reza, S., & Srinivas, M. B. (2013). E-learning for empowering the rural people in Bangladesh opportunities and challenges. In *Proceedings of the 2nd International Conference on E-Learning and E-Technologies in Education (ICEEE)* (pp. 323-328). 10.1109/ICeLeTE.2013.6644397

Niyigena, J.-P., Jiang, Q., Hasan, A. S. M. T., Ziou, D., Chen, H., & Wang, P. (2018). ICT Usage and Attitudes among EAC Undergraduate Students - A Case Study. *IEEE Access: Practical Innovations, Open Solutions*, *6*, 42661–42674. doi:10.1109/ACCESS.2018.2854925

Norris, P. (2001). *Digital Divide: civic engagement, information poverty, and the internet worldwide*. Cambridge University Press. doi:10.1017/CBO9781139164887

Ogembo, J. G., Ngugi, B., & Pelowski, M. (2012). Computerizing primary schools in rural kenya: Outstanding challenges and possible solutions. *The Electronic Journal on Information Systems in Developing Countries*, *52*(1), 52. doi:10.1002/j.1681-4835.2012.tb00371.x

Patton, M. Q. (2014). *Qualitative Research & Evaluation Methods. Integrating Theory and Practice* (4th ed.). Sage.

Potter, C., & Naidoo, G. (2009). Use of low-end ICT's as a platform for teacher development: An evaluative case study of an interactive radio programme in South African primary schools. In *Proceedings of the 3rd International Multi-Conference on Society, Cybernetics and Informatics* (*vol. 1*, pp. 58-63). Academic Press.

Prahalad, C. K. (2004). *The Fortune at the Bottom of the Pyramid. Eradicating Poverty through Profits*. Wharton School Publishing.

Prince Machado, M. S., Tenorio Sepúlveda, G. C., & Ramirez Montoya, M. S. (2016). Educational innovation and digital competencies: The case of OER in a private Venezuelan university. *International Journal of Educational Technology in Higher Education*, *13*(1), 1–10. doi:10.118641239-016-0006-1

Pruet, P., Ang, C. S., & Farzin, D. (2016). Understanding tablet computer usage among primary school students in underdeveloped areas: Students' technology experience, learning styles and attitudes. *Computers in Human Behavior*, *55*, 1131–1144. doi:10.1016/j.chb.2014.09.063

Rodrigo, M. M. T. (2003). Tradition or transformation? An evaluation of icts in metro manila schools. *Information Technology for Development*, *10*(2), 95–122. doi:10.1002/itdj.1590100205

Schulte, B. (2015). (Dis)Empowering technologies: ICT for education (ICT4E) in China, past and present. *Chinese Journal of Communication*, *8*(1), 59–77. doi:10.1080/17544750.2014.990909

Stratton, C., Bailey, D. E., & Leonardi, P. M. (2019). Translating national discourse into teaching and learning outcomes: Portability and connectivity in developing countries' ICT in education (ICT4E) initiatives. *New Media & Society*, *22*(12), 2083–2107. doi:10.1177/1461444819884373

Tabira, Y., & Otieno, F. X. (2017). Integration and implementation of sustainable ICT-based education in developing countries: Low-cost, en masse methodology in Kenya. *Sustainability Science*, *12*(2), 221–234. doi:10.100711625-017-0422-8

Tedre, M., Hansson, H., Mozelius, P., & Lind, S. (2011). Crucial considerations in one-to-one computing in developing countries. In *2011 IST-Africa Conference Proceedings* (pp. 1-11). IEEE.

Tranfield, D., Denyer, D., & Smart, P. (2003). Towards a methodology for developing evidence-informed management knowledge by means of systematic review. *British Journal of Management*, *14*(3), 207–222. doi:10.1111/1467-8551.00375

Viswanathan, D., & Blom, J. (2010). New metaphors from old practices - mobile learning to revitalize education in developing regions of the world. *IEEE Transactions on Learning Technologies*, *3*(1), 18–23. doi:10.1109/TLT.2010.5

Wagner, D. A. (2018). Technology for education in low-income countries: Supporting the UN sustainable development goals. In I. Lubin (Ed.), *ICT-Supported Innovations in Small Countries and Developing Regions: Perspectives and Recommendations for International Education* (pp. 51–74). Springer. doi:10.1007/978-3-319-67657-9_3

Wang, Z., & Li, X. (2010). Chinese schools modern distance education project in rural Areas. *British Journal of Educational Technology*, *41*(4), 612–613. doi:10.1111/j.1467-8535.2010.01073.x

Warschauer, M. (2004). *Technology and Social Inclusion. Rethinking the digital divide.* The MIT Press. doi:10.7551/mitpress/6699.001.0001

Wilkinson, R., & Pickett, K. (2009). *The Spirit Level: Why more equal societies almost always do better*. Allen Lane.

ENDNOTES

All tables have been elaborated by authors basing on systematic literature review and on data collected for case studies

1 **See** https://www.globalinnovationexchange.org/global-development-innovation-data

APPENDIX

Table 4. List of data sources for selected case studies

N. Cases	Product	Company	Main sources
1	Kitkit School	Enuma	• https://www.globalinnovationexchange.org/innovation/enuma • http://kitkitschool.com/ • https://enuma.com/ • KitKit School Handbook • Tanzania case study; Kenya case study; Rwanda case study • Bangladesh feasibility study
2	Can't Wait to Learn	War Child Holland	• https://www.globalinnovationexchange.org/innovation/can-t-wait-to-learn • https://www.warchildholland.org/projects/cwtl/ • Research Report e-learning Sudan phases I &II
3	School BeLL	Open Learning Exchange Ghana	• https://www.globalinnovationexchange.org/innovation/ghana-reads • http://ghanareads.oleghana.org/ • Ghana Reads documentary
4	Ubongo Kids	Ubongo	• https://www.globalinnovationexchange.org/innovation/ubongo • https://www.ubongo.org/shows/ubongo-kids/ • Ubongo Annual Report 2019 • Ubongo Blog, Adapting edutainment for the classroom with Silverleaf • Ubongo blog, Ubongo Kids Club: Bringing Edutainment to Off-Grid Areas with USAID
5	OER2GO	World Possible	• https://www.globalinnovationexchange.org/innovation/rachel-connecting-offline-learners-to-the-world-s-knowledge • https://worldpossible.org/oer2go • www.worlpossible/chapters • Mobile Learning Lab – project evaluation report-Sierra Leone
6	Broad Class – Listen to Learn	Power99 Foundation	• https://www.globalinnovationexchange.org/innovation/broadclass-listen-to-learn • http://power99.foundation/projects-programs/ • https://hundred.org/en/innovations/broad-class-listen-to-learn-interactive-radio-instruction-program

Source: Author's own elaboration based on systematic literature review

Chapter 15
Study of Blended Learning in Higher Education and the Role of Social Media Applications With Special Reference to Vietnam

Thanh Hong Lam
https://orcid.org/0000-0002-3097-7264
University of Economics and Law, Vietnam National University, Vietnam

Jaheer Mukthar K. P.
https://orcid.org/0000-0002-7888-0242
Kristu Jayanti College (Autonomous), Bengaluru, India

Lanh Thanh Le
https://orcid.org/0000-0002-6970-7819
Dong Nai Technology University, Vietnam

Hien Thanh Le
https://orcid.org/0000-0002-1380-3406
Dong Nai Technology University, Vietnam

Nam Duy Nguyen
Dong Nai Technology University, Vietnam

Bao Quoc Do
Dong Nai Technology University, Vietnam

ABSTRACT

The present study aims to examine the effect of the combination of learning methods, in which diverse IT resources are applied to facilitate study activities of Vietnamese undergraduate students. The main focus of this study is that in the blended learning context of Vietnam education, the combination of various communication means such as F2F and traditional education technologies can enable the level of engagement of students with the blended courses. The study measured the level of students' engagement in the blended learning program, in which physical classrooms and different IT resources are implemented. The authors distinguish two kinds of IT resources: traditional education technologies and social media applications. It is proposed that while F2F classrooms and traditional education technologies can enable students' engagement, which leads to stronger satisfaction and motivation. Meanwhile, social media applications can intensify those relationships.

DOI: 10.4018/978-1-7998-7184-2.ch015

INTRODUCTION

Blended learning was initially built from distance education (Brody, 2006) in which ICT resources such as sound and video recording, television and computer are implemented broadly in teaching (Akkoyunlu & Soylu, 2008). While there is debate around just how to define blended learning, researchers such as (Bonk, Graham, Cross, & Moore, 2006; Kaur, 2013; Voos, 2003) suggested that it is now commonly associated with being a combination of different modes of delivery, models of teaching and styles of learning which are exercised in an interactively meaningful learning environment. Meanwhile, Garrison (2004) stated similarly that blended learning includes courses that combine online and classroom learning activities and optimally uses resources in order to improve students' learning outcomes and to address critical institutional issues to enhance effectiveness and socialization opportunities of the classroom and the technologically active learning possibilities of the online environment (Garrison, 2004). More and more institutions, teachers and learners are choosing blended learning over other learning options including fully online (Bonk et al., 2006; Kim & Bonk, 2006). Educational technology capabilities (ETC) provide complementary insights to identify the best approach when aligning learning goals in technology-based implementations (Robin Castro 2019)

Blended learning have been firstly applying in many universities in developed countries and brought some benefits such as: expanding access, improving quality, serving diverse student populations, reducing time to graduation, addressing student desire for technology in education, and greater insight and tracking of student progress (Porter, Graham, Spring, & Welch, 2014). Service quality, course quality, and student–instructor interaction have indirect and positive effects on learners' continuance intentions for online learning, while the variable of perceived value is a significant mediator for online learners' retention and has a direct influence on their continuance intentions. Student–student interaction and student–content interaction do not have direct or indirect effects on online learners' continuance intentions.(Yiwen Li 2021)

This study aims to examine the effect of the combination of learning methods, in which diverse IT resources are applied to facilitate study activities of Vietnamese undergraduate students. The main point of this study is that in the blended learning context of Vietnam education, the combination of various communication means such as F2F and traditional education technologies can enable the level of engagement of students with the blended courses. It is proposed that the positive attitude of openness when using social media applications for learning purposes before and after class can have an impact on the engagement. Student's enjoyment of sharing information related to study, which obtains when using social media application can also enhance the relationship among blended learning strategies and student's learning experience. Student's good experience, in result, is believed that can lead to better learning attitude such as satisfaction and motivation.

First, the study adds a different view of this research field by having a look at the perspectives of students from Asia. Second, an extensive look into students' behavior and attitude in a new form of learning in Vietnam education is also provided. With the implementation and engagement, the students show various responses both positive and negative towards the implementation of blended learning. It is believed that this study provided insights into student views and impact on blended learning practices in similar contexts in Vietnam. In particular, as it presents a sample of student views, it can help inform the further development and implementation of blended learning in Vietnamese universities. It could, for example, enable university managers and faculty to have a better understanding of the student experience in these environments, which are very new to stakeholders. Finally, by providing a picture of student experience of blended courses at a university in Vietnam, it may assist instructor and educators as they seek to answer questions relating to the effectiveness and suitability of blended programs in a Vietnamese context.

RESEARCH MODEL AND HYPOTHESES

One of the challenges for educators when implementing blended learning as an official teaching method for undergraduate students is that to ensure the engagement and positive perception of students toward this new method. Since the most significant purposes to apply any kind of instructional design is to bring better performance for students. Students' engagement is believed can obtain this. The greater the students' involvement, the greater is the probability that the students will achieve better performance (Hwang & Francesco, 2010; Li, Tarafdar, & Subba Rao, 2012; Lin & Shao, 2000). However, in practice, while some students prefer more time for F2F classes, other students like to take more time for online learning. This is a crucial problem since if students are not satisfied with this blended learning program, probably they will not engage with the courses and do not want to take the next course with a similar method. This means that the implementation perhaps fails to attract or benefit the students' learning experiences. Engagement is very important according to Cluskey, Hodges, and Smith (2006) reported that with the blended model over either F2F or online learning environments, the academic performance appeared to be roughly equal (Clusky Jr, Hodges, & Smith, 2006), while the level of engagement with F2F or online can lead to different outcomes (Arbaugh & Benbunan-Fich, 2007).

To the best of our knowledge, while different IT resources in blended learning have been received many attentions from research, the role of F2F has been undertaken. This study aims to research the impact of both traditional F2F classes and the usage of technologies in a blended learning environment for undergraduate students.

The study is guided by the following research question:

- Does the combination of traditional F2F classes and the use of traditional education technologies in the blended learning impact on students' engagement and its outcomes?
- Can social media applications amplify the impact of a combination of F2F classes and the use of traditional education technology on students' engagement?

Different from many previous studies, in which the use of IT resources is mainly investigated in a traditional pedagogical (only containing F2F classes), we are focusing on both the effectiveness of the physical class time and some technologies used by students for learning purposes. Our study also focuses on the amplifying role of social media applications, which receives little attention from previous studies.

From different literature review, we obtain our proposed conceptual model for this research, which is presented in Figure 1 below

RESEARCH DESIGN

We motivated the choice of quantitative study as a research method. Since the data collection was performed via a questionnaire, we went into detail on the development of the questionnaire and the

Figure 1. Conceptual model

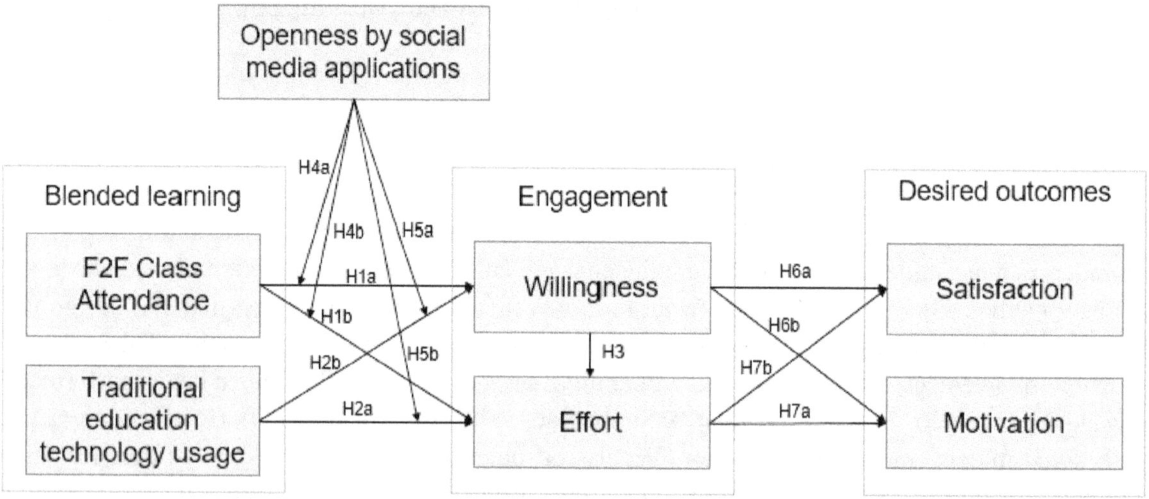

measurement items used to measure the constructs in this case. After explaining the data collection, we provided a description of the target population. The last part of the methodology section will clarify the statistical method used in this study. The research design is important in any research study, as it represents the framework that drives the conduct of the research study through the search to find the answers to the research questions (Cooper & Schindler, 2011). The conceptual model and hypotheses were developed to answer the research questions, based on the understanding gained from the literature review. The constructs used in the model were adapted and modified for the questionnaire development. The statistical methods can be used to identify facts and relationships among variables (Creswell, 2003).

This research instrument used a questionnaire research method. Our questionnaire using Vietnamese language and was divided into 7 sections as follow: Introduction, general information, frequency and importance of blended learning, openness in social media applications, students' willingness and engagement, students' satisfaction and motivation, other comments/ recommendations. The constructs used in the model were adapted from previous studies and modified for the questionnaire development.

Data Collection and Analysis

Data collection: an online survey approach was used in this study. Participants in a university in Vietnam were required to fill the questionnaire through Google Form. Data were collected from 1st, March 2019 until 29th, March 2019. Students' participation in the online survey was voluntary. However, in order to increase the response rate, we asked the university's' management to help us to spread the questionnaire.

Data analysis: The data was analyzed using a variance-based structural equation modeling (SEM) statistical technique, such as partial least squares (PLS) path modeling using SmartPLS version 3 (Ringle, Wende, & Becker, 2014), to estimate the relationships between the different parameters of the research model. SEM tests theoretical models using hypothesis testing to understand the simultaneous modeling of relationships among various independent and dependent variables (Schumacker & Lomax, 2010). PLS-SEM consist of outer and inner models, respectively measurement and structural models (Hair Jr, Sarstedt, Hopkins, & Kuppelwieser, 2014), which is demonstrated in Figure 2

Figure 2. **A PLS path model (Hair Jr et al., 2014)**

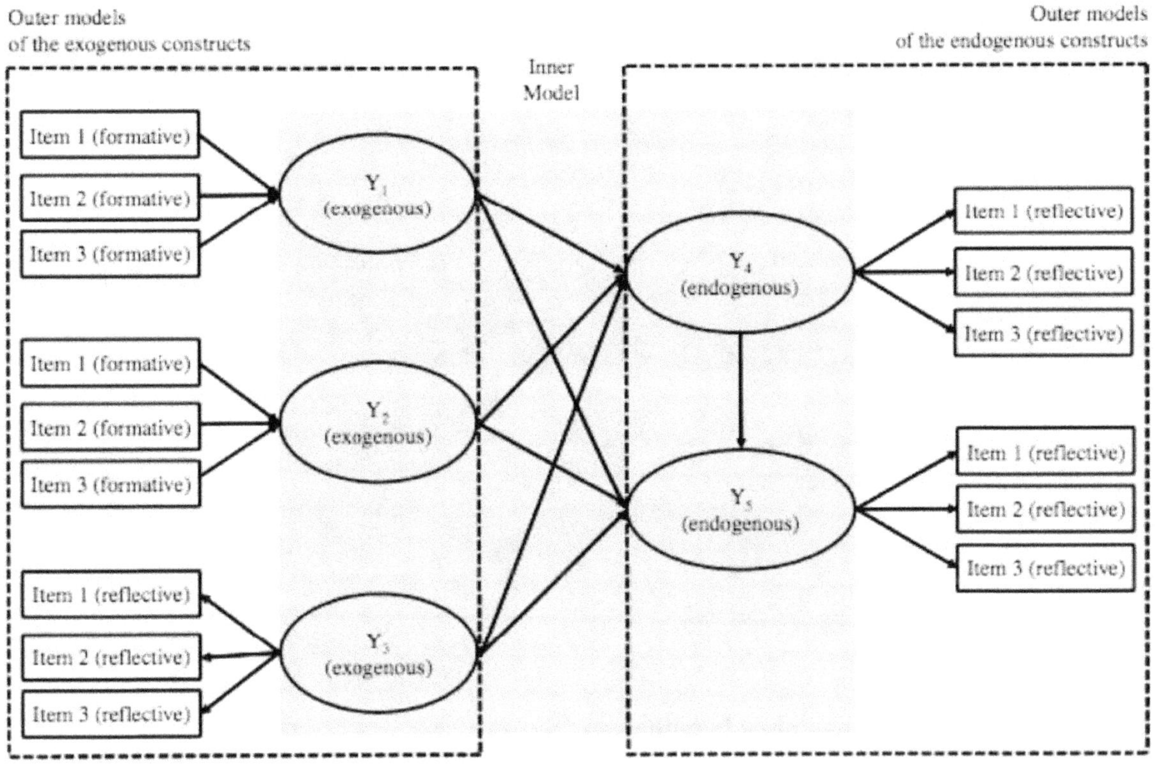

Moderating effects: The moderating effects of Openness of Social media applications on constructs were performed using the product indicator approach. The product indicator approach by (Chin, Marcolin, & Newsted, 2003) refers to the products of each indicator of the independent latent construct with each indicator of the moderator construct. This approach is considered as the most promising technique to determine the moderating effects (Henseler & Fassott, 2010), in particular when the moderator variable is reflective (Henseler & Chin, 2010). In this study, the moderating constructs of culture are modeled as reflective. An example of the product indicator approach is shown in Figure 3, adapted from (Henseler & Chin, 2010). The summary of our proposed hypotheses is shown in Table 1

RESULTS

Respondents' demographic profiles: Some of demographic items that are considered in this study including gender, education background and the ratio between F2F learning and online learning in the blended program implementing in the university. The results give insight into the demographic profiles of respondents who participated in the online questionnaire. Based on the analysis, the response rate was 99.8% (509 responses/531 views). Among these respondents, 45.58% were male and 54.42% were female. Hence, the gender ratio is quite balanced. About education background, 40.8% of the respondents are freshman, which is quite dominant. This also means that most of the respondents (59.2%) have at

Figure 3. Product indicator approach (Henseler & Chin, 2010)

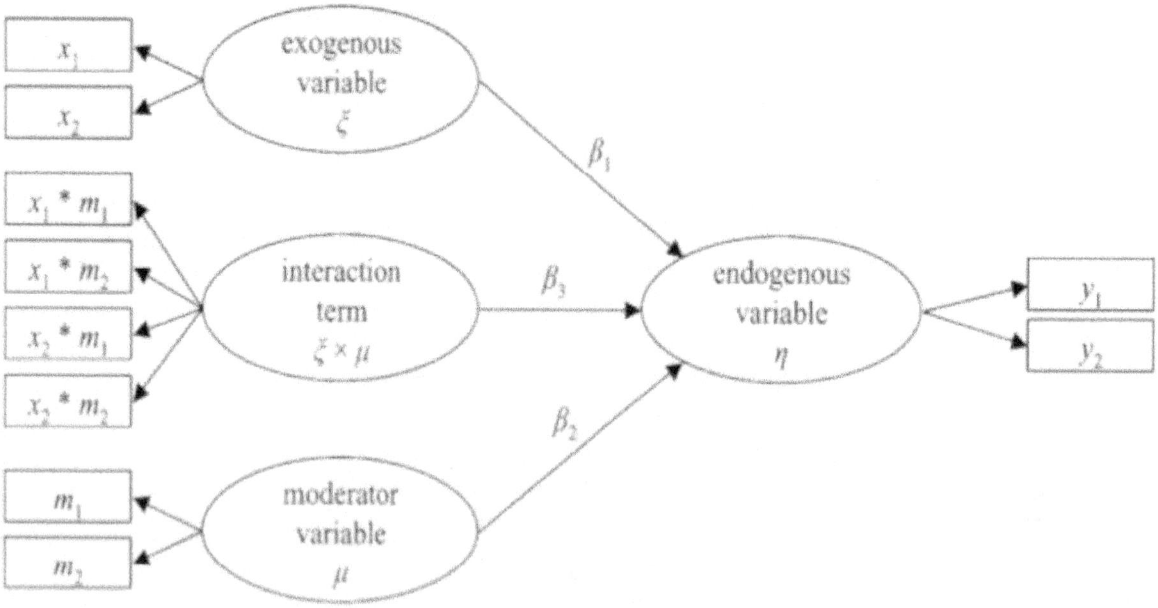

Table 1. **Summary of our proposed hypotheses**

Hypotheses	Descriptions
H1a	Attending F2F class in blended learning can positively impact students' willingness to engage
H1b	Attending F2F class in blended learning can positively impact students' practical effort
H2a	Using traditional education technologies in blended learning can positively impact students' willingness to engage
H2b	Using traditional education technologies in blended learning can positively impact students' practical effort
H3	Students' willingness to engage can positively impact students' practical effort
H4a	Openness of social media applications positively leverage the relationship between attending F2F class in blended learning and students' willingness to engage
H4b	Openness of social media applications positively leverage the relationship between attending F2F class in blended learning and students' practical effort
H5a	Openness of using social media applications positively leverage the relationship between using traditional education technologies in blended learning and students' willingness to engage
H5b	Openness of social media applications positively leverage the relationship between using traditional education technologies in blended learning and students' practical effort
H6a	Students' willingness to engage have a positive impact on students' satisfaction with the blended learning method
H6b	Students' willingness to engage have a positive impact on students' motivation to use blended learning method
H7a	Students' practical effort has a positive impact on students' satisfaction with the blended learning method
H7b	Students' practical effort has a positive impact on students' motivation to use the blended learning method

least more than a year of experience in blended learning. The analysis also showed that the allocation of students' major is evenly distributed among the respondents.

The majority of respondents (55.4%) answered that they have to spend from 30% to 50% of total course length for using traditional education technology for learning activities (the rest is for F2F classes) according to instructors' requirement, while 16.9% with 10% to 30% and 17.88% with 51% to 70% of the total course length. Only 9.82% of respondents said that they have to spend less than 10% the time for online learning. This analysis showed that blended learning programs have been well implemented, in which almost half of the course length is spent for technological pedagogy such as learning through e-learning websites or using email and instructors' websites, while the time for traditional classes still remains from 50% to 70%. Therefore, it can be concluded that our responses data can be used for our hypothesis testing.

Students' frequency of blended learning: Regarding to students' self-evaluation about their frequency of attending F2F class and using IT resource, we summarized the results below:

Figure 4. Students' frequency of blended learning

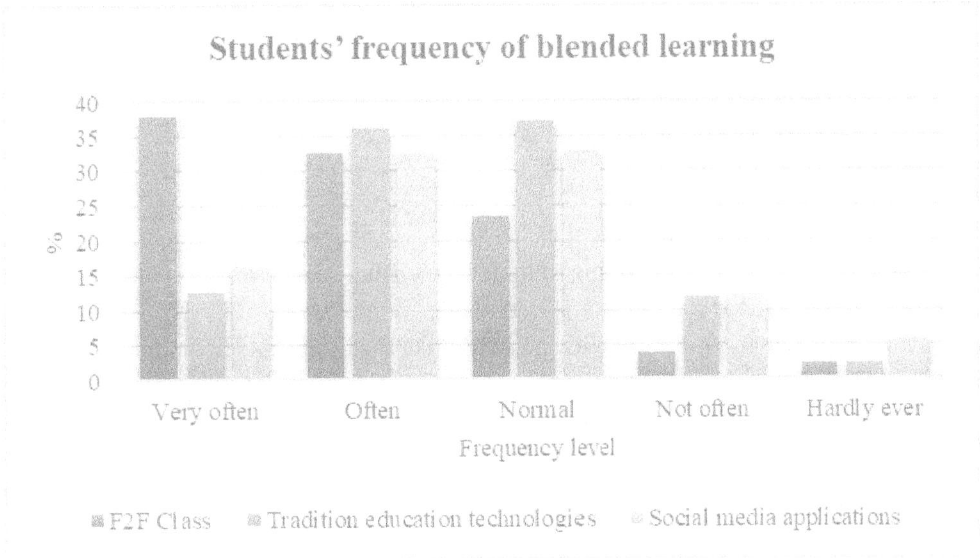

From Figure 4, we observed that the respondents very often attend F2F class, while they still often using traditional education technologies and social media applications. However, from the Figures 4, it is obvious that attending F2F class is quite dominated in the case since the majority of respondents answered that they very often come to class.

Students' activities and perception of blended learning: The students' online learning activities are shown in Figure 5 below. Comparing between traditional education technologies and social media applications, it can be seen that while the majority of respondents focus on attending the online lecture with Edmodo, downloading and exchanging materials and submitting homework by traditional education technologies, social media applications are mostly used for communicating with instructors and classmates and getting course notifications. This reinforces our proposal for the openness of social

Figure 5. Students' online academic activities

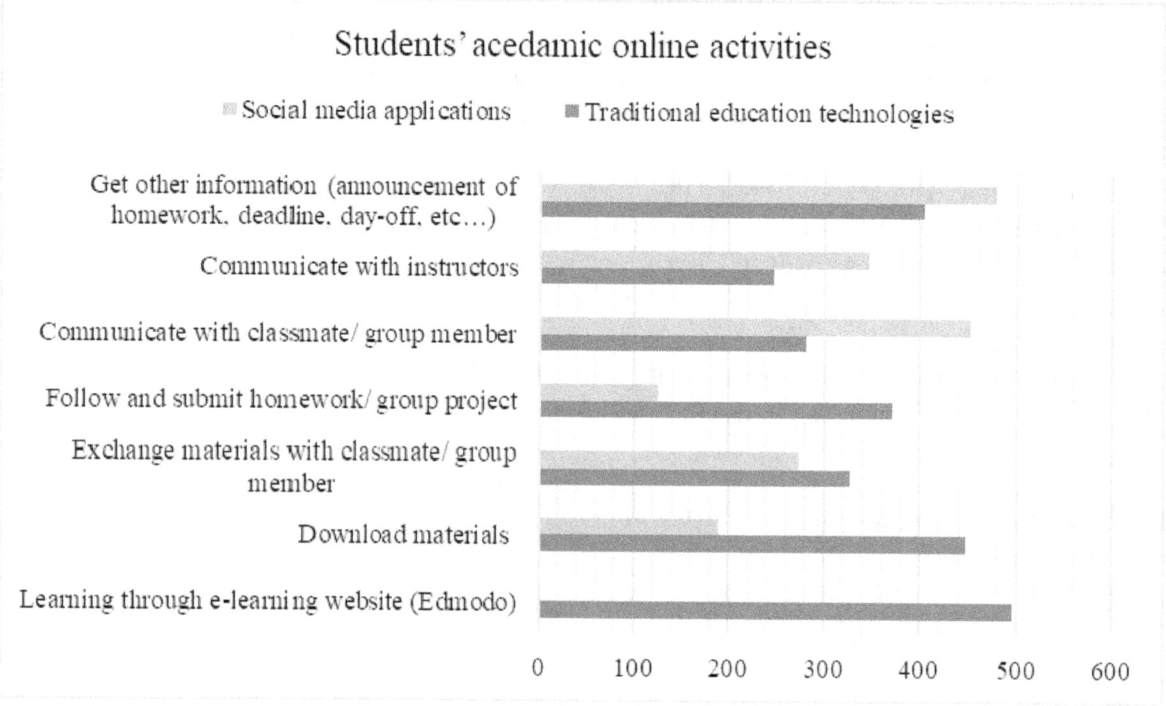

networking applications. Students might feel easier when sharing and communicating on social media applications since they feel deeply belonging to their own virtual world, which is less threatening learning community (Rasiah, 2014).

Student's perception: Concerning students' perception of the importance of attending class and using technology in a blended learning environment according to the results, to the students, attending F2F class is considered as one of the most important learning activities (76%). Meanwhile, related to using technologies for study purposes, while email and e-learning website (i.e. Edmodo) are the most crucial traditional education technologies (68%), instructors' website is not so important (42% of respondents thinks this is normal). YouTube and Facebook Messenger are the two social media applications that students considered as very important for their learning because students refer to YouTube for one of the learning channels for their self-study and Messenger is the main online communication tools since both students and instructors have used it daily. Facebook and Zalo are also important with students (33% and 39%) because they can create some learning group with their group members or friends to discuss before and after class or exchange learning material.

Hypotheses testing: Figure 6 shown the result of our hypotheses testing with the effect of moderators the use of Social Media Applications. It can be see a clear influence of the use of traditional education technology on Students' willingness to engage. Another important relationship is the influence of Students' willingness to engage on Students' engagement. The effects between Willingness and Practical Engagement on Students' satisfaction and motivation also be accepted. However, we must reject the hypothesis that Attending F2F class has an effect on Willingness and Practical Engagement. The relationship between using traditional education technologies and students' practical engagement is not supported also because that is not getting significant level.

Figure 6. Research model with moderator effect of openness

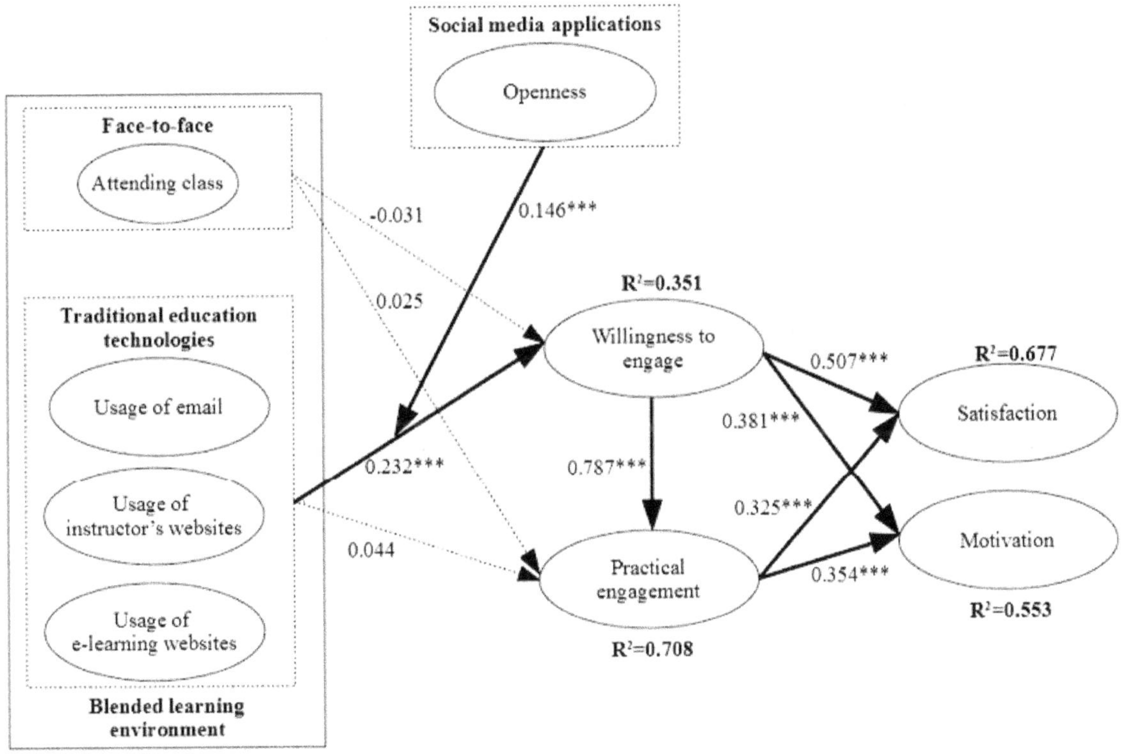

DISCUSSION

Blended Learning and Student's Engagement

From the analysis, it is shown that students who had more time spent online indicated a significantly higher positive willingness of the blended learning course. Therefore, we found that in a blended learning environment, the role of technology-enhanced is very important for students' learning activities. First, using traditional education technologies such as email, instructor's website, and e-learning website helps to increase student's engagement by providing students with flexibility and convenience in timing. For instance, through e-learning platform (i.e. Edmodo), course syllabus and learning materials and are represented in a well-organized way and delivered in a timely way, thus can meet student's expectations about the learning resources. Moreover, since Edmodo is not limited in time and space, course information is also updated, and questions are answered quickly than only have F2F classes, leads students to spend more time for self-study, thus keeps them always involved in learning activities. This idea is also support by (Purnawarman, Susilawati, & Sundayana, 2016), which stated that the usage of Edmodo can enable student's engagement by allowing students to work independently, concerning their work' quality and taking part in group discussion.

Student's Willingness to Engage

From our data analysis, there is a strong relationship between Willingness and Practical Engagement. Students who have a positive sense that they can perform well an academic task and perceive that the task has value or interest to them, will experience enjoyment and willingness considered as emotional engagement to exert more practical effort toward the activity ((Manwaring, Larsen, Graham, Henrie, & Halverson, 2017; Pekrun & Linnenbrink-Garcia, 2012) which is practical engagement.

F2F Classes and Student's Engagement

Meanwhile, in terms of F2F session, from the statistical analysis, we are not able to find any evidence that attending F2F class related to student's engagement. However, from the descriptive data, most of the respondents (76%) still considered attending class is very important and important for their learning. This result is also unified with previous literature, which is stated that student's expectations is blended learning is dominated by the level of interaction between students and instructors or peers (Ireland, Covin, & Kuratko, 2009; Paechter & Maier, 2010). Study of Ireland et al. (2009) confirmed that students do not want the F2F session to be minimized (Ireland et al., 2009).

It is significant to note that besides instructional design can generate different level of engagement in a blended learning environment (Dringus & Seagull, 2013; Garrison, 2004; Graham & Robison, 2007), student's characteristics are also challenges for blended learning engagement. Several personal characteristics that make engagement difficult, such as low self-study ability, low adaptability, and low self-regulation, regardless to any learning approach settings. For instance, more proactive students will find it is easier to talk in class and to communicate with instructors or friends, thus those students tend to be more engaged with the class session. In contrast, students are more inactive find more difficulties to make engagement since they are not willing to adapt to this learning method, which is a student-centered approach and needs more self-efforts. More energetic students, meanwhile, likely tend to prepare well before and after class thanks to the support of traditional education technologies, thus such students are more confident and willing to involve in learning activities both seat-time or online time.

Moreover, this new finding is also shown in the student's responses to the open question of our survey: "For me, online learning is quite effective and convenient. However, because Vietnamese students are so familiar with studying under the guidance of their instructors, the spirit of self-study is poor and students are more dependable, so learning by this method leads students to become less enthusiastic, lazy and usually copy other's works". "I think it's easier to learn online now than to study F2F. People who are busy can still submit homework and project online"

Regarding student's F2F class session, from descriptive data, we also found that 38% of students very often and 32,8% often attend class. The reason is student's attendance may be controlled by instructors, and the lecture's quality may be undertaken in this case.

The positive outcomes of student engagement are investigated for many years despite any kind of learning context. Findings from those studies showed that higher student engagement with the course have a significant and positive impact on students' learning and satisfaction (Luaran, Yusof, Jain, Alias, & Hussin, 2015; Marks, Sibley, & Arbaugh, 2005; Sher, 2009) while higher students' motivation and learning outcomes could also be obtained if students are more engaged with the course (Du, Havard, & Li, 2005; Lam, Fai Cheng, & McNaught, 2005; Sargeant, Curran, Allen, Jarvis-Selinger, & Ho, 2006).

The Role of Social Media Applications

In related to IT resources used in a blended learning environment, we proposed the amplifying role of social media applications such as Facebook, Messenger, YouTube, Zalo in the relationship of blended learning teaching method and student's engagement. This role of social media applications is clearly demonstrated in student's interaction and communication. For instance, students join to a learning group created by instructors through Zalo since other group members participate too so that the student is more engaged with the course. Similarly, when instructors post a question on an e-learning platform and ask students to solve it before the next lecture, students usually discuss with their friends through Facebook group or self-study by YouTube, thus become more involved in learning activities.

CONCLUSION

While educators in Asia still have a lot of worries about applying different online and social media applications in teaching, our research provides instructors and educators a positive sign that blended learning or e-learning contains a potential development in the future. The case of blended learning implementation showed that students' engagement could be generated and facilitated by using traditional education technologies such as Edmodo learning platforms, email or instructors' websites despite lack of direct communication with instructors or classmates. If instructors can provide their students with good and enough materials resources, practices and discussions, students will be tightly engaged with the learning processes even less or without F2F classes. Actively engaged students invest more effort and time in achieving learning, leads them to be satisfied and motivated since they acquire new knowledge and develop skill during the learning process. In other word, students who truly learn in a blended course will obtain higher satisfaction and motivation. Therefore, appropriately choosing the best traditional education technology and carefully invest in the content provided online are thus critical to engage students and increase their satisfaction and motivation.

This study also provides a new notion in terms of blended learning. While previous studies showed the negative impact of social media applications, our research proved that those technologies could positively enhance students' engagement. Facebook, Messenger, YouTube, Zalo can be used by students and instructors to facilitate their communication before and after class. Social media applications help instructors to keep in touch and stay close with their students in real-time. Moreover, with students who are more inactive and less engaged, instructors can motivate their self-learning. Therefore, it is logical to say that social media applications can be used as a complementary tool with traditional education technologies to amplify students' engagement in blended learning. Educators now can be confident in the future of development and the potential to attract students of e-learning models and distance learning. The next important issue that educators should focus on is choosing the model that is appropriate for each subject, and the learning environment to bring the highest efficiency to students.

As from the data analysis, while F2F classes are still very significant to students, we cannot find any impact on their engagement. This finding opens up new avenues to investigate the effect of students' characteristics as well as lecture quality on the level of engagement. We believe that future researchers should investigate how the class environment affects engagement in different students' characteristic and lecture quality and the role of social media applications in this context.

Data Availability: The data are not publicly available due to their containing information that could compromise the privacy of research participants

Conflicts of Interest: the authors declare that they have no conflicts of interest.

Response to Reviewers Feedback: As per Reviewers Feed Back, I have Included Discussion and Conclusion in separate segment

I also Included latest references including 2021 published article related to this topic and cited with in text there by strengthen the background information related to the study. This was a major feedback by one of the reviewer.

As per another reviewer feedback I have cited with in text and indirectly also referred articles which are publisher after 2010.

REFERENCES

Akkoyunlu, B., & Soylu, M. Y. (2008). A Study of Student's Perceptions in a Blended Learning Environment Based on Different Learning Styles. *Journal of Educational Technology & Society*, *11*(1), 183–193.

Arbaugh, J. B., & Benbunan-Fich, R. (2007). The importance of participant interaction in online environments. *Decision Support Systems*, *43*(3), 853–865. doi:10.1016/j.dss.2006.12.013

Ata, R. (2016). An exploration of higher education teaching in second life in the context of blended learning. *The Turkish Online Journal of Educational Technology*, *15*(3), 9–26.

Bonk, C. J., Graham, C. R., Cross, J., & Moore, M. G. (2006). *The Handbook of Blended Learning: Global Perspectives*. Local Designs.

Brody, T. (2006). Blended learning: A recipe for the future. *Carolina TESOL*, *30*(2).

Castro, R. (2019). Blended learning in higher education: Trends and capabilities. *Education and Information Technologies*, *24*(4), 2523–2546. doi:10.100710639-019-09886-3

Chin, W. W., Marcolin, B. L., & Newsted, P. R. (2003). A partial least squares latent variable modeling approach for measuring interaction effects: Results from a Monte Carlo simulation study and an electronic-mail emotion/adoption study. *Information Systems Research*, *14*(2), 189–217. doi:10.1287/isre.14.2.189.16018

Clusky, G. Jr, Hodges, C. W., & Smith, S. (2006). The impact of online quizzing on student success in an introductory financial accounting class. *Journal of College Teaching and Learning*, *3*(7), 13–18. doi:10.19030/tlc.v3i7.1697

Cooper, D., & Schindler, P. (2011). *Business Research Methods* (11th ed.). McGraw Hill.

Creswell, J. W. (2003). *Research Design: Qualitative, Quantitative, and Mixed Methods Approaches*. SAGE Publications.

Crompton, H., Olszewski, B., & Bielefeldt, T. (2016). The mobile learning training needs of educators in technology-enabled environments. *Professional Development in Education*, *42*(3), 482–501. doi:10.1080/19415257.2014.1001033

Dringus, L. P., & Seagull, A. B. (2013). *A five-year study of sustaining blended learning initiatives to enhance academic engagement in computer and information sciences campus courses*. CEC Faculty Books and Book.

Du, J., Havard, B., & Li, H. (2005). *Dynamic online discussion: Task-oriented interaction for deep learning* (Vol. 42). Academic Press.

Garrison, D. R., & Kanuka, H. (2004). Blended learning: Uncovering its transformative potential in higher education. *The Internet and Higher Education*, *7*(2), 95–105. doi:10.1016/j.iheduc.2004.02.001

Graham, C. R., & Robison, R. (2007). Realizing the transformational potential of blended learning: Comparing cases of transforming blends and enhancing blends in higher education. In A. G. Picciano & C. D. Dziuban (Eds.), Blended Learning: Research Perspectives (pp. 83–110). Academic Press.

Hair, J. F., Jr., Sarstedt, M., Hopkins, L., & Kuppelwieser, V. (2014). Partial least squares structural equation modeling (PLS-SEM) An emerging tool in business research. *European Business Review*, *26*(2), 106–121. doi:10.1108/EBR-10-2013-0128

Henseler, J., & Chin, W. W. (2010). A Comparison of Approaches for the Analysis of Interaction Effects Between Latent Variables Using Partial Least Squares Path Modeling. *Structural Equation Modeling*, *17*(1), 82–109. doi:10.1080/10705510903439003

Henseler, J., & Fassott, G. (2010). Testing Moderating Effects in PLS Path Models: An Illustration of Available Procedures. In V. Esposito Vinzi, W. W. Chin, J. Henseler, & H. Wang (Eds.), *Handbook of Partial Least Squares: Concepts, Methods and Applications* (pp. 713–735). Springer Berlin Heidelberg. doi:10.1007/978-3-540-32827-8_31

Hwang, A., & Francesco, A. M. (2010). *The Influence of Individualism–Collectivism and Power Distance on Use of Feedback Channels and Consequences for Learning* (Vol. 9). Academic Press.

Ireland, R. D., Covin, J. G., & Kuratko, D. F. (2009). Conceptualizing corporate entrepreneurship strategy. *Entrepreneurship Theory and Practice*, *33*(1), 19–46. doi:10.1111/j.1540-6520.2008.00279.x

Kaur, M. (2013). Blended Learning - Its Challenges and Future. *Procedia: Social and Behavioral Sciences*, *93*, 612–617. doi:10.1016/j.sbspro.2013.09.248

Kicheva, M., & Dimitrova, B. T. K. (2021) Distance Education During the 2020 Global Crisis Lockdown. *SHS Web of Conferences, 92*.

Kim, K. J., & Bonk, C. J. (2006). The future of online teaching and learning in higher education: The survey says.... *EDUCAUSE Quarterly*, *29*(4), 22–30.

Lam, P., Fai Cheng, K., & McNaught, C. (2005). *Asynchronous Online Discussion: Empirical Evidence on Quantity and Quality*. Academic Press.

Li, Y., Nishimura, N., Yagami, H., & Park, H.-S. (2021). An Empirical Study on Online Learners' Continuance Intentions in China. *Sustainability, 13*(2), 889. doi:10.3390u13020889

Li, Y., Tarafdar, M., & Subba Rao, S. (2012). *Collaborative knowledge management practices: Theoretical development and empirical analysis*. doi:10.1108/01443571211223077

Lin, W. T., & Shao, B. B. M. (2000). The relationship between user participation and system success: A simultaneous contingency approach. *Information & Management, 37*(6), 283–295. doi:10.1016/S0378-7206(99)00055-5

Luaran, J. E., Yusof, N. Y. M., Jain, J., Alias, R., & Hussin, A. A. (2015). *Blended learning: Examining student satisfaction, willingness, and stress in learning English*. Academic Press.

Manwaring, K. C., Larsen, R., Graham, C. R., Henrie, C. R., & Halverson, L. R. (2017). Investigating student engagement in blended learning settings using experience sampling and structural equation modeling. *The Internet and Higher Education, 35*, 21–33. doi:10.1016/j.iheduc.2017.06.002

Marks, R. B., Sibley, S. D., & Arbaugh, J. B. (2005). A Structural Equation Model of Predictors for Effective Online Learning. *Journal of Management Education, 29*(4), 531–563. doi:10.1177/1052562904271199

Martin, F., & Whitmer, J. C. (2016). Applying learning analytics to investigate timed release in online learning. *Technology. Knowledge and Learning, 21*(1), 59–74. doi:10.100710758-015-9261-9

Paechter, M., & Maier, B. (2010). Online or face-to-face? Students' experiences and preferences in e-learning. *The Internet and Higher Education, 13*(4), 292–297. doi:10.1016/j.iheduc.2010.09.004

Pekrun, R., & Linnenbrink-Garcia, L. (2012). Academic Emotions and Student Engagement. In S. L. Christenson, A. L. Reschly, & C. Wylie (Eds.), *Handbook of Research on Student Engagement* (pp. 259–282). Springer US. doi:10.1007/978-1-4614-2018-7_12

Porter, W. W., Graham, C. R., Spring, K. A., & Welch, K. R. (2014). Blended learning in higher education: Institutional adoption and implementation. *Computers & Education, 75*, 185–195. doi:10.1016/j.compedu.2014.02.011

Purnawarman, P., Susilawati, S., & Sundayana, W. (2016). The use of Edmodo in teaching writing in a blended learning setting. Indonesian Journal of Applied Linguistics. doi:10.17509/ijal.v5i2.1348

Ringle, C., Wende, S., & Becker, J. (2014). SmartPLS 3. *Academy of Management Review, 9*, 419–445.

Sargeant, J., Curran, V., Allen, M., Jarvis-Selinger, S., & Ho, K. (2006). *Facilitating interpersonal interaction and learning online: Linking theory and practice* (Vol. 26). Academic Press.

Schumacker, R. E., & Lomax, R. G. (2010). *A beginner's guide to structural equation modeling* (3rd ed.). Routledge/Taylor & Francis Group.

Sher, A. (2009). Assessing the Relationship of Student-Instructor and Student-Student Interaction to Student Learning and Satisfaction in Web-Based Online Learning Environment %J. *Journal of Interactive Online Learning, 8*(2), 102–120.

Voos, R. (2003). Blended learning—What is it and where might it take us? *Sloan-C View, 2*(1), 2–5.

Chapter 16
Implications of Knowledge Management Adoption Within Higher Education Institutions:
Business Process Reengineering Approach

Fadzliwati Mohiddin
https://orcid.org/0000-0002-7332-209X
University of Technology Brunei, Brunei

Heru Susanto
https://orcid.org/0000-0002-1823-357X
University of Technology Brunei, Brunei & The Indonesian Institute of Sciences, Indonesia

Fahmi Ibrahim
University of Technology Brunei, Brunei

ABSTRACT

The aim and objective of this research is to get a better understanding on the knowledge management system (KMS) practices and perception within higher education institutions (HEIs). This research will focus on three main aspects. The first aspect will be on identifying management tools used at the organizational level. Second, will be the supportive and hindrance factors on the adoption of KMS and the user perception and practices of KMS in the institution. A mix of methodologies is adapted to generate findings for this research. Both quantitative and qualitative methods will be used for this research through a questionnaire approach. The questionnaire is constructed in such a way that closed-ended questions and open-ended questions are included. The research has led to several important outcomes for the implementation of KMS in HEIs. This study has proposed a conceptual framework and support from other research outcomes (i.e., identification of the management tools used, the support and barriers for implementation, and user perception and practices for the KMS implementations).

DOI: 10.4018/978-1-7998-7184-2.ch016

INTRODUCTION

The main task is to conduct research on medium to large organization and identify the impacts of introduction of business process reengineering in their businesses as well as the benefits they gained from it. Recent literature is also employed to reinforce the results of the findings and to obtain a better understanding of the topic. The prospect of Business Process Re-engineering (BPR) was originally introduced by Michael Hammer in the 1990's. BPR comprises of altering the structures and the procedures that are carried out within the organization's surrounding. The progress and the outcomes of a company most likely rely upon the people, technology used as well as the processes. BPR may cause alterations to different aspects within the company such as the technological side, the company's structures as well as the employees. The process causes companies to rebuild or remove any ineffective management tier, eliminate any excess and redesign the procedures to operate in other ways. BPR is otherwise also known as process innovation or rather a core process redesign.

Rojahonka (2010) stated that business processes are activities that generate a particular product for the customer and processes that are crucial for success are often referred as "business processes" or "core processes". Normal core processes as stated by Laamanen and Tinnila (as cited in Rojahonka, 2010) are customer support, order fulfillments and product as well as service development. According to Goll (as cited in Huang, Lee, Chiu & Yen, 2014) BPR allows transformations of business process to achieve improvements in the performance of the business as well as, according to Petrozzo and Stepper, (as cited by Huang et al., 2014) the betterment of company's goods and services. Information Technology (IT), as agreed by Gunasekaran and Nath (as cited in Huang et al., 2014) serves as a significant support to the implementation of BPR in businesses for the reason that IT can provide information regarding company goals and strategies to close precision. BPR can offer a number of benefits to businesses.

Due to globalization and the rapid changes occurring in the marketplace, companies have to constantly monitor and come up with solutions in order to handle the numerous challenges that causes uncertainty and inconsistency in which therefore will affect all the areas that is in the business environment. This challenge requires the company to make changes which will alter the different areas within the organization in order to keep up with the constantly evolving marketplace. The main aim of BPR is to alter the companies to be more adaptable, responsive, productive and capable to cater all of their stakeholders.

LITERATURE REVIEW

Today, most of the organizations in the world have adopted and implemented Business Process Reengineering (BPR). Some have also decided to use it as a corporate strategy. This proves that the act of redesigning and restructuring business processes is important for a company in order for the company to improve its performance, as demonstrated by Al-Mashari and Zairi (1999). However, according to Mir-Ghaderi; Habib (as cited in Omidi & Koshtinat, 2016) 70% of BPR projects encountered failure, as it is considered a high risk project. This literature review will discover the topic of BPR in depth, and additionally introduces IS concept as this research aimed to bring to light the implementation of BPR as a corporate strategy through information systems tools.

From the research that has been done, various authors have given different definitions of BPR. As stated by Goll (as cited in Huang, Lee, Chiu & Yen, 2014), BPR is defined as "an approach for business process transformation and unconstrained reshaping of all business process transformation and unconstrained reshaping of all business processes, involved technologies, and related management systems, as well as the accompanied organizational structure and values, to achieve considerable advances in performance throughout the business" (p.1). Valentine and Knights; Simpson, Kondouli and Wai (as cited in Subramoniam, Tounsi and Krishnankutty, 2009), however, say that BPR only means a change from being role-based to operation-based and have also categorized BPR into two types: "radical BPR and revisionist BPR" (p.654). The former holds the meaning of having the whole company restructured while the latter, only a small part of the company's business process is modified (Subramoniam, Tounsi & Krishnankutty, 2009). On the other hand, Gunasekaran and Ichimura (as cited in Tsai, Chen, Hwang & Hsu, 2010) states that BPR includes the taking on of the task views of a company. Hammer and Champy (as cited in Yin, 2010) has a similar definition to Tsai, Chen, Hwang and Hsu's (2010) definition of BPR and believes that BPR "represents a fundamental rethinking of organizations and radical redesign of business processes to achieve dramatic improvements in critical, contemporary measures of performance, such as cost, quality, service and speed" (p.27).

Alter (as cited in Yin, 2010) has also defined BPR as a systematic procedure that requires information technology to repair business processes in a whole which results in achieving the company's main objectives. Information Technology System is "a system where people and technology, having their own constituents and associated activities, communicate for the same reason" (Soltanmohammadi, Asadi & Ithnin, 2013, p.330).

Corporate's Strategies: BPR Approaches

There are several reasons as to why companies decide to use BPR as a corporate strategy. Companies have goals and objectives that they wish to attain and BPR may be used as a mean of way to accomplish them. According to Huang, Lee, Chiu and Yen (2014), companies that wants to adopt BPR have the goal to "restructure and simplify business process" with the purpose of that it allows "the managers or line workers to use a well-designed process" (p.3). With the use of BPR, companies are also able to "rationalise, innovate and adapt to the changing circumstances" (Subhas, Kumar & Kumar, 2008, p.65). Furthermore, Subramoniam, Tounsi and Krishnankutty (2009) state that BPR was implemented in companies so that the cycle time used is reduced, quality of the products and services provided by the company is enhanced and that customer service is improved. The objectives of organizations in implementing BPR are mainly improve in performance which results in an increase in profit in the company and become a competitive advantage to benefit the company in the long term.

Taken from the journal of "*Business Process Reengineering A review of recent literature, Technovation*", it states that BPR must be viewed as a crucial, multi- purpose venture that should be incorporated with different parts of management in the event that it is able to contribute to the organization in which the important condition is that managers comprehend all aspects of the present business practices prior to commencing the BPR venture. The journal also states that the utilization of IT can support significant enhancements in the operations of the system of the business, and taking everything in mind as the crucial element of reengineering activity is that it must be combined with the demands of every stakeholder as the top of the priority list.

With all the different elements that need to be considered that will in any way bring upon a change either before or after the process, companies need to take into account if it is really beneficial and important for them to implement BPR. According to Panda (2013), he stated that the driving factor for BPR is to acknowledge powerful changes by essentially reconsidering how an organization's function should be done rather than the minor process changes that centers around practical and accumulative change.

Vesely (2011) stated that the main aim of BPR is to improve on the ways in which an organization functions by adopting specific values of a more successful organization. Knights and Wilmott (as cited in Borgianni, Cascini. & Rotini, 2015) claimed that BPR applications have been aimed at conserving resources. The application of BPR reduces time consumption and cost of production, which indirectly improves the efficiency and effectiveness of the productivity of the workforce. As commented by Lee, Chu and Tseng (2009), production costs will be reduced. Panda (2013) believes that this will result in an improvement in productivity, as less work is needed to do a single task. Bond and Guimaraes; Choi and Chan (as cited in Yin, 2010) described the role of BPR as redesigning business process, dramatic discontinuous improvement as to cease practicing the obsolete rules and fundamental beliefs that underlie operations. Choi and Chan (as cited in Yin, 2010) further elaborated that the role of BPR is to increase effectiveness of accomplishment of the company's management, administrative and operational tasks. Yin (2010) also stated that the structure reorganization that is implemented in the company to adapt the new process will help the organization to focus on processes which in turn results to the flexibility and efficiency. Glykas and Valiris asserted that one of the main positive traits of BPR to the organization is the focus on core business processes (as cited in Yin, 2010). Using IT will help to build a robust network environment which improve the company's competitiveness (Yin, 2010). Lastly, the organization would benefit from BPR such as "productivity, decreased cycle time, inventory or cost, profitability (and) increased economic growth" after the successful application of BPR (Yin, 2010, p.97).

As indicated by Huang, Lee, Chiu and Yen (2014), BPR can help in the improvement the business processes in terms of quality, reduction in costs and shortening of the product development cycle and thus, helps companies to gain a competitive advantage. The integration of IT with BPR can help organizations to improve the communication of information about business objectives and business strategies in terms of speed and accuracy of information transmitted (Gunasekaran and Nath, as cited in Huang, Lee, Chiu and Yen, 2014). Departmental managers and staff from different divisions are also able to communicate and share information and knowledge with ease and convenience with the application of BPR (Ramirez, Melville & Lawler, 2010). According to Huang, Lee, Chiu and Yen (2014), organizations need to train employees so that they are able to make wise decisions and choices and react to unforeseen events. Therefore, the application of BPR can also raise the morale of the employees in an organization as well as its labor productivity (Guimaraes and Bond, as cited in Huang, Lee, Chiu and Yen, 2014).

Success of BPR as a Corporate Strategy

BPR as a corporate strategy has proved to be successful in various literature and case studies. Several authors such as Davenport, Peppard and Ward and Scheer and Habermann (as cited in Morris and Venkatesh, 2010) contended that success or failure of an ERP system implementation is determined by the job and process redesign. According to Hall, Rosenthal and Wade, since BPR applications were mainly focused on reducing cost it has underestimated the importance of the value delivered to end users. However Terziovski, Fitzpatrick and O'Neill think otherwise as they regard such practices as a determinant for BPR efforts to be successful (as cited in Borgianni, Cascini and Rotini, 2015) and thus the success of BPR is customer-driven. A case study agrees with the topic where BPR improved the performance of the company. In addition, overall quality of service improved and thus making the company more competitive by regaining back market share and prolong its business life (Budiono & Loice, 2012). This shall be further elaborated in the discussion of the research findings.

Although BPR has its advantages, a misuse in BPR may lead to the failure of companies' operations. As indicated by Bhattacherjee and Ma (2009), a failure in the IT system may be due to resistance by the users or employees and their inability to use it to its fullest potential. Kwahk and Lee (2008) also agree with Bhattacherjee and Ma as they believe that the failure rate of BPR is between 60% to 90% where the reason lie in the resistance of the users to change as the success depends of willingness of the employee to change. It was further supported by Chou and Chang (2008) as around 40% to 60% failures were due to the difference in interests between customer organizations and ERP vendors and also mentioned that the BPR implementation fails due to certain uncertainties; organizational misfit, organizational resistance, adaptation problems and differentiation among sub-units.

Companies may sometimes "underestimate or misunderstand the risks such as spending a considerable amount in its investment, not considered as part of ERP system initiation and the lack of consistency between system and business process in ERP package selection" (Tsai, Chen, Hwang & Hsu, 2010, p.27). Other failures may include the difficulties of the staff to cope with the new system (Morris and Venkatesh, 2010) and the fact that BPR is a risk-taking decision in which large amount of investments are needed to execute it, leading to a large uncertainty with the success of the business (Subhas, Khumar & Khumar, 2008).

Despite the fact that there are some failures during the application of BPR as a corporate strategy, there are several methods that researchers have found to minimize the risks of BPR. According to Subhas, Kumar and Kumar (2008), "effective management", "modeling of risks", "predicting and estimating the risks [which is known as risk management]" are a few of the ways a company can do in order to minimize the risk of BPR implementation (p.66). In addition, Soltanmohammadi, Asadi and Ithnin (2013) have also mentioned that the information system and the user must be able to operate together efficiently as well. On the other hand, Chou and Chang (2008) have stated that Organizational Information Processing Theory (OIPT) was used for the management of activities that serves to minimize the uncertainties that may occur after implementing BPR or using BPR as its corporate strategy.

As cited by Kwahk and Lee (2008), Piderit asserted that the solution for reducing resistance to BPR is by creating readiness for change. Parasuraman also stated that technology readiness as a mentality that affected "people's [natural behaviors to accept and use new technologies for realizing objectives]..." (p.475). In addition, Walczuch, Lemmink and Streukens further elaborated that more innovative individuals were claimed to have a smoother shift into a new technology without much cognitive struggle. Users must overcome knowledge barriers and disregard the previous operations (Kwakh & Lee, 2008). As for Yin (2010), employees need to be trained to instill awareness among them for the need of continuous improvement and crucial rethinking. This would guarantee that the BPR philosophy will continue to flourish in the organization as a result. Proper communication, coordination and control would be established in the organization.

In order to adopt BPR as a corporate strategy in the company, there are different steps in which it can be done and phases that it goes through. Vesely (2011) has identified some of the methods in the restructuring process;

1. Analyze target site for problems and room for improvements with regards to meeting the organization's goals
2. Find exemplars of working practices that appear superior

3. "Explanation" to know and understand why it works
4. "Extrapolation"-to apply the best practice to the target site. (Vesely, 2011, p.103)

However, Yin (2010) identified two phases in BPR; initiation phase and definition phase.

In initiation phase, recognition and inspection of the capacity of major business operations to be refined are done. This is also where the "acquisition process of prototype parts" was pinpointed as an important activity in within the development. This enables the staff in the company to develop their concentration in their future tasks. For the second and last phase, definition phase, the staff tried to consider and understand the cause and search for solutions through the act of teamwork. This will develop a "teamwork atmosphere" in the company. Here, the staff "[rearranges] the structure to adapt the new process". This will develop an operation-based organization and enables the organization to improve in flexibility and efficiency. (Yin, 2010, p.97)

BPR Awareness

Gunasekaran and Nath (1997) assert that BPR is meant for organizations that are eager and determined to enhance their performance significantly. Terziovski, Fitzpatrick and O'Neill (2003) also stated that since last decade, organizations are keen with new means and tools to achieve competitive advantage in te fluctuating business environment. Ligus (as cited in Terziovski et al., 2003) demonstrated that implementation of BPR can results in the reduction of costs, reduction of delivery time, reduction of inventories, reduction of cost of quality as well as increase in market share. On the other hand, Cummings (as cited in Terziovski et al., 2003) illustrates the advantages of BPR exercise to be the growth of sales and revenue, enhancement in customer services, quicker processes and improvements in quality.

According to Gunasekaran and Nath (1997), IT enhanced accuracy by elimination error that can be caused by humans when they perform tasks that are difficult and repetitive, in addition to time-saving. Moreover, IT can also save money due to the reduction of time and errors in a tasks. Overall, a competitive advantage can be achieves through the use of IT. They (as cited in Terziovski et al., 2003) also states that the usage of IT in BPR enables cycle times to be reduced due to the lesser tasks that are needed in order to perform the process. Furthermore, Hammer; Hammer and Champy, Gunasekaran and Nath (as cited in Terziovski et al., 2003) illustrates IT as a tool to create new processes.

Additionally, the role of IT in reengineering can be viewed from two viewpoints: the role of the IT function, such as the Internet, CAD, CAM; and the role of technology, for instance ATM and fiber optics. The role of IT plays an important part in the successfulness and offers enormous advantages of the whole reengineering strategy. Davenport and short; Hewitt believes that organizations' information management should stimulate their employees to grow and improve their skills and knowledge in computer-aided systems engineering (as cited in Gunasekaran and Nath, 1997) These authors also assert that a wide variety of IT can be utilised to enhance the merging of different working divisions to aid in the smooth running of information throughout an organization.

Information systems (IS) awareness is important because it encompasses the internal environment of an organization. Since information system is supported by people and procedures, employees need to know and be aware of the IS their organization employs. They need to know what type of IS it is, what it does, among others. The purpose of IS are to support organizations in solving problems, making decisions and other day-to-day business activities (Sousa & Oz, 2015).

Governments are the largest user of IS, since they exist to serve the population (*Government Information Systems: A Guide to Effective Use of Information Technology in the Public Sector of Developing Countries*, 1995). Therefore, they process a large number of data and information. IS help governments in data collection, storing of data, processing the data, circulating and employing the data (*Government Information Systems: A Guide to Effective Use of Information Technology in the Public Sector of Developing Countries*, 1995). In private organizations, the purpose of IS is to process raw data into information that is useful, which can then be utilize for better decision making ("What Are Information Systems? - Definition & Types", n.d.)

Mitra and Chaya (1996) discovered that the results of investing on IT corresponds to lower average production costs and total costs, but it will also lead to higher average fixed costs. According to Gurbaxani and Whang (1991), information systems can directly influence the productivity of manufacturing and service operations.

Attaining a secure system is bound to be costly but yet, information security is oftentimes an underrated element in technology (Soltanmohammadi, Asadi & Ithin, 2013). Users of IS need to be aware of the standard security application used in an organization and also the fact that human component, i.e. human errors, is usually the initial setback that creates a hole in the Information Technology system security. A secure system is not guaranteed by the existence of security systems, similar to how protection of data is not secured even though it is in the relevant security-oriented arrangement (Soltanmohammadi, Asadi & Ithin, 2013). According to these authors, the evaluation of human's factors are crucial during security employment, as intrusion can upset an organization's security goals. Human factors are the focus of analysis and investigation, instead of technological criteria, should there be any security issues that occur.

More than 80% of accidents in workplaces are caused by human errors, ranging from air transport operations to nuclear power plants (Harper et al., 2011 and Hollnagel, 1993). If we humans simply predict that our errors and mistakes on security practices is two-thirds of safety accidents, the fact that human error is the majority cause of these accidents is alarming. Information security inspectors focusing on the abovementioned issue produced statistics that indicated that they make up a huge part of complications raised in computer security. Ahmed et al. (2012) discovered in his research, as revealed by the Global Financial Services Industry (GFSI) According to a survey in Brostoff, Fischer and Hubner study (as cited in Soltanmohammadi et al., 2013) the majority of respondents, at 86%, stated that the main reason there is information systems failure was because of human mistakes. 65% of economic loss resulted by information security breaches was because of human error, as compared to only 3% which originated from outsiders. Additionally, Brostoff and Spruit et al. (as cited in Soltanmohammadi et al. 2013) found that 41% of security disturbances were caused by human mistakes and errors; at the same time, only 9% were because of intended crimes.

Information security threats can be caused by human or non-human malefactor, both internally and externally (Chen, Shaw, Yang 2016) intentionally and unintentionally as stated by Kreicberge; Siponen et al. (as cited in Soltanmohammadi, Asadi, Ithin, 2013). External threat includes natural disaster and hackers. Internal includes staff malpractice, security error,_carelessness, and attacks (Chen et al, 2016) and poor users behavior such as mistakes and negligence, mentioned by Leach (as cited in_Soltanmohammadi et al, 2013). If an organization not aware of these threats, they can be prone to its attack (Chen et al, 2016). They believed that the security problems faced today is as a result of lack of security awareness, and can be lessen even without sophisticated technologies, as the human factor plays a more significant role. The implementation of security measures like firewall, antivirus software, proxy server did not gave much protection, but aggravates the threats. According to a Computer Crime and Computer Security survey, co-conducted by Computer Security Institute and the Federal Bureau of Investigation in 2005, stated by Gordon, Loeb, Lucyshyn, & Richardson, as cited in Chen et al (2016), 73% of security threats consists of virus infection. Contrastingly,, Boujettif and Wand, as cited by Soltanmohammadi et al. (2013) found that 4 out of 5 security incidents in organization are caused by internal threats

METHODOLOGY

The aim of this subtopic is to describe the research methodology of the survey questionnaire. It includes the sample selection of participants/respondents in the survey questionnaire, description of the procedure used in performing this survey and the method applied in data collection as well as a clear explanation of the statistical procedures used to analyze the data.

Sample Size

A total of 4 medium-to-large sized companies, two (2) private agencies and two (2) government sectors, with a total sample of 40 staff from the four agencies were either interviewed according to the survey questions or merely answer the questionnaire through the Google Forms link we have created.

Data Analysis

Initially we received the permission letter from the School of Business and Economics (SBE) before we sent them to the selected companies by email. Then, the companies would select their staff to answer the survey questionnaire.

The data from the survey will be analyzed and categorized under three points under the results and findings section: Information System Awareness, Attitudes to Information Security System and BPR Awareness. The steps in data analysis consist of examining the surveys for its accuracy and completeness, keying the data into Microsoft Excel and performing an analysis according to the statistical frequencies using charts and graphs.

RESULT AND DISCUSSION

From the graph above, it show that both the government and private organizations are utilizing information system in their operation with all of them agreeing on utilizing information system in their management. This prove that information system play an important role in the organization.

Figure 2 above shows the frequency of IT usage in both private organizations and government agencies. On the left-hand side is the graph showing private organizations' feedback while the right-hand side shows government agencies' feedback. From the graph above, it shows that DHL always uses IT (at 100% usage) while BAG Networks uses IT always (at 80%) and often (at 20%) respectively. DARE (Darussalam Enterprise) always uses IT (at 100% usage) while the Printing Department always (50%) and often (50%) uses Information Technology.

Figure 1. Utilization of information system

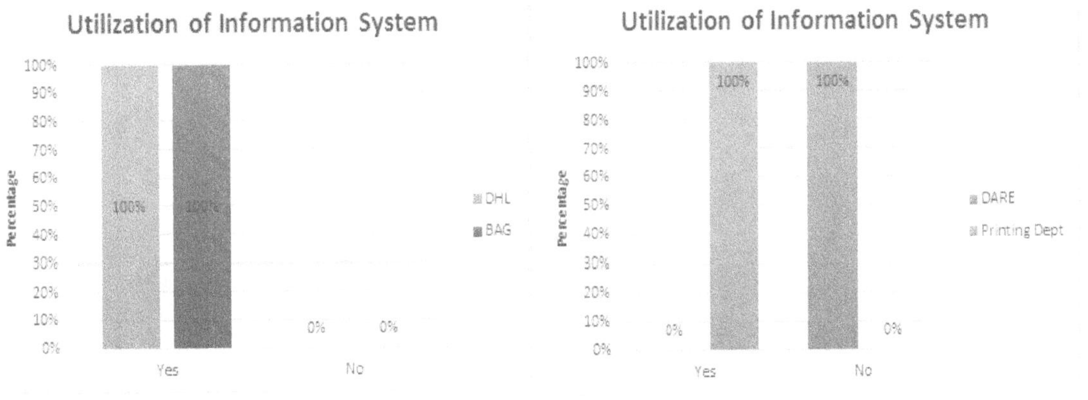

This indicates that information technology usage are progressively important since at least half of the respondents from both the private and government organization always use it in their management and operations.

The graph above illustrated that 100% of the government organisations selected in this research reviewed their information systems at hourly interval. On the other hand, private organisations, particularly DHL, reviewed their IS at daily interval; meanwhile only 40% of respondents from BAG do so. The remaining respondents, i.e. 60% reviewed at frequency other than the suggested intervals in the questionnaire. On the other hand, only 20% of respondents from BAG reviewed their IS one in a month.

Reviewing MIS in an organization either hourly, daily or often (once in a month) imply that how often an organization are checking on the performance of their information system in the organization, since it can affect the management and operation of the business.

From the graph above, it is found that DARE had implemented IT in their organisations for around six month to a year, meanwhile for Printing Department, they have utilised IT for two years or more, similar to the two private organisations. On the other hand, only 10% from BAG indicated that they have use IT for approximately one to two years.

Figure 2. Frequency Usage of IT

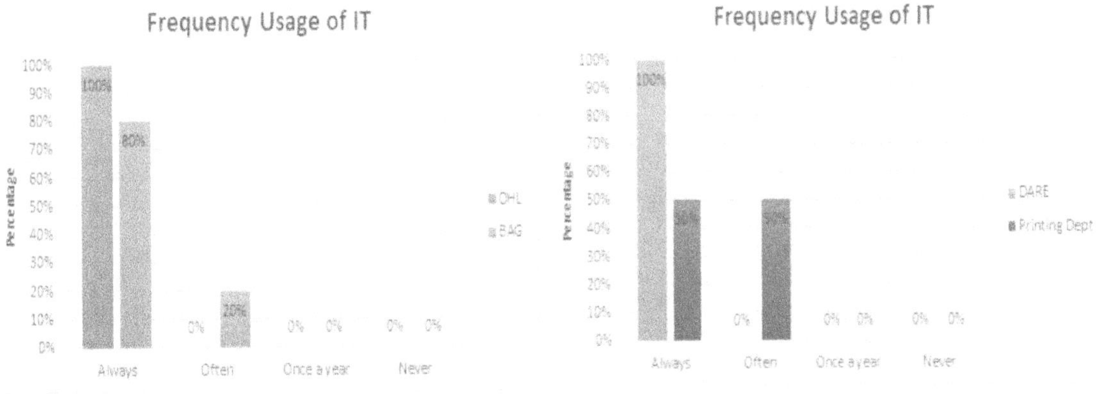

Figure 3. Frequency of reviewing MIS

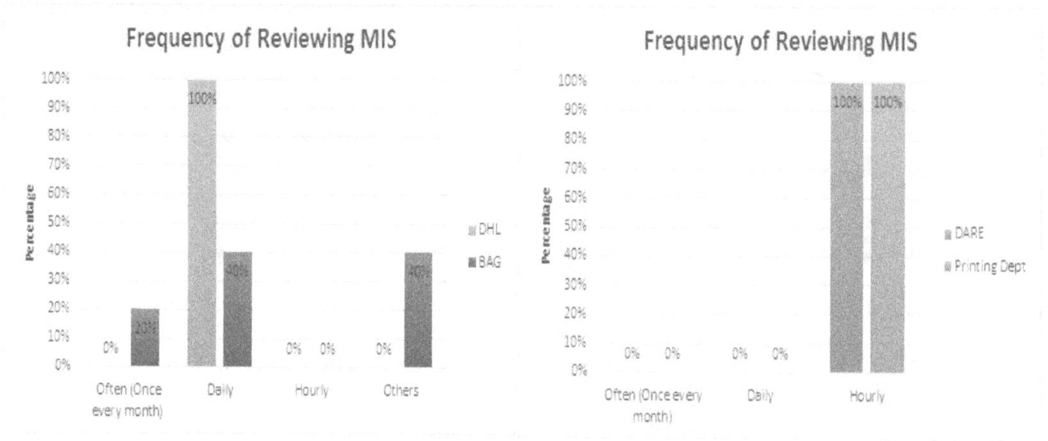

Figure 4. Duration of IT implementation

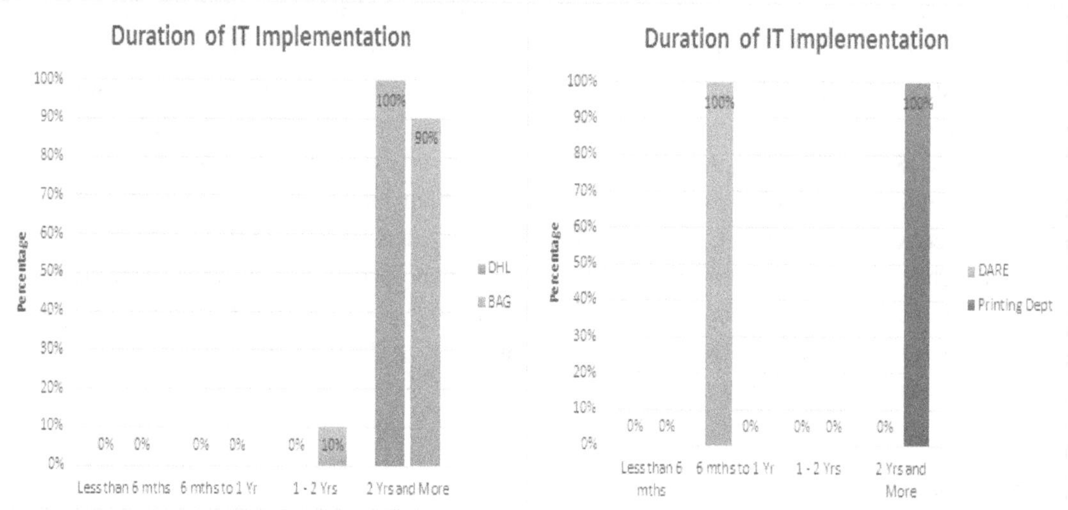

Organization such as DHL, BAG and Printing departments had been implementing IT more than 2 years in their operation which prove that IT help in their management and operation of the business.

The graph above shows that 100% respondents from the Printing Department and DHL have the authorization to access the documents in their IS. At the same time, only 80% of respondents from BAG networks stated that they have the authorization. Only 20% from BAG said otherwise. Whereas, 100% respondents from DARE did not have authorization to access documents in IS.

From the graph above, it can be demonstrated that Printing Department had encountered security breaches such as system failure or data corruption, infection by viruses or malicious software as well as attack by an unauthorized outsider or hacked systems, stated by 50% of the respondents. Meanwhile,

Figure 5. Authorization to access documents in IS

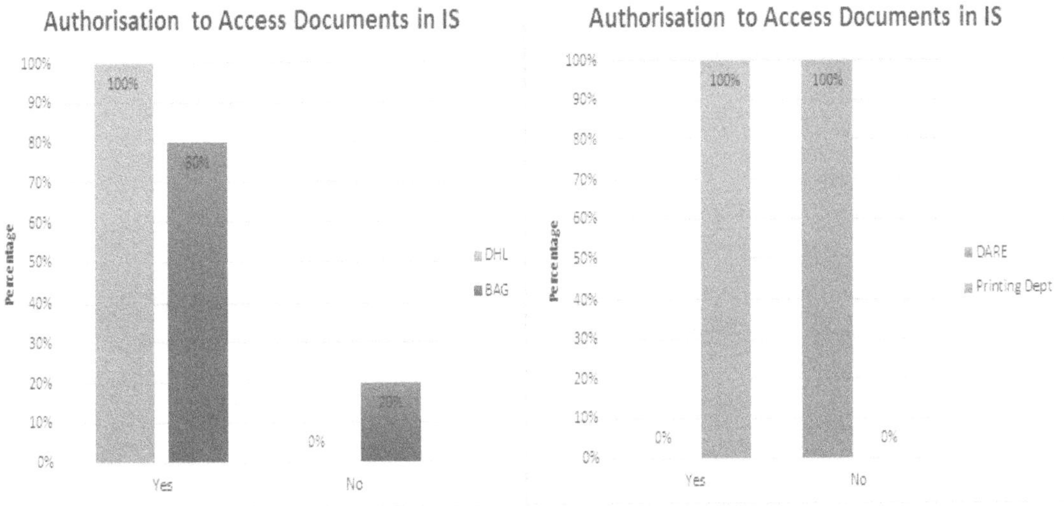

Figure 6. Information security breaches encountered by organization

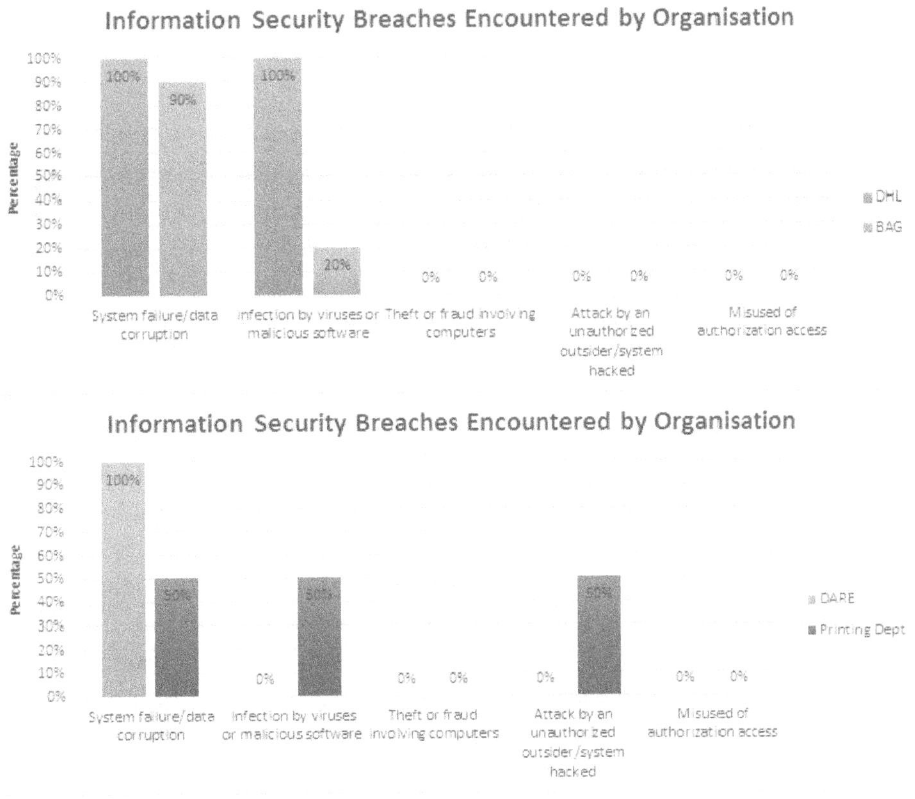

DARE stated that they had encounter system failure or data corruption. At the same time,100% of respondents from DHL exhibit that they have encountered system failure or data corruption and from infection by viruses or malicious software. As for BAG, 90% of the respondents revealed that they encountered systems failure or data corruption, and only 20% of the respondents choose infection by viruses or malicious software.

Figure 7. Organization outsource to external providers for information security system

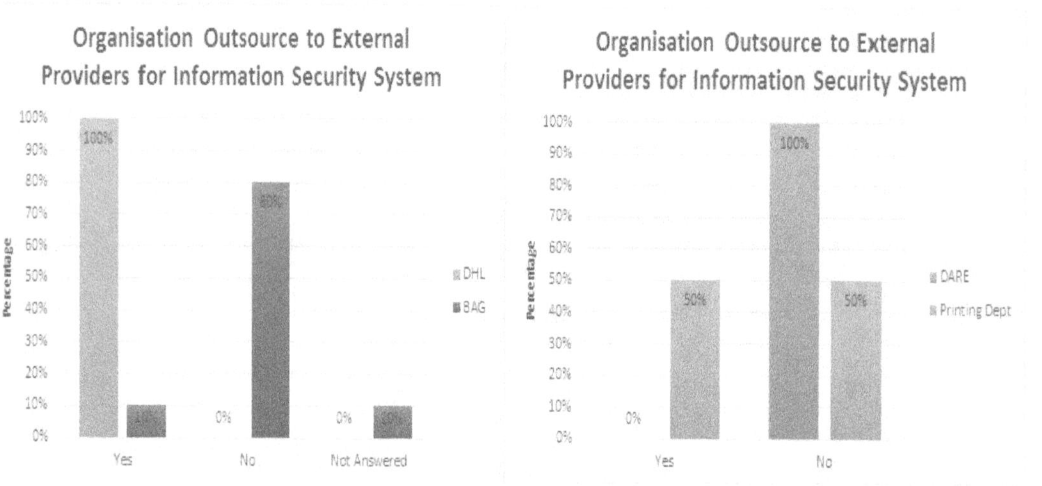

Figure 7 shows that DHL chooses to outsource when it comes to their information security system, as stated by 100% of the respondents. At the same time only half of the respondents from Printing Department said yes, while the remaining stated otherwise. Additionally, it is revealed that DARE did not choose to outsource. On the other hand, 80% of the responses from BAG indicate they did not, too.

From the figure above, it can be seen that BAG provided a couple of IS trainings such as IS basics, application information management or life cycle management and implementation training, management and implementation training in IS, risk management and contingency planning in which the former is selected by 40% of the respondents. Meanwhile, DHL only stated application information management or Life cycle management as the training that is provided to the staff. DARE, also, only disclose IS basics training as the training that is provided to their staff. On the other hand, 50% of the respondents from Printing Department revealed that the training that are provided includes IS basics and management and implementation training in IS respectively.

It is found that, DARE implemented accounts and passwords individually as the standard procedure followed for their information security systems, stated by 100% of the respondents from the organisation. Meanwhile, 90% of respondents from Printing Department stated that they implemented antivirus;at the same time 50% indicated that they installed firewall and implement AAA respectively. On the other hand, DHL implemented firewall, antivirus, AAA as well as accounts and passwords individually, as stated by all of the respondents. As for BAG, they implement the same standard procedure as DHL, in addition to formal written information security policy documented.

Figure 8. IS training provided to the staff by the organisation

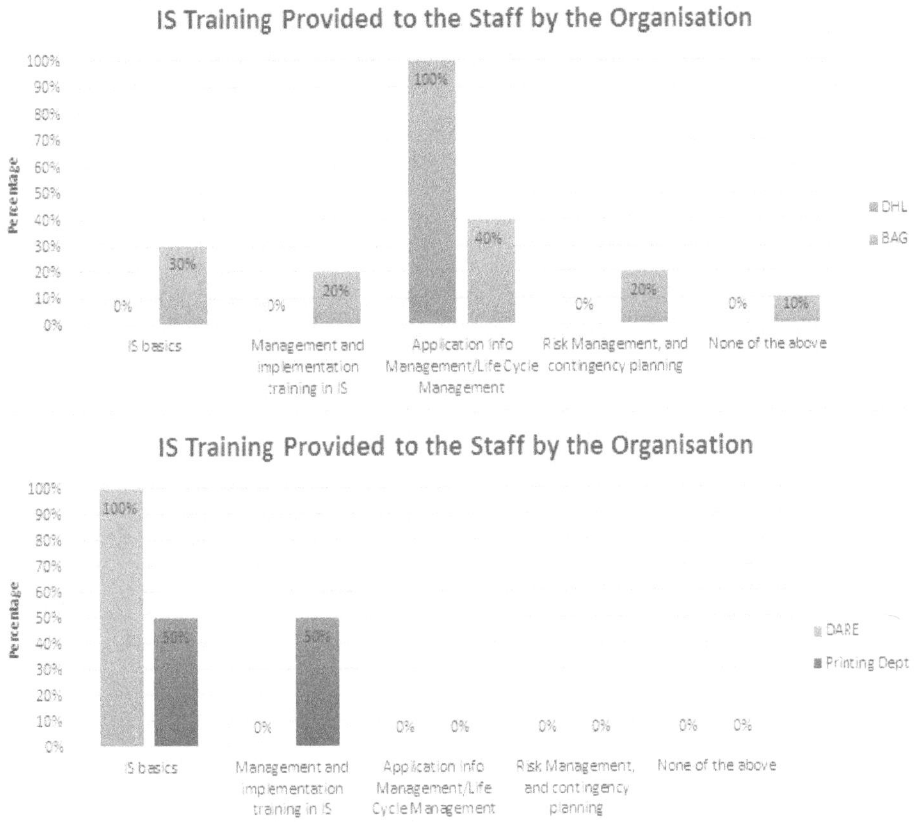

DARE revealed that, in order for them to mitigate information security breaches, they have blocked the access to inappropriate websites. On the other hand, the measures that are taken by Printing Departments includes blocking access to social networking sites and also monitoring of website or social through logs., revealed by 50% out of 10 respondent respectively. As for DHL, the measures that were taken by them are by, blocking access to inappropriate websites and to social networking sites and, restrict access to the internet at work as well as monitoring of website or socials through logs, which are agreed by all of the respondents. It is also found that BAG also implemented the same measure, in which 90% of the 10 respondents from BAG have stated the former; the last two measures stated by 70% out of 10 respondents and 30% out of 10 respondents respectively.

The figure above shows how both government and private organisations reacted to the issues on information security systems. DHL reacts by improving their information security policy, as agreed by all of the 10 respondents. BAG also reacts the same way, stated by 60% of the 10 respondents, in addition to70% of the respondents that revealed their organisations give training on information security system. DARE also does the same. On the other hand, Printing department shows that they react by improving their information security policies as well as investing more on information security systems, stated by 50% of the respondents respectively.

Figure 12 identify the different types of business process that involves the usage of IT in both the government and private organisations. All respondents from DHL and BAG specified that in their or-

Figure 9. Standard procedure followed for information security system

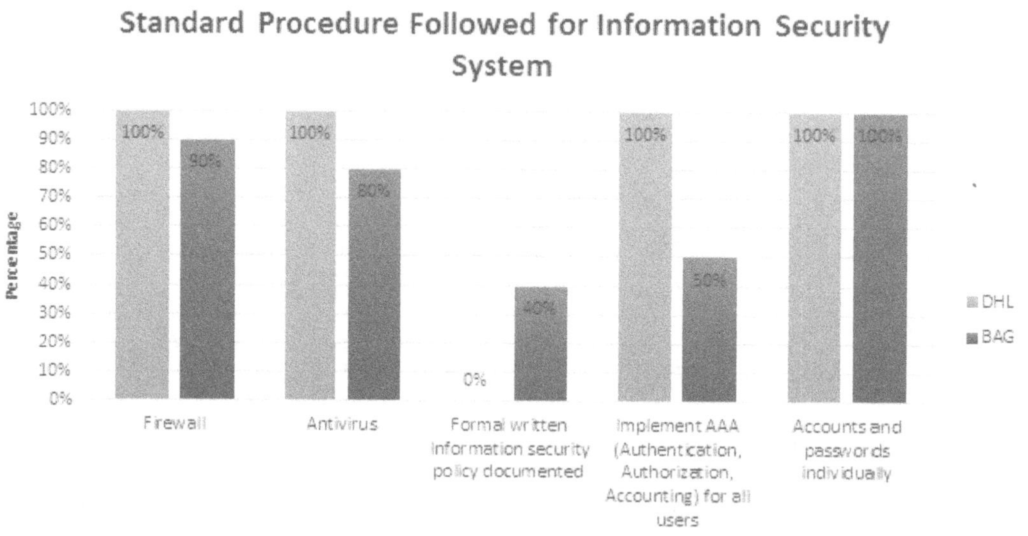

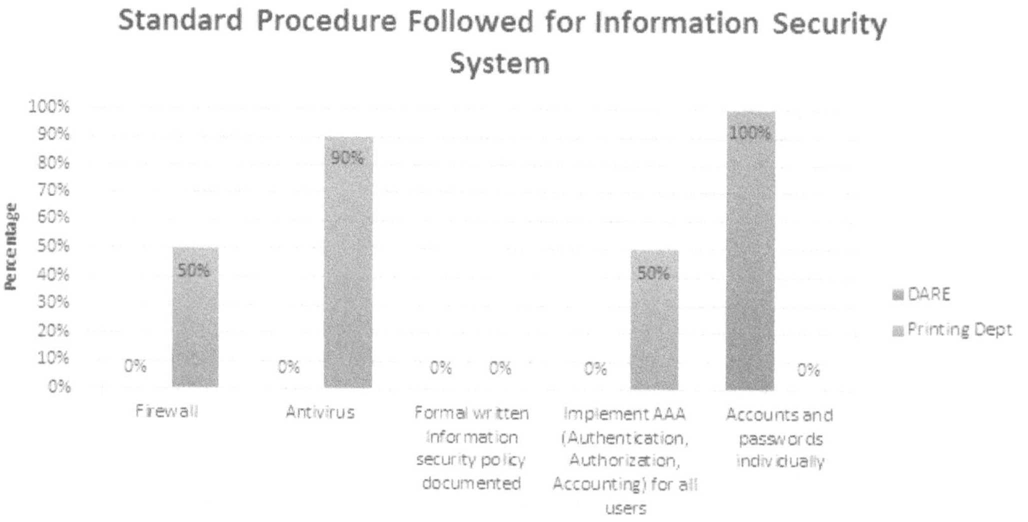

ganisations, corporate website, corporate email, payment processing, payroll processing, sales and/or marketing, customer transaction processing, finance and accounting, office tools (e.g. word processing) and data storage involves IT. As for government organisations, all the respondents from DARE stated that its corporates email are the business process that involve the use of IT. Meanwhile, for Printing Department, the business process includes corporate websites, payroll processing as well as finance and accounting.

From the graph above, it show that all of the respondent from DARE and Printing department of government organization and DHL of private organization agreed that they used 100% of authentication IDs for its employee. However, only 90% of respondents from BAG networks used authentication IDs

Figure 10. Measures taken to mitigate information security system breach

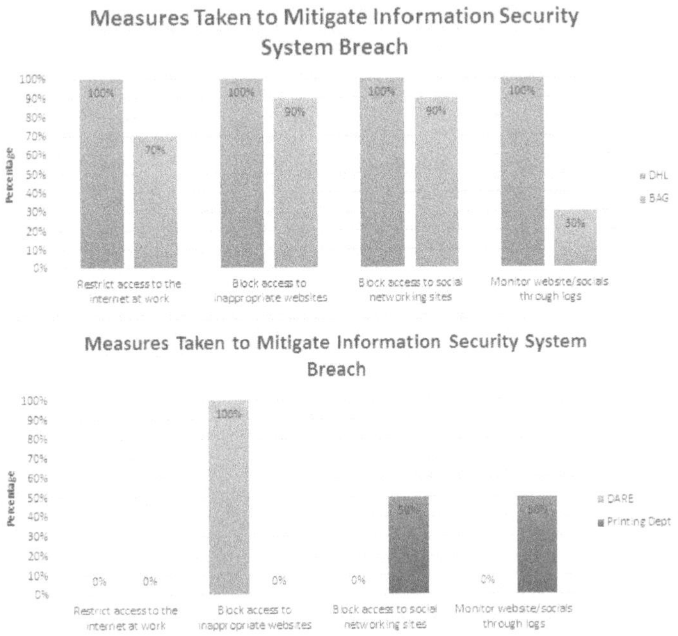

and 10% did not use authentication IDs. This could suggest that they are from different department which only require specific department to use authentication IDs and some did not have to use IDs.

This graph indicate that private organization; BAG had detected 10% unauthorised access from role-based access into system and 20% from surveillance cameras while DHl did not provide answer to the question asked. Meanwhile, 50% of respondents from printing departments detected unauthorized access through biometrics and the rest 50% did not answer the question, on the other hand DARe did not answer the question asked.

The graph states most respondents utilize the use of remote access network servers. All of the respondents from both DHL from the private sector as well as DARe from the public sector utilizes remote

Figure 11. Reaction to issues on information security system

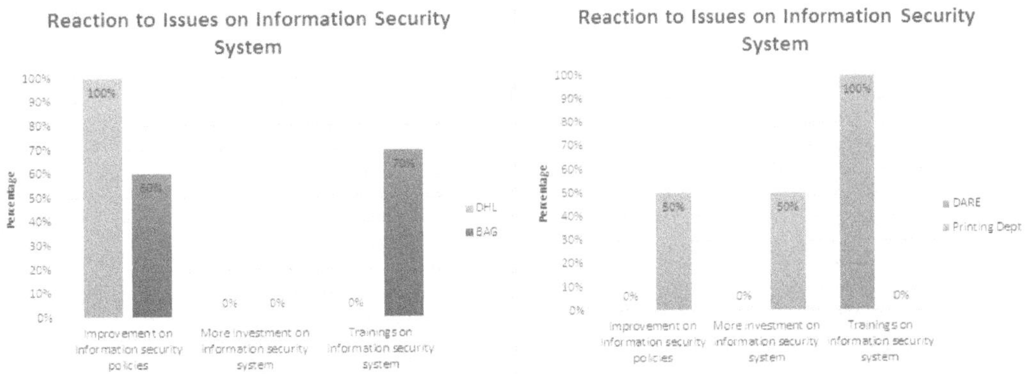

Figure 12. Business processes involving IT

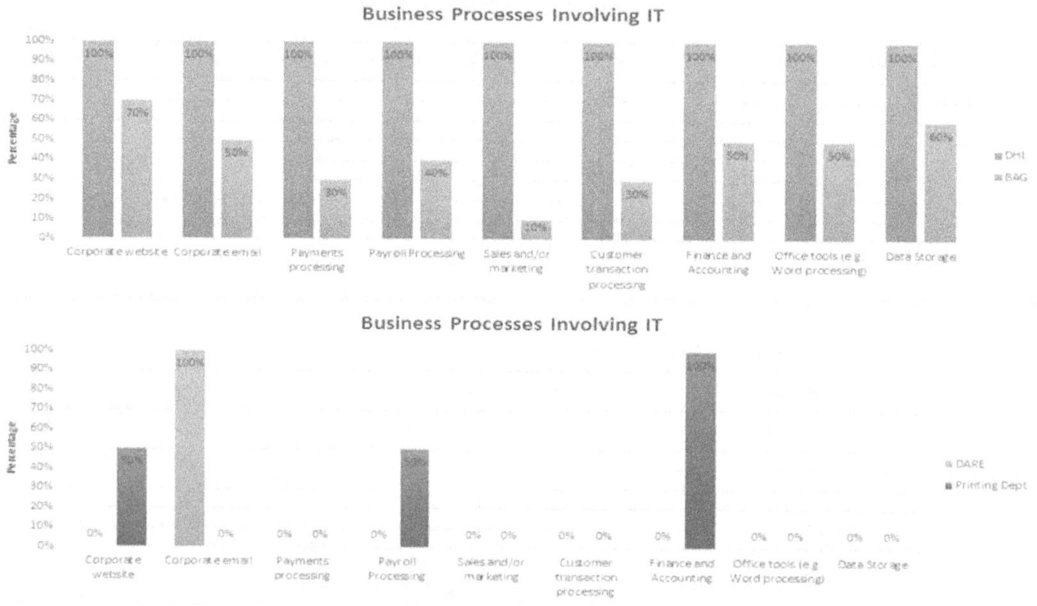

access network serves in their operations. Meanwhile only 80% of respondents from BAG make use of remote access network servers and only half of the respondents from the printing department do so.

Most of the respondents from the private organizations opt to use virtual private network as their choice of remote server with only 20% of the respondents from BAG chooses to work with Wi-Fi. On the other hand from the government organizations side, all the respondents from DARe and half of the respondents from the printing department opt to work with WiFi as their remote server. The other half of the printing department work with Dial-Up.

For the government sector, the printing department complied COBIT in accordance to their global security standards, however the respondents from DARe are uncertain of which global security standards

Figure 13. Usage of authentication IDs or access card for employees to track unauthorised access

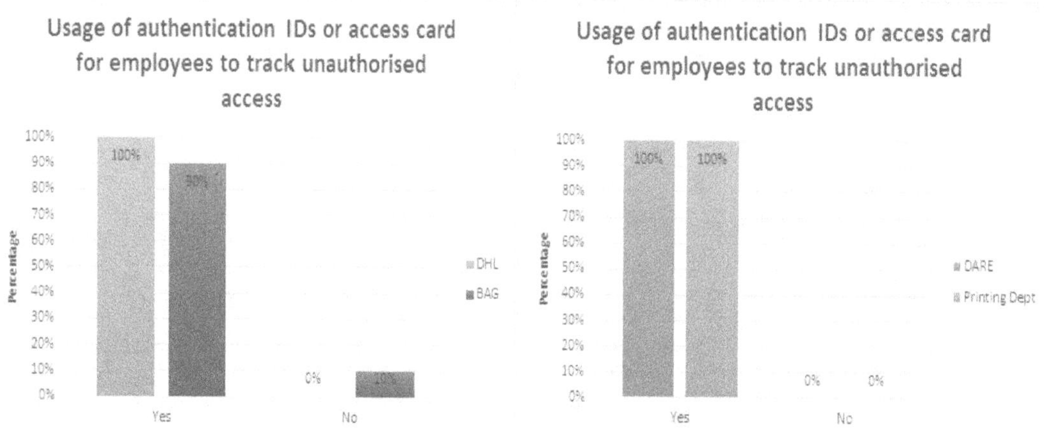

Figure 14. Detection of unauthorized access

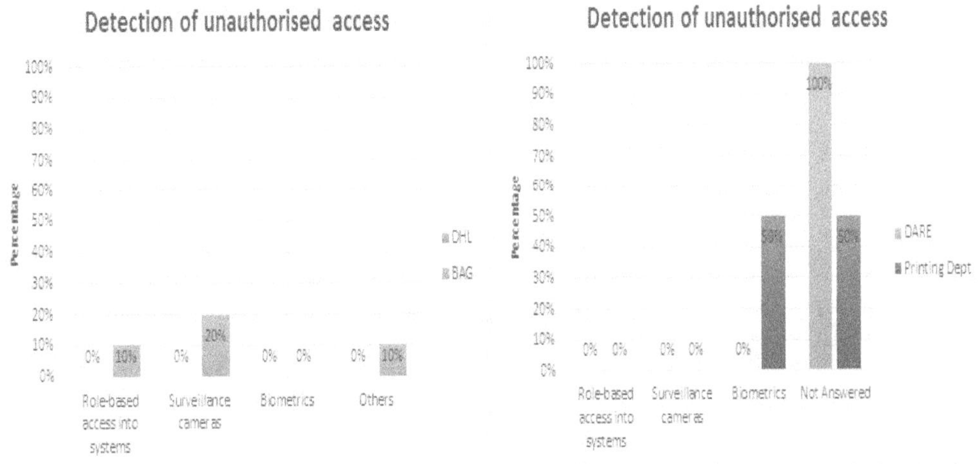

Figure 15. Use of remote access network servers

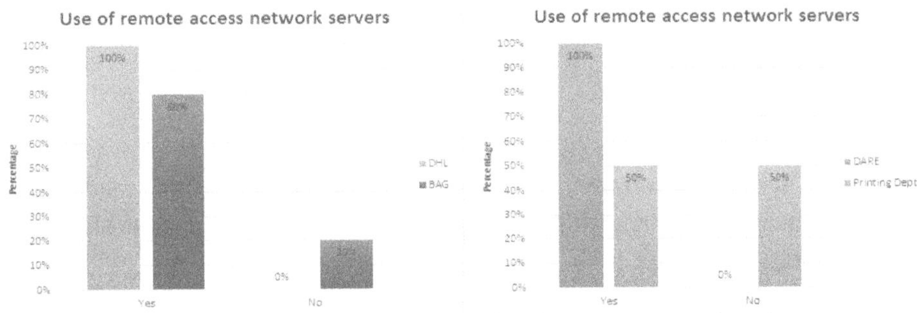

Figure 16. Types of remote access network server

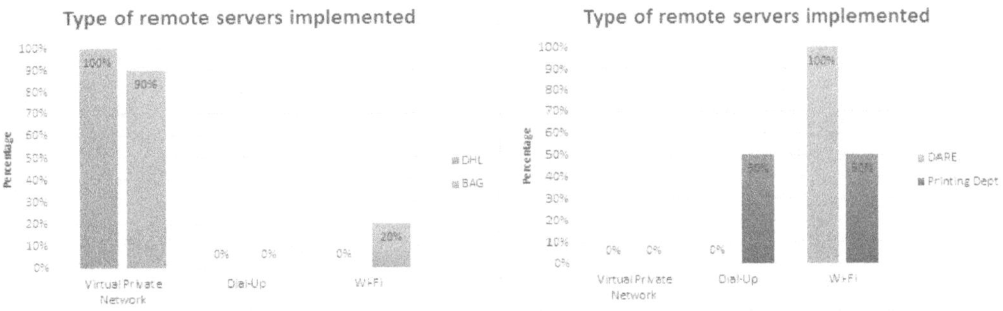

Figure 17. Choice of global security standards

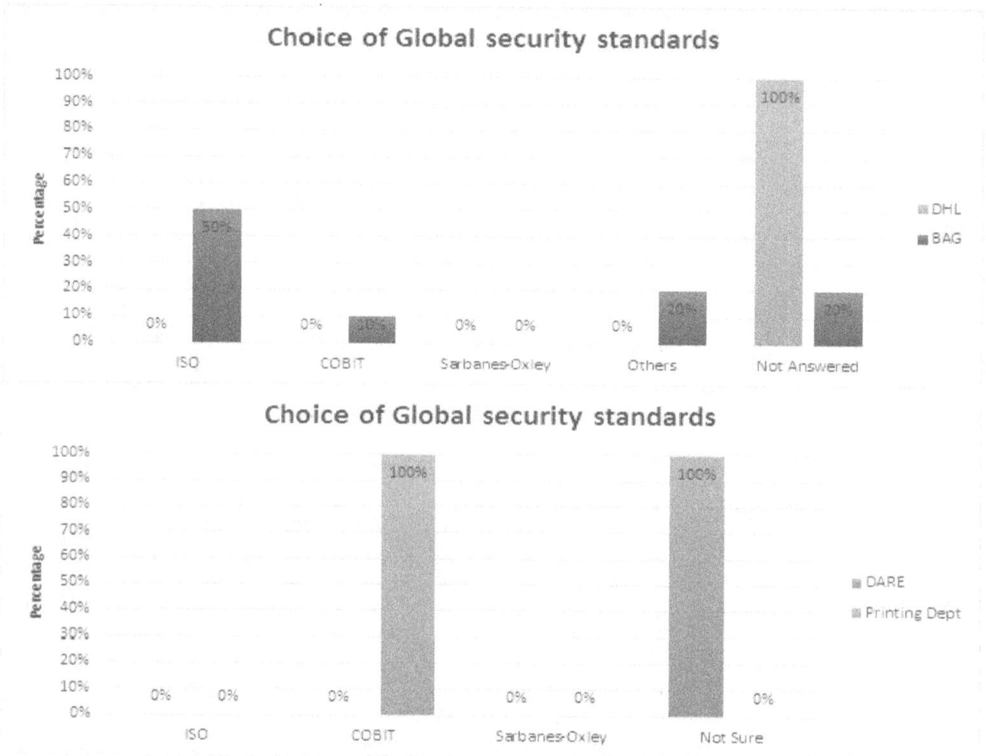

their company comply to. In the private sector, 50% of the respondents from BAG follow the standards of ISO, 10% of the respondents comply to COBIT, 20% others follow other standards that were not mentioned and the remaining respondents did not give their answer. With this said, all of the respondents from DHL choose not to answer the question.

For the private sectors, database technology that have been applied by DHL are PeopleSoft which is chosen by all of the respondents from DHL, Meanwhile, for BAG they applied Oracle, PeopleSoft and

Figure 18. Database technology applied

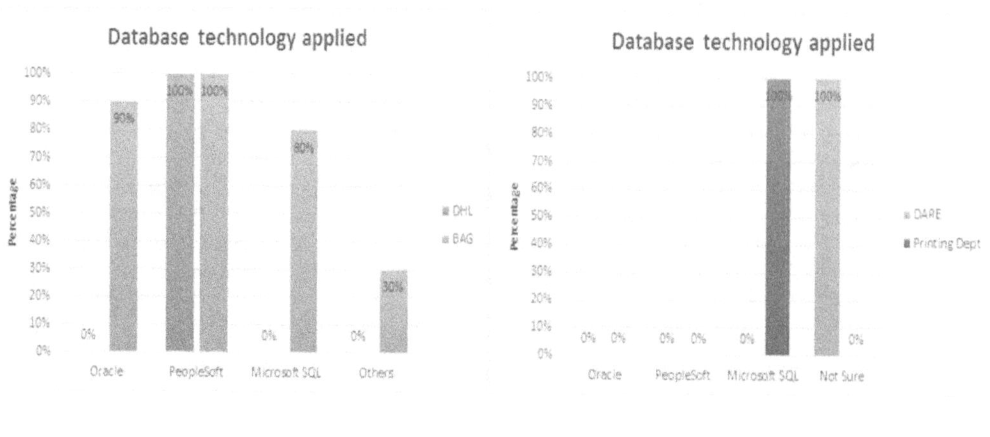

Figure 19. Reason for choice(s) of database technology

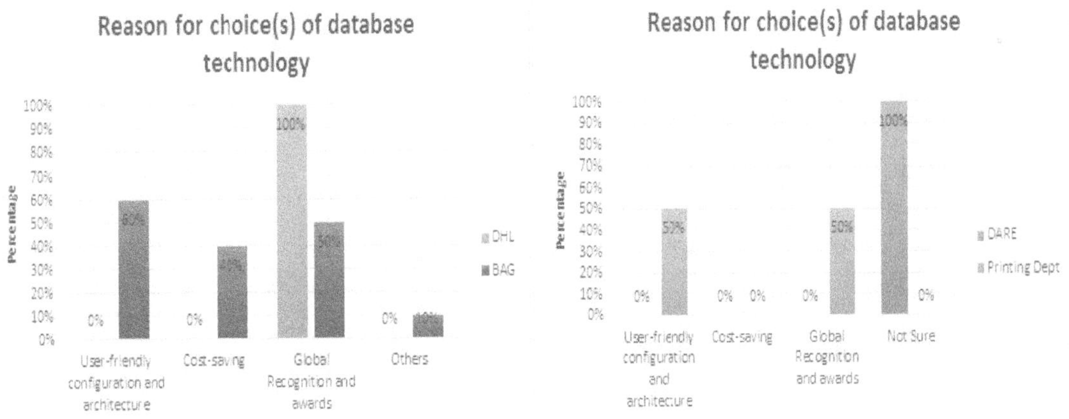

Microsoft SQL for their Database technology of 90%,100% and 80% respectively. On the other hand, for the government sectors, Printing departments applied 100% of Microsoft SQL database in their management whereas all of the respondents from DARE are not sure on which database that they are using.

The reason for choosing of database technology from DHL perspectives are because of global recognition and awards, which is agreed by all of the them, and from BAG perspectives, their reason for choosing the database are because of it user-friendly configuration and architecture of 60%, cost-saving of 40% and global recognition and awards of 50%. Whereas, from government sectors, their reason for choosing the database are because of it user-friendly configuration and architecture of 50% and because of Global recognition and awards of 50%. But DARE did not surre the reason for choices of database technology.

Figure 20. Security issues faced in recent years

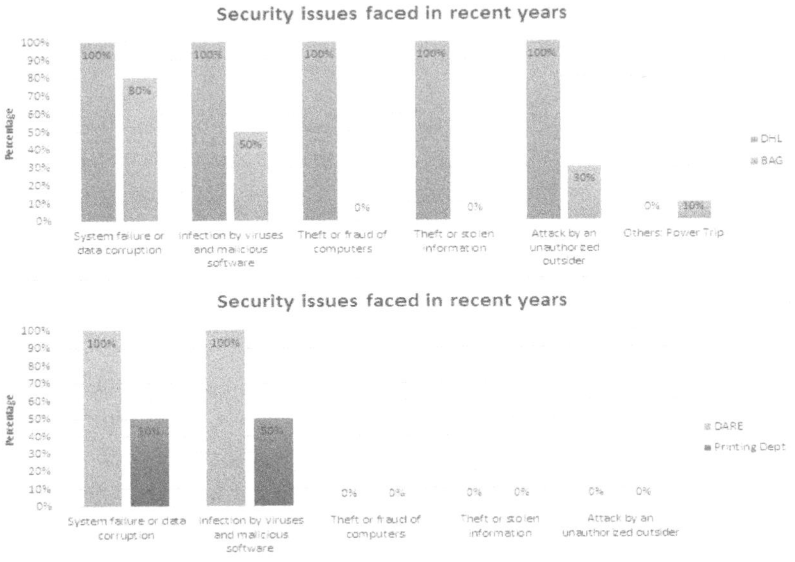

Figure 21. Staff-related incidents that occurred in recent years

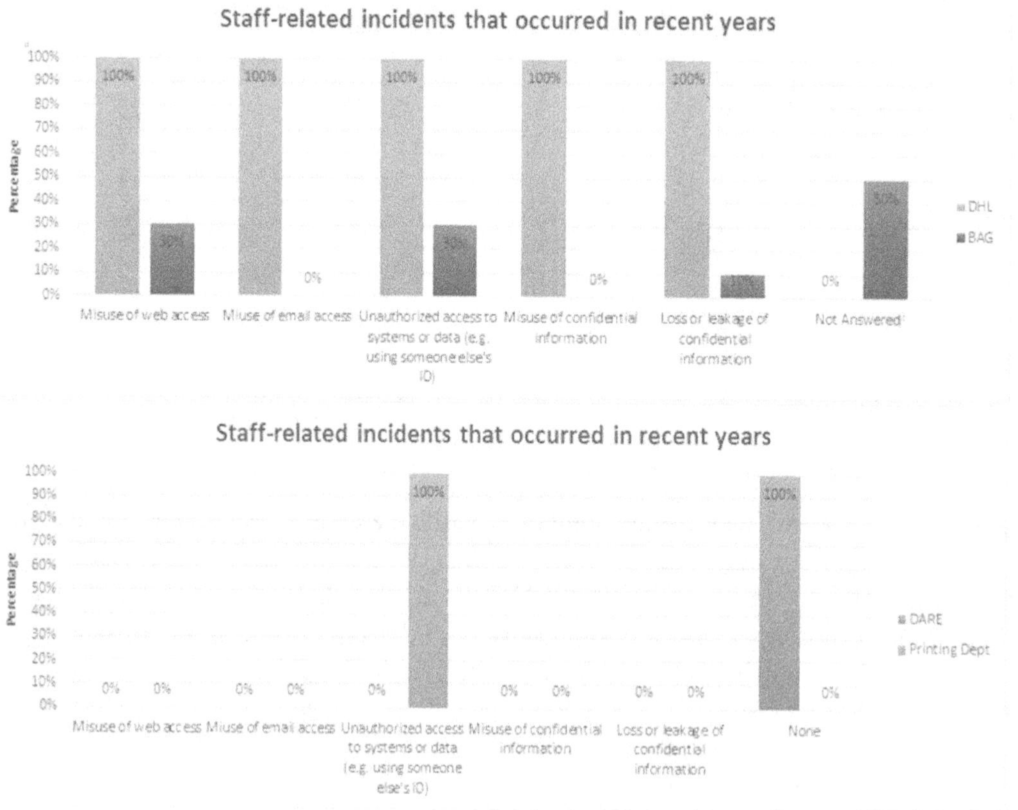

In the government organizations their problems in relation to the security of information system concentrates mostly on either system failures or data corruption and through infection by viruses and malicious software. All the respondents from DARe selected system failure or data corruption as well as infection by viruses and malicious software. Whereas half of the respondents from the printing department experience system failure or data corruption with the other half experiencing infection by viruses and malicious software.

All the responses from one of the private organization, DHL, states that they deal with all the problems mentioned which are system failure or data corruption, infection by viruses and malicious software, theft or fraud of both computers and information as well as attacks by an unauthorized outsider. For BAG, 80% of the respondent experiences system failure or data corruption, 50% deals with infection by viruses and malicious software, 30% have been attacked by an unauthorized outsider and 10% suffers from power trips.

For the Private Organization, the staff- related incidents that occurred in recent years for DHl are they had encountered 100% of misuse of web access, misuse of email access, unauthorised access to system or data, misuse of confidential informations, and loss or leakage of confidential information.Whereas, for BAG, they encountered 30% of misuse of web access, 30% of unauthorised access to systems or data and 10% from loss or leakage of confidential information. On the other hands, Printing departments only encountered 100% from unauthorised access to system or data, and none from Dare.

Figure 22. Frequency of anti-virus update

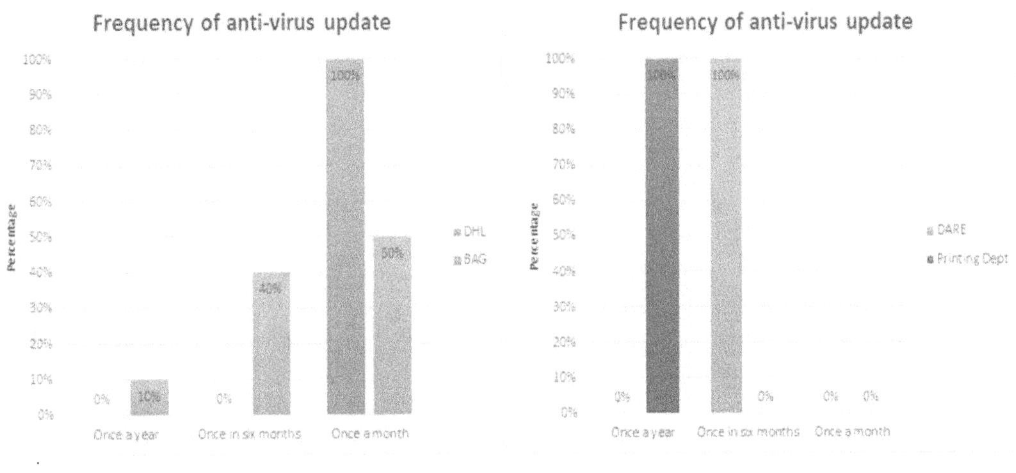

From the table above, it state that, all of the respondents from DARE update their anti-virus once in a month, whereas from BAG, the frequency of anti-virus update are 10% once in a year, 40% once in six months and 50% of the respondents update once in a month. However, all of the respondents from DARE update their anti- virus once in a years, and at the same time, all of the respondents from Printing departments also update their anti-virus once in a years.

Figure 23. Introduction of BPR in the company/business

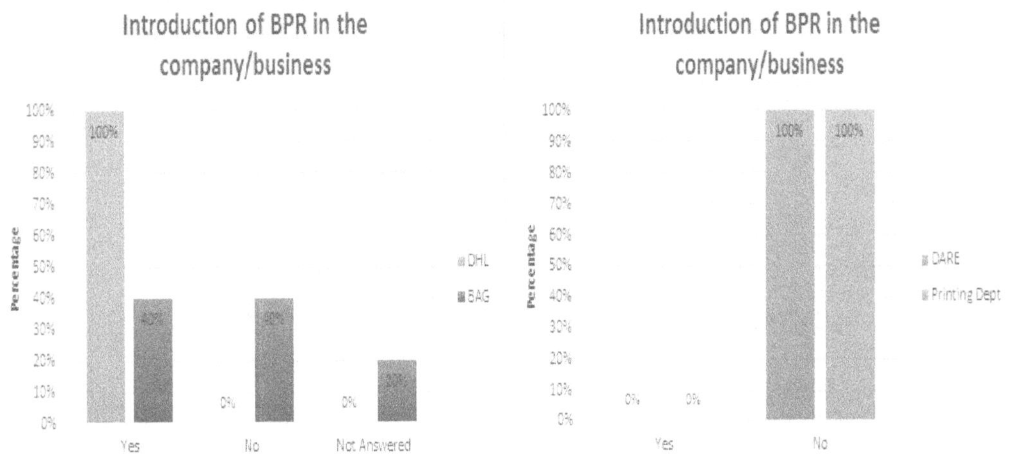

From the graph above, it illustrated that all of the respondents from DHL, DARE and Printing departments had introduced BPR in their company. Whereas from BAG responses, only 40% of the the respondents had introduced BPR in the company, 40% said otherwise and the remaining of 20% did not answer the question given.

Figure 24. How BPR exercise was undertaken

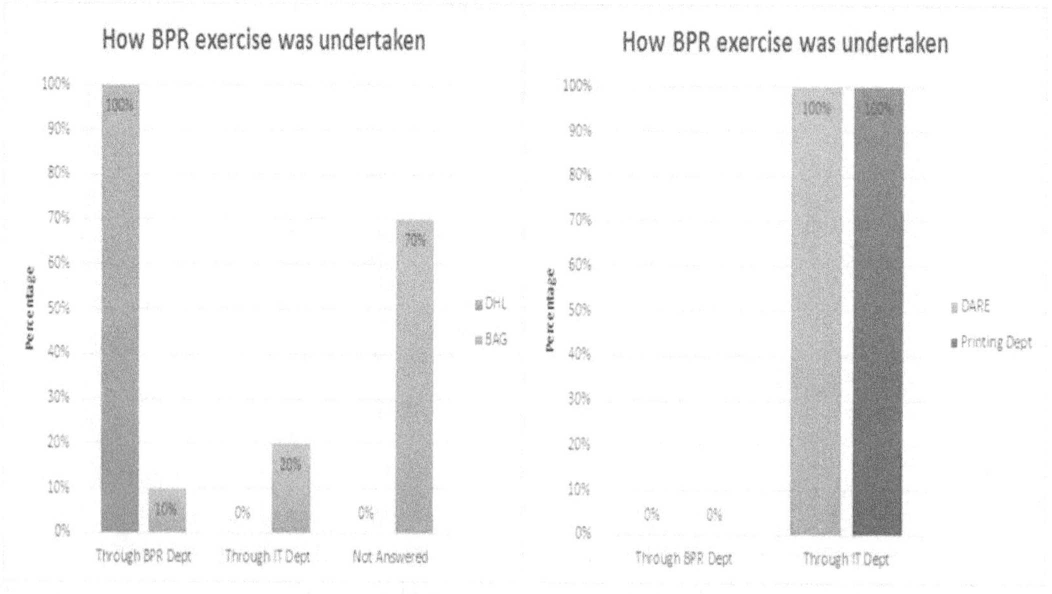

The graph above indicate how BPR exercise was undertaken in the organization, DHL stated that they implemented it through BPR departments, while from Bag, 10% through BPR departments, 20% through IT departments and the rest 70% did not answered the question. However, all of the respondents from DARE and Printing departments stated that their organization exercise BPR through IT departments.

All the respondents from DHL stated that generic process is the new process that is launched when BPR is implemented. 50% of the respondents from BAG, on the other hand, stated the same as DHL. The remaining 30% of BAG respondents specified core process and the rest 20% choose not to answer.

Figure 25. New processes launched when BPR was implemented

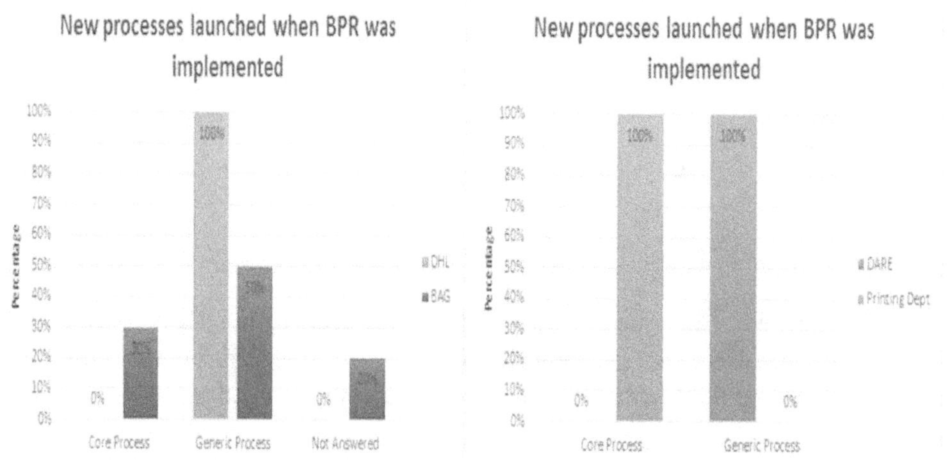

Figure 26. Processes affected in BPR exercise

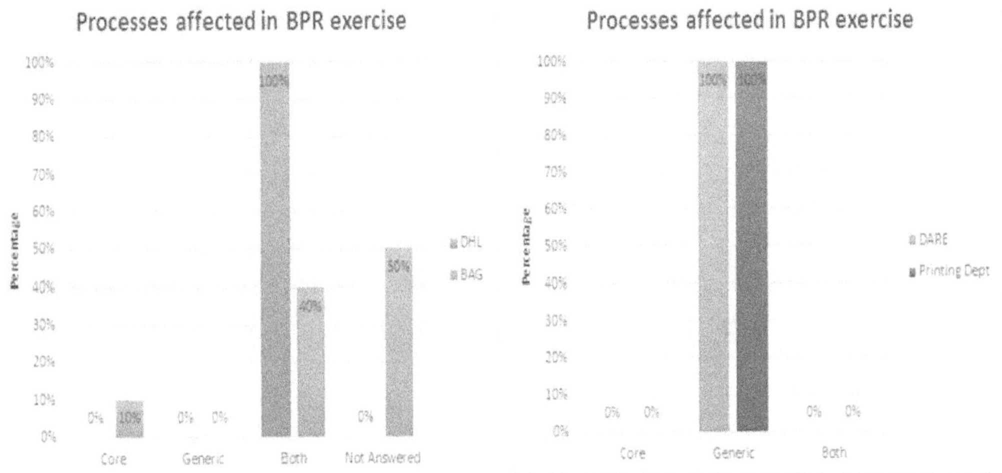

Additionally, all the respondents from DARE specified generic process, and Printing Department stated core process.

The graph above demonstrate that both generic and core processes are affected in BPR exercise, as stated by all the respondents from DHL. Meanwhile, only 40% of the respondents from BAG said so; the remaining did not respond to this question. On the other hand, all respondents from both the government organisations, DARE and Printing Department revealed that only generic process was effected in BPR exercise.

Figure 27. Changes in core and generic process by bringing in technology

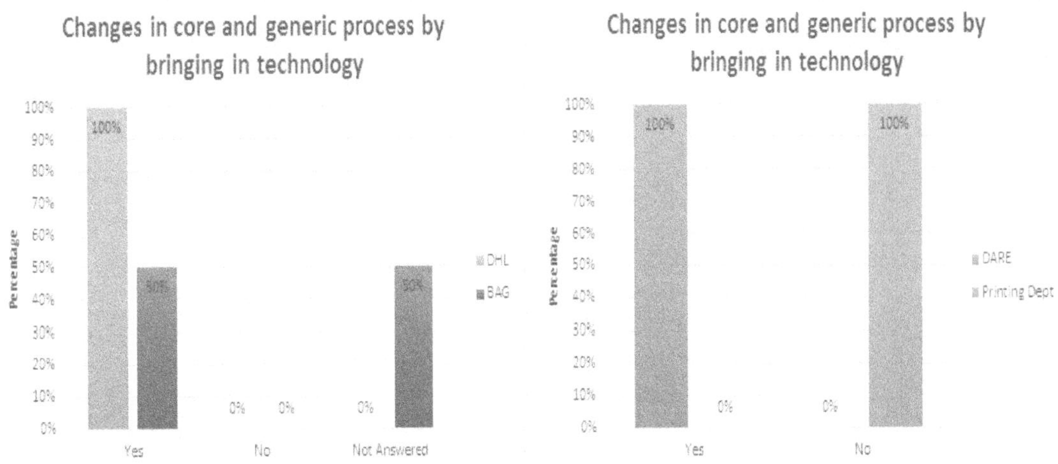

100% of the 10 respondents from BPR said that technology does changes their core and generic process; the response garnered from DARE also illustrate the same. As for BAG, half of the respondents

Figure 28. Role of IT in BPR

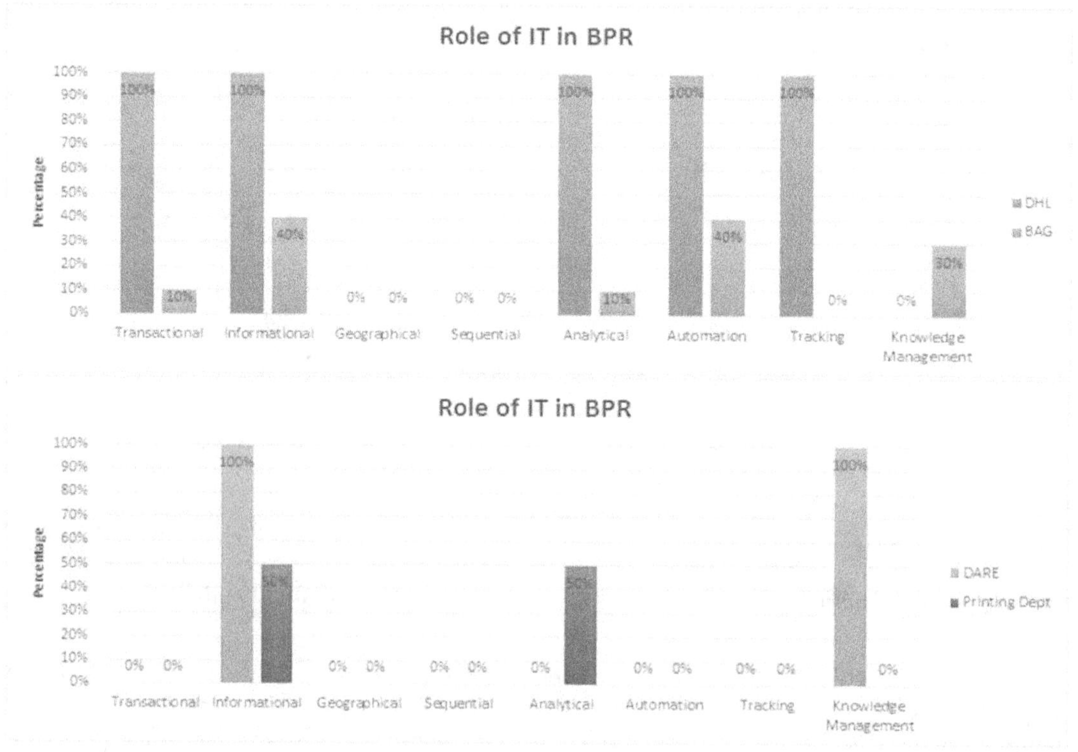

said so;the remaining 50% did not contribute their answers. On the other hand, all of the respondents from Printing Department stated that technology did not bring any changes in the mentioned processes.

From the graph above, all of the respondents from DHL affirmed IT plays the transactional, informational analytical, automation and tracking role in the newer process under BPR. 40% of the 10 respondents from BAG stated that IT plays the transactional and automation role respectively. Only 10% of the respondents stated that IT plays transactional and analytical role. The remaining 40% of the respondents from BAG indicate that IT plays the role of knowledge management. As for DARE, all of the

Figure 29. Usage of software solution for the BPR

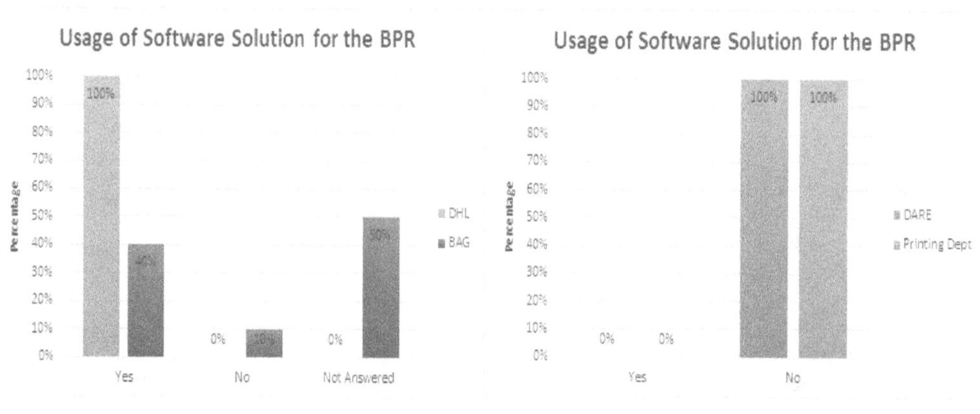

Figure 30. Hiring of external consultants

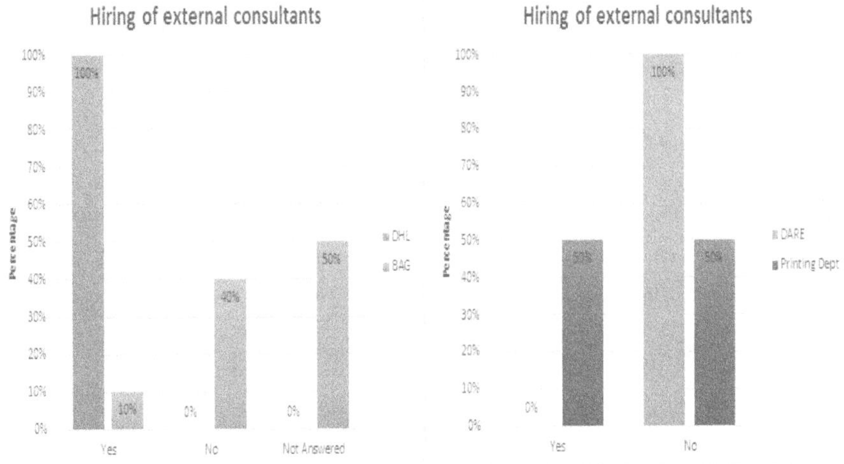

respondents agreed that, IT plays both the informational and knowledge management role. Meanwhile, 50% of the respondents from Printing Department revealed that IT plays informational and analytical role respectively.

It is found from the graph above that DHL implement the use of Software Solution for BPR. 40% of the 10 respondents from BAG also said so. Meanwhile, only 10% of the respondents from BAG indicate no. The rest of the respondents omitted this question. On the other hand, both DARE and Printing Department stated that they did not use Software Solution in BPR.

All of the respondents from DHL revealed that they hires external consultants for the implementation of BPR. On the other hand, only 10% of the respondents from BAG said so. 40% of them stated no, and the remaining 50% of the respondents did not provide their answer. All of the respondents from DARE

Figure 31. Type of cost affected due to the introduction of BPR

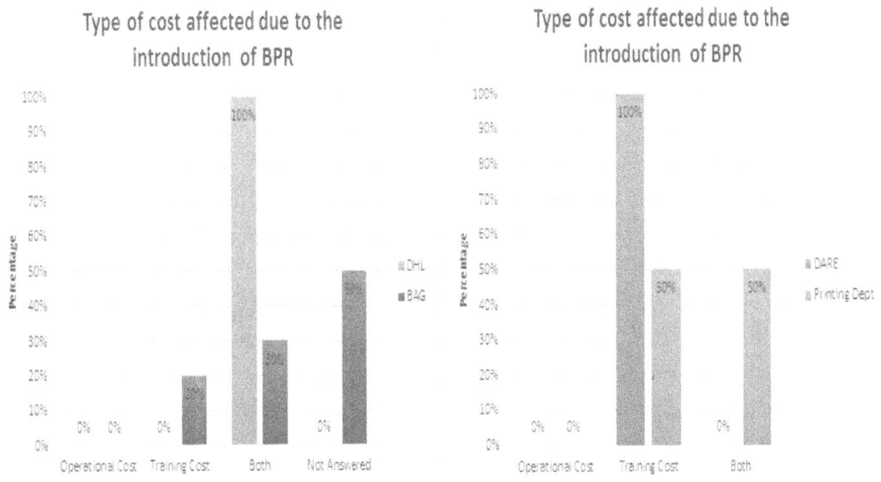

confirms that they hire external consultant for BPR, along with half of the respondents from Printing Department. The remaining half of the respondents from this private organisation said otherwise.

The figure above shows that BAG encountered both training and operational cost, stated by 30% out of 10 respondents, as the type of cost affected due to the introduction of BPR, similar to DHL, in which all their respondents have stated that their organisations encounter both type of cost. . Meanwhile, only 20% of the respondents indicate that they only experienced training cost. The remaining 50% of the respondents did not provide their response on this question. As for DARE, 100% of the 10 respondents indicate that training cost is the type of cost that is affected due to the implementation of BPR. On the other hand, only half of the respondents from Printing Department indicate that they encountered only training cost, and the other remaining 50% of the respondents stated that both training and operational cost are affected.

Figure 32. Reduction in cost after the implementation of BPR

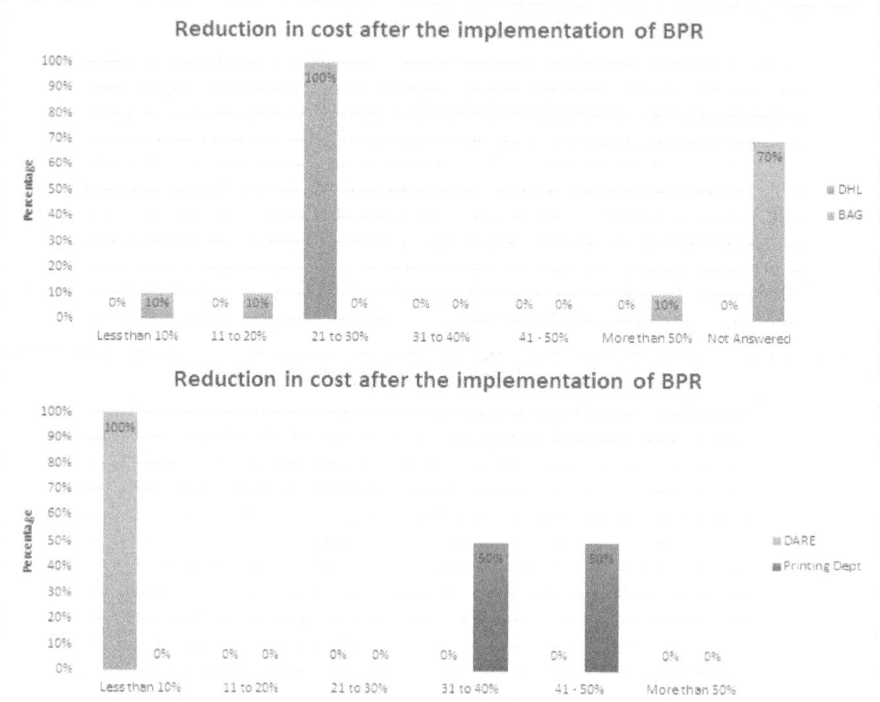

In the graph above, it can be found that, 100% of the 10 respondents from DHL stated that there in a 21 to 30% cost reduction after the implementation of BPR. As for DHL, 10% of the 10 respondents observes less than 10%, 11 to 21% as well as more than 10% reduction respectively. Meanwhile, the rest of the respondents did not specify their answer. DARE, on the other hand, have all their respondence observes a reduction of less than 10% in cost. For Printing Department, half of the respondents note a 31 to 41% and 41 to 50% cost reduction respectively.

The graph above indicate the increase of revenue in both the selected private and government organisation after the implementation of BPR. For BAG, 20% of the 10 respondents declared that they observes

Figure 33. Increase in revenue after the implementation of BPR

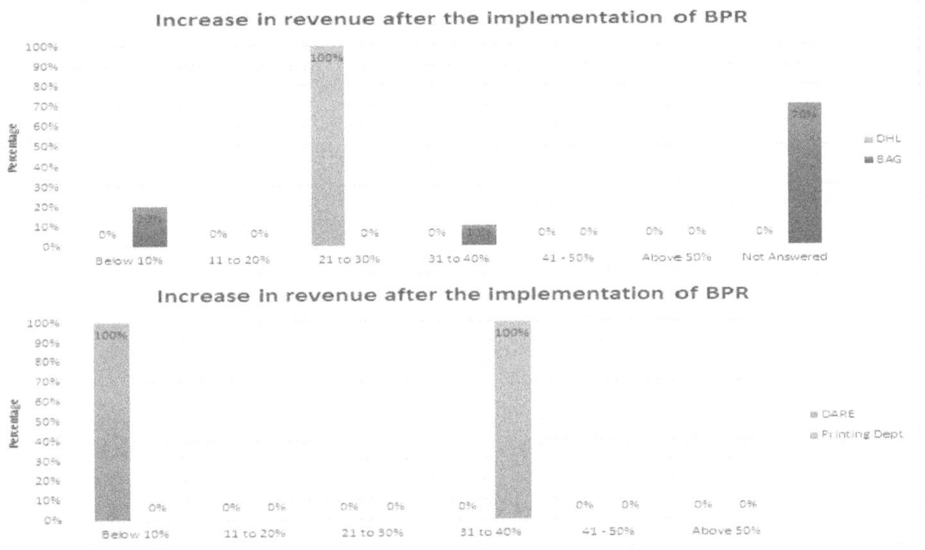

below 10% increase of revenue after its implementation. Only 10% of the respondents revealed that there are 31 to 41% increase in revenue. The rest of the respondents did not provide their feedback. All of the employees from DHL, on the other hand, stated that there are 21 to 30% increase in revenue. On

Figure 34. Number of customers increase after the implementation of BPR

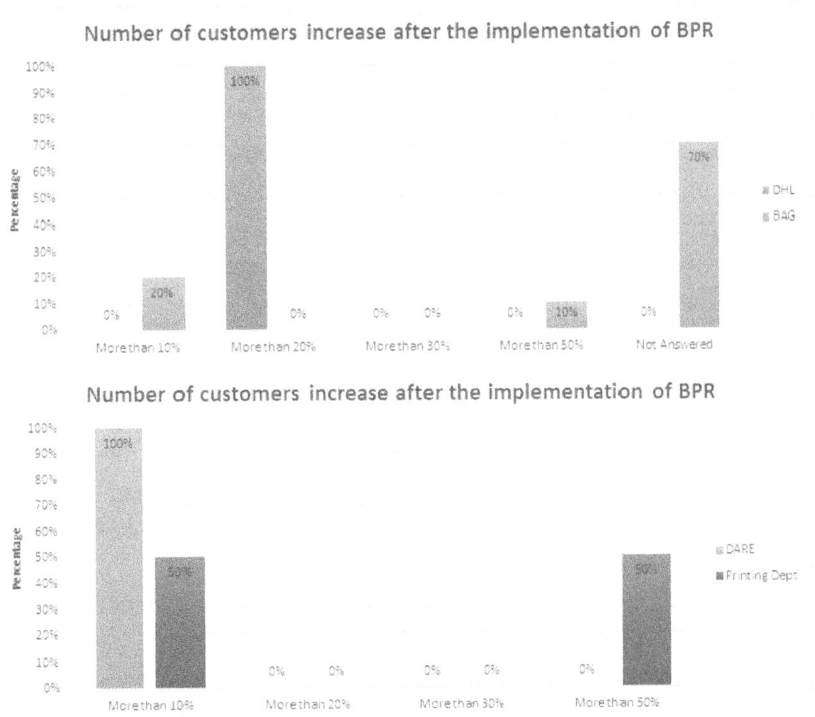

the other hand, all of the respondents in DARE noticed more than 10% increase in revenue, meanwhile 100% of the 10 respondents from Printing Department stated that there are 31 to 40% increase in revenue.

The figure above shows the amount of increase in customers after the implementation of BPR in their organisations. All of the respondents from DHL observes that there are more than 20% increase of customer. Meanwhile, for BAG, 20% of the 10 respondents revealed more than 10% increase. Only10% of the respondents sees more than 50% increase. The remaining 70% of the respondents from BAG did not provide the feedback to this question. As for DARE, all of the respondents stated that more than 10% increase in customers. On the other hand, 505 of the respondents from Printing Department stated that there are more than 10% and more than 50% increase of customers respectively

DISCUSSION

Section 1: Information System Awareness (Figure 1 - Figure 12)

(Figure 1 and 2) Both public sectors (DARE & Printing Department) are utilizing information systems in their organizations. Information systems is a system that collects, stores and processes data in order to provide the organization with enough information and knowledge. In addition, the information and knowledge obtained will be beneficial to the organization. Adeoti-Adekeye (1997) stated that the progression and the adaptation of information system in an organization provide an information that can contribute to a more effective planning, better decision making and better results. Moreover, IS becoming a more concerning factors in dynamic and forward-looking organization, where it require detailed and accurate procedure for the formation, management and utilization of organization's database.

By using their organization's information systems, it allows the employees to keep track of the data and handle the records in the system. This is to ensure that the employees work more effectively and efficiently in order to handle a large amount of storage data. Most of the private sectors use information system to help the employees in terms of better decisions as well as to record any activities in the organization. The reason for the organization utilizing information system is because it enables them to record any daily activities by accessing into the system. In contrast to the public sectors, both private sectors (DHL & Bag Network) utilize the information system in their organizations. According to the chart in Figure 1, DHL utilizes and implements organization's information system as it helps the employees to do their work in the department. Almost all the employees in private sectors are reviewing the information system on a daily basis. This is mainly because either upgrading their system to a newer version or adding an information in their system.

Both public sectors have an hourly review on the management information system in order to prevent their data from being outdated and to keep their system up-to-date from time to time. As the public sectors have been dealing with the development of the country, reviewing the management information system hourly is a daily routine for the organization. While on the other hand, mostly the private sectors reviews their management information system in a daily basis to ensure on the smoothness of their management information system.(see figure 3)

Public sectors have been implementing information systems in each organization for more than one year and two years, which are DARE and Printing Department respectively. (see figure 4) As compared to public sectors, private sectors have been implementing information system in their organization for more than two years. This is mainly because implementing information system in the organization has helped the employees to manage and improve their work efficiency. The implementation of information systems in the public sectors has given the authority to all employees to access the data and information in the system. Thus, this will give all the employees in the organization the ability to share and enhance their knowledge with each other. One of the disadvantages of using information system as an open culture knowledge is security breaches. Straub demonstrated that organization need to take thoughtful/serious interest in implementing IS security effectiveness as it can provide restriction from unauthorised access and prevent misuse of IS (as cited in Kankanhalli et al., 2003).

As compared to public sectors, in Figure 5 shows that almost all of the respondents from private sectors have the authorization to access the document in the information system. However, only 20% of the respondents do not have the access to the information system.Kankanhalli et al (2003) demonstrated that security level can be seen in two levels: basic level and in intermediate level. At basic level he stated that the software security installed in operating system can provide user's access control to organization's specialized database and files such as using user passwords and IDS to enter to a specific database. Whereas at intermediate level the software security installed provide the user s with access control at specific records and fields in organization database. For example, it give restriction to view or to access certain files in database and give restriction to change or to revise database. Most importantly it prevent from unauthorized access to database.

System failures and data corruption are the most common type of security breaches that DARE,BAG and DHL encounters. A system failure may occur due to the system stopping from functioning as there might be problems on the software or hardware problems which can bring a big impact to the system. As for the data corruption, this may happen when unauthorized sites gain access to the system, in which losing data in the system may occur. As a solution, there are many ways in order to prevent the management's information security breaches such that the public sectors may block unknown websites from accessing to their system. However, it is well-known by the population that public sectors have the most confidential system in the country. One of the best ways to prevent their data from being hacked or stolen by unauthorized users is by strengthening their information system policies. In relation to the security factor, there are two types of information system breaches that are mostly encountered in the organization which are system failure or data corruption and system gets infected by viruses and malicious software. As compared to public sector, 80% of the respondents from private sectors do not outsource their information to the external providers. This is mainly because the public sectors could be at risk if they were to expose their confidential data and information to outsiders. For instance, if this happens, they might lose their ideas to the competitors if their confidential data and information were being leaked. Since the private sectors do not outsource their information security system to external providers, the organization provides different types of information security system training to the employees.

Based on figure 7 in the result section, both public sectors outsource the information security system to the external providers as it can be beneficial to the organization. As stated by Schaffhauser (2005), outsourcing is defined as a collaboration in order to do a particular task with other parties. Outsourcing the information system to the experts can lead the employees to focus more on their work without any distractions on the organization's security system. The most common reason of outsourcing to external providers is because it can save costs in terms of recruiting staffs to be trained in order to ensure the security of an organization's information system. By outsourcing, the organization does not have to spend money to purchase tools and technologies to recruit security system. Moreover, outsourcing can help the organization to focus more on the goals and business objectives by letting the experts solve any issues regarding information systems that may rise in the organization.

According to Figure 8 in the results section, it shows that the public sectors provide training on the information system to the employees in the organization. As public sectors outsource their work to external providers, the employees in DARE are being trained for the basic information system. As shown in the chart, 50% of the employees in Printing Department are being trained in terms of management and implementation training in information system. This is because they have been dealing with the surface area of information system. Even though, the organizations are outsourcing their information system to external providers, the organization still needs to implement security procedures in a way to protect the data and information in the organization's system. Another way to prevent information leakage is by applying the information security system standard procedure. Almost all the employees in DARE protect their data by setting up their accounts and passwords individually as a step-in procedure for information system as most of the employees are given personal email for the ease of their contacts. (see figure 9) In addition, passwords can protect the employees' identities on their email accounts, websites and many more. However, the chances of their data being hacked are high and losses of data may happen, creating a secure passwords is one of the most common ways to avoid identity theft. Changing password for at least every two months is another way to prevent the data being hacked. According to the chart, 50% of the respondents in Printing Department have been implementing Firewall in the system as it is another best way to prevent any unauthorized users from accessing to the network in the organization. Securework (2015) states that Firewall is a software that can detect and block any untrusted websites from reaching the network or system in the organization. On the other hand, according to the data, most of the private sector invest in the use of Anti-virus. Anti-virus is a program that will prevent viruses and protect the computer or the system. And as shown in the chart in Figure 8, the employees are given training on the basics of information system. Not only the basics, they are also being trained on the management and implementation in information system. Apart from that, the employees are also being trained on the application into management or life-cycle management as well as risk management and contingency planning. By giving these types of training to the employees, this can help the organization to reduce cost in terms of implementing a security system which may be cost-efficient. This training given to the employees will help them to increase their productivity in the organization such as managing and operating the information system in a good manner.

Dhillon and Backhouse, (2000), illustrated that with the increased of computer's user and knowledge in using computer as well as the advancement of computer software appliance will eventually increase the possibility of IS security breach in the coming years. Therefore, the organization need to seriously implement it IS security in their organization. Moreover according to Barsanti (1999), she stated that IS security abuse/ breach can provide negative issues in the organization such as reducing organizational activity and growth which can lead to a competitive disadvantage as well as give negative image to the organization. (as cited in Kankanhalli et al., (2003). Actions taken by the public sectors to mitigate the information security system breach is by blocking access to inappropriate websites which does not have any relation to their work. Another action taken is by blocking access to social networking sites such as Facebook and Instagram. (see figure 10) As the use of social media has increased, the higher the misuse of social networking in the organization which can become a serious issue in the future. The misuse of social network can bring a bigger impact to the organization. By restricting the access of social media in the workplace can help the employees to work effectively and efficiently. InfoSec (2013) says that the time wasted on the social network can be used to complete any task given by the top-level managers. One of the most taken measures in order to prevent leakage of information is by providing trainings on information security system as the issues related to information system are breached. Another issue related to this and the action taken is by making and investing in improvement on the information security policies. In addition, when the securities are stronger placed in the information system, it is difficult for the information to be leaked by unwanted thefts. The processes that are involved in the public sectors are corporate email, finance and accounting, payroll processing and corporate website.

Figure 11 from the result section state on the reaction issues of Information system security. All of the 4 company from both the government and the private organization really emphasized on the improvement in information security policies, more investments on information security systems and providing training on information security systems. In relation with the issue on training on information security system. Mitchell, R at el. (1999) stated that the BS7799 Code of Practice propose that the employee of the organization should be given training in information system security procedure and policies where the employee should know their responsibilities towards the use of security software packages, and their responsibilities to report for any security incident that occurred in the organization.

Figure 12 from the result section above it talk on the the business process that are involved by using the information system for the government organization and the private organization. As can be seen all of the business process required an information system involvement. This is because in today worlds all organization and business management, activities and process need to work through both online and offline to ensure their business activities running effectively and efficiently.

Section 2: Attitudes to Information Systems Awareness (Figure 13 - figure 22)

This section will further explain on the organization's attitude towards information system awareness both for the government and the private organizations .From figure 13 and 14 above, it illustrate on the authentication IDs or access card to track unauthorized access. Both of the government organization, DARE and Printing department and from private organization of DHL and BAG network assigned Authentication IDs or access card in order to track unauthorised access. This prove that authentication IDs plays an important role as it provide safety and protection of data against unauthorised access.Obaidat and Sadoun, 1998; Bours and Barghouthi, 2009 stated that authentication IDs provide a person with the ability or permission to access data or information in an organization. And in addition according to Davaanaym et al. (2009), he illustrated that the best ways in providing electronic authentication today is by using username and passwords. It can be seen that other than authentication IDs, the organizations also use Role- based access into systems, surveillance cameras and through biometrics method to detect unauthorised access. Unauthorised access to information system can be harmful to the organization as it can lead to misconduct and the misuse of information in the organization. Figure 15 and 16 explains about remote access network server. It can be seen that all of the organizations had implemented remote access network server in their management, with DARE and DHL stating that they are implementing the server and only about 80% from BAG and 50% from Printing departments stated that they are using the server. Remote access network server provides the organization with the power to control to access

Figure 17 shows which global security standards each organization follows. It is said that the choice of security standard will affect the information system security. COBIT that was picked by all respondents from printing department as well as 10% of the respondents from BAG was the most chosen standard. COBIT concentrates more towards the managerial side, it assists organizations to boost in value that were obtained from IT, empowers the arrangement and clarify the execution of the business IT administration and control structure. Half of the respondents from BAG utilize ISO instead. ISO are seen as strategic tools that can help to lessen cost by limiting waste and mistakes as well as making things to be more efficient. However, all respondents from DARe and DHL as well as 20% of the respondents from BAG were not able to answer the question.

Figure 18 & 19 explains about Database technology used as well as the reasons for using the chosen databases. A database is basically where systemized collection of data are stored for future use. A database server is seen as an important way of taking care of data management in which they are able to store, control, alter, find and draw out any information that are present inside the databases. With so many different types of database, companies also have to take note that is crucial to select the database software which works well with their business needs without causing much difficulties. The different factors companies must consider before settling on a database are the database architecture, the management needed for the database, the flexibility of the database as well as the challenges that may arise while formatting the database. The architecture of the database is concentrates around the outline, improvement, usage and the upkeep of computer programs that maintains and arrange data for organizations, offices and establishments.

According to the survey, it has been discovered the different types of databases each organization have applied into their systems. All respondents from DHL have uses PeopleSoft with their reasons for utilizing it is because the software have received global recognition and it fits with their system. PeopleSoft started out by creating functions only for HR and finance departments. Throughout the years, it has created instruments and appliances for common business procedures, examples being equipment in assisting management and e-business, it is also providing for specialized enterprises.

Currently BAG utilizes different types of software with PeopleSoft chosen by all, Oracle follows with 90%, Microsoft SQL next with 30% as well as other types of software at 30%. The reasons for adapting each types of software also differs with 60% of the respondents utilizing their chosen software due to the user-friendly configuration as well as the database architecture, 50% works with their chosen software because it has global recognition, another 40% have chosen their software in order to save cost, whereas further 10% have other unmentioned reason for utilizing their chosen software. Oracle is the primary database intended for big business grid computing, it is the best adaptable and financially savvy approach to oversee data and applications. Microsoft SQL aim is to assist in a big assortment processing exchange, business intelligence (BI) as well as the examination applications in corporate IT conditions. The printing department stated that they chose to work with Microsoft SQL reasons being it has a user friendly configuration and architecture as well as due to the global recognition the database has received.

Figure 20 questions about the different security issues that companies have faced within the recent years. According to O'Neill & Sohal (1999) IT has the ability to support the methods in order to carry out progressive achievements in organizational frameworks. Regardless of the size of the organization, it is important for companies that utilizes information system to have security over their data and information. The reason being that the data itself brings value to the organization especially now that the market is at a digital age where data and information can be easily obtained and used to help solve problems. With the rise of data driven companies, data and information will play a big part in their daily operation and with that companies increasingly will find any possible way to obtain as much data as they can in order to gain an advantage in the marketplace. The main problem that organizations deals with is when it concerns system failures or data corruption. Another problem is regarding the infections through viruses and malicious software as well as theft or fraud of information. Kankanhalli et al., (2003) state that an investment of IS security in the organization are important as it can help to prevent from misconduct of IS used which can cause competitive disadvantage. Additionally (Zviran & Haga, 1999) expressed that with the lack of organization interest in IS security can lead to an undesirable of security misuse in operation. (as cited in Kankanhalli et al., (2003)

Companies have to strengthen the security for their systems in order to minimize these problems from happening. One way could be that companies need to have backup data installed. However, companies also have to manage the backup data to ensure that it is can be accessed and used. When there are problems occurred that affects the system, the systems and application used can also be restored however it may be proven quite challenging to recover original data. For extra protection, companies can also choose to encrypt the data so that only selected people can access it. Companies also need to have a strategy for the data just in case the company experiences hardware problems examples could include people who have unauthorized access destroying the data that was kept in the computers. A way to do that could be safeguarding copies of necessary data or information at a different and secure place.

Figure 21 from the result section above, mention on the types of staff related incidents that happened in recent years. Staff related incidents can be in the form of misuse of web access, misuse of email access, unauthorized access to system or data, misuse of confidential information and loss or leakage of confidential information. It can be assumed that the most common incident that happened is unauthorised access to systems or data while DHL had experience with all of the incidents mentioned earlier. Lack of Information systems security in the organization will lead to IS breaches and abuses.

It can be seen that organization from the government and the private update their antivirus software differently, with government organization update their antivirus in between once in six months to once in a years. (see figure 22) While private organization, DHL updated their antivirus software once in a month and BAG usually update their antivirus in a range of once in a month to once in a six month. The survey of Computer Security Institute (2010) gathered from 1999 to 2010, illustrate that computer viruses are likely to spread through emails, instant messaging and from online social networking. The surveys also stated that one of the leading Information security threat are from computer viruses. (as cited in (Sung, Ku and Su, 2014)

Section 3: BPR Awareness (Figure 23 - figure 34)

This sections aims to discuss the awareness of BPR in both the selected government and private organisations. Both the private organisations DHL and BAG stated that BPR was introduced into their organisation. Meanwhile, both of the government organisation, DARE and Printing Department deny its introduction, (see Figure 23.) The reason being can be, both organisations may not be ready for the implementation of BPR, as according to Abdolvand, Albadvi and Ferdowsi (2008) BPR is very complex, high risk, time-consuming, costly and tend to fail. Chiplunkar et al., 2003 and Dennis et al., illustrated as cited in Abdolvand et al. (2008) findings from surveys that indicate 60 to 80% of BPR attempts are faced with failures. Meanwhile, Hammer and Champy (as cited in Al-Mashari & Zairi, 1999) 70% of the organisations that exercise BPR were not successful in their attempts.

The practise of BPR can be implemented through IT department and BPR department of an organisation. In government organisations, (Dare and Printing Department) IT department are majorly responsible for the BPR exercise (see figure 24.) This is mainly because they have strong IT infrastructure, as IT is an enabler of BPR; they may also be surrounded by IT culture and have top management that is familiar with IT, which too, are the driver of BPR processes (Lobontiu and Big, 2006) Meanwhile for private organisation, particularly DHL. BPR implementation is undertaken by its BPR departments. Al-Mashari and Zaini (1999) believes that BPR success lies on its cross-functional BPR team. This suggests that

BPR departments from DHL are highly trained, according to Carr (as cited by Al-Mashari & Zaini, 1999), which are one of the BPR success factors. Meanwhile, for BAG network, mainly IT departments are responsible. This implies that majority of the organisations prefer the implementation of BPR to be managed by their IT Departments. However, contradictingly, when asked, DARE and Printing department did not affirmed to the introduction of BPR in their respective organisations, but manage to answer the set of questions that are related to BPR. This may means that the organisations may have been implementing BPR, however are not aware of this term.

Olalla (2000) demonstrated that BPR support changes, the introduction of new process and working styles. When BPR exercises takes place both of the selected organisations in this research, it results in the introduction of new processes in generic and core processes, as Core business processes are essential for the running of the business while generic processes are the ones that supports these core processes (Pooja, 2013). All of the respondents from DARE and DHL, and majority from BAG indicated that generic processes are the new processes introduced. Meanwhile, Printing Department and other 30% of respondents from BAG specified core process as the new process (refer figure 25). It can be seen that the process redesign have introduce these new process to further enhance effectiveness and efficiencies of the organisation in order to achieving their organisational goals.. Meanwhile, figure 26 demonstrated which of these two processes are affected in both organisations during BPR implementations, For government organisations, DARE and Printing Department, additionally private organisation DHL, and 40% of the respondents from BAG stated that generic process are affected. This may imply that both of the core and generic processes, prior to BPR implementation are not as effective and efficient, therefore, resulting in its redesign.

Figure 27 demonstrated whether technology has bring changes to both the core and generic processes. Both DARE, DHL along with 50% of the respondents from BAG affirmed to this. Again, this concludes that the previously these processes may be inefficient, and technology further assist to enhance its performance. However only Printing Department disagree to this. This may be because, Printing Department, as mentioned above, have strong IT culture in their organisations, so it can be that they have utilised the best technologies, and their performance are already maximised, so they did not observed further improvements to its already efficient and effective performance.

Figure 28 concerns about the role that IT plays in BPR practice, which includes transactional, informational, geographical, sequential, analytical, automation, tracking and last but not least, knowledge management. DHL informed that IT plays transactional, informational, analytical, automation and tracking. This holds true as DHL is a courier service, it needs to be efficient in tracking and monitoring the delivery of parcels, the processing of online transactions or billing, it needs to be informational in terms of the customers' location and items, improve business performance through the analysis of data of its stakeholders, and automation of its packaging process. Meanwhile, for BAG, they specified that IT plays transactional, informational, analytical, automation and knowledge management. These roles are imperative to allow them to offer better and enhanced services to their customers. DARE, on the other hand mentioned informational and knowledge management role. This is important for DARE as they deal with data and information from businesses and startups that they manage. Printing department selected informational and analytical role, which are crucial for decision making process.

The usage of software solution for BPR is illustrated in figure 29. It is found that both of the government organisations did not utilised Software Solution in the implementation of BPR, along with 10% of respondents from BAG. Meanwhile, DHL affirmed to utilising it. Software Solutions assists organisations with problems pertaining IS.

Organisations are able to focus on their core business should they hire external consultants (Boddy, Bonstra & Kennedy, 2009) for the implementation of BPR. In addition, they will have highly skilled consultants to assist them with the implementation of BPR (Boddy et al. 2009). These may be the reason why DHL, half of the respondents from Printing Department and 10% of BAG respondents said that they outsourced their BPR practise to external service provider (see figure 30). On the other hand, 40% of respondents from BAG said no, similar to 50% of Printing Department's respondents. The reason why organisations are often reluctant to the idea of outsourcing are because they may lose control and depend too much on the service provider, they might lose their existing skilled employees, and they might be paying more than what they should pay for the service, which Boddy et al. (2009) illustrated as the risks of outsourcing.

Champy illustrated (as cited in Neill & Sohal, 1999) that, BPR can led to improvements in cost, service, quality and speed. The type of cost affected in BPR implementations includes training costs and operational costs. Both the government organisations DARE and half of the respondents from Printing Department, as well as 20% of the respondents from BAG indicate that the type of cost they encounter is training cost. This indicate that they spend more on training their staff to achieve competitive advantage; training and education is also one of the success factors of BPR (Al-Mashari & Zairi, 1999). Meanwhile, half of the respondents from Printing Department, DHL and 30% of the respondents from BAG indicate both operational cost and training cost are encountered (refer figure 31). Figure 32 observes the extent to how much cost is reduced after the implementation of BPR. BAG and Printing Departments experience a 41 to 50% of cost reduction after BPR implementation. This shows how that these two organisations achieve the most efficiencies in terms of cost. Meanwhile, the other organisation, DHL, experience 21 to 30% reduction of cost, also with Printing department, as stated by half of their respondents.

Figure 33 shows the extent to which BPR has contributed to the increase of revenues in an organisations. Printing Departments sees the most highest increase, i.e. 31 to 40%, similar to BAG network as mentioned by 10% of their respondents. This means that Printing Departments and BAG yield the most efficiencies as a consequence of its BPR implementations. DARE, on the other hand, experienced increase of below 10%. Meanwhile, figure 34 shows how much the customer of these organisations has increased after BPR implementations. 505 of the respondents from Printing department, and 10% of BAG's respondents claimed that they experienced more than 50% of increase in customers, indicating the effectiveness and efficiency of its BPR exercise are higher compared to the other organisations. DARE, and 20% of the respondents from BAG garnered the lowest number of customer increase in this survey at more than 10%.

Table 1. Business process at workshop X

Administration	Finance	Sales and service	Warehouse and purchase
Managing price list Recording employee payroll Recording purchases	Accounts receivable collection Invoice payment Employee salary payment	Motorcycle service Sales of spare part Return damaged or inappropriate spare parts.	Procurement Receiving Storage
Recording sales and services activity	Other expenses payment		Inventory control
	Payment receipt		Return to supplier

Table 2. Customers need for B2B and B2C segments

No	B2B Segment	B2C Segment
1	Competitive prices	Fair price
2	Rapid sales service	Friendly service
3	Delivery facility	Proper product recommendation
4	Completeness of products	Completeness of products
5	Bonus for loyal customers	Warranty provision

Case Study: BPR in Motorcycle Workshop X for Business Sustainability

In this case study about a motorcycle workshop in Indonesia (Budiono & Loice, 2012), specifically the motorcycle spare part business where the business processes were categorised into four as shown in Table below.

There were weak points in business processes which were identified and they were:

1. Sales of spare parts process for the segment Business-to-Business (B2B) and segment Business-to-Consumers (B2C) was the same business process.
2. The approximate service time for customers who made purchases over 10 types of goods was 30 to 60 minutes. Sales transaction records were done manually.
3. Stock out rate experienced by the company is about 70%.

A focus group discussion was conducted to identify the needs of consumers with several corporate customers involving ten loyal customers and former customers who were no longer doing business with workshop X. The result of the discussion is shown in the table 8 below.

The gap analysis focused on customer needs of B2B segment was conducted to establish whether those needs were met in the current business processes. Gaps that happen are grouped into three groups: no gap, performance gap, and the process gap. No gap is a situation in which consumer needs are already

Table3. Gap analysis

No	Customer need	Current Process	Gap
1	Competitive prices	The company has been providing a competitive price compared to local competitors.	No Gap
2	Rapid sales service	The average time of service to consumers who make purchases over 10 types of goods ranging from 30-60minutes	Performance Gap
3	Delivery facility	Current business processes do not have the delivery function	Process Gap
4	Completeness of products	The company provides a wide range of standards spare parts of motor vehicle and is currently the most comprehensive provider of spare parts in the region.	Performance Gap
5	Bonus for loyal customers	The Company does not have a loyalty and incentive program for loyal customers.	Process Gap

satisfied, the performance gap is a situation in which the consumer needs unmet by the current process, and process gap is a condition where there was not a process that facilitated those needs at the current business processes. The table 9 below shows the result of the gap analysis.

The business process redesign of the sales process was undertaken to improve the service performance in the B2B segment. The goal is to reduce the service time of 30-60 minutes to less than 15 minutes and provide delivery to meet customer needs. The new sales process intensively using computers to hasten activities in the sales business process. The main differences with initial process are:

- The new system can facilitate bookings via SMS / Phone / Fax
- Faster preparation of customer orders with the help of computers and parallel processing of multiple stages
- Availability of delivery facility

Table 4. IT capabilities and their organisational impacts

Capability	Organizational Impact/Benefit
Transactional	The unstructured stock control and procurement could be transformed into routinized transactions process.
Automational	IT can be used in inventory management to make a list of items running out and number of stock to be ordered as the input for the purchase process. IT can be used to make a sales note and automatically calculate the amount should be paid by customers.
Analytical	Could help the process of supplier selection
Informational	The search process of a spare part price can be faster than the manual search. IT could provide information of stock availability, product substitution, and storage location
Sequential	IT can enable changes in the sequence of tasks in sales process
Knowledge Management	IT allows the capture and dissemination of product knowledge from experienced labor to minimize error and improved overall service quality
Tracking	IT allows the detailed tracking of task status, inputs, and outputs in sales and service process.

Table above illustrates the various organisational impact for various capabilities

The main problems facing the company were the performance of the sales process and poor inventory control. After the reengineering process, the average service time decreased by 75% while the availability rate of the products also increased significantly by 20%. Improved performance in the sales

Table 5. Comparison of performance before and after BPR

	Prior BPR	After BPR
Sales Service time	30-60 minutes	Less than 15 minutes
Availability rate	70%	90%
Additional Cost (annually)	-	About 30 million
Cost Saving (annually)	-	About 70 million

process, combined with increased availability of the product can improve the overall quality of service so that workshop X can seize market share that has been lost and maintain its business continuity.[2]

CONCLUSION

In conclusion, IS is essential for businesses in this era of technological advancement to be used as a competitive advantage. There are roles that BPR and ERP play in organisations. The success and failure of BPR are highly dependent on the internal and external forces of the organisation. There are also several ways where the risks of BPR application can be minimised as well. IS benefits the organisations in many ways but it all lies on the organisation ability to implement it cautiously. Moreover, the nature of jobs nowadays mostly require IS as part of their systems in a way that it helps in processing business transactions while producing an accurate and reliable outcomes. However, security measures are needed to be taken to protect one's own information system as one may not expect when the stored data could be invaded, which may in turn cause leakage or loss of data.

On the case study on the motorcycle workshop in Indonesia, it shows that BPR sped up the sales process and decreased chances of stock out can heighten the competitiveness level of the business and thus making the business likely to be ahead of its competitors in the market. Productivity is closely linked together with efficiency which means doing things right; and effectiveness, doing the right things. Panda (2013) believes that the administration of IT in BPR has an influence over the productivity of a business. The effect is an increase in the productivity of the workforce, as little work is needed to complete a particular task. As an illustration, a single task - packaging a finished product, for instance - must be done by five workers. However, with the implementation of IT, the task can be completed with just one technologically advanced, operative machine employed in BPR, which in this case is an automated robot arm. The cost of production, as suggested by Lee, Chu and Tseng (2009) will therefore be reduced. This is agreed by Wymer and Regan; Sarkar and Singh; Ziaul, Faizul and Ken (as cited in Lee, Chu & Tseng, 2009) as they stated that IT allows organisations to function efficiently with less manpower. As a whole, the application of IT in businesses will first lessen the time consumed in the production department, which will then cause the production costs to also be reduced. The finance department will observe a cut in costs, which will be of benefit to the business as the money saved can be reserved for future needs, or even for the pay of its employees. As a result, the employees of a business will be more motivated to work even harder, which results in an increase in efficiency and effectiveness of the workforce productivity. It is a never-ending cycle but IT must be constantly injected in the input of BPR for the business to be able to progress in this dynamic business environment.

RECOMMENDATION

Since IT and IS are improving rapidly and plays a significant role in organisations, some improvements are required to fully utilised the uses. Here are some suggestions on improving it.

1. Train the employees on how to use new IT systems introduced to the organisation through workshops and courses to enhance and upgrade their skills on IT (Mlay et.al, 2013). Mlay et.al (2013) further supported this by organising workshops for the staff. Through this workshop, the staff would be

informed on the significance of IT and IS in BPR in assisting the organisation to achieve its mission and goals. This would reduce the level of resistance of the staff in using IT and IS. They will be more willing to accept changes made by the senior management.

2. Senior managers should be committed and present throughout the whole process of the implementation of BPR and external consultants can be hired to assist the transformation process (Kadre, 2011.).
3. BPR requires good strategic planning. This can be done by investing the most advance IT and IS systems in BPR to enable and support new business processes, which may be the basis for changing an organisation's competitive position (Subashish, William & James, 2010). Strategic goals can be easily achieved with more advanced technologies being used in the organisation. It is also expected that both external (the market) and internal (the efficiency) strategic arrangements are able to cope up with the present IT and IS competencies and the infrastructure of the organisation.

LIMITATION

Throughout the progress on doing the research, several limitations were encountered. Firstly, due to the small sample size, the data collected were unreliable. Secondly, due to the requirement of the companies to answer the survey questions by pen and paper method, the staff experienced diluteness in certain questions of the survey, the accuracy of the data collected might not be fully reflected. The third reason is due to the low response rate from the organizations, especially the last section of the questionnaire: BPR Awareness. The survey questionnaires may contain reliable questions, but there can still be serious problems. For example, respondents, i.e, the staff may elect to leave one or more questions unanswered either without knowledge or because they feel inhibited in responding to items dealing with sensitive questions regarding their company. Missing data can have big impact on statistical analyses based on the survey responses, including biased parameter estimates, as the majority of the statistical procedures require complete data for data analysis and data charting. In this case, one approach to deal with the issue is the imputation method, where missing data are simulated or replicated with other respondents' answers.

ACKNOWLEDGMENT

Heru Susanto as main contributor, and Fadzliwati Mohiddin as contributor. All authors review then approved final version of this manuscript.

REFERENCES

Abdolvand, N., Albadvi, A., & Ferdowsi, Z. (2008). Assessing readiness for business process reengineering. *Business Process Management Journal*, *14*(4), 497–511. doi:10.1108/14637150810888046

Al-Mashari, M., & Zairi, M. (1999). BPR implementation process: An analysis of key success and failure factors. *Business Process Management Journal*, *5*(1), 87–112. doi:10.1108/14637159910249108

Attaran, M. (2004). Exploring the relationship between information technology and business process reengineering. *Information & Management, 41*(5), 585–596. doi:10.1016/S0378-7206(03)00098-3

Boddy, D., Boonstra, A., & Kennedy, G. (2009). *Managing Information Systems: Strategy and Organisation* (3rd ed.). FT Prentice Hall.

Borgianni, Y., Cascini, G., & Rotini, F. (2015). Business Process Reengineering driven by customer value: A support for undertaking decisions under uncertainty conditions. *Computers in Industry, 68*, 132–147. doi:10.1016/j.compind.2015.01.001

Budiono, A., & Loice, R. (2012). Business Process Reengineering in Motorcycle Workshop X for Business Sustainability. *Procedia Economics and Finance, 4*, 33–43. doi:10.1016/S2212-5671(12)00318-8

Business Process Reengineering (BPR) – Definition, Steps, and Examples. (n.d.). *Kissflow*. Retrieved Oct 7, 2017 from https://kissflow.com/bpm/business-process-reengineering/

Chen, C. C., Shaw, R. S., & Yang, S. C. (2006). Mitigating information security risks by increasing user security awareness: A case study of an information security awareness system. *Information Technology, Learning and Performance Journal, 24*(1), 1.

Chou, S., & Chang, Y. (2008). The implementation factors that influence the ERP (enterprise resource planning) benefits. *Decision Support Systems, 46*(1), 149–157. doi:10.1016/j.dss.2008.06.003

COBIT 4.1: Framework for IT Governance and Control. (n.d.). *ISACA*. Retrieved Oct 19, 2017 from https://www.isaca.org/Knowledge-Center/COBIT/Pages/Overview.aspx

Government Information Systems: A Guide to Effective Use of Information Technology in the Public Sector of Developing Countries. (1995). Retrieved from http://unpan1.un.org/intradoc/groups/public/documents/un/unpan000155.pdf

Gunasekaran, A., & Nath, B. (1997). The role of information technology in business process reengineering. *International Journal of Production Economics, 50*(2-3), 91–104. doi:10.1016/S0925-5273(97)00035-2

Gurbaxani, V., & Whang, S. (1991). The impact of information systems on organizations and markets. *Communications of the ACM, 34*(1), 59–73. doi:10.1145/99977.99990

Hal.inria.fr. (2017). *A Review on Authentication Methods*. Available at: https://hal.inria.fr/hal-00912435/document

Huang, S. Y., Lee, C., Chiu, A., & Yen, D. C. (2014). *How business process reengineering affects information technology investment and employee performance under different performance measurement*. doi:10.100710796-014-9487-4

InfoSec Institute. (2013). *Restricting social media at work*. Retrieved on October 18, 2017 from http://resources.infosecinstitute.com/restricting-social-media-at-work/#gref

International Organization for Standardization. (n.d.). Retrieved Oct 19, 2017 from https://www.iso.org/about-us.html

Kadre, S. (2011). *Going corporate: A geek's guide*. Retrieved from https://books.google.com.bn/books?id=BR3jx1dUUaMC&pg=PA161&lpg=PA161&dq=business+process+reengineering+analysis+and+recommendations&source=bl&ots=oud3A13Jqy&sig=Q7GISS-X4J-Hgs8KSDuBrhRghno&hl=en&sa=X&ei=TPPpVObBB8_g8AWW94DIAw&ved=0CDQQ6AEwBDgK#v=onepage&q=business%20process%20reengineering%20analysis%20and%20recommendations&f=false

Kankanhalli, A., Teo, H., Tan, B., & Wei, K. (2003). An integrative study of information systems security effectiveness. *International Journal of Information Management*, *23*(2), 139–154. doi:10.1016/S0268-4012(02)00105-6

Kwahk, K., & Lee, J. (2008). The role of readiness for change in ERP implementation: Theoretical bases and empirical validation. *Information & Management*, *45*(7), 474–481. doi:10.1016/j.im.2008.07.002

Lee, Y., Chu, P., & Tseng, H. (2009). Exploring the relationships between information technology adoption and business process reengineering. *Journal of Management & Organization*, *15*(2), 170–185. doi:10.5172/jmo.837.15.2.170

Leu, F.Y., Liu, C.Y., Liu, J.C., Jiang, F.C., & Susanto, H. (2015). S-PMIPv6: An intra-LMA model for IPv6 mobility. *J. Netw. Comput. Appl.*, *58*, 180–191.

Liu, J. C., Leu, F. Y., Lin, G. L., & Susanto, H. (2018). An MFCC-based text-independent speaker identification system for access control. *Concurr. Comput. Pract. Exp.*, *30*(2), e4255. doi:10.1002/cpe.4255

Lobontiu, G., & Big, R. (2006). Implementing Business Process Reengineering. Scientific Bulletin Series C: Fascicle Mechanics, Tribology. *Machine Manufacturing Technology*, *20*, 231.

Microsoft S. Q. L. Server. (n.d.). *TechTarget*. Retrieved Oct 19, 2017 from https://searchsqlserver.techtarget.com/definition/SQL-Server

Mitchell, R. C., Marcella, R., & Baxter, G. (1999). Corporate information security management. *New Library World*, *100*(5), 213–227. doi:10.1108/03074809910285888

Mitra, S., & Chaya, A. (1996). Analyzing Cost-Effectiveness of Organizations: The Impact of Information Technology Spending. *Journal of Management Information Systems*, *13*(2), 29–57. doi:10.1080/07421222.1996.11518122

Mlay, S. V., Zlotnikov, I., & Watundu, S. (2013). A quantitative analysis of business process engineering and organizational resistance: The case of Uganda. *The African Journal of Information Systems*, *5*(1). http://digitalcommons.kennesaw.edu/cgi/viewcontent.cgi?article=1116&context=ajis

Morris, M. G., & Venkatesh, V. (2010). Job characteristics and job satisfaction: Understanding the role of enterprise resource planning system implementation. *Management Information Systems Quarterly*, *34*(1), 162. doi:10.2307/20721418

Ramirez, R., Melville, N., & Lawler, E. (2010). Information technology infrastructure, organizational process redesign, and business value: An empirical analysis. *Decision Support Systems*, *49*(4), 417–429. doi:10.1016/j.dss.2010.05.003

Schaffhauser. (2005). *Outsourcing – What is Outsourcing?* Retrieved on October 18, 2017 from https://www.sourcingmag.com/what-is-outsourcing/

Secureworks. (2016). *What is Firewall Security?* Retrieved on October 20, 2017 from https://www.secureworks.com/blog/firewall-security

Soltanmohammadi, S., Asadi, S., & Ithnin, N. (2013). Main human factors affecting information system security. *Interdisciplinary Journal of Contemporary Research in Business, 5*, 329–354.

Subashish, G., William, J. K., & James, T. C. T. (2010). *Process Reengineering. The IS Manager's Enabling Role in Business*. Retrieved from https://www.google.com.bn/url?sa=t&source=web&rct=j&ei=Sj_sVPblBIbf8AXdvYCAAw&url=http%3A%2F%2Fwww.ittoday.info%2FAIMS%2FInformation_Management%2F1-03-10.pdf&ved=0CBoQFjAA&usg=AFQjCNEHzJMsuWgCC5flzbA_O9k-3KU5iPw

Subhas, C., Kumar, M. U., & Kumar, V. (2008). Modelling strategic actor relationships for risk management in organizations undergoing business process reengineering due to information systems adoption. *Business Process Management Journal, 14*(1), 65–84. doi:10.1108/14637150810849418

Subramoniam, S., Tounsi, M., & Krishnankutty, K. V. (2009). The role of BPR in the implementation of ERP systems. *Business Process Management Journal, 15*(5), 653–668. doi:10.1108/14637150910987892

Sun, Y., Bhattacherjee, A., & Ma, Q. (2009). Extending technology usage to work settings: The role of perceived work compatibility in ERP implementation. *Information & Management, 46*(6), 351–356. doi:10.1016/j.im.2009.06.003

Sung, P., Ku, C., & Su, C. (2014). Understanding the propagation dynamics of multipartite computer virus. *Industrial Management & Data Systems, 114*(1), 86–106. doi:10.1108/IMDS-04-2013-0197

Susanto, H. (2017). Electronic Health System: Sensors Emerging and Intelligent Technology Approach. In *Smart Sensors Networks* (pp. 189–203). Elsevier. doi:10.1016/B978-0-12-809859-2.00012-7

Susanto, H. (2018). Smart mobile device emerging Technologies: An enabler to Health Monitoring system. In *High-Performance Materials and Engineered Chemistry* (pp. 241–264). Apple Academic Press. doi:10.1201/9781315187860-8

Susanto, H., & Almunawar, M. N. (2015). Managing Compliance with an Information Security Management Standard. In *Encyclopedia of Information Science and Technology* (3rd ed., pp. 1452–1463). IGI Global. doi:10.4018/978-1-4666-5888-2.ch138

Susanto, H., & Almunawar, M. N. (2018). *Information Security Management Systems: A Novel Framework and Software as a Tool for Compliance with Information Security Standard*. CRC Press. doi:10.1201/9781315232355

Susanto, H., Almunawar, M. N., Leu, F. Y., & Chen, C. K. (2016). Android vs iOS or Others? SMD-OS Security Issues: Generation Y Perception. *International Journal of Technology Diffusion, 7*(2), 1–18. doi:10.4018/IJTD.2016040101

Susanto, H., & Chen, C. K. (2017). Information and Communication Emerging Technology: Making Sense of Healthcare Innovation. In *Internet of Things and Big Data Technologies for Next Generation Healthcare* (pp. 229–250). Springer. doi:10.1007/978-3-319-49736-5_10

Susanto, H., Chen, C. K., & Almunawar, M. N. (2018). Revealing Big Data Emerging Technology as Enabler of LMS Technologies Transferability. In *Internet of Things and Big Data Analytics Toward Next-Generation Intelligence* (pp. 123–145). Springer. doi:10.1007/978-3-319-60435-0_5

Susanto, H., Leu, F.-Y., Caesarendra, W., Ibrahim, F., Haghi, P. K., Khusni, U., & Glowacz, A. (2020). Managing Cloud Intelligent Systems over Digital Ecosystems: Revealing Emerging App Technology in the Time of the COVID19 Pandemic. *Appl. Syst. Innov.*, *3*(3), 37. doi:10.3390/asi3030037

What Is Database Architecture? (n.d.). Retrieved Oct 19, 2017 from https://learn.org/articles/What_is_Database_Architecture.html

Yin, G. L. (2010). BPR application. *Modern Applied Science*, *4*(4), 96–101. http://www.ccsenet.org/journal/index.php/mas/article/view/5655. doi:10.5539/mas.v4n4p96

ADDITIONAL READING

Adeoti-Adekeye, W. B. (1997). The importance of management information systems. *Library Review*, *46*(5), 318–327. doi:10.1108/00242539710178452

O'Neill, P., & Sohal, A. S. (1999). Business Process Reengineering A review of recent literature. *Technovation*, *19*(9), 571–581. doi:10.1016/S0166-4972(99)00059-0

Olalla, M. F. (2000). Information Technology in Business Process Reengineering. *IEAR*, *6*(3), 581–589.

Omidi, A., & Khoshtinat, B. (2016). Factors Affecting the Implementation of Business Process Reengineering: Taking into Account the Moderating Role of Organizational Culture (Case Study: Iran Air). *Procedia Economics and Finance*, *36*, 425–432. doi:10.1016/S2212-5671(16)30058-2

Panda, M. (2013). IT Enabled Business Process Reengineering, *International Journal of Information Technology & Management Information System (IJITMIS), 4*(3), 85-95. Retrieved from https://pdfs.semanticscholar.org/0368/dae6236e223eea1fddd75b19b31a0857139f.pdf

Panda, M. (2013). IT enabled business process reengineering. *International Journal of Information Technology & Management Information System*, *4*(3), 89–95.

Soltanmohammadi, S., Asadi, S., & Ithnin, N. (2013). Main human factors affecting information system security. *Interdisciplinary Journal of Contemporary Research in Business*, *5*(7), 329–354.

Sousa, K., & Oz, E. (2015). *Management Information Systems* (7th ed.). Cengage Learning.

Terziovski, M., Fitzpatrick, P., & O'Neill, P. (2003). Successful predictors of business process reengineering (BPR) in financial services. *International Journal of Production Economics*, *84*(1), 35–50. doi:10.1016/S0925-5273(02)00378-X

Tsai, W. H., Chen, S. P., Hwang, E., & Hsu, J. L. (2010). A study of the impact of business process on the ERP system effectiveness. *International Journal of Business and Management*, *5*(9), 26. doi:10.5539/ijbm.v5n9p26

Veselý, A. (2011). Theory and methodology of best practice research: A critical review of the current state. *Central European Journal of Public Policy*, *5*(2), 98–117.

KEY TERMS AND DEFINITIONS

Assistive Technology: Is assistive, adaptive, and rehabilitative devices for People with disability or the elderly population. People with disability often have difficulty performing activities of daily living (ADLs) independently, or even with assistance. ADLs are self-care activities that include toileting, mobility (ambulation), eating, bathing, dressing, grooming, and personal device care. Assistive technology can ameliorate the effects of disabilities that limit the ability to perform ADLs. Assistive technology promotes greater independence by enabling people to perform tasks they were formerly unable to accomplish, or had great difficulty accomplishing, by providing enhancements to, or changing methods of interacting with, the technology needed to accomplish such tasks.

Awareness Training: Helps employees to understand risks and identify potential attacks they may encounter as they receive email and use the web. Awareness training also acquaints employees with best practices for avoiding risk.

Business Re-Engineering Systems: Involves the radical redesign of core business processes to achieve dramatic improvements in productivity, cycle times and quality.

Corporate Strategy: Corporate strategy encompasses a firm's corporate actions with the aim to achieve company objectives while achieving a competitive advantage.

Education Technology: Commonly abbreviated as EduTech, or EdTech, is the combined use of computer hardware, software, and educational theory and practice to facilitate learning. When referred to with its abbreviation, EdTech, it is often referring to the industry of companies that create educational technology.

Encapsulation: Encapsulation is one of the fundamental concepts in object-oriented programming (OOP). It describes the idea of bundling data and methods that work on that data within one unit, e.g., a class in Java. This concept is also often used to hide the internal representation, or state, of an object from the outside.

Information Systems: Information Systems is an academic study of systems with a specific reference to information and the complementary networks of hardware and software that people and organizations use to collect, filter, process, create and also distribute data. Information systems help to control the performance of business processes.

Information Technology Apps for Learning: The Apps enable students to acquire lecture materials, take online quizzes or assessments, submit tutorials or assignments, view results, view course materials, see news and announcements, online interaction, anytime and anywhere without any geographical or time barriers. However, the key to effective apps -learning is not from its multimedia, design or user-friendliness, but on how the individuals are engaged by the content. Although the use of apps-learning provides notable benefits for students as a whole, the effectiveness of the use of the system depends on the level of acceptance and use of students. The goals of apps-learning will not be achieved if there is lag and resistance to the use of new technology. The process of implementing apps-learning in the institution might face several factors that constraints the effective use of apps-learning as a learning medium, such as infrastructure issues, the willingness and readiness of the institutions and students.

IT Emerging Technology: Emerging technology is a term generally used to describe a new technology, but it may also refer to the continuing development of an existing technology; it can have slightly different meaning when used in different areas, such as media, business, science, or education. The term commonly refers to technologies that are currently developing, or that are expected to be available within the next five to ten years, and is usually reserved for technologies that are creating, or are expected to create, significant social or economic effects.

Knowledge Management System: A knowledge management system is any kind of IT system that stores and retrieves knowledge to improve understanding, collaboration, and process alignment. Knowledge management systems can exist within organizations or teams, but they can also be used to center your knowledge base for your users or customers.

Compilation of References

Abasheva, C. (2010). Specifics of the English Language Education in the Study Groups with Different Mother Tongues. In *Proceedings of the 5th International Scientific Conference Theory for Practice in the Education of Contemporary Society*. Riga: Riga Teacher Training and Educational Management Academy.

Abdolvand, N., Albadvi, A., & Ferdowsi, Z. (2008). Assessing readiness for business process reengineering. *Business Process Management Journal, 14*(4), 497–511. doi:10.1108/14637150810888046

Abdullah, F., Ward, R., & Ahmed, E. (2016). Investigating the influence of the most commonly used external variables of TAM on students' Perceived Ease of Use (PEOU) and Perceived Usefulness (PU) of e-portfolios. *Computers in Human Behavior, 63*, 75–90. doi:10.1016/j.chb.2016.05.014

Abu Bakar, R. (2020). *Brunei reports first COVID-19 case*. Retrieved from https://thescoop.co/2020/03/09/brunei-reports-first-COVID-19-case/

Adams, D., Sumintono, B., Mohamed, A., & Noor, N. S. M. (2018). E-Learning Readiness among Students of Diverse Backgrounds in a Leading Malaysian Higher Education Institution. *Malaysian Journal of Learning and Instruction, 15*(2), 227–256.

Adzaho, G. (2013, December 19). *Diplo*. Retrieved from Can technology help preserve elements of culture in the digital age: https://www.diplomacy.edu/blog/can-technology-help-preserve-elements-culture-digital-age

Affouneh, S., Salha, S., & Khlaif, Z. (2020). Designing Quality E-Learning Environments for Emergency Remote Teaching in Coronavirus Crisis. *Interdisciplinary Journal of Virtual Learning in Medical Sciences, 11*. Advance online publication. doi:10.30476/ijvlms.2020.86120.1033

Aftab, P. (2010). *Stop cyberbullying: What's the parent's role in this?* Retrieved June 22, 2010, from http://www.stopcyberbullying.org/prevention/parents_role.html

Agarwal, R., & Prasad, J. (1998). A conceptual and operational definition of innovativeness in the domain of information technology. *Information Systems Research, 9*(2), 204–215. doi:10.1287/isre.9.2.204

Agatston, P., Kowalski, R., & Limber, S. (2007). Students perspectives on cyberbullying. *The Journal of Adolescent Health, 41*(6), S59–S60. doi:10.1016/j.jadohealth.2007.09.003 PMID:18047946

Ahrens, A., & Zaščerinska, J. (2014a). Students' Attitude to Interdisciplinary Research. Society, Integration, Education. *Proceedings of the International Scientifical Conference*. Volume I*: Higher Education Institutions Pedagogy, School Pedagogy, Pre-School Pedagogy*, 13-23.

Ahrens, A., & Zaščerinska, J. (2015a). A Comparative Study of Business and Engineering Students' Attitude to Mobile Technologies in Distance Learning. In Assessing the Role of Mobile Technologies and Distance Learning in Higher Education (pp. 29-59). IGI Global.

Ahrens, A., & Zaščerinska, J. (2015b). Principles of Sampling in Educational Research in Higher Education. *Proceedings of the International Scientifical Conference Society, Integration, Education, Volume 1 Higher Education Pedagogy*, 25-35. http://journals.ru.lv/index.php/SIE/issue/view/23

Ahrens, A., & Zascerinska, J. (2020). Post-COVID-19 University Governance in Germany. In Education Reform: Education Content Research and Implementation Problems (vol. 2, pp. 7-16). Rezekne: Rezekne Academy of Technologies. doi:10.17770/er2020.2.5336

Ahrens, A., Foerster, M., Zaščerinska, J., & Wasser, I. (2020). European Accreditation Agency's View on Kazakhstan's Engineering and Information Technology Higher Education. *Society. Integration. Education Proceedings of the International Scientific Conference, 5*, 15-25. 10.17770ie2020vol1.4861

Ahrens, A., Gruenwald, N., Bassus, O., Zaščerinska, J., & Melnikova, J. (2017). Master Programme "Information and Electrical Engineering" for International Students at Hochschule Wismar: Theoretical Framework. In *Conference Proceedings of 8th Balkan Region Conference on Engineering and Business Education (BRCEBE) and 10th International Conference on Engineering and Business Education (ICEBE) "Creating a mindset for growth and socio-economic development* (pp. 175-182). Lucian Blaga University of Sibiu. 10.1515/cplbu-2017-0023

Ahrens, A., Grünwald, N., Bassus, O., Andreeva, N., Zaščerinska, J., & Melnikova, J. (2018). Impact of Master Programme "Information and Electrical Engineering" for International Students at Hochschule Wismar on Regional Economics: Theoretical Modelling. In *Scientific Printed Works of the 8th International Scientific Conference Perspectives of Economics of Kaliningrad Region and EU Development* (pp. 6-9). Kaliningrad State Technical University.

Ahrens, A., Purvinis, O., Zaščerinska, J., Miceviciene, D., & Tautkus, A. (2018). *Burstiness Management for Smart, Sustainable and Inclusive Growth: Emerging Research and Opportunities*. IGI Global.

Ahrens, A., & Zaščerinska, J. (2014b). *Factors that Influence Sample Size in Educational Research. In 2014 ATEE Spring University proceedings Changing Education in a Changing Society*. Klaipeda University.

Ajnaware. (2009, October 6). *Ajnaware's Weblog*. Retrieved from Sun Seeker – Seeing the Light with Augmented Reality: https://ajnaware.wordpress.com/2009/10/06/sun-seeker-seeing-the-light-with-augmented-reality/

Akareem, H., & Hossain, S. (2012). Perception of education quality in private universities of Bangladesh: A study from students' perspective. *Journal of Marketing for Higher Education, 22*(1), 11–33. doi:10.1080/08841241.2012.705792

Akkoyunlu, B., & Soylu, M. Y. (2008). A Study of Student's Perceptions in a Blended Learning Environment Based on Different Learning Styles. *Journal of Educational Technology & Society, 11*(1), 183–193.

Alavi, M., & Leidner, D. E. (2001, March). Knowledge Management And Knowledge Management Systems: Conceptual Foundations And Research Issues. *MIS Quaterly, 25*(1), 107–136. doi:10.2307/3250961

Al-drees, A. A., Khalil, M. S., Irshad, M., & Abdulghani, H. M. (2015). *Students' perception towards the problem based learning tutorial session in a system-based hybrid curriculum*. doi:10.15537mj.2015.3.10216

Ale, K., Loh, Y. A.-C., & Chib, A. (2017). Contextualized-OLPC education project in rural India: Measuring learning impact and mediation of computer self-efficacy. *Educational Technology Research and Development, 65*(3), 769–794. doi:10.100711423-017-9517-2

Alemdag, E., & Erdem, M. (2017). Designing an e-mentoring program for novice teachers in Turkey and investigating online interactions and program outcomes. *Mentoring & Tutoring, 25*(2), 1–28. doi:10.1080/13611267.2017.1327394

Al-Fraihat, D., Joy, M., Masa'deh, R., & Sinclair, J. (2017). Identifying success factors for e-learning in higher education. In *International conference on e-learning* (pp. 247-255). Academic Conferences International Limited.

Alhammad, F., Al Faori, S., & Abu Husan, L. S. (2009). Knowledge sharing in the Jordanian universities. *Journal of Knowledge Management, 10*(3), 1–9.

Alharthi, A. D., Spichkova, M., & Hamilton, M. (2019). Sustainability requirements for eLearning systems: A systematic literature review and analysis. *Requirements Engineering, 24*(4), 523–543. doi:10.100700766-018-0299-9

Alhumaid, K., Ali, S., Waheed, A., Zahid, E., & Habes, M. (2020). COVID-19 & Elearning. *Perceptions & Attitudes Of Teachers Towards E-Learning Acceptance in The Developing Countries., 6*. Advance online publication. doi:10.5281/zenodo.4060121

Ali, A. (2015). Integrating Blended Learning in Higher Education. *Procedia: Social and Behavioral Sciences, 186*, 600–603. doi:10.1016/j.sbspro.2015.04.086

Al-Kurdi, O., El-Haddadeh, R., & Eldabi, T. (2018). Knowledge sharing in higher education institutions: A systematic review. *Journal of Enterprise Information Management, 31*(2), 226–246. doi:10.1108/JEIM-09-2017-0129

Allan, B., Hunter, B., & Lewis, D. (2006). Four years on: a longitudinal study assessing the impact of membership of a virtual community of practice. In *Fifth International Conference on Networked Learning*. Lancaster University.

Al-Mashari, M., & Zairi, M. (1999). BPR implementation process: An analysis of key success and failure factors. *Business Process Management Journal, 5*(1), 87–112. doi:10.1108/14637159910249108

Alsaaty, F. M., Carter, E., Abrahams, D., & Alshameri, F. (2016). Traditional versus online learning in institutions of higher education: Minority business students' perceptions. *Business and Management Research, 5*(2), 31–41. doi:10.5430/bmr.v5n2p31

Alspaugh, J. W. (1999). The Relationship between the Number of Students per Computer and Educational Outcomes. *Journal of Educational Computing Research, 21*(2), 141–150. doi:10.2190/RBRX-39G9-LHAP-7DT3

Alsulimani, T., & Kaabi, H. (2018). The effect of E-Learning on Teachers' Motivation: A case study in Jeddah University. *International Journal of Management and Information Technology, 14*(1), 3316–3327.

Altrichter, H., Feldman, A., Posch, P., & Somekh, B. (2008). *Teachers investigate their work; An introduction an action research across the professions* (2nd ed.). Routledge.

Álvarez, B. (2012). Flipping the Classroom: Homework in class, lessons at home. *Journal of Education Digest: Essential Readings Condensed for Quick Review, College Student Personnel, 77*(8), 18–21. Retrieved from https://eric.ed.gov/?id=EJ982505

Al-Zahrani, A. M. (2014). Challenges and Obstacles to the Effective Integration of Technology : A Qualitative Investigation of the Policymakers Perspective in Saudi Pre-Service Teacher Education. *Saudi Journal of Educational Technology Research*, 1-12.

AmadeoK. (2020). Retrieved from https://www.thebalance.com/what-is-unemployment-3306222

Amayah, A. T. (2013). Determinants of knowledge sharing in a public sector organization. *Journal of Knowledge Management, 17*(3), 454–471. doi:10.1108/JKM-11-2012-0369

Amin, N. A. H. N., Hasnan, A. S., Besar, N. N., & Almunawar, M. N. (2016). Knowledge Sharing Using Web 2.0: Preferences, Benefits and Barriers in Brunei Darussalam's Tertiary Education. *International Journal of Asian Business and Information Management, 7*(4), 1–18. doi:10.4018/IJABIM.2016100101

Amu, A. (n.d.). *Smarter Brunei*. Retrieved from https://www.smarterbrunei.com/

Anderson, J. (2005). IT, E-Learning and Teacher Development. *International Education Journal, 5*(5), 1–14.

Andersson, U., Dasi, A., Mudambi, R., & Pederson, T. (2016). Technology, innovation and knowledge: The importance of international connectivity. *Journal of World Business*, *51*(1), 153–162. doi:10.1016/j.jwb.2015.08.017

Anshari, M., Almunawar, M. N., Shahrill, M., Wicaksono, D. K., & Huda, M. (2017). Smartphones usage in the classrooms: Learning aid or interference? *Education and Information Technologies*, *22*(6), 3063–3079. doi:10.100710639-017-9572-7

Antoniadou, N., Kokkinos, C. M., & Markos, A. (2016). Possible common correlates between bullying and cyber-bullying among adolescents. *Psicologia dell'Educazione*, *22*(1), 27–38. doi:10.1016/j.pse.2016.01.003

Arbaugh, J. B., & Benbunan-Fich, R. (2007). The importance of participant interaction in online environments. *Decision Support Systems*, *43*(3), 853–865. doi:10.1016/j.dss.2006.12.013

Argentin, G., Gui, M., Tamanini, C. (2013). Ascuola di competenza digitale. Il ruolo degli insegnanti nell'uso delle ICT degli student. *Scuola democratica, 1.*

ASEAN Today. (2018, April 30). Retrieved from https://www.aseantoday.com/2018/04/bruneis-equal-opportunities-problem/

Ashton, P. B., Koch, L., & Rothberg, A. (2014). The influence of blended learning on student performance in an undergraduate occupational therapy curriculum. *South African Journal of Occupational Therapy*, *44*(1), 75–80. Retrieved November 4, 2018, from http://www.scielo.org.za/pdf/sajot/v44n1/15.pdf

Asia & the Pacific. (2019, December). Retrieved from https://www.asia-pacific.undp.org/content/rbap/en/home/blog/2019/ensuring-an-accessible-future-for-people-with-print-disabilities.html

Asociación Nacional de Universidades e Instituciones de Educación Superior (2020b). *Anuarios estadísticos de la educación superior, ciclo escolar 2018-2019. Licenciatura y posgrado.* ANUIES.

Asociación Nacional de Universidades e Instituciones de Educación Superior. (2020a). *Acuerdo Nacional por la Unidad en la Educación Superior frente a la emergencia sanitaria provocada por el covid-19.* Retrieved from http://www.anuies.mx/media/docs/avisos/pdf/200424155500Acuerdo+Nacional+frente+al+COVID-19.pdf

Association of Colleges and University Educators. (2020). *Effective online teaching practices.* https://acue.org/programs/catalog/

Assudani, R. H. (2005). Catching the chameleon: Understanding the elusive term knowledge. *Journal of Knowledge Management*, *9*(2), 31–44. doi:10.1108/13673270510590209

Ata, R. (2016). An exploration of higher education teaching in second life in the context of blended learning. *The Turkish Online Journal of Educational Technology*, *15*(3), 9–26.

Attaran, M. (2004). Exploring the relationship between information technology and business process reengineering. *Information & Management*, *41*(5), 585–596. doi:10.1016/S0378-7206(03)00098-3

Attorney General's Chambers. (2019). Retrieved from http://www.agc.gov.bn/Theme/Home.aspx

Aubert, B. A., Barki, H., Patry, M., & Roy, V. (2008). A multi-level, multi-theory perspective of information technology implementation. *Information Systems Journal*, *18*(1), 45–72. doi:10.1111/j.1365-2575.2007.00279.x

Autio, E. (2017). *Digitalisation, ecosystems, entrepreneurship, and policy.* Perspectives into topical issues in society and ways to support political decision making. Government's Analysis, Research and Assessment Activities. Helsinki, Policy Brief, 20/2017.

Autio, E., Szerb, L., Komlósi, E., & Tiszberger, M. (2018). *The European Index of Digital Entrepreneurship Systems.* JRC Technical Reports. Publications Office of the European Union.

Autism Spectrum Disorder: Communication Problems in Children. (n.d.). Retrieved from https://www.nidcd.nih.gov/health/autism-spectrum-disorder-communication-problems-children

Autism Spectrum Disorder: MedlinePlus. (n.d.). Retrieved from https://medlineplus.gov/autismspectrumdisorder.html

Ayebi-Arthur, K. (2017). E-learning, resilience and change in higher education: Helping a university cope after a natural disaster. *E-Learning and Digital Media, 14*(5), 259–274. doi:10.1177/2042753017751712

Azaraimy, H. (2017). *3G modasys*. Retrieved from https://3g.modasys.net/index.php/news-events/around-brunei/local-news/29409-centre-for-capacity-building-to-begin-training-programmes-in-september.html

Babu, N., & Reddy, D. (2015). Challenges and Opportunity of E-Learning in Developed and Developing Countries-A Review. *International Journal of Emerging Research in Management and Technology, 4*, 2278–9359.

Bakar, R. H. (2019). *The Scoop*. Retrieved from https://thescoop.co/2019/01/02/unemployment-in-brunei-rises-to-9-3-higher-among-men/

BakarR. (2019). Retrieved from https://thescoop.co/2019/01/02/unemployment-in-brunei-rises-to-9-3-higher-among-men/

Baker, N., & Jacobs, K. (2003). The nature of working in the United States: an occupational therapy perspective Work. In *A journal of Prevention* (pp. 53–61). Assessment and Rehabilitation.

Baldiris-Navarro, S., Zervas, P., Gesa, R., & Sampson, D. (2016). Developing teachers' competences for designing inclusive learning experiences. *Journal of Educational Technology & Society, 19*(1), 17–27. https://csula-primo.hosted.exlibrisgroup.com/permalink/f/117sn1j/TN_cdi_csuc_recercat_oai_recercat_cat_2072_324273

Banco Mundial. (2003). *Construir sociedades de conocimiento: Nuevos desafíos para la educación terciaria*. Banco Mundial. Retrieved from http://siteresources.worldbank.org/TERTIARYEDUCATION/Resources/Documents/Constructing-Knowledge-Societies/CKS-spanish.pdf

Bandura, A. (1997). *Self-efficacy: The exercise of control*. W.H. Freeman.

Barhoumi, C. (2016). User Acceptance of the e-Information Service as Information Resource: A NewExtension of the Technology Acceptance Model. *New Library World, 117*(9/10), 626–643. doi:10.1108/NLW-06-2016-0045

Barnett, R. (1990). *The idea of higher education*. McGraw-Hill Education.

Barron, A., Hogarty, K., Kromrey, J., & Lenkway, P. (1999). An Examination of the Relationships between Student Conduct and the Number of Computers per Student. *Journal of Research on Computing in Education, 32*(1), 108–127. doi:10.1080/08886504.1999.10782271

Basilaia, G., Dgebuadze, M., Kantaria, M., & Chokhonelidze, G. (2020). Replacing the Classic Learning Form at Universities as an Immediate Response to the COVID-19 Virus Infection in Georgia. *International Journal for Research in Applied Science and Engineering Technology, 8*(3), 2321–9653. doi:10.22214/ijraset.2020.3021

Bassus, O., & Zaščerinska, J. (2012). *Innovation and Higher Education*. Mensch & Buch.

Beaman, L., Ariel, B., Jeremy, M., & Musfiq, M. A. (2018). Can Network Theory-Based Targeting Increase Technology Adoption? *Evolution*, 1–14.

Beetham, H. (2004). *Review: developing e-learning models for the JISC practitioner communities: A report for the JISC e-pedagogy programme*. Joint Information Systems Committee (JISC).

Beetham, H., & Sharpe, P. (2007). *Rethinking Pedagogy for a Digital Age: Designing and delivering e-learning*. Routledge. doi:10.4324/9780203961681

Benke, I. (2019). Social Augmentation of Enterprise Communication Systems for Virtual Teams using Chatbots. *Proceedings of 17th European Conference on Computer-Supported Cooperative Work - Doctoral Colloquium. Reports of the European Society for Socially Embedded Technologies*, *2*(3).

Bentivenga, J. (2009). Escenarios mundiales de la educaciòn superior: Anàlisis global y estudios de casos. *Propuesta Educativa (Buenos Aires)*, 31.

Bermejo, S. (2005). Cooperative electronic learning in virtual laboratories through forums. *IEEE Transactions on Education*, *48*(1), 140–149. doi:10.1109/TE.2004.837045

Berna-Martinez, J. & Maciá Pérez, F. (2012). Overcoming resistance to change in business innovation processes. *IACSIT International Journal of Engineering and Technology*, *4*, 148.

Besar, N. A. (2009). *Impact in ICT in Brunei Darussalam System of Education*. Universiti Brunei Darussalam.

Bhatia, M. (2018, September 5). *Human of Data*. Retrieved from Your Guide to Qualitative and Quantitative Data Analysis Methods: https://humansofdata.atlan.com/2018/09/qualitative-quantitative-data-analysis-methods/

Bhusry, M., & Ranjan, J. (2011). Knowledge Collaboration in Higher Educational Institutions in India: Charting a Knowledge management Solution. *International Journal of Computational Science*, *8*(5), 332–341.

Biggs, J. B. (1999). *Teaching for Quality Learning at University*. SRHE and Open University Press.

Bitrián, P., Buil, I., & Catalán, S. (2020). Flow and business simulation games: A typology of students. *International Journal of Management Education*, *18*(1), 100365. doi:10.1016/j.ijme.2020.100365

Blazic, A. J., & Arh, T. (2013). *Immersive business simulation games: An innovative pedagogical approach to e-learning and education*. Paper presented at the 30th Ascilite Conference, Macquarie University.

Blazic, A. J., & Blazic, B. D. J. (2015). Exploring and upgrading the educational business-game taxonomy. *Journal of Educational Computing Research*, *52*(3), 303–340. doi:10.1177/0735633115572959

Blazic, A. J., Ribeiro, C., Fernandes, J., Pereira, J., & Arh, T. (2012). Analysing the required properties of business simulation games to be used in E-learning and education. *Intelligent Information Management*, *4*(06), 348–356. doi:10.4236/iim.2012.46039

Boddy, D., Boonstra, A., & Kennedy, G. (2009). *Managing Information Systems: Strategy and Organisation* (3rd ed.). FT Prentice Hall.

Boekaerts, M. (2002). Bringing about change in the classroom: Strengths and weaknesses of the self-regulated learning approach. *Learning and Instruction*, *12*(6), 589–604. doi:10.1016/S0959-4752(02)00010-5

Bond, M., Marín, V. I., Dolch, C., Bedenlier, S., & Zawacki-Richter, O. (2018). Digital transformation in German higher education: Student and teacher perceptions and usage of digital media. *International Journal of Educational Technology in Higher Education*, *15*(1), 48. doi:10.118641239-018-0130-1

Bonk, C. J., Graham, C. R., Cross, J., & Moore, M. G. (2006). *The Handbook of Blended Learning: Global Perspectives*. Local Designs.

Bonk, C., & Zhang, K. (2006). Introducing the R2D2 model: Online learning for the diverse learners of this world. *Distance Education*, *27*(2), 249–264. doi:10.1080/01587910600789670

Borgianni, Y., Cascini, G., & Rotini, F. (2015). Business Process Reengineering driven by customer value: A support for undertaking decisions under uncertainty conditions. *Computers in Industry*, *68*, 132–147. doi:10.1016/j.compind.2015.01.001

Borko, H. (2004). Professional development and teacher learning: Mapping the terrain. *Educational Researcher, 33*(8), 3–15. doi:10.3102/0013189X033008003

Bourne, J., & Moore, J. (2003). *Elements of Quality Online Education*. Babson College.

Boursicot, K., Kemp, S., Ong, T., Wijaya, L., Goh, S., Freeman, K., & Curran, I. (2020). Conducting a high-stakes OSCE in a COVID-19 environment. *MedEdPublish, 9*(1). Advance online publication. doi:10.15694/mep.2020.000054.1

Boyle, S. (2011). *Teaching toolkit: An introduction to games based learning*. UCD Teaching and Learning/ Resources.

BozkurtA.SharmaR. (2020). *Emergency remote teaching in a time of global crisis due to CoronaVirus pandemic. 15*, i–vi. doi:10.5281/zenodo.3778083

Braun, V., & Clarke, V. (2012). Thematic analysis. In H. Cooper, P. M. Camic, D. L. Long, A. T. Panter, D. Rindskopf & K. J. Sher (Eds), APA Hand- book of Research Methods in Psychology, Vol. 2: Research Designs: quantitative, qualitative, neuropsychological and biological (pp. 57-71). Washington, DC: American Psychological Association. doi:10.1037/13620-004

Brito, C. C., & Oliveira, M. T. (2013). Bullying and self-esteem in adolescents from public schools. *Jornal de Pediatria, 89*(6), 601–607. doi:10.1016/j.jped.2013.04.001 PMID:24029549

Broadbent, B. (2002). *ABCs of e-learning: Reaping the benefits and avoiding the pitfalls*. Jossey-Bass.

Brody, T. (2006). Blended learning: A recipe for the future. *Carolina TESOL, 30*(2).

Brookfield, S. D. (1986). *Understanding and Facilitating Adult Learning*. Jossey-Bass.

Brooks, C. F. (2010). Toward ‘hybridized’ faculty development for the twenty-first century: Blending online communities of practice and face-to-face Meetings in instructional and professional support programmes. *Innovations in Education and Teaching International, 47*(3), 261–270. doi:10.1080/14703297.2010.498177

Brunei Computer Emergency Response Team (BruCERT). (2020). *Survey on Learning / Working from Home*. Author.

Buchal, R., & Songsore, E. (2019). Using Microsoft Teams to support collaborative knowledge building in the context of sustainability assessment. *Proceedings of the Canadian Engineering Education Association (CEEA-ACEG) Conference*.

Budde, R. (2005). *Mexican and Central American L.A. Garment Workers: Globalized Industries and their economic constraints*. LIT Verlag Münster.

Budiono, A., & Loice, R. (2012). Business Process Reengineering in Motorcycle Workshop X for Business Sustainability. *Procedia Economics and Finance, 4*, 33–43. doi:10.1016/S2212-5671(12)00318-8

Budoya, C. M., Kissaka, M. M., & Mtebe, J. S. (2019). Towards Developing Interactive Content for Enhancing Life Skills Education in Tanzania: Possibilities and Pitfalls. *IFIP Advances in Information and Communication Technology, 552*, 374–385. doi:10.1007/978-3-030-19115-3_31

Burns, M. (2011). *Distance Education for Teacher Training: Modes, Models, and Methods*. Education Development Center.

Burton-Jones, A., & Hubona, G. (2005). Individual differences and usage behavior: Revisiting a Technology Acceptance Model assumption. *ACM SIGMIS Database, 36*(2), 58–77. doi:10.1145/1066149.1066155

Business Process Reengineering (BPR) – Definition, Steps, and Examples. (n.d.). *Kissflow*. Retrieved Oct 7, 2017 from https://kissflow.com/bpm/business-process-reengineering/

Cabero, J., Marín, V. & Castaño, C. (2015). Validación de la aplicación del modelo TPACK para la formación del profesorado en TIC. *Revista d´innovació Educativa Universitat de Valéncia, 14,* 13-22. doi:10.7203/attic.14.4001

Cabero, J. (2013). *Nuevos modelos, recursos y diseño de programas en la práctica docente*. Ediciones CEF.

Cabrera, L. (2020). Efectos del coronavirus en el sistema de enseñanza: Aumenta la desigualdad de oportunidades educativas en España. *Research in Sociology of Education, 13*(2), 114–139. doi:10.7203/RASE.13.2.17125

Cabrol, M., & Severin, E. (2010). *ICT to improve quality in education—A conceptual framework and indicators in the use of information communication technology for education (ICT4E). In Assessing the effects of ICT in education*. Publications Office of the European Union.

Calvete, E., Orue, I., Estévez, A., Villardón, L., & Padilla, P. (2010). *Cyberbullying in adolescents: Modalities and aggressors' profile*. Academic Press.

Capitano, J., DiRenzo, M. S., Aten, K. J., & Greenhaus, J. H. (2017). Role identity salience and boundary permeability preferences: An examination of enactment and protection effects. *Journal of Vocational Behavior, 102*, 99–111. doi:10.1016/j.jvb.2017.07.001

Capitano, J., & Greenhaus, J. H. (2018). When work enters the home: Antecedents of role boundary permeability behavior. *Journal of Vocational Behavior, 109*, 87–100. doi:10.1016/j.jvb.2018.10.002

Carey, K. (2020). Is everybody ready for the big migration to online college? Actually no. *The New York Times*. http://www.nytimes.com

Carey, K. (2020, March 13). Everybody Ready for the Big Migration to Online College? Actually, No. *The New York Times*. Retrieved from https://www.nytimes.com/2020/03/13/upshot/coronavirus-online-college-classes-unprepared.html

Casany, M. J., Alier, M., & Barcelo, M. (2012). Integration of M-learning and LMS: A sustainability approach. In *2012 International Symposium on Computers in Education (SIIE 2012)* (pp. 1-6). Andorra la Vella.

Castaño, J., Redecker, C., Vuorikari, R., & Punie, Y. (2014). Open Education 2030: Planning the future of adult learning in Europe. *Open Learning, 28*(3), 171–186. doi:10.1080/02680513.2013.871199

Castillo, J., & Castillo, A. (2021). El impacto de la COVID-19 en el profesorado de educación superior y sus concepciones sobre la evaluación. *Campus Virtuales, 10*(19), 89-101. Retrieved from http://www.uajournals.com/campusvirtuales/journal/18/7.pdf

Castro, R. (2019). Blended learning in higher education: Trends and capabilities. *Education and Information Technologies, 24*(4), 2523–2546. doi:10.100710639-019-09886-3

Cavas, B., Cavas, P., Karaoglan, B., & Kisla, T. (2009). A study on science teachers' attitudes toward information and communication technologies in education. *The Turkish Online Journal of Educational Technology, 8*(2), 20–32.

CEDEFOP. (2014). *Terminology of European education and training policy. A selection of 130 key terms* (2nd ed.). Retrieved from: http://www.cedefop.europa.eu/ en/publications-and-resources/publications/4117

Čehlova, Z. (2002). *Izziņas aktivitāte mācībās* [Cognitive activity in learning]. RaKa.

Chandavimol, P., Natakuatoong, O., & Tantrarungroj, P. (2013). Knowledge Management and Action Learning in Blended Training Activities. *Creative Education, 4*(9), 51–55. doi:10.4236/ce.2013.49B010

Chehaibar, L. (2020). Flexibilidad curricular. Tensiones en tiempos de pandemia. In H. Casanova (Coord.), Educación y pandemia. Una visión académica (pp. 83-91). UNAM.

Chen, T. F. (2016). E-learning 3.0: Technologies, applications, benefits, trends and challenge. In S. Kadry & A. El Hami (Eds.), E-Systems for the 21st Century: Concept, Developments, and Applications - Volume 2: E-Learning, E-Maintenance, E-Portfolio, E-System, and E-Voting (pp. 105-176). New York: Apple Academic Press.

Chen, C. C., Shaw, R. S., & Yang, S. C. (2006). Mitigating information security risks by increasing user security awareness: A case study of an information security awareness system. *Information Technology, Learning and Performance Journal, 24*(1), 1.

Cheng, M. Y., Ho, J. S. Y., & Lau, P. M. (2009). Knowledge Sharing in Academic Institutions: A Study of Multimedia University Malaysia. *Electronic Journal of Knowledge Management, 7*(3), 313–324.

Chikumba, P. A. (2011). Student performance in computer studies in secondary schools in Malawi. In R. Popescu-Zeletin, I. A. Rai, K. Jonas, & A. Villafiorita (Eds.), *E-Infrastuctures and E-Services for Developing Countries. AFRICOMM 2010. Lecture Notes of the Institute for Computer Sciences, Social Informatics and Telecommunications Engineering* (Vol. 64). Springer. doi:10.1007/978-3-642-23828-4_11

Chin, W. W., Marcolin, B. L., & Newsted, P. R. (2003). A partial least squares latent variable modeling approach for measuring interaction effects: Results from a Monte Carlo simulation study and an electronic-mail emotion/adoption study. *Information Systems Research, 14*(2), 189–217. doi:10.1287/isre.14.2.189.16018

Chopra, G., Madan, P., Jaisingh, P., & Bhaskar, P. (2019). Effectiveness of e-learning portal from students' perspective: A structural equation model (SEM) approach. *Interactive Technology and Smart Education, 16*(2), 94–116. doi:10.1108/ITSE-05-2018-0027

Chou, S., & Chang, Y. (2008). The implementation factors that influence the ERP (enterprise resource planning) benefits. *Decision Support Systems, 46*(1), 149–157. doi:10.1016/j.dss.2008.06.003

Christmann, E., & Badgett, J. (1999). A Comparative Analysis of the Effects of Computer-Assisted Instruction on Student Achievement in Differing Science and Demographical Areas. *Journal of Computers in Mathematics and Science Teaching, 18*, 135 43.

Churchill, R., Ferguson, P., Godinho, S., Johnson, N. F., Keddie, A., Letts, W., Mackay, J., McGill, M., Moss, J., Nagel, M. C., Nicholson, P., & Vick, M. (2011). *Teaching: Making a difference*. John Wiley and Sons.

Chuttur, M. (2009). Overview of the Technology Acceptance Model: Origins, Developments and Future Directions. *Sprouts: Working Papers on Information Systems, 9*.

Clark, R., & Mayer, R. (2003). e-Learning and the Science of Instruction. San Francisco CA: Jossey-Bass/Pfeiffer.

Clusky, G. Jr, Hodges, C. W., & Smith, S. (2006). The impact of online quizzing on student success in an introductory financial accounting class. *Journal of College Teaching and Learning, 3*(7), 13–18. doi:10.19030/tlc.v3i7.1697

COBIT 4.1: Framework for IT Governance and Control. (n.d.). *ISACA*. Retrieved Oct 19, 2017 from https://www.isaca.org/Knowledge-Center/COBIT/Pages/Overview.aspx

Coenen, M., & Kok, R. A. W. (2014). Workplace flexibility and new product development performance: The role of telework and flexible work schedules. *European Management Journal, 32*(4), 564–576. doi:10.1016/j.emj.2013.12.003

Cohen, L., Manion, L., & Morrison, K. (2003). *Research Methods in Education*. Routledge/Falmer Taylor & Francis Group.

Cojocariu, V.-M., Lazar, I., Nedeff, V., & Lazar, G. (2014). SWOT Anlysis of E-learning Educational Services from the Perspective of their Beneficiaries. *Procedia: Social and Behavioral Sciences, 116*, 1999–2003. doi:10.1016/j.sbspro.2014.01.510

Colegio de Ciencias y Humanidades. (2020). *Cuadernillo de orientaciones 2020-2021*. https://www.cch.unam.mx/sites/default/files/Cuadernillo_Orientaciones_2020-2021.pdf

Cole, M., & Griffin, P. (Eds.). (1987). *Contextual Factors in Education: Improving Science and Mathematics Education for Minorities and Women.* Wisconsin Center for Education Research.

Conceição, P. (2019). Human Development Report 2019. United Nations Development Program.

Conger, S., Krauss, K., & Simuja, C. (2015). Human Factors Issues in Developing Country Remote K-12 Education. *Procedia Manufacturing, 3*, 1566–1573. doi:10.1016/j.promfg.2015.07.441

Cook, S. D. N., & Brown, J. S. (1999). Bridging epistemologies: The generative dance between organizational knowledge and organizational knowing. *Organization Science, 10*(4), 381–400. doi:10.1287/orsc.10.4.381

Cooper, D., & Schindler, P. (2011). *Business Research Methods* (11th ed.). McGraw Hill.

Corral, Y. (2009). Validez y confiabilidad de los instrumentos de investigación para la recolección de datos. *Revista Ciencias de la Educación, 19*(33), 229-247. http://servicio.bc.uc.edu.ve/educacion/revista/n33/art12.pdf

Creemers, B., Kyriakides, L., & Antoniou, P. (2013). *Teacher professional development for improving quality of teaching.* Springer Publication. doi:10.1007/978-94-007-5207-8

Creswell, J. W. (2003). *Research Design: Qualitative, Quantitative, and Mixed Methods Approaches.* SAGE Publications.

Creswell, J. W. (2015). *Educational Research: Planning, Conducting, and Evaluating Quantitative and Qualitative Research.* Pearson.

Crompton, H., Olszewski, B., & Bielefeldt, T. (2016). The mobile learning training needs of educators in technology-enabled environments. *Professional Development in Education, 42*(3), 482–501. doi:10.1080/19415257.2014.1001033

Czerniewiez, L., & Brown, C. (2010). *Born into the digital age in the South of Africa: the reconfiguration of the "digital citizen". Proceedings ot the 7th International Confernces on Networked Learning 2010.*

Daniel, S. J. (2020). Education and the COVID-19 pandemic. *Prospects, 49*(1-2), 91–96. doi:10.100711125-020-09464-3 PMID:32313309

Darling-Hammond, L., Wei, R. C., Andree, L. A., Richardson, N., & Orphanos, S. (2009). *Professional learning in the learning profession: A status report on teacher development in the US and abroad.* National Staff Development Council.

Davenport, T. H., & Prusak, L. (1998). *Working Knowledge: Managing What Organization Knows.* Harvard Business School Press.

Davis, F. D. (1985). *A Technology Acceptance Model for Empirically Testing New End-User Information Systems: Theory and Results (Ph.D in Management Disertation).* Massachusetts Institute of Technology, Sloan School of Management.

Davis, F. D. (1989). Perceived usefulness, perceived ease of use, and user acceptance of information technology. *Management Information Systems Quarterly, 13*(3), 319–340. doi:10.2307/249008

Davis, P. E., Fox, C. J., DeBode, J. D., & Peterson, L. T. (2021). Is avoiding the appearance of incompetence the key to success? An examination of team goal orientation and performance in a simulation environment. *Journal of Educational Computing Research, 58*(8), 1562–1585. doi:10.1177/0735633120940955

De Janasz, S. C., & Godshalk, V. M. (2013). The role of e-mentoring in proteges' learning and satisfaction. *Group & Organization Management, 38*(6), 743–774. doi:10.1177/1059601113511296

Delone, W. H., & McLean, E. R. (2003). The Delone and McLean Model of information systems success: A Ten-Year update. *Journal of Management Information Systems, 19*(4), 9–30. doi:10.1080/07421222.2003.11045748

Demirbilek, M. (2014). *The "Digital Natives" Debate: An Investigation of the Digital Propensities of University Students*. Retrieved December 25, 2020, from https://www.researchgate.net/publication/287248663_The_'Digital_Natives'_Debate_An_Investigation_of_the_Digital_Propensities_of_University_Students

Denzin, N. K. (1989). *The Research Act: A theoretical Introduction to Sociological Methods*. Prentice-Hall.

Dhamdhere, S. N. (2015). Importance of Knowledge Management. In *The Higher Educational Institutes, Turkish Online. Journal of Distance Education*, *6*(1), 162–183. doi:10.17718/tojde.34392

Dhawan, S. (2020). Online Learning: A Panacea in the Time of COVID-19 Crisis. *Journal of Educational Technology Systems*, *49*(1), 5–22. doi:10.1177/0047239520934018

Di Maggio, P., Hargittai, E., Celeste, C., & Shafer, S. (2004). Digital inequality. From unequal access to differentiated use: A literature review and agenda for research on digital inequality. In *Neckerman K. (a cura di), Social inequality*. Russell Sage.

Diaz, L. A., & Entonado, F. B. (2009). Are the functions of teachers in e-learning and face-to-face learning environments really different? *Journal of Educational Technology & Society*, *12*(4), 331–343.

Dominici, G., & Palumbo, F. (2013). How to Build an E-Learning Product: Factors for Student/Customer Satisfaction. *Business Horizons*, *56*(1), 87–96. doi:10.1016/j.bushor.2012.09.011

Dringus, L. P., & Seagull, A. B. (2013). *A five-year study of sustaining blended learning initiatives to enhance academic engagement in computer and information sciences campus courses*. CEC Faculty Books and Book.

Du, J., Havard, B., & Li, H. (2005). *Dynamic online discussion: Task-oriented interaction for deep learning* (Vol. 42). Academic Press.

Durodolu, O. (2016). *Technology Acceptance Model as a predictor of using information system to acquire information literacy skills*. Academic Press.

Dziuban, C., & Moskal, P. (2011). A course is a course is a course: Factor invariance in student evaluation of online, blended and face-to-face learning environments. *The Internet and Higher Education*, *14*(4), 236–241. doi:10.1016/j.iheduc.2011.05.003

Eilon, S. (1963). Management games. *The Journal of the Operational Research Society*, *14*(2), 137–149. doi:10.1057/jors.1963.22

Ellis, R. A., Ginns, P., & Piggott, L. (2009). E-learning in higher education: Some key aspects and their relationship to approaches to study. *Higher Education Research & Development*, *28*(3), 303–318. doi:10.1080/07294360902839909

Empson, L. (2001). Introduction: Knowledge Management in Professional Service Firms. *Human Relations*, *54*(7), 811–817. doi:10.1177/0018726701547001

Er, E., Ozden, M., & Arifoglu, A. (2009). A blended e-learning environment: A model proposition for integration of asynchronous and synchronous e-learning. *International Journal of Learning*, *16*(2), 449.

Escudero, A. (2018). Redefinición del "aprendizaje en red" en la cuarta revolución industrial. *Apertura (Guadalajara, Jal.)*, *10*(1), 149–163.

European University Association. (2011). *Impact of the economic crisis on European universities*. European University Association. https://eua.eu/downloads/publications/impact%20of%20the%20economic%20crisis%20on%20european%20universities%20january%202011.pdf

Fahey, L., & Prusak, L. (1998). The eleven deadliest sins of knowledge management. *California Management Review, 41*(3), 265–276. doi:10.2307/41165954

Faria, A. J. (1987). 'A survey of the use of business games in academia and business. *Simulation & Games, 18*(2), 207–224. doi:10.1177/104687818701800204

Faria, A. J. (1996). Business simulation games: Current usage levels - A ten year update. *Developments In Business Simulation & Experiential Exercises, 23*, 22–28.

Faria, A. J. (1998). Business simulation games: Current usage levels - An update. *Simulation & Gaming, 29*(3), 295–308. doi:10.1177/1046878198293002

Faria, A. J., Hutchinson, D., Wellington, W. J., & Gold, S. (2009). Developments in business gaming: A review of the past 40 years. *Simulation & Gaming, 40*(4), 464–487. doi:10.1177/1046878108327585

Faria, A. J., & Wellington, W. J. (2004). A survey of simulation game users, former-users, and never-users. *Simulation & Gaming, 35*(2), 178–207. doi:10.1177/1046878104263543

Farrell, C. (2020). Do international marketing simulations provide an authentic assessment of learning? A student perspective. *International Journal of Management Education, 18*(1), 100362. doi:10.1016/j.ijme.2020.100362

Felix, A. (2020). *Awareness of Students towards E-Learning in Education*. Academic Press.

Ferrari, A. (2012). *Digital competence in practce: An analysis of frameworks*. Publications Office. Retrieved from https://data.europa.eu/doi/10.2791/82116

Ferreira, S. M., Gouin-Vallerand, C., & Hotte, R. (2016) Game based learning: A case study on designing an educational game for children in developing countries. In *2016 8th International Conference on Games and Virtual Worlds for Serious Applications, VS-Games*. Barcelona: IEEE.

Fishbane, L., & Tomer, A. (2020, March 20). *As classes move online during COVID-19, what are disconnected students to do?* Retrieved December 25, 2020, from Brookings website: https://www.brookings.edu/blog/the-avenue/2020/03/20/as-classes-move-online-during-covid-19-what-are-disconnected-students-to-do/

Fitzgerald, G., & Werner, J. (1996). The Use of the Computer to Support Cognitive Behavioral Interventions for Students with Behavioral Disorders. *Journal of Computing in Childhood Education, 7*, 127–148.

Frenette, M., Frank, K., Deng, Z. (2020). School closures and the online preparedness of children during the Covid-19 pandemic. *Economic Insights, 103.*

Fry, K. (2001). E-learning markets and providers: Some issues and prospects. *Education + Training, 43*(4/5), 233–239. doi:10.1108/EUM0000000005484

Fullan, M. G. (1991). *The new meaning of educational change* (2nd ed.). Teachers College Press.

Fullan, M. G. (1995). The limits and the potential of professional development. In T. R. Guskey & M. Huberman (Eds.), *Professional development in education: New paradigms and practices* (pp. 253–267). Teachers College Press.

Fullan, M., & Hargreaves, A. (1992). Teacher development and educational change. In M. Fullan & A. Hargreaves (Eds.), *Teacher Development and Educational Change* (pp. 1–9). Falmer Press.

Galilee-Belfer, M. (2010). *Higher Education and the New Economy: Crisis or Opportunity? Summary and Recommendations*. The University of Arizona College of Education.

García, F., Corell, A., Abella, V., & Grande, M. (2020). La evaluación online en la educación superior en tiempos de la COVID-19. *Education in the Knowledge Society*, *21*(0), 1–26. doi:10.14201/eks.23013

Garrison, D. R., & Kanuka, H. (2004). Blended learning: Uncovering its transformative potential in higher education. *The Internet and Higher Education*, *7*(2), 95–105. doi:10.1016/j.iheduc.2004.02.001

Gedik, N., Kiraz, E., & Ozden, M. Y. (2013). Design of a blended learning environment: Considerations and implementation issues. *Australasian Journal of Educational Technology*, *29*(1), 1–19. doi:10.14742/ajet.6

Geithner, S., & Menzel, D. (2016). Effectiveness of learning through experience and reflection in a project management simulation. *Simulation & Gaming*, *47*(2), 228–256. doi:10.1177/1046878115624312

George, D., & Mallery, P. (2011). *SPSS for Windows Step by Step: A simple guide and reference*. Allyn y Bacon.

George, G., Howard-Grenville, J., Joshi, A., & Tihanyi, L. (2016). Understanding and tackling societal grand challenges through management research. *Academy of Management Journal*, *59*(6), 1880–1895. doi:10.5465/amj.2016.4007

George, G., McGahan, A. M., & Prabhu, J. (2012). Innovation for inclusive growth: Towards a theoretical framework and a research agenda. *Journal of Management Studies*, *49*(4), 661–683. doi:10.1111/j.1467-6486.2012.01048.x

Gérvas, J., & Meneu, R. (2010, December). Las crisis de salud pública en una sociedad desarrollada. Aciertos y limitaciones en España. Informe SESPAS 2010. *Gaceta Sanitaria*, *24*, 33–36. doi:10.1016/j.gaceta.2010.06.009 PMID:21094562

Gewin, V. (2020). Five tips for moving teaching online as COVID-19 takes hold. *Nature*, *580*(7802), 295–296. doi:10.1038/d41586-020-00896-7 PMID:32210377

Giovanis, K. (2015). Keep it simple: Challenges, solutions, and best practices for global eLearning initiatives. *International Journal of Advanced Corporate Learning*, *8*(2), 47–49. doi:10.3991/ijac.v8i2.4622

Glazer, E. M., & Hannafin, M. J. (2006). The collaborative apprenticeship model: Situated professional development within school settings. *Teaching and Teacher Education*, *22*(2), 179–193. doi:10.1016/j.tate.2005.09.004

Glood, S. H., Hussein, R. M., & Kamil, W. A. (2018). The effects of information quality, service quality, and compatibility on continue use of M-learning among students in the public universities of Iraqi. *Journal of Theoretical and Applied Information Technology*, *96*(12), 3739–3755.

Goi, C. L. (2019). The use of business simulation games in teaching and learning. *Journal of Education for Business*, *94*(4), 342–349. doi:10.1080/08832323.2018.1536028

Gonella, L., & Panto, E. (2008). Didactic architectures and organization models. *eLearning Papers*. Retrieved from: https://www.researchgate.net/publication/28264179_Didactic_architectures_and_organization_models_a_process_of_mutual_adaptation

Gonen, A., Brill, E., & Frank, M. (2009). Learning through business games – An analysis of successes and failures. *Horizon*, *17*(4), 356–367. doi:10.1108/10748120910998434

González, C., Infante, A., & Infante, J. (2020). Implementation of e-proctoring in online teaching: A study about motivational factors. *Sustainability*, *12*(8), 3488. Advance online publication. doi:10.3390u12083488

González, C., Marco, E., & Medina, T. (2020). *Informe de iniciativas y herramientas de evaluación online universitaria en el contexto del COVID-19*. Ministerio de Universidades.

Goode, J. (2010). Mind the gap: The digital dimension of college access. *The Journal of Higher Education*, *81*(5), 583–618. doi:10.1080/00221546.2010.11779068

Government Information Systems: A Guide to Effective Use of Information Technology in the Public Sector of Developing Countries. (1995). Retrieved from http://unpan1.un.org/intradoc/groups/public/documents/un/unpan000155.pdf

Grabovska, R. (2006). *Ilgtspējības principa īstenošana skolotāju izglītībā* [Implementation of principle of sustainability in teacher education] [Unpublished doctoral dissertation]. Univeristy of Daugavpils, Latvia.

Graham, C. R., & Robison, R. (2007). Realizing the transformational potential of blended learning: Comparing cases of transforming blends and enhancing blends in higher education. In A. G. Picciano & C. D. Dziuban (Eds.), Blended Learning: Research Perspectives (pp. 83–110). Academic Press.

Grandon, E., Alshare, O., & Kwan, O. (2005). Factors influencing student intention to adopt online classes: A cross-cultural study. *Journal of Computing Sciences in Colleges*, *20*, 46–56.

Gray, L., Thomas, N., & Lewis, L. (2010). Teachers' us of educational technology in U.S. Public Schools: 2009 (NCES 2010-040) National Center for Education Statistic. Institute of Education Sciences, U.S. Development of Education.

Greenlaw, P. S., Herron, L. W., & Rawdon, R. H. (1962). *Business simulation in industrial and university education*. Prentice-Hall.

Gruenwald, N., Ahrens, A., Zaščerinska, J., Melnikova, J., & Andreeva, N. (2018). Socio-Cultural Adaptation of International Students of Master Programme "Information and Electrical Engineering" at Hochschule Wismar. In *Proceedings of the 5th International Scientific Conference on "Modern Economics"*. University of Wismar.

Gruenwald, N., Pfaffenberger, K., Zascerinska, J., & Ahrens, A. (2017). A Study on Digital Teaching Competence of Trainers from South Africa within the PEESA Project. In *Proceedings of Riga Teacher Training and Educational Management Academy's 12th International Young Scientist Conference*, (pp. 116–124). Riga: Riga Teacher Training and Educational Management Academy.

Grundy, S. (1987). *Curriculum: Product or Praxis?* The Falmer Press.

Grundy, S., & Kemmis, S. (1988). Educational Action Research in Australia: The state of the art (an overview). In St. Kemmis & R. McTaggart (Eds.), *The Action Research Planner* (pp. 321–335). Deakin University Press.

Gülbahar, Y., & Madran, R. O. (2009). Communication and Collaboration, Satisfaction, Equity, and Autonomy in Blended Learning Environments: A Case from Turkey. *International Review of Research in Open and Distance Learning*, *10*(2), 1–22.

Gunasekaran, A., & Nath, B. (1997). The role of information technology in business process reengineering. *International Journal of Production Economics*, *50*(2-3), 91–104. doi:10.1016/S0925-5273(97)00035-2

Gunderman, R. B. (2019). *Educating Learners about the Pros and Cons of Telework*. Elsevier Science Inc.

Guragain, N. (2016). *E-learning benefits and applications*. Helsinki University of Applied Sciences Thesis.

Gurbaxani, V., & Whang, S. (1991). The impact of information systems on organizations and markets. *Communications of the ACM*, *34*(1), 59–73. doi:10.1145/99977.99990

Gutiérrez, I. (2014). Perfil del profesor universitario español en torno a las competencias en tecnologías de la información y la comunicación. *Pixel-Bit. Revista de Medios y Educación*, *44*, 51–65.

Güzera, B., & Canera, H. (2014). The past, present and future of blended learning: An in depth analysis of literature. *Procedia: Social and Behavioral Sciences*, *116*, 4596–4603. doi:10.1016/j.sbspro.2014.01.992

Hair, J. F., Jr., Sarstedt, M., Hopkins, L., & Kuppelwieser, V. (2014). Partial least squares structural equation modeling (PLS-SEM) An emerging tool in business research. *European Business Review*, *26*(2), 106–121. doi:10.1108/EBR-10-2013-0128

Hal.inria.fr. (2017). *A Review on Authentication Methods*. Available at: https://hal.inria.fr/hal-00912435/document

Halloluwa, H. K. T. C., Usoof, H., & Hewagamage, K. P. (2014). Stimulating learners' motivation in primary education in Sri Lanka - A literature review. *International Journal of Emerging Technologies in Learning*, *9*(1), 47–52. doi:10.3991/ijet.v9i1.2964

Halloluwa, T., Vyas, D., Usoof, H., & Hewagamage, K. P. (2018). Gamification for development: A case of collaborative learning in Sri Lankan primary schools. *Personal and Ubiquitous Computing*, *22*(2), 391–407. doi:10.100700779-017-1073-6

Hall, T., Connolly, C., Ó Grádaigh, S., Burden, K., Kearney, M., Schuck, S., Bottema, J., Cazemier, G., Hustinx, W., Evens, M., Koenraad, T., Makridou, E., & Kosmas, P. (2020). Education in precarious times: A comparative study across six countries to identify design priorities for mobile learning in a pandemic. *Information and Learning Sciences*, *121*(5/6), 433–442. doi:10.1108/ILS-04-2020-0089

Halverson, L. R., Graham, C. R., Spring, K. J., Drysdale, J. S., Curtis, R., & Henrie, C. R. (2014). A thematic analysis of the most highly cited scholarship in the first decade of blended learning research. *The Internet and Higher Education*, *20*, 20–34. doi:10.1016/j.iheduc.2013.09.004

Han, S., & Abu Bakar, R. (2020). Brunei proceeds to final phase of de-escalation plan on July 27. *The Scoop*. Retrieved from https://thescoop.co/2020/07/23/brunei-proceeds-to-final-phase-of-de-escalation-plan-o n-july-27/

Hargittai, E. (2008). *The digital reproduction of inequality, Social Stratification, a cura di D. Grunsky*. Westview Press.

Harris, J., Mishra, P., & Koehler, M. (2009). Teachers' technological pedagogical content knowledge and learning activity types: Curriculum-based technology integration reframed. *Journal of Research on Technology in Education*, *41*(4), 393–416. doi:10.1080/15391523.2009.10782536

Hayashi, A., Chen, C., Ryan, T., & Wu, J. (2004). The role of social presence and moderating role of computer self efficacy in predicting the continuance usage of e-learning system. *Journal of Information Systems Education*, *15*(2).

Hayes, H. (2010). *Curriculum 21: Essential education for a changing world*. ASCD.

Haythornthwaite, C. (2007). Digital Divide and Elearning. In R. Andrews & C. Haythornthwaite (Eds.), *Handbook of Elearning Research*. Sage.

Heeks, R. (2008). ICT4D 2.0: The next phase of applying ICT for International Development. *Computer*, *41*(6), 26–31. doi:10.1109/MC.2008.192

Heeks, R. (2020). ICT4D 3.0? Part 1—The Components of an Emerging 'digital-for-Development' Paradigm. *The Electronic Journal on Information Systems in Developing Countries*, *1*(1), 1–15. doi:10.1002/j.1681-4835.2016.tb00563.x

Heldt, J. P., Agrawal, A., Loeb, R., Richards, M., Castillo, E. G., & DeBonis, K. (2021). We're not sure we like it but we still want more: Trainee and faculty perceptions of remote learning during the COVID-19 pandemic. *Academic Psychiatry*. Advance online publication. doi:10.100740596-021-01403-4 PMID:33594628

Henseler, J., & Chin, W. W. (2010). A Comparison of Approaches for the Analysis of Interaction Effects Between Latent Variables Using Partial Least Squares Path Modeling. *Structural Equation Modeling*, *17*(1), 82–109. doi:10.1080/10705510903439003

Henseler, J., & Fassott, G. (2010). Testing Moderating Effects in PLS Path Models: An Illustration of Available Procedures. In V. Esposito Vinzi, W. W. Chin, J. Henseler, & H. Wang (Eds.), *Handbook of Partial Least Squares: Concepts, Methods and Applications* (pp. 713–735). Springer Berlin Heidelberg. doi:10.1007/978-3-540-32827-8_31

Hepp, P., & Laval, E. (2003). ICT for rural education: A developing country perspective. *IFIP Advances in Information and Communication Technology*, *113*, 115–125. doi:10.1007/978-0-387-35668-6_12

Hernández, R., Fernández, C., & Baptista, P. (2010). *Metodología de la investigación*. McGraw-Hill.

Herrington, J. (2006). Authentic e-learning in higher education: Design principles for authentic learning environments and tasks. *E-Learn: World Conference on E-Learning in Corporate, Government, Healthcare, and Higher Education*, 3164–3173.

Hershberg, E., Flinn-Palcic, A., & Kambhu, C. (2020). The COVID-19 pandemic and Latin American universities. *Center for Latin America & Latino Studies*. https://www.american.edu/centers/latin-american-latino-studies/upload/la-higher-ed-covid-final.pdf

Hess, F. M., & Leal, D. L. (2001). A shrinking "Digital Divide"? The provision of classroom computers across urban school system. *Social Science Quarterly*, *82*(4), 765–778. doi:10.1111/0038-4941.00058

Hicks, M., Reid, I., & George, R. (2001). Enhancing on-line teaching: Designing responsive learning environments. *The International Journal for Academic Development*, *6*(2), 143–151. doi:10.1080/713769258

Hill, E. J., & Holmes, E. K. (2019). Families and workplaces. In *APA handbook of contemporary family psychology: Applications and broad impact of family psychology* (Vol. 2, pp. 379–395). American Psychological Association. doi:10.1037/0000100-024

Hislop, D. (2005). *Knowledge Management in Organisations*. Oxford University Press.

Hislop, D. (2013). *Knowledge Management in Organisations: a critical introduction*. Oxford University Press.

Hodges, C., Moore, S., Lockee, B., Trust, T., & Bond, A. (2020). The differences between emergency remote teaching and online learning. *Educause Review*. Available at: https://er.educause.edu/article/2020/3/the-difference-between-emergency-remote-teaching-and-online-learning

Hollow, D., & Masperi, P. (2009). An evaluation of the use of ICT within primary education in Malawi. In *Proceedings of the 3rd international conference on Information and Communication Technologies and Development (ICTD 2009)* (pp. 27-34). IEEE. 10.1109/ICTD.2009.5426707

Horton, W. (2001). *Leading e-Learning*. American Society for Training and Development.

Horton, W., & Horton, K. (2003). *E-learning tools and Technologies: A consumer's guide for trainers, teachers, educators, and instructional designers*. Wiley Publishing.

Hou, H. T., Chang, K. E., & Chang, Y. T. (2010). What kinds of knowledge do teachers share on blogs? A quantitative content analysis of teachers' knowledge sharing on blogs. *British Journal of Educational Technology*, *41*(6), 963–967. doi:10.1111/j.1467-8535.2009.01040.x

Howard, L., Remenyi, Z., & Pap, G. (2006). Adaptive Blended Learning Environments. *Proceedings 9th International Conference on Engineering*, 11–16.

Hrastinski, S. (2008). *Asynchronous and Synchronous E-Learning*. Retrieved December 20, 2020, from https://er.educause.edu/articles/2008/11/asynchronous-and-synchronous-elearning

Hrastinski, S. (2008). Asynchronous & synchronous e-learning. *EDUCAUSE Quarterly*, *31*(4), 51–55.

Huang, S. Y., Lee, C., Chiu, A., & Yen, D. C. (2014). *How business process reengineering affects information technology investment and employee performance under different performance measurement*. doi:10.100710796-014-9487-4

Huang, R. H., Liu, D. J., Tlili, A., Yang, J. F., & Wang, H. H. (2020). *Handbook on Facilitating Flexible Learning During Educational Disruption: The Chinese Experience in Maintaining Undisrupted Learning in COVID-19 Outbreak*. Smart Learning Institute of Beijing Normal University.

Hubackova, S. (2015). History and perspectives of elearning. *Procedia: Social and Behavioral Sciences*, *191*, 1187–1190. doi:10.1016/j.sbspro.2015.04.594

Hubbard, M., & Bailey, M. J. (2018). *Mastering Microsoft Teams: End User Guide to Practical Usage, Collaboration, and Governance*. Apress. doi:10.1007/978-1-4842-3670-3

Huda, M., Maseleno, A., Atmotiyoso, P., Ahamad, R., Nor Muhammad, N. H., Jasmi, K. A., Nasrul Hisyam Nor Muhamad, N. H. N., Mustari, M. I., & Basiron, B. (2018). Big Data Emerging Technology: Insights into Innovative Environment for Online Learning Resources. *International Journal of Emerging Technology in Learning*, *13*(1), 23–36. doi:10.3991/ijet.v13i01.6990

Huong, P. T. T. (2018). Applying Blended Learning Method in Teaching English at the University of Da Nang, Vietnam. *The Educational Review, USA*, *3*(1), 16–21.

Hu, P. J., Chau, P. Y. K., Sheng, O. R. L., & Tam, K. Y. (1999). Examining the technology acceptance model using physical acceptance of telemedicine technology. *Journal of Management Information Systems*, *16*(2), 91–112. doi:10.1080/07421222.1999.11518247

Husniyah, A. I. (2019). *Blended Learning in Efl Classrooms With Slow Internet: Insights From Teachers and Students*. https://www.researchgate.net/publication/330400197_BLENDED_LEARNING_IN_EFL_CLASSROOMS_WITH_SLOW_INTERNET_INSIGHTS_FROM_TEACHERS_AND_STUDENTS

Hussain, J. (2018). Three common barriers to success in the flipped classroom model. *Teach Thought*. Retrieved from https://www.teachthought.com/learning/3-common-barriers-to-success-in-a-flipped-classroom-model/

Hutchison, A., & Colwell, J. (2012). Using a wiki to facilitate an online professional learning community for induction and mentoring teachers. *Education and Information Technologies*, *17*(3), 273–289. doi:10.100710639-011-9159-7

Hwang, A., & Francesco, A. M. (2010). *The Influence of Individualism–Collectivism and Power Distance on Use of Feedback Channels and Consequences for Learning* (Vol. 9). Academic Press.

Hwang, G., Chu, H., Lin, Y., & Tsai, C. (2011). A knowledge acquisition approach to developing mindtools for organizing and sharing differentiating knowledge in a ubiquitous learning environment. *Computers & Education*, *57*(1), 1368–1377. doi:10.1016/j.compedu.2010.12.013

Iahad, N., Dafoulas, G. A., Milankovic-Atkinson, M., & Murphy, A. (2004). E-Learning in developing countries: Suggesting a methodology for enabling computer-aided assessment. In *Proceedings of the 4th IEEE International Conference on Advanced Learning Technologies* (pp. 983-987). IEEE. 10.1109/ICALT.2004.1357734

Ibrahim, F., & Ali, D. N. (2021). Evaluating Knowledge Management Practices in Higher Education Institutions (HEIs): Towards KMPro Framework Guidelines. In S. Zyngier (Ed.), *Handbook of Research on Knowledge Management Tools in Higher Education* (pp. 221–245). IGI Global.

Ibrahim, F., & Barr, S. (2009). Reconfiguring IT and the Cultural Dimension in Knowledge Management Practices, International *Journal of Knowledge. Culture and Change Management*, *9*(11), 27–43.

Ibrahim, F., & Reid, V. (2010). Integrated Use of Information Technology and People Involvement for Knowledge Management. *International Journal of Technology, Knowledge and Society*, *6*(2), 163–180. doi:10.18848/1832-3669/CGP/v06i02/56086

Ibrahim, F., & Reid, V. (2010). Unpacking Knowledge Management: Management Fad or Real Business Practice? *Enterprise Risk Management*, *2*(1), 25–38.

Ibrahim, F., & Salleh, N. M. (2019). Embedding Knowledge Management Theory in Learning and Teaching Approach. *International Journal of Learning and Development*, *9*(1), 20–40. doi:10.5296/ijld.v9i1.13786

Ibrahim, F., Susanto, H., Haghi, P. K., & Desi Setiana, D. (2020). Shifting Paradigm of Education Landscape in Time of the COVID-19 Pandemic: Revealing of a Digital Education Management Information System. *Applied Systems Innovation*, *3*(4), 1–21.

IESALC. (2020a). *Coronavirus COVID-19 and Higher Education: Impact and recommendations.* UNESCO. Retrieved from http://www.iesalc.unesco.org/en/2020/03/09/coronavirus-covid-19-and-higher-education-impact-and-recommendations/

IESALC. (2020b). *COVID-19 and higher education: Today and tomorrow. Impact analysis, political responses and recommendations.* UNESCO. Retrieved from http://www.iesalc.unesco.org/en/wp-content/uploads/2020/04/COVID-19-EN-090420-2.pdf

IGN. (2002). *Trevor Chan's Capitalism II.* Retrieved from https://www.ign.com/articles/2002/01/17/trevor-chans-capitalism-ii

Ilag, B. N. (2018). *Introducing Microsoft Teams: Understanding the New Chat-Based Workspace in Office 365.* Apress. doi:10.1007/978-1-4842-3567-6

InfoSec Institute. (2013). *Restricting social media at work.* Retrieved on October 18, 2017 from http://resources.infosecinstitute.com/restricting-social-media-at-work/#gref

Instituto Nacional de Estadística y Geografía. (2020). *Encuesta Nacional sobre la Disponibilidad y Uso de las Tecnologías en los Hogares.* México: INEGI. Retrieved from https://www.inegi.org.mx/programas/dutih/2019/

Instituto Politécnico Nacional (2020b). *Comunicado 53. Registra alrededor de 166 mil visitas virtuales la plataforma de continuidad académica del IPN.* Author.

Instituto Politécnico Nacional. (2020a). *Plan virtual de continuidad académica.* Retrieved from https://elementosdeaprendizaje.ipn.mx/

International Labour Office. (1990). *Economically active population, employment, unemployment and hours of work (household surveys).* Author.

International Organization for Standardization. (n.d.). Retrieved Oct 19, 2017 from https://www.iso.org/about-us.html

Ireland, R. D., Covin, J. G., & Kuratko, D. F. (2009). Conceptualizing corporate entrepreneurship strategy. *Entrepreneurship Theory and Practice*, *33*(1), 19–46. doi:10.1111/j.1540-6520.2008.00279.x

Jackson, C., & Keirstead, C. (2020). *Schools' first and forever responders: Preparing and supporting teachers in the time of COVID-19.* National Comprehensive Center at Westat.

JAPEM. (n.d.). Retrieved from http://www.japem.gov.bn/Themed/english/FAQ/Alternative%20Channels%20to%20Provide%20Contribution%20to%20People%20with%20Special%20Needs.htm

Jerman, B. A., & Arh, T. (2013). *Immersive business simulation games: an innovative pedagogical approach to E-learning and education.* Paper presented at the 30th ascilite Conference, Macquarie University.

Johnson, R., Kemp, E., Kemp, R., & Blakey, P. (2007). The learning computer: Low bandwidth tool that bridges digital divide. *Journal of Educational Technology & Society, 10*(4), 143–155.

Jr, H., Celsi, M., Money, A., Samouel, P., & Page, M. (2015). *The essentials of business research methods* (3rd ed.)., doi:10.4324/9781315716862

Kabir, F.S., & Kadage, A.T. (2017). ICTS and Educational Development: The Utilization of Mobile Phones in Distance Education in Nigeria. *The Turkish Online Journal of Distance Education, 18*(1), 63–76.

Kadre, S. (2011). *Going corporate: A geek's guide*. Retrieved from https://books.google.com.bn/books?id=BR3jx1dUUaM-C&pg=PA161&lpg=PA161&dq=business+process+reengineering+analysis+and+recommendations&source=bl&ots=oud3A13Jqy&sig=Q7GISS-X4J-Hgs8KSDuBrhRghno&hl=en&sa=X&ei=TPPpVObBB8_g8AWW94DIAw&ved=0CDQQ6AEwBDgK#v=onepage&q=business%20process%20reengineering%20analysis%20and%20recommendations&f=false

Kahiigi, E., Ekenberg, L., Hansson, H., Tusubira, F., & Danielson, M. (2008). Exploring the e-Learning State of art. *The Electronic Journal of e-Learning, 6.*

Kankanhalli, A., Teo, H., Tan, B., & Wei, K. (2003). An integrative study of information systems security effectiveness. *International Journal of Information Management, 23*(2), 139–154. doi:10.1016/S0268-4012(02)00105-6

Karim, A., & Hussain, F. (2019). 'When will you start teaching the REAL curriculum?': Challenges and innovations in education for Rohingya Refugees. In P. Nielsen & H. C. Kimaro (Eds.), *Information and Communication Technologies for Development. Strengthening Southern-Driven Cooperation as a Catalyst for ICT4D* (pp. 675–686). Springer. doi:10.1007/978-3-030-18400-1_55

Kauppinen, M., Kainulainen, J., Hökkä, P., & Vähäsantanen, K. (2020). Professional agency and its features in supporting teachers' learning during an in-service education programme. *European Journal of Teacher Education, 43*(3), 384–404. doi:10.1080/02619768.2020.1746264

Kaur, M. (2013). Blended Learning - Its Challenges and Future. *Procedia: Social and Behavioral Sciences, 93*, 612–617. doi:10.1016/j.sbspro.2013.09.248

Kazekami, S. (2020). Mechanisms to improve labor productivity by performing telework. *Telecommunications Policy, 44*(2), 101868. doi:10.1016/j.telpol.2019.101868

Kebritchi, M., Lipschuetz, A., & Santiague, L. (2017). Issues and Challenges for Teaching Successful Online Courses in Higher Education: A Literature Review. *Journal of Educational Technology Systems, 46*(1), 4–29. doi:10.1177/0047239516661713

Keeton, M. (2004). Best online instructional practices: Report of phase I of an ongoing study. *Journal of Asynchronous Learning Networks, 8*(2), 75–100. doi:10.24059/olj.v8i2.1829

Kelly, K., Clark, B., & Vivienne Brown, J. S. (2003). Good practice in the conduct and reporting of survey research. *International Journal for Quality in Health Care, 15*(3), 261–266. doi:10.1093/intqhc/mzg031 PMID:12803354

Kenechukwu, M., Newman, C., Kramer, I. I. D., & Pearson, M. (2009). The changing landscape in higher education. In S. Harper & S. J. Quaye (Eds.), *Student engagement in higher education* (pp. 137–154). Springer Publishing.

KentonW. (2019). Retrieved from https://www.investopedia.com/terms/o/one-tailed-test

Khan, A. U. (2020). *The ASEAN post*. Retrieved from https://theaseanpost.com/article/bruneis-youth-facing-unemployment

Kicheva, M., & Dimitrova, B. T. K. (2021) Distance Education During the 2020 Global Crisis Lockdown. *SHS Web of Conferences, 92.*

Kidwell, J. J., Vander Linde, K. M., & Johnson, S. (2001). Applying corporate knowledge management practices in higher education. In G. Bernbom (Ed.), *Information alchemy: The art and science of knowledge management* (pp. 1–24). Jossey-Bass.

Kim, J. B., & Watson, E. F. (2018). *Flow in business simulation games: Comparison between online and face-to-face MBA*. Paper presented at the 51st Hawaii International Conference on System Sciences, Hilton Waikoloa Village, HI. 10.24251/HICSS.2018.004

Kim, K. J., & Bonk, C. J. (2006). The future of online teaching and learning in higher education: The survey says.... *EDUCAUSE Quarterly*, *29*(4), 22–30.

Kim, K., Bonk, C. J., & Oh, E. (2008). The present and future state of Blended Learning in Workplace Learning Settings in United States. *Performance Improvement*, *47*(8), 5–16. doi:10.1002/pfi.20018

Kim, Y. (2018). The Framework of cloud e-learning system for strengthening ICT competence of teachers in Nicaragua. *International Journal on Advanced Science, Engineering and Information Technology*, *8*(1), 62–67. doi:10.18517/ijaseit.8.1.2700

Kirschner, P., & Paas, F. (2001). Web-enhanced higher education: A Tower of Babel. *Computers in Human Behavior*, *17*(4), 347–354. doi:10.1016/S0747-5632(01)00009-7

Kivunja, C., & Wood, D. (2012). Multigrade pedagogy and practice: Accelerating millennium development goals for sub-saharan Africa. *International Journal of Learning*, *18*(11), 17–32. doi:10.18848/1447-9494/CGP/v18i11/47811

Klees, S. (2012). *The economic crisis and education: key issues*. Retrieved on June 26, 2014 from http://www.educationincrisis.net/blog/item/403-the-economic-crisis-and-education-key-issues

Knowles, M. (1998). *The Adult Learner: The Definitive Classic in Adult Education and Human Resource Development*. Gulf Publishing Company.

Knox, A. B. (1977). *Adult development and learning*. Jossey-Bass.

Kok, A. (2007). Intellectual Capital Management as Part of Knowledge Management Initiatives at Institutions of Higher Learning. *Electronic Journal of Knowledge Management*, *5*(2), 181–192.

Kokkinos, C. M., Antoniadou, N., & Markos, A. (2014). Cyber-bullying: An investigation of the psychological profile of university student participants. *Journal of Applied Developmental Psychology*, *35*(3), 204–214. doi:10.1016/j.appdev.2014.04.001

Koper, R. (2004). Learning technologies: an integrated domain model. In *W. Jochems, J. Van Merrienboer & R. Koper, Integrated eLearning: Implications for Pedagogy, Technology and Organization* (pp. 64–79). Routledge.

Koper, R., & Olivier, B. (2004). Representing the learning design of units of learning. *Journal of Educational Technology & Society*, *7*(3), 97–111.

Kopp, M., Gröblinger, O., & Adams, S. (2019, March 12). *Five common assumptions that prevent digital transformation at higher education institutions*. Academic Press.

Kothari, C. (2004). *Research Methodology: methods & techniques* (Vol. 1). New Age International (P) Ltd.

Kowalski, R. M., & Limber, S. P. (2013). Psychological, Physical, and Academic Correlates of Cyberbullying and Traditional Bullying. *The Journal of Adolescent Health*, *53*(1), S13–S20. Advance online publication. doi:10.1016/j.jadohealth.2012.09.018 PMID:23790195

Kowalski, R., Limber, S., & Agatston, P. (2012). Cyber Bullying: Bullying. In *The Digital Age* (2nd ed., pp. 27–39). John Wiley & Sons.

Kramer, B. J., Klebl, M., & Zobel, A. (2010). Sharing educational knowledge and best practices in edu-sharing. *Proceedings of the 2010 Second International Conference on Mobile, Hybrid and On-Line Learning*, 53-9. 10.1109/eLmL.2010.27

Kriz, W. C. (2017). Historical roots and new fruits of gaming and simulation. *Simulation & Gaming*, *48*(5), 583–587. doi:10.1177/1046878117732845

Kroplijs, A., & Raščevska, M. (2004). *Kvalitatīvās pētniecības metodes sociālajās zinātnēs* [Qualitative research methods in social sciences]. RaKa.

Krueger, R. A., & Casey, M. A. (2000). *Focus Groups: A Practical Guide for Applied Research* (3rd ed.). Sage Publications.

Kurdi, B. (2019, March 26). *PNAS*. Retrieved from Model-free and model-based learning processes in the updating of explicit and implicit evaluations: https://www.pnas.org/content/116/13/6035

Kwahk, K., & Lee, J. (2008). The role of readiness for change in ERP implementation: Theoretical bases and empirical validation. *Information & Management*, *45*(7), 474–481. doi:10.1016/j.im.2008.07.002

Lam, P., Fai Cheng, K., & McNaught, C. (2005). *Asynchronous Online Discussion: Empirical Evidence on Quantity and Quality*. Academic Press.

Lamberigts, R., & Dīpenbroks, J.-V. (2004). Aktīvās mācības kooperatīvā mācību vidē: eksperimenta īstenošana un rezultāti [Active learning in cooperative learning environment: conducting of an experiment and its results]. In *Kooperatīvā mācīšanās* (pp. 106–116). RaKa.

Lansmann, S., Schallenmuller, S., & Rigby, M. (2019). Teams Everywhere - Investigating the Impact of Microsoft Teams on Knowledge Worker. *Proceedings of the Pre-ICIS 2019, 8th International Workshop on The Changing Nature of Work.*

Lapointe, L., & Rivard, S. (2005). A Multilevel Model of Resistance to Information Technology Implementation. *Management Information Systems Quarterly*, *29*(3), 461–491. doi:10.2307/25148692

Latin America. (2020). Retrieved from american.edu

Lawrence. (2019, June). Retrieved from https://www.helpguide.org/articles/relationships-communication/nonverbal-communication.htm

Lee, J., Burnett, G., Vandegrift, M., Baeg, J. H., & Morris, R. (2015). Availability and accessibility in an open access institutional repository: a case study. *Information Research, 20*(1). Retrieved from http://InformationR.net/ir/20-1/paper661.html

Lee, K. (2012). *Augmented Reality in Education and Training*. University of Northern Colorado. doi:10.100711528-012-0559-3

Lee, Y., Chu, P., & Tseng, H. (2009). Exploring the relationships between information technology adoption and business process reengineering. *Journal of Management & Organization*, *15*(2), 170–185. doi:10.5172/jmo.837.15.2.170

Legris, P., Ingham, J., & Collerette, P. (2003). Why do people use information technology? A critical review of the technology acceptance model. *Information & Management*, *40*(3), 191–204. doi:10.1016/S0378-7206(01)00143-4

Leszczyński, P., Charuta, A., Łaziuk, B., Gałązkowski, R., Wejnarski, A., Roszak, M., & Kołodziejczak, B. (2018). Multimedia and interactivity in distance learning of resuscitation guidelines: A randomised controlled trial. *Interactive Learning Environments*, *26*(2), 151–162. doi:10.1080/10494820.2017.1337035

Leu, F. Y., Chiang, P. J., Susanto, H., Hung, R. T., & Huang, H. L. (2020). Mobile Physiological Sensor Cloud System for Long-term Care. *Internet of Things*.

Leu, F. Y., Ko, C. Y., Lin, Y. C., Susanto, H., & Yu, H. C. (2017). Fall Detection and Motion Classification by Using Decision Tree on Mobile Phone. In Smart Sensors Networks (pp. 205-237). Academic Press.

Leu, F.Y., Liu, C.Y., Liu, J.C., Jiang, F.C., & Susanto, H. (2015). S-PMIPv6: An intra-LMA model for IPv6 mobility. *J. Netw. Comput. Appl., 58*, 180–191.

Leu, F. Y., Susanto, H., Tsai, K. L., & Ko, C. Y. (2020). A channel assignment scheme for MIMO on concentric-hexagon-based multi-channel wireless networks. *International Journal of Ad Hoc and Ubiquitous Computing, 35*(4), 205–221. doi:10.1504/IJAHUC.2020.111462

Li, Y., Tarafdar, M., & Subba Rao, S. (2012). *Collaborative knowledge management practices: Theoretical development and empirical analysis*. doi:10.1108/01443571211223077

Liao, H. L., & Lu, H. P. (2008). Richness Versus Parsimony Antecedents of Technology Adoption Model for E-Learning Websites. In F. Li, J. Zhao, T. K. Shih, R. Lau, Q. Li, D. McLeod (Eds.), Advances in Web Based Learning - ICWL 2008. ICWL 2008. Lecture Notes in Computer Science, (vol. 5145). Berlin: Springer.

Lieberman, M. (2020). Coronavirus prompting e-learning strategies. *Education Week, 39*(24), 11.

Li, F. W., Lau, R. W., & Dharmendran, P. (2009). A three-tier pro ling framework for adaptive e-learning. *Proceedings of the 8th International Conference on Advances in Web Based Learning*, 235-244.

Light, G., Cox, R., & Calkins, S. (2009). *Learning and Teaching in Higher Education* (2nd ed.). Sage.

Lindfors, P. L., Kaltiala-Heino, R., & Rimpelä, A. H. (2012). Cyberbullying among Finnish adolescents – a population-based study. *BMC Public Health, 12*(1), 1027. Advance online publication. doi:10.1186/1471-2458-12-1027 PMID:23176715

Lin, W. T., & Shao, B. B. M. (2000). The relationship between user participation and system success: A simultaneous contingency approach. *Information & Management, 37*(6), 283–295. doi:10.1016/S0378-7206(99)00055-5

Li, Q. (2010). Cyberbullying in High Schools: A Study of Students Behaviors and Beliefs about This New Phenomenon. *Journal of Aggression, Maltreatment & Trauma, 19*(4), 372–392. doi:10.1080/10926771003788979

Li, S., Yamaguchi, S., Sukhbaatar, J., & Takada, J.-I. (2019). The influence of teachers' professional development activities on the factors promoting ICT integration in Primary Schools in Mongolia. *Education Sciences, 9*(2), 78. doi:10.3390/educsci9020078

Li, S., Yamaguchi, S., & Takada, J. I. (2018). The influence of interactive learning materials on self-regulated learning and learning satisfaction of primary school teachers in Mongolia. *Sustainability (Switzerland), 10*(4), 1–19. doi:10.3390u10041093

Liu, H., Macintyre, R., & Ferguson, R. (2012). Exploring qualitative analytics for e-mentoring relationships building in an online social learning environment. In *Proceedings of the 2nd International Conference on Learning Analytics and Knowledge* (pp. 179-183). ACM. 10.1145/2330601.2330646

Liu, J. C., Leu, F. Y., Lin, G. L., & Susanto, H. (2018). An MFCC-based text-independent speaker identification system for access control. *Concurr. Comput. Pract. Exp., 30*(2), e4255. doi:10.1002/cpe.4255

Liu, Y., & Wang, H. (2009). A comparative study on e-learning technologies and products: From the East to the West. *Systems Research and Behavioral Science, 26*(2), 191–209. doi:10.1002res.959

Li, Y., Nishimura, N., Yagami, H., & Park, H.-S. (2021). An Empirical Study on Online Learners' Continuance Intentions in China. *Sustainability*, *13*(2), 889. doi:10.3390u13020889

Liyanagunawardena, T. R., Adams, A. A., Rassool, N., & Williams, S. A. (2014). Developing government policies for distance education: Lessons learnt from two Sri Lankan case studies. *International Review of Education*, *60*(6), 821–839. doi:10.100711159-014-9442-0

Llorens, F. (2020b). *Transformación digital versus digitalización*. Universidad. Retrieved from https://www.universidadsi.es/transformacion-digital-versus-digitalizacion/

Lobo, R. A. (2014). *Augmented Reality for educative and collaborative environments*. Bogoto: University Pompeu Fabra.

Lobontiu, G., & Big, R. (2006). Implementing Business Process Reengineering. Scientific Bulletin Series C: Fascicle Mechanics, Tribology. *Machine Manufacturing Technology*, *20*, 231.

Lohmann, R. (2019). Taking a Glimpse Into the Future by Playing? *Simulation & Gaming*, *50*(3), 377–392. doi:10.1177/1046878119848133

Lopez, L. L. (2016, March 24). *L3*. Retrieved from Virtual Reality And Augmented Reality In Education: https://elearningindustry.com/virtual-reality-augmented-reality-education

López, M., & Andrés, S. (2020). Trayectorias escolares en la educación superior ante la pandemia ¿continuar, interrumpir o desistir? In H. Casanova (Coord.), Educación y pandemia. Una visión académica (pp. 66-74). UNAM.

Love, N., & Fry, N. (2006). Accounting Students' Perceptions of a Virtual Learning Environment: Springboard or Safety Net? *Accounting Education*, *15*(2), 151–166. doi:10.1080/06939280600609201

Luaran, J. E., Yusof, N. Y. M., Jain, J., Alias, R., & Hussin, A. A. (2015). *Blended learning: Examining student satisfaction, willingness, and stress in learning English*. Academic Press.

Luka, I., Ludborza, S., & Maslo, I. (2009). *Effectiveness of the use of more than two languages and quality assurance in European interuniversity master studies*. Paper presented at the European Conference on Educational Research, University of Vienna. https://www.eera-ecer.de/ecer-programmes/conference/2/contribution/3411/

Luthra, P., & Mackenzie, S. (2020). *4 ways COVID-19 could change how we educate future generations*. Retrieved from https://www.weforum.org/agenda/2020/03/4-ways-covid-19-education-future-generations/

Lytras, M. D., & Pouloudi, A. (2006). Towards the development of a novel taxonomy of knowledge management systems from a learning perspective: An integrated approach to learning and knowledge infrastructures. *Journal of Knowledge Management*, *10*(6), 64–80. doi:10.1108/13673270610709224

Lytras, M. D., Pouloudi, A., & Poulymenakou, G. (2002). A framework for technology convergence in learning and working. *Journal of Educational Technology & Society*, *5*(2), 99–106.

Machumu, H., & Zhu, C. (2019). Students' conceptions of learning approaches and their engagement in blended learning environments. *International Journal of Technology Enhanced Learning*, *11*(3), 304–322. doi:10.1504/IJTEL.2019.100490

Mahesh, V., & Woll, C. (2007). Blended learning in high tech manufacturing: A case study of cost benefits and production efficiency. *Journal of Asynchronous Learning Networks*, *11*(2), 43–60.

Malhotra, N. K. (n.d.). *Marketing Research: An applied orientation, Sixt Edition*. Pearson Education Inc.

Malhotra, N. K., & Birks, D. F. (2003). *Marketing Research; an applied approach* (2nd European Edition). Pearson Education.

Mansell, R. (2017). Inequality and digitally mediated communication: divides, contradictions and consequences. *Javnost- the Public*, *24*(2), 146-161.

Manwaring, K. C., Larsen, R., Graham, C. R., Henrie, C. R., & Halverson, L. R. (2017). Investigating student engagement in blended learning settings using experience sampling and structural equation modeling. *The Internet and Higher Education*, *35*, 21–33. doi:10.1016/j.iheduc.2017.06.002

Marks, R. B., Sibley, S. D., & Arbaugh, J. B. (2005). A Structural Equation Model of Predictors for Effective Online Learning. *Journal of Management Education*, *29*(4), 531–563. doi:10.1177/1052562904271199

Martin, M., & Furiv, U. (2020). *COVID-19 shows the need to make learning more flexible.* University World News. Retrieved from https://www.universityworldnews.com/post.php?story=20200324115802272

Martin, F., & Whitmer, J. C. (2016). Applying learning analytics to investigate timed release in online learning. *Technology. Knowledge and Learning*, *21*(1), 59–74. doi:10.100710758-015-9261-9

Martin, L., & Tapp, D. (2019). Teaching with Teams: An introduction to teaching an undergraduate law module using Microsoft Teams. *Innovative Practice in Higher Education*, *3*(3), 58–66.

Masie, E. (2001). *E-Learning: If we Build It, Will They Come?* American Society for Training and Development.

Maslo, E. (2007). Transformative Learning Space for Life-Long Foreign Languages Learning. In D. Rumpite, K. Makinen, & T. S. Piskozub (Eds.), *International Nordic-Baltic Region Conference of FIPLV Innovations in Language Teaching and Learning in the Multicultural Context*. Rīga: SIA "Izglītības soļi".

Maslo, I. (2006). *No zināšanām uz kompetentu darbību* [From knowledge to Competent Performance]. Latvijas Universitātes Akadēmiskais apgāds.

Mason, R., & Rennie, F. (2006). *Elearning: The Key Concepts*. Routledge. doi:10.4324/9780203099483

Mawere, T., & Sai, K. O. S. (2018). An investigation on e-resource utilisation among university students in a developing country: A case of Great Zimbabwe University. *South African Journal of Information Management*, *20*(01), 1–7. doi:10.4102ajim.v20i1.860

Mayring, P. (2000). Qualitative Content Analysis. *Forum Qualitative Social Research*, *1*(2), 20.

Mayring, P. (2004). Qualitative Content Analysis. In U. Flick, E. Von Kardoff, & I. Steinke (Eds.), *A Companion to Qualitative Research* (pp. 266–269). SAGE.

Mazey, S., & Richardson, J. (2020). Lesson-Drawing from New Zealand and Covid-19: The need for anticipatory policy making. *The Political Quarterly*, *91*(3), 561–570. doi:10.1111/1467-923X.12893 PMID:32836413

Mazzola, C. (2019). *Microsoft Teams as Digital Community of Practice in Higher Education?* Retrieved from: https://www.researchgate.net/publi-cation/333451072

McBrien, J. L., Cheng, R., & Jones, P. (2009). *Virtual spaces: Employing a synchronous online classroom to facilitate student engagement in online learning*. doi:10.19173/irrodl.v10i3.605

McCallum, S., Schultz, J., Sellke, K., & Spartz, J. (2015). An Examination of the Flipped Classroom Approach on College Student Academic Involvement. *International Journal on Teaching and Learning in Higher Education*, *27*(1), 42–55. https://www.isetl.org/ijtlhe/pdf/IJTLHE1880.pdf

McElroy, M. (2003). *The New Knowledge Management: Complexity, Learning, and Sustainable Innovation*. Butterworth-Heinemann.

McGlynn-Stewart, M., Brathwaite, L., Hobman, L., Maguire, N., Mogyorodi, E., & Park, Y. U. (2017). Inclusive Teaching with Digital Technology: Supporting Literacy Learning in Play-Based Kindergartens. LEARNing Landscapes, 11(1), 199-216.

McLaughlin, M. W., & Talbert, J. (2006). *Building school-based teacher learning communities: Professional strategies to improve student achievement*. Teachers College Press.

McLoughlin, C., Brady, J., Lee, M. J., & Russell, R. (2007). *Peer-to-peer: An e-mentoring approach to developing community, mutual engagement and professional identity for pre-service teachers*. Australian Association for Research in Education (AARE) Conference, Fremantle, Australia.

Mesquita, A., & Silva, P. (2020). Are we ready for the job market?: The role of business simulation in the preparation of youngsters. In J.-É. Pelet (Ed.), *Handbook of Research on User Experience in Web 2.0 Technologies and Its Impact on Universities and Businesses* (pp. 19–36). IGI Global.

Mevarech, Z., & Bracha, K. (2017). *Matemáticas críticas para las sociedades innovadoras. El papel de las pedagogías metacognitivas*. OECD – IPN. doi:10.1787/9789264273078-es

Meza-Cordero, J. A. (2017). Learn to Play and Play to Learn: Evaluation of the One Laptop per Child Program in Costa Rica. *Journal of International Development*, *29*(1), 3–31. doi:10.1002/jid.3267

Microsoft S. Q. L. Server. (n.d.). *TechTarget*. Retrieved Oct 19, 2017 from https://searchsqlserver.techtarget.com/definition/SQL-Server

Miller, D. R. (2015). *The University of Arizona*. Retrieved from Implementing Augmented Reality in the Classroom: https://journals.uair.arizona.edu/index.php/itet/article/view/18601/18526

Mills, G. E. (2011). *Action research: a guide for the teacher researcher* (4th ed.). Pearson/Allyn & Bacon.

Ministry of Education. (2018). *Brunei Darussalam - Special Education Unit*. Retrieved from http://www.moe.gov.bn

Ministry of Education. (2021). *Ministry of Education, Brunei Darussalam*. Retrieved February 17, 2021, from https://www.moe.gov.bn/SitePages/News.aspx

Ministry of Health. (2020). *The Current Situation of the COVID-19 Infection in Brunei Darussalam* [Press Release]. Retrieved from http://www.moh.gov.bn/SitePages/pressreleaseCOVID-19.aspx

Ministry of Religious Affairs. (2015). Retrieved from http://www.mora.gov.bn/Lists/Titah/NewDisplayItem.aspx?ID=176

Mitchell, D. (2014). *What really works in special and inclusive education: Using evidence-based teaching strategies* (2nd ed.). Routledge. doi:10.4324/9780203105313

Mitchell, R. C., Marcella, R., & Baxter, G. (1999). Corporate information security management. *New Library World*, *100*(5), 213–227. doi:10.1108/03074809910285888

Mitra, S., & Chaya, A. (1996). Analyzing Cost-Effectiveness of Organizations: The Impact of Information Technology Spending. *Journal of Management Information Systems*, *13*(2), 29–57. doi:10.1080/07421222.1996.11518122

Mlay, S. V., Zlotnikov, I., & Watundu, S. (2013). A quantitative analysis of business process engineering and organizational resistance: The case of Uganda. *The African Journal of Information Systems*, *5*(1). http://digitalcommons.kennesaw.edu/cgi/viewcontent.cgi?article=1116&context=ajis

Moe, M., & Rajendran, V. (2020). Dawn of the age of digital learning: An acceleration of trends that have building for year. *GSV Ventures*. https://medium.com/gsv-ventures/dawn-of-the-age-of-digital-learning-4c4e38784226

Mohamedbhai, G. (2020). *COVID-19: What consequences for higher education? University World News*. Africa Edition. Retrieved from https://www.universityworldnews.com/post.php?story=20200407064850279

Mohapatra, S., & Roy, R. (2009). Impact of ICT on primary education. *World Academy of Science, Engineering and Technology*, *38*, 1316–1324.

Molbæk, M. (2017). Inclusive teaching strategies – dimensions and agendas. *International Journal of Inclusive Education*, *22*(3), 1–14. doi:10.1080/13603116.2017.1414578

Monks, C. P., Mahdavi, J., & Rix, K. (2016). The emergence of cyberbullying in childhood: Parent and teacher perspectives. *Psicologia dell'Educazione*, *22*(1), 39–48. doi:10.1016/j.pse.2016.02.002

Moore, M. G. (1983). On a theory of independent study. In D. Sewart, D. Keegan, & B. Holmberg (Eds.), *Distance education: International perspectives* (pp. 68–94). Croom Helm, St. Martin's Press.

Moore, M. G., & Diehl, W. (2019). *Handbook of Distance Education*. Routledge.

Moore, M. G., & Kearsley, G. (2012). *Distance education: A systems view of online learning* (3rd ed.). Wadsworth Cengage Learning.

Morris, M. G., & Venkatesh, V. (2010). Job characteristics and job satisfaction: Understanding the role of enterprise resource planning system implementation. *Management Information Systems Quarterly*, *34*(1), 162. doi:10.2307/20721418

Mozelius, P. (2014). Education for all by ICT4D hubs: A Sri Lankan case study. In *Proceedings of the European Conference on e-Learning (ECEL 2014)* (pp. 354-361). Academic Conferences and Publishing International Limited.

Mpungose, C. B. (2020). Emergent transition from face- to-face to online learning in a South African University in the context of the Coronavirus pandemic. *Humanties and Social Sciences Communications*, *7*(1), 113. doi:10.105741599-020-00603-x

Mridha, M., Nihlen, G., Erlandsson, B.-E., Khan, A. A., Islam, M. S., Sultana, N., Reza, S., & Srinivas, M. B. (2013). E-learning for empowering the rural people in Bangladesh opportunities and challenges. In *Proceedings of the 2nd International Conference on E-Learning and E-Technologies in Education (ICEEE)* (pp. 323-328). 10.1109/ICeLeTE.2013.6644397

Mulyani, M. A., Razzaq, A., Ridho, S. L. Z., & Anshari, M. (2019). Smartphone and Mobile Learning to Support Experiential Learning. *2019 International Conference on Electrical Engineering and Computer Science (ICECOS)*, 6–9. 10.1109/ICECOS47637.2019.8984501

Murillo, J. & Duk, C. (2020). El Covid-19 y las Brechas Educativas. *Revista latinoamericana de educación inclusiva, 14*(1), 11-13. doi:10.4067/S0718-73782020000100011

N, A. (2019). Retrieved from http://nda.ie/Resources/Accessibility-toolkit/Provide-disability-equality-training-to-staff/

Nadikattu, R. R. (2020). *Information Technologies: Rebooting the World Activities during COVID-19* (*SSRN* Scholarly Paper No. ID 3622733). Rochester, NY: Social Science Research Network. doi:10.2139srn.3622733

NAEDS. (n.d.). Retrieved from https://www.neads.ca/en/about/projects/inclusion/guide/pwd_01.php

Nawaz, M. N., & Gomez, A. M. (2014). Review of Knowledge Management in Higher Education Institutions. *European Journal of Business and Management*, *6*(7), 71–79.

Nazarenko, A. L. (2015). Blended learning vs traditional learning: What works?(a case study research). *Procedia: Social and Behavioral Sciences*, *200*, 77–82. doi:10.1016/j.sbspro.2015.08.018

Newell, S., Robertson, M., Scarborough, H., & Swan, J. (2002). *Managing Knowledge Work*. Palgrave Macmillan.

NewGenApps. (2017, November 23). *newgenapps*. Retrieved from Know the Augmented Reality Technology: https://www.newgenapps.com/blog/augmented-reality-technology-how-ar-works

Ng, E., & Lai, Y. (2012). An exploratory study on using wiki to foster student teachers' learner-centered learning and self and peer assessment. *Journal of Information Technology Education: Innovations in Practices*, *11*, 71–84. https://eric.ed.gov/?id=EJ971761

Nielsen, N. J. (2018). *Community college professors' engagement and perceptions of professional development in remote environments*. ProQuest Dissertations Publishing.

Ņikiforovs, O. (1994). *Lomu mijiedarbības sistēma „Skolotājs-skolēns" ietekme uz skolēnu tuvākās attīstības zonas kognitīvajiem komponentiem* [Impact of role "teacher-student" in the interaction system on pupil proximal zone of development's cognitive components] [Unpublished doctoral dissertation]. Rīgā, Latvia: University of Latvia.

Ning, A., & Corcoran, B. (2020). How China schools are getting through COVID-19. *Ed Surge Global Education*. Retrieved from https://www.edsurge.com/news/2020-04-20-how-china-s-schools-are-getting-through-covid-19

Ningsih, S. K., & Mulyono, H. (2019). Digital assessment resources in primary and secondary school classrooms. Teachers' Use and Perceptions. IJIM, 13(8).

Niyigena, J.-P., Jiang, Q., Hasan, A. S. M. T., Ziou, D., Chen, H., & Wang, P. (2018). ICT Usage and Attitudes among EAC Undergraduate Students - A Case Study. *IEEE Access: Practical Innovations, Open Solutions*, *6*, 42661–42674. doi:10.1109/ACCESS.2018.2854925

Njenga, J. K. (2018). Digital literacy: The quest of an inclusive definition. *Reading & Writing (Cape Town, South Africa)*, *9*(1), 1–7. doi:10.4102/rw.v9i1.183

Nonaka, I., & Takeuchi, H. (1995). *The Knowledge Creating Company: How Japanese Companies Create the Dynamics of Innovation*. Oxford University Press.

Noor-Ul-Amin. (2013). *An effective use of ICT for education and learning by drawing on worldwide knowledge, research and experience: ICT as a change agent for education (A Literature review)*. Retrieved December 21, 2020, from https://www.researchgate.net/publication/312197085_An_effective_use_of_ICT_for_education_and_learning_by_drawing_on_worldwide_knowledge_research_and_experience_ICT_as_a_change_agent_for_education_A_Literature_review

Norris, P. (2001). *Digital Divide: civic engagement, information poverty, and the internet worldwide*. Cambridge University Press. doi:10.1017/CBO9781139164887

Odhaib, M. F. (2018). Does E-Learning Give a Better Result than Traditional Learning? *International Journal of Computer Science and Mobile Computing*, *7*(9), 29–36.

OECD. (2019). *Economic Outlook for Southeast Asia, China and India 2019 – Update: Responding to Environmental Hazards in Cities*. OECD Publishing.

OECD. (2020). *Teachers' training and use of information and communications technology in the face of the COVID-19 crisis. Teaching in Focus, No. 35*. OECD Publishing. doi:10.1787/696e0661-

OECD. (2020a). *A Helping Hand: Education Responding to the Coronavirus Pandemic*. Retrieved from https://oecdedutoday.com/education-responding-coronavirus-pandemic/

OECD. (2020b). *Education Disrupted - Education Rebuilt: Some Insights from PISA on the Availability and Use of Digital tools for Learning*. Retrieved from https://oecdedutoday.com/coronavirus-education-digital-tools-for-learning/

Ogembo, J. G., Ngugi, B., & Pelowski, M. (2012). Computerizing primary schools in rural kenya: Outstanding challenges and possible solutions. *The Electronic Journal on Information Systems in Developing Countries*, *52*(1), 52. doi:10.1002/j.1681-4835.2012.tb00371.x

Okoli, C., & Pawlovski, S. (2004). The Delphi Method as a Research Tool: An example, design considerations and applications. *Information & Management*, *42*(1), 15–29. doi:10.1016/j.im.2003.11.002

Omerzel, D. G., Biloslavo, R., & Trnavcevic, A. (2011). Knowledge management and organisational culture in higher education institutions. *Journal for East European Management Studies*, *16*(2), 111–139. doi:10.5771/0949-6181-2011-2-111

Organisation for Economic Co-operation and Development (OECD). (2013). *Education Indicators in Focus*. The Organisation for Economic Co-operation and Development (OECD) Publishing. https://www.oecd.org/education/skills-beyond-school/educationindicatorsinfocus.htm

Osberg, D. (2008) *Education, Emergence and the Idea of "Non- Normative Normativity"*. The European Conference of Educational Research, Gothenburg, Sweden. https://www.eera-ecer.de/ecer-programmes/conference/1/contribution/509/

Owen, H. (2014). Putting the PLE into PLD: Virtual Professional Learning and Development. *Journal of Educators Online*, *11*(2). Advance online publication. doi:10.9743/JEO.2014.2.1

Owens, E., & Hersholt, W. (1996). Differences among urban, suburban, and rural schools on technology access and use in Eighth- Grade mathematics classrooms. *Journal of Educational Technology Systems*, *24*(1), 83–92. doi:10.2190/PAP0-HJTM-95JU-RE2W

Ożadowicz, A. (2020). Modified Blended Learning in Engineering Higher Education during the COVID-19 Lockdown—Building Automation Courses Case Study. *Education Sciences*, *10*(10), 292. doi:10.3390/educsci10100292

Paechter, M., & Maier, B. (2010). Online or face-to-face? Students' experiences and preferences in e-learning. *The Internet and Higher Education*, *13*(4), 292–297. doi:10.1016/j.iheduc.2010.09.004

Palmunen, L.-M., Lainema, T., & Pelto, E. (2021). Towards a manager's mental model: Conceptual change through business simulation. *International Journal of Management Education*, *19*(2), 100460. doi:10.1016/j.ijme.2021.100460

Parkes, M., Stein, S., & Reading, C. (2014). Student preparedness for university e-learning environments. *The Internet Higher education*, *25*, 1–10. doi:10.1016/j.iheduc.2014.10.002

Parlamento Europeo. (2006). Raccomandazione del Parlamento Europeo e del Consiglio del 18 dicembre 2006 relativa a competenze chiave per l'apprendimento permanente. *Gazzetta Ufficiale dell'Unione Europea.*

Partlow, K. M., & Gibbs, W. J. (2003). Indicators of constructivist principles in internet-based courses. *Journal of Computing in Higher Education*, *14*(2), 68–97. doi:10.1007/BF02940939

Patton. (1990). *Qualitative evaluation and research methods* (2nd ed.). Academic Press.

Patton, M. Q. (2014). *Qualitative Research & Evaluation Methods. Integrating Theory and Practice* (4th ed.). Sage.

Pavlis-Korres, M. (2017). The Positive Effect of Evaluation on Improving E-learning Courses Addressed to Adults: A Case Study on the Evolution of the GSLLLY Courses in Greece over a Decade. *Journal of Education and Training Studies*, *5*(1), 1-11. doi:10.11114/jets.v5i1.1940

Pavlis-Korres, M., Karalis, T., Leftheriotou, P., & Garcia Barriocanal, E. (2009). Integrating adults' characteristics and the requirements for their effective learning in an e-learning environment. In M. D. Lytras, P. Ordonez de Pablos, E. Damiani, D. Avison, A. Naeve, & D. G. Horner (Eds.), *Best practices for the knowledge society. Knowledge, learning, development and technology for all. WSKS 2009* (pp. 570–584). Springer. doi:10.1007/978-3-642-04757-2_61

Pavlis-Korres, M., & Leftheriotou, P. (2016). Building interaction in adults' online courses: A case study on training e-educators of adults. In L. Kyei-Blankson, J. Blankson, E. Ntuli, & C. Agyeman (Eds.), *Handbook of research on strategic management of interaction, presence and participation in online courses* (pp. 185–215). IGI Global. doi:10.4018/978-1-4666-9582-5.ch008

Pekrun, R., & Linnenbrink-Garcia, L. (2012). Academic Emotions and Student Engagement. In S. L. Christenson, A. L. Reschly, & C. Wylie (Eds.), *Handbook of Research on Student Engagement* (pp. 259–282). Springer US. doi:10.1007/978-1-4614-2018-7_12

Pérez, I. (2017). Creación de recursos educativos digitales: Reflexiones sobre Innovación Educativa con TIC. *The International Journal of Social Education, 6*(2), 244–268. doi:10.17583/rise.2017.2544

Perraton, H. (1988). A theory for distance education. In D. Sewart, D. Keegan, & B. Holmberg (Eds.), *Distance education: International perspectives* (pp. 34–45). Routledge Press.

Perraton, H. (Ed.). (1993). *Distance education for teacher training*. Routledge Press. doi:10.4324/9780203304075

Persatuan KACA Brunei. (n.d.). Retrieved from http://kacabrunei.blogspot.com/

Petillion, R. J., & McNeil, W. S. (2020). Student experiences of emergency remote teaching: Impacts of instructor practice on student learning, engagement, and well-being. *Journal of Chemical Education, 97*(9), 2486–2493. doi:10.1021/acs.jchemed.0c00733

Phillips, D. (2006). Comparative Education: Method. *Research in Comparative and International Education, 1*(4), 304–319. doi:10.2304/rcie.2006.1.4.304

Picciano, A. G. (2009). Blending with purpose: The multimodal model. *Journal of Asynchronous Learning Networks, 13*(1), 7–18.

Picciano, A. G. (2016). Research in Online and Blended Learning: New Challenge and New Opportunity. In C. Dziuban, A. G. Picciano, C. R. Graham, & P. D. Moskal (Eds.), *Conducting research in online and blended learning environments: New pedagogical frontiers*. Routledge, Taylor & Francis Group.

Pilon, M. (2015). Monopoly's inventor: The progressive who didn't pass 'go'. *The New York Times*. Retrieved from https://www.nytimes.com/2015/02/15/business/behind-monopoly-an-inventor-who-didnt-pass-go.html

Porter, W. W., Graham, C. R., Bodily, R. G., & Sandberg, D. S. (2016). Internet and Higher Education A qualitative analysis of institutional drivers and barriers to blended learning adoption in higher education. *The Internet and Higher Education, 28*, 17–27. doi:10.1016/j.iheduc.2015.08.003

Porter, W. W., Graham, C. R., Spring, K. A., & Welch, K. R. (2014). Blended learning in higher education: Institutional adoption and implementation. *Computers & Education, 75*, 185–195. doi:10.1016/j.compedu.2014.02.011

Portillo, J., Garay, U., Tejada, E., & Bilbao, N. (2020). Self-perception of the digital competences of educators during the Covid-19 pandemic: a cross- analysis of different educational stages. *Sustainability, 12*, 1-128.

Portillo, J., Garay, U., Tejada, E., & Bilbao, N. (2020). Self-Perception of the digital competence of educators during the COVID-19 pandemic: A cross-analysis of different educational stages. *Sustainability. (Basel, Switzerland), 12*(10128), 10128. doi:10.20944/preprints202011.0426.v1

Potter, C., & Naidoo, G. (2009). Use of low-end ICT's as a platform for teacher development: An evaluative case study of an interactive radio programme in South African primary schools. In *Proceedings of the 3rd International Multi-Conference on Society, Cybernetics and Informatics* (*vol. 1*, pp. 58-63). Academic Press.

Prahalad, C. K. (2004). *The Fortune at the Bottom of the Pyramid. Eradicating Poverty through Profits*. Wharton School Publishing.

Prensky, M. (2001). Digital Natives, Digital Immigrants Part 1. *On the Horizon*, *9*(5), 1–6. doi:10.1108/10748120110424816

Prince Machado, M. S., Tenorio Sepúlveda, G. C., & Ramirez Montoya, M. S. (2016). Educational innovation and digital competencies: The case of OER in a private Venezuelan university. *International Journal of Educational Technology in Higher Education*, *13*(1), 1–10. doi:10.118641239-016-0006-1

Probst, G., Raub, S., & Romhardt, K. (2000). *Managing Knowledge: Building Blocks for Success*. John Wiley & Sons.

Program Ace. (2020, February 7). *Program Ace*. Retrieved from Augmented Reality in Education: The Future is Already Here: https://program-ace.com/blog/augmented-reality-in-education/

Pruet, P., Ang, C. S., & Farzin, D. (2016). Understanding tablet computer usage among primary school students in underdeveloped areas: Students' technology experience, learning styles and attitudes. *Computers in Human Behavior*, *55*, 1131–1144. doi:10.1016/j.chb.2014.09.063

Psarras, J. (2006). Education and training in the knowledge-based economy. *VINE: The Journal of Information and Knowledge Information Systems*, *36*(1), 85-96.

Purnawarman, P., Susilawati, S., & Sundayana, W. (2016). The use of Edmodo in teaching writing in a blended learning setting. Indonesian Journal of Applied Linguistics. doi:10.17509/ijal.v5i2.1348

Pusat Ehsan Al-Ameerah Al-Hajjah Maryam. (n.d.). Retrieved from https://www.pusatehsan.org.bn/

Putterman, L. (2013). Institutions, social capability, and economic growth. *Economic Systems*, *37*(3), 345–353. doi:10.1016/j.ecosys.2012.12.002

Quality Matters. (2020). *Why QM*. Retrieved from https://www.qualitymatters.org/why-quality-matters/impact

Quirós, E. (2009). Recursos didácticos digitales: Medios innovadores para el trabajo colaborativo en línea. *Revista Electrónica Educare*, *13*(2), 47–62. doi:10.15359/ree.13-2.4

Rai, L. (2018). Offline sport model for low bandwidth users to survive in MOOCs. *International Journal of Emerging Technologies in Learning*, *13*(10), 270–277. doi:10.3991/ijet.v13i10.8595

Ramirez, R., Melville, N., & Lawler, E. (2010). Information technology infrastructure, organizational process redesign, and business value: An empirical analysis. *Decision Support Systems*, *49*(4), 417–429. doi:10.1016/j.dss.2010.05.003

Ramsden, P. (2003). *Learning to Teach in Higher Education* (2nd ed.). Routledge Flamer., doi:10.4324/9780203507711

Rasidah. (2018, December 4). *The Scoop*. Retrieved from https://thescoop.co/2018/12/04/smarter-brunei-launches-employment-programme-new-bistro-cafe/

Rasidah. (2019). Retrieved from https://thescoop.co/2019/01/09/moe-wants-to-introduce-work-quotas-for-individuals-with-disabilities/

Razzaq, A., Samiha, Y. T., & Anshari, M. (2018). Smartphone habits and behaviors in supporting students self-efficacy. *International Journal of Emerging Technologies in Learning*, *13*(02), 94–109. doi:10.3991/ijet.v13i02.7685

Reddy, P., Sharma, B., & Chaudhary, K. (2020). Digital literacy: A review of literature. *International Journal of Technoethics*, *11*(2), 65–94. doi:10.4018/IJT.20200701.oa1

Reimers, F. M., & Schleicher, A. (2020). *A framework to guide an education response to the COVID-19 Pandemic of 2020*. The Harvard Graduate School of Education, OECD.

Renshaw, J. R., & Heuston, A. (1957). *The game Monopologs*. US Air Force Project Rand Retrieved from https://www.rand.org/content/dam/rand/pubs/research_memoranda/2007/RM1917-1.pdf

Repetto, M., & Trentin, G. (2011). *Faculty training for web enhanced learning*. Nova Science, Incorporated.

Ribeiro, R. (2020). *How University Faculty Embraced the Remote Learning Shift*. Retrieved December 25, 2020, from Technology Solutions That Drive Education website: https://edtechmagazine.com/higher/article/2020/04/how-university-faculty-embraced-remote-learning-shift

Rieley, J. B. (2020). *Corona virus and its impact on higher education*. Research Gate.

Ringle, C., Wende, S., & Becker, J. (2014). SmartPLS 3. *Academy of Management Review*, *9*, 419–445.

Ritzko, J. M., & Robinson, S. (2006). Using games to increase active learning. *Journal of College Teaching and Learning*, *3*(6), 45–50.

Robbins, D. (2007). Vygotsky's and Leontiev's Non-classical Psychology Related to Second Language Acquisition. In *International Nordic-Baltic Region Conference of FIPLV Innovations in Language Teaching and Learning in the Multicultural Context*. Rīga: SIA "Izglītības soļi".

Robert, S. (2005). On demand learning: Blended learning for today's evolving workforce. *IBM Learning Solutions*, (September), 24.

Roblyer, M. (2014). *Integrating Educational Technology into Teaching*. Pearson.

Rodrigo, M. M. T. (2003). Tradition or transformation? An evaluation of icts in metro manila schools. *Information Technology for Development*, *10*(2), 95–122. doi:10.1002/itdj.1590100205

Rodriguez, D. R. (2020, April 28). *aim*. Retrieved from Augmented Reality And The Future Of Education: https://analyticsindiamag.com/augmented-reality-and-the-future-of-education/

Rogero, J. (2020). *Ficción educativa en tiempos de confinamiento*. El Diario de la Educación. Retrieved from https://eldiariodelaeducacion.com/2020/03/25/ficcion-educativa-en-tiempos-de-confinamiento/

Rogers, R. R. (2001). Reflection in Higher Education: A Concept Analysis. *Innovative Higher Education*, *26*(1), 37–57. doi:10.1023/A:1010986404527

Rogmans, T., & Abaza, W. (2019). The impact of international business strategy simulation games on student engagement. *Simulation & Gaming*, *50*(3), 393–407. doi:10.1177/1046878119848138

Román, M. P., Román, A. P., & Gil, I. P. (2021). Business simulation as a tool to develop the scenario analysis capacity. *Journal of Management and Business Education*, *4*(1), 1–17.

Rosenberg, M. J. (2000). e-Learning. McGraw-Hill.

Rosenberg, M. (2001). *E-learning: strategies for delivering knowledge in the digital age*. McGraw-Hill.

Rosen, L., & Weil, M. (1995). Computer Availability, Computer Experience, and Technophobia among Public School Teachers. *Computers in Human Behavior*, *11*(1), 9–31. doi:10.1016/0747-5632(94)00018-D

Roungas, B., Bekius, F., & Meijer, S. (2019). The game between game theory and gaming simulations: Design choices. *Simulation & Gaming*, *50*(2), 180–201. doi:10.1177/1046878119827625

Rouse, M. (2016, July). *TechTarget*. Retrieved from CGI (computer-generated imagery): https://whatis.techtarget.com/definition/CGI-computer-generated-imagery

Rudzinska, I. (2008). The Quality of Aim Setting and Achieved Results in English for Specific Purposes-Study Course in Lecturers and Students' Opinion. In *Proceedings of the ATEE Spring University Conference Teacher of the 21st Century: Quality Education for Quality Teaching* (pp. 366-373). Riga, Latvia: University of Latvia.

Rupesh Kumar, A. (2009). E-Learning 2.0: Learning Redefined. *Library Philosophy and Practice (e-journal).* Retrieved from: https://digitalcommons.unl.edu/libphilprac/284/

Saba, F. (2005). Is distance education losing its identity? Or what should our field be called these days? *XXth Annual Conference on Distance Teaching and Learning.*

Saba, F., & Shearer, R. L. (1994). Verifying key theoretical concepts in a dynamic model of distance education. *American Journal of Distance Education, 8*(1), 36–59. doi:10.1080/08923649409526844

Safi, F., Wenzel, T., & Trimble Spalding, L. A. (2020). Remote Learning Community: Supporting Teacher Educators During Unprecedented Times. *Journal of Technology and Teacher Education, 28*(2), 211–222.

Salceanu, C. (2020). Higher Education Challenges During COVID-19 Pandemic. A Case Study. *Revista Universitară de Sociologie, 16*(1).

Sanders, K. (2001). *Fast Path to Success with Centra.* Centra.

Sandkuhl, K., & Lehmann, H. (2017). *Digital Transformation in Higher Education – The Role of Enterprise Architectures and Portals—Digitale Bibliothek—Gesellschaft für Informatik e.V.* Retrieved December 17, 2020, from https://dl.gi.de/handle/20.500.12116/119

Sangra, A., Vlachopoulos, D., & Cabrera, N. (2012). Building an inclusive definition of elearning: An approach to the conceptual framework. *International Review of Research in Open and Distance Learning, 13*(2), 145–159. doi:10.19173/irrodl.v13i2.1161

Sankey, M., Campbell, C., & Poulsen, S. (2019). The semi-formal benchmarking of TEL practice: Helping the TEL community get its act together. In Y. W. Chew, K. M. Chan & A. Alphonso (Eds.), Personalized Learning. Diverse Goals. One Heart. ASCILITE 2019 Singapore (pp. 541-545). ASCILITE.

Sargeant, J., Curran, V., Allen, M., Jarvis-Selinger, S., & Ho, K. (2006). *Facilitating interpersonal interaction and learning online: Linking theory and practice* (Vol. 26). Academic Press.

Sarrab, M., Alzahrani, A., Al Alwan, N., & Alfarraj, O. (2014). From traditional learning into mobile learning in education at the university level: Undergraduate students perspective. *International Journal of Mobile Learning and Organisation, 8*(3–4), 167–186. doi:10.1504/IJMLO.2014.067014

Sathishkumar, V., Radha, R., Saravanakumar, A., & Mahalakshmi, K. (2020). E-Learning during Lockdown of Covid-19 Pandemic: A Global Perspective. *International Journal of Control and Automation, 13*, 1088–1099.

Save the Children. (2014). *No child left behind, Education in crisis in the Asia-Pacific Region Victoria.* Author.

Sayer, P., & Braun, D. (2020). The disparate impact of COVID-19 remote learning on English learners in the United States. *TESOL Journal, 11*(3). Advance online publication. doi:10.1002/tesj.546

Scammell, R. (2020, February 27). *Verdict.* Retrieved from Augmented reality media trends: https://www.verdict.co.uk/augmented-reality-media-trends/

Schaffhauser. (2005). *Outsourcing – What is Outsourcing?* Retrieved on October 18, 2017 from https://www.sourcing-mag.com/what-is-outsourcing/

Schulte, B. (2015). (Dis)Empowering technologies: ICT for education (ICT4E) in China, past and present. *Chinese Journal of Communication*, *8*(1), 59–77. doi:10.1080/17544750.2014.990909

Schumacher, C. (2018). Supporting Informal Workplace Learning Through Analytics. In D. Ifenthaler (Ed.), *Digital Workplace Learning* (pp. 43–61). Springer., doi:10.1007/978-3-319-46215-8_4

Schumacker, R. E., & Lomax, R. G. (2010). *A beginner's guide to structural equation modeling* (3rd ed.). Routledge/ Taylor & Francis Group.

Schwarzer, R., & Luszczynska, A. (2008). Reactive, anticipatory, preventive, and proactive coping: A theoretical distinction. *Prevention Researcher*, *15*(4), 22.

Secretaría de Educación Pública (2019). *Principales cifras del Sistema Educativo Nacional, 2018-2019*. México: SEP.

Secretaría de Educación Pública. (2020). *Boletín No. 239 El sector educativo se impuso a los efectos de la pandemia: Esteban Moctezuma Barragán*. Retrieved from https://www.gob.mx/sep/articulos/boletin-no-239-el-sector-educativo-se-impuso-a-los-efectos-de-la-pandemia-esteban-moctezuma-barragan?idiom=es

Secureworks. (2016). *What is Firewall Security?* Retrieved on October 20, 2017 from https://www.secureworks.com/blog/firewall-security

Selkie, E. M., Kota, R., Chan, Y. F., & Moreno, M. (2015). Cyberbullying, depression, and problem alcohol use in female college students: A multisite study. *Cyberpsychology, Behavior, and Social Networking*, *18*(2), 79–86. doi:10.1089/cyber.2014.0371 PMID:25684608

Selwyn, N. (2014). The Internet and Education. In Y. Benkler (Ed.), *Change: 19 Key Essays on How the Internet Is Changing Our Lives*. Turner Publicaciones.

Selwyn, N. (2015). The discursive construction of education in the digital age. In R. H. Jones, A. Chik, & C. A. Hafner (Eds.), *Discourse and digital practices: Doing discourse analysis in the digital age* (p. 226). Routledge.

Serban, A. M., & Luan, J. (2002). Overview of Knowledge Management. In Knowledge Management: Building a Competitive Advantage in Higher Education. Wiley Periodicals. doi:10.1002/ir.34

Serban, A. M., & Luan, J. (2002). *Knowledge management: Building a competitive advantage in higher education: New Directions for Institutional Research*. Jossey-Bass.

Sewart, D., Keegan, D., & Holmberg, B. (Eds.). (1988). *Distance education: International perspective*. Routledge.

Shahzad, A., Hassan, R., Aremu, A. Y., Hussain, A., & Lodhi, R. N. (2020). Effects of COVID-19 in E-learning on higher education institution students: The group comparison between male and female. *Quality & Quantity*. Advance online publication. doi:10.100711135-020-01028-z PMID:32836471

Sher, A. (2009). Assessing the Relationship of Student-Instructor and Student-Student Interaction to Student Learning and Satisfaction in Web-Based Online Learning Environment %J. *Journal of Interactive Online Learning*, *8*(2), 102–120.

Sierra, J. (2020). The potential of simulations for developing multiple learning outcomes: The student perspective. *International Journal of Management Education*, *18*(1), 100361. doi:10.1016/j.ijme.2019.100361

Silvio, J. (2006). Hacia una educación virtual de calidad, pero con equidad y pertinencia. *Revista Universitaria y Sociedad del Conocimiento*, *3*(1), 1–14.

Simonson, M., Schlosser, C., & Orellana, A. (2011). Distance education research: A review of the literature. *Journal of Computing in Higher Education*, *23*(2), 124–142. doi:10.100712528-011-9045-8

Simonson, M., Smaldino, S., Albright, M., & Zvacek, S. (2012). *Teaching and learning at a distance: Foundations of distance education* (5th ed.). Pearson.

Singh, G., & Hardaker, G. (2014). Barriers and Enablers to Adoption and Diffusion of ELearning. *Education + Training, 56*(2/3), 105–121. doi:10.1108/ET-11-2012-0123

Singh, V., & Thurman, A. (2019). How Many Ways Can We Define Online Learning? A Systematic Literature Review of Definitions of Online Learning (1988-2018). *American Journal of Distance Education, 33*(4), 289–306. doi:10.1080/08923647.2019.1663082

Singla, A., Sethi, A., & Ahuja, I. S. (2018). A study of transitions between technology push and demand pull strategies for accomplishing sustainable development in manufacturing industries. *World Journal of Science. Technology and Sustainable Development, 15*(4), 302–312. doi:10.1108/WJSTSD-09-2017-0028

Skoumpopoulou, D., Wong, A. K. L., & Ng, P. M. L. (2018). Factors That Affect the Acceptance of New Technologies in the Workplace: a Cross Case Analysis Between UK and Hong Kong. *Ukais 2018.* http://nrl.northumbria.ac.uk/id/eprint/34489

Smarter Brunei. (n.d.). Retrieved from https://www.smarterbrunei.com/

Smedley, J. (2010). *Modelling the impact of knowledge management using technology.* Retrieved December 25, 2020, from https://www.researchgate.net/publication/220438594_Modelling_the_impact_of_knowledge_management_using_technology

Smith, C., & Gillespie, M. (2007). Research on professional development and teacher change: implications for adult basic education. In J. Comings, B. Garner & C. Smith (Eds.), Review of Adult Learning and Literacy, Volume 7: Connecting Research, Policy and Practice (pp. 205-245). Lawrence Erlbaum Associates.

Sobaih, A., Elnasr, E., Hasanein, A. M., Elnasr, A., & Ahmed, E. (2020). Responses to COVID-19 in higher education: Social media usage for sustaining formal academic communication in developing countries. *Sustainability. (Basel, Switzerland), 12*(16), 6520. doi:10.3390u12166520

Sokol, A. (2008). *The Thinking Approach. Introductory Information.* www.thinking-approach.org

Soltanmohammadi, S., Asadi, S., & Ithnin, N. (2013). Main human factors affecting information system security. *Interdisciplinary Journal of Contemporary Research in Business, 5*, 329–354.

Song, L., & McNary, S. W. (2011). Understanding students' online interaction: Analysis of discussion board postings. *Journal of Interactive Online Learning, 10*(1), 1–14.

Song, L., Singleton, E. S., Hill, J. R., & Koh, M. H. (2004). Improving online learning: Student perceptions of useful and challenging characteristics. *The Internet and Higher Education, 7*(1), 59–70. doi:10.1016/j.iheduc.2003.11.003

Soni, V. D. (2020). Global Impact of E-learning during COVID 19. SSRN *Electronic Journal, 12.* doi:10.2139srn.3630073

Sowter, B., Reggio, D., & Hijazi, S. (2017). QS World University Rankings. *Research Analytics: Boosting University Productivity and Competitiveness through. Scientometrics*, 121–136.

Speech and Language Impairment Defined | Special Education. (n.d.). Retrieved from https://www.specialeducationguide.com/disability-profiles/speech-and-language-impairments/

Spellings, M. (2006). *A test of leadership: Charting the future of US higher education.* US Department of Education.

Srivastava, S., Malik, H., Sood, Y. R., & Ahmad, A. (2018). *Applications of artificial intelligence techniques in engineering. In Sigma* (Vol. 1). Springer.

StadlerD. (2019). Retrieved from https://www.shrm.org/resourcesandtools/hr-topics/behavioral-competencies/global-and-cultural-effectiveness/pages/4-ways-to-hire-more-people-with-disabilities.aspx

Stockwell, B. R., Stockwell, M. S., Cennamo, M., & Jiang, E. (2015). Blended Learning Improves Science Education. *Cell*, *162*(5), 933–936. doi:10.1016/j.cell.2015.08.009 PMID:26317458

Stratton, C., Bailey, D. E., & Leonardi, P. M. (2019). Translating national discourse into teaching and learning outcomes: Portability and connectivity in developing countries' ICT in education (ICT4E) initiatives. *New Media & Society*, *22*(12), 2083–2107. doi:10.1177/1461444819884373

Stringer, E. T. (2013). *Action research* (4th ed.). Sage Publications.

Subashish, G., William, J. K., & James, T. C. T. (2010). *Process Reengineering. The IS Manager's Enabling Role in Business*. Retrieved from https://www.google.com.bn/url?sa=t&source=web&rct=j&ei=Sj_sVPblBIbf8AXdvYCAAw&url=http%3A%2F%2Fwww.ittoday.info%2FAIMS%2FInformation_Management%2F1-03-10.pdf&ved=0CBoQFjAA&usg=AFQjCNEHzJMsuWgCC5flzbA_O9k3KU5iPw

Subhas, C., Kumar, M. U., & Kumar, V. (2008). Modelling strategic actor relationships for risk management in organizations undergoing business process reengineering due to information systems adoption. *Business Process Management Journal*, *14*(1), 65–84. doi:10.1108/14637150810849418

Subramoniam, S., Tounsi, M., & Krishnankutty, K. V. (2009). The role of BPR in the implementation of ERP systems. *Business Process Management Journal*, *15*(5), 653–668. doi:10.1108/14637150910987892

Sumra, H. (2018, April 25). *wareable*. Retrieved from Augmented reality explained: What is AR and what's coming next?: https://www.wareable.com/ar/everything-you-need-to-know-about-augmented-reality

Sung, P., Ku, C., & Su, C. (2014). Understanding the propagation dynamics of multipartite computer virus. *Industrial Management & Data Systems*, *114*(1), 86–106. doi:10.1108/IMDS-04-2013-0197

Sun, Y., Bhattacherjee, A., & Ma, Q. (2009). Extending technology usage to work settings: The role of perceived work compatibility in ERP implementation. *Information & Management*, *46*(6), 351–356. doi:10.1016/j.im.2009.06.003

Susanto, H. (2017). Electronic Health System: Sensors Emerging and Intelligent Technology Approach. In Smart Sensors Networks (pp. 189-203). Academic Press.

Susanto, H., Yie, L. F., Rosiyadi, D., Basuki, A. I., & Setiana, D. Data Security for Connected Governments and Organisations: Managing Automation and Artificial Intelligence. In Web 2.0 and Cloud Technologies for Implementing Connected Government (pp. 229-251). IGI Global.

Susanto, H., Yie, L. F., Setiana, D., Asih, Y., Yoganingrum, A., Riyanto, S., & Saputra, F. A. (2020). Digital Ecosystem Security Issues for Organizations and Governments: Digital Ethics and Privacy. In Web 2.0 and Cloud Technologies for Implementing Connected Government (pp. 204-228). IGI Global.

Susanto, H. (2017). Electronic Health System: Sensors Emerging and Intelligent Technology Approach. In *Smart Sensors Networks* (pp. 189–203). Elsevier. doi:10.1016/B978-0-12-809859-2.00012-7

Susanto, H. (2018). Smart mobile device emerging Technologies: an enabler to Health monitoring system. In *High-Performance Materials and Engineered Chemistry* (pp. 241–264). Apple Academic Press.

Susanto, H. (2018). Smart mobile device emerging Technologies: An enabler to Health Monitoring system. In *High-Performance Materials and Engineered Chemistry* (pp. 241–264). Apple Academic Press. doi:10.1201/9781315187860-8

Susanto, H., & Almunawar, M. N. (2015). Managing Compliance with an Information Security Management Standard. In *Encyclopedia of Information Science and Technology* (3rd ed., pp. 1452–1463). IGI Global. doi:10.4018/978-1-4666-5888-2.ch138

Susanto, H., & Almunawar, M. N. (2016). Security and Privacy Issues in Cloud-Based E-Government. In *Cloud Computing Technologies for Connected Government* (pp. 292–321). IGI Global.

Susanto, H., & Almunawar, M. N. (2018). *Information Security Management Systems: A Novel Framework and Software as a Tool for Compliance with Information Security Standard.* CRC Press. doi:10.1201/9781315232355

Susanto, H., Almunawar, M. N., Leu, F. Y., & Chen, C. K. (2016). Android vs iOS or Others? SMD-OS Security Issues: Generation Y Perception. *International Journal of Technology Diffusion*, *7*(2), 1–18. doi:10.4018/IJTD.2016040101

Susanto, H., & Chen, C. K. (2017). Information and Communication Emerging Technology: Making Sense of Healthcare Innovation. In *Internet of Things and Big Data Technologies for Next Generation Healthcare* (pp. 229–250). Springer. doi:10.1007/978-3-319-49736-5_10

Susanto, H., Chen, C. K., & Almunawar, M. N. (2018). Revealing Big Data Emerging Technology as Enabler of LMS Technologies Transferability. In *Internet of Things and Big Data Analytics Toward Next-Generation Intelligence* (pp. 123–145). Springer. doi:10.1007/978-3-319-60435-0_5

Susanto, H., Ibrahim, F., Nazmudeen, S. H., Mohiddin, F., & Setiana, D. (2020). Human-Centred Design to Enhance the Usability, Human Factors, and User Experience Within Digital Destructive Ecosystems. In *Global Challenges and Strategic Disruptors in Asian Businesses and Economies* (pp. 76–94). IGI Global.

Susanto, H., Leu, F. Y., & Chen, C. K. (2019). *Business Process Reengineering: An ICT Approach.* CRC Press.

Susanto, H., Leu, F. Y., Chen, C. K., & Mohiddin, F. (Eds.). (2019). *Managing Human Capital in Today's Globalization: A Management Information System Perspective.* CRC Press.

Susanto, H., Leu, F.-Y., Caesarendra, W., Ibrahim, F., Haghi, P. K., Khusni, U., & Glowacz, A. (2020). Managing Cloud Intelligent Systems over Digital Ecosystems: Revealing Emerging App Technology in the Time of the COVID19 Pandemic. *Applied System Innovation*, *3*(3), 37–55. doi:10.3390/asi3030037

Sutherland, I. E. (2017). Learning and growing: Trust, leadership, and response to crisis. *Journal of Educational Administration*, *55*(1), 2–17. doi:10.1108/JEA-10-2015-0097

Sveiby, K. E. (1989). *Managing Know how: Add value by Valuing Creativity.* Bloomsbury.

Tabak, F., & Nguyen, N. T. (2013). Technology Acceptance and Performance in Online Learning Environments: Impact of Self-Regulation. UBD study shows Bruneians interested in online learning. *Brunei Times.* https://btarchive.org/news/national/2016/02/06/ubd-study-showsbruneians-interested-online-learning

Tabira, Y., & Otieno, F. X. (2017). Integration and implementation of sustainable ICT-based education in developing countries: Low-cost, en masse methodology in Kenya. *Sustainability Science*, *12*(2), 221–234. doi:10.100711625-017-0422-8

Tabung Amanah Pekerja. (n.d.). Retrieved from www.tap.com.bn

Tedre, M., Hansson, H., Mozelius, P., & Lind, S. (2011). Crucial considerations in one-to-one computing in developing countries. In *2011 IST-Africa Conference Proceedings* (pp. 1-11). IEEE.

Thamarana, S. (2016, August 27). *Role of E-learning and Virtual Learning Environment in English language learning.* doi:10.13140/RG.2.1.4665.1122

The ASEAN post. (2018a, June 17). Retrieved from https://theaseanpost.com/article/bringing-inclusivity-brunei

The ASEAN post. (2018b, october 27). Retrieved from https://theaseanpost.com/article/bruneis-unevenly-distributed-income

The ASEAN post. (2018c). Retrieved from https://theaseanpost.com/article/digitalising-brunei

The European Council by the Reflection Group on the Future of the EU 2030. (2010). *Project Europe 2030 Challenges and Opportunities*. Luxembourg: Publications Office of the European Union. https://www.consilium.europa.eu/media/30776/qc3210249enc.pdf

Tibok, R. P., & Hiew, W. (2019). Higher Education Systems and Institutions. Academic Press.

Tiļļa, I. (2003). *Development of adolescents' social culture competence within the second foreign language studies* [Unpublished doctoral dissertation]. University of Latvia, Riga, Latvia.

Tiļļa, I. (2006). Sociālkultūras mācīšanās konstruktīvistiskā sistēma [The constructive system of social culture learning]. In I. Maslo (Ed.), *No zināšanām uz kompetentu darbību. Latvijas Universitātes Akadēmiskais apgāds* (pp. 161–170).

Timperley, H. (2008). *Teacher professional learning and development*. International Academy of Education.

Tranfield, D., Denyer, D., & Smart, P. (2003). Towards a methodology for developing evidence-informed management knowledge by means of systematic review. *British Journal of Management*, *14*(3), 207–222. doi:10.1111/1467-8551.00375

Trust, T. (2015). Deconstructing an online community of practice: Teachers' actions in the edmodo math subject community. *Journal of Digital Learning in Teacher Education*, *31*(2), 73–81. doi:10.1080/21532974.2015.1011293

Trust, T., & Horrocks, B. (2017). I never feel alone in my classroom: Teacher professional growth within a blended community of practice. *Professional Development in Education*, *43*(4), 645–665. doi:10.1080/19415257.2016.1233507

Tsiligiris, V. (2012). The impact of the economic crisis on higher education. *University World News*, (213).

Turns, A. (2020). *'The world is changing now': why education and climate activism go hand in hand.* Retrieved from https://www.theguardian.com/education/2020/jan/27/the-world-is-changing-now-why-education-and-climate-activism-go-hand-in-hand

Tzima, S. (2019). *Augmented Reality Applications in Education: Teachers Point of View*. University of Patras.

Umek, L., Keržič, D., Aristovnik, A., & Tomaevic, N. (2016). Implications of blended learning on students' performance in public administration education. *Proceedings - 8th International Conference on U- and E-Service, Science and Technology, UNESST 2015*, 39–44. 10.1109/UNESST.2015.18

Ünal, Y., Alır, G., & Soydal, İ. (2013, September). Students readiness for e-learning: an assessment on Hacettepe University Department of Information Management. In *International Symposium on Information Management in a Changing World* (pp. 137-147). Springer.

UNESCO IESALC. (2020). *COVID-19 and higher education: Today and tomorrow*. UNESCO. http://www.iesalc.unesco.org/en/wp-content/uploads/2020/04/COVID-19-EN-090420-2.pdf

UNESCO. (2014). *Políticas TIC en los sistemas educativos de América Latina*. UNESCO.

UNESCO. (2020). *Consecuencias negativas del cierre de las escuelas*. Retrieved from https://es.unesco.org/covid19/education-response/consecuencias

United Nations. (2020). *Policy brief: Education during COVID-19 and beyond*. Retrieved from https://www.un.org/development/desa/dspd/wp-content/uploads/sites/22/2020/08/sg_policy_brief_covid-19_and_education_august_2020.pdf

Universidad Autónoma de México. (2020). *Recomendaciones para la transición a la docencia no presencial.* Retrieved from https://cuaieed.unam.mx/descargas/Recomendaciones-para-la-transicion-a-la-docencia-no-presencial.pdf

Urdan, T. A., & Weggen, C. C. (2000). *Corporate e-learning: Exploring a new frontier.* WR Hambrecht.

Van Dam, N. (2005). *The Business Impact of e-Learning* (PhD Thesis). Nyenrode Business University.

Van Deursen, A. J., & Van Dijk, J. A. (2019). The first- level digital divide shifts from inequalities in physical access to inequalities in material access. *New Media & Society*, *21*(2), 354–375. doi:10.1177/1461444818797082 PMID:30886536

Van Dijk, J. (2017). Digital divede: impact of access. In P. Rossler (Ed.), *The International Encyclopedia of Media Effect.* Wiley. doi:10.1002/9781118783764.wbieme0043

Van Dijk, J. (2020). *Il Digital Divide Cambridge*, Polity Press. *Communication, 2020.* Advance online publication. doi:10.1515/commun-2020-0026

Vanhoucke, M., & Wauters, M. (2015). Blended learning in project management experiences on busineß games and case studies. *CSEDU 2015 - 7th International Conference on Computer Supported Education Proceedings*, *2*, 267–276.

Vaughan, N., & Garrison, D. R. (2006). How blended learning can support a faculty development community of inquiry. *Journal of Asynchronous Learning Networks*, *10*(4), 139–152.

Venzin, M., von Krogh, G., & Roos, J. (1998). Future research into Knowledge Management, In Knowing in Firms: Understanding, Managing and Measuring Knowledge. Sage Publications. doi:10.4135/9781446280256.n3

Victoria. (2019, January 18). *RubyGarage*. Retrieved from Use Cases of Augmented Reality in Education and Training: https://rubygarage.org/blog/augmented-reality-in-education-and-training

Villanueva, J. (2015). Flipped Inclusion Classroom. *Action Research*, 1–16. http://128.171.57.22/handle/10125/40822

Viswanathan, D., & Blom, J. (2010). New metaphors from old practices - mobile learning to revitalize education in developing regions of the world. *IEEE Transactions on Learning Technologies*, *3*(1), 18–23. doi:10.1109/TLT.2010.5

Vongkulluksn, V. W., Xie, K., and Bowman, M. A. (2018). The role of value on teachers' internalization of external barriers and externalization of personal beliefs for classroom technology integration. *Computers and Education*, *118*(November), 70–81. doi:10.1016/j.compedu.2017.11.009

Voos, R. (2003). Blended learning—What is it and where might it take us? *Sloan-C View*, *2*(1), 2–5.

Vosniadou, S. (1994). *Technology-Based Learning Environments.* Springer. doi:10.1007/978-3-642-79149-9

Wagner, D. A. (2018). Technology for education in low-income countries: Supporting the UN sustainable development goals. In I. Lubin (Ed.), *ICT-Supported Innovations in Small Countries and Developing Regions: Perspectives and Recommendations for International Education* (pp. 51–74). Springer. doi:10.1007/978-3-319-67657-9_3

Wagner, N., Hassanein, K., & Head, M. (2008). Who is Responsible for E-Learning Success in Higher Education? A Stakeholders' Analysis. *Journal of Educational Technology & Society*, *11*, 26–36.

Waheed, M., & Hussain, M. F. (2010). Empirical study of e-learner contentment towards e-Learning: Influential role of key factors. *The 2010 MIT LINC Conference in Stratton Center on the MIT Campus.*

Walker, S. (2002). *Insight: Distance education learning environments survey.* https:// insight.southcentralrtec.org/ilib/delesa/delesainfo.html

Wang, A. (2018, April 16). *Gearbrain*. Retrieved from Genesis Augmented Reality — your one stop shop for warriors, beasts and gods: https://www.gearbrain.com/genesis-augmented-reality-app-review-2556535762.html

Wang, C. H., Shannon, D. M., & Ross, M. E. (2013). Students' characteristics, self-regulated learning, technology self-efficacy, and course outcomes in online learning. *Distance Education, 34*(3), 302–323. doi:10.1080/01587919.2013.835779

Wang, G., Cheng, Z., Yue, X., & McAleer, M. (2020). Risk Management of COVID-19 by Universities in China. *Journal of Risk and Financial Management, 13*(2), 36. doi:10.3390/jrfm13020036

Wang, M. (2018). *E-Learning in the Workplace: Performance Oriented Approach*. Springer. doi:10.1007/978-3-319-64532-2

Wang, Y. Y., Wang, Y. S., & Jian, S. E. (2020). Investigating the determinants of students' intention to use business simulation games. *Journal of Educational Computing Research, 58*(2), 433–458. doi:10.1177/0735633119865047

Wang, Z., & Li, X. (2010). Chinese schools modern distance education project in rural Areas. *British Journal of Educational Technology, 41*(4), 612–613. doi:10.1111/j.1467-8535.2010.01073.x

Warschauer, M. (2004). *Technology and Social Inclusion. Rethinking the digital divide*. The MIT Press. doi:10.7551/mitpress/6699.001.0001

Washbush, J. B., & Gosen, J. (1998). Total enterprise simulation performance and participant learning. *Journal of Workplace Learning, 6/7*(6/7), 314–319. doi:10.1108/13665629810236264

Webster-Wright, A. (2009). Reframing Professional Development through Understanding Authentic Professional Learning. *Review of Educational Research, 79*(2), 702–739. doi:10.3102/0034654308330970

Wei R. C., Andree, A., & Darling-Hammond, L. (2009). How nations invest in teachers. *Educational Leadership: Journal of the Department of Supervision and Curriculum Development, 66*(5), 28-33.

Wellington, W. J., Hutchinson, D. B., & Faria, A. J. (2017). Measuring the impact of a marketing simulation game: Experience on perceived indecisiveness. *Simulation & Gaming, 48*(1), 56–80. doi:10.1177/1046878116675103

Wenger, E., McDermott, R., & Snyder, W. (2002). *Cultivating Communities of Practice*. Harvard Business School Press.

What Is Database Architecture? (n.d.). Retrieved Oct 19, 2017 from https://learn.org/articles/What_is_Database_Architecture.html

Whitcomb, J., Borko, H., & Liston, D. (2009). Growing talent promising professional development models and practices. *Journal of Teacher Education, 60*(3), 207–212. doi:10.1177/0022487109337280

Wilbanks, J. E. (2014). E-mentoring: Examining the feasibility of electronic, online, or distance mentoring. *Journal of Higher Education Theory and Practice, 14*(5), 24.

Wilkinson, R., & Pickett, K. (2009). *The Spirit Level: Why more equal societies almost always do better*. Allen Lane.

Williams, E. (1996). *So... you want to teach adults*. Pippin Publishing Corporation.

Willig, C. (2013). *Introducing qualitative research in psychology: Adventures in theory and method* (3rd ed.). McGraw-Hill Education.

Witze, A. (2020). Universities will never be the same after the coronavirus crisis. *Nature, 582*(7811), 162–164. doi:10.1038/d41586-020-01518-y PMID:32504014

Woen, A.,, Sylvia, C.,, & Handoko, H., & Abdurachman, E. (2018). E-learning acceptance analysis using technology acceptance model (Tam) (case study: Stmik mikroskil). *Journal of Theoretical and Applied Information Technology, 96*, 6292–6305.

Wolfe, J. (1993). A history of business teaching games in English-speaking and Post-Socialist countries: The origination and diffusion of a management education and development technology. *Simulation & Gaming*, *24*(4), 446–463. doi:10.1177/1046878193244003

Woodall J. (2020). COVID-19 and the role of health promoters and educators. *Emerald Open Res, 2*(28).

Woolfolk, A. (2014). *Educational Psychology*. Pearson Education Limited.

World Health Organization. (2020a). *Coronavirus disease (COVID-19) pandemic.* Retrieved from https://www.euro.who.int/en/health-topics/health-emergencies/coronavirus-COVID-19/n ovel-coronavirus-2019-ncov

World Health Organization. (2020b, September 17). *COVID-19 in Brunei Darussalam.* Retrieved from https://www.who.int/brunei/emergencies/coronavirus-disease-(COVID-19)-in-brunei

World Health Organization. (2020c, September 16). *WHO Coronavirus Disease (COVID-19) Dashboard.* Retrieved on November 03, 2020 from https://COVID19.who.int/

Yang, R. (2020). China's higher education during the COVID-19 pandemic: Some preliminary observations. *Higher Education Research & Development*, *39*(7), 1317–1321. doi:10.1080/07294360.2020.1824212

Yeh, Y. C., Huang, L. Y., & Yeh, Y. L. (2011). Knowledge management in blended learning: Effects on professional development in creativity instruction. *Computers & Education*, *56*(1), 146–156. doi:10.1016/j.compedu.2010.08.011

Yeh, Y. M. C. (2005). The Implementation of Knowledge management system in Taiwan's Higher Education. *Journal of College Teaching and Learning*, *2*(9), 35–42. doi:10.19030/tlc.v2i9.1861

Yen, W. C., & Lin, H. H. (2020). Investigating the effect of flow experience on learning performance and entrepreneurial self-efficacy in a business simulation systems context. *Interactive Learning Environments*, 1–16. doi:10.1080/10494820.2020.1734624

Yeou, M. (2016). An Investigation of Students ' Acceptance of Moodle in a Blended Learning Setting Using Technology Acceptance Model. *Journal of Educational Technology Systems*, *44*(3), 300–318. doi:10.1177/0047239515618464

Yie, L. F., Susanto, H., & Setiana, D. (2020). Collaborating Decision Support and Business Intelligence to Enable Government Digital Connectivity. In *Web 2.0 and Cloud Technologies for Implementing Connected Government* (pp. 95–112). IGI Global.

Yildirim, I., & Kurt, S. C. (2018). The Students' Perceptions on Blended Learning. *Educational Sciences: Theory and Practice*, *18*(2), 427–446. doi:10.12738/estp.2018.2.0002

Yin, G. L. (2010). BPR application. *Modern Applied Science*, *4*(4), 96–101. http://www.ccsenet.org/journal/index.php/mas/article/view/5655. doi:10.5539/mas.v4n4p96

Zaar, M., & García, M. (2020). El COVID-19 en España y sus primeras consecuencias. *Espaço e Economia*, *17*(17). Advance online publication. doi:10.4000/espacoeconomia.10142

Zafra, I. (2020). La desesperada búsqueda de los alumnos que se han quedado desconectados del sistema educativo. *El País*. Retrieved from https://elpais.com/sociedad/2020-04-12/la-desesperada-busqueda-de-los-alumnos-que-se-han-quedado-desconectados-del-sistema-educativo.html

Zaščerinska, J. (2010). Professional Environment for Teacher Professional Development. *Proceedings of 5th International scientific conference Theory for Practice in the Education of Contemporary Society of Riga Teacher Training and Educational Management Academy*. Riga: Riga Teacher Training and Educational Management Academy.

Zaščerinska, J., & Ahrens, A. (2013). E-business Applications to Students' Blended Learning in Higher Education. In *Proceedings of the 4th International Conference on Data Communication Networking (DCNET 2013), 10th International Conference on e-Business (ICE-B 2013) and 4th International Conference on Optical Communication Systems (OPTICS 2013)*. SciTePress - Science and Technology Publications. Printed in Portugal.

Zaščerinska, J., & Ahrens, A. (2015). A Comparative Study of Teacher and Student Use of Social Media for Interaction with Other People. In Impact of Economic Crisis on Education and the Next-Generation Workforce. IGI Global. doi:10.4018/978-1-4666-9455-2

Zascerinska, J., Aleksejeva, L., Zascerinskis, M., Gukovica, O., & Aleksejeva, A. (2020). The Impact of COVID-19 on the Improvement of Teaching Skills on Problem-Solving Learning. *International Journal for 21st Century Education, 7*(1), 42-59. https://www.uco.es/ucopress/ojs/index.php/ij21ce/article/view/13074/12073

Ziemba, E. (2016). Factors affecting the adoption and usage of ICT's within polish household. *Interdisciplinary Journal of Information. Knowledge and Management*, *11*, 89–113.

Zirawaga, V. S., Olusanya, A. I., & Maduku, T. (2017). Gaming in education: Using games as a support tool to teach history. *Journal of Education and Practice*, *8*(15), 55–64.

Zulfiqar, S., Al-reshidi, H. A., Al-Moteri, M. A., Feroz, H. M. B., Yahya, N., & Al-Rahmi, W. M. (2021). Understanding and predicting students' entrepreneurial intention through business simulation games: A perspective of COVID-19. *Sustainability*, *13*(4), 1–27. doi:10.3390u13041838

Zulfiqar, S., Sarwar, B., Aziz, S., Chandia, K. E., & Khan, M. K. (2018). An analysis of influence of business simulation games on business school students' attitude and intention toward entrepreneurial activities. *Journal of Educational Computing Research*, *57*(1), 106–130. doi:10.1177/0735633117746746

Сорокин, Н. А. (1974). Дидактика [Didactics]. Издательство "Просвещение" Москва.

About the Contributors

Patricia Ordóñez de Pablos is a professor in the Department of Business Administration in the Faculty of Business and Economics at The University of Oviedo (Spain). She completed her education in The London School of Economics (UK). Her teaching and research interests focus on the areas of strategic management, knowledge management, organizational learning, human resource management, intellectual capital, information technologies, with special interest in Asia (Bhutan, China, Laos, Myanmar). She is Editor-in-Chief of the International Journal of Learning and Intellectual Capital (IJLIC) and International Journal of Asian Business and Information Management (IJABIM), respectively. She has edited books for IGI-Global, Routledge and Springer.

Mohammad Nabil Almunawar is currently an associate professor at the School of Business and Economics, Universiti of Brunei Darussalam (UBDSBE), Brunei Darussalam. He received his bachelor's degree in 1983 from Bogor Agricultural University, Indonesia, master's degree (MSc) from the Department of Computer Science, University of Western Ontario, London, Canada in 1991, and Ph.D. from the University of New South Wales in 1998. Dr. Almunawar has published more than 100 papers in refereed journals, books, book chapters, and international conference proceedings. He has more than 30 years of teaching experience in the area of information systems. His overall research interests include applications of IT in management, e-business/commerce, digital marketplace/platform, digital business ecosystem, health informatics, information security, and cloud computing. Currently, he focuses his research on digital platform and digital business ecosystem.

Kwok Tai Chui received the B.Eng. degree in electronic and communication engineering - Business Intelligence Minor and Ph.D. degree from City University of Hong Kong. He had industry experience as Senior Data Scientist in Internet of Things (IoT) company. He joined the Department of Technology, School of Science and Technology, at The Open University of Hong Kong as Research Assistant Professor. He was the recipient of 2nd Prize Award (Postgraduate Category) of 2014 IEEE Region 10 Student Paper Contest. Also, he received Best Paper Award in IEEE The International Conference on Consumer Electronics-China, in both 2014 and 2015. He has more than 45 research publications including edited books, book chapters, journal papers, and conference papers. His research interests include computational intelligence, data science, energy monitoring and management, intelligent transportation, smart metering, healthcare, machine learning algorithms and optimization.

Maniam Kaliannan, PhD, is an Associate Professor of Human Resource Management with School of Business, University of Nottingham Malaysia. He has more than 20 years of experience in teaching and corporate training. He has presented his research work in international conferences and published his work in international journals.

* * *

Andreas Ahrens received the Dipl.-Ing. degree in electrical engineering from the University of Rostock in 1996. From 1996 to 2008, he was with the Institute of Communications Engineering of the University of Rostock, from which he received the Dr.-Ing. and Dr.-Ing. habil. degree in 2000 and 2003, respectively. In 2008, he became a Professor for Signal and System theory at the Hochschule Wismar, University of Technology, Business and Design, Germany. His main fields of interest are error correcting codes, multiple-input multiple-output systems and iterative detection for both wireline and wireless communication.

Muhammad Anshari is researcher and academic staff at School of Business & Economics, Universiti Brunei Darussalam. His professional experience started when he was IT Business Analyst at Astra International. Research Fellowship from The Government Republic of China (Taiwan) at National Taiwan University (Jan-Dec, 2014). Research Fellowship from King Saud University - the Kingdom of Saudi Arabia 2009. Senior Associate Researcher of Informatics Department, Universitas Islam Negeri Yogyakarta, Indonesia.

Siti Norainna Besar is currently a lecturer at Academy of Brunei Studies, Universiti Brunei Darussalam. She completed her BA Education (Islamic Studies) from the Sultan Hassanal Bolkiah Institute of Education (SHBIE) at Universiti Brunei Darussalam in 2006. In 2007, she was appointed as a tutor at the Academy of Brunei Studies and later promoted to lecturer. She holds a MA degree in Education from the University of Leeds, United Kingdom in 2008. In 2016, she has been awarded with the degree of PhD in Education from the University of Manchester, United Kingdom. Her research interests are in Education specifically on Technology Education.

Parulkumari Bhati holds a Ph.D in Human resources Management in the area of HRM practices and Job satisfaction. She brings in a vast academic and administrative experience of 12 years. Currently she is associated with NIrma University, Ahmedbad. She has also worked as a faculty with Saurashtra University Gujarat Technological University and Gujarat University, guiding PG-UG Students in areas of Human resources, Organizational behavior and General Management. Dr. Bhati holds a certificate in AMT (Accredited management Teacher) awarded by AIMA (All India Management Association), New Delhi in the area of Human resource Management. She has qualified NET (National eligibility Test) examination conducted by CSIR and UGC. She is a member of Board of Studies, Atmiya University, Rajkot has three books and several research papers to her credit. She has attended various conferences National and International repute. She has been awarded best professor award by Indian Society of Concept Management. She was mentor for MBA and engineering students for International Exchange Program for Wismar University, Germany and Poland.

Edgar Cardoso Espinosa, PhD, is Professor - Researcher since 2009 on Division of Postgraduate Studies and Research of the Superior School of Commerce and Administration (ESCA) of the National Polytechnic Institute (IPN), Mexico City. In his position conducts research projects focused on the management and development of education in educational programs at senior level. He teaches courses Methodological Seminar I, II, III and Statistics for Educational Research to Master's and Research Seminars I, II and III as well as Research Visits I, II, III and IV to PhD level. Dr. Cardoso earned his doctorate at the IPN. He has a master of science in management and development of education in the ESCA-IPN. His research includes evaluation of educational programs and executive education. He belongs to the National System of Researchers with the level I distinction in the CONACyT of Mexico. He has directed several research projects in the area of educational management. He has conducted thesis addresses at the master's and doctoral level in the educational area.

Jésica Alhelí Cortés Ruiz, PhD, is a Professor - Researcher and is a member of the National System of Researchers on la Sección de Estudios de Posgrado e Investigación of the Escuela Superior de Comercio y Administración (ESCA) of the Instituto Politécnico Nacional (IPN), Mexico City. PhD in Administrative Sciences from the Higher School of Commerce and Administration, Master of Science in Systems Engineering from the Higher School of Mechanical and Electrical Engineering. She is a specialist in transdisciplinary systemic and has been the author of chapters of dissemination books, as well as various articles in research journals. Her systemic training and dedication to the knowledge society has allowed her to teach In the International Business Degree, the Master in Administration in Management and Development of Education, The Master in Business Administration for Sustainability And the Master of Science in Business Administration.

Alessandra Corti graduated with honors from the Catholic University of Milan in 2016 (BSc in "Languages for Foreign Relations") with a dissertation about the British Referendum and "Brexit". After having successfully completed an internship at the Italian Chamber of Commerce for Germany (ITKAM) in Berlin, Alessandra is about to conclude a Double Degree Master Program involving both the University of Insubria in Varese (Global Entrepreneurship, Economics and Management (GEEM), with a specialization in "International Business and Entrepreneurship"), and the Friedrich Schiller University in Jena (Economics with a specialization in "Innovation and Change").

Rafaela Gjergji is a Postdoctoral Researcher at School of Economics & Management, Università Cattaneo - LIUC (Castellanza, Italy). Her research interests are focused on innovation and open innovation in family businesses. Her research activity mainly employs quantitative methods and it has been published in academic journals including International Journal of Entrepreneurship and Small Business, International Journal of Technology Intelligence and Planning, Management Research: The Journal of Iberoamerican Academy of Management, Journal of Business Strategy and the Environment.

Fahmi Ibrahim (PhD) is Assistant Professor of School of Business, Universiti Teknologi Brunei (UTB), Brunei Darussalam. He gained his PhD from Glasgow Caledonian University, Glasgow, UK and MSc in Business Information Technology Systems (BITS) from University of Strathclyde, Glasgow, UK. He has a wide range of academic experience, gained in further and higher education establishments in the Brunei Darussalam and UK. This experience includes module and programme development, programme leadership, and international collaboration. His current teaching and research areas are in the field of Strategic Management, Knowledge Management, and Intellectual Capital Management, Management Information Systems (MIS), Operations Management within public, private and SMEs organisations. His consultancy experience is in the area of Business Transformation particularly in SMEs. The consultancy expertise is supported by and complemented by his research interests. His research output includes book chapters, journal articles and conference papers. In recent years his research interest has evolved to be contextualised around the strategic development of organisations in complex and transitional environments. Also he has developed research interest on learning and teaching drawing from cross-disciplinary initiatives. He is currently on the editorial board of four international journals. In addition, he regularly contributes to conference organising committees and acts as keynote speaker and a reviewer for a range of conferences.

Antonios Kokkonos is an Educational Work Coordinator at Peloponnese Regional Educational Planning Center, Greece. He is Ph.D. candidate of Educational Leadership in Digital Age at University of Peloponnese, Greece. He holds a Master Degree in e-learning from the University of Piraeus, Greece, a Master Degree in Educational Leadership and Policy from Open University of Cyprus, Cyprus, and a Master Degree in Adults' Education from Hellenic Open University, Greece. He has served as teacher in public and private Primary Schools and as School Principal of Primary Schools. He has published articles about e-learning and educational leadership, has made presentations at conferences, seminars and training programs, and has been actively engaged in research projects about e-learning. His research interests focus on educational leadership in digital age and on the utilization of digital collaboration and communication environments for teachers' training and educational work support.

Alena Leshchenko is a professor, Doctor of Phylosophy, Professor of Department of Social and Humanitarian Disciplines and Innovative Pedagogy of Kherson State Maritime Academy and Director of the Science Park of KSMA "Maritime Industry Innovations". The Science Park performs work related to realization of scientific developments and implementation of innovations into industrial activities and participates in formation of policy according to the latest developments of education. Her research is focused on human resources management, decision-making processes, improvement of educational process by means of digital technologies etc. She is the author of over 60 scientific publications, including 2 monographs and 3 student's books.

Fadzliwati Mohiddin is a Deputy Dean, School of Business, Brunei University of Technology, Brunei Darussalam.

Nena Padilla-Valdez is currently a Senior Asst. Professor in the Centre for Communication Learning and Teaching, Universiti Teknologi Brunei, Brunei Darussalam. Her main research interests and publications are in the areas of eco-tourism and cultural preservation, learner diversity and learning engagement, STEM inquiry practice, curriculum development, pedagogy, teacher empowerment and reflective practice, early childhood care and development, and school counselling. She is an AKEPT Master Trainer of Trainers, module writer, and researcher on 'Learner Diversity' and inclusive teaching, and a primary trainer of vocational education enhancement program for chief executives and educators of Cambodia, Bangladesh, and the Philippines, to name a few. Prior to her current position, she charted more than 30 years' experience in the academe holding various positions as a Vice President for Academic Affairs, Continuing and Alternative Education Director, Guidance and Counselling University Head, and Teacher Education Supervisor on top of a handful of ministerial and external designations as a book writer-evaluator and multi-media instructional materials evaluator of the Department of Education, an ETEEAP Technical Panel of the Commission of Higher Education, Philippines, and a consultant locally and abroad on TVET Ladderized Education, Ford Foundation-Assisted government projects, and equivalency and alternative programs in Hong Kong, Taiwan, Singapore, Vietnam, and the Philippines. She graduated a Bachelor of Science degree in General Science, masters in Guidance & Counselling, and a doctorate in Development Study.

Maria Pavlis-Korres obtained a university degree in Political Science in Athens. From 1983 until 2018 she worked on Adult Education in the Greek Ministry of Education. Since 2005 her research interests are focused on e-learning and she became a PhD student in the University of Alcalá, Spain. In 2008 she obtained her Advance Studies Degree from the Computer Science Department of the University of Alcalá and in 2010 she obtained her PhD with honors. Since 2012 she is a member of the scientific staff of Hellenic Open University and teaches in "Adult Education" and "Education Science" postgraduate programs. In June 2017 she has been elected Associate Professor in the Pedagogical Sector of the Aristotle University of Thessaloniki to teach "Lifelong Learning and non-Formal Education". She has published several articles, chapters and books on Roma, adult education and e-learning. Her current interests are focused on design, development and evaluation of educational projects for adults, face to face and e-learning, as well as the group dynamics in an online environment and the appropriate use of communication tools in order to promote interaction in an online environment.

Alessia Pisoni is Assistant Professor at the Department of Economics - University of Insubria, where she teaches Innovation, Technologies and Operations Management. She holds a Ph.D. in Economics of Production and Development, and coordinates the research unit of the Research Centre for Innovation and Life Sciences Management (CRESIT). Since 2010, she has also been collaborating with Mind the Bridge Foundation's research activities on European ICT startup ecosystems. Nowadays, her research interests are in the area of innovation, internationalization and entrepreneurship. She is author of an extensive list of articles and books in the fields of innovation, entrepreneurship, corporate governance and international business.

Desi Setiana received a BSc and MSc in Psychology Behavior of Information Technology, respectively from University of Indonesia and University of Brunei. She is researcher at the Ministry of Law and Human Right, Republic of Indonesia. Her research interests are in the areas of Psychology of Information Security, User Behaviour toward Cyberbullying, IT Emerging Technology for Psychology Education. She is now in-pipeline to pursuing Ph.D in IT Psychology for Cyberbullying and Security Protection for Prisoners.

Mina Richards holds a Ph.D. in Computer Information Systems from Nova Southeastern University, an MBA, and a Masters in MIS from Claremont Graduate University. She is a professor of Information Systems and Business Administration courses at traditional and online universities. She teaches for the California State University system and chairs doctoral students in the DBA program for Trident University at AIU. Previously, she served as a director of Academic Assessment to support regional accreditation efforts. Her research interests are varied and include emerging technologies to improve user productivity, information security, business analytics, blockchain, and assessment. She has earned certificates in data science, cybersecurity, Internet of Things, Quality Matters, and many others in SAP and teaching competencies. She also held leadership positions in the IT industry as a project manager in systems development and integration projects for banking and financial systems.

Graziella Sicoli is a researcher in Accounting at University of Calabria. Her main research interests are intellectual capital, corporate governance family business. She attended many national and international conferences.

Heru Susanto is currently Researcher at Research Center for Informatics, the Indonesian Institute of Sciences. At present he is an Honorary Professor, Department of Information Management, College of Management, Tunghai University, Taichung, Taiwan, and also Visiting Scholar at School of Business, University Technology of Brunei. Dr. Susanto has worked as an IT professional in several roles, including Web Division Head of IT Strategic at Indomobil Group, and Prince Muqrin Chair for Information Security Technologies. His research interests are in the areas of Information Security, 5G Technologies, Grid Application, Big Data, Business Process Re-engineering, and e-Marketing. Dr. Susanto received a BSc in Computer Science; an MBA in Marketing Management; an MSc in Information Systems; and a PhD in Information Security, from IPB University, King Saud University and Tunghai University, respectively. Nowadays, Dr. Heru Successfully authoring more than 35 books published by Francis & Taylor Group; including 8 full authored books and 30 book chapters, and more than 60 international publication in peer review journal and high impact journal; Scopus, Science Direct, Springer, ISI, and Global Indexed, such as: Information Security Management Systems, Business Process Reengineering An ICT Approach, The Emerging Technology of Big Data, Human Capital through ICT, Chemical Technology and Informatics in Chemistry with Applications.

Jeļena Zaščerinska was awarded Dr. paed. Degree from the University of Latvia, Riga, Latvia, in 2011. In January 2012 she became a leading researcher at the Centre for Education and Innovation Research, Riga, Latvia. Dr. paed. Jeļena Zaščerinska has been awarded a number of research grants. In 2012 Dr. paed. Jeļena Zaščerinska was bestowed expert rights by the Latvian Council of Science, Riga, Latvia. In December 2013 Dr. paed. Jeļena Zaščerinska was awarded expert rights by Horizon 2020 – the Framework Programme for Research and Innovation, the European Commission, Brussels, Belgium. Since 2013 Dr. paed. Jeļena Zaščerinska has been actively acting as the Editorial Board Member and Reviewer in such international scientific journals as the Journal of Information Technology Research (JITR), International Journal of Modern Education Research (IJMER), International Journal of Learning, Teaching and Educational Research (IJLTER), International Journal of Modern Education Forum (IJMEF), etc. Dr. Jeļena Zaščerinska is a member of international research teams focused on interdisciplinary investigations.

Mihails Zascerinskis is a founder of Centre for Education and Innovation Research (CEIR). He is CEIR Board Member and deputy director. He also works as a CEIR scientific assistant. His scientific focus is on implementation of teacher training in use of ICT in education, integration of entrepreneurship into education, use of multimedia in educational process, etc. He teaches webdesign and multimedia, information security and safety, intelligent internet in English and Latvian to adults and youth. He actively participates in national and international projects. He has received an extensive experience in managing international projects within Erasmus+, TEMPUS, DAAD and other programmes. Mihails Zascerinskis closely cooperates with a couple of higher education institutions. His major research results reflected in a number of publications have been indexed by well-acknowledged international research publication databases such as Thomson Reuters Conference Proceedings Citations Index, DBLP, Library of Congress and others.

María Zepeda Hurtado is a researcher professor at the Instituto Politécnico Nacional, CECyT 11, México, with thirty-five years of teaching experience, instructor of courses, workshops, seminars, designer of teacher training actions in the pedagogical area.

Index

A

B

C

D

P

Q

R

S

T

U

V

W

www.ingramcontent.com/pod-product-compliance
Lightning Source LLC
Chambersburg PA
CBHW081632240426
43735CB00046B/575